Lecture Notes in Computer Science 8663

Commenced Publication in 1973
Founding and Former Series Editors:
Gerhard Goos, Juris Hartmanis, and Jan van Leeuwen

More information about this series at http://www.springer.com/series/7407

Santiago Escobar (Ed.)

Rewriting Logic and Its Applications

10th International Workshop, WRLA 2014
Held as a Satellite Event of ETAPS
Grenoble, France, April 5–6, 2014
Revised Selected Papers

 Springer

Editor
Santiago Escobar
Departamento de Sistemas Informáticos y
    Computación
Universitat Politècnica de València
Valencia
Spain

ISSN 0302-9743   ISSN 1611-3349 (electronic)
Lecture Notes in Computer Science
ISBN 978-3-319-12903-7   ISBN 978-3-319-12904-4 (eBook)
DOI 10.1007/978-3-319-12904-4

Library of Congress Control Number: 2014954581

LNCS Sublibrary: SL1 – Theoretical Computer Science and General Issues

Springer Cham Heidelberg New York Dordrecht London

Printed on acid-free paper

Springer International Publishing AG Switzerland is part of Springer Science+Business Media
(www.springer.com)

Preface

This volume contains a selection of the papers presented at the 10th International Workshop on Rewriting Logic and its Applications (WRLA 2014), held during April 5–6, 2014 in Grenoble, France.

Rewriting logic (RL) is a natural model of computation and an expressive semantic framework for concurrency, parallelism, communication, and interaction. It can be used for specifying a wide range of systems and languages in various application fields. It also has good properties as a metalogical framework for representing logics. In recent years, several languages based on RL (ASF+SDF, CafeOBJ, ELAN, Maude) have been designed and implemented. The aim of the workshop is to bring together researchers with a common interest in RL and its applications, and to give them the opportunity to present their recent works, discuss future research directions, and exchange ideas. The previous meetings were held at Asilomar (USA) 1996, Pont-à-Mousson (France) 1998, Kanazawa (Japan) 2000, Pisa (Italy) 2002, Barcelona (Spain) 2004, Vienna (Austria) 2006, Budapest (Hungary) 2008, Paphos (Cyprus) 2010, and Tallinn (Estonia) 2012.

Typically, the topics of interest include (but are not restricted to):

- foundations and models of RL;
- languages based on RL, including implementation issues;
- RL as a logical framework;
- RL as a semantic framework, including applications of RL to

  - object-oriented systems,
  - concurrent and/or parallel systems,
  - interactive, distributed, open ended and mobile systems,
  - specification of languages and systems;

- use of RL to provide rigorous support for model-based software engineering;
- formalisms related to RL, including

  - real-time and probabilistic extensions of RL,
  - rewriting approaches to behavioral specifications,
  - tile logic;

- verification techniques for RL specifications, including

  - equational and coherence methods,
  - verification of properties expressed in first-order, higher-order, modal and temporal logics,
  - narrowing-based analysis and verification;

- comparisons of RL with existing formalisms having analogous aims;
- application of RL to specification and analysis of

  - distributed systems,
  - physical systems.

The last editions of WRLA were held as a satellite event of the European Joint Conferences on Theory & Practice of Software (ETAPS). This year's edition was a satellite event of ETAPS 2014.

There were 21 original contributions to the workshop and the Program Committee selected 13 papers for publication, and revised versions of these selected papers are included in this volume. Each contribution was reviewed by at least three Program Committee members. This volume also includes three invited contributions by Francisco Durán from the University of Málaga, Spain, Alberto Lluch Lafuente from the IMT Institute for Advanced Studies Lucca, Italy, and Peter Ölveczky from the University of Oslo, Norway. We would like to thank them for having accepted our invitation for both presentation at the workshop and this volume.

We would also like to thank all the members of the Program Committee and all the referees for their careful work in the review process. Finally, I express our gratitude to all members of the local organization of ETAPS 2014 and the Easychair system, whose work has made the workshop possible.

August 2014   Santiago Escobar

Organization

Program Committee

Mark van den Brand	Eindhoven University of Technology, The Netherlands
Roberto Bruni	Università di Pisa, Italy
Manuel Clavel	Universidad Complutense de Madrid, Spain
Francisco Durán	University of Málaga, Spain
Santiago Escobar	Universitat Politècnica de València, Spain
Kokichi Futatsugi	JAIST, Japan
Alexander Knapp	Universität Augsburg, Germany
Alberto Lluch Lafuente	IMT Institute for Advanced Studies Lucca, Italy
Dorel Lucanu	Alexandru Ioan Cuza University, Romania
Narciso Martí Oliet	Universidad Complutense de Madrid, Spain
Jose Meseguer	University of Illinois at Urbana-Champaign, USA
Ugo Montanari	Università di Pisa, Italy
Pierre-Etienne Moreau	École des Mines de Nancy and Inria Nancy, France
Kazuhiro Ogata	JAIST, Japan
Peter Ölveczky	University of Oslo, Norway
Miguel Palomino	Universidad Complutense de Madrid, Spain
Grigore Rosu	University of Illinois at Urbana-Champaign, USA
Vlad Rusu	Inria Lille Nord-Europe, France
Mark-Oliver Stehr	SRI International, USA
Carolyn Talcott	SRI International, USA
Martin Wirsing	Ludwig-Maximilians-Universität München, Germany

Additional Reviewers

Abd Alrahman, Yehia	Martin, Oscar
Aguirre, Luis	Riesco, Adrián
Asavoae, Irina Mariuca	Sakai, Masahiko
Bodei, Chiara	Sammartino, Matteo
Bosnacki, Dragan	Stefanescu, Andrei
Calvès, Christophe François Olivier	Vandin, Andrea
Gadducci, Fabio	Wijs, Anton

Contents

Composition of Graph-Transformation-Based DSL Definitions by Amalgamation

Francisco Durán[✉]

University of Málaga, Málaga, Spain
duran@lcc.uma.es

Abstract. Given a graph-grammar formalization of DSLs, we build on graph transformation system morphisms to define parameterized DSLs and their instantiation by an amalgamation construction. Results on the protection of the behavior along the induced morphisms allow us to safely combine definitions of DSLs to build more complex ones. We illustrate our proposal on our e-Motions definition of the Palladio DSL. The resulting DSL allows us to carry on performance analysis on Palladio models.

1 Introduction

In Model-Driven Engineering (MDE) [43], models are used to specify, simulate, analyze, modify, and generate code. One of the key ingredients making this approach particularly attractive is the use of domain-specific languages (DSLs) [49] for the definition of such models. DSLs offer concepts specifically targeted at a particular domain, which allow experts in such domains to express their problems and requirements in their own languages. On the other hand, the higher amount of knowledge embedded in these concepts allows for much more complete and specialized generation of executable solution code from DSL models [30].

The application of these techniques to different domains has resulted in the proliferation of DSLs of very different nature: the more specific for a particular domain a DSL is, the more effective it is. However, DSLs are only viable if their development can be made efficient. With this goal in mind, DSLs are often defined by specifying their syntax in some standard formalisms, such as MOF, thus facilitating the use of generic frameworks for the management of models, including their composition, the definition of model transformations, use of model editors, etc.

Syntax is however just part of the story. Without a definition of the operational behavior of the defined DSLs, we will not be able to simulate or analyze the defined models. In recent years, different formalisms have been proposed for the definition of the behavior of DSLs, including UML behavioral models [19,22], abstract state machines [3,10], or in-place model transformations [9,39]. Between all these approaches, we find the use of in-place model transformations particularly powerful, not only because its expressiveness, but also because it facilitates its integration with the rest of the MDE environment and tools.

© Springer International Publishing Switzerland 2014
S. Escobar (Ed.): WRLA 2014, LNCS 8663, pp. 1–20, 2014.
DOI: 10.1007/978-3-319-12904-4_1

While we have reasonably good knowledge of how to modularize DSL syntax, the modularization of language semantics is an as yet unsolved issue. Given a graph-grammar [6,14,42] formalization of DSLs, we build on graph transformation system (GTS) morphisms to define composition operations on DSLs. Specifically, we define parameterized GTSs, that is, GTSs which have other GTSs as parameters. The instantiation of such parameterized GTSs is then provided by an amalgamation construction. We present formal results about GTSs and GTSs morphisms between them. Specifically, we are interested on how these morphisms preserve or protect behavior, and what behavior-related properties may be guaranteed on the morphisms induced by the amalgamation construction defining the instantiation of parameterized GTSs. Of particular interest for our goals is the identification of the circumstances in which we can guarantee protection of behavior when DSLs get instantiated.

In the rest of the paper, we propose the use of parameterized DSLs, we present their implementation in the e-Motions system, and show its potential presenting the definition of the e-Motions implementation of a significant part of the Palladio DSL. Although we motivate and illustrate our approach using the e-Motions language [37], our proposal is language-independent, and all the results are presented for GTSs and adhesive HLR systems [16,34]. e-Motions graphical specifications are translated into Maude specifications [38]. Given this transformation, models in DSLs developed in e-Motions, may be "simulated" in accordance to the given semantics. Since the resulting specification is a valid theory in rewriting logic, Maude's formal tools, as its reachability analysis tool or its model checker, may be used on it.

The rest of the paper is structured as follows. Section 2 introduces behavior-reflecting and -protecting GTS morphisms, the construction of amalgamations in the category of GTSs and GTS morphisms, and several results on these amalgamations. Section 3 presents the e-Motions definition of the Palladio DSL and how the composition operations presented in Sect. 2 are used to provide mechanisms to carry on performance-related monitoring and analysis of systems. The paper presents some related work in Sect. 4 and finishes with some conclusions and future work in Sect. 5.

2   Graph Transformation and GTS Amalgamations

Graph transformation [14,42] is a formal, graphical and natural way of expressing graph manipulation based on rewriting rules. In graph-based modelling (and meta-modelling), graphs are used to define the static structures, such as class and object ones, which represent visual alphabets and sentences over them. A more detailed presentation of the results in this section may be found in [11].

2.1   Rules, Rule Morphisms, and Rule Amalgamations

Our formalisation is developed for weak adhesive high-level replacement (HLR) categories [14], making it much more general. The concepts of adhesive and (weak) adhesive HLR categories abstract the foundations of a general class of models, and come together with a collection of general semantic techniques [16,34]. Thus, e.g., given proofs for adhesive HLR categories of general results such as the Local Church-Rosser, or the Parallelism and Concurrency Theorem, they are automatically valid for any category which is proved an adhesive HLR category. The category of typed attributed graphs, the one of interest to us, was proved to be adhesive HLR in [18].

In the DPO approach to graph transformation, a rule with application conditions p is of the form $(L \xleftarrow{l} K \xrightarrow{r} R, ac)$ with graphs L, K, and R, called, respectively, left-hand side, interface, and right-hand side, some kind of monomorphisms (typically, inclusions) l and r, and ac a *(nested) application condition* on L. A graph transformation system (GTS) is a pair (P, π) where P is a set of rule names and π is a function mapping each rule name p into a rule $(L \xleftarrow{l} K \xrightarrow{r} R, ac)$.

An application of a rule $p = (L \xleftarrow{l} K \xrightarrow{r} R, ac)$ to a graph G via a match $m : L \to G$, such that m satisfies ac, written $m \models ac$, is constructed as two gluings (1) and (2), which are pushouts in the corresponding graph category, leading to a direct transformation $G \xRightarrow{p,m} H$.

$$ac \quad \triangleright \quad L \xleftarrow{\;l\;} K \xrightarrow{\;r\;} R$$
$$m \downarrow \quad (1) \quad \downarrow \quad (2) \quad \downarrow$$
$$G \longleftarrow D \longrightarrow H$$

Application conditions may be positive or negative. Positive application conditions have the form $\exists a$, for a monomorphism $a : L \to C$, and demand a certain structure in addition to L. Negative application conditions of the form $\nexists a$ forbid such a structure. A match $m : L \to G$ satisfies a positive application condition $\exists a$ if there is a monomorphism $q : C \to G$ satisfying $q \circ a = m$. A matching m satisfies a negative application condition $\nexists a$ if there is no such monomorphism. Given an application condition $\exists a$ or $\nexists a$, for a monomorphism $a : L \to C$, another application condition ac can be established on C, giving place to nested application conditions [25]. Given an application condition ac on L and a monomorphism $t : L \to L'$, then there is an application condition $\mathsf{Shift}(t, ac)$ on L' such that for all $m' : L' \to G$, $m' \models \mathsf{Shift}(t, ac) \leftrightarrow m = m' \circ t \models ac$.

$$ac \triangleright L \xrightarrow{\;t\;} L' \triangleleft \mathsf{Shift}(t, ac)$$
$$m \searrow \quad \swarrow m'$$
$$G$$

To improve readability, we assume projection functions ac, lhs and rhs, returning, respectively, the application condition, left-hand side and right-hand side of a rule. Thus, given a rule $r = (L \xleftarrow{l} K \xrightarrow{r} R, ac)$, $ac(r) = ac$, $lhs(r) = L$, and $rhs(r) = R$.

We only consider injective matches, that is, monomorphisms. If the matching m is understood, a DPO transformation step $G \xrightarrow{p,m} H$ will be simply written $G \Rightarrow H$. A transformation sequence $\rho = \rho_1 \ldots \rho_n : G \Rightarrow^* H$ via rules $p_1, \ldots, p_n$ is a sequence of transformation steps $\rho_i = (G_i \xrightarrow{p_i, m_i} H_i)$ such that $G_1 = G$, $H_n = H$, and consecutive steps are composable, that is, $G_{i+1} = H_i$ for all $1 \le i < n$. The category of transformation sequences over an adhesive category $\mathbf{C}$, denoted by $\mathbf{Trf}(\mathbf{C})$, has all graphs in $|\mathbf{C}|$ as objects and all transformation sequences as arrows.

Parisi-Presicce proposed in [36] a notion of rule morphism very similar to the one below, although we consider rules with application conditions, and require the commuting squares to be pullbacks instead of pushouts.

Definition 1 (From [11], Rule morphism). *Given graph transformation rules $p_i = (L_i \xleftarrow{l_i} K_i \xrightarrow{r_i} R_i, ac_i)$, for $i = 0, 1$, a rule morphism $f : p_0 \to p_1$ is a tuple $f = (f_L, f_K, f_R)$ of graph monomorphisms $f_L : L_0 \to L_1$, $f_K : K_0 \to K_1$, and $f_R : R_0 \to R_1$ such that the squares with the span morphisms l_0, l_1, r_0, and r_1 are pullbacks, as in the diagram below, and such that $ac_1 \Rightarrow Shift(f_L, ac_0)$.*

$$
\begin{array}{ccccc}
p_0 & : & ac_0 \,\triangleright\, L_0 \xleftarrow{l_0} K_0 \xrightarrow{r_0} R_0 \\
f \downarrow & & f_L \downarrow \quad pb \; f_K \downarrow \quad pb \quad \downarrow f_R \\
p_1 & : & ac_1 \,\triangleright\, L_1 \xleftarrow{l_1} K_1 \underset{r_1}{\rightrightarrows} R_1
\end{array}
$$

Asking that the two squares are pullbacks means, precisely, to preserve the "structure" of objects. I.e., we preserve what should be deleted, what should be added, and what must remain invariant. Of course, pushouts also preserve the created and deleted parts, but they reflect this structure as well, which we do not want in general. With componentwise identities and composition, rule morphisms define the category **Rule**.

A key concept in the constructions in Sect. 2.3 is that of *rule amalgamation* [2]. The amalgamation of two rules p_1 and p_2 glues them together into a single rule $\tilde{p}$ to obtain the effect of the original rules. I.e., the simultaneous application of p_1 and p_2 yields the same successor graph as the application of the amalgamated rule $\tilde{p}$. The possible overlapping of rules p_1 and p_2 is captured by a rule p_0 and rule morphisms $f : p_0 \to p_1$ and $g : p_0 \to p_2$.

Definition 2 (From [11], Rule amalgamation). *Given graph transformation rules $p_i = (L_i \xleftarrow{l_i} K_i \xrightarrow{r_i} R_i, ac_i)$, for $i = 0, 1, 2$, and rule morphisms $f : p_0 \to p_1$ and $g : p_0 \to p_2$, the amalgamated production $p_1 +_{p_0} p_2$ is the production $(L \xleftarrow{l} K \xrightarrow{r} R, ac)$ in the diagram below, where subdiagrams (1), (2) and (3) are pushouts, l and r are induced by the universal property of (2) so that all subdiagrams commute, and $ac = Shift(\widehat{f_L}, ac_2) \wedge Shift(\widehat{g_L}, ac_1)$.*

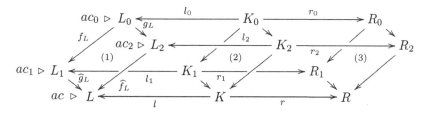

Notice that in the above diagram all squares are either pushouts or pullbacks (by the van Kampen property [34]) which means that all their arrows are monomorphisms (by being an adhesive HLR category).

2.2 Typed Graph Transformation Systems

A (directed unlabeled) *graph* $G = (V, E, s, t)$ is given by a set of nodes (or vertices) V, a set of edges E, and source and target functions $s, t\colon E \to V$. Given graphs $G_i = (V_i, E_i, s_i, t_i)$, with $i = 1, 2$, a graph homomorphism $f\colon G_1 \to G_2$ is a pair of functions $(f_V : V_1 \to V_2, f_E : E_1 \to E_2)$ such that $f_V \circ s_1 = s_2 \circ f_E$ and $f_V \circ t_1 = t_2 \circ f_E$. With componentwise identities and composition this defines the category **Graph**.

Given a distinguished graph TG, called *type graph*, a *TG-typed graph* (G, g_G), or simply *typed graph* if TG is known, consists of a graph G and a typing homomorphism $g_G : G \to TG$ associating with each vertex and edge of G its type in TG. However, to enhance readability, when the typing morphism g_G can be considered implicit, we will often refer to a typed graph (G, g_G) just as G. A TG-typed graph morphism between TG-typed graphs $(G_i, g_i : G_i \to TG)$, with $i = 1, 2$, denoted $f\colon (G_1, g_1) \to (G_2, g_2)$, is a graph morphism $f\colon G_1 \to G_2$ which preserves types, i.e., $g_2 \circ f = g_1$. **Graph**$_{TG}$ is the category of TG-typed graphs and TG-typed graph morphisms, which is the comma category **Graph** over TG.

If the underlying graph category is adhesive (resp., adhesive HLR, weakly adhesive) then so are the associated typed categories [14], and therefore all definitions in Sect. 2.1 apply to them. A TG-typed graph transformation rule $p = (L \xleftarrow{l} K \xrightarrow{r} R, ac)$ is a span of injective TG-typed graph morphisms and a (nested) application condition on L. Given TG-typed graph transformation rules $p_i = (L_i \xleftarrow{l_i} K_i \xrightarrow{r_i} R_i, ac_i)$, with $i = 1, 2$, a typed rule morphism $f\colon p_1 \to p_2$ is a tuple (f_L, f_K, f_R) of TG-typed graph monomorphisms such that the squares with the span monomorphisms l_i and r_i, for $i = 1, 2$, are pullbacks, and such that $ac_2 \Rightarrow \mathsf{Shift}(f_L, ac_1)$. TG-typed graph transformation rules and typed rule morphisms define the category **Rule**$_{TG}$, which is the comma category **Rule** over TG.

Following [6], we use forward and backward retyping functors to deal with graphs over different type graphs. A graph morphism $f\colon TG \to TG'$ induces a forward retyping functor $f^> : \mathbf{Graph}_{TG} \to \mathbf{Graph}_{TG'}$, with $f^>(g_1) = f \circ g_1$ and $f^>(k\colon g_1 \to g_2) = k$ by composition, as shown in the diagram in Fig. 1(a). Similarly, such a morphism f induces a backward retyping functor $f^< : \mathbf{Graph}_{TG'} \to$

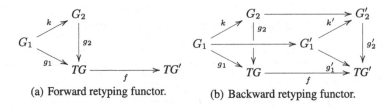

(a) Forward retyping functor.   (b) Backward retyping functor.

Fig. 1. Forward and backward retyping functors.

Graph$_{TG}$, with $f^<(g_1') = g_1$ and $f^<(k' : g_1' \to g_2') = k : g_1 \to g_2$ by pullbacks and mediating morphisms as shown in the diagram in Fig. 1(b). Since, as said above, we refer to a TG-typed graph $G \to TG$ just by its typed graph G, leaving TG implicit, given a morphism $f : TG \to TG'$, we may refer to the TG'-typed graph by $f^>(G)$.

A typed graph transformation system over a type graph TG, is a graph transformation system where the given graph transformation rules are defined over the category of TG-typed graphs. Since we deal with GTSs over different type graphs, we will make explicit the given type graph. This means that, from now on, a typed GTS is a triple (TG, P, π) where TG is a type graph, P is a set of rule names and π is a function mapping each rule name p into a rule $(L \xleftarrow{l} K \xrightarrow{r} R, ac)$ typed over TG.

The set of transformation rules of a GTS specifies a behavior in terms of the derivations obtained via such rules. A GTS morphism defines then a relation between its source and target GTSs by providing an association between their type graphs and rules.

Definition 3 (From [11], GTS morphism). *Given typed graph transformation systems* $GTS_i = (TG_i, P_i, \pi_i)$, *for* $i = 0, 1$, *a GTS morphism* $f : GTS_0 \to GTS_1$, *with* $f = (f_{TG}, f_P, f_r)$, *is given by a morphism* $f_{TG} : TG_0 \to TG_1$, *a surjective mapping* $f_P : P_1 \to P_0$ *between the sets of rule names, and a family of rule morphisms* $f_r = \{f^p : f_{TG}^>(\pi_0(f_P(p))) \to \pi_1(p)\}_{p \in P_1}$.

Given a GTS morphism $f : GTS_0 \to GTS_1$, each rule in GTS_1 extends a rule in GTS_0. However if there are internal computation rules in GTS_1 that do not extend any rule in GTS_0, we can always consider that the empty rule is included in GTS_0, and assume that those rules extend the empty rule. Notice that to deal with rule morphisms defined on rules over different type graphs we retype one of the rules. Typed GTSs and GTS morphisms define the category **GTS**.

2.3   GTS Amalgamations and Preservation of Behavior

Given a GTS morphism $f : GTS_0 \to GTS_1$, we say that it *reflects* behavior if for any derivation that may happen in GTS_1 there exists a corresponding derivation in GTS_0.

Definition 4 (From [11], Behavior-reflecting GTS morphism). *Given transformation systems* $GTS_i = (TG_i, P_i, \pi_i)$, *for* $i = 0, 1$, *a GTS morphism* $f: GTS_0 \to GTS_1$ *is behavior-reflecting if for all graphs* G, H *in* $|\mathbf{Graph}_{TG_1}|$, *all rules* p *in* P_1, *and all matches* $m: lhs(\pi_1(p)) \to G$ *such that* $G \overset{p,m}{\Longrightarrow} H$, *then* $f^<_{TG}(G) \xrightarrow{f_P(p), f^<_{TG}(m)} f^<_{TG}(H)$ *in* GTS_0.

We call *extension morphisms* to those morphisms between GTSs that only add to the transformation rules elements not in their source type graph. All extension GTS morphisms are behavior-reflecting [11].

Definition 5 (From [11], Extension GTS morphism). *Given graph transformation systems* $GTS_i = (TG_i, P_i, \pi_i)$, *for* $i = 0, 1$, *a GTS morphism* $f: GTS_0 \to GTS_1$, *with* $f = (f_{TG}, f_P, f_r)$, *is an extension morphism if* f_{TG} *is a monomorphism and for each* $p \in P_1$, $\pi_0(f_P(p)) \equiv f^<_{TG}(\pi_1(p))$.

When a DSL is extended with alien elements that do not interfere with its behavior, e.g., to measure or to verify some property, we need to guarantee that such an extension does not change the semantics of the original DSL. Specifically, we need to guarantee that the behavior of the resulting system is exactly the same, that is, that any derivation in the source system also happens in the target one (behavior preservation), and any derivation in the target system was also possible in the source one (behavior reflection). The following definition of behavior-protecting GTS morphism captures the intuition of a morphism that both reflects and preserves behavior, that is, that establishes a bidirectional correspondence between derivations in the source and target GTSs.

Definition 6 (From [11], Behavior-protecting GTS morphism). *Given transformation systems* $GTS_i = (TG_i, P_i, \pi_i)$, *for* $i = 0, 1$, *a GTS morphism* $f: GTS_0 \to GTS_1$ *is behavior-protecting if for all graphs* G *and* H *in* $|\mathbf{Graph}_{TG_1}|$, *all rules* p *in* P_1, *and all matches* $m: lhs(\pi_1(p)) \to G$, $g^<_{TG}(G) \xrightarrow{g_P(p), g^<_{TG}(m)} g^<_{TG}(H) \iff G \overset{p,m}{\Longrightarrow} H$

We find in the literature definitions of behavior-preserving morphisms as morphisms in which the rules in the source GTS are included in the set of rules of the target GTS (see, e.g., [24,28]). Although these morphisms trivially preserve behavior, they are not useful for our purposes. Notice that, in our case, in addition to adding new rules, we are enriching the rules themselves.

GTS amalgamation provides a very convenient way of composing GTSs. Theorem 1 below establishes behavior-related properties on the induced morphisms.

Definition 7 (From [11], GTS Amalgamation). *Given typed graph transformation systems* $GTS_i = (TG_i, P_i, \pi_i)$, *for* $i = 0, 1, 2$, *and GTS morphisms* $f: GTS_0 \to GTS_1$ *and* $g: GTS_0 \to GTS_2$, *the amalgamated GTS* $\widehat{GTS} = GTS_1 +_{GTS_0} GTS_2$ *is the GTS* $(\widehat{TG}, \widehat{P}, \widehat{\pi})$ *constructed as follows. We first construct the pushout of typing graph morphisms* $f_{TG}: TG_0 \to TG_1$ *and* $g_{TG}: TG_0 \to TG_2$, *obtaining morphisms* $\widehat{f}_{TG}: TG_2 \to \widehat{TG}$ *and* $\widehat{g}_{TG}: TG_1 \to \widehat{TG}$. *The pullback of set morphisms* $f_P: P_1 \to P_0$ *and* $g_P: P_2 \to P_0$ *defines morphisms* $\widehat{f}_P: \widehat{P} \to P_2$

and $\widehat{g}_P \colon \widehat{P} \to P_1$. Then, for each rule p in $\widehat{P}$, the rule $\widehat{\pi}(p)$ is defined as the amalgamation of rules $\widehat{f}_{TG}^{>}(\pi_2(\widehat{f}_P(p)))$ and $\widehat{g}_{TG}^{>}(\pi_1(\widehat{g}_P(p)))$ with respect to the kernel rule $\widehat{f}_{TG}^{>}(g_{TG}^{>}(\pi_0(g_P(\widehat{f}_P(p)))))$.

$$
\begin{array}{ccc}
GTS_0 & \xrightarrow{\;\;f\;\;} & GTS_1 \\
{\scriptstyle g}\downarrow & \widehat{f} & \downarrow{\scriptstyle \widehat{g}} \\
GTS_2 & \dashrightarrow & \widehat{GTS}
\end{array}
$$

The following result gives conditions under which behavior-related guarantees can be established on the morphisms induced by the amalgamation construction.

Theorem 1 (From [11]). *Given typed transformation systems $GTS_i = (TG_i,$ $P_i, \pi_i)$, for $i = 0, 1, 2$, and the amalgamation $\widehat{GTS} = GTS_1 +_{GTS_0} GTS_2$ of GTS morphisms $f \colon GTS_0 \to GTS_1$ and $g \colon GTS_0 \to GTS_2$, if f is a behavior-reflecting GTS morphism, then $\widehat{f}$ is a monomorphism, and if g is an extension and behavior-protecting morphism, then $\widehat{g}$ is behavior-protecting as well.*

$$
\begin{array}{ccc}
GTS_0 & \xrightarrow{\;\;f\;\;} & GTS_1 \\
{\scriptstyle g}\downarrow & \widehat{f} & \downarrow{\scriptstyle \widehat{g}} \\
GTS_2 & \dashrightarrow & \widehat{GTS}
\end{array}
$$

3 Non-functional Properties as Parameterized Domain Specific Languages

In previous work [12, 48], we have explored the modular definition of non-functional properties as parameterized DSLs in the e-Motions framework [37]. These ideas were further exploited in [35] to provide a modular reimplementation of a substantive part of the Palladio Architecture Simulator [26] to perform predictive analysis of architectural software models. In particular, we re-implemented the Palladio Component Model [1], its workload model, and parts of its stochastic expressions model.

We explicitly modeled simulations as graph transformations in the e-Motions framework, and then, each NFP to be analyzed was modeled as an independent, parameterized DSL ready to be composed with the base Palladio model. The modular definition of NFPs as separate, parameterized DSLs allows its reuse, but also makes it easy to define additional NFPs to be analyzed. For a particular analysis problem, the relevant NFP DSLs can then be selected from a library and composed as required.

The results presented in Sect. 2.3 provides guarantees for preservation of semantics under composition, that is, the consideration of additional NFPs (satisfying certain restrictions) do not change the behavior of the system being modeled.

In this section, we introduce Palladio, e-Motions, and then the definition of the Palladio DSL in the e-Motions system. We pay special attention to the definition of observers and how they are 'woven' with the Palladio system to enrich the definition of its behavior for the observation of NFPs.

3.1 The Palladio DSL

The Palladio Architecture Simulator [26] is a predictive software analysis tool. It consists of a number of metamodels, foremost the Palladio Component Model (PCM) [1], that allow the high-level modeling of component-based architectures and their properties relevant for performance and reliability analysis. Palladio supports predictive analyses by transformation into a program that runs a simulation of the architecture's behavior, and by transforming to formalisms more amenable to analysis—e.g., Queuing Petri Nets.

Figure 2 shows the usage model and the component specification of a very simple example, provided as part of the distribution of the Palladio Architecture Simulator. The usage model in Fig. 2(a) specifies the way tasks arrive into the system. In Palladio, the work load may be either closed or open. To be *closed* (ClosedWorkload object) means that the number of requests is fixed by the population attribute, and their corresponding inter-arrival rate given by the think time attribute. Alternatively, an OpenedWorkload object represents an infinite stream of arrivals. According to the usage model in Fig. 2(b), each work arriving to the system consists on a system call action to a component, AnInterface.do, and then a delay with a fixed time of 1.0 time units.

Figure 2(b) shows the specification of the component, in which the control flow may branch into one of two flows. Each branch is associated with a particular branch probability to indicate the likelihood of a particular branch being taken. Finally, resource demands, i.e. CPU or HDD, are expressed as probability distributions. This is the kind of information required to perform execution-time analysis on the component's behavior as is standard in software performance engineering (see, e.g., [45]). In addition, we could model failure information to support reliability analysis.

The Palladio Simulator offers the results of the analysis of performance and reliability of the system being analyzed in different formats.

3.2 The e-Motions System

e-Motions [37] is a graphical framework that supports the specification, simulation, and formal analysis of real-time systems. It provides a way to graphically specify the dynamic behavior of DSLs using their concrete syntax, making this task very intuitive. The abstract syntax of a DSL is specified as an Ecore metamodel, which defines all relevant concepts—and their relations—in the language. Its concrete syntax is given by a GCS (Graphical Concrete Syntax) model, which attaches an image to each language concept. Then, its behavior is specified with (graphical) in-place model transformations.

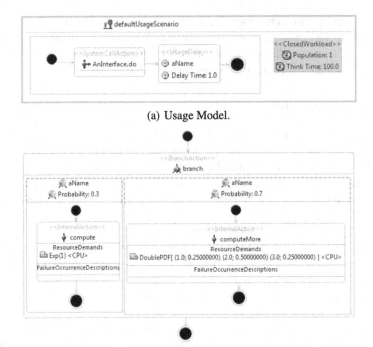

(a) Usage Model.

(b) Resource-Demanding Service-Effect specification (RDSEFF).

Fig. 2. *Minimum Example*: Workload and component specification in Palladio.

In-place transformations are defined by rules, each of which represents a possible *action* of the system. These rules are of the form [NAC]* × LHS → RHS, where LHS (left-hand side), RHS (right-hand side) and NAC (negative application conditions) are model patterns that represent certain (sub-)states of the system. The LHS and NAC patterns express the conditions for the rule to be applied, whereas the RHS represents the effect of the corresponding action. A LHS may also have positive conditions, which are expressed, as any expression in the RHS, using OCL [40]. Thus, a rule can be applied, i.e., triggered, if a match of the LHS is found in the model, its conditions are satisfied, and none of its NAC patterns occurs. If several matches are found, one of them is non-deterministically chosen and applied, giving place to a new model where the matching objects are substituted by the appropriate instantiation of its RHS pattern. The transformation of the model proceeds by applying the rules on sub-models of it in a non-deterministic order, until no further transformation rule is applicable.

e-Motions provides a model of time, supporting features like duration, periodicity, etc., and mechanisms to state action properties. There are two types of rules to specify time-dependent behavior, namely, *atomic* and *ongoing* rules. Atomic rules represent atomic actions with a duration. Atomic rules with duration zero are called *instantaneous* rules. Ongoing rules represent actions that progress continuously over time while the rule's preconditions (LHS and not NACs) hold. Both atomic and ongoing rules can be scheduled, or be given an execution interval. From a DSL definition, e-Motions generates an executable Maude [5] specification which can be used for simulation and analysis [38]. Other tools in the Maude formal environment, as its model checker or its reachability analysis tool, can also be used on this specification.

3.3   An e-Motions Re-implementation of Palladio

As for any DSL, the definition of the PCM includes its abstract syntax, its concrete syntax and its behavior. Since Palladio has been developed following MDE principles, and specifically it is implemented using the Eclipse Modeling Framework, its metamodel may be used as abstract syntax definition of Palladio in e-Motions.[1] Palladio models consists of several views, namely UsageModel, System, etc., corresponding to the different developer roles participating in the architecture of a system. These models are conformant to metamodels Core PCM, StoEx, Units, . . . used by the different Eclipse plug-ins in the PCM Bench. As we will see in Sect. 3, using the PCM as abstract syntax will allow us to take models generated in the Palladio Simulator into e-Motions, and to use them to perform simulations in the e-Motions definition of Palladio.

The concrete syntax is provided by a GCS model in which each concept in the abstract syntax of the DSL being defined is linked to an image. Since these images are used to graphically represent Palladio models in e-Motions, we have used the same images that the Palladio Simulator uses to represent these concepts. This way, we maintain the PCM's look in the e-Motions definition (see rules in Fig. 3).

In e-Motions, we describe how systems evolve by describing all possible changes of the models by corresponding visual time-aware in-place transformation rules. We may visualize each execution of a Palladio model has a token moving around such model. An action with a token has the control of execution. In fact, there might be several concurrent executions, since new tasks may keep arriving to the system, depending on its work load. The execution of each of these tasks proceeds independently, as far as the required resources are available.

For illustration purposes, Fig. 3 shows two of the rules defining the behavior of Palladio in e-Motions. As above explained, an open workload specifies an infinite stream of tasks arriving at the system with some inter-arrival time given by a random variable with some probability distribution. Each generated task executes the specified scenario, and then leave the system. Figure 3(a) shows the OpenWorkloadSpec rule, which specifies the behavior of a UsageScenario usSc with an OpenWorkload ow. When the rule is triggered, a new token is added to the first action of the system, i.e., the start action. The rule is fired every owRate, which is a local variable whose value is given by ow's random variable.

A ScenarioBehavior, which is included in a UsageScenario, as the one shown in Fig. 2, describes the behavior of the system components by using actions Start,

---

[1] The actual metamodel used is a conservative extension of the PCM to include additional concepts such as tokens, see below. The interested reader is referred to [35] for details.

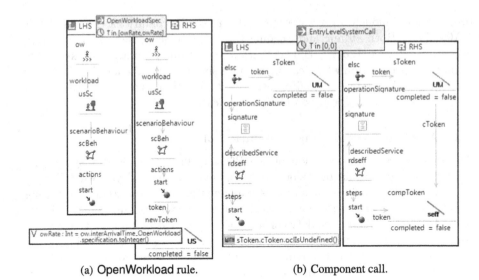

(a) OpenWorkload rule.   (b) Component call.

Fig. 3. New task rule specification.

Stop, EntryLevelSystemCall, Branch, and Loop. Figure 3(b) models the EntryLevel-SystemCall action, which is used to invoke an operation in a component. If a (sub)-state matches the LHS of the rule, the SToken object associated to the EntryLevelSystemCall action remains in this action, while a new CToken is created and linked to the start action of the invoked component (effectively building up a call stack). As the rule's header shows, this rule is instantaneous (it takes zero time).

The complete e-Motions definition of the Palladio DSL is available at http://atenea.lcc.uma.es/Palladio.

Once the whole DSL has been defined, and given a model as initial state, it may be simulated by applying the rules describing its behavior. This model does not collect information on NFPs, and therefore is not ready for performance analysis. We enrich them later, as explained in the following section.

3.4 Parameterized DSL for NFP Observation

Troya, Rivera and Vallecillo proposed in [47] an approach for the specification and monitoring of non-functional properties of DSLs using *observers*. Observers are objects with which we extend the e-Motions definition of systems for the analysis of NFPs by simulation, such as mean and maximum cycle times, busy and idle cycles of operation units, throughput, mean-time between failures, etc. We explored in [12, 48] how to define observers generically and independently from any system, so that they can afterwards be woven and merged with different systems. Given systems described as DSLs and generic DSLs defining the different observers, we can use the composition mechanisms presented in Sect. 2.3 to combine them. The result is that we can use the combined enriched system DSL to monitor NFPs of our systems. Theorem 1 proves that, given very natural requirements on the observers and the instantiating mappings, the system thus obtained is a conservative enrichment of the original system, in the sense that the observers added *do not change the behavior of the system.*

Given an e-Motions definition of Palladio as the one presented in Sect. 3.3, we can then enrich it with the definition of the observers we wish, which can be selected from a library of generically specified observers. Specifically, we can select those observers that monitor the properties available in the Palladio Simulator, but also others that monitor other properties. The NFPs chosen can then be analysed by simulation.

Let us consider a generic DSL for monitoring the *response time*, which is one of the properties available in Palladio. Response time can be defined as the time that elapses since a request arrives to a system until it is served. Hence, the same generic notion allows us to measure the response time of information packets being delivered through a network, of cars being manufactured in a production line, or of passengers checking-in in an airport. Given a system description, to measure response time, we just need to register the time at which requests arrive to the system, and the time at which they are completed. With this data and a simple calculation, we can easily get the response time.

A generic DSL achieving this is shown in Fig. 4. Its abstract syntax (the metamodel in Fig. 4(a)) contains three generic and two concrete classes—generic classes are shown with a shaded background. System, Server and Request are parameter classes to be instantiated by specific classes, as explained below. The System class represents the whole system, which is composed of a set of Servers. These, in turn, can have Requests that they have to process. The class RespTimeOb represents the observer for measuring the response time. Note that there is yet another observer in this metamodel, TimeStampOb, used to store the times at which Requests arrive.

The behavior of this DSL is defined by the three in-place transformation rules in Fig. 4, in which parametric concepts have no concrete syntax, they are depicted as boxes, and have a shaded background. Observer objects have a concrete syntax, that will also be used to depict them in the woven rules (see below). Rule CreateRespTOb deals with the creation of the response time observer. Its LHS includes a condition that avoids the creation of new observer objects if there is one, ensuring that only one of these observers is created per instantiated object. The observer is associated to the system in its RHS. Rule RequestArrives generates a time stamp observer whenever a new Request appears. The observer gets associated to the Request and keeps the time at which it appears in the system—note the presence of the system object Clock, which provides the current time. Finally, rule CompletedRequest computes the response time every time a Request is consumed—the Request and its associated observer have disappeared in the RHS. Attribute counter of RespTimeOb keeps the number of completed Requests, while tAcc contains the addition of cycle times of all Requests, i.e., the time they have spent in the system. Finally, attribute respT uses the former two attributes to calculate the response time of the System.

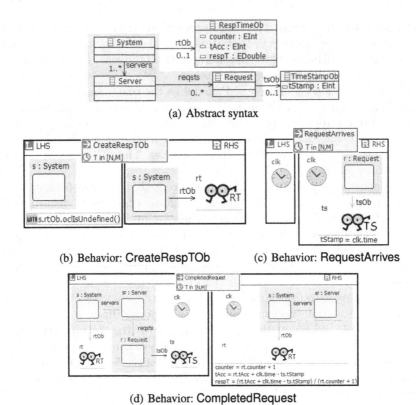

(a) Abstract syntax

(b) Behavior: CreateRespTOb   (c) Behavior: RequestArrives

(d) Behavior: CompletedRequest

Fig. 4. Response Time observer DSL definition.

3.5   Adding Observers to System Specifications

To add observers to our e-Motions specifications, we may compose the observer DSLs with the DSL of our system, the e-Motions definition of Palladio in our case. Let us use the amalgamation construction in Sect. 2.3 for it. Let us call $DSL_{Observer}$ to the Response Time DSL from Sect. 3.4, and let us consider the inclusion morphism from its parameter sub-DSL, DSL_{Par}. Given this inclusion morphism and a binding morphism B from DSL_{Par} to the Palladio DSL, $DSL_{Palladio}$, we can build its amalgamation as shown in Fig. 5. The result are morphisms $\hat{i}$ and $\widehat{B}$ to the DSL $\widehat{Palladio}$, which is the Palladio DSL extended with the response-time observer objects. Its metamodel is the Palladio metamodel enriched with the additional classes as indicated in the mappings, and the rules defining its behavior enriched with the observer objects.

The morphism B is just a mapping from elements in the parameter DSL into elements in the Palladio DSL. This is done by defining a correspondences model (see [12]). For example, for weaving the metamodel of response time with the metamodel of our Palladio implementation in e-Motions, the Request class is mapped to Token. Regarding rules, we basically need to map each rule in the

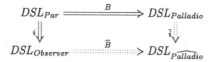

Fig. 5. Amalgamation in the category **GTS**.

source DSL to a rule in the target one. The mapping defined for the metamodel does most of the rest. The RequestArrives rule (Fig. 4(c)) is woven with the Open-WorkloadSpec rule of our Palladio system (Fig. 4(a)), that represents the arrival of a new Token in the system. Rule CreateRespTOb of the observer DSL is woven with an identity rule, triggering the creation of observer objects if they were not already created. Finally, rule CompletedRequest (Fig. 4(d)) is woven with the StopUsageModel rule, which just models the elimination of a token upon its arrival to a stop action.

Theorem 1 provides a checkable condition for verifying the conservative nature of an extension in our example, namely if B is a behavior-reflecting GTS morphism and i is an extension and behavior-protecting morphism, then $\hat{i}$ is behavior-protecting as well.

Once the observers DSL are defined and checked, they can be used as many times as wished. To use them, we just need to provide the morphism binding the parameter DSL and the target system.

4 Related Work

Graph transformation systems (GTSs) were proposed as a formal specification technique for the rule-based specification of the dynamic behavior of systems [13]. Different approaches exist for modularization in the context of the graph-grammar formalism [6,14,42]. All of them have followed the tradition of modules inspired by the notion of algebraic specification module [17]. A module is thus typically considered as given by an export and an import interface, and an implementation body that realizes what is offered in the export interface, using the specification to be imported from other modules via the import interface. For example, Große-Rhode, Parisi-Presicce, and Simeoni introduce in [24] a notion of *module* for typed graph transformation systems, with interfaces and implementation bodies; they propose operations for union, composition, and refinement of modules. Other approaches to modularization of graph transformation systems include PROGRES Packages [44], GRACE Graph Transformation Units and Modules [33], and DIEGO Modules [46]. See [29] for a discussion on these proposals. For the kind of systems we deal with, the type of module we need is much simpler. For us, a module is just the specification of a system, a GTS, without import and export interfaces. Then, we build on GTS morphisms to compose these modules, and specifically we define parameterized GTSs.

We find different forms of GTS morphisms in the literature, taking one form or another depending on their concrete application. Thus, we find proposals centered on refinements [23, 24, 28], views [21], and substitutability [20]. See [20] for a first attempt to a systematic comparison of the different proposals and notations. None of these notions fit our needs, and none of them coincide with our behavior-aware GTS morphisms.

As far as we know, parameterized GTSs and GTS morphisms, as we discuss them, have not been studied before. Heckel and Cherchago introduce parameterized GTSs in [27], but their notion has little to do with our parameterized GTSs. In their case, the parameter is a signature, intended to match service descriptions. They however use a double-pullback semantics, and have a notion of substitution morphism which is related to our behavior preserving morphism.

The way in which we think about composition of reusable DSL modules is related to work in aspect-oriented modeling (AOM). In particular, our ideas for expressing parameterized metamodels are based on the proposals in [4, 32]. Most AOM approaches use syntactic notions to automate the establishment of mappings between different models to be composed, often focusing primarily on the structural parts of a model. While our mapping specifications are syntactic in nature, we focus on composition of behaviors and provide semantic guarantees. In this sense, our work is perhaps most closely related to the work on MATA [50] or semantic-based weaving of scenarios [31].

The idea of generic DSL has also been used in the context of model management by different authors. E.g., [8, 41] use generic metamodel *concepts* as an intermediate, abstract metamodel over which model management specifications are defined, enabling the application of the operations thus defined to any metamodel satisfying the requirements imposed by the concept.

5 Conclusions

Our work was originally motivated by the specification of non-functional properties (NFPs), such as performance or throughput, in DSLs. We have been looking for ways in which to encapsulate the ability to specify non-functional properties into reusable DSL modules. Troya et al. used the concept of observers in [47, 48] to model non-functional properties of systems described by GTSs in a way that could be analyzed by simulation. In [12, 48], we have built on this work to allow the modular encapsulation of such observer definitions in a way that can be reused in different DSL specifications. We then formalized and generalized the composition operations needed in [11], were we provided a full formal framework of such language extensions.

In [35], we addressed the performance analysis problem by presenting a modular, model-based partial reimplementation of one well-known analysis framework—the Palladio Architecture Simulator. We have specified key DSLs from Palladio in e-Motions, describing the basic simulation semantics as a set of graph-transformation rules. Different properties to be analyzed have been encoded as separate, parameterized DSLs, independent of the definition of Palladio. We have then composed these DSLs with the base Palladio DSL to generate specific simulation environments. Models created in the Palladio IDE can be fed directly into our simulation environment for analysis.

We have demonstrated two main benefits of our approach: (1) The semantics of the simulation and the non-functional properties to be analyzed are made explicit in the respective DSL specifications, and (2) because of the compositional definition, it is easy to add definitions of new non-functional properties and their analyses. More importantly, our proposal provides a place were to experiment with new features and tailor solutions for specific problems at a very low development cost.

As future work, we plan to provide methods to check the preconditions of Theorem 1, and automatically checkable conditions that imply these, so that behavior protection of an extension can be checked effectively. This will enable the development of tooling to support the validation of language or transformation compositions. We also plan to study relaxations of our definitions so as to allow cases where there is a less than perfect match between the base DSL and the DSL to be woven in.

We plan to incorporate additional features to our definition of Palladio, as, for example, full resource models, and failures and reliability analysis. Indeed, we foresee generic definitions of selectable features, such as resource handling and deployment strategies, etc. We also plan to experiment with other NFPs, such as reliability or security, and to use our flexible setting for the analysis of dynamic systems, where components and resources are dynamically added to or removed from the system under study.

Acknowledgements. This work is an overview of work developed in collaboration with A. Moreno-Delgado, F. Orejas, J. Troya, A. Vallecillo, and S. Zschaler. I am grateful to all of them. This work is partially funded by Project TIN2011-23795 and by U. de Málaga, Campus de Excelencia Intl. Andalucía Tech.

References

1. Becker, S., Koziolek, H., Reussner, R.: Model-based performance prediction with the Palladio component model. In: Proceedings of 6th International Workshop on Software and Performance (WOSP'07). ACM (2007)
2. Boehm, P., Fonio, H.-R., Habel, A.: Amalgamation of graph transformations with applications to synchronization. In: Ehrig, H., Floyd, C., Nivat, M., Thatcher, J. (eds.) TAPSOFT 1985. LNCS, vol. 185, pp. 267–283. Springer, Heidelberg (1985)
3. Chen, K., Sztipanovits, J., Abdelwalhed, S., Jackson, E.: Semantic anchoring with model transformations. In: Hartman, A., Kreische, D. (eds.) ECMDA-FA 2005. LNCS, vol. 3748, pp. 115–129. Springer, Heidelberg (2005)
4. Clarke, S., Walker, R.J.: Generic aspect-oriented design with Theme/UML. In: Aspect-Oriented Software Development, pp. 425–458. Addison-Wesley (2005)
5. Clavel, M., Durán, F., Eker, S., Lincoln, P., Martí-Oliet, N., Meseguer, J., Talcott, C. (eds.): All About Maude. LNCS, vol. 4350. Springer, Heidelberg (2007)
6. Corradini, A., Ehrig, H., Löwe, M., Montanari, U., Padberg, J.: The category of typed graph grammars and its adjunctions with categories of derivations. In: Cuny, J., et al. [7], pp. 56–74
7. Cuny, J., Ehrig, H., Engels, G., Rozenberg, G. (eds.): Graph Grammars 1994. LNCS, vol. 1073. Springer, Heidelberg (1996)

8. de Lara, J., Guerra, E.: From types to type requirements: genericity for model-driven engineering. Softw. Syst. Model. **12**(3), 453–474 (2013)
9. de Lara, J., Vangheluwe, H.: Automating the transformation-based analysis of visual languages. Formal Asp. Comput. **22**(3–4), 297–326 (2010)
10. Di Ruscio, D., Jouault, F., Kurtev, I., Bézivin, J., Pierantonio, A.: Extending AMMA for supporting dynamic semantics specifications of DSLs. Technical report 06.02, Laboratoire d'Informatique de Nantes-Atlantique (LINA), April 2006
11. Durán, F., Orejas, F., Zschaler, S.: Behaviour protection in modular rule-based system specifications. In: Martí-Oliet, N., Palomino, M. (eds.) WADT 2012. LNCS, vol. 7841, pp. 24–49. Springer, Heidelberg (2013)
12. Durán, F., Zschaler, S., Troya, J.: On the reusable specification of non-functional properties in DSLs. In: Czarnecki, K., Hedin, G. (eds.) SLE 2012. LNCS, vol. 7745, pp. 332–351. Springer, Heidelberg (2013)
13. Ehrig, H.: Introduction to the algebraic theory of graph grammars. In: Claus, V., Ehrig, H., Rozenberg, G. (eds.) Graph Grammars 1978. LNCS, vol. 73, pp. 1–69. Springer, Heidelberg (1979)
14. Ehrig, H., Ehrig, K., Prange, U., Taentzer, G.: Fundamentals of Algebraic Graph Transformation. Springer, Heidelberg (2005)
15. Ehrig, H., et al. (eds.): Handbook of Graph Grammars and Computing by Graph Transformation. Applications, Languages and Tools, vol. II. World Scientific, Singapore (1999)
16. Ehrig, H., Habel, A., Padberg, J., Prange, U.: Adhesive high-level replacement categories and systems. In: Ehrig, H., Engels, G., Parisi-Presicce, F., Rozenberg, G. (eds.) ICGT 2004. LNCS, vol. 3256, pp. 144–160. Springer, Heidelberg (2004)
17. Ehrig, H., Mahr, B.: Fundamentals of Algebraic Specification 2. Module Specifications and Constraints. Springer, Heidelberg (1990)
18. Ehrig, H., Prange, U., Taentzer, G.: Fundamental theory for typed attributed graph transformation. In: Ehrig, H., Engels, G., Parisi-Presicce, F., Rozenberg, G. (eds.) ICGT 2004. LNCS, vol. 3256, pp. 161–177. Springer, Heidelberg (2004)
19. Engels, G., Hausmann, J.H., Heckel, R., Sauer, S.: Dynamic meta modeling: a graphical approach to the operational semantics of behavioral diagrams in UML. In: Evans, A., Caskurlu, B., Selic, B. (eds.) UML 2000. LNCS, vol. 1939, pp. 323–337. Springer, Heidelberg (2000)
20. Engels, G., Heckel, R., Cherchago, A.: Flexible interconnection of graph transformation modules. In: Kreowski, H.-J., Montanari, U., Orejas, F., Rozenberg, G., Taentzer, G. (eds.) Formal Methods in Software and Systems Modeling. LNCS, vol. 3393, pp. 38–63. Springer, Heidelberg (2005)
21. Engels, G., Heckel, R., Taentzer, G., Ehrig, H.: A combined reference model- and view-based approach to system specification. Intl. J. Softw. Eng. Knowl. Eng. **7**(4), 457–477 (1997)
22. Fischer, T., Niere, J., Torunski, L., Zündorf, A.: Story diagrams: a new graph rewrite language based on the unified modeling language and java. In: Ehrig, H., Engels, G., Kreowski, H.-J., Rozenberg, G. (eds.) TAGT 1998. LNCS, vol. 1764, pp. 296–309. Springer, Heidelberg (2000)
23. Große-Rhode, M., Parisi-Presicce, F., Simeoni, M.: Spatial and temporal refinement of typed graph transformation systems. In: Brim, L., Gruska, J., Zlatuška, J. (eds.) MFCS 1998. LNCS, vol. 1450, pp. 553–561. Springer, Heidelberg (1998)
24. Große-Rhode, M., Parisi-Presicce, F., Simeoni, M.: Formal software specification with refinements and modules of typed graph transformation systems. J. Comput. Syst. Sci. **64**(2), 171–218 (2002)

25. Habel, A., Pennemann, K.-H.: Correctness of high-level transformation systems relative to nested conditions. Math. Struct. Comput. Sci. **19**(2), 245–296 (2009)
26. Happe, J., Koziolek, H., Reussner, R.: Facilitating performance predictions using software components. IEEE Softw. **28**(3), 27–33 (2011)
27. Heckel, R., Cherchago, A.: Structural and behavioural compatibility of graphical service specifications. J. Logic Algebraic Program. **70**(1), 15–33 (2007)
28. Heckel, R., Corradini, A., Ehrig, H., Löwe, M.: Horizontal and vertical structuring of typed graph transformation systems. Math. Struct. Comput. Sci. **6**(6), 613–648 (1996)
29. Heckel, R., Engels, G., Ehrig, H., Taentzer, G.: Classification and comparison of modularity concepts for graph transformation systems. In: Ehrig et al. [15], chap. 17, pp. 669–690
30. Hemel, Z., Kats, L.C.L., Groenewegen, D.M., Visser, E.: Code generation by model transformation: a case study in transformation modularity. Softw. Syst. Modell. **9**(3), 375–402 (2010)
31. Klein, J., Hélouët, L., Jézéquel, J.-M.: Semantic-based weaving of scenarios. In: Proceedings of 5th International Conference on Aspect-Oriented Software Development (AOSD'06). ACM (2006)
32. Klein, J., Kienzle, J.: Reusable aspect models. In: Proceedings of Aspect-Oriented Modeling Workshop (2007)
33. Kreowski, H., Kuske, S.: Graph transformation units and modules. In: Ehrig et al. [15], chap. 15, pp. 607–638
34. Lack, S., Sobociński, P.: Adhesive categories. In: Walukiewicz, I. (ed.) FOSSACS 2004. LNCS, vol. 2987, pp. 273–288. Springer, Heidelberg (2004)
35. Moreno-Delgado, A., Durán, F., Zschaler, S., Troya, J.: Modular DSLs for flexible analysis: an e-Motions reimplementation of palladio. In: Cabot, J., Rubin, J. (eds.) ECMFA 2014. LNCS, vol. 8569, pp. 132–147. Springer, Heidelberg (2014)
36. Parisi-Presicce, F.: Transformations of graph grammars. In: Cuny et al. [7], pp. 428–442
37. Rivera, J.E., Durán, F., Vallecillo, A.: A graphical approach for modeling time-dependent behavior of DSLs. In: Proceedings of IEEE Symposium on Visual Languages and Human-Centric Computing (VL/HCC'09), pp. 51–55. IEEE (2009)
38. Rivera, J.E., Durán, F., Vallecillo, A.: On the behavioral semantics of real-time domain specific visual languages. In: Ölveczky, P.C. (ed.) WRLA 2010. LNCS, vol. 6381, pp. 174–190. Springer, Heidelberg (2010)
39. Rivera, J.E., Guerra, E., de Lara, J., Vallecillo, A.: Analyzing rule-based behavioral semantics of visual modeling languages with maude. In: Gašević, D., Lämmel, R., Van Wyk, E. (eds.) SLE 2008. LNCS, vol. 5452, pp. 54–73. Springer, Heidelberg (2009)
40. Roldán, M., Durán, F.: Dynamic validation of OCL constraints with mOdCL. ECEASST, 44 (2011)
41. Rose, L.M., Guerra, E., de Lara, J., Etien, A., Kolovos, D.S., Paige, R.F.: Genericity for model management operations. Softw. Syst. Model. **12**(1), 201–219 (2013)
42. Rozenberg, G. (ed.): Handbook of Graph Grammars and Computing by Graph Transformations. Foundations, vol. I. World Scientific, Singapore (1997)
43. Schmidt, D.C.: Model-driven engineering. IEEE Comput. **39**(2), 25–31 (2006)
44. Schürr, A., Winter, A., Zündorf, A.: The PROGRES-approach: language and environment. In: Ehrig et al. [15], chap. 13, pp. 487–550
45. Smith, C.U., Williams, L.G. (eds.): Performance Solutions: A Practical Guide to Creating Responsive, Scalable Software. Object-Technology Series. Addison-Wesley, Boston (2002)

46. Taentzer, G., Schürr, A.: DIEGO, another step towards a module concept for graph transformation systems. Electron. Notes Theoret. Comput. Sci. **2**, 277–285 (1995)
47. Troya, J., Rivera, J.E., Vallecillo, A.: Simulating domain specific visual models by observation. In: Proceedings of Spring Simulation Multiconference (SpringSim'10), pp. 128:1–128:8. ACM (2010)
48. Troya, J., Vallecillo, A., Durán, F., Zschaler, S.: Model-driven performance analysis of rule-based domain specific visual models. Inf. Softw. Technol. **55**(1), 88–110 (2013)
49. van Deursen, A., Klint, P., Visser, J.: Domain-specific languages: an annotated bibliography. SIGPLAN Not. **35**(6), 26–36 (2000)
50. Whittle, J., Jayaraman, P., Elkhodary, A., Moreira, A., Araújo, J.: MATA: a unified approach for composing UML aspect models based on graph transformation. In: Katz, S., Ossher, H., France, R., Jézéquel, J.-M. (eds.) Transactions on AOSD VI. LNCS, vol. 5560, pp. 191–237. Springer, Heidelberg (2009)

Can We Efficiently Check Concurrent Programs Under Relaxed Memory Models in Maude?

Yehia Abd Alrahman[1], Marina Andric[1], Alessandro Beggiato[1],
and Alberto Lluch Lafuente[1,2(✉)]

[1] IMT Institute for Advanced Studies Lucca, Lucca, Italy
[2] DTU Compute, Technical University of Denmark, Lyngby, Denmark
albl@dtu.dk

Abstract. Relaxed memory models offer suitable abstractions of the actual optimizations offered by multi-core architectures and by compilers of concurrent programming languages. Using such abstractions for verification purposes is challenging in part due to their inherent non-determinism which contributes to the state space explosion. Several techniques have been proposed to mitigate those problems so to make verification under relaxed memory models feasible. We discuss how to adopt some of those techniques in a Maude-based approach to language prototyping, and suggest the use of other techniques that have been shown successful for similar verification purposes.

1 Introduction

As we enter the so called *multi-core era*, electronic devices made of multiple computational units that work over shared memory are becoming more and more ubiquitous. The demand of performance on such systems is likewise increasing but, unfortunately, *the free lunch is over* [1,2], that is, it is getting harder and harder to develop more performant and energy efficient single computational units. This has lead compiler constructors and hardware designers to develop sophisticated optimization techniques that in some cases may affect the intended semantics of programs. A prominent example are optimizations that give up memory consistency to accelerate memory operations. Typically, such optimizations do not affect the meaning of sequential programs, but the situation is different for concurrent programs as different threads may have subtly different (inconsistent) views of the shared memory and thus their execution may result in an unexpected (non-sequentially consistent) behaviour.

As a motivating example, consider the pseudocode in Fig. 1 which may be seen as the initial part of Dekker's algorithm for mutual exclusion. There are two threads, 1 (left) and 2 (right), whose programs are symmetric. Initially, all variables are assumed to have value 0. When thread 1 tries to enter the critical section it sets `flag1` to 1, and checks the value of `flag2`. If the value for `flag2`

Research supported by the European projects IP 257414 ASCENS and STReP 600708 QUANTICOL, and the Italian PRIN 2010LHT4KM CINA.

S. Escobar (Ed.): WRLA 2014, LNCS 8663, pp. 21–41, 2014.
DOI: 10.1007/978-3-319-12904-4_2

$$\left[\begin{array}{l} \texttt{flag1 := 1} \\ \texttt{if (flag2 = 0) then} \\ \quad \texttt{//critical section} \end{array}\right] \quad \left[\begin{array}{l} \texttt{flag2 := 1} \\ \texttt{if (flag1 = 0) then} \\ \quad \texttt{//critical section} \end{array}\right]$$

Fig. 1. Can both threads enter the critical section?

is 0, it assumes that thread 2 has not yet attempted to enter the critical section and proceeds to enter it. Thread 2 proceeds similarly. Under the usual model of shared memory (i.e. sequential consistency) the algorithm guarantees mutual exclusion: either one thread enters the critical section or none of them does. However, under some of the mentioned relaxations of memory consistency, it is possible for both threads to enter the critical section. Indeed, as we shall see, it may be also the case that updates on memory are delayed, so that both threads execute their updates and then read the old value 0 on each other's flag, proceeding then together into the critical section. As a matter of fact, a direct implementation of the above algorithm on Intel or AMD x86 multiprocessors yields an incorrect program.

As we shall see, many authors have developed formal semantics for these optimizations which relax the standard sequential consistency of programs. Very often this has been done by defining appropriate abstract models of shared memory called *relaxed memory models*. Using such abstractions for verification purposes is challenging in part since they introduce yet another source of nondeterminism, thus contributing to the state space explosion.

As an example consider the graph in Fig. 2. The vertical axis presents the size of the state space in terms of number of states while in the horizontal axis we have the results obtained on 1-entry versions of four mutual exclusion algorithms (Dekker, Peterson, Lamport and Szymanski) and, for each of them, three cases: the algorithm under the usual sequential consistency memory model (Sc), and two versions of the algorithms under a relaxed memory model (namely, Tso). The first of

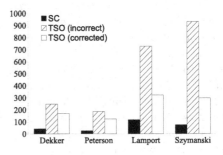

Fig. 2. State-Space Size: Sc vs Tso

these relaxed versions is incorrect, while the second one is a correct variant obtained by adding some synchronization points referred as *fences*. The results provide evidence of the state space increase due to relaxed memory models, even in the case of correct algorithms. The situation is worse if one considers that even the simple program `while true do x:=0` has an infinite state space under some memory models.

Several verification techniques that have been proposed to mitigate those problems in the last years aimed at making verification under relaxed memory models feasible. Some of them are described and discussed in Sects. 2 and 5. Unfortunately, those techniques are sometimes language- or model-specific and not directly applicable in the verification tasks typical of language design activities. We adopt in this work the perspective of a language designer who is willing to prototype a new language for concurrent programs under some relaxed memory model. We assume that the language designer has chosen Maude as a framework due to its suitability both as a *semantic framework* where different styles (SOS, CHAM, K, etc.) can be easily adopted [3] and as a *verification framework* featuring several tools (e.g. reachability analysis, LTL model checking, etc.). We assume that the language designer is interested in performing simple verification tasks using Maude's `search` command for the sake of testing the semantics of the language being prototyped by checking reachability properties of concurrent programs. We further assume that he is certainly not willing to modify Maude's engine for the sake of a more efficient verification and would rather resort to verification optimizations that can be realized in Maude itself. We assume that he is not willing to implement an existing technique before the language is mature enough for the development of sophisticated applications that will require state-of-the art verification techniques.

We discuss in this paper how to adopt in Maude some simple techniques to optimize the verification of concurrent programs under relaxed memory models. Some of the techniques are based or inspired by approaches to the verification of relaxed memory models or by other approaches that have been shown to be successful for similar verification purposes. We start the paper by providing in Sect. 2 a gentle introduction to relaxed memory models, mainly aimed at readers not familiar with this topic. We next introduce in Sect. 3 a running example consisting of the language PIMP, a simple language for concurrent programs, for which we provide a relaxed semantics. In Sect. 4 we discuss three families of techniques for mitigating the state space explosion due to relaxed memory models: approximations (Sect. 4.2), partial-orders (Sect. 4.3) and search strategies (Sect. 4.4). Last we discuss some of the most relevant verification techniques for relaxed memory models in Sect. 5 and draw some concluding remarks and future research in Sect. 6.

2   Relaxed Memory Models

A *memory consistency model* is a formal specification of the semantics of a shared memory, which can be a hardware-based shared-memory multiprocessor or a large-scale distributed storage. In what follows we will mainly refer to the former due to the focus on concurrent programing in our paper, but some of the inherent ideas apply to distributed settings as well. The simplest and, arguably, the most intuitive memory model is *sequential consistency* which can be seen as an extension of the uniprocessor model to multiple processors. As defined by Lamport [4], a multiprocessor is sequentially consistent if the result of any execution is the same as if the operations of all the processors were executed in some sequential order, and the operations of each individual processor appear in this sequence in the order specified by its program. Such model imposes two requirements: (1) *write atomicity*, that is, memory operations must execute atomically with respect to each other and (2) *total program order*, which means that program order is maintained between operations from individual processors.

Sequential consistency provides a clear and well-understood model of shared memory to programmers but, on the other hand, it may affect the performance of concurrent programs since it constrains many common hardware and compiler optimizations. For instance, a common hardware optimization one can consider are write buffers with bypass capability which are used to mitigate the latency of write operations. The idea is that when a processor wants to perform a write operation, it inserts it into a write buffer and continues executing without waiting for the write to be completed. In a multiprocessor system each processor may buffer its write operations thus allowing subsequent read operations to bypass the write as long as the addresses being read differ from the address of any of the buffered writes. This clearly leads to a violation of total program order and write atomicity and hence the resulting programs are no more sequentially consistent.

Relaxed memory models provide an abstraction of the result of applying similar consistency-relaxing optimizations. If we let $X, Y \in \{Read, Write\}$, then *X-to-Y* denotes the relaxation that allows to violate the program order by performing a Y operation before an X operation that appears before in the program. The instances of this relaxation are *Write-to-Read*, *Write-to-Write*, *Read-to-Read* and *Read-to-Write*. Two common relaxations of write atomicity are *Read other's write early*, which allows a read operation to return the value of another processor's write before the write is made visible to all other processors, and *Read own's write early* which allows a read operation to return the value of its own previous write, before it is made visible to other processors.

Figure 3 depicts a hierarchy of memory models [5] and how they relate to each other based the relaxations they allow. The strictest model is sequential consistency (Sc) which does not allow any relaxation. In the second category fall *total store order* (Tso), *processor consistency* (PC) and IBM-370 as they allow the *Write-to-Read* relaxation, all other program orders are maintained. The third category comprises of *partial store order* (Pso) that allows both

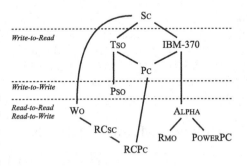

Fig. 3. Hierarchy of relaxations

Write-to-Read and *Write-to-Write* relaxations. The models at the bottom of the hierarchy also allow *Read-to-Read* and *Read-to-Write* reorderings and hence are the least strict.

The formalization of memory models has been mainly motivated by the fact that many processor vendors often do not provide clear architectural specifications of the underlying memory models [6]. Instead, the documentation is typically given in (sometimes ambiguous) informal prose, which makes it hard to program above or to reason about. The formalization of memory models has been tackled by several authors in different styles: e.g. axiomatic and operational. Some examples are the axiomatic x86-Tso model [7], which is sound with respect to the Intel and AMD architectures, the axiomatic models for Java and C++ languages [8,9], and the operational models of relaxed memories for programming languages [10,11]. It is also worth to remark the efforts towards unifying frameworks to capture most memory models [12] and the theory of memory models of [13].

We focus in this work on the Tso model which we introduce first informally, following the usual operational description based on the architectural view depicted in Fig. 4: (i) each processor has a write buffer for storing write operations, and each processor corresponds to one thread; (ii) a thread that performs a read operation must read its most recent buffered write if there is one, otherwise reads are taken from shared memory; (iii) a thread can see its own writes before they are made visible to other threads by committing the pending writes to

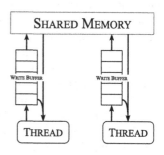

Fig. 4. Tso architecture

memory; (iv) delayed updates are committed from the buffer to the memory non-deterministically by the multiprocessor system, one-by-one and respecting their arrival order; (v) the programmer can use the `mfence` instruction to wait until a buffer is fully committed, so to enforce memory order between preceding and succeeding instructions. The next section will present a formal semantics of a language running under this memory model.

3   A Simple Language with Relaxed Concurrency

We introduce in this section a simple language called PIMP that we shall use as a case study and as a running example. Basically, PIMP is a simple imperative language reminiscent of the WHILE and IMP languages [14] enriched with some few concurrency features including shared memory communication, and blocking wait and fence operations. In few words, PIMP allows one to specify sequential threads that communicate over shared memory.

Definition 1 (threads). *The programs of* PIMP *threads are terms generated by S in the following grammar:*

$$S ::= skip \mid x := u \mid mfence \mid S \ ; \ S' \mid if\ B\ then\ S\ else\ S' \mid while\ B\ do\ S \mid wait\ B$$

were $\mathcal{X}$ is a set of variables, $x \in \mathcal{X}$, $u \in \mathbb{N}$ and B is a Boolean expression on $\mathcal{X}$.

Most of the syntactic constructs of the language are rather standard. We just mention here the `mfence` primitive (used to block a thread until its local view of memory is consistent) and the `wait` primitive (used to specify blocking guards). The construct `skip` is used to denote (immaterial) complete computations.

Definition 2 (programs). *The programs of* PIMP *are terms generated by* T *in the following grammar:*

$$P ::= \langle T, M \rangle \qquad\qquad T ::= [S \,/\, N]_i \mid T \parallel T'$$
$$N ::= \emptyset \mid x \mapsto u \mid N \bullet N \qquad M ::= \emptyset \mid x \mapsto u \mid M, M$$

where $x \in \mathcal{X}$, *and* $i, u \in \mathbb{N}$.

Programs are obtained by the parallel composition of sequential threads (denoted by juxtaposition). Each thread is indexed with a unique identifier i. Such identifier is later used to ease the presentation of some concepts but we often drop it when unnecessary. Each thread comes equipped with a (possibly empty) local memory N made of a composition of memory updates. In the case of TSO, N models a buffer. Programs are turned into *program configurations* (i.e. terms generated by P) by equipping them with a shared memory M, which we assume to denote a function $M \in (\mathcal{X} \twoheadrightarrow \mathbb{N})$ which may be partial on $\mathcal{X}$ but is certainly total on the variables of the program. In the definition above $\_,\_$ is considered to be associative, commutative and idempotent with $\emptyset$ as identity and with no two maps on the same variable. We shall also use the concept of *thread configuration*, i.e. tuples $\langle S, N, M \rangle$, where S is the program of the thread, N is its local memory (buffer), and M is the global (shared) memory. Thread configurations ease the presentation of the semantics, by allowing us to focus on individual threads thanks to the interleaving semantics of parallel composition.

Memory Views. An important concept that eases the presentation of the semantics is the *memory view*, which allow us to formalize the thread's local view on memory. More precisely, threads perceive memory as a particular composition of the shared memory M and their local memory N. We shall see that in the case of the SC model there is in practice no local memory, and threads will only perceive M as the available memory. In the case of TSO, the thread's view on memory will be $M \circ M'$, where M' is obtained by rewriting N as a set (denoted $N \to_{\mathcal{F}} M'$) and $\circ$ is a composition operation defined by

$$M \circ \emptyset = M$$
$$(M, x \mapsto u) \circ (M', x \mapsto v) = (M, x \mapsto v) \circ M'$$
$$M \circ (M', x \mapsto v) = (M, x \mapsto v) \circ M' \qquad \text{if } M(x) = \bot$$

Rewriting a local memory N as a memory M is formalized by the following rule to be applied top-down

$$\frac{N \longrightarrow_{\mathcal{F}} M}{N \bullet x \mapsto u \longrightarrow_{\mathcal{F}} M \circ x \mapsto u}$$

Note that, in principle, $\longrightarrow_{\mathcal{F}}$ has a functional behavior, i.e. for a given local memory N there is only one possible rewrite $N \longrightarrow_{\mathcal{F}} M$. In this case we may use $\mathcal{F}(N)$ to denote M. Later, however, we shall consider variants of local memories where $\bullet$ obeys some axioms and since we consider terms up to structural

Table 1. Rules of the operational semantics of PIMP

$$(\textsc{Par}) \qquad \dfrac{\langle S,N,M\rangle \overset{a}{\longrightarrow}_{\mathcal{M}} \langle S',N',M'\rangle}{\langle [S|N]_i \; T_2,M\rangle \overset{i\vdash a}{\longrightarrow}_{\mathcal{M}} \langle [S'|N']_i \; T_2,M'\rangle}$$

$$(\textsc{Comp}) \qquad \dfrac{\langle S,N,M\rangle \overset{a}{\longrightarrow}_{\mathcal{M}} \langle S'',N',M'\rangle}{\langle S;S',N,M\rangle \overset{a}{\longrightarrow}_{\mathcal{M}} \langle S'' \; ; \; S',N',M'\rangle}$$

$$(\textsc{Skip}) \qquad \dfrac{}{\texttt{skip} \; ; \; S = S}$$

$$(\textsc{IfT}) \qquad \dfrac{N\longrightarrow_{\mathcal{F}} N' \qquad [\![B]\!]_{M\circ N'} = \texttt{true}}{\langle \texttt{if } B \texttt{ then } S \texttt{ else } S',N,M\rangle \overset{\tau}{\longrightarrow}_{\mathcal{M}} \langle S,N,M\rangle}$$

$$(\textsc{IfF}) \qquad \dfrac{N\longrightarrow_{\mathcal{F}} N' \qquad [\![B]\!]_{M\circ N'} = \texttt{false}}{\langle \texttt{if } B \texttt{ then } S \texttt{ else } S',N,M\rangle \overset{\tau}{\longrightarrow}_{\mathcal{M}} \langle S',N,M\rangle}$$

$$(\textsc{WhileT}) \qquad \dfrac{N\longrightarrow_{\mathcal{F}} N' \qquad [\![B]\!]_{M\circ N'} = \texttt{true}}{\langle \texttt{while } B \texttt{ do } S,N,M\rangle \overset{\tau}{\longrightarrow}_{\mathcal{M}} \langle S \; ; \texttt{ while } B \texttt{ do } S,N,M\rangle}$$

$$(\textsc{WhileF}) \qquad \dfrac{N\longrightarrow_{\mathcal{F}} N' \qquad [\![B]\!]_{M\circ N'} = \texttt{false}}{\langle \texttt{while } B \texttt{ do } S,N,M\rangle \overset{\tau}{\longrightarrow}_{\mathcal{M}} \langle \texttt{skip},N,M\rangle}$$

$$(\textsc{Wait}) \qquad \dfrac{N\longrightarrow_{\mathcal{F}} N' \qquad [\![B]\!]_{M\circ N'} = \texttt{true}}{\langle \texttt{wait } B,N,M\rangle \overset{\tau}{\longrightarrow}_{\mathcal{M}} \langle \texttt{skip},N,M\rangle}$$

$$(\textsc{AssSc}) \qquad \dfrac{}{\langle \texttt{x := u},\emptyset,M\rangle \overset{\texttt{x := u}}{\longrightarrow}_{\textsc{Sc}} \langle \texttt{skip},\emptyset,M\circ(\texttt{x} \mapsto u)\rangle}$$

$$(\textsc{AssTso}) \qquad \dfrac{}{\langle \texttt{x := u},N,M\rangle \overset{\texttt{x := u}}{\longrightarrow}_{\textsc{Tso}} \langle \texttt{skip},N\bullet(\texttt{x} \mapsto u),M\rangle}$$

$$(\textsc{Commit}) \qquad \dfrac{}{\langle S,(\texttt{x} \mapsto u)\bullet N,M\rangle \overset{\tau}{\longrightarrow}_{\mathcal{M}} \langle S,N,M\circ(\texttt{x} \mapsto u)\rangle}$$

$$(\textsc{Mfence}) \qquad \dfrac{}{\langle \texttt{mfence},\emptyset,M\rangle \overset{\tau}{\longrightarrow}_{\mathcal{M}} \langle \texttt{skip},\emptyset,M\rangle}$$

equivalence $\longrightarrow_{\mathcal{F}}$ may have a non-functional behavior. An example of this will be used later to model non-deterministic evaluations of Boolean expressions for abstract local memories, where $\bullet$ enjoys the axioms of sets.

PIMP *Semantics.* The semantics of PIMP under a memory model $\mathcal{M} \in \{\textsc{Sc}, \textsc{Tso}\}$ is a labeled transition system whose states are program configurations and whose transitions $\rightarrow_{\mathcal{M}} \subseteq P \times A \times P$ are defined by the rules of Table 1. In the presented rules, program and thread configurations are to be intended up to a structural equivalence relation induced by the axiomatization of programs as multisets of threads (i.e. juxtaposition $\_ \, \_$ is AC), memories as sets of updates (i.e. memory composition $\_,\_$ is ACI with identity $\emptyset$) and buffers as lists of updates (i.e. buffer composition $\_\bullet\_$ is A with identity $\emptyset$). The labels in A are used for the only purpose of decorating the semantics with information that will be useful in the verification techniques presented in later sections. At this point it is sufficient to understand that A contains labels of the form $i \vdash a$, where i is either a thread or buffer identifier and a is some action associated to the rules of the semantics, essentially used to record in some cases the statement associated to the transition. Label τ is used to denote some transition whose origin is not relevant. We sometimes drop labels from transitions.

Rule PAR is the only rule for program configurations and specifies the interleaving semantics of the language. The rest of the rules specify then how individual threads evolve independently based on (and possibly modifying) the shared memory M and their local buffer N. Rule COMP is defined as usual. It is however worth to remark that `skip` is treated as the left identity of sequential composition to get rid of completed executions. The semantics of control flow constructs is rather standard and defined by rules IFT, IFF, WHILET and WHILEF. Such rules are defined in a big-step style, i.e. the evaluation of a binary expression B in some local view of memory M', denoted by $[\![B]\!]_{M'}$ is performed atomically as one thread transition. It is worth to remark that such evaluation is done based on the thread's view of the available memory (i.e. $M \circ N'$). Note that in the case of SC, N' is always $\emptyset$ so that threads observe M directly. Rule WAIT specifies the semantics of the `wait` primitive which blocks the execution until the binary condition B holds. The evaluation of the binary condition B is done in the same manner as for control flow constructs. The semantics of assignments depends on the memory model under consideration. We actually consider two cases defined respectively by rules ASSSC (for SC) and ASSTSO (for TSO). Rule ASSIGNSC is as usual: an update is directly performed on the shared memory M. In the case of TSO, the story is totally different. Indeed, rule ASSTSO models the fact that updates are delayed by appending them to the thread's buffer N. The delayed updates in the buffers can be non-deterministically committed to memory in the order in which they arrived. This is specified by rule COMMIT. A memory commit consists in removing the update $(\mathtt{x} \mapsto u)$ at the beginning of the write buffer of any thread and updating the value of variable $\mathtt{x}$ in memory. Finally, rule MFENCE specifies the semantics of the `mfence` primitive, which blocks the thread until its write buffer becomes empty.

We assume that the reader has some familiarity with the canonical approaches to encode operational semantic styles in rewriting logic and Maude are detailed [3]. We hence do not provide a detailed explanation on how to specify a Maude interpreter for PIMP. In few words, the main idea is to specify a rewrite theory $\mathcal{R}_{\text{PIMP}} = \langle \Sigma, E \cup A, R \rangle$ as a Maude module where (i) signature Σ models syntactic categories as sorts and contains all function symbols used in terms, (ii) equations and axioms $E \cup A$ model the above mentioned structural equivalence on terms, and (iii) rules R model the rules of the operational semantics. The obtained encoding is faithful in the sense that there is a one-to-one correspondence between transitions and 1-step rewrites of configuration-sorted terms.

4   Tackling the State Space Explosion

This section presents a number of techniques to tackle the state space explosion caused by relaxed memory models. More precisely, Sect. 4.2 deals with approximation techniques, focusing mostly in avoiding the generation of infinite state spaces due to the potentially unlimited growth of store buffers; Sect. 4.3 presents a partial order reduction technique aimed at reducing the number of interleavings introduced by the non-deterministic nature of relaxed memory models, and Sect. 4.4 discusses heuristic search strategies that can be adopted in order to detect bugs in a more efficient way by guiding the search towards error states and thus exploring a smaller portion of the state space.

4.1 Preliminaries

We introduce here some basic notation that we shall use in the rest of this section. First, we shall consider Kripke structures as semantic model for verification problems. These are obtained as usual, i.e. by enriching transition systems with observations on states, so to abstract away from concrete representation of states (as program configurations) and by restricting to reachable configurations only.

Definition 3 ($\mathcal{M}$-Kripke structure). *An $\mathcal{M}$-Kripke structure is a Kripke structure $(S, s_0, \rightarrow, \mathcal{L}, AP, \mathcal{M})$ where: $S \subseteq P$ is the set of s_0-reachable configurations, i.e. $\{s \in P \mid s_0 \rightarrow^*_{\mathcal{M}} s\}$; $s_0 \in P$ is the initial state; $\rightarrow \subseteq S \times A \times S$ is a transition relation defined as $(P \times A \times P) \cap \rightarrow_{\mathcal{M}}$, i.e. the restriction of $\rightarrow_{\mathcal{M}}$ to reachable states; $\mathcal{L} : S \rightarrow 2^{AP}$ a labeling function for the states; AP is a set of atomic propositions; and $\mathcal{M} \in \{\textsc{Tso}, \textsc{Sc}\}$ is a memory model.*

$\mathcal{M}$-Kripke structures are like ordinary Kripke structures with an explicit reference to the underlying memory model $\mathcal{M}$ and the corresponding transition system semantics $\rightarrow_{\mathcal{M}}$. In what follows we shall often fix $\mathcal{M}$ to be $\textsc{Tso}$ unless stated otherwise. We shall also use the term *initial Kripke structure* for some program T to denote some Kripke structure whose initial state is an *initial configuration* $\langle T, M \rangle$, i.e. a configuration where M maps all variables of T to 0.

Some of the techniques we shall consider allow us to obtain for a given Kripke structure another (possibly smaller one) which is semantically related. We assume familiarity with the usual notions of state-based equivalences and preorders, such as weak/strong (bi)simulation and (stuttering) trace equivalence. Those semantic relations with respect to the observations on states specified by the labelling function $\mathcal{L}$ and the proposed techniques depend on the properties of $\mathcal{L}$. For a labelling function $\mathcal{L}$ we denote by $\equiv_{\mathcal{L}} \subseteq P \times P$ the equivalence relation on program configurations induced by labelling equality. Often, we shall require that $\mathcal{L}$ cannot distinguish states identified by some other equivalence relation R, i.e. that $\equiv_{\mathcal{L}} \supseteq R$. For example, consider the smallest congruence relation induced by axiom $[S, N] = [S, N']$, denoted $\equiv_{[S,N]=[S,N']}$, which identifies program configurations up to their local memories. Then requiring $\equiv_{\mathcal{L}} \supseteq \equiv_{[S,N]=[S,N']}$ amounts to require that $\mathcal{L}$ cannot observe local memories.

4.2 Approximations

Consider the simple sequential thread $p \triangleq$ while true do x:=0 and the initial configuration $s = \langle [p \mid \emptyset], x \mapsto 0 \rangle$. Any initial Kripke structure $(S, s, \rightarrow, \mathcal{L}, AP, \textsc{Sc})$ is clearly finite-state and just composed of state s with a self loop $s \rightarrow s$. However, the same program under TSO has an infinite state space, i.e. Kripke structures $(S, s, \rightarrow, \mathcal{L}, AP, \textsc{Tso})$ have infinitely many states since it is possible to iterate the body of the while infinitely many times, each time adding an entry to the buffer: $s \rightarrow \langle [x:=0;p \mid \emptyset], x \mapsto 0 \rangle \rightarrow \langle [p \mid x \mapsto 0], x \mapsto 0 \rangle \rightarrow \langle [x:=0;p \mid x \mapsto 0], x \mapsto 0 \rangle \rightarrow \langle [p \mid x \mapsto 0 \bullet x \mapsto 0], x \mapsto 0 \rangle \rightarrow \ldots$ The unbounded growth of buffers is indeed one of the most challenging issues in the verification of concurrent programs under relaxed memory models and several approaches have been proposed in the literature as we shall discuss later in Sect. 5. In this section we discuss one simple approach that one may easily adopt in Maude. For the sake of illustration we present as well some simple ideas that cannot be easily turned into useful sound approximations.

Simple Approximations. We shall consider in this section a simple approach to realize approximations based on equating program configurations. This kind of approximations can be easily implemented in Maude by language designers since they require minimal changes in the formal specification of the language, such as changing the equational attributes of some function symbols or introducing some equations. Moreover, the Maude literature offers approaches, such as equational abstractions [15] and c-reductions [16], to realize such kind of approximations in a disciplined way, and to use possibly tool-based proof techniques to prove their soundness and eventually correct them.

In this paper we will essentially follow an approach based on equational abstractions [15]. The main idea is to consider some axioms A of the form $t = t'$ where t, t' are terms denoting part of the program or thread configurations. Such laws will then be then used to specify a rewrite theory $R_{\text{PIMP}/A}$ which specifies the approximated semantics. This is realized in Maude by introducing the axioms of A as equational attributes or as equations in R_{PIMP}, the Maude specification of PIMP. The effect is that for a Kripke structure K we obtain an approximated Kripke structure K_A that, under some reasonable conditions on $\mathcal{L}$ (e.g. not being able to distinguish states identified by A), should simulate K. In some cases concrete transitions may not have an approximated counterpart, a situation that we can repair by introducing additional rules in the semantics. The final effect of the approximations is that more states will be identified thus resulting in smaller state spaces.

Buffers as Ordered Maps. Let us start considering the following simple approach to get rid of the unbounded growth of TSO buffers. The idea is to keep in the buffer just the latest update for each variable removing older updates. The rationale would be that by doing so we still preserve the order of write operations and all write operations will certainly have their chance to be committed to memory. We are just forbidding to delay updates on the same variable too much. This can be formalized by considering the following simple equation

$$\text{OM} \triangleq (x \mapsto u) \bullet N \bullet (x \mapsto v) = N \bullet (x \mapsto v)$$

The question is whether this would result in a useful approximation. We shall see that this is not the case. Let us consider first the PIMP program T in Fig. 5(a) and let K be some initial Kripke structure for it. It is easy to see that in K it is not possible to reach a state in which z takes the value 1, while this is possible in K_{OM}. The reason is, of course, that there exists an approximated execution in which the commit of $(x \mapsto 1)$ is discarded, and thus never visible to the second thread. For the same reason deadlock states can be introduced as well.

Of course, obtaining new *spurious* behaviors is usual when considering over-approximations. However, one would expect then that no concrete behavior is lost.

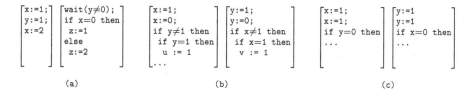

Fig. 5. Some concurrent programs

We can also observe that this is unfortunately not the case. Consider, a concurrent program T of the form in Fig. 5(b) and some initial Kripke structure K for it. It is easy to see that in K we can reach a configuration where both u and v have value 1. This can happen if both threads perform and delay their first two assignments, then enter the first branch of their first if statement, then commit their first pending write and finally enter the first branch of their second if statement thus proceeding to the update of u and v. Such behavior is however not possible in K_{OM}. Essentially, the considered approximation implies a loss of information that could only be recovered by considering an approximated semantics that would take into account all potentially (infinitely many) pending updates that could have been removed. Therefore, while simple, the idea of removing old updates from buffers is unlikely to provide a useful approximation.

Forced-commit Approximation. Let us consider now a similar idea, based on handling updates on the same variables in a slightly different way. Suppose we allow more than one update on the same variable with one exception: if the head of the buffer is an update $x \mapsto u$ on a variable x for which there is another update $x \mapsto v$ on the tail of the buffer, we remove the update $x \mapsto u$ but this time we commit it to memory. This time the equation under consideration is

$$\mathrm{Fc} \triangleq \langle P, (x \mapsto u) \bullet N \bullet (x \mapsto v), M \rangle = \langle P, N \bullet (x \mapsto v), M \circ (x \mapsto u) \rangle$$

Can we exploit Fc to build a useful approximation? It can be shown that under some reasonable constraints on $\mathcal{L}$ no observable behavior is introduced, but unfortunately, this approximation does not solve the problem of infinite state spaces as illustrated by the simple program y:=0; while true do x:=0. Clearly, there is an execution that delays and never commits the pending update $(y \mapsto 0)$ while cumulating repeated updates $(x \mapsto 0)$. Moreover, this approximation loses some behaviours. This can be seen by a program T such as the one in Fig. 5(c). In the initial Kripke structure K for T, it is possible for both threads to execute the **then** branch of the if statement. However, in the corresponding approximated Kripke structure K_{FC} it is no longer possible to reach a state in which both threads execute the **then** branch of the if statement.

Buffers as Set of Updates. What would then be a simple and still sound approximation? A simple idea to get rid of multiple copies of a same commit in a buffer is to approximate the buffer with a set of updates. This amounts to consider those axioms Us that make the $\bullet$ operation become associative, commutative and idempotent, with identity $\emptyset$. Even if it may seem that we are again losing information, in particular about the order and multiplicity of pending updates, this is not exactly true. The reason is that now the evaluation of expressions automatically becomes non-deterministic due to the non-deterministic nature of $\rightarrow_{\mathcal{F}}$ that would consider all possible orderings among updates. What is left is the multiplicity of updates, which can be easily handled by introducing the rule

$$(\textsc{CommitUs})\ \ \langle S,(\mathrm{x}\ \mapsto\ \mathrm{u})\bullet N,M\rangle\ \xrightarrow{\tau}_{\textsc{Tso}}\ \langle S,(\mathrm{x}\ \mapsto\ \mathrm{u})\bullet N,M\circ(\mathrm{x}\ \mapsto\ \mathrm{u})\rangle$$

in the semantics. The rationale is that any update can be committed to memory but still kept in the buffer as it may represent an arbitrary number of copies of the same update. An advantage of this approximation is that it can be easily realized in Maude by changing the equational attributes of $\bullet$ and by adding a rule modeling rule CommitUs. The obtained approximation may exhibit "spurious" behaviours, but we are guaranteed to not miss any concrete behaviour provided that we do not want to observe too much information on states.

Proposition 1. *Let K be a* Tso-*Kripke structure whose labeling function $\mathcal{L}$ is such that $\equiv_{\mathcal{L}} \supseteq \equiv_{[S,N]=S[S,N']}$. Then K_{Us} simulates K.*

Experiments. Figure 6 presents the results of some of our experiments. The vertical axis corresponds to the size of the state space in terms of number of states. In the horizontal axis we have our four mutual exclusion algorithms and, for each of them, the result obtained without (1st column) and with the above discussed approximations: Om (2nd column), Fc (3rd column), and Us

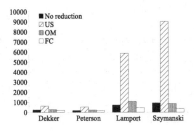

Fig. 6. Approximated state spaces

(4th column). Clearly, not all explorations make sense since some of the approximations are unsound or incomplete but we included them here for a more comprehensive presentation of our experiments. The most relevant observation is that simple approximations such as Us, do provide finite state spaces but may enormously contribute to the state space explosion. This is evident in the considered mutual exclusion programs which are finite-state since they are 1-entry instances of the algorithms (i.e. with no loop). Section 5 discusses several sophisticated techniques that can provide more efficient approximations.

4.3   Partial-Order Reduction

As we have seen, relaxed memory models introduce a large amount of non-determinism in the state space of concurrent programs. In the case of the Tso, this is due to the introduction of buffers, which delay updates that are non-deterministically committed at any time. Such non-determinism may lead to an increase of the interleaving of actions some of which may be equivalent. A popular and successful family of techniques to cope with this problem is *Partial Order Reduction* (POR) [17–19]. These techniques have been extended and implemented in several ways and are often part of the optimization features of verification tools such as model checkers, and they have been already successfully applied in the verification of programs under relaxed memory models [20,21].

POR in Maude. An easy way to adopt POR in Maude-based verification is to instantiate the generic language-independent approach described in [22], that we shall refer to as PORM. The method discharges relatively little requirements on a language designer: (i) a formal executable specification of the semantics of the programming language L under consideration (PIMP in our case) as a rewrite theory $\mathcal{R}_L$ satisfying some reasonable conditions explained below, and (ii) the specification of some properties of the language (e.g. an approximation of dependencies between actions). The latter, of course, may require some manual proof. The advantages of the method are that no additional proof is needed to guarantee the correctness of the approach, and that no change in the underlying verification capabilities of Maude are necessary.

We recall that the main idea underlying the ample set approach to POR [18], considered in PORM, is to prune *redundant* parts of the state space, avoiding the exploration of paths that do not bring additional information. This is done by considering at each state s a subset of its successors called *ample* set. For presentation purposes, we recall now some useful definitions. Let K be the Kripke structure under consideration. We denote with *enabled*(s) the set of all the enabled transitions in state $s \in S$, i.e. *enabled*(s) = $\{s \xrightarrow{\alpha} s'\}$. We sometimes use the notation $t(s)$ to denote the target s' of transition $t = s \xrightarrow{\alpha} s'$. Two fundamental concepts in POR are those of *invisibility* of actions and *independence* between actions and between transitions.

Definition 4 (invisibility). *Let K be a Kripke structure. A transition $s \xrightarrow{\alpha} s'$ is invisible in K iff $\mathcal{L}(s) = \mathcal{L}(s')$. Similarly, an action α is invisible if all transitions $s \xrightarrow{\alpha} s'$ are invisible.*

Definition 5 (independence). *Two transition t_0, t_1 are independent if for each state s such that $t_0 \in$ enabled(s) and $t_1 \in$ enabled(s) it holds: $t_1 \in$ enabled($t_0(s)$), $t_0 \in$ enabled($t_1(s)$), and $t_0(t_1(s)) = t_1(t_0(s))$. We define the independence relation $\mathcal{I} \subseteq T \times T$ as $\{(t_0, t_1) \mid t_0$ and t_1 are independent$\}$.*

In words, independent transitions do not disable each other, and their execution commutes. If two transitions are not independent, we say that they are *dependent*. We let $\mathcal{D}$ be simply defined as $\mathcal{D} = (T \times T) \setminus \mathcal{I}$.

Instantiating PORM to PIMP. We recall that the PORM approach imposes some restrictions on the language under consideration as well as on the approximation of the dependency relation. The conditions on the language are: *"(1) In each program there are entities equivalent to threads, or processes, which can be uniquely identified by a thread identifier. The computation is performed as the combination of local computations inside individual threads, and communication between these threads through any possible discipline such as shared memory, synchronous and asynchronous message passing, and so on. (2) In any computational step (transition) a single thread is always involved. In other words, threads are the entities that carry out the computations in the system. (3) Each thread has at most one transition enabled at any moment."* Clearly, PIMP satisfies those conditions by viewing buffers as independent computation entities (whose only actions are to commit updates to memory).

The strategies to compute ample sets discussed in [22] guarantee correctness given that the language designer provides a safe approximation of dependencies between transitions, and a correct specification of visibility. Regarding visibility, the idea we propose here for PIMP relies on the fact that, as long as the properties of interest do not concern the local memories or the program itself, all the transitions caused by assignments are invisible. This leads to the first lemma needed to ensure the correct instantiation of the PORM approach.

Lemma 1 (invisibility of assignments). *Let K be a Kripke structure. If $\mathcal{L}$ is such that $\equiv_\mathcal{L} \supseteq \equiv_{[S,N]=[S',N']}$ then all actions $\alpha = i \vdash x := u$ are invisible in K.*

Furthermore, it is easy to convince ourselves that the only way a transition could be dependent on an assignment transition, is to be generated by the execution of an instruction of the same thread following the assignment itself. Indeed, we hence define the following over-approximation of $\mathcal{D}$.

Definition 6 (dependency approximation). *Let K be a Kripke structure and let $F \subseteq A \times A$ be the relation on actions made of all pairs of actions (α, β) or (β, α) such that $\alpha = (i \vdash x := u)$, $\beta = (j \vdash a)$ and $i \neq j$. We define $D \subseteq T \times T$ as the set $(T \times T) \setminus \{(s \xrightarrow{\alpha} s', s'' \xrightarrow{\beta} s''') \mid (\alpha, \beta) \in F\}$.*

Lemma 2 (approximation of dependency). *Let K be a Kripke structure. We have $\mathcal{D} \subseteq D$.*

Of course, D is a very simple and coarse approximation but it serves well our illustrative purposes and can be easily implemented. Indeed, the simplest strategy of PORM consists of considering single transitions as candidates for ample sets. For a single transition t to be accepted as ample set it must be invisible (C2 in [22]), such that no other thread has a transition in the future that is dependent on t (C1' in [22]) and should not close a cycle in the state space (C3 in [22]). In our case, our approximation of dependency makes transitions corresponding to assignments obvious candidates. If we denote by $ample : P \to 2^P$ the function computing ample sets that the simplest strategy of PORM implements and if we let $K = (S, s_0, \to, \mathcal{L}, AP, \mathcal{M})$ be an $\mathcal{M}$-Kripke structure, then the PORM reduction of K is $K_{\text{PORM}} = (S, s_0, \to \cap \{(s, s') \mid s' \in ample(s)\}, \mathcal{L}, AP, \mathcal{M})$.

Proposition 2 (Soundness). *Let K be a Kripke structure whose labeling function $\mathcal{L}$ is such that $\equiv_\mathcal{L} \supseteq \equiv_{[S,N]=[S',N']}$, then K and K_{PORM} are stuttering bisimilar.*

The correctness of Proposition 2 trivially follows from Theorem 1 of [22] and Lemmas 1 and 2.

Experiments. Figure 7 presents the results of our experiments. The vertical axis corresponds to the size of the state space in terms of number of states. In the horizontal axis we have our four mutual exclusion algorithms and, for each of them, the result obtained without (left) and with (right) POR. The obtained result provides evidence of the advantages of applying POR even in the simple form presented here.

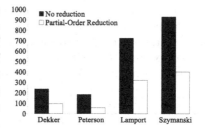

Fig. 7. Reduction with POR

4.4 Search Strategies

Verification tools based on explicit-state state space traversal often use quite simple but efficient search algorithms based on depth-first and breadth-first strategies. This is indeed the case of the standard verification capabilities of Maude: the search command performs a breadth-first search traversal of the state space of a rewrite theory, while the Maude LTL model checker [23] applies the usual nested depth-first search algorithm for checking emptiness of ω-regular languages. However, as many authors have noticed, using *smart* search strategies can provide better verification performances, both in the time and the memory consumed by the verification tool. The application of such techniques is often known in the model checking community by *directed model checking*, a term originally coined in [24], and made popular by its adoption in several model checkers such as SPIN [25] and Java Path Finder [26].

The main idea underlying such techniques is the use of search algorithms whose exploration strategy depends on some heuristics that aim at exploring a portion of the state space that is as small as possible for the required verification task. The archetypal example is the use of standard AI algorithms such as A* and best-first search in combination with heuristics that rank the states according to their likelihood to lead to a violation of the property being verified. Bug-finding, indeed, rather than verification, is the killer application of such techniques.

Search strategies are not novel in the Maude community. Indeed, they have been thoroughly investigated in [27]. In the proof-of-concept spirit of this work we have followed a very simple approach to give evidence of the advantages of using heuristically guided search algorithms in the verification of concurrent programs under relaxed memory models. In particular, we have implemented and evaluated the best-first search algorithm in combination with simple heuristics.

We recall that the best-first search algorithm works by maintaining two sets of states: a set of *closed* states (i.e. visited states whose transitions have been already explored) and a set of *open* states (i.e. visited states whose transitions are yet to be explored). The algorithm starts with an initially empty set of closed states and only the initial state in the open set, and iteratively selects one open state to be *expanded* and moved to the close set. Expanding a state means exploring the states immediately reachable through outgoing transitions and putting them in the open set if they have been never visited before. The choice of the open state to be expanded depends on some heuristic function that ranks the states according to some rationale. Our implementation is rather canonical and exploits the reflective capabilities of the Maude language. Since Maude's meta-level module offers a `metaSearch` command to obtain the outgoing transitions of a state, the implementation of best-first search in a declarative way is almost straightforward.

Our heuristics are inspired by the work of Groce and Visser on so-called *structural* heuristics for directed model checking in the Java Path Finder model checker [26]. Such heuristics are based on inherently structural causes of errors in concurrent software. For instance, some of the heuristics tend to promote the exploration of executions with more context-switches or interleavings with the rationale that programmers tend to think sequentially and bugs such as race conditions often are due to unexpected interleavings. With this spirit we have designed three simple heuristics tailored for finding bugs in concurrent programs to be run under relaxed memory models, all of which map program configurations into natural numbers with the idea that program configurations with higher values are more likely to lead to a bug. The heuristics respectively count the number of non-empty buffers (NEB), the number of pending writes (Pw), i.e. the sum of the sizes of all buffers, and the number of *inconsistent* pending writes (IPW), i.e. the number of pending writes $x \mapsto u$ that map a variable x to a value u different from the value v assigned to x by the shared memory. These heuristics are measures of the level of memory inconsistency.

Figure 8 presents the results of our experiments. As usual, the vertical axis presents the number of states that were explored. In this case we were looking for violations of the mutual exclusion property and the verification stopped once the first violation was found. In the horizontal axis we have our four mutual exclusion algorithms and, for each of them, four cases: the usual breadth-

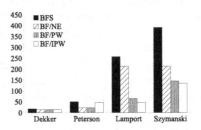

Fig. 8. Bug-finding with heuristics

first (BFS) search and best-first (BF) search in combination with the three heuristics. Without entering into details, the main observation is that the heuristically guided search for errors is in general more space efficient than the standard algorithm. Of course, there is a slight time overhead in our implementation since breadth-first search is implemented in Maude itself (using the meta-level) and the search command is provided by the Maude (C++) engine directly. However, our main point here is to show the potential of heuristically guided search strategies that may be prototyped using the meta-level (as we do here) and eventually implemented as extensions of the Maude engine if high time performance is needed.

5   Related Works

We discuss here some approaches, focusing the discussion on those that have inspired the techniques we have adopted in our case study and describing as well some archetypal examples of alternative techniques.

Partial order reduction techniques have been applied to the verification of concurrent programs under relaxed consistency by several authors. For instance, the authors of [20] use the SPIN model checker and exploit SPIN's POR based on the ample set approach [18], while the authors of [21] combine different techniques (some discussed below) which include an implementation of the persistent set approach to POR [17]. Those works should not be confused with the *partial order* models used [28], whose authors address the problem of program verification under relaxed memory (Tso, Pso, Rmo and Power) by using partial orders to model executions of finite-state programs. Those models are then analyzed using a SAT-based technique called *symbolic decision procedure for partial orders*, implemented in the *Bounded Model Checker for ANSI-C programs (CBMC)* [29]. The key idea is the partial order model, which is a graph whose nodes are the read/write operations of the program and whose directed arcs model the data and control dependency between operations. While the data dependency cannot be relaxed, the control dependency is relaxed according to the memory model under consideration. The absence of undesirable properties (e.g. possibility of reading certain values) is reduced to checking the presence of cycles in the graph.

Several approximation techniques for concurrent programs under relaxed consistency can be found in the literature (e.g. [30–32]). A representative example is described in [33], whose authors propose a verification approach for concurrent programs under Tso. The key idea is to approximate the (possibly unbounded) store buffers in a way that not only makes verification under Tso feasible, but also reduces the reachability problem under Tso to a reachability problem under Sc, thus enabling the use of off-the-shelf Sc analysis tools (as other authors do, e.g. [34]). The approach is based on *context-bounded analysis* [35]. A *context* is a computation segment where only one thread is active. All memory updates within a context are the result of committing delayed updates in the store buffer of the active thread. The authors prove that for every concurrent program P, it is possible to construct another concurrent program P' such that when P' runs under Sc, the reachable states of P' are exactly the same of the reachable states of P running under Tso with at most k context-switches for each thread. Their translation is done with a limited overhead, i.e. a polynomial increase in the size of the original program. The authors show that it is possible to use only a k-dependent fixed number of additional copies of the shared variables as local variables to simulate the store buffers, even if they are unbounded. The key assumption is that each store operation produced by some thread cannot stay in its store buffer for more than a bounded number of context switches of that thread. As a consequence, for a finite-state program, the context-bounded analysis of Tso programs is decidable. Such sort of bounded verification is proposed by other authors and there are also approaches that address the infinite state space by resorting to predicate abstractions (e.g. [36]) or symbolic approaches (see e.g. [37–40])). A prominent example are *buffer automata* [41].

Apart from the already mentioned CBMC [29] several other verification tools have been conceived with the aim of supporting the development of correct and efficient C programs under relaxed memory models. For instance, *Check-Fence* [42] is a tool that statically checks the consistency of a data type implementation for a given bounded test program and memory model (TSO or RMO). The tool checks all concurrent executions of a given C program under relaxed consistency and produces a counterexample if it finds an execution that is not sequentially consistent. Another example is the tool *DFence* [43] which implements a technique that, given a C program, a safety property and a memory model (TSO or PSO), checks for violations of the property and infers fences to constrain problematic reorderings causing the violations. Finally, it is worth mention that the specification of KernelC in the K framework [44] includes as well a x86-TSO semantics of the memory models [45] which allow one to use the K tools (some of which are Maude-based) for verification purposes.

6   Conclusion

This paper addresses one of the problems that a language designer may encounter when prototyping a language for concurrent programs with a weak shared memory model, namely the state space explosion due to relaxed consistency. We have discussed how the flexibility of the Maude framework can be exploited to adopt some efficient verification techniques proposed in the literature. We have essentially focused on reachability analysis, since it plays an important role in the development of concurrent programming languages and programs, not only for verification purposes but also in techniques for automatically porting programs from sequential consistency memories to relaxed ones (e.g. by fence-insertion techniques [21,32,46,47]). The kind of verification techniques we have discussed are approximations, partial order reduction and heuristic search strategies. While approximations and partial order reduction have been proposed before, as far as we know, the use of directed model checking techniques in the domain of relaxed concurrency is a novelty. However, rather than proposing novel verification techniques, our aim was to provide evidence of the flexibility of Maude for adopting techniques that ease verification and language design task in presence of relaxed consistency. We believe that there are still many developments that can be carried out to provide language designers with a powerful verification-based framework, in particular in what regards the automatization of correctness proofs for the adopted verification techniques.

References

1. Sutter, H.: The free lunch is over: a fundamental turn toward concurrency in software. Dr. Dobbs J. **30**(3), 202–210 (2005)

2. Sutter, H., Larus, J.R.: Software and the concurrency revolution. ACM Queue **3**(7), 54–62 (2005)
3. Serbanuta, T.F., Rosu, G., Meseguer, J.: A rewriting logic approach to operational semantics. Inf. Comput. **207**(2), 305–340 (2009)
4. Lamport, L.: How to make a correct multiprocess program execute correctly on a multiprocessor. IEEE Trans. Comput. **46**(7), 779–782 (1997)
5. Memory consistency models, csc/ece 506 spring 2013/10c ks (2013). http://wiki. expertiza.ncsu.edu/index.php/CSC/ECE_506_Spring_2013/10c_ks
6. Zappa Nardelli, F., Sewell, P., Ševčík, J., Sarkar, S., Owens, S., Maranget, L., Batty, M., Alglave, J.: Relaxed memory models must be rigorous. In: Exploiting Concurrency Efficiently and Correctly, CAV 2009 Workshop, June 2009
7. Sewell, P., Sarkar, S., Owens, S., Nardelli, F.Z., Myreen, M.O.: x86-TSO: a rigorous and usable programmer's model for x86 multiprocessors. Commun. ACM **53**(7), 89–97 (2010)
8. Manson, J., Pugh, W., Adve, S.V.: The Java memory model. In: Palsberg, J., Abadi, M. (eds.) POPL, pp. 378–391. ACM (2005)
9. Gupta, R., Amarasinghe, S.P. (eds.) Proceedings of the ACM SIGPLAN 2008 Conference on Programming Language Design and Implementation. ACM, Tucson, 7–13 June 2008
10. Boudol, G., Petri, G.: Relaxed memory models: an operational approach. In: Shao, Z., Pierce, B.C. (eds.) POPL, pp. 392–403. ACM (2009)
11. Petri, G.: Studying operational models of relaxed concurrency. In: Abadi, M., Lluch Lafuente, A. (eds.) TGC 2013. LNCS, vol. 8358, pp. 254–272. Springer, Heidelberg (2014)
12. Adve, S., Hill, M.D.: A unified formalization of four shared-memory models. IEEE Trans. Parallel Distrib. Syst. **4**, 613–624 (1993)
13. Saraswat, V.A., Jagadeesan, R., Michael, M.M., von Praun, C.: A theory of memory models. In: Yelick, K.A., Mellor-Crummey, J.M. (eds.) PPOPP, pp. 161–172. ACM (2007)
14. Nielson, H.R., Nielson, F.: Semantics with Applications: An Appetizer. Undergraduate Topics in Computer Science. Springer, London (2007)
15. Meseguer, J., Palomino, M., Martí-Oliet, N.: Equational abstractions. Theor. Comput. Sci. **403**(2–3), 239–264 (2008)
16. Lluch Lafuente, A., Meseguer, J., Vandin, A.: State space c-reductions of concurrent systems in rewriting logic. In: Aoki, T., Taguchi, K. (eds.) ICFEM 2012. LNCS, vol. 7635, pp. 430–446. Springer, Heidelberg (2012)
17. Godefroid, P., Wolper, P.: A partial approach to model checking. Inf. Comput. **110**(2), 305–326 (1994)
18. Peled, D.: Combining partial order reductions with on-the-fly model-checking. In: Dill, D.L. (ed.) CAV 1994. LNCS, vol. 818, pp. 377–390. Springer, Heidelberg (1994)
19. Valmari, A.: A stubborn attack on state explosion. In: Clarke, E., Kurshan, R.P. (eds.) CAV 1990. LNCS, vol. 531, pp. 156–165. Springer, Heidelberg (1991)
20. Jonsson, B.: State-space exploration for concurrent algorithms under weak memory orderings: (preliminary version). SIGARCH Comput. Archit. News **36**(5), 65–71 (2008)
21. Linden, A., Wolper, P.: A verification-based approach to memory fence insertion in PSO memory systems. In: Piterman, N., Smolka, S.A. (eds.) TACAS 2013 (ETAPS 2013). LNCS, vol. 7795, pp. 339–353. Springer, Heidelberg (2013)
22. Farzan, A., Meseguer, J.: Partial order reduction for rewriting semantics of programming languages. Electr. Notes Theor. Comput. Sci. **176**(4), 61–78 (2007)

23. Eker, S., Meseguer, J., Sridharanarayanan, A.: The maude ltl model checker. Electr. Notes Theor. Comput. Sci. **71**, 162–187 (2002)
24. Reffel, F., Edelkamp, S.: Error detection with directed symbolic model checking. In: Wing, J.M., Woodcock, J. (eds.) FM 1999. LNCS, vol. 1708, p. 195. Springer, Heidelberg (1999)
25. Edelkamp, S., Leue, S., Lluch-Lafuente, A.: Directed explicit-state model checking in the validation of communication protocols. STTT **5**(2–3), 247–267 (2004)
26. Groce, A., Visser, W.: Heuristics for model checking java programs. STTT **6**(4), 260–276 (2004)
27. Martí-Oliet, N., Meseguer, J., Verdejo, A.: A rewriting semantics for maude strategies. Electr. Notes Theor. Comput. Sci. **238**(3), 227–247 (2009)
28. Alglave, J., Kroening, D., Tautschnig, M.: Partial orders for efficient bounded model checking of concurrent software. In: Sharygina, N., Veith, H. (eds.) CAV 2013. LNCS, vol. 8044, pp. 141–157. Springer, Heidelberg (2013)
29. Clarke, E., Kroning, D., Lerda, F.: A tool for checking ANSI-C programs. In: Jensen, K., Podelski, A. (eds.) TACAS 2004. LNCS, vol. 2988, pp. 168–176. Springer, Heidelberg (2004)
30. Abdulla, P.A., Atig, M.F., Chen, Y.-F., Leonardsson, C., Rezine, A.: Counterexample guided fence insertion under TSO. In: Flanagan, C., König, B. (eds.) TACAS 2012. LNCS, vol. 7214, pp. 204–219. Springer, Heidelberg (2012)
31. Kuperstein, M., Vechev, M.T., Yahav, E.: Partial-coherence abstractions for relaxed memory models. In: Hall, M.W., Padua, D.A. (eds.) PLDI, 187–198. ACM (2011)
32. Kuperstein, M., Vechev, M.T., Yahav, E.: Automatic inference of memory fences. In:Bloem, R., Sharygina, N. (eds.) FMCAD, pp. 111–119. IEEE (2010)
33. Atig, M.F., Bouajjani, A., Parlato, G.: Getting rid of store-buffers in TSO analysis. In: Gopalakrishnan, G., Qadeer, S. (eds.) CAV 2011. LNCS, vol. 6806, pp. 99–115. Springer, Heidelberg (2011)
34. Alglave, J., Kroening, D., Nimal, V., Tautschnig, M.: Software verification for weak memory via program transformation. In: Felleisen, M., Gardner, P. (eds.) Programming Languages and Systems. LNCS, vol. 7792, pp. 512–532. Springer, Heidelberg (2013)
35. Musuvathi, M., Qadeer, S.: Iterative context bounding for systematic testing of multithreaded programs. ACM SIGPLAN Not. **42**(6), 446–455 (2007)
36. Dan, A.M., Meshman, Y., Vechev, M., Yahav, E.: Predicate abstraction for relaxed memory models. In: Logozzo, F., Fähndrich, M. (eds.) Static Analysis. LNCS, vol. 7935, pp. 84–104. Springer, Heidelberg (2013)
37. Burckhardt, S., Musuvathi, M.: Effective program verification for relaxed memory models. In: Gupta, A., Malik, S. (eds.) CAV 2008. LNCS, vol. 5123, pp. 107–120. Springer, Heidelberg (2008)
38. Burckhardt, S., Alur, R., Martin, M.M.K.: Bounded model checking of concurrent data types on relaxed memory models: a case study. In: Ball, T., Jones, R.B. (eds.) CAV 2006. LNCS, vol. 4144, pp. 489–502. Springer, Heidelberg (2006)
39. Gopalakrishnan, G.C., Yang, Y., Sivaraj, H.: QB or not QB: an efficient execution verification tool for memory orderings. In: Alur, R., Peled, D.A. (eds.) CAV 2004. LNCS, vol. 3114, pp. 401–413. Springer, Heidelberg (2004)
40. Burnim, J., Sen, K., Stergiou, C.: Sound and complete monitoring of sequential consistency for relaxed memory models. In: Abdulla, P.A., Leino, K.R.M. (eds.) TACAS 2011. LNCS, vol. 6605, pp. 11–25. Springer, Heidelberg (2011)

41. Linden, A., Wolper, P.: An automata-based symbolic approach for verifying programs on relaxed memory models. In: van de Pol, J., Weber, M. (eds.) Model Checking Software. LNCS, vol. 6349, pp. 212–226. Springer, Heidelberg (2010)
42. Burckhardt, S., Alur, R., Martin, M.M.K.: Checkfence: checking consistency of concurrent data types on relaxed memory models. In: Ferrante, J., McKinley, K.S. (eds.) PLDI, pp. 12–21. ACM (2007)
43. Liu, F., Nedev, N., Prisadnikov, N., Vechev, M.T., Yahav, E.: Dynamic synthesis for relaxed memory models. In: Vitek, J., Lin, H., Tip, F. (eds.) PLDI, pp. 429–440. ACM (2012)
44. Rosu, G., Serbanuta, T.F.: An overview of the K semantic framework. J. Log. Algebr. Program. **79**(6), 397–434 (2010)
45. Şerbănuţă, T.F.: A Rewriting Approach to Concurrent Programming Language Design and Semantics. Ph.D. Thesis, University of Illinois at Urbana-Champaign, December 2010. https://www.ideals.illinois.edu/handle/2142/18252
46. Linden, A., Wolper, P.: A verification-based approach to memory fence insertion in relaxed memory systems. In: Groce, A., Musuvathi, M. (eds.) SPIN Workshops 2011. LNCS, vol. 6823, pp. 144–160. Springer, Heidelberg (2011)
47. Kuperstein, M., Vechev, M.T., Yahav, E.: Automatic inference of memory fences. SIGACT News **43**(2), 108–123 (2012)

Real-Time Maude and Its Applications

Peter Csaba Ölveczky$^{(\boxtimes)}$

University of Oslo, Oslo, Norway
`peterol@ifi.uio.no`

Abstract. Real-Time Maude extends the rewriting-logic-based Maude system to support the executable formal modeling and analysis of real-time systems. Real-Time Maude is characterized by its general and expressive, yet intuitive, specification formalism, and offers a spectrum of formal analysis methods, including: rewriting for simulation purposes, search for reachability analysis, and both untimed and metric temporal logic model checking. Real-Time Maude is particularly suitable for specifying real-time systems in an object-oriented style, and its flexible formalism makes it easy to model different forms of communication.

This modeling flexibility, and the usefulness of both Real-Time Maude simulation and model checking, has been demonstrated in many advanced state-of-the-art applications, including both distributed protocols of different kinds and industrial embedded systems. Furthermore, Real-Time Maude's expressiveness has also been exploited to define the formal semantics of a number of modeling languages for real-time/embedded systems. Real-Time Maude thereby provides formal analysis for these languages for free, and such analysis has been integrated into the tool environment of a number of modeling languages.

This paper gives an informal overview of Real-Time Maude and some of its applications.

1 Introduction

Real-Time Maude is a rewriting-logic-based formal specification language and simulation and model checking tool that extends Maude to support the formal modeling and analysis of real-time systems. Being an extension of Maude, Real-Time Maude inherits Maude's key features:

- a simple and intuitive formalism;
- expressiveness and generality; and
- providing a natural model of object-based real-time systems.

In Real-Time Maude the data types are user-defined as an algebraic equational specification; that is, the user declares her sorts and functions on those sorts. Some functions are "constructors" that together define the "elements" of the sorts, and the other functions are defined by (first-order) conditional equations. Local transitions that are assumed to take zero time are specified by (possibly conditional) *rewrite rules* of the form `crl` [l] : $t \Rightarrow t'$ `if` *cond*, where t

© Springer International Publishing Switzerland 2014
S. Escobar (Ed.): WRLA 2014, LNCS 8663, pp. 42–79, 2014.
DOI: 10.1007/978-3-319-12904-4_3

and t' are two terms, possibly containing variables, denoting (sets of) local state fragments. Finally, time elapse is modeled explicitly using *tick rewrite rules* of the form `crl [l]: {t} => {t'} in time` Δ `if` *cond*; this ensures uniform time elapse in all parts of the system, since the *entire state* should have the form $\{u\}$. The duration of the transition is given by the term Δ, which may contain variables, including variables not appearing in t. The time domain can be discrete or dense.

Some key features of Real-Time Maude, which distinguish it from other real-time formalisms and formal analysis tools, include:

- Expressiveness and flexibility. Any computable data type can be defined as an algebraic specification [18]. In particular, we may have "advanced" functions, unbounded data structures, etc. Likewise, the rewrite rules can define very sophisticated transition patterns.
- Object-based distributed real-time systems can be naturally modeled in Real-Time Maude, including features such as
  - dynamic object creation and deletion, and
  - *hierarchical* objects, which may contain entire dynamic subsystems.
- Real-Time Maude is not based on a fixed model of communication, into which other models of communication have to be encoded. Instead, the desired form of communication can be specified directly in the logic.
- Simple and intuitive formalism. Both static, dynamic, and real-time aspects are specified in a simple and intuitive framework (equations and rewrite rules), that should make Real-Time Maude a low-threshold tool for developers with limited formal methods experience.
- A range of automatic formal analyses, including simulation and different kinds of timed and untimed temporal logic model checking.
- The possibility of defining *parametrized* atomic propositions.

Real-Time Maude provides a number of automated explicit-state analyses, including:

- timed rewriting for simulation,
- timed reachability analysis,
- untimed—but possibly time-bounded—LTL model checking, and
- timed CTL (TCTL) model checking.

The price to pay for this modeling convenience is that key system properties are *undecidable*: the above analysis methods are *in general* not sound and complete.

Real-Time Maude should be seen as complementing the highly successful timed automaton formalism [6]—which is a fairly restricted formalism to ensure that key system properties are always decidable—and its equally successful tools such as UPPAAL [14] (and RED [63]), by focussing on expressiveness and modeling convenience. Real-Time Maude can also be seen to complement languages such as IF [21] and BIP [13] by having (essentially) a single formalism instead of being composed of three fairly different formalisms for three different aspects, by supporting the specification of any data type in a logic instead of in Java, by not being based on a fixed communication model, and by supporting the dynamic creation and deletion of (possibly hierarchical) objects.

The key question concerning Real-Time Maude is of course whether all these features are needed or useful. That is:

> **Question 1.** Are there interesting systems where the above features of Real-Time Maude are needed/useful, and where meaningful Real-Time Maude analysis is still possible?

Since Real-Time Maude analyses are in general not sound and complete, an important part of answering **Question 1** is to answer the following question:

> **Question 2.** Are there interesting classes of systems for which Real-Time Maude analyses are guaranteed to be sound and complete?

The goal of this paper is to briefly and informally introduce Real-Time Maude and its applications. In particular, Sect. 2 introduces modeling in Real-Time Maude. Section 3 explains how Real-Time Maude specifications are executed, and gives an overview of the tool's analysis features. Section 4 addresses **Question 2** by presenting classes of systems for which LTL and TCTL model checking is indeed sound and complete. The main part of the paper is Sect. 5, which summarizes some applications of Real-Time Maude. Section 6 discusses extensions of Real-Time Maude, and Sect. 7 gives some concluding remarks.

The formal treatment of Real-Time Maude and its semantics is given in [49]; the underlying real-time rewrite theory model is presented in [47]; and early summaries of some of the uses of Real-Time Maude to define the semantics of modeling languages were presented in [43,44].

Finally, Real-Time Maude is a Maude program that is available free of charge at http://ifi.uio.no/RealTimeMaude.

2 Specification in Real-Time Maude

A Real-Time Maude module tmod M is (Σ, E, IR, TR) endtm specifies a real-time rewrite theory [47], where Σ is an algebraic signature declaring sorts (keywords sort and sorts) subsorts (subsort), and function symbols. A function declaration has the form op f : $s_1 \ldots s_n$ -> s [atts], which declares a function f with n arguments of sorts $s_1, \ldots, s_n$, respectively, that gives an element of sort s. The optional set atts of function attributes could declare f to be a *constructor* symbol that constructs the elements of the sort s, or could declare the function—in case it is a binary function—to be *associative* (assoc), *commutative* (comm), and/or to have an identity element, or declare that f is a *frozen* operator, so that rewrites cannot take place in its subterms. E is a set of (possibly conditional) equations of the form eq $t = t'$ and ceq $t = t'$ if *cond*; the terms t and t' could contain mathematical variables, which are declared with the keyword var or vars. IR is a set of declarations of *instantaneous* rewrite rules rl [l] : t => t' and crl [l] : t => t' if *cond*, where l is a label; such rules define local transitions that are assumed to take zero time. Finally, TR is a set of *tick*

(rewrite) rules of the form `rl [l]` : `{t} => {t'}` in `time` u and `crl [l]` : `{t} =>`
`{t'}` in `time` Δ if *cond* that are used to model time advance in the system.

The equational specification (Σ, E) must contain a specification of a time
domain, which may be dense or discrete. Real-Time Maude has predefined
useful time domains such as `NAT-TIME-DOMAIN` (unbounded natural numbers)
and `POSRAT-TIME-DOMAIN` (unbounded nonnegative rational numbers), and their
extensions `NAT-TIME-DOMAIN-WITH-INF` and `POSRAT-TIME-DOMAIN-WITH-INF`
that add a supersort `TimeInf` of `Time` with an "infinity" element `INF`.

The global state of the system must always have the form `{u}`, where u is a
term of sort `System`. The form of the tick rule then ensures that time advances
uniformly in all parts of the system.

We illustrate specification in Real-Time Maude with a small example borrowed from [49].

Example 1. The following module models a *"retrograde" clock* with a dense
time domain. The clock may be running (in which case the system is in state
`{clock(r)}` for r the time shown by the clock) or may have stopped
(in which case the system is in state `{stopped-clock(r)}` for r the clock value
when it stopped). When the clock shows 24 it must be reset to 0 immediately:

```
(tmod DENSE-CLOCK is protecting POSRAT-TIME-DOMAIN .
  ops clock stopped-clock : Time -> System [ctor] .
  vars R R' : Time .
  crl [tickWhenRunning] :
      {clock(R)} => {clock(R + R')} in time R' if R' <= 24 - R [nonexec] .
  rl [tickWhenStopped] :
      {stopped-clock(R)} => {stopped-clock(R)} in time R' [nonexec] .
  rl [reset] :    clock(24) => clock(0) .
  rl [batteryDies] :    clock(R) => stopped-clock(R) .
endtm)
```

The two tick rules model the effect of time elapse on a system by increasing the
clock value of a running clock according to the time elapsed, and by leaving a
stopped clock unchanged. The rules `reset` and `batteryDies` are instantaneous
rules modeling events that take zero time.

To specify *all possible behaviors* in a dense time domain, the duration of the
tick rules is given by a variable (`R'`) that is not present in the lefthand sides of
the rules. This means that time may elapse by *any* amount less than $24 - r$ from
a state `{clock(r)}`, and by any amount from a state `{stopped-clock(r)}`.

Tick rules—especially in dense time domains—typically have the forms

```
rl [l]  : {t} => {t'} in time x .
crl [l] : {t} => {t'} in time x  if cond .
crl [l] : {t} => {t'} in time x  if x <= u .
crl [l] : {t} => {t'} in time x  if x <= u /\ cond .
```

where x is a variable that does not appear in t and is not instantiated in the
condition. Section 3 explains how such tick rules are executed.

2.1 Object-Oriented Specifications

In Real-Time Maude, we can declare *classes* in object-oriented timed modules ((tomod M is ... endtom)). A class declaration

    class C | att_1 : s_1, ... , att_n : s_1 .

declares a class C with attributes att_1 to att_n of sorts s_1 to s_n, respectively. An *object* of class C in a given state is represented as a term

    < O : C | att_1 : val_1, ..., att_n : val_n >

of sort Object, where O, of sort Oid, is the object's *identifier*, and where val_1 to val_n are the current values of the attributes att_1 to att_n. A *message* m with parameters p_1, ..., p_n of sorts s_1, ..., s_n can be represented as a term $m(p_1, ..., p_n)$ of sort Msg; such messages are declared

    msg m : s_1 ... s_n -> Msg .

A *configuration* is term of the sort Configuration, and is a *multiset* of objects and messages. Multiset union for configurations is denoted by a juxta-position operator (empty syntax) that is associative and commutative, so that rewriting is *multiset rewriting* supported directly in Real-Time Maude. Since a class attribute may have sort Configuration, we can have *hierarchical* objects which contain a subconfiguration of other (possibly hierarchical) objects and messages.

The dynamic behavior of concurrent object systems is axiomatized by specifying each of its transition patterns by a rewrite rule. For example, the rule

```
rl [1]  :  m(O,w)
           < O : C | a1 : x, a2 : O', a3 : z >
        =>
           < O : C | a1 : x + w, a2 : O', a3 : z >
           m'(O',x) .
```

defines a parameterized family of transitions (one for each substitution instance) in which a message m, with parameters O and w, is read and consumed by an object O of class C, the attribute a1 of the object O is changed to x + w, and a new message m'(O',x) is generated. The message m(O,w) is *removed* from the state by the rule, since it does *not* occur in the right-hand side of the rule. Likewise, the message m'(O',x) is *generated* by the rule, since it *only* occurs in the right-hand side of the rule. Attributes whose values do not change and do not affect the next state of other attributes or messages, such as a3, need not be mentioned in a rule. Similarly, attributes whose values influence the next state of other attributes or the values in messages, but are themselves unchanged, such as a2, can be omitted from right-hand sides of rules.

A *subclass* inherits all the attributes and rules of its superclasses.

Messaging delay can be modeled by sending a "delayed" message dly(m, d), where d is the remaining delay of the message. When the remaining delay is 0, the message is "ripe" and becomes m. The dly wrapper can be declared as follows (the sort NEConfiguration denotes non-empty configurations):

```
sort DlyMsg .
subsorts Msg < DlyMsg < NEConfiguration .

op dly : Msg Time -> DlyMsg [ctor right id: 0] .
```

Most object-oriented Real-Time Maude specifications use the tick rule

```
var T : Time .    var SYSTEM : Configuration .

crl [tick] :
    {SYSTEM} => {timeEffect(SYSTEM, T)} in time T if T <= mte(SYSTEM) .
```

where

- the function `mte` defines the *m*aximum *t*ime that may *e*lapse before some (instantaneous) event must take place, and
- the function `timeEffect` defines how the passage of a certain amount of time affects the state of the system.

These functions typically distribute over the elements (objects and messages) in a configuration as follows:

```
vars T T1 T2 : Time .    vars C1 C2 : Configuration .    vars M : Msg .

op mte : Configuration -> TimeInf [frozen (1)] .
eq mte(none) = INF .      --- infinity value
ceq mte(C1 C2) = min(mte(C1), mte(C2)) if C1 =/= none and C2 =/= none .

op timeEffect : Configuration Time -> Configuration [frozen (1)] .
eq timeEffect(none, T) = none .
ceq timeEffect(C1 C2, T) = timeEffect(C1, T)  timeEffect(C2, T)
    if C1 =/= none and C2 =/= none .

eq timeEffect(dly(M, T1), T2) = dly(M, T1 monus T2) .
```

where the built-in operator **monus** is defined by x **monus** $y = \max(x - y, 0)$. If a message must be read exactly when it becomes "ripe", i.e., when its remaining delay is 0, `mte` is defined as follows:

```
eq mte(dly(M, T)) = T .
```

However, if the message delay instead denotes the *minimum* delay, and the message can be read *at any time* after the messaging delay has expired, the following definition of `mte` on messages should be used instead:

```
eq mte(dly(M, T)) = INF .
```

To fully specify the timing behavior an object-oriented real-time system it is then enough to define `mte` and `timeEffect` on *single* objects, as illustrated in the following example, which is also borrowed from [49].

Example 2. We illustrate object-oriented specification with a simple protocol for computing *round trip times* (i.e., the time it takes for a message to travel from a given node to another node, and back) between pairs of nodes in a network.

The protocol is straightforward: A message findRtt(*initiator, neighbor*) kicks off the protocol and indicates that the node *initiator* wants to find the round trip time to the *neighbor* node. An initiator cannot participate in multiple runs of the protocol, as an initiator, at the same time.

The *initiator* node has a local clock and starts a run of the protocol by sending an rttReq message to its neighbor *neighbor* with its current time stamp r (rule startSession). When the neighbor receives the rttReq message, it replies with an rttResp message containing the received time stamp r (rule rttResponse). When the initiator reads the rttResp message with its original time stamp r, the rtt value is just its current clock value minus r (rule treatRttResp).

Since the transmission times might depend on factors such as network traffic, we assume that the messaging delay of a single message could be *any* value greater than or equal to MIN-DELAY. If the initiator does not receive a response in time less than MAX-RTT, it initiates another round of the protocol exactly time MAX-RTT after its first attempt (rule tryAgain). The process is repeated until an rtt value less than MAX-RTT is found. The rule ignoreOldResp ignores responses from earlier rounds of the protocol.

In the following specification, each Node object uses a timer attribute to ensure that a new attempt is initiated at every MAX-RTT time units, until an rtt value is found. If the timer has value r, it must "ring" in time r from the current time. The timer is turned off when its value is INF. The class Node has the attributes nbr, which denotes the node whose rtt value it is interested in (and is noOid otherwise), and a clock attribute denoting the value of its local clock. The rtt attribute stores the rtt to its neighbor:

```
(tomod RTT is protecting NAT-TIME-DOMAIN-WITH-INF .
  ops MIN-DELAY MAX-RTT : -> Time .
  eq MIN-DELAY = 1 .     eq MAX-RTT = 4 .

  op noOid : -> Oid [ctor] .     ---"null" object name

  class Node | clock : Time, rtt : TimeInf, nbr : Oid, timer : TimeInf .

  msgs rttReq rttResp : Oid Oid Time -> Msg .
  msg  findRtt : Oid Oid -> Msg .                   --- start a run

  vars O O' : Oid .   vars R R' : Time .   var TI : TimeInf .

  --- start a session, and set timer:
  rl [startSession] :
    findRtt(O, O')
    < O : Node | clock : R >
    =>
    < O : Node | timer : MAX-RTT, nbr : O' >
    dly(rttReq(O', O, R), MIN-DELAY) .

  --- respond to request:
```

```
    rl [rttResponse] :
       rttReq(O, O', R)
       < O : Node | >
      =>
       < O : Node | >
       dly(rttResp(O', O, R), MIN-DELAY) .


    --- received resp within time MAX-RTT; record rtt value and turn off timer:
    crl [treatRttResp] :
       rttResp(O, O', R)
       < O : Node | clock : R' >
      =>
       < O : Node | rtt : (R' monus R), timer : INF >
     if (R' monus R) < MAX-RTT .


    --- ignore and discard too old message:
    crl [ignoreOldResp] :
       rttResp(O, O', R)
       < O : Node | clock : R' >
      =>
       < O : Node | >
     if (R' monus R) >= MAX-RTT .


    --- start new round and reset timer when timer expires:
    rl [tryAgain] :
       < O : Node | timer : O, clock : R, nbr : O' >
      =>
       < O : Node | timer : MAX-RTT >
       dly(rttReq(O', O, R), MIN-DELAY) .


    ...     --- the tick rule, dly, mte, and timeEffect are defined as above
            --- and are not shown
    eq timeEffect(< O : Node | clock : R, timer : TI >, R') =
            < O : Node | clock : R + R', timer : TI monus R' > .

    eq mte(< O : Node | timer : TI >) = TI .
    eq mte(dly(M, T)) = INF .
endtom)
```

This use of timers, clocks, and the functions `mte` and `timeEffect` is fairly typical
for object-oriented real-time specifications. The following timed module defines
an initial state with three nodes **n1**, **n2**, and **n3**:

```
(tomod RTT-I is including RTT .
  ops n1 n2 n3 : -> Oid [ctor] .
  op initState : -> GlobalSystem .
  eq initState =
       {findRtt(n1, n2)   findRtt(n2, n3)   findRtt(n3, n1)
         < n1 : Node | clock : 0, timer : INF, nbr : noOid, rtt : INF >
         < n2 : Node | clock : 0, timer : INF, nbr : noOid, rtt : INF >
         < n3 : Node | clock : 0, timer : INF, nbr : noOid, rtt : INF >} .
endtom)
```

3 Formal Analysis

This section gives an overview of the formal analyses supported by the Real-Time Maude tool.

3.1 Time Sampling Strategies

Maude specifications are *executable* under reasonable conditions. However, as explained above, in dense time domains, tick rules will typically have the forms

```
crl [l] : {t} => {t'} in time x  if cond [nonexec] .
crl [l] : {t} => {t'} in time x  if x <= u /\ cond [nonexec] .
```

(where *cond* might be omitted), where x a variable not occurring in t and not initialized in *cond*, which allows any moment in time to be "visited." Such tick rules are not directly executable (`[nonexec]`). Timed automata "discretize" dense time by defining "clock regions," so that all states in the same clock region satisfy the same properties [6]. The clock region construction cannot be employed in the much more expressive Real-Time Maude formalism. The Real-Time Maude approach to such tick rules is to provide a set of *time sampling strategies* that define how to instantiate the variable x in the tick rules:

- The *default* time sampling strategy increases time by a user-given value.
- The *maximal* time sampling strategy advances time *as much as possible* (as given by u). If there is no bound on the time elapse, time is advanced by a user-given value.

The user selects her time sampling strategy by giving either the command (`set tick def r .`) or the command (`set tick max def r .`).

   All applications of time-nondeterministic tick rules—whether it is for rewriting, search, or model checking—are performed using the given time sampling strategy. This means that some behaviors in the system, namely those obtained by applying the tick rules differently, are not analyzed. The result of a Real-Time Maude analysis should be understood as being in general incomplete: counterexamples are true counterexamples, but (except for the case of discrete time when all states are visited) satisfaction of a property only shows that it holds for the states visited. Section 4 shows that Real-Time Maude analyses are, nevertheless, sound and complete for many interesting systems.

3.2 Analysis Commands

Simulation. The *timed rewrite* command

```
(tfrew t₀ in time <= r .)
```

simulates *one* behavior of the system from initial state t_0 up to a total duration less than or equal to the `Time` value r. The time bound can also have the forms `in time < r` and `with no time limit`. Real-Time Maude's *tracing* facilities allow us to trace the steps in a timed rewrite sequence (see [42] for details).

Example 3. Before we can analyze our retrograde clock, we need to define a time sampling strategy. Since the clock may stop at any time, we use the time sampling strategy that increases time by one time unit in each tick rule application:

Maude> *(set tick def 1 .)*

We can then simulate one behavior of the clock system up to time 100:

Maude> *(tfrew {clock(0)} in time <= 100 .)*

Result ClockedSystem :   {stopped-clock(0)} in time 100

Reachability Analysis. Explicit-state *timed search* can be used to analyze not just *one* behavior, but to analyze *all* behaviors from a given initial state, relative to the chosen time sampling strategy. The syntax variations of the timed search command—which is used to search for states which match a *search pattern* and which are reachable in a given time interval—are:

(tsearch t_0 *arrow pattern* with no time limit .)
(tsearch t_0 *arrow pattern* in time $\sim r$.)
(tsearch t_0 *arrow pattern* in time-interval between $\sim' r$ and $\sim'' r'$.)

where t_0 is the initial state, *pattern* is either t or has the form t such that *cond*, for a term t and a semantic condition *cond*, $\sim$ is either <, <=, >, or >=, $\sim'$ is either >= or >, $\sim''$ is either <= or <, and r and r' are ground terms of sort Time. The *arrow* is either =>1, =>*, and =>+, which searches for states reachable from t_0 in, respectively, one, zero or more, and one or more rewrite steps. The arrow =>! is used to search for states which cannot be further rewritten. The search command can be parametrized by the number of solutions sought ((tsearch [n] ...)). As explained in Sect. 3.3, timed search maintains a "system clock" in the state. The set of reachable "timestamped states" will therefore be infinite even when the reachable state space is finite. Therefore, the *untimed search* command

(utsearch t_0 *arrow pattern* .)

which abstracts from the "system clock," can be used when the reachable state space is finite.

Example 4. We continue analyzing our retrograde clock with the time sampling strategy chosen above. Although the time domain is dense, the reachable state space (from {clock(0)}) should be finite when the time sampling strategy is taken into account. We check whether it is possible to reach a bad state where a running clock shows 25 or more:

Maude> *(utsearch [1]*
            {clock(0)} => {clock(T:Time)} such that T:Time >= 25 .)*

No solution

Checking whether it is possible to reach a state where the running clock shows 1/2 also returns "No solution":

```
Maude> (utsearch [1] {clock(0)} =>* {clock(1/2)} .)
```

```
No solution
```

In this case, our time-sampling-based analysis is incorrect, since in the model it is indeed possible to reach the state {clock(1/2)}.

Example 5. The reachable state space from initState is infinite in our round trip time protocol, since the (local) clock values may grow beyond any bound and since the state may contain any number of old messages. Search should therefore be *time-bounded* to ensure termination. We set the time sampling strategy with the command (set tick def 1 .) to cover the discrete time domain.

The command

```
Maude> (tsearch [1]
           initState =>* {< O:Oid : Node | rtt : T:Time > REST:Configuration}
           such that T:Time > 4  in time <= 9 .)
```

```
No solution
```

then checks whether a state with a rtt value > 4 can be reached within time 9.

LTL Model Checking. Real-Time Maude extends Maude's explicit-state LTL model checker to timed modules. *Atomic propositions* are terms of sort Prop. A useful feature is the possibility to define *parametrized* atomic propositions $p(t_1, \ldots, t_n)$ as follows:

```
op p : s₁ ... sₙ -> Prop [ctor] .
```

The semantics of such state propositions are given by equations of the forms

$$\texttt{eq } \{statePattern\} \mathrel{|=} p(t_1, \ldots, t_n) = b$$

and

$$\texttt{ceq } \{statePattern\} \mathrel{|=} p(t_1, \ldots, t_n) = b \texttt{ if } condition,$$

for b a term of sort Bool, which defines the state proposition $p(u_1, \ldots, u_n)$ to hold in all states $\{t\}$ where $\{t\} \mathrel{|=} p(u_1, \ldots, u_n)$ evaluates to true.

Real-Time Maude also supports the definition of "clocked" atomic propositions, whose semantics can depend on the elapsed time in the system:

$$\texttt{eq } \{statePattern\} \texttt{ in time } t \mathrel{|=} p(t_1, \ldots, t_n) = b$$

and

$$\texttt{ceq } \{statePattern\} \texttt{ in time } t \mathrel{|=} p(t_1, \ldots, t_n) = b \texttt{ if } condition.$$

An LTL formula is constructed by state propositions and temporal logic operators such as True, ~ (negation), /\, \/, -> (implication), [] ("always"), <> ("eventually"), and U ("until"). Then, the *unbounded* (resp., *time-bounded*) LTL model checking commands

$$\text{(mc } t_0 \text{ |=u } \varphi \text{ .)} \qquad \text{and} \qquad \text{(mc } t_0 \text{ |=t } \varphi \text{ in time <= } \tau \text{ .)}$$

check whether the formula φ holds in all behaviors from the initial state t_0 (resp., in all behaviors up to time τ). Only *time-bounded* model checking may involve clocked propositions. If the formula does not hold, the model checker returns a behavior that does not satisfy the formula.

The module TIME-MODEL-CHECKER should be imported by the modules defining the atomic propositions.

Example 6. The following module defines the *state* propositions clock-dead (which holds for all stopped clocks) and clock-is(r) (which holds if a *running* clock shows r), and the *clocked* proposition clockEqualsTime (which holds if the running clock shows the time elapsed in the system):

```
(tmod MODEL-CHECK-DENSE-CLOCK is including TIMED-MODEL-CHECKER .
  protecting DENSE-CLOCK .
  ops clock-dead clockEqualsTime : -> Prop [ctor] .
  op clock-is : Time -> Prop [ctor] .
  vars  R R' : Time .
  eq {stopped-clock(R)}       |=   clock-dead = true .
  eq {clock(R)}               |=   clock-is(R') = (R == R') .
  eq {clock(R)} in time R'    |=   clockEqualsTime = (R == R') .
endtm)
```

A natural correctness requirement is that the clock shows the elapsed time in the system, either until time 24 is reached or until the clock stops:

```
Maude> (mc {clock(0)} |=t clockEqualsTime U (clock-dead \/ clock-is(24))
            in time <= 50 .)
```

Result Bool :   true

Timed CTL Model Checking. Real-Time Maude has recently been equipped with an explicit-state *Timed CTL* (TCTL) model checker for *timed* temporal logic properties such as "every request will be followed by a response *within 100 ms*" or "the minimum time between two p-states is *10 s*" [34,35].

In TCTL, the temporal modalities are annotated with time intervals: $\square_{\leq 5} \phi$, $\Diamond_{>8} \phi$, and $\phi_1 \, \mathcal{U}_{[2,9]} \, \phi_2$, and so on. We refer to [35] for the full syntax of TCTL in Real-Time Maude. The model checker uses the logical operators not, and, or, implies, and so on. A formula $\forall \square_{\leq 20} \phi$ is written AG[<= than 20] ϕ, a formula $\exists \Diamond_{>11} \phi$ is written EF[> than 11] ϕ, and a formula $\forall \phi_1 \, \mathcal{U}_{[2,9]} \, \phi_2$ is written A ϕ_1 U[c 2, 9 c] ϕ_2.

The TCTL model checking has the syntax

(mc-tctl t_0 |= *formula*.)

At the moment, the model checker only gives a "yes/no" answer, and does not have a "time-bounded" version to deal with systems with infinite reachable state space. The module TCTL-MODEL-CHECKER should be imported when using the TCTL model checker.

Example 7. We check whether from any state where the running clock shows 5, it is possible to reach, in exactly 24 time units, a state where the running clock also shows 5:

Maude> *(mc-tctl*
     {clock(0)} |= AG (clock-is(5) implies EF[c 24,24 c] clock-is(5)).)

Property satisfied

Other Commands. Real-Time Maude also provides commands for finding the shortest time it takes a desired state, and the longest time it takes to find the desired state for the first time.

3.3   Implementation

Real-Time Maude is implemented in Maude as an extension of Full Maude [22]. For efficiency purposes, all simulation, search, and LTL model checking commands have been implemented by transforming a Real-Time Maude module M, a time sampling strategy s, an initial state t_0, and a Real-Time Maude command C into a core Maude module M', an initial state t_0', and a Maude command C' that is then executed in Maude [49]. The results from Maude are then transformed back into suitable Real-Time Maude output.

The target Maude module M' is a function of *both* the Real-Time Maude command and the time sampling strategy used. For the *unbounded* search (utsearch) and LTL model checking ((mc ... |=u ... .)) commands, the transformation abstracts from the "system clock". Therefore, if the reachable state space is finite in the original model, it will remain so in the transformed Maude model M'. However, simulation and *time-bounded* search (tsearch) and LTL model checking ((mc ... |=t ...)) need to keep track of elapsed time; therefore, the states in the resulting Maude module M' have the form t in time r, where t is the state component, and r is the "time stamp" (or "system clock"). A single state t in M can then lead to multiple "time-stamped states" t in time r_1, t in time $r_2, \ldots$, in M', which leads to an infinite reachable timestamped state space; however, with an appropriate time sampling strategy, the set of such states reachable within a given upper time bound should be finite.

The other commands (find earliest/latest and TCTL model checking) cannot be transformed into Maude commands and are implemented directly using Maude's meta-level.

4   Sound and Complete Real-Time Maude Analysis

Section 3 explains that the time-sampling-based explicit-state reachability analysis and temporal logic model checking methods used by Real-Time Maude are in general not sound and complete, since only a subset of all possible behaviors are explored. Section 4.1 shows that maximal-time-sampling-based reachability and LTL model checking analyses *are* sound and complete for many interesting systems encountered in practice, and for which there were previously no such soundness/completeness results. Section 4.2 discusses the semantics of TCTL and soundness and completeness of TCTL model checking in Real-Time Maude.

4.1   Sound and Complete Reachability Analysis and LTL Model Checking in Real-Time Maude

Explicit-state model checking in a dense time domain cannot visit all moments in time. If the time domain is discrete, all behaviors can be explored by applying the time sampling strategy that advances time by the smallest time unit in each application of a tick rule. However, in many applications, this would be prohibitively expensive. For example, in the wireless sensor network algorithm analyzed in [52] and mentioned in Sect. 5, the time domain is *milliseconds*, while each round of the algorithm is *1000 s*. Most of the time the system is idling. Clearly, visiting each single moment in time yields a very inefficient simulation, and the large number of states encountered would make any model checking analysis unfeasible. Therefore, using maximal time sampling is in practice necessary also for many discrete-time systems.

An important question, posed as **Question 2** in the introduction, is whether there are interesting classes of systems for which maximal-time-sampling-based Real-Time Maude analysis is guaranteed to give the correct result. In [48], José Meseguer and I answer this question affirmatively by identifying classes of real-time rewrite theories for which maximal-time-sampling-based reachability analysis and LTL model checking are sound and complete analysis methods. In particular, we show that such analyses are sound and complete when:

- The system is *time-robust*, which means that no instantaneous action can take place after a tick step that does not advance time as much as possible.
- The atomic propositions appearing in the formula are *tick-invariant*, which means that their valuation is not affected by applying a tick rule.

More precisely, if $\mathcal{R}$ is a time-robust real-time rewrite theory, and $\mathcal{R}^{mts}$ is the theory obtained by applying the tick rules in $\mathcal{R}$ according to the maximal time sampling strategy, then for any CTL^* formula ϕ excluding the next-state operator $\bigcirc$ and involving only tick-invariant atomic propositions, we have

$$\mathcal{R}, t_0 \models \phi \qquad \text{if and only if} \qquad \mathcal{R}^{mts}, t_0 \models \phi.$$

The paper [48] also gives soundness and completeness results with somewhat weaker restrictions. Furthermore, it gives some easily checkable conditions for time-robustness of object-oriented Real-Time Maude specifications.

Although time-robustness and tick-invariance seem to be fairly restrictive conditions, many systems encountered in practice satisfy these conditions. For example, in many network protocols, actions are triggered either by the expiration of a timer or by the reception of a message with fixed delay; these systems are time-robust. Tick-invariance is almost always satisfied in practice, since the tick rules typically only affect timers and local clocks, which almost never affect the valuation of an atomic proposition.

Our retrograde clock is *not* time-robust, since the rule `batteryDies` can be applied at any time—including after non-maximal tick steps. Likewise, our round trip time example is not time-robust, since a message can be received at any time after its minimum delay has expired. If we replace the equation

```
eq mte(dly(M:Msg, T)) = INF .
```

with

```
eq mte(dly(M:Msg, T)) = T .
```

then the system is time-robust, since every message now has a fixed deadline (since time cannot advance when there is an unread ripe message in the state).

Among the large applications mentioned in Sect. 5, the OGDC wireless sensor network algorithm, the AER/NCA active network multicast protocol, Ptolemy II DE models, Timed Rebeca models, etc., are all time-robust. All of the these systems/languages go beyond the class of systems that can be captured by timed automata. Our results therefore yield sound and complete model checking procedures for dense-time systems beyond timed automata. On the other hand, the class of timed automata include many non-time-robust systems.

4.2   Sound and Complete TCTL Model Checking

In contrast to untimed LTL model checking, TCTL model checking using maximal time sampling is *not* sound and complete for time-robust real-time rewrite theories. Assume, for example, that from a state {f(0)}, the next event will take place after time 3; that is, we have the tick rule

```
crl [tick] : {f(T)} => {f(T + T')} in time T' if T' <= 3 - T .
```

Consider the property $\exists \Diamond_{[1,2]}$ **true**; that is, it is possible to reach a state in some time $t \in [1,2]$ where **true** holds. This property holds from initial state {f(0)}, since there is a non-maximal tick step to {f(1)} in time 1, and **true** holds in {f(1)}. However, maximal time sampling would rewrite {f(0)} in one step to {f(3)}, and hence the above property would *not* be satisfied.

Now consider the property $\forall \Diamond_{[1,2]}$ **true**; that is, in *all* behaviors we can reach a state some time in the time interval [1, 2]. Does this property hold in our specification? If we only consider all possible behaviors in the system, this property clearly does *not* hold, since time can advance from {f(0)} to {f(3)} in *one* tick step that advances time by 3 time units. However, it may be natural to understand the above tick rule as modeling a "continuous process" from {f(0)} to {f(3)}. In that case, this second property should hold.

These two ways of interpreting a real-time rewrite theory are called, respectively, the *pointwise* semantics and the *continuous* semantics.

In [35], Daniela Lepri, Erika Ábrahám, and I show that we can obtain sound and complete TCTL model checking of time-robust theories in *both* the pointwise and the continuous semantics, by advancing time by a value r_0 in each tick step. This value r_0 is "half the greatest common divisor" of the following values:

- all the tick durations obtained by applying the tick rules according to the maximal time sampling strategy; and
- all the non-zero time bounds occurring in the TCTL formula being analyzed.

Such TCTL model checking can be performed by giving the command

    (mc-tctl-gcd t_0 |= ϕ .)

5   Some Real-Time Maude Applications

This section gives a brief overview of some Real-Time Maude applications, thereby answering **Question 1** in the introduction: are there interesting systems where the expressiveness and the more advanced modeling features of Real-Time Maude are needed, and where Real-Time Maude analysis still can provide useful results? In particular, Sect. 5.1 summarizes some "concrete" applications of Real-Time Maude. Real-Time Maude has been particularly useful to provide a formal semantics and formal analysis capabilities to domain-specific modeling languages for real-time systems; such applications are discussed in Sect. 5.3. Other applications of Real-Time Maude are mentioned in Sects. 5.2 and 5.4.

5.1   Some Concrete Applications

This section gives an overview of some "concrete" applications of Real-Time Maude.

Wireless Sensor Network Algorithms. OGDC [65] is a sophisticated state-of-the-art density control algorithm for wireless sensor networks developed at UIUC. The goal of a density control algorithm is to maximize the lifetime of a wireless sensor network by periodically turning nodes on and off while maintaining coverage of the entire area. The OGDC algorithm is based on always trying to turn on the "best placed" node, w.r.t. nodes that are already turned on, next. The OGDC developers used the ns-2 network simulator with a wireless extension to show that OGDC outperforms other density control algorithms.

Wireless sensor networks pose(d) many challenges to formal methods, including new forms of communication (area broadcast with delays, possibly sent with different signal strength), the need to analyze both performance and correctness, and so on. OGDC adds the need to deal with geometrical areas, angles, amount of overlap between multiple coverage areas, and so on.

Thorvaldsen and I model and analyze OGDC in [52]. The key Real-Time Maude features were the ability to easily define the new form of communication, defining data types for geometrical areas, and defining complex functions on such areas. To the best of our knowledge, the Real-Time Maude analysis of OGDC was the first formal analysis of an advanced wireless sensor network algorithm.

We performed a series of simulations of OGDC with up to 800 sensor nodes. The Real-Time Maude simulations gave performance figures very similar to the ns-2 simulations when we did *not* consider transmission delays. Since the OGDC developers did not include delays in their simulations, this indicates that *Real-Time Maude simulations provide quite accurate performance estimates of OGDC*. However, messaging delays play a crucial role in the OGDC algorithm. Real-Time Maude simulations *with delays* showed that the performance of OGDC is actually more than twice as bad as in the ns-2 simulations. Furthermore, we found a significant flaw in OGDC that explains its bad performance.

The techniques in [52] were then used and extended by Katelman, Meseguer, and Hou in their definition of the LMST topology control algorithm for wireless sensor networks in [31]. The goal is to minimize power consumption by adjusting the broadcast signal strength while maintaining network connectivity. Real-Time Maude was used to verify network connectivity by model checking a number of 4-node configurations. Their Real-Time Maude model was then extended with a number of probabilistic "implementation" features, such as quartz clock drift and 802.11 MAC contention, and the resulting probabilistic rewrite theory was subjected to *statistical model checking* using the VeStA [59] tool.

Mobile Ad Hoc Networks. Wireless mobile ad hoc networks (MANETs) combine wireless communication with node mobility. However, it is quite challenging to provide realistic models of mobility combined with wireless communication, since both the sender and a potential receiver may move—possible into or out of transmission range—*during* the "transmission time." In [37], Si Liu, José Meseguer, and I define a framework for modeling popular node mobility models together with wireless communication in Real-Time Maude.

In [38], we used our framework to model and analyze the well known leader election protocol for MANETs by Vasudevan, Kurose, and Towsley [62]. Our more detailed and flexible model of MANETs allowed us to study the protocol under various mobility and communication scenarios, including unidirectional communication links resulting from transmitting with different signal strength.

Scheduling Algorithms. The CASH algorithm is a sophisticated state-of-the-art scheduling algorithm developed by Marco Caccamo at UIUC. The idea is that tasks that do not need all of their allocated CPU time can put the unused budgets into a queue, so that other tasks can use that CPU time for improved system performance. Caccamo and I used Real-Time Maude to model and analyze a proposed optimization of CASH [46]. Real-Time Maude simulation showed that the queue of unused budgets can grow beyond any bound; since unbounded data structures are needed, the algorithm cannot be modeled by, e.g., timed automata. Real-Time Maude search uncovered a subtle behavior in the proposed optimization that led to missed hard deadlines. Furthermore, by using a pseudo-random function, we could generate tasks with "random" arrival and execution times, and use rewriting to perform "Monte-Carlo simulations." Extensive such simulation indicated that it is unlikely that the missed deadline could be found by simulation alone.

Prabhakar, Liu, and I have shown in [51] how resource-sharing algorithms, such as the priority inheritance and the priority ceiling protocol, can be formalized and analyzed using Real-Time Maude.

Embedded Car Software. Real-Time Maude has been used by a Japanese research institute to find several time-dependent bugs in embedded car software used by major car makers. The time sampling approach of Real-Time Maude was supposedly crucial to detect the bugs, which could not be found by the usual model-checking tools employed in industry.

Timing Features in AUTOSAR OS. *AUTOSAR* (AUTomotive Open System ARchitecture) is automotive open system architecture standard intended to unify and standardize automotive software development methodologies. The core group defining AUTOSAR includes BMW, Bosch, Daimler, General Motors, Toyota, and Volkswagen. In [66], Longfei Zhu and others use Real-Time Maude to formalize and analyze a number of timing properties in a part of the AUTOSAR operating system. In particular, many tasks are scheduled by the OS on a specific electronic control unit (ECU): tasks with different priorities as well as interrupts that must be handled. Zhu *et al.* model the task scheduling in AUTOSAR OS and use Real-Time Maude to analyze the following properties:

– schedulability, by searching for a task that misses its deadline;
– non-fault-propagation: other tasks should not miss their deadlines if the execution time of one task is longer than expected; and
– consistent configuration of components.

Google's Megastore and Its Extension. Cloud systems need to replicate data to ensure scalability and high availability. Unfortunately, combining wide-area replication with data consistency is quite hard. Some applications, such as Facebook and online newspapers, can tolerate low levels of consistency. However, to be able to use a cloud infrastructure also for consistency-critical applications such as stock exchange systems, online auctions, and banking and medical systems, replicated data stores must provide *transactions*. Megastore, developed at Google and used for, e.g., Gmail, Android Market, Google+, and Google App-Engine, is one of very few data stores that provide transactions. The problem is that the only publicly available description of Megastore is short and informal.

To facilitate the widespread study, adoption, and further development of Megastore's novel approach to transactions on replicated data, a much more detailed and precise description is needed.

In [29], Jon Grov and I develop a fairly detailed Real-Time Maude model of Megastore consisting of 56 rewrite rules. Since our starting point was a brief and informal overview paper, we had to in essence develop our own version of Megastore. We used Real-Time Maude simulation and model checking extensively throughout our development of this very complex system to improve our model to the point where we could not find any flaws during model checking. One Real-Time Maude feature that made this work possible was the ability to define complex atomic propositions; this allowed us to model check the serializability property of distributed concurrent transactions (as well as data consistency).

Megastore combines high performance, availability, and consistency by partitioning data into *entity groups*, and only guarantees data consistency if each transaction only accesses data from a single entity group. Grov and I define in [30] Megastore-CGC, an extension of Megastore that provides consistency also for transactions accessing data from multiple entity groups, thereby increasing the applicability of such cloud data stores. Megastore-CGC achieves this extra consistency without introducing significant additional message exchanges. We use Real-Time Maude to verify key properties, but also to compare the performance of Megastore with that of Megastore-CGC.

Avionics Systems. To smoothly turn an airplane, the airplane's ailerons and its rudder need to move in a synchronized way. (An aileron is a flap attached to the end of each wing, and a rudder is a flap attached to the plane's vertical tail.) A *turning algorithm* takes the desired next direction from the pilot as input, and should give commands to the aileron and rudder controllers to achieve a smooth turn in the desired direction.

In [10], Kyungmin Bae, Joshua Krisiloff, José Meseguer, and I formalize and analyze in Real-Time Maude a textbook turning algorithm for smaller aircrafts. Real-Time Maude simulations revealed that the turning algorithm failed to ensure a smooth turn: the (undesired) *adverse yaw* can become greater than 1.5° when the pilot gives a sharp turn command. We then modified the turning algorithm, and verified using Real-Time Maude model checking that, with the new turning algorithm, the plane will reach the desired direction fairly quickly and that the adverse yaw angle is less than 1.0° throughout the turn.

José Meseguer and I analyze a different avionics system in [39]: the *active standby* system developed by Steve Miller and Darren Cofer at Rockwell-Collins. In integrated modular avionics (IMA), a *cabinet* is a chassis with a power supply, internal bus, and general purpose computing, I/O, and memory cards. There are always two or more cabinets that are physically separated on the aircraft so that physical damage does not take out the computer system. The active standby system considers the case of two cabinets and focuses on the logic for deciding which side is *active*. Each side could fail, and can recover after failure. In case one side fails, the non-failed side should be the active side. In addition, the pilot can toggle the active status of these sides. The architecture of the system is shown in Fig. 1. The active standby system is *virtually synchronous*: it proceeds in rounds, and in each round, the components get an input in all their input channels (depicted as arrows in Fig. 1). LTL model checking showed that the desired properties were not satisfied. However, we could verify weakened versions of the desired requirements, which turned out to be exactly the same properties discovered independently by Cofer and Miller during their NuSMV analysis.

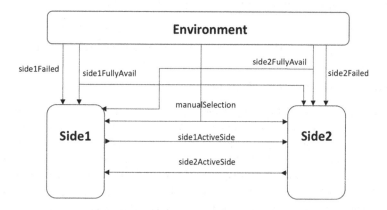

Fig. 1. The architecture of the active standby system.

Multicast Protocols. AER/NCA is a suite of protocols aimed at achieving network-friendly and reliable multicast in *active networks*. The informal specification of AER/NCA that was the starting point of the Real-Time Maude modeling and analysis effort described in [50] consisted of more than 50 pages of prose and informal "use-case" descriptions. Some of the challenges—apart from the sheer size of the protocol suite—included the need to analyze the protocols both in isolation and in combination, a detailed communication model that took packet size, link capacity, etc., into account, and sophisticated functions to update various parameters based on measures such networks congestion.

Class inheritance techniques allowed us analyze both single protocols and different combinations of protocols without modifying the protocols significantly. Another key feature was that Real-Time Maude allowed us to easily define the desired low-level model of communication very easily. In particular, we could analyze the protocols under many different link scenarios by just modifying a few parameters of the link objects. Thanks to this flexibility, our Real-Time Maude analysis—mostly simulation—found *all* the errors that the protocol developers had discovered independently using network simulators and testbeds, but had not told us about. Furthermore, our Real-Time Maude analysis revealed a significant error in the protocols that essentially invalidated the protocol, and that the protocol developers were *not* aware of.

Elisabeth Lien and I used many of the same techniques to model and analyze parts of an earlier version of the NORM multicast protocol developed by the

IETF [36]. Our model checking efforts uncovered a few errors; however, those had been corrected in later versions of NORM.

Some Other Applications. Minyoung Kim *et al.* use Real-Time Maude rewriting in [33] to estimate the performance of several power management schemes for an MPEG video streaming client. Shin Nakajima explains in [41] how Real-Time Maude can be used to model check *power consumption automata* to analyze power consumption in smartphones. Finally, in [64] Martin Wirsing *et al.* model pervasive user-centric applications—in particular, an interactive advertising board that monitors whether a person is standing in front of the board and acts accordingly—and verify them using timed temporal logic model checking.

5.2   Formalizing Formal Patterns

José Meseguer describes *formal patterns* as the formal counterparts of the well known *design patterns* in software engineering [40]. Formal patterns provide solutions to frequently occurring problems in system design, but are in additional formally specified and verified. The point is that the effort spent on verifying a formal pattern is amortized over all the instances of the pattern; they all satisfy the correctness properties. A formal pattern can be seen as a theory transformation $\mathcal{P}$ transforming a system T, with additional parameters Γ, into a system $\mathcal{P}(T, \Gamma)$ that satisfies the correctness properties of the pattern. Real-Time Maude has been used to formalize a number of formal patterns, including the following.

The Command Shaper Pattern for Medical Devices. The *command shaper* pattern developed by Mu Sun, Meseguer, and Lui Sha aims at ensuring the safe operation of medical devices connected to patients [61]. The pattern transforms a controller T that sends commands to a medical device to a new controller $\mathcal{CS}(T, \Gamma)$ to ensure that:

- the patient is not in a *stress situation* for too long; and
- the time between stress periods is sufficiently long.

The developers mention three instances of their pattern:

1. Modern pacemakers are flexible and allow a faster heart rate for limited durations, e.g., when a person is exercising. The command shaper pattern transforms a system T controlling the heart rate, together with parameters Γ denoting the durations of the stress periods, rest times, etc., into the device controller $\mathcal{CS}(T, \Gamma)$ that ensures that the pacemaker does not provide heart rates above normal for too long, and that the rest time between strenuous activities is sufficiently long.
2. A patient in pain can control an infusion pump to administer, e.g., morphine. To avoid the patient overdosing by operating the infusion pump incorrectly, her commands can go through the command shaper to ensure that morphine

is only pumped for certain durations, and that the time between infusions is sufficiently long.

3. A mechanical *ventilator* helps a patient breathing, e.g., during surgery. However, it sometimes needs to be turned off, for example to avoid blurry pictures when taking X-rays. The command shaper pattern can ensure that the ventilator is not turned off for too long, and that the time between each pause of the ventilator is sufficiently long.

The PALS and Multirate PALS Synchronizers for Cyber-Physical Systems. Many cyber-physical systems, such as avionics, automotive, and robotics systems, are *virtually synchronous*: they proceed logically in rounds, and in each round they read input, update their local states, and produce outputs. However, such distributed systems are hard to design because of asynchrony, clock skews, and network delays. Furthermore, the model checking verification of such systems quickly becomes unfeasible due to the state space explosion caused by asynchrony. The idea of the PALS pattern [3]—developed by Steve Miller and Darren Cofer at Rockwell-Collins, Lui Sha, José Meseguer, Mu Sun, and Abdullah Al-Nayeem at UIUC, and myself—is to reduce the design and verification of a virtually synchronous CPS to designing and verifying its much simpler underlying synchronous design. Formally, PALS is a pattern transforming a synchronous design T and performance bounds Γ on the network delays, clock skews, execution times into the corresponding distributed real-time system PALS(T, Γ), that satisfy the same temporal logic properties as T [39].

The benefits of PALS can be illustrated by the active standby avionics system mentioned in Sect. 5.1. The synchronous system has 185 reachable states, whereas the number of reachable states in the simplest possible distributed version, with perfect clocks and no network delays, is 3,047,832. If the network delay can be either 0 and 1, then no model checking is feasible. Other instances of PALS include the LMST wireless sensor network protocol [32] and, presumably, the well known steam-boiler controller benchmark [1].

One limitation of PALS and other synchronizers is the assumption that all components share the same period. However, different controllers may operate at different rates. For example, the aileron controllers and the rudder controller of an airplane typically operate with different periods, yet they must synchronize to turn an airplane. Bae, Meseguer, and I therefore extended PALS to the Multirate PALS pattern to deal with virtually synchronous hierarchical multirate control systems [7]. Figure 2 shows the hierarchical multirate nature (with the period of each subsystem given in parenthesis) of the airplane turning system mentioned in Sect. 5.1. The number of states reachable in 3 s in the synchronous version of this system is 2,111, whereas the number of states reachable in 3 s is 4,415,784 in the much simplified asynchronous setting.

5.3   Semantics and Formal Analysis of Modeling Languages

Most modeling languages for real-time embedded systems (RTESs) that are used in industry currently lack a formal semantics, which not only limits unambiguous

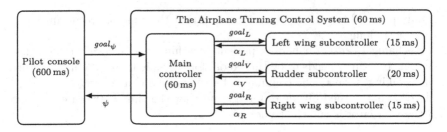

Fig. 2. The architecture of our airplane turning control system.

communication between model developers, but also implies that models described in such languages cannot be subjected to formal analysis. Furthermore, some modeling languages are not executable, which limits the possibility to even simulate their models. There is therefore a clear need for:

- A formal semantic framework in which the precise semantics of a modeling language for RTESs can be defined in a natural way; and
- associated simulation and formal analysis tools which support the automated formal analysis of models in such languages.

To be useful for model-based system engineering in practice, the formal analysis framework should also:

1. Allow model developers to define analysis commands without understanding the formal language or the formal representation of their models; and
2. provide formal analysis results, such as counterexamples in temporal logic model checking, that the model developer can easily understand.

A number of advanced modeling tools provide a code generation infrastructure to support the generation of deployment code from a design model. Once the formal semantics of a modeling language has been defined, we can leverage this code generation infrastructure to automatically generate a *formal verification model* from the informal design model, enabling a *formal model-engineering* process that combines the convenience of modeling using an informal but intuitive modeling language with formal analysis.

An important point is that informal modeling languages invariably are fairly expressive; all of the languages mentioned in this section are Turing-complete. Therefore, they cannot be given a semantics using a decidable formalism. However, Real-Time Maude, with its natural model of time and its expressiveness, should make it a suitable semantic framework for modeling languages for RTESs. Furthermore, since it provides both rewriting and model checking, it should also be a suitable simulation and formal analysis back-end for such languages.

Real-Time Maude addresses the desiderata (1) and (2) above as follows:

1. *Parametric* atomic state propositions allow us to (pre-)define useful parametric state propositions in the Real-Time Maude interpreter of a language, making it easy for the user to define temporal logic formulas.

2. A key requirement to (i) understanding the results of Real-Time Maude analyses, and (ii) being able to map them back into the original modeling formalism is to have, respectively, a small *representational distance* between the original models and their formal counterparts, and a one-to-one correspondence between these models. Since hierarchical composition and encapsulation play key roles in modeling languages for industrial systems, the possibility of defining *hierarchical* objects enable us to achieve both small representational distance and the above one-to-one correspondence.

This section summarizes some uses of Real-Time Maude to define the semantics and provide a formal analysis back-end for RTESs modeling languages.

Ptolemy II Discrete-Event Models. Ptolemy II [23] is a well-established graphical modeling language and simulation tool for real-time and embedded systems used in industry. In Ptolemy II, real-time systems are modeled as *discrete-event* (DE) models. Like many graphical modeling languages, Ptolemy II DE models lack formal verification capabilities.

A Ptolemy II model consists of a set of *actors* with *input ports* and *output ports* used to pass *events* between actors. There are different kinds of actors, including clocks that generate events, timers, *delay* actors that output their input event after a fixed delay, and finite state machine (FSM) actors; furthermore, a Ptolemy II model can be encapsulated as a *composite* actor. Each event has a *timestamp* denoting the model time at which the event occurs.

An *event queue* is used for the execution. In each iteration of the system, the events in the queue with the smallest timestamp are executed. All components with input execute *synchronously*. Since connections are instantaneous and the components execute in lock-step, we must compute the *fixed point* of the input for each component in the round before its execution; this input comes from the output of another actor's execution in the same synchronous round. Figure 3 shows a hierarchical Ptolemy II model of a fault-tolerant traffic light system, consisting of one car light and one pedestrian light, at a pedestrian crossing.

Defining the formal semantics of Ptolemy II DE models is challenging; in addition to FMSs with unbounded variables, it involves unbounded queues, and, in particular, computing fixed points in hierarchical systems. Kyungmin Bae and others define the Real-Time Maude semantics of Ptolemy II DE models in [11].

We have used Ptolemy II's code generation infrastructure to integrate both the synthesis of a Real-Time Maude model from a Ptolemy II model as well as Real-Time Maude model checking of the synthesized model into Ptolemy II itself. When the blue `RTMaudeCodeGenerator` button in a Ptolemy II DE model is double-clicked, Ptolemy II opens a dialog window (shown in Fig. 4) which allows the user to give model checking commands to formally analyze her model.

We have also predefined in our model checker useful atomic propositions. For example, the proposition

$$actorId \mid var_1 = value_1, \dots, var_n = value_n$$

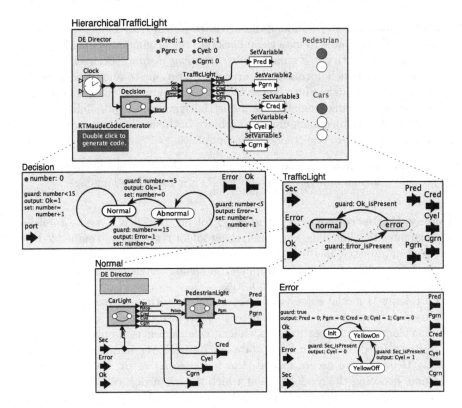

Fig. 3. A hierarchical fault-tolerant traffic light system in Ptolemy II.

holds if the value of the parameter var_i of the actor *actorId* equals $value_i$. Similarly, *actorId* | port p is *value* and *actorId* | port p is *status* hold if, respectively, the port p of actor *actorId* has the value *value* and status *status*.

The Real-Time Maude formalization of a Ptolemy II DE model is time-robust, and the above atomic propositions are tick-invariant; Real-Time Maude model checking using the efficient maximal time sampling strategy therefore yields a sound and complete model checking procedure for Ptolemy II DE models.

In the traffic light system, the following *timed* CTL property states that the car light will turn yellow, *and only yellow*, within 1 time unit of a failure:

```
AG (('HierarchicalTrafficLight . 'Decision | port 'Error is present) implies
    AF[<= than 1] ('HierarchicalTrafficLight | 'Cyel = 1, 'Cgrn = 0, 'Cred = 0))
```

Model checking shows that this property is not satisfied (see Fig. 4), which made us aware of a previously unknown error: the car light may show red or green in addition to blinking yellow during a failure.

AADL. The *Architecture Analysis & Design Language* (AADL) [28,58] is an industrial modeling standard used in avionics, aerospace, automotive, medical

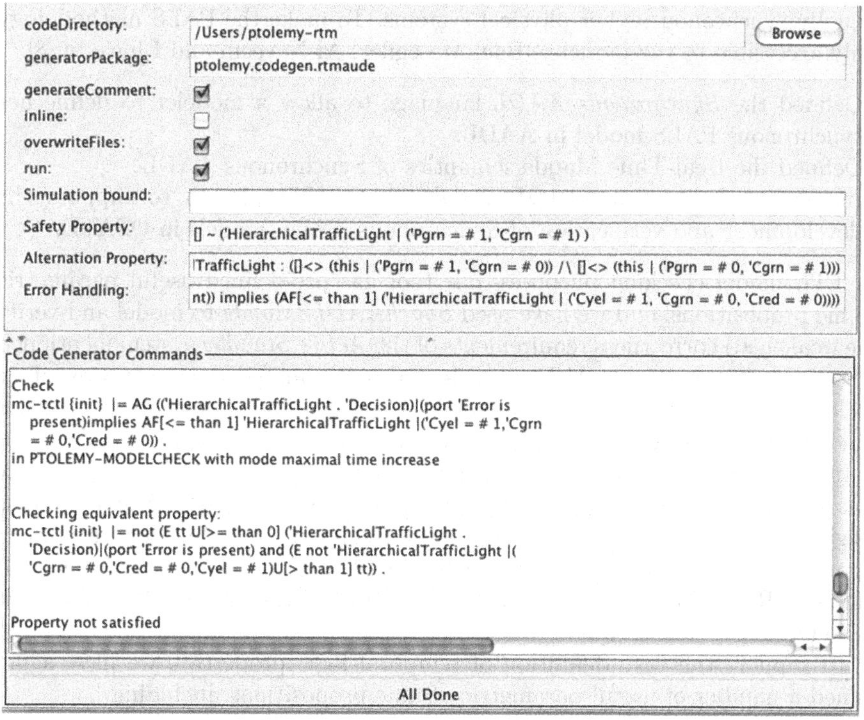

codeDirectory:	/Users/ptolemy-rtm	Browse
generatorPackage:	ptolemy.codegen.rtmaude	
generateComment:	☑	
inline:	☐	
overwriteFiles:	☑	
run:	☑	
Simulation bound:		
Safety Property:	[] ~ ('HierarchicalTrafficLight	('Pgrn = # 1, 'Cgrn = # 1))	
Alternation Property:	'TrafficLight : ([]<> (this	('Pgrn = # 1, 'Cgrn = # 0)) /\ []<> (this	('Pgrn = # 0, 'Cgrn = # 1)))	
Error Handling:	nt)) implies (AF[<= than 1] ('HierarchicalTrafficLight	('Cyel = # 1, 'Cgrn = # 0, 'Cred = # 0))))	

┌─Code Generator Commands──────────────────────────────────────

```
Check
mc-tctl {init} |= AG (('HierarchicalTrafficLight . 'Decision)|(port 'Error is
   present)implies AF[<= than 1] 'HierarchicalTrafficLight |('Cyel = # 1,'Cgrn
   = # 0,'Cred = # 0)) .
in PTOLEMY-MODELCHECK with mode maximal time increase


Checking equivalent property:
mc-tctl {init} |= not (E tt U[>= than 0] ('HierarchicalTrafficLight .
   'Decision)|(port 'Error is present) and (E not 'HierarchicalTrafficLight |(
   'Cgrn = # 0,'Cred = # 0,'Cyel = # 1)U[> than 1] tt)) .

Property not satisfied
```

                              All Done

Fig. 4. Dialog window for the Real Time Maude code generation and analysis.

devices, and robotics communities—including Honeywell, Rockwell-Collins, Lockheed Martin, General Dynamics, Airbus, the European Space Agency, Dassault, EADS, Ford, and Toyota—to describe an embedded real-time system as an assembly of software components mapped onto an execution platform. The OSATE modeling environment provides a set of Eclipse plug-ins for AADL.

The AADL standard is defined using English prose, which makes it ambiguous and also fails to make explicit important assumptions. In joint work with José Meseguer, I have defined the Real-Time Maude semantics of a subset of the *software components* of AADL [45]. This subset defines the architectural and behavioral specification of a system as a set of hierarchical components with ports and connections, with the thread behaviors given by Turing-complete transitions systems defined in AADL's *behavior annex*. Together with Artur Boronat, we have also developed an OSATE plug-in that generates a Real-Time Maude specification from an AADL model.

Papers by Belala *et al.* describe other efforts to define the semantics of a subset of behavioral AADL models in Real-Time Maude [15,16].

Synchronous AADL and Multirate Synchronous AADL. As mentioned in Sect. 5.2, the PALS pattern can greatly simplify the design and verification of virtually synchronous cyber-physical systems. To make the PALS methodology easily accessible to the modeler, Bae, Meseguer, Al-Nayeem and I have in [8]:

- Defined the *Synchronous AADL* language to allow a modeler to define her synchronous PALS model in AADL.
- Defined the Real-Time Maude semantics of Synchronous AADL.
- Implemented the *SynchAADL2Maude* [9] OSATE plug-in to support the development and verification of Synchronous AADL models in OSATE.

For LTL model checking purposes, our tool has pre-defined useful parametric atomic propositions, and we have used *SynchAADL2Maude* to model and verify (the weakened) correctness requirements of the *Active Standby* system mentioned in Sect. 5.1. Furthermore, Al-Nayeem has also automated the generation of an AADL model of the real-time system PALS(T, Γ) from a synchronous PALS model T defined using Synchronous AADL.

In the same way, Bae, Meseguer, and I have defined the *Multirate Synchronous AADL* language to support the modeling of Multirate PALS synchronous designs in AADL [12]. We have defined the Real-Time Maude semantics of our language, and have integrated the *MR-SynchAADL* tool to support the modeling and Real-Time Maude analysis of Multirate Synchronous AADL models inside OSATE.

To support the easy definition of temporal logic properties, we have again defined a number of useful parametric atomic propositions, including

full component name | boolean expression

which holds if *boolean expression* evaluates to *true* in the given component.

Figure 5 shows the MR-SynchAADL window for the airplane turning algorithm system in Sect. 5.1. In the editor part, two system requirements, `safety` (the yaw angle is always less than 1.0°) and `safeTurn` (the yaw angle is less than 1.0° until we eventually reach the goal direction and the plane is stable) are specified using the requirement specification language and listed in the "AADL Property Requirement" table. The `Constraints Check`, the `Code Generation`, and the `Perform Verification` buttons are used to perform, respectively, the syntactic validation of the model, the Real-Time Maude code generation, and the LTL model checking. The `Perform Verification` button has been clicked and the results are shown in the "Maude Console."

Both Synchronous AADL and Multirate Synchronous AADL models are time-robust and the predefined atomic propositions are tick-invariant, so that Real-Time Maude analyses are sound and complete.

Timed Rebeca. Timed Rebeca [2] is an actor-based modeling language with a Java-like syntax and a simple and intuitive message-driven and object-based computational model. In addition to a statement language with (nondeterministic) assignments, conditionals, and loops, Timed Rebeca also supports the dynamic creation of new actors. Zeynab Sabahi-Kaviani and others define the Real-Time Maude semantics of Timed Rebeca and integrate formal analysis in

Fig. 5. MR-SynchAADL window in OSATE.

the Rebeca toolset in [56,57]. Real-Time Maude's possibility of creating new objects dynamically is key to define the semantics of Timed Rebeca. It is again worth mentioning that the resulting Real-Time Maude specifications are time-robust.

Timed Model Transformations Frameworks. The MOMENT2 [20] formal model transformation framework is based on a formalization of MOF meta-models in rewriting logic. The static semantics of a system is given as a class diagram (or meta-model) describing the set of valid system states (or models) that are represented as object diagrams, and the dynamics of a system is defined as an *in-place model transformation*. In joint work with Artur Boronat, I have extended MOMENT2 to support the definition of timed behaviors by providing a set of basic constructs such as clocks and timers [19], and have defined the semantics of such timed model transformations in Real-Time Maude [19].

The e-Motions model transformation framework [55] for domain-specific visual languages is also based on EMF. Although the specification of behaviors is based on in-place model transformations, e-Motions does not use ("low-level") constructs such as clocks and timers to support timed model transformations. Instead, timed behaviors are defined by different kinds of *timed model transformation rules* of the form

$$[NAC]^* \times LHS \stackrel{[t_{min}, t_{max}]}{\longrightarrow} RHS$$

where *LHS* (its left-hand side), *RHS* (its right-hand side), and the optional *NAC*s (negative application conditions) are model patterns that represent state fragments, and the interval $[t_{min}, t_{max}]$ defines the possible *durations* of the rule. A rule "instance" is *triggered* as soon as it is enabled, and is *executed* some time $t \in [t_{min}, t_{max}]$ after being triggered. An atomic rule can also be declared to be *soft*, which means that it is not triggered eagerly, and/or may be declared to be *periodic*, in which case it is triggered periodically (for each instance) as long it is enabled. *Ongoing rules* do not have a fixed duration but are applied as long as the precondition holds. These are powerful constructs that typically imply that many different rules are being applied simultaneously to an object. This also means that a Real-Time Maude semantics is clearly needed, and is indeed provided by Rivera, Dúran, and Vallecillo in [54,55].

A Modeling Language for Handset Software. In [4], Musab AlTurki and researchers at DOCOMO USA Labs give a Real-Time Maude semantics to a simple but powerful specification language, called $\mathcal{L}$, that is claimed to be well suited for describing a spectrum of behaviors of various software systems. The language provides flexible SDL-inspired timing constructs that yield a more expressive language for timed behaviors than Erlang.

The language has an expression language, imperative features for describing sequential computations, and asynchronously communicating processes that can be dynamically created or destroyed. It is worth remarking that already the dynamic process creation places $\mathcal{L}$ outside the class of systems that can be represented as timed automata; so does its expression language and imperative features which make $\mathcal{L}$ Turing-complete.

5.4 Analysis of Distributed Maude Programs

(Core) Maude provides support for communication with external objects by means of TCP sockets. In this way multiple Maude processes running on different machines can be connected, giving rise to distributed Maude programs. Since such a program cannot be model checked directly, it must be related to a more abstract non-distributed (Real-Time) Maude model for formal analysis purposes. For real-time systems, this involves relating logical time in a Real-Time Maude specification to real physical time in a distributed implementation. This section summarizes three papers that verify Real-Time Maude abstractions of distributed Maude implementations.

Implementing and Analyzing the EIGRP Routing Protocol. In [53], Adrían Riesco and Alberto Verdejo provide a distributed formalization/"implementation" of the *Enhanced Interior Gateway Routing Protocol* (EIGRP), which is a CISCO proprietary distance-vector routing protocol, in Maude.

EIGRP is a *real-time* protocol: a router periodically broadcasts "hello" messages to its one-hop neighbors; if a router does not hear a "hello" message for a certain amount of time, it assumes that the link to that router is down. Since Maude does not provide support for distributed real-time application directly, Riesco and Verdejo use another external object, a Java object with access to real time, for timing purposes as follows: a Maude object can send a message wait(n) to this external Java "clock" object, asking that object to reply back with a tick message after n milliseconds of real time have elapsed.

For analysis purposes, Riesco and Verdejo transform their distributed model back to a single Real-Time Maude system. A key technique here is to formalize the properties of Maude's socket features, so that the specification being model checked resembles the original distributed system as closely as possible.

Two of the advantages of EIGRP compared to other routing protocols is that EIGRP has loop-free routing and fast convergence. Riesco and Verdejo use Real-Time Maude's *find latest* command to analyze the convergence time, its search command to check whether all routes are always loop-free, and its LTL model checker to check whether the best routes are eventually found. No errors in EIGRP were discovered during this analysis.

Generating and Analyzing Distributed Implementations of Orc Programs. Orc is an elegant and powerful programming language for orchestrating web services. In [5], Musab AlTurki and José Meseguer show how (i) one can go from an Orc specification to a distributed Maude implementation of the Orc specification, using their Maude semantics of Orc and Maude sockets; and (ii) how such distributed implementations can be model checked using Real-Time Maude. Orc is a timed language, and, as in [53], AlTurki and Meseguer integrate physical time in their distributed implementations by each distributed node having a local clock object. This clock is a Java object that uses the built-in Java classes Timer and Socket to send a "tick" message every t time units to the co-located Maude process.

To formally analyze a distributed implementation, AlTurki and Meseguer also formally specify in Real-Time Maude both the internet sockets supporting the distributed implementation and the local clock objects. They illustrate their methodology by taking an Orc specification of a simplified online auction management system, generating the distributed Maude implementation of the system, executing the distributed Maude program using the erew command in Maude, transforming this distributed Maude implementation into a Real-Time Maude specification using formal specification of the behaviors of the sockets and external clocks, and, finally, model checking the resulting specification using Real-Time Maude.

Real-Time Emulation of Verified Medical Device Controllers. Mu Sun and José Meseguer go the other way in [60]: from verified Real-Time Maude models to concrete systems operating with their environments in real time. More precisely, they create executable *emulations* of medical device controllers from Real-Time Maude models that are instances of their command shaper pattern. These emulations can be connected to real devices to validate the safety of the device in a real environment. Essentially, an execution "wrapper" around the Real-Time Maude model deals with handling time and messages to and from the external world. Model time is again related to physical time by interacting with a

Java thread. Sun and Meseguer advance time maximally by sending a "time-out request" to the time thread; however, they can also deal with "interrupts" from external devices which may happen at any time. They analyze the time that the "instantaneous" transitions and message passing take (never more than 0.2 s), and make sure that any skew is not multiplied over time.

Sun and Meseguer present two case studies, where the safe device controllers are instances of the command shaper pattern. The first case study is a pacemaker controller. Sun and Meseguer connect their device controller emulator to

- a "user" that sends a "dangerous" sequence of pacemaker commands to the device controller; and
- a Java widget that simulates a pacemaker by receiving pacemaker commands (from the device controller) and drawing the corresponding ECG trace.

The ECG trace shows that the device controller ensured a safe heart rate. In their second case study they actually connect their wrapped Real-Time Maude model of a safe syringe pump controller to a real Multi-Phaser NE-500 syringe pump, and validate their controller by weighing the amount of liquid infused from the syringe pump.

6   Extensions of Real-Time Maude

This section presents two extensions of Real-Time Maude, namely, to hybrid systems and priced timed systems.

6.1   HI-Maude: Object-Oriented Modeling and Formal Analysis of Continuously Interacting Hybrid Systems

Section 5 shows that Real-Time Maude's expressiveness and modeling flexibility have made it possible to successfully apply the tool to a number of large and complex applications, all of which have been modeled in an object-oriented style. An important question is whether Real-Time Maude can also successfully model and analyze complex *hybrid* systems in an object-oriented way.

It is a nightmare to define the continuous dynamics of many hybrid systems, since different components may influence each other's continuous behaviors; we call such systems *(continuously) interacting hybrid systems*. Consider the problem of keeping track of the temperature of a hot cup of coffee in a colder room. The temperature of the coffee will continuously decrease *and* the temperature of the room will continuously *increase* due to heat transfer from the coffee. Although the continuous behaviors of the single components and the heat flow between them are well known, it is very hard to define the continuous behavior of the entire system "in one shot," which is what current formal models of hybrid systems require. Existing formalisms therefore also do not support the object-oriented specification of continuously interacting hybrid systems, since the continuous behavior must be completely redefined for each new configuration of objects (for example, if we have *three* cups of coffee), and therefore cannot be defined at the class level.

Muhammad Fadlisyah, Erika Ábrahám, and I have addressed the formal modeling and analysis of interacting hybrid systems in [24–27]. In our object-oriented modeling methodology, which is based on the *effort/flow* method, *both* the *physical entities* and the *physical interactions* between the entities are modeled explicitly as objects. For example, heat flows from the coffee and the cup to the room through heat *convection*, and heat flows between the coffee and the cup through heat *conduction*. This approach is applicable to different kinds of systems, including mechanical translation systems, mechanical rotation systems, electrical systems, fluidic systems, and thermal systems.

Our modeling methodology is supported by the HI-Maude tool [24], which extends Real-Time Maude. In HI-Maude, one can define the continuous dynamics of *single* physical component objects and *single* interaction objects. HI-Maude then computes the continuous dynamics of the entire system. This enables object-oriented modeling, since both the discrete and the continuous dynamics are defined at the class level, and since the dynamic creation/deletion of physical components is supported. For example, to add another cup of coffee, one could just add (possibly dynamically) a new coffee object, a new cup object, and three new interaction objects to the state.

To analyze hybrid systems—and HI-Maude targets complex systems whose continuous dynamics may be defined by differential equations that are not analytically solvable—we have adapted different numerical methods (the Euler method and the Runge-Kutta methods of 2nd and 4th order) to our modeling methodology to give approximate solutions to coupled differential equations. These approximations are then used in HI-Maude simulation, reachability analysis, and linear temporal logic model checking. For example, HI-Maude's hybrid *rewrite* command is used to simulate one behavior of the system from a given initial state *initState* up to duration *timeLimit*:

(**hrew** *initState* **in time <=** *timeLimit* **using** *numMethod* **stepsize** *stepSize* .)

where *numMethod* $\in$ {**euler, rk2, rk4**} is the numerical approximation method used and *stepSize* is the time increment used in the approximations.

Since the numerical methods only approximate the real continuous behaviors, *HI-Maude analyses are in general not sound and complete*. The main value of HI-Maude is therefore to formally define and simulate complex hybrid systems.

Case Study: Modeling the Human Thermoregulatory System. The *human thermoregulatory system* (HTS) attempts to ensure human survival and comfort in different environments. The HTS has been studied extensively—sometimes by experimentation on live subjects—to analyze how long a person can survive in cold water, how long he can exercise in hot weather without succumbing to heat stroke, and how to provide the most comfortable environment for pilots, astronauts, and airplane passengers, and so on.

In the HTS, the hypothalamus part of the brain enables the following mechanisms to support *heat loss* from the body when needed: increasing the diameter of blood vessels to let more blood flow underneath the skin (*vasodilation*),

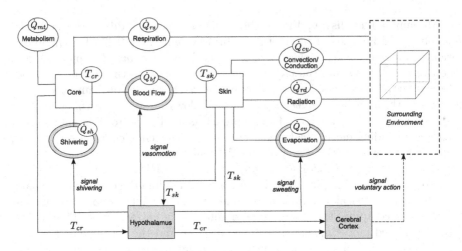

Fig. 6. Effort/flow model of the human thermoregulatory system.

which promotes heat loss by radiation, convection, and conduction; and increasing sweat production, which promotes heat loss by evaporation. When the body temperature is decreasing, the hypothalamus may decrease the diameter of blood vessels to let less blood flow underneath the skin (*vasoconstriction*) to reduce heat loss, and may stimulate the skeletal muscles to cause shivering to increase heat production. Behavioral thermoregulation (e.g., putting on or taking off a jacket) is related to a part of the brain called the cerebral cortex.

In [27] we define a HI-Maude model of the human thermoregulatory system according to accepted physiological facts and models, where the *body core* and the *skin* are two main components. Heat flows between them through blood flows where the diameter of the blood vessels changes continuously. The main forms of heat exchange between skin and environment are by conduction/convection, radiation, and evaporation of sweat; between core and environment heat flows mainly through respiration. Figure 6 shows the physical entities (boxes) and interactions (ovals) in our model, where heat production by metabolism and by shivering are represented as one-sided interactions.

We can connect our fairly sophisticated model to different environments. We chose to analyze possible causes of the accident at the 2010 Sauna World Championships, which ended in a tragedy when the two finalists collapsed with severe burn injuries after about six minutes; one of them died the next day. The cause of this tragedy is still under investigation. Our HI-Maude analyses show that even the average person should endure 12 min in the sauna before the onset of major injuries. We also used HI-Maude to analyze what scenarios could cause major injuries to a five-time world champion in around 6 min [27].

Priced-Timed Maude. Reasoning about the accumulated *cost* (say, *price* or *energy usage*) during behaviors is crucial in embedded systems and sensor networks where minimizing overall energy consumption is critical. The *Priced-Timed Maude* tool [17] extends Real-Time Maude to support the formal modeling of non-hierarchical object-oriented priced and timed systems by adding *priced* rules of the form c => c' with cost u if *cond*, where c and c' are terms of sort Configuration, and priced tick rules of the form $\{t\}$ => $\{t'\}$ in time τ with cost u if *cond*. Apart from extending Real-Time Maude's analysis commands in the expected way, Priced-Timed Maude also adds commands for finding *optimal* solutions, such as the cheapest behavior leading to a desired state.

Although Priced-Timed Maude has been applied to benchmarks such as energy task graph scheduling, the airplane landing problem, and to the slightly larger problem of efficiently routing passengers within a subway network while minimizing power consumption of the trains, the tool has not been applied to state-of-the-art applications.

7   Concluding Remarks

Real-Time Maude is an expressive modeling language and a formal analysis tool that is particularly useful for defining distributed real-time systems in an object-oriented way. Indeed, virtually all the Real-Time Maude applications summarized in Sect. 5 have been object-oriented Real-Time Maude specifications. I have shown that Real-Time Maude features such as user-definable data types, hierarchical objects, dynamic object creation, unbounded data structures, and the possibility to easily define the appropriate communication model have all been needed to apply the tool on a number of advanced state-of-the-art applications and to define the formal semantics of several modeling languages.

Despite the size and complexity of the applications, Real-Time Maude analysis – both simulation and model checking – could still be used to discover significant previously unknown flaws in many of the applications, as well as to provide formal analysis capabilities for the modeling languages. Furthermore, many of those applications and modeling languages are formalized as time-robust Real-Time Maude specifications, which means that their Real-Time Maude analyses are guaranteed to be sound and complete.

Many large real-time systems are *probabilistic* systems, either because their algorithms are probabilistic in nature or because there is a need to analyze their performance in an environment which can be seen as probabilistic. Real-Time Maude should therefore be extended to model probabilistic behaviors. This would also enable useful and scalable analysis by means of statistical model checking. Finally, Real-Time Maude should also incorporate symbolic analysis techniques, including the use of SMT solvers, to increase the efficiency and analytic power of Real-Time Maude model checking.

Acknowledgments. I thank all my coauthors for very nice collaborations which have motivated, improved, and validated Real-Time Maude. In particular, I would like to thank José Meseguer, who has been part of the entire Real-Time Maude journey, Martin Wirsing, who initiated this journey, and Kyungmin Bae. I am also grateful to Santiago Escobar for inviting me to give an invited talk at WRLA 2014 and for patiently waiting for this paper to be finished.

References

1. Abrial, J.-R., Börger, E., Langmaack, H. (eds.): Formal Methods for Industrial Applications: Specifying and Programming the Steam Boiler Control. LNCS, vol. 1165. Springer, Heidelberg (1996)
2. Aceto, L., Cimini, M., Ingólfsdóttir, A., Reynisson, A.H., Sigurdarson, S.H., Sirjani, M.: Modelling and simulation of asynchronous real-time systems using Timed Rebeca. In: Proceedings of FOCLASA'11, vol. 58. EPTCS (2011)
3. Al-Nayeem, A., Sun, M., Qiu, X., Sha, L., Miller, S.P., Cofer, D.D.: A formal architecture pattern for real-time distributed systems. In: RTSS'09. IEEE (2009)
4. AlTurki, M., Dhurjati, D., Yu, D., Chander, A., Inamura, H.: Formal specification and analysis of timing properties in software systems. In: Chechik, M., Wirsing, M. (eds.) FASE 2009. LNCS, vol. 5503, pp. 262–277. Springer, Heidelberg (2009)
5. AlTurki, M., Meseguer, J.: Dist-Orc: A rewriting-based distributed implementation of Orc with formal analysis. In: Proceedings of RTRTS'10, vol. 36. EPTCS (2010)
6. Alur, R., Dill, D.L.: A theory of timed automata. Theoret. Comput. Sci. **126**(2), 183–235 (1994)
7. Bae, K., Meseguer, J., Ölveczky, P.C.: Formal patterns for multirate distributed real-time systems. Sci. Comput. Programm. **91(A)**, 3–44 (2014)
8. Bae, K., Ölveczky, P.C., Al-Nayeem, A., Meseguer, J.: Synchronous AADL and its formal analysis in Real-Time Maude. In: Qin, S., Qiu, Z. (eds.) ICFEM 2011. LNCS, vol. 6991, pp. 651–667. Springer, Heidelberg (2011)
9. Bae, K., Ölveczky, P.C., Meseguer, J., Al-Nayeem, A.: The SynchAADL2Maude tool. In: de Lara, J., Zisman, A. (eds.) Fundamental Approaches to Software Engineering. LNCS, vol. 7212, pp. 59–62. Springer, Heidelberg (2012)
10. Bae, K., Krisiloff, J., Meseguer, J., Ölveczky, P.C.: Designing and verifying distributed cyber-physical systems using Multirate PALS: an airplane turning control system case study. Sci. Comput. Programm. (2014, to appear). doi: 10.1016/j.scico.2014.09.011
11. Bae, K., Ölveczky, P.C., Feng, T.H., Lee, E.A., Tripakis, S.: Verifying hierarchical Ptolemy II discrete-event models using Real-Time Maude. Sci. Comput. Program. **77**(12), 1235–1271 (2012)
12. Bae, K., Ölveczky, P.C., Meseguer, J.: Definition, semantics, and analysis of Multirate Synchronous AADL. In: Jones, C., Pihlajasaari, P., Sun, J. (eds.) FM 2014. LNCS, vol. 8442, pp. 94–109. Springer, Heidelberg (2014)
13. Basu, A., Bensalem, S., Bozga, M., Combaz, J., Jaber, M., Nguyen, T.H., Sifakis, J.: Rigorous component-based system design using the BIP framework. IEEE Softw. **28**(3), 41–48 (2011)
14. Behrmann, G., David, A., Larsen, K.G.: A tutorial on UPPAAL. In: Bernardo, M., Corradini, F. (eds.) SFM-RT 2004. LNCS, vol. 3185, pp. 200–236. Springer, Heidelberg (2004)
15. Belala, F., Benammar, M., Barkaoui, K., Hicheur, A.: Formal modeling and analysis of AADL threads in Real-Time Maude. J. Softw. Eng. Appl. **5**, 187–192 (2012)
16. Benammar, M., Belala, F.: How to make AADL specification more precise. Int. J. Comput. Appl. **8**(10), 16–23 (2010)
17. Bendiksen, L., Ölveczky, P.C.: The Priced-Timed Maude tool. In: Kurz, A., Lenisa, M., Tarlecki, A. (eds.) CALCO 2009. LNCS, vol. 5728, pp. 443–448. Springer, Heidelberg (2009)
18. Bergstra, J.A., Tucker, J.V.: Algebraic specification of computable and semicomputable data types. Theoret. Comput. Sci. **50**, 137–181 (1987)

19. Boronat, A., Ölveczky, P.C.: Formal real-time model transformations in MOMENT2. In: Rosenblum, D.S., Taentzer, G. (eds.) FASE 2010. LNCS, vol. 6013, pp. 29–43. Springer, Heidelberg (2010)

20. Boronat, A., Heckel, R., Meseguer, J.: Rewriting logic semantics and verification of model transformations. In: Chechik, M., Wirsing, M. (eds.) FASE 2009. LNCS, vol. 5503, pp. 18–33. Springer, Heidelberg (2009)

21. Bozga, M., Graf, S., Ober, I., Ober, I., Sifakis, J.: The IF toolset. In: Bernardo, M., Corradini, F. (eds.) SFM-RT 2004. LNCS, vol. 3185, pp. 237–267. Springer, Heidelberg (2004)

22. Clavel, M., Durán, F., Eker, S., Lincoln, P., Martí-Oliet, N., Meseguer, J., Talcott, C. (eds.): All About Maude - A High-Performance Logical Framework. LNCS, vol. 4350. Springer, Heidelberg (2007)

23. Eker, J., Janneck, J.W., Lee, E.A., Liu, J., Liu, X., Ludvig, J., Neuendorffer, S., Sachs, S., Xiong, Y.: Taming heterogeneity–the Ptolemy approach. Proc. IEEE 91(2), 127–144 (2003)

24. Fadlisyah, M., Ölveczky, P.C.: The HI-Maude tool. In: Heckel, R., Milius, S. (eds.) CALCO 2013. LNCS, vol. 8089, pp. 322–327. Springer, Heidelberg (2013)

25. Fadlisyah, M., Ölveczky, P.C., Ábrahám, E.: Formal modeling and analysis of hybrid systems in rewriting logic using higher-order numerical methods and discrete-event detection. In: Proceedings of CSSE'11. IEEE (2011)

26. Fadlisyah, M., Ölveczky, P.C., Ábrahám, E.: Object-oriented formal modeling and analysis of interacting hybrid systems in HI-Maude. In: Barthe, G., Pardo, A., Schneider, G. (eds.) SEFM 2011. LNCS, vol. 7041, pp. 415–430. Springer, Heidelberg (2011)

27. Fadlisyah, M., Ölveczky, P.C., Ábrahám, E.: Formal modeling and analysis of interacting hybrid systems in HI-Maude: What happened at the 2010 Sauna World Championships? Sci. Comput. Programm. (2014). http://dx.doi.org/10.1016/j.scico.2014.06.010

28. Feiler, P.H., Gluch, D.P.: Model-Based Engineering with AADL. Addison-Wesley, Upper Saddle River (2012)

29. Grov, J., Ölveczky, P.C.: Formal modeling and analysis of Google's Megastore in Real-Time Maude. In: Iida, S., Meseguer, J., Ogata, K. (eds.) Specification, Algebra, and Software. LNCS, vol. 8373, pp. 494–519. Springer, Heidelberg (2014)

30. Grov, J., Ölveczky, P.C.: Increasing consistency in multi-site data stores: Megastore-CGC and its formal analysis. In: Giannakopoulou, D., Salaün, G. (eds.) SEFM 2014. LNCS, vol. 8702, pp. 159–174. Springer, Heidelberg (2014)

31. Katelman, M., Meseguer, J., Hou, J.: Redesign of the LMST wireless sensor protocol through formal modeling and statistical model checking. In: Barthe, G., de Boer, F.S. (eds.) FMOODS 2008. LNCS, vol. 5051, pp. 150–169. Springer, Heidelberg (2008)

32. Katelman, M., Meseguer, J.: Using the PALS architecture to verify a distributed topology control protocol for wireless multi-hop networks in the presence of node failures. In: Proceedings of RTRTS'10, vol. 36. EPTCS (2010)

33. Kim, M., Dutt, N., Venkatasubramanian, N.: Policy construction and validation for energy minimization in cross layered systems: a formal method approach. In: Proceedings of IEEE RTAS'06 Work-in-Progress Session, pp. 4–7 (2006)

34. Lepri, D., Ábrahám, E., Ölveczky, P.C.: A timed CTL model checker for Real-Time Maude. In: Heckel, R., Milius, S. (eds.) CALCO 2013. LNCS, vol. 8089, pp. 334–339. Springer, Heidelberg (2013)

35. Lepri, D., Ábrahám, E., Ölveczky, P.C.: Sound and complete timed CTL model checking of timed Kripke structures and real-time rewrite theories. Sci. Comput. Program. (2014). http://dx.doi.org/10.1016/j.scico.2014.06.006

36. Lien, E., Ölveczky, P.C.: Formal modeling and analysis of an IETF multicast protocol. In: Proceedings of SEFM'09. IEEE (2009)

37. Liu, S., Ölveczky, P., Meseguer, J.: A framework for mobile ad hoc networks in Real-Time Maude. In: Escobar, S. (ed.) WRLA 2014. LNCS, vol. 8663, pp. 162–177. Springer, Heidelberg (2014)

38. Liu, S., Ölveczky, P., Meseguer, J.: Formal analysis of leader election in MANETs using Real-Time Maude. In: Festschrift honoring Martin Wirsing. LNCS. Springer, Heidelberg (2015)

39. Meseguer, J., Ölveczky, P.C.: Formalization and correctness of the PALS architectural pattern for distributed real-time systems. Theoret. Comput. Sci. **451**, 1–37 (2012)

40. Meseguer, J.: Taming distributed system complexity through formal patterns. Sci. Comput. Program. **83**, 3–34 (2014)

41. Nakajima, S.: Model-based power consumption analysis of smartphone applications. In: Proceedings of ACESMB@MoDELS, CEUR Workshop Proceedings, vol. 1084. CEUR-WS.org (2013)

42. Ölveczky, P.C.: Real-Time Maude 2.3 Manual (2007). http://ifi.uio.no/RealTimeMaude/

43. Ölveczky, P.C.: Formal model engineering for embedded systems using Real-Time Maude. In: Proceedings of AMMSE'11, vol. 56. EPTCS (2011)

44. Ölveczky, P.C.: Semantics, simulation, and formal analysis of modeling languages for embedded systems in Real-Time Maude. In: Agha, G., Danvy, O., Meseguer, J. (eds.) Formal Modeling: Actors, Open Systems, Biological Systems. LNCS, vol. 7000, pp. 368–402. Springer, Heidelberg (2011)

45. Ölveczky, P.C., Boronat, A., Meseguer, J.: Formal semantics and analysis of behavioral AADL models in Real-Time Maude. In: Hatcliff, J., Zucca, E. (eds.) FMOODS 2010, Part II. LNCS, vol. 6117, pp. 47–62. Springer, Heidelberg (2010)

46. Ölveczky, P.C., Caccamo, M.: Formal simulation and analysis of the CASH scheduling algorithm in Real-Time Maude. In: Baresi, L., Heckel, R. (eds.) FASE 2006. LNCS, vol. 3922, pp. 357–372. Springer, Heidelberg (2006)

47. Ölveczky, P.C., Meseguer, J.: Specification of real-time and hybrid systems in rewriting logic. Theoret. Comput. Sci. **285**, 359–405 (2002)

48. Ölveczky, P.C., Meseguer, J.: Abstraction and completeness for Real-Time Maude. ENTCS **176**(4), 5–27 (2007)

49. Ölveczky, P.C., Meseguer, J.: Semantics and pragmatics of Real-Time Maude. Higher-Order Symbolic Comput. **20**(1–2), 161–196 (2007)

50. Ölveczky, P.C., Meseguer, J., Talcott, C.L.: Specification and analysis of the AER/NCA active network protocol suite in Real-Time Maude. Formal Methods Syst. Des. **29**(3), 253–293 (2006)

51. Ölveczky, P.C., Prabhakar, P., Liu, X.: Formal modeling and analysis of real-time resource-sharing protocols in Real-Time Maude. In: Proceedings of IPDPS'08. IEEE (2008)

52. Ölveczky, P.C., Thorvaldsen, S.: Formal modeling, performance estimation, and model checking of wireless sensor network algorithms in Real-Time Maude. Theoret. Comput. Sci. **410**(2–3), 254–280 (2009)

53. Riesco, A., Verdejo, A.: Implementing and analyzing in Maude the Enhanced Interior Gateway Routing Protocol. ENTCS **238**(3), 249–266 (2009)

54. Rivera, J.E.: On the semantics of real-time domain specific modeling languages. Ph.D. thesis, Universidad de Málaga (2010)
55. Rivera, J.E., Durán, F., Vallecillo, A.: On the behavioral semantics of real-time domain specific visual languages. In: Ölveczky, P.C. (ed.) WRLA 2010. LNCS, vol. 6381, pp. 174–190. Springer, Heidelberg (2010)
56. Sabahi-Kaviani, Z., Khosravi, R., Ölveczky, P.C., Khamespanah, E., Sirjani, M.: Formal semantics and efficient analysis of Timed Rebeca in Real-Time Maude (2014, submitted for publication)
57. Sabahi-Kaviani, Z., Khosravi, R., Sirjani, M., Ölveczky, P.C., Khamespanah, E.: Formal semantics and analysis of Timed Rebeca in Real-Time Maude. In: Artho, C., Ölveczky, P.C. (eds.) FTSCS 2013. CCIS, vol. 419, pp. 178–194. Springer, Heidelberg (2014)
58. SEA International: Architecture Analysis & Design Language (AADL). Standard AS5506, Revision B, September 2012. http://standards.sae.org/as5506b/
59. Sen, K., Viswanathan, M., Agha, G.A.: VeStA: a statistical model-checker and analyzer for probabilistic systems. In: Proceedings of QEST'05. IEEE (2005)
60. Sun, M., Meseguer, J.: Distributed real-time emulation of formally-defined patterns for safe medical device control. In: Proceedings of RTRTS'10. vol. 36. EPTCS (2010)
61. Sun, M., Meseguer, J., Sha, L.: A formal pattern architecture for safe medical systems. In: Ölveczky, P.C. (ed.) WRLA 2010. LNCS, vol. 6381, pp. 157–173. Springer, Heidelberg (2010)
62. Vasudevan, S., Kurose, J.F., Towsley, D.F.: Design and analysis of a leader election algorithm for mobile ad hoc networks. In: Proceedings of ICNP'04. IEEE (2004)
63. Wang, F.: Efficient verification of timed automata with BDD-like data structures. Softw. Tools Technol. Trans. 6(1), 77–97 (2004)
64. Wirsing, M., Bauer, S.S., Schroeder, A.: Modeling and analyzing adaptive user-centric systems in Real-Time Maude. In: Proceedings of RTRTS'10, vol. 36. EPTCS (2010)
65. Zhang, H., Hou, J.C.: Maintaining sensing coverage and connectivity in large sensor networks. Wirel. Ad Hoc Sens. Netw. Int. J. 1(1–2), 89–124 (2005)
66. Zhu, L., Liu, P., Shi, J., Wang, Z., Zhu, H.: A timing verification framework for AUTOSAR OS component development based on Real-Time Maude. In: Proceedings of TASE'13. IEEE (2013)

Conditional Narrowing Modulo in Rewriting Logic and Maude

Luis Aguirre[✉], Narciso Martí-Oliet, Miguel Palomino, and Isabel Pita

Facultad de Informática, Universidad Complutense de Madrid, Madrid, Spain
{luisagui,narciso,miguelpt,ipandreu}@ucm.es

Abstract. This work studies the relationship between verifiable and computable answers for reachability problems in rewrite theories with an underlying membership equational logic. These problems have the form

$$(\exists \bar{x}) s(\bar{x}) \rightarrow^* t(\bar{x})$$

with $\bar{x}$ some variables, or a conjunction of several of these subgoals. A calculus that solves this kind of problems has been developed and proved correct. Given a reachability problem in a rewrite theory, this calculus can compute any normalized answer that can be checked by rewriting, or a more general one. Special care has been taken in the calculus to keep membership information attached to each term, using this information whenever possible.

Keywords: Maude · Narrowing · Reachability · Rewriting logic · Unification · Membership equational logic

1 Introduction

Rewriting logic is a computational logic that has been around for more than twenty years [Mes90], whose semantics [BM06] has a precise mathematical meaning allowing mathematical reasoning for property proving, providing a more flexible framework for the specification of concurrent systems. It turned out that it can express both concurrent computation and logical deduction, allowing its application in many areas such as automated deduction, software and hardware specification and verification, security, etc. One important property of rewriting logic is reflection [CM96]. Intuitively, reflection means representing a logic's metalevel at the object level, allowing the definition of strategies that guide rule application in an object-level theory.

Reachability problems have the form

$$(\exists \bar{x}) s(\bar{x}) \rightarrow^* t(\bar{x})$$

Research supported by MINECO Spanish project StrongSoft (TIN2012–39391–C04–04) and Comunidad de Madrid program PROMETIDOS (S2009/TIC-1465).

© Springer International Publishing Switzerland 2014
S. Escobar (Ed.): WRLA 2014, LNCS 8663, pp. 80–96, 2014.
DOI: 10.1007/978-3-319-12904-4_4

with $\bar{x}$ some variables, or a conjunction of several of these subgoals. They can be solved by model checking methods for finite state spaces. A technique known as *narrowing* [Fay78] that was first proposed as a method for solving equational goals (*unification*), has been extended to cover also reachability goals [MT07], leaving equational goals as a special case of reachability goals. In recent years the idea of *variants of a term* has been applied to narrowing. A strategy for order-sorted unconditional rewrite theories known as *folding variant narrowing* [ESM12], which computes a complete set of variants of any term, has been developed by Escobar, Sasse and Meseguer, allowing unification *modulo* a set of equations and axioms. The strategy terminates on any input term on those systems enjoying the *finite variant property*, and it is *optimally terminating*. It is being used for cryptographic protocol analysis [MT07], with tools like Maude-NPA [EMM05], termination algorithms modulo axioms [DLM+08], and algorithms for checking confluence and coherence of rewrite theories modulo axioms, such as the Church-Rosser (CRC) and the Coherence (ChC) Checkers for Maude [DM12].

This work explores narrowing for membership conditional rewrite theories, going beyond the scope of folding variant narrowing which works on order-sorted unconditional rewrite theories. A calculus that computes answers to reachability problems in membership conditional rewrite theories has been developed and proved correct with respect to idempotent normalized answers.

The work is structured as follows: in Sect. 2 all needed definitions and properties for rewriting and narrowing are introduced. Section 3 introduces the first part of the narrowing calculus, the one that deals with equational unification. Section 4 introduces the part of the calculus dealing with reachability and its proof of correctness. Section 5 shows the calculus at work. In Sect. 6, related work, conclusions and current lines of investigation for this work are presented. An extended version of this paper, with all the missing proofs, can be found at http://maude.sip.ucm.es/cnarrowing/, together with a previous version of this work with transformation rules and a prototype.

2 Preliminaries

We assume familiarity with rewriting logic [BM06]. There are several language implementations of rewriting logic, including Maude [CDE+07]. Rewriting logic is parameterized by an underlying equational logic. In Maude's case this logic is membership equational logic [Mes97].

2.1 Tower of Hanoi Example

Throughout this paper the Tower of Hanoi puzzle will be used as a motivating example to explain the definitions in a less abstract way. We have Rods a, b and c, and Disks 1, 2, 3 and 4 which can slide onto any Rod. We call a Rod with zero or more stacked Disks (written juxtaposed) a Tower. If smaller Disks are always stacked on top of bigger Disks we have a ValidTower (abbreviated VT).

A set of valid towers (written separated by commas) is a State (abbreviated St). A move between a Pair of towers (written separated by a − symbol) is defined by the rules: 1) only one Disk may be moved at a time, 2) each move consists of taking the upper Disk from one Tower and placing it on top of another Tower, and 3) Disk X may be placed on top of Disk Y only if X is smaller than Y (written $X < Y =$ t, where t is the *true* Boolean value). The goal of the puzzle is to reach a desired State from a given initial State.

2.2   Membership Equational Logic

A *membership equational logic* (MEL) *signature* [BM06] is a triple $\Sigma = (K, \Omega, S)$, with K a set of *kinds*, $\Omega = \{\Sigma_{w;k}\}_{(w;k)\in K^*\times K}$ a many-kinded algebraic signature, and $S = \{S_k\}_{k\in K}$ a K-kinded family of disjoint sets of sorts. For simplicity, we only allow overloading of operators whenever the result belongs in the same kind. The kind of a sort s is denoted by $[s]$. The sets $T_{\Sigma,s}$, $T_\Sigma(X)_s$, $T_{\Sigma,k}$ and $T_\Sigma(X)_k$ denote, respectively, the set of ground Σ-terms with sort s, the set of Σ-terms with sort s over the set X of *sorted* variables, the set of ground Σ-terms with kind k and the set of Σ-terms with kind k over the set X of *sorted* variables. We write T_Σ, $T_\Sigma(X)$ for the corresponding term algebras. $Var(t) \subseteq X$ denotes the set of variables in $t \in T_\Sigma(X)$.

In the Tower of Hanoi puzzle, $\Sigma = (K, \Omega, S)$ is:

- $K = \{\text{TS}, \text{P}, \text{D}, \text{B}\}$,
- $\Omega = \{\cdot_{\text{D TS;TS}}, ,_{\text{TS TS;TS}}, -_{\text{TS TS;P}}, \text{move}_{\text{P;P}}, <_{\text{D D;B}}\}$,
- $S = \{S_{\text{TS}}, S_{\text{P}}, S_{\text{D}}, S_{\text{B}}\}$, where
  $S_{\text{TS}} = \{\text{Rod}, \text{VT}, \text{Tower}, \text{St}\}$, $S_{\text{P}} = \{\text{Pair}\}$, $S_{\text{D}} = \{\text{Disk}\}$, $S_{\text{B}} = \{\text{Boolean}\}$.

Finally, $\{\text{a}, \text{b}, \text{c}\}$, $\{1, 2, 3, 4\}$, and $\{\text{t}\}$ are the *atoms* with sort Rod, Disk, and Boolean respectively.

Positions in a term t: we represent the root of t as ϵ and the other positions as strings of nonzero natural numbers in the usual way, considering t as a tree. The set of positions of a term is written $Pos(t)$. $t|_p$ is the subtree below position p. $t[u]_p$ is the replacement in t of the subterm at position p with term u.

A *substitution* $\sigma : Y \rightarrow T_\Sigma(X)$ is a function from a finite set of sorted variables $Y \subseteq X$ to $T_\Sigma(X)$ such that $\sigma(y)$ has the same or lower sort as that of the variable $y \in Y$ ($s_1 \leq s_2$, formally defined in the next paragraph). Substitutions are written as $\sigma = \{x_1 \mapsto t_1, \ldots, x_n \mapsto t_n\}$ where $Dom(\sigma) = \{x_1, \ldots, x_n\}$ and $Ran(\sigma) = \bigcup_{i=1}^n Var(t_i)$. The identity substitution is *id*. The restriction of σ to a set of variables V is $\sigma|_V$. Composition of two substitutions is denoted by $\sigma\sigma'$. For substitutions σ and σ' where $Dom(\sigma) \cap Dom(\sigma') = \emptyset$, we denote their union by $\sigma \cup \sigma'$.

A MEL theory [BM06] is a pair $(\Sigma, \mathcal{E})$, where Σ is a MEL signature and $\mathcal{E}$ is a finite set of MEL sentences, either conditional equations or conditional memberships of the forms:

$$(\forall X)\ t = t' \text{ if } \bigwedge_i A_i, \quad (\forall X)\ t{:}s \text{ if } \bigwedge_i A_i$$

for $t, t' \in T_\Sigma(X)_k$ and $s \in S_k$, the latter stating that t is a term of sort s, provided the condition holds, and each A_i can be of the form $t=t'$, $t:s$, or $t:=t'$ (a *matching* equation). Matching equations are treated as ordinary equations, but they impose a limitation in the syntax of admissible MEL theories, as we will see. We also admit unconditional sentences in $\mathcal{E}$. Order-sorted (*sugared*) notation $s_1 \leq s_2$ can be used instead of $(\forall x:[s_1])\ x:s_2$ if $x:s_1$. An operator declaration $f : s_1 \times \cdots \times s_n \to s$ corresponds to declaring f at the kind level and giving the membership axiom $(\forall x_1:[s_1], \ldots, x_n:[s_n])\ f(x_1, \ldots, x_n):s$ if $\bigwedge_{1 \leq i \leq n} x_i:s_i$. Given a MEL sentence ϕ, we denote by $\mathcal{E} \vdash \phi$ that ϕ can be deduced from $\mathcal{E}$ using the rules in Fig. 1, where $=$ can be either $=$ or $:=$ as explained before [BM12]. The rules of Fig. 1 specify a sound and complete calculus. A MEL theory $(\Sigma, \mathcal{E})$ has an *initial algebra*, denoted by $T_{\Sigma/\mathcal{E}}$, whose elements are the equivalence classes $[t]_{\mathcal{E}} \subseteq T_\Sigma$ of ground terms identified by the equations in $\mathcal{E}$.

$$\frac{t \in T_\Sigma(X)}{(\forall X)t = t} \ \textbf{Reflexivity} \qquad \frac{(\forall X)t = t'}{(\forall X)t' = t} \ \textbf{Symmetry}$$

$$\frac{(\forall X)t_1 = t_2 (\forall X)t_2 = t_3}{(\forall X)t_1 = t_3} \ \textbf{Transitivity} \qquad \frac{(\forall X)t':s \ \ (\forall X)t=t'}{(\forall X)t:s} \ \textbf{Membership}$$

$$\frac{f \in \Sigma_{k_1 \cdots k_n, k} \ (\forall X)t_i = t'_i \ \ t_i, t'_i \in T_\Sigma(X)_{k_i}, 1 \leq i \leq n}{(\forall X)f(t_1, \ldots, t_n) = f(t'_1, \ldots, t'_n)} \ \textbf{Congruence}$$

$$\frac{((\forall X)\ A_0 \text{ if } \bigwedge_i A_i) \in E \ \ \theta : X \to T_\Sigma(Y) \ \ (\forall Y)A_i\theta}{(\forall Y)A_0\theta} \ \textbf{Replacement}$$

Fig. 1. Deduction rules for membership equational logic.

The MEL theory for the Tower of Hanoi puzzle consists of $\Sigma = (K, \Omega, S)$ and the following set $\mathcal{E}$ of MEL sentences where we omit the universal quantifiers:

$X : \mathsf{St}$ *if* $X : \mathsf{VT}$; $X : \mathsf{Tower}$ *if* $X : \mathsf{VT}$;
$X : \mathsf{St}$ *if* $X : \mathsf{Rod}$; $X : \mathsf{Tower}$ *if* $X : \mathsf{Rod}$;
$X : \mathsf{St}$ *if* $X : \mathsf{Rod}$; $X : \mathsf{VT}$ *if* $X : \mathsf{Rod}$;
$XY : \mathsf{Tower}$ *if* $X : \mathsf{Disk} \wedge Y : \mathsf{Tower}$;
$X, Y : \mathsf{St}$ *if* $X : \mathsf{St} \wedge Y : \mathsf{St}$;
$X, Y = Y, X$ (commutativity);
$(X, Y), Z = X, (Y, Z)$ (associativity);
$X - Y : \mathsf{Pair}$ *if* $X : \mathsf{Tower} \wedge Y : \mathsf{Tower}$;
$X - Y = Y - X$ (commutativity);
$X < Y : \mathsf{Boolean}$ *if* $X : \mathsf{Disk} \wedge Y : \mathsf{Disk}$;
$XR : \mathsf{VT}$ *if* $X : \mathsf{Disk} \wedge R : \mathsf{Rod}$;
$XYT : \mathsf{VT}$ *if* $X : \mathsf{Disk} \wedge Y : \mathsf{Disk} \wedge T : \mathsf{Tower} \wedge X{<}Y = \mathsf{t} \wedge YT : \mathsf{Vt}$;
$1 < 2 = \mathsf{t}$; $1 < 3 = \mathsf{t}$; $1 < 4 = \mathsf{t}$;
$2 < 3 = \mathsf{t}$; $2 < 4 = \mathsf{t}$; $3 < 4 = \mathsf{t}$;
$\mathsf{move}(XT - R) = T - XR$ *if* $X : \mathsf{Disk} \wedge T : \mathsf{Tower} \wedge R : \mathsf{Rod}$;

$move(XT - YT') = T - XYT'$ if X : Disk $\land Y$: Disk $\land T$: Tower $\land$
$\land\, T'$: Tower $\land$ X < Y = t; $move(X)$: Pair *if* X : Pair.

A single Disk stacked on a Rod is always a ValidTower. For multiple Disks, we compare them recursively. The operator move distinguishes between two cases: if one Tower is empty, i.e. a Rod, then we can stack any Disk on it; else the sizes of the top Disks on each Tower must be compared (<) and we can stack the smaller one on top of the other.

2.3 Rewriting Logic

A rewrite theory $\mathcal{R} = (\Sigma, \mathcal{E}, R)$ consists of a MEL theory $(\Sigma, \mathcal{E})$ together with a finite set R of *conditional rewrite rules* each of which has the form

$$(\forall X)\, l \rightarrow r \text{ if } \bigwedge_i p_i{=}q_i \land \bigwedge_j w_j{:}s_j \land \bigwedge_k l_k \rightarrow r_k,$$

where l, r are Σ-terms of the same kind and = can be either = or :=. Rewrite rules can also be unconditional.

Such a rewrite rule specifies a *one-step transition* from a state $t[l\theta]_p$ to the state $t[r\theta]_p$, denoted by $t[l\theta]_p \rightarrow^1_R t[r\theta]_p$, provided the condition holds. The subterm $t|_p$ is called a *redex*.

In the example, R has as only element the conditional rewrite rule: $D, E \rightarrow F, G$ if D : Tower $\land E$: Tower $\land F - G := move(D - E) \land F$: Tower $\land G$: Tower.

F and G are new variables on the right side of the rule. They are instantiated by matching on the conditional part of the rule.

The inference rules in Fig. 2 for rewrite theories can infer all possible computations in the system specified by $\mathcal{R}$ [BM12]. We can *reach* a state v from a state u if we can prove $\mathcal{R} \vdash u \rightarrow v$.

The relation $\rightarrow^1_{R/\mathcal{E}}$ on $T_\Sigma(X)$ is $=_\mathcal{E} \circ \rightarrow^1_R \circ =_\mathcal{E}$. $\rightarrow^1_{R/\mathcal{E}}$ on $T_\Sigma(X)$ induces a relation $\rightarrow^1_{R/\mathcal{E}}$ on $T_{\Sigma/\mathcal{E}}(X)$, the equivalence relation modulo $\mathcal{E}$, by $[t]_\mathcal{E} \rightarrow^1_{R/\mathcal{E}} [t']_\mathcal{E}$ iff $t \rightarrow^1_{R/\mathcal{E}} t'$. The transitive (resp. transitive and reflexive) closure of $\rightarrow^1_{R/\mathcal{E}}$ is denoted $\rightarrow^+_{R/\mathcal{E}}$ (resp. $\rightarrow^*_{R/\mathcal{E}}$). We say that a term t is $\rightarrow_{R/\mathcal{E}}$-*irreducible* (or just $R/\mathcal{E}$-irreducible) if there is no term t' such that $t \rightarrow^1_{R/\mathcal{E}} t'$.

$$\frac{t \in T_\Sigma(X)}{(\forall X)t \rightarrow t} \text{ Reflexivity} \qquad \frac{(\forall X)t_1 \rightarrow t_2,\ (\forall X)t_2 \rightarrow t_3}{(\forall X)t_1 \rightarrow t_3} \text{ Transitivity}$$

$$\frac{f \in \Sigma_{k_1 \cdots k_n,k}\ (\forall X)t_i \rightarrow t_i'\ \ t_i, t_i' \in T_\Sigma(X)_{k_i}, 1 \leq i \leq n}{(\forall X)f(t_1, \ldots, t_n) \rightarrow f(t_1', \ldots, t_n')} \text{ Congruence}$$

$$\frac{((\forall X)\, l \rightarrow r \text{ if } \bigwedge_i p_i{=}q_i \land \bigwedge_j w_j{:}s_j \land \bigwedge_k l_k \rightarrow r_k) \in R}{\theta{:}X{\rightarrow}T_\Sigma(Y)\ \ \bigwedge_i \mathcal{E} \vdash (\forall Y)p_i\theta{=}q_i\theta\ \ \bigwedge_j \mathcal{E} \vdash (\forall Y)w_j\theta{:}s_j\ \ \bigwedge_k (\forall Y)l_k\theta \rightarrow r_k\theta}{(\forall Y)l\theta \rightarrow r\theta} \text{ Replace}$$

Fig. 2. Deduction rules for rewrite theories.

A rewrite rule $l \to r$ if $cond$, is *sort-decreasing* if for each substitution σ, we have that for any sort s if $l\sigma \in T_\Sigma(X)_s$ and $(cond)\sigma$ is verified implies $r\sigma \in T_\Sigma(X)_s$. A Σ-equation $t = t'$ is *regular* if $Var(t) = Var(t')$. It is *sort-preserving* if for each substitution σ, we have $t\sigma \in T_\sigma(X)_s$ implies $t'\sigma \in T_\sigma(X)_s$ and vice versa.

A substitution is called *$\mathcal{E}$-normalized* (or normalized) if $x\sigma$ is $\mathcal{E}$-irreducible for all $x \in V$.

The relation $\to^1_{R/\mathcal{E}}$ is *terminating* if there are no infinite rewriting sequences. The relation $\to^1_{R/\mathcal{E}}$ is *operationally terminating* if there are no infinite well-formed proof trees. The relation $\to^1_{R/\mathcal{E}}$ is *confluent* if whenever $t \to^*_{R/\mathcal{E}} t'$ and $t \to^*_{R/\mathcal{E}} t''$, there exists a term t''' such that $t' \to^*_{R/\mathcal{E}} t'''$ and $t'' \to^*_{R/\mathcal{E}} t'''$. In a confluent, terminating, sort-decreasing, and operationally terminating membership rewrite theory, for each term $t \in T_\Sigma(X)$, there is a unique (up to $\mathcal{E}$-equivalence) $R/\mathcal{E}$-irreducible term t' obtained by rewriting to *canonical* form, denoted by $t \to^!_{R/\mathcal{E}} t'$, or $t \downarrow_{R/\mathcal{E}}$ when t' is not relevant, which we call $can_{R/\mathcal{E}}(t)$.

2.4   Executable Rewrite Theories

For a rewrite theory $\mathcal{R} = (\Sigma, \mathcal{E}, R)$, whether a one step rewrite $t \to^1_{R/\mathcal{E}} t'$ holds is undecidable in general. We impose additional conditions, similar to those required for functional and system modules in Maude, under which we can decide if $t \to^1_{R/\mathcal{E}} t'$ holds. We decompose $\mathcal{E}$ into a disjoint union $E \cup A$, with A a set of equational axioms (such as associativity, and/or commutativity, and/or identity). We define the relation $\to^1_{E,A}$ on $T_\Sigma(X)$ as follows: $t \to^1_{E,A} t'$ if there is a position $\omega \in Pos(t)$, an equation $l = r$ if $cond \in E$, and a substitution σ such that $t|_\omega =_A l\sigma$ (A-matching), $(cond)\sigma$ is satisfied, and $t' = t[r\sigma]_\omega$. The relation $\to^1_{R,A}$ is similarly defined. We define $\to^1_{R \cup E,A}$ as $\to^1_{R,A} \cup \to^1_{E,A}$. A rewrite theory $\mathcal{R} = (\Sigma, E \cup A, R)$ is *executable* if each kind k in Σ is nonempty, E, A, and R are finite and the following conditions hold:

1. E and R are *operationally terminating* and *admissible* [CDE+07]. Then we have a *deterministic 3-CTRS* [Ohl02]. Any new variable in the conditions will be instantiated by matching. New variables are distinguished in Maude by using a := symbol instead of = in the condition. They appear on the left terms of these *matching equations*. Conditions in deterministic 3-CTRS's *must* be solved in left to right order.

2. Equality modulo A is decidable and there exists a finite *matching algorithm modulo A* producing a finite number of A-matching substitutions, or failing otherwise.

3. The equations in E are *sort-decreasing*, and *terminating and confluent modulo A* when we consider them as oriented rules, where $\to^1_{E/A}$ is defined in the same way as we did for $\to^1_{R/\mathcal{E}}$.

4. $\to_{E,A}$ is *coherent with* A, i.e., $\forall t_1, t_2, t_3$ we have $t_1 \to_{E,A}^+ t_2$ and $t_1 =_A t_3$ implies $\exists t_4, t_5$ such that $t_2 \to_{E,A}^* t_4, t_3 \to_{E,A}^+ t_5$ and $t_4 =_A t_5$ [MT07].

$$
\begin{array}{ccc}
t_1 & \to_{E,A}^+ t_2 & \to_{E,A}^* t_4 \\
\| A & & \| A \\
t_3 & \xrightarrow{}_{E,A}^+ & t_5
\end{array}
$$

5. $\to_{R,A}$ is $\mathcal{E}$-*consistent with* A, i.e., $\forall t_1, t_2, t_3$ we have $t_1 \to_{R,A} t_2$ and $t_1 =_A t_3$ implies $\exists t_4$ such that $t_3 \to_{R,A} t_4$ and $t_2 =_{\mathcal{E}} t_4$. Also $\to_{R,A}$ is $\mathcal{E}$-*consistent with* $\to_{E,A}$, i.e., $\forall t_1, t_2, t_3$ we have $t_1 \to_{R,A} t_2$ and $t_1 \to_{E,A}^* t_3$ implies $\exists t_4, t_5$ such that $t_3 \to_{E,A}^* t_4$ and $t_4 \to_{R,A} t_5$ and $t_2 =_{\mathcal{E}} t_5$. In both cases the $\to_{R,A}$ rewriting steps from t_3 and t_4 must be performed with the *same* rule that was applied to t_1 [MT07].

$$
\begin{array}{cc}
t_1 \to_{R,A} t_2 & \\
\| A \qquad \| \mathcal{E} & \\
t_3 \to_{R,A} t_4 &
\end{array}
\qquad\qquad
\begin{array}{cccc}
t_1 & \xrightarrow{}_{R,A} & & t_2 \\
\downarrow_{E,A}^* & & & \| \mathcal{E} \\
t_3 & \to_{E,A}^* t_4 & \to_{R,A} & t_5
\end{array}
$$

(a) $\mathcal{E}$-consistency of $\to_{R,A}$ with A (b) $\mathcal{E}$-consistency of $\to_{R,A}$ with $\to_{E,A}$

Technically, what coherence means is that the weaker relation $\to_{E,A}^1$ becomes semantically equivalent to the stronger relation $\to_{E/A}^1$, so we can decide $t \to_{R/\mathcal{E}}^1 t'$ by finding t'' such that $can_{E,A}(t) \to_R^1 t''$ and $can_{E,A}(t') =_A can_{E,A}(t'')$, which is decidable, since the number of rules is finite and A-matching is decidable and finite.

Under these conditions we can implement $\to_{R/\mathcal{E}}$ on terms using $\to_{R \cup E,A}$ [MT07]. This lemma links $\to_{R/\mathcal{E}}$ with $\to_{E,A}$ and $\to_{R,A}$. Patrick Viry gave a proof for unsorted unconditional rewrite theories [Vir94], which can easily be lifted to our membership conditional case.

Lemma 1. *Let* $\mathcal{R} = (\Sigma, \mathcal{E}, R)$ *be an executable rewrite theory, that is, it has all the properties specified in Sect. 2.4. Then* $t_1 \to_{R/\mathcal{E}} t_2$ *if and only if* $t_1 \to_{E,A}^* \to_{R,A} t_3$ *for some* $t_3 =_{\mathcal{E}} t_2$.

The rewrite theory for the Tower of Hanoi puzzle is executable if we decompose $\mathcal{E}$ in the following way: the set A has as elements the associative equation and the commutative equations in $\mathcal{E}$; the set E has as elements the rest of equations and all memberships in $\mathcal{E}$, and we add to R the following rule needed for $\mathcal{E}$-consistency:

$$
\begin{aligned}
D, E, S &\to F, G, S \text{ if } D : \mathsf{Tower} \wedge E : \mathsf{Tower} \wedge S : \mathsf{State} \wedge \\
&\wedge F - G := \mathtt{move}(D - E) \wedge F : \mathsf{Tower} \wedge G : \mathsf{Tower}.
\end{aligned}
$$

2.5   Unification

Given a rewrite theory $\mathcal{R} = (\Sigma, \mathcal{E}, R)$, a Σ-*equation* is an expression of the form $t = t'$ where $t, t' \in T_\Sigma(X)_s$ for an appropriate s. The $\mathcal{E}$-*subsumption* preorder

$\ll_{\mathcal{E}}$ on $T_{\Sigma}(X)_s$ is defined by $t \ll_{\mathcal{E}} t'$ if there is a substitution σ such that $t =_{\mathcal{E}} t'\sigma$. For substitutions σ, ρ and a set of variables V we define $\sigma|_V \ll_{\mathcal{E}} \rho|_V$ if there is a substitution η such that $\sigma|_V =_{\mathcal{E}} (\rho\eta)|_V$. Then we say that ρ is more general than σ with respect to V. When V is not specified, we assume that $V = Dom(\sigma) = Dom(\rho)$ and we say that ρ is more general than σ.

A *system of equations* F is a conjunction of the form $t_1 = t'_1 \wedge \ldots \wedge t_n = t'_n$ where for $1 \leq i \leq n$, $t_i = t'_i$ is a Σ-equation. We define $Var(F) = \bigcup_i Var(t_i) \cup Var(t'_i)$. An *$\mathcal{E}$-unifier* for F is a substitution σ such that $t_i\sigma =_{\mathcal{E}} t'_i\sigma$ for $1 \leq i \leq n$. For $V = Var(F) \subseteq W$, a set of substitutions $CSU_{\mathcal{E}}^W(F)$ is said to be a *complete set of unifiers modulo $\mathcal{E}$* of F away from W if

- each $\sigma \in CSU_{\mathcal{E}}^W(F)$ is an $\mathcal{E}$-unifier of F;
- for any $\mathcal{E}$-unifier ρ of F there is a $\sigma \in CSU_{\mathcal{E}}^W(F)$ such that $\rho|_V \ll_{\mathcal{E}} \sigma|_V$;
- for all $\sigma \in CSU_{\mathcal{E}}^W(F)$, $Dom(\sigma) \subseteq V$ and $Ran(\sigma) \cap W = \emptyset$.

An $\mathcal{E}$-unification algorithm is *complete* if for any given system of equations it generates a complete set of $\mathcal{E}$-unifiers, which may not be finite. A unification algorithm is said to be *finite* and complete if it terminates after generating a finite and complete set of solutions.

2.6 Reachability Goals

Given a rewrite theory $\mathcal{R} = (\Sigma, \mathcal{E}, R)$, a *reachability goal* G is a conjunction of the form $t_1 \rightarrow^* t'_1 \wedge \ldots \wedge t_n \rightarrow^* t'_n$ where for $1 \leq i \leq n$, $t_i, t'_i \in T_{\Sigma}(X)_{s_i}$ for appropriate s_i. We define $Var(G) = \bigcup_i Var(t_i) \cup Var(t'_i)$. A substitution σ is a *solution* of G if $t_i\sigma \rightarrow^*_{R/\mathcal{E}} t'_i\sigma$ for $1 \leq i \leq n$. We define $E(G)$ to be the system of equations $t_1 = t'_1 \wedge \ldots \wedge t_n = t'_n$. We say σ is a *trivial solution* of G if it is an $\mathcal{E}$-unifier for $E(G)$. We say G is trivial if the identity substitution id is a trivial solution of G.

For goals $G : t_1 \rightarrow^* t_2 \wedge \ldots \wedge t_{2n-1} \rightarrow^* t_{2n}$ and $G' : t'_1 \rightarrow^* t'_2 \wedge \ldots \wedge t'_{2n-1} \rightarrow^* t'_{2n}$ we say $G =_{\mathcal{E}} G'$ if $t_i =_{\mathcal{E}} t'_i$ for $1 \leq i \leq 2n$. We say $G \rightarrow_R G'$ if there is an odd i such that $t_i \rightarrow_R t'_i$ and for all $j \neq i$ we have $t_j = t'_j$. That is, G and G' differ only in one subgoal ($t_i \rightarrow t_{i+1}$ vs $t'_i \rightarrow t_{i+1}$), but $t_i \rightarrow t'_i$, so when we rewrite t_i in G to t'_i we get G'. The relation $\rightarrow_{R/\mathcal{E}}$ over goals is defined as $=_{\mathcal{E}} \circ \rightarrow_R \circ =_{\mathcal{E}}$.

2.7 Narrowing

Let t be a Σ-term and W be a set of variables such that $Var(t) \subseteq W$. The R, A-*narrowing* relation on $T_{\Sigma}(X)$ is defined as follows: $t \leadsto_{p,\sigma,R,A} t'$ if there is a non-variable position $p \in Pos_{\Sigma}(t)$, a rule $l \rightarrow r$ if *cond* in R, properly renamed, such that $Var(l) \cap W = \emptyset$, and a unifier $\sigma \in CSU_A^{W'}(t|_p = l)$ for $W' = W \cup Var(l)$, such that $t' = (t[r]_p)\sigma$ and $(cond)\sigma$ holds. Similarly E, A-narrowing and $R \cup E$, A-narrowing relations are defined.

2.8 Associated Rewrite Theory

Any executable MEL theory $(\Sigma, E \cup A)$ has a corresponding rewrite theory $\mathcal{R}_E = (\Sigma', A, R_E)$ associated to it [DLM+08]: we add a fresh new kind *Truth* with a constant tt to Σ, and for each kind $k \in K$ an operator $eq : k\ k \rightarrow Truth$. $\top$ represents a conjunction of any number of tt's. There are rules $eq(x{:}k, x{:}k) \rightarrow tt$ for each kind $k \in K$. For each conditional equation or membership in E the set R_E has a conditional rule or membership of the form

$$t \rightarrow t' \ if \ A_1^\bullet \wedge \ldots \wedge A_n^\bullet \qquad t{:}s \ if \ A_1^\bullet \wedge \ldots \wedge A_n^\bullet$$

where if A_i is a membership then $A_i^\bullet = A_i$, if $A_i \equiv t_i := t_i'$ then $A_i^\bullet$ is $t_i' \rightarrow t_i$, and if $A_i \equiv t = t'$ then $A_i^\bullet$ is $eq(t, t') \rightarrow tt$.

$$\frac{t_1 \rightarrow^1 t_2, \ t_2 \rightarrow t_3}{t_1 \rightarrow t_3} \ \textbf{Transitivity} \qquad \frac{t \rightarrow^1 t', t' : s}{t : s} \ \textbf{Subject Reduction}$$

$$\frac{t =_A t'}{t \rightarrow t'} \ \textbf{Reflexivity} \qquad \frac{t_i \rightarrow^1 t_i'}{f(t_1, \ldots, t_i, \ldots, t_n) \rightarrow^1 f(t_1, \ldots, t_i', \ldots, t_n)} \ \textbf{Congruence}$$

$$\frac{t \rightarrow t' \ if \ A_1^\bullet \ldots A_n^\bullet \in R_E \ and \ u =_A t\sigma \quad A_1^\bullet \sigma \ldots A_n^\bullet \sigma}{u \rightarrow^1 t'\sigma} \ \textbf{Replacement}$$

$$\frac{t : s \ if \ A_1^\bullet \ldots A_n^\bullet \in R_E \ and \ u =_A t\sigma \quad A_1^\bullet \sigma \ldots A_n^\bullet \sigma}{u : s} \ \textbf{Membership}$$

Fig. 3. Inference rules for membership rewriting.

Systems of equations in $(\Sigma, E \cup A)$ with form $G \equiv \bigwedge_{i=1}^m (s_i = t_i)$ become reachability goals in R_E of the form $\bigwedge_{i=1}^m eq(s_i, t_i) \rightarrow tt$. A substitution σ is a solution of G if there are derivations for $\bigwedge_{i=1}^m (s_i\sigma = t_i\sigma)$, or $\bigwedge_{i=1}^m eq(s_i\sigma, t_i\sigma)$ rewrites to $\top$.

The *inference rules for membership rewriting in* R_E are the ones in Fig. 3, adapted from [DLM+08, Fig. 4, p. 12], where the rules are defined for context-sensitive membership rewriting.

3   Conditional Narrowing Modulo Unification

Narrowing allows us to assign values to variables in such a way that a reachability goal holds. We implement narrowing using a calculus that has the following properties:

1. If σ is an $R/\mathcal{E}$-normalized idempotent solution for a reachability goal G, the calculus can compute a more general answer $\sigma \ll_\mathcal{E} \sigma'$ for G.
2. If the calculus computes an answer σ for G, then σ is a solution for G.

That is, we want to compute a complete set of answers for G, a set that includes a generalization of any possible solution for G, with respect to $R/\mathcal{E}$-normalized substitutions.

We are going to split this task into two subtasks: first we will solve the part of the calculus that deals with unification; second, we will solve the part that deals with reachability.

3.1   Calculus Rules for Unification

We assume we are working with an executable rewrite theory named M. We refer to the set of equations and memberships in M as E, to the set of rules as R and to the set of axioms as A. We also assume that we have an A-unification algorithm that returns a CSU for any pair of terms.

A unification equation is a term $s{:}S = t{:}T$, which is a shorthand for the system of equations $s = t \wedge s = X_S \wedge t = Y_T$ (we will also write $s = t$, $s{:}S$, $t{:}T$). This means that we intend to unify s and t, with resulting sorts S and T respectively. A unification goal is a sequence (understood as conjunction) of unification equations.

Admissible goals, or simply goals, are any sequence of $s{:}S{=}t{:}T$, $s{:}S{:=}t{:}T$, $s{:}S{\rightarrow}t{:}T$, $s{:}S{\rightarrow}^1 t{:}T$ and $t{:}T$. Any condition in an equation, of the form $s{=}t$ or $s{:=}t$ is turned into an admissible goal by adding inferred sorts to it. If any term s is a variable or a constant, we use the sort of s as inferred sort. If the term is of the form $f(\bar{s})$, we use the kind of any membership for f.

Our calculus is defined by the following set of inference rules derived from those in Fig. 3. The first two rules, $[u]$ and $[x]$, transform *equational* problems into *rewriting* problems modulo axioms, rule $[u]$ playing the part of the added rules $eq(x{:}k, x{:}k) \rightarrow tt$ in the associated rewrite theory; rule $[n]$ describes one step of unification narrowing where the conditions on the applied rule are turned into subgoals and the instantiated right side of the rule $(r\theta)$ is required to have a sort which is a common subsort of S and T; rule $[t]$ allows us to apply several unification narrowing steps; rule $[i]$ decomposes a term allowing rule $[n]$ to be applied to any subterm of it; rule $[r]$ allows instantiation of variables on unificable terms; rule $[m1]$ solves the membership problem for variables, and rules $[s]$ and $[m2]$ for the rest of terms, using the membership conditions in E:

– $[u]$ *unification*

$$\frac{s{:}S = t{:}T, G'}{s{:}S' \rightarrow X_{S'}{:}S', t{:}S' \rightarrow X_{S'}{:}S', G'}$$

where $X_{S'}$ fresh variable, $S' \leq S, S' \leq T$.

– $[x]$ *matching*

$$\frac{s{:}S := t{:}T, G'}{t{:}S' \rightarrow s{:}S', G'}$$

where $S' \leq S, S' \leq T$.

– $[n]$ *narrowing*

$$\frac{s{:}S \rightarrow^1 X{:}T, G'}{((c,)X{:}S', G')\rho\theta}$$

where s is not a variable, $(c)eq\ l{=}r\ (if\ c) \in E$ has fresh variables,
$S' \leq S, S' \leq T,\ \theta \in CSU_A(s = l),\ \rho{=}\{X \mapsto r\}$.

– $[t]$ *transitivity*

$$\frac{s{:}S \to t{:}T, G'}{s{:}S' \to^1 X_{S'}{:}S', X_{S'}{:}S' \to t{:}S', G'}$$

where $X_{S'}$ fresh variable, $S' \leq S, S' \leq T$.

– $[i]$ *imitation*

$$\frac{f(\bar{s}{:}\bar{S}){:}S \to^1 X{:}T, G'}{G'\theta, s_i{:}S_i \to^1 X'_{S_i}{:}S_i, X\theta{:}S', G''\theta}$$

with $X \notin Var(s), \theta = \{X \mapsto f((s_1, \ldots, s_{i-1}, X'_{S_i}{:}S_i, s_{i+1}, \ldots, s_n))\}$,

X'_{S_i} fresh variable, $S' \leq S, S' \leq T$.

– $[r]$ *removal of equations*

$$\frac{s{:}S \to t{:}T, G'}{(G', s{:}S', G')\theta}$$

with $\theta \in CSU_A(s = t), S' \leq S, S' \leq T$

– $[s]$ *subject reduction*

$$\frac{s{:}S, G'}{s{:}[S] \to^1 X_S{:}S, G'}$$

X_S fresh variable.

– $[m1]$ *membership*

$$\frac{X_S{:}T, G'}{(G')\theta}$$

where $\theta = \{X_S \mapsto X'_{S'}\}$ with $X'_{S'}$ fresh variable and $S' \leq S, S' \leq T$.

– $[m2]$ *membership*

$$\frac{s{:}S, G'}{((c,)\, G')\theta}$$

where $(c)mb\ t{:}T\ (if\ c)$ is a fresh variant, with $T \leq S$, of a (conditional) membership in E, and $\theta \in CSU_A(s = t)$.

From a unification equation u a derivation is made applying rules of the calculus. If the derivation ends in the empty goal, denoted by $\square$, then the composition of the substitutions used on each derivation step, restricted to those variables appearing in u, is a computed answer for u.

Theorem 1. *The calculus for unification is sound and weakly complete.*

That is, given a unification goal G, if $G \rightsquigarrow^*_\sigma \square$ then $G\sigma$ can be derived, so σ is a solution for G in $\to_{E/A}$, and if ρ is an E/A-normalized idempotent answer of G ($G\rho \to^*_{E/A} \top$), then there is ρ' idempotent, with $\rho \ll_A \rho'$, such that $G \rightsquigarrow_{\rho'} \square$.

Proof. We prove correctness of the calculus with respect to E/A-normalized idempotent substitutions for the executable MEL theory $(\Sigma, E \cup A)$ and the corresponding rewrite theory $\mathcal{R}_E = (\Sigma', A, R_E)$ associated to it.

1. Soundness: by structural induction on the calculus rule for unification applied.
2. Completeness: by induction on the length of inferences in $\mathcal{R} = (\Sigma', A, R_E)$, looking at the last inference rule used.

4 Reachability by Conditional Narrowing

Conditional narrowing relies on conditional unification. As we have used the symbol $\rightarrow$ in the calculus rules for unification, we will use a different symbol $\Rightarrow$ in the calculus rules for reachability. Our goal, given a reachability problem $\bigwedge_i s_i{:}S_i \Rightarrow t_i{:}T_i$, is to find a solution σ (ground or not) such that $\bigwedge_i s_i\sigma{:}S_i \Rightarrow_{R/\mathcal{E}} t_i\sigma{:}T_i$. For executable rewrite theories this is equivalent to $\bigwedge_i s_i\sigma{:}S_i \Rightarrow_{R\cup E,A} \bigwedge_i t_i\sigma{:}T_i$. These new calculus rules deal with the $\leadsto_{R,A}$ part. Narrowing, we call it *replacement* here, takes place only at position ϵ of terms, thanks to new transitivity and imitation calculus rules.

Reachability goals are any sequence (understood as conjunction) of subgoals of the form $s{:}S \Rightarrow t{:}T$. Admissible goals, or simply goals, are now extended to be any sequence of $s{:}S\Rightarrow t{:}T$, $s{:}S\Rightarrow^1 t{:}T$, $s{:}S=t{:}T$, $s{:}S\rightarrow t{:}T$, $s{:}S\rightarrow^1 t{:}T$, $s{:}S{:}{=}t{:}T$ and $t{:}T$. If the calculus derives the empty goal from a reachability goal G with a substitution σ, then σ is a computed answer for G.

As for unification, any reachability subgoal in our calculus of the form of $s{:}S \Rightarrow^{(1)} t{:}T$ is equivalent to the admissible goal $s \Rightarrow^{(1)} t$, $s{:}S$, $t{:}T$.

4.1 Calculus Rules for Reachability

Reachability by conditional narrowing is achieved using the calculus rules presented in Sect. 3, extended with the following calculus rules, based on the deduction rules for rewrite theories in Fig. 2. Rule $[X]$ solves reachability problems by unification; rule $[R]$ applies one step of reachability narrowing; rule $[T]$ enables reachability narrowing modulo and multiple steps of reachability narrowing. It is a direct consequence of Lemma 1; rule $[I]$ allows us to imitate narrowing at non root term positions, replacing the rewriting rule for congruence, that can now be achieved by transitivity and imitation. Recall that narrowing steps for reachability ($\Rightarrow^1$), which are generated by rule $[T]$, impose no sort within the given kind on the right side of the step:

– $[X]$ *reflexivity*

$$\frac{s{:}S \Rightarrow t{:}T, G'}{s{:}S = t{:}T, G'}$$

– $[R]$ *replacement*

$$\frac{s{:}S \Rightarrow^1 X_{[S]}{:}[S], G'}{(s{:}S, (c,), G')\rho\theta}$$

where s is not a variable, $(c)rl\ l \Rightarrow r\ (if\ c)$ is a fresh variant of a (conditional)rule in R, $\rho = \{X_{[S]} \mapsto r\}$, $\theta \in CSU_A(s = l)$.

– $[T]$ *transitivity*

$$\frac{s{:}S \Rightarrow t{:}T, G'}{s{:}S \rightarrow X'_S{:}S, X'_S{:}S \Rightarrow^1 X''_{[S]}{:}[S], X''_{[S]}{:}[S] \Rightarrow t{:}T, G'}$$

where X'_S and $X''_{[S]}$ are fresh variables.

– [I] *imitation*

$$\frac{f(\bar{s}{:}\bar{S}){:}S \Rightarrow^1 X_{[S]}{:}[S], G'}{s_i{:}S_i \Rightarrow^1 X'_{S_i}{:}S_i, f(\bar{s}{:}\bar{S}){:}S, G'\theta}$$

where $X_{[S]} \notin Var(s), \theta = \{X_{[S]} \mapsto f((s_1, \ldots, X'_{S_i}{:}S_i, \ldots, s_n))\}$, X'_{S_i} fresh variable.

From a reachability goal r a derivation is made applying rules of the calculus. Each application of the *reflexivity* rule generates a unification equation. These unification equations as well as any generated membership goals must be solved using the calculus rules for unification. If the derivation ends with an *empty goal*, written $\Box$, then the composition of the substitutions used on each derivation step, restricted to those variables appearing in r, is a computed answer for r.

Theorem 2. *The calculus for reachability is sound and weakly complete.*

That is, given a reachability goal G, if $G \leadsto^*_\sigma \Box$ then $G\sigma$ can be derived, so σ is a solution for G in $\rightarrow_{R/\mathcal{E}}$, and if θ is an $R/\mathcal{E}$-normalized idempotent answer for a reachability problem G in $\rightarrow_{R/\mathcal{E}}$, then there is σ idempotent, with $\theta \ll_\mathcal{E} \sigma$, such that $G \leadsto^*_\sigma \Box$.

Proof. We prove correctness of the calculus for reachability with respect to $R/\mathcal{E}$-normalized (equivalently $R \cup E, A$) idempotent substitutions for the executable rewrite theory $\mathcal{R} = (\Sigma, \mathcal{E}, R)$ in $\rightarrow_{R/\mathcal{E}}$.

1. Soundness: By structural induction on the calculus rule for reachability applied.
2. Completeness: We prove that for $R/\mathcal{E}$-normalized idempotent answers $\Rightarrow^1$ solves $\rightarrow^1_{R,A}$ reachability problems and $\Rightarrow$ solves $\rightarrow^*_{R/\mathcal{E}}$ reachability problems, according to [MT07, Theorem 3] and Lemma 1. Then it follows that if θ is an $R/\mathcal{E}$-normalized idempotent answer for a reachability problem G in $\rightarrow_{R/\mathcal{E}}$, then there is σ idempotent, with $\theta \ll_\mathcal{E} \sigma$, such that $G \leadsto^*_\sigma \Box$. Inferred sorts are treated as in the proof of completeness of the calculus for unification (see extended version). We don't show the inferred sorts here.
   (a) We prove that if $s\rho \rightarrow^1_{R,A} t$ then $s \Rightarrow^1 t' \leadsto^*_\sigma \Box$, with $\rho \ll_\mathcal{E}\sigma$ and $t \ll_\mathcal{E} t'$. By definition there is a position p in $s\rho$, a rule $l \rightarrow r$ if $c \in R$ and a matching θ such that $s\rho|_p = l\theta$, $c\theta$ can be derived and $t \equiv (s\rho)[r\theta]_p$. By the same reasoning we used for the completeness of the calculus for unification, p must be a nonvariable position in s. Otherwise ρ would not be $R/\mathcal{E}$-normalized. From $s \Rightarrow^1 X$, by imitation we can reach position p, turning our reachability problem into $s|_p \Rightarrow^1 X^p$ with $\eta = \{X \mapsto s[X^p]_p\}$. Applying replacement, as $s\rho|_p = l\theta$, there is $\sigma (\equiv \rho' \cup \theta') \in CSU_A(s\rho|_p = l)$, with $\rho \ll_\mathcal{E} \rho'$, $\theta \ll_\mathcal{E} \theta'$ and $t' \equiv X\eta\sigma \equiv (s\rho')[r\theta']_p$.
   It is important to remember, again, that ACU-coherence completion allows A-unification of the left term of the ACU-coherence completed version of the rule, l, with the whole $s\rho|_p$ whenever the original left term l can be A-unified with some subterm of a recombination of $s\rho|_p$.
   (b) We prove that if $s\rho \rightarrow^*_{R/\mathcal{E}} t\rho$, ρ is a solution, then $s \Rightarrow t \leadsto^*_\sigma \Box$, with $\rho \ll_\mathcal{E} \sigma$. We distinguish two cases:

- Reflexive case: $s\rho =_{\mathcal{E}} t\rho$. Then $s{\Rightarrow}t \leadsto_{[X]} s{=}t \leadsto_\sigma^* \square$, with $\rho \ll_{\mathcal{E}} \sigma$ by correctness of the calculus for unification.
- Rest of the cases: According to [MT07, Lemmas 7 and 8] and the Lemma in Sect. 2.4 it suffices to show that $(\leadsto_{E,A}^* \leadsto_{R,A})^+ =_{\mathcal{E}}$ is implemented by $\Rightarrow$. This is done in the transitivity rule

$$\frac{s{:}S \Rightarrow t{:}T, G'}{s{:}S \rightarrow X_S'{:}S, X_S'{:}S \Rightarrow^1 X_{[S]}''{:}[S], X_{[S]}''{:}[S] \Rightarrow t{:}T, G'}$$

$s{:}S \rightarrow X_S'$ implements $\leadsto_{E,A}^*$ as proved in the calculus for unification. $X_S'{:}S \Rightarrow^1 X_{[S]}''{:}[S]$ implements $\leadsto_{R,A}$ as proved in the previous point. $X_{[S]}''{:}[S] \Rightarrow t{:}T$ allows iteration (the $^+$ part) through several uses of the transitivity rule ending with the $=_{\mathcal{E}}$ part through the use of the reflexivity rule, which is the only rule that enables us to exit the loop generated by the transitivity rule.

Finally, correct typing is ensured because $s{:}S$ and $t{:}T$ are included as conditions.

5   Example

As an example of our calculus we use the specification of the Tower of Hanoi puzzle in Sect. 2 and the reachability problem

$$(3T_T^0, b, c){:}S \Rightarrow (a, b, T_T^1){:}S$$

where from a `State` composed of one `Tower` with `Disk` 3 on top of it and two `Towers` with `Rods` b and c alone respectively we want to reach a `State` composed of two `Towers` with `Rods` a and b alone respectively and another `Tower`. The subindex of each variable means its type (sort or kind) and we write D, R, V, T, P, S instead of `Disk`, `Rod`, `ValidT`, `Tower`, `Pair`, `State` for readability.:

1. $\underline{(3T_T^0, b, c){:}S \Rightarrow (a, b, T_T^1){:}S} \leadsto_{[T]}$
   Transitivity decomposes reachability into several rewriting narrowing steps.
2. $\underline{(3T_T^0, b, c){:}S \rightarrow X_S^1{:}S}, X_S^1{:}S \Rightarrow^1 X_{[S]}^2{:}[S], X_{[S]}^2{:}[S] \Rightarrow (a, b, T_T^1){:}S$
   $\leadsto_{[r],\{T_T^0 \mapsto a, X_S^1 \mapsto (3a,b,c)\}} T_T^0$ is instantiated through rule $[r]$.
3. $\underline{(3a, b, c){:}S}, (3a, b, c){:}S \Rightarrow^1 X_{[S]}^2{:}[S], X_{[S]}^2{:}[S] \Rightarrow (a, b, T_T^1){:}S$
   We focus on the first subgoal.
4. $\underline{(3a, b, c){:}S} \leadsto_{[m2],S_{[S]}^1,S_{[S]}^2{:}S} \text{ if } S_{[S]}^1{:}S \wedge S_{[S]}^2{:}S, \{S_{[S]}^1 \mapsto (3a,b), S_{[S]}^2 \mapsto c\}$
5. $\underline{c{:}S}, (3a, b){:}S \leadsto \ldots$
6. $\underline{3a{:}S} \leadsto_{[m2],X_{[D]}R_{[R]}{:}V} \text{ if } X_{[D]}{:}D \wedge R_{[R]}{:}R, \{X_{[D]} \mapsto 3, R_{[R]} \mapsto a\}.$ OK because $V \le S$.
7. $\underline{3{:}D}, a{:}R \leadsto \ldots$ similar to previous steps. First subgoal finished.
8. $\underline{(3a, b, c){:}S} \Rightarrow^1 X_{[S]}^2{:}[S], X_{[S]}^2{:}[S] \Rightarrow (a, b, T_T^1){:}S.$ We focus on the first subgoal.

9. $(3a, b, c){:}S \Rightarrow^1 X^2_{[S]}{:}[S] \rightsquigarrow_{[R],D_{[T]},E_{[T]},X_{[S]} \rightarrow F_{[T]},G_{[T]},X_{[S]}}$ if

$\overline{D_{[T]}{:}T \wedge E_{[T]}{:}T \wedge X_{[S]}{:}S \wedge F_{[T]}{:}T \wedge G_{[T]}{:}T \wedge F_{[T]} - G_{[T]} := move(D_{[T]} - E_{[T]})}$,
$\theta = \{D_{[T]} \mapsto 3a, E_{[T]} \mapsto c, X_{[S]} \mapsto b\}, \rho = \{X^2_{[S]}{:}[S] \mapsto F_{[T]}, G_{[T]}, X_{[S]}\}$ Narrowing step.

10. $(3a, b, c){:}S, 3a{:}T, c{:}T, b{:}S, (F_{[T]} - G_{[T]}){:}[P] := move(3a - c){:}[P] \rightsquigarrow \ldots$

11. $\overline{F_{[T]} - G_{[T]}{:}[P] := move(3a - c){:}[P]} \rightsquigarrow_{[x]}$

12. $move(3a - c){:}[P] \rightarrow F_{[T]} - G_{[T]}{:}[P] \rightsquigarrow_{[t]}$

Transitivity decomposes unification into several unification narrowing steps.

13. $move(3a - c){:}[P] \rightarrow^1 Y_{[P]}{:}[P], Y_{[P]}{:}[P] \rightarrow F_{[T]} - G_{[T]}{:}[P] \rightsquigarrow_{[n]}$,

$move(X_{[D]}T_{[T]} - R_{[R]}) = T_{[T]} - X_{[D]}R_{[R]}$ if $X_{[D]}{:}D \wedge T_{[T]}{:}T \wedge R_{[R]}{:}R$,
$\theta = \{X_{[D]} \mapsto 3, T_{[T]} \mapsto a, R_{[R]} \mapsto c\}, \rho = \{Y_{[P]} \mapsto T_{[T]} - X_{[D]}R_{[R]}\}$

Unification narrowing step. $Y_{[P]}$ is instantiated to a ground term.

14. $a - 3c{:}[P], 3{:}[D], a{:}[T], c{:}[R], a - 3c{:}[P] \rightarrow F_{[T]} - G_{[T]}{:}[P] \rightsquigarrow \ldots$

15. $a - 3c{:}[P] \rightarrow F_{[T]} - G_{[T]}{:}[P] \rightsquigarrow_{[r], \theta_1 = \{F_{[T]} \mapsto a, G_{[T]} \mapsto 3c\}}$ Removal of equations.

16. $a - 3c{:}[P] \rightsquigarrow \ldots$ We omit this and go back to the second subgoal on step 8.

17. $(a, 3c, b) : [S] \Rightarrow (a, b, T^1_T){:}S \rightsquigarrow_{[X]} \cdots$

18. $(a, 3c, b) : S \rightarrow X_S{:}S, (a, b, T^1_T){:}S \rightarrow X_S{:}S \rightsquigarrow_{[r], \{X_S \mapsto (a, 3c, b)\}}$

19. $(a, 3c, b) : S, (a, b, T^1_T){:}S \rightarrow (a, 3c, b){:}S \rightsquigarrow \ldots$

20. $(a, b, T^1_T){:}S \rightarrow (a, 3c, b){:}S \rightsquigarrow_{[r], \{T^1_T \mapsto 3c\}}$ T^1_T is instantiated through rule $[r]$.

21. $(a, b, 3c) : S \rightsquigarrow \ldots \square$

From the substitutions in steps 2 and 20 the answer $\{T^1_T \mapsto 3c, T^0_T \mapsto a\}$ is computed. The calculus has found the solution $(3a, b, c){:}S \Rightarrow (a, b, 3c){:}S$ which is an instance of the given reachability problem $(3T^0_T, b, c){:}S \Rightarrow (a, b, T^1_T){:}S$.

6   Related Work, Conclusions and Future Work

A classic reference in equational conditional narrowing modulo is the work of Bockmayr [Boc93]. The topic is addressed here for Church-Rosser equational CTRS with empty axioms, but non terminating axioms (like ACU) are not allowed. Non conditional narrowing modulo order-sorted equational logics is covered by Meseguer and Thati [MT07], the reference for recent development in this area, which is actively being used for cryptographic protocol analysis. This work is partially based on the work of Viry [Vir94] where $R/\mathcal{E}$ rewriting is defined in terms of R, A and E, A for unsorted rewrite theories. Another topic addressed by the present work, membership equational logic, is defined by Meseguer [Mes97]. An equivalent rewrite system for MEL theories is presented by Durán, Lucas et al. [DLM+08], allowing unification by rewriting. Strategies, which also play a main role in narrowing, have been studied by Antoy, Echahed and Hanus [AEH94]. Their needed narrowing strategy, for inductively sequential rewrite systems, generates only narrowing steps leading to a computed answer. The use of this lazy narrowing strategy has been explained by Alpuente, Lucas and Escobar [ALE99] inside the programming language Curry. Recently Escobar,

Sasse, and Meseguer [ESM12] have developed the concepts of variant and folding variant, a narrowing strategy for order-sorted unconditional rewrite theories that terminates on those theories having the *finite variant property*. As an extension to rewrite theories Bruni and Meseguer [BM06] have defined *generalized rewrite theories* that support context-sensitive rewriting, thus allowing rewrites only on certain positions of terms.

In this work we have developed a narrowing calculus for unification in membership equational logic and a narrowing calculus for reachability in rewrite theories with an underlying membership equational logic. The main features in these calculi are that they make use of membership information whenever possible, reducing the state space, and also that they only allow steps leading to a different state, no mutual cancelling steps are allowed. The calculi have been proved correct. This work is part of a bigger effort where we attempt to explore the possibilities of performing conditional narrowing with constraint solvers. A transformation for rules and goals that will make both calculi strongly complete is under study. Strong completeness of reachability for topmost rewrite theories, Russian dolls configurations and linear theories are also under study. Finally, decidability of the calculus for unification in the case of *operationally terminating* MEL theories with a finitary and complete A-unification algorithm [LM09], using the required strategy for deterministic 3-CTRS's of solving subgoals from left to right, is being studied.

Our current line of investigation also intends to study the extension of the calculi to handle constraints and their connection with external constraint solvers for domains such as finite domains, integers, Boolean values, etc., that could greatly improve the performance of any implementation. We also plan on the extension of the calculi, adding support for generalized rewrite theories. Better strategies that may help reducing the state space will also be studied. All the improvements will have new sets of transformation rules that will allow their implementation on Maude.

Acknowledgments. We are very grateful to Santiago Escobar and the referees for their helpful comments and suggestions to improve this paper. Santiago also deserves special thanks for many conversations about narrowing and everything else.

References

[ALE99] Alpuente, M., Lucas, S., Escobar, S.: An incremental needed narrowing calculus for curry. In: Meo, M.C., Ferro, M.V. (eds.) APPIA-GULP-PRODE, pp. 75–88 (1999)

[AEH94] Antoy, S., Echahed, R., Hanus, M.: A needed narrowing strategy. In: Boehm, H.-J., Lang, B., Yellin, D.M. (eds.) POPL, pp. 268–279. ACM Press (1994)

[BM06] Bruni, R., Meseguer, J.: Semantic foundations for generalized rewrite theories. Theor. Comput. Sci. **360**(1–3), 386–414 (2006)

[BM12] Bae, K., Meseguer, J.: Model checking LTLR formulas under localized fairness. In: Durán, F. (ed.) WRLA 2012. LNCS, vol. 7571, pp. 99–117. Springer, Heidelberg (2012)

[Boc93] Bockmayr, A.: Conditional narrowing modulo a set of equations. Appl. Algebra Eng. Commun. Comput. **4**, 147–168 (1993)

[CDE+07] Clavel, M., Durán, F., Eker, S., Lincoln, P., Martí-Oliet, N., Meseguer, J., Talcott, C. (eds.): All About Maude - A High-Performance Logical Framework. LNCS, vol. 4350. Springer, Heidelberg (2007)

[CM96] Clavel, M., Meseguer, J.: Reflection and strategies in rewriting logic. Electron. Notes Theor. Comput. Sci. **4**, 126–148 (1996)

[DLM+08] Durán, F., Lucas, S., Marché, C., Meseguer, J., Urbain, X.: Proving operational termination of membership equational programs. High. Order Symbolic Comput. **21**(1–2), 59–88 (2008)

[DM12] Durán, F., Meseguer, J.: On the Church-Rosser and coherence properties of conditional order-sorted rewrite theories. J. Logic Algebraic Program. **81**(7–8), 816–850 (2012)

[EMM05] Escobar, S., Meadows, C., Meseguer, J.: A rewriting-based inference system for the NRL protocol analyzer: grammar generation. In: Atluri, V., Samarati, P., Küsters, R., Mitchell, J.C. (eds.) FMSE, pp. 1–12. ACM (2005)

[ESM12] Escobar, S., Sasse, R., Meseguer, J.: Folding variant narrowing and optimal variant termination. J. Logic Algebraic Program. **81**(7–8), 898–928 (2012)

[Fay78] Fay, M.J.: First-Order Unification in an Equational Theory. University of California, Santa Cruz (1978)

[LM09] Lucas, S., Meseguer, J.: Operational termination of membership equational programs: the order-sorted way. Electr. Notes Theor. Comput. Sci. **238**(3), 207–225 (2009)

[Mes90] Meseguer, J.: Rewriting as a unified model of concurrency. In: Baeten, J.C.M., Klop, J.W. (eds.) CONCUR '90. LNCS, vol. 458, pp. 384–400. Springer, Heidelberg (1990)

[Mes97] Meseguer, J.: Membership algebra as a logical framework for equational specification. In: Parisi-Presicce, F. (ed.) WADT 1997. LNCS, vol. 1376, pp. 18–61. Springer, Heidelberg (1998)

[MT07] Meseguer, J., Thati, P.: Symbolic reachability analysis using narrowing and its application to verification of cryptographic protocols. High. Order Symbolic Comput. **20**(1–2), 123–160 (2007)

[Ohl02] Ohlebusch, E.: Advanced Topics in Term Rewriting. Springer, New York (2002)

[Vir94] Viry, P.: Rewriting: an effective model of concurrency. In: Halatsis, C., Philokyprou, G., Maritsas, D., Theodoridis, S. (eds.) PARLE 1994. LNCS, vol. 817, pp. 648–660. Springer, Heidelberg (1994)

Language Definitions as Rewrite Theories

Andrei Arusoaie[1]([✉]), Dorel Lucanu[1], Vlad Rusu[2], Traian-Florin Şerbănuţă[1,3], Andrei Ştefănescu[4], and Grigore Roşu[4]

[1] Alexandru Ioan Cuza University, Iaşi, Romania
andrei.arusoaie@gmail.com
[2] Inria Lille Nord Europe, Lille, France
[3] University of Bucharest, Bucharest, Romania
[4] University of Illinois at Urbana-Champaign, Champaign, USA

Abstract. $\mathbb{K}$ is a formal framework for defining the operational semantics of programming languages. It includes software tools for compiling $\mathbb{K}$ language definitions to Maude rewrite theories, for executing programs in the defined languages based on the Maude rewriting engine, and for analyzing programs by adapting various Maude analysis tools. A recent extension to the $\mathbb{K}$ tool suite is an automatic transformation of language definitions that enables the symbolic execution of programs, i.e., the execution of programs with symbolic inputs. In this paper we investigate the theoretical relationships between $\mathbb{K}$ language definitions and their translations to Maude, between symbolic extensions of $\mathbb{K}$ definitions and their Maude encodings, and how the relations between $\mathbb{K}$ definitions and their symbolic extensions are reflected on their respective representations in Maude. These results show, in particular, how analyses performed with Maude tools can be formally lifted up to the original language definitions.

1 Introduction

$\mathbb{K}$ [11] is a framework for formally defining the semantics of programming languages. The current version of $\mathbb{K}$ includes options that have Maude [3] as a backend: the $\mathbb{K}$ compiler transforms any $\mathbb{K}$ definition into a Maude module; then, the $\mathbb{K}$ runner uses Maude to run or analyze programs in the defined language.

Recently, $\mathbb{K}$ has been extended with symbolic execution support [2]. Briefly, a $\mathbb{K}$ language definition is automatically transformed into a *symbolic-language* definition, such that the concrete executions of programs using the symbolic definition are symbolic executions of programs using the original language definition. The transformation amounts to incorporating *path conditions* in program configurations, and to changing the language's semantic rules so that they match on *symbolic configurations* and that they automatically update the path conditions.

Symbolic executions are called *feasible* if their path conditions are satisfiable. Two results relating concrete and symbolic program executions are proved in [2]: *coverage*, saying that for each concrete execution there is a feasible symbolic one taking the same path on the program; and *precision*, saying that for each feasible symbolic execution there is a concrete one taking the same program path.

© Springer International Publishing Switzerland 2014
S. Escobar (Ed.): WRLA 2014, LNCS 8663, pp. 97–112, 2014.
DOI: 10.1007/978-3-319-12904-4_5

In this paper we propose two ways of representing $\mathbb{K}$ language definitions in Maude: a *faithful* representation and an *approximate* one. We then study the relationships between $\mathbb{K}$ language definitions (including the symbolic ones, obtained by the above-described transformation) and their representations in Maude. We also show how the coverage and precision results, which relate a language $\mathcal{L}$ and its symbolic extension $\mathcal{L}^s$, are reflected on their respective representations in Maude. These results show, in particular, how (symbolic) analyses performed with Maude tools on the (faithful and approximate) Maude representations of languages can be lifted up to the original language definitions. The various results that we have obtained can be graphically depicted as in following diagram (dashed arrows show the results proved in the paper):

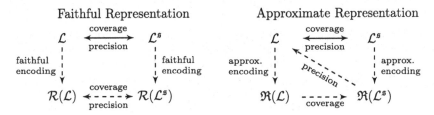

Faithful Representation   Approximate Representation

In the faithful encoding, each semantic rule of the language definition $\mathcal{L}$ is translated into a rewrite rule of the rewrite theory $\mathcal{R}(\mathcal{L})$. Equations are only introduced in order to express equality in the data domain. The resulting rewrite theory is proved to be *executable* by Maude, and the transition system generated by the language definition is shown to be isomorphic to the one generated by the rewrite theory. Some variations of this encoding are also discussed, all of which satisfy the executability and faithfulness properties. As a consequence, both positive and negative results of reachability analyses, obtained on rewrite theories (i.e., by using the Maude *search* command) also hold on the original language definitions. Moreover, all symbolic reachability analysis results obtained on the rewrite-theory representation $\mathcal{R}(\mathcal{L}^s)$ of a symbolic language $\mathcal{L}^s$ also hold on the rewrite-theory representation $\mathcal{R}(\mathcal{L})$ of the language $\mathcal{L}$. The latter property is analoguous to the results obtained in [10], where *rewriting modulo SMT* is shown to be related to (usual) rewriting in a *sound* and *complete* way.

For nontrivial language definitions, the faithful encoding is not very practical, because it typically generates a huge state-space that is not amenable to reachability analysis. This is why we introduce approximate representations of language definitions as *two-layered rewrite theories*. These approximations are obtained by splitting the semantic rules of the language into two sets, called *layers*, such that the first layer forms a terminating rewrite system. The one-step rewriting in such a theory is obtained by computing an irreducible form w.r.t. rules from the first layer (according to a given strategy), and then applying a rule from the second layer. A simple example of a two-layered rewrite theory is a Maude module consisting of equations and rules, where the equations (denoting the first layer) are only required to be terminating, and both the equations and rules (which form the second layer) specify transitions in the underlying transition-system model of the theory.

In an (approximating) two-layered rewrite theory $\mathfrak{R}(\mathcal{L})$, only a subset of the executions of programs in the original language $\mathcal{L}$ are represented. The consequence is that only positive results of reachability analyses on the two-layered rewrite theories can be lifted up to the corresponding language definitions. In addition to reducing the state-space to be explored, the approximate encoding of a language by a two-layered rewrite theory can also be seen as the output of a *compiler* that solves some semantic choices left by the language definition at compile-time. For example, in C, the order in which the operands of addition are evaluated is a compile-time choice. By turning the operand-evaluation rules into first-layer rules, and by letting Maude automatically execute these rules in various orders according to certain strategies, one can reproduce the various design compile-time choices for the evaluation of arguments.

We note that approximating two-layered rewrite theories have some limitations: only the coverage property relating the language definition $\mathcal{L}$ to its symbolic version $\mathcal{L}^s$ also holds on their respective approximate encodings theories; the precision property holds only in some restricted cases. However, the precision property between the approximate symbolic encoding $\mathfrak{R}(\mathcal{L}^s)$ and the language definition $\mathcal{L}$ always holds. Hence, one can trace symbolic reachability analyses (performed on $\mathfrak{R}(\mathcal{L}^s)$) back to programs in $\mathcal{L}$, and also (in some restricted cases) to the representation of programs in $\mathfrak{R}(\mathcal{L})$, which, as discussed above, can be seen as compiled programs where some semantic choices are left to the compiler.

Organisation. In Sect. 2 we present our working examples, which are two programs belonging to the CinK kernel of C++, which was specified in $\mathbb{K}$ [7]. A partial description of the $\mathbb{K}$ definition for CinK is included. In Sect. 3 we introduce a formal notion of a language-definition framework, which allows us to make our approach independent of the $\mathbb{K}$ language definitional framework and to abstract away some particular implementation details of $\mathbb{K}$. For the same reason, we will be using rewrite theories (instead of their implementations as Maude modules) for the encodings of language definitions. We also briefly present the language-independent symbolic execution approach [2] and recap some essential notions related to the executability of rewrite theories.

Section 4 presents the faithful and the approximate representations of language definitions into a rewrite theory and the various relations between them (graphically depicted in the above diagram). Section 5 presents the applications of these representations to the compilation of $\mathbb{K}$ language definitions as Maude modules. Finally, Sect. 6 presents conclusions and related work.

2 Running Example

Our running example is CinK [7], a kernel of the C++ programming language. The $\mathbb{K}$ definition of CinK can be found on the $\mathbb{K}$ Framework Github repository: http://github.com/kframework/cink-semantics. As any $\mathbb{K}$ definition, it consists of the language syntax, given using a BNF-style grammar, and of its semantics, given using rewrite rules on configurations. In this paper we only exhibit a small part of the $\mathbb{K}$ definition of CinK, whose syntax is shown in Fig. 1. Some of the grammar productions are annotated with $\mathbb{K}$-specific attributes.

$$
\begin{array}{lll}
Exp & ::= Id \mid Int & \\
& \mid \ \text{++} \ Exp & [strict, prefinc] \\
& \mid \ \text{--} \ Exp & [strict, predec] \\
& \mid \ Exp \ / \ Exp & [strict(all(context(rvalue))), divide] \\
& \mid \ Exp \ \text{+} \ Exp & [strict(all(context(rvalue))), plus] \\
& \mid \ Exp \ \text{>} \ Exp & [strict(all(context(rvalue)))] \\
Stmt & ::= Exps \ ; & [strict] \\
& \mid \ \{Stmts\} & \\
& \mid \ \text{while} \ (Exp)Stmt & \\
& \mid \ \text{return} \ Exp \ ; & [strict(all(context(rvalue)))] \\
& \mid \ \text{if} \ (Exp)Stmt \ \text{else} \ Stmt & [strict(1(context(rvalue)))]
\end{array}
$$

Fig. 1. CinK syntax

A major feature of C++ expressions is that given by the "sequenced before" relation [1], which defines a partial order over the evaluation of subexpressions. This can be easily expressed in $\mathbb{K}$ using the *strict* attribute to specify an evaluation order for an operation's operands. If the operator is annotated with the *strict* attribute then its operands will be evaluated in a nondeterministic order. For instance, all the binary operations are strict. Hence, they may induce nondeterminism in programs because of possible side-effects in their arguments.

Another feature is given by the classification of expressions into *rvalues* and *lvalues*. The arguments of binary operations are evaluated as rvalues and their results are also rvalues, while, e.g., both the argument of the prefix-increment operation and its result are lvalues. The *strict* attribute for such operations has a sub-attribute *context* for wrapping any subexpression that must be evaluated as an rvalue. Other attributes (*funcall, divide, plus, minus,...*) are names associated to each syntactic production, which can be used for referring to them.

The $\mathbb{K}$ framework uses *configurations* to store program states. A configuration is a nested structure of cells, which typically include the program to be executed, input and output streams, values for program variables, and other additional information. The configuration of CinK (Fig. 2) includes the $\langle \rangle_k$ cell containing the code that remains to be executed, which is represented as a list of computation tasks $C_1 \curvearrowright C_2 \curvearrowright \ldots$ to be executed in the given order. Computation tasks are typically statements and expression evaluations. The memory is modeled using two cells $\langle \rangle_{env}$ (which holds a map from variables to addresses) and $\langle \rangle_{state}$ (which holds a map from addresses to values). The configuration also includes a cell for the function call stack and another one for the return values of functions.

$$
\langle \ \langle \$PGM \rangle_k \ \ \langle \cdot \rangle_{env} \ \ \langle \cdot \rangle_{store} \ \ \langle \cdot \rangle_{stack} \ \ \langle \cdot \rangle_{return} \ \rangle_{cfg}
$$

Fig. 2. CinK configuration

When the configuration is initialised at runtime, a CinK program is loaded in the $\langle\rangle_k$ cell, and all the other cells remain empty. A $\mathbb{K}$ *rule* is a topmost rewrite rule specifying transitions between configurations. Since usually only a small part of the configuration is changed by a rule, a *configuration abstraction* mechanism is used, allowing one to only specify the parts transformed by the rule. For instance, the (abstract) rule for addition, shown in Fig. 3, represents the (concrete) rule

$$\langle\langle I_1{+}I_2 \curvearrowright C\rangle_k\langle E\rangle_{env}\langle S\rangle_{store}\langle T\rangle_{stack}\langle V\rangle_{return}\rangle_{cfg}$$
$$\Rightarrow$$
$$\langle\langle I_1 +_{Int} I_2 \curvearrowright C\rangle_k\langle E\rangle_{env}\langle S\rangle_{store}\langle T\rangle_{stack}\langle V\rangle_{return}\rangle_{cfg}$$

$I_1{:}Int + I_2{:}Int \Rightarrow I_1 +_{Int} I_2$	[*plus*]
$I_1{:}Int \,/\, I_2{:}Int \Rightarrow I_1 /_{Int} I_2$ **requires** $I_2 \neq_{Int} 0$	[*division*]
if(*true* **)** *St:Stmt* **else** _ $\Rightarrow St$	[*if-true*]
if(*false* **)** _ **else** *St:Stmt* $\Rightarrow St$	[*if-false*]
while(*B:Exp* **)** *St:Stmt* $\Rightarrow$ **if(** *B* **){** *St* **while(** *B* **)** *St* **else {}}**	[*while*]
$V{:}Val$ **;** $\Rightarrow \cdot$	[*instr-expr*]
$\langle{\tt ++lval(}\ L{:}Loc\ {\tt)} \Rightarrow {\tt lval(}\ L\ {\tt)}\ \cdots\rangle_k\langle\cdots\ L \mapsto (V{:}Int \Rightarrow V +_{Int} 1\ \cdots\rangle_{store}$	[*inc, memw*]
$\langle{\tt --lval(}\ L{:}Loc\ {\tt)} \Rightarrow {\tt lval(}\ L\ {\tt)}\ \cdots\rangle_k\langle\cdots\ L \mapsto (V{:}Int \Rightarrow V -_{Int} 1\ \cdots\rangle_{store}$	[*dec, memw*]
$\langle\langle{\tt lval(}\ L{:}Loc\ {\tt)}{=}\ V{:}Val \Rightarrow V\ \cdots\rangle_k\langle\cdots\ L \mapsto \_ \Rightarrow V\ \cdots\rangle_{store}\ \cdots\rangle_{cfg}$	[*update, memw*]
$\langle\langle{\tt \$lookup(}\ L{:}Loc\ {\tt)} \Rightarrow V\ \cdots\rangle_k\langle\cdots\ L \mapsto V{:}Val\ \cdots\rangle_{store}\ \cdots\rangle_{cfg}$	[*lookup, memr*]
{ *Sts:Stmts* **}** $\Rightarrow Sts$	[*block*]

Fig. 3. Subset of rules from the K semantics of CinK

where $+_{Int}$ is the mathematical operation for addition. Note that the ellipses in a cell (e.g., $\langle\cdots\rangle_k$) represent the part of the cell not affected by the rule.

The rule for division has a side condition which restricts its application. The conditional statement **if** has two corresponding rules, one for each possible evaluation of the condition expression. The rule for the **while** loop is unrolled into an **if** statement. The increment and update rules have side effects in the $\langle\rangle_{store}$ cell, modifying the value stored at a specific address. Finally, the reading of a value from the memory is specified by the lookup rule, which matches a value in the $\langle\rangle_{store}$ and places it in the $\langle\rangle_k$ cell. The auxiliary construct $\tt \$lookup$ is used, e.g., when a program variable is evaluated as an rvalue.

In addition to these rules (writtten by the $\mathbb{K}$ user), the $\mathbb{K}$ framework automatically generates so-called *heating* and *cooling* rules, which are induced by *strict* attributes. We show only the case of division, which is strict in both arguments:

$$A_1 \,/\, A_2 \Rightarrow rvalue(A_1) \curvearrowright \square \,/\, A_2 \quad (1) \qquad rvalue(I_1) \curvearrowright \square \,/\, A_2 \Rightarrow I_1 \,/\, A_2 \quad (3)$$

$$A_1 \,/\, A_2 \Rightarrow rvalue(A_2) \curvearrowright A_1 \,/\, \square \quad (2) \qquad rvalue(I_2) \curvearrowright A_1 \,/\, \square \Rightarrow A_1 \,/\, I_2 \quad (4)$$

where $\square$ is a special symbol, destined to receive the result of an evaluation.

We shall be using the following two programs in the sequel. The program `counter` in Fig. 4 is nondeterministic; nondeterminism arises from the undefined

```
int counter = 1;
int inc() {
  return ++counter;
}
int dec() {
  return --counter;
}
int main() {
  return  inc() + dec();
}
```
a) The program **counter**

```
int main() {
int k, x;
  x = A:Int;   //A:Int is a symbolic value
  k = 0;
  while (x > 0) {
    ++k;
    x = x / 2;
  }
}
```
b) The program **log**

Fig. 4. Two C++ programs

evaluation order for the arguments of the + operation and from the side-effects in its arguments. The program log in the same figure is a symbolic one because A:Int is a symbolic value, which can denote any integer value. When it is completed the variable k holds $[\log_2(A)]$ where $[\_]$ denotes the integer part of a real number. In Sect. 5 we show how the behaviours of these programs can be analysed using our encodings of the CinK language as Maude programs.

3 Background

3.1 The Ingredients of a Language Definition

In this section we identify the ingredients of language definitions in an algebraic and term-rewriting setting. The concepts are explained on the $\mathbb{K}$ definition of CinK. We assume the reader is familiar with the basics of algebraic specification and rewriting. A language $\mathcal{L}$ can be defined as a triple $(\Sigma, \mathcal{T}, \mathcal{S})$, consisting of:

1. A many-sorted algebraic signature Σ, which includes at least a sort *Cfg* for *configurations* and a sort *Bool* for *constraint formulas*. For the sake of presentation, we assume in this paper that the constraint formulas are Boolean terms built with a subsignature $\Sigma^{\mathsf{Bool}} \subseteq \Sigma$ including the boolean constants and operations. Σ may also include other subsignatures for other data sorts, depending on the language $\mathcal{L}$ (e.g., integers, identifiers, lists, maps,...). Let Σ^{Data} denote the subsignature of Σ consisting of all *data* sorts and their operations. We assume that the sort *Cfg* and the syntax of $\mathcal{L}$ are not data, i.e., they are defined in $\Sigma \setminus \Sigma^{\mathsf{Data}}$. Let T_Σ denote the Σ-algebra of ground terms and $T_{\Sigma,s}$ denote the set of ground terms of sort s. Given a sort-wise infinite set of variables *Var*, let $T_\Sigma(Var)$ denote the free Σ-algebra of terms with variables, $T_{\Sigma,s}(Var)$ denote the set of terms of sort s with variables, and $var(t)$ denote the set of variables occurring in the term t.
2. A Σ^{Data}-model $\mathcal{D}$, which interprets the data sorts and operations. For convenience, we assume that $\mathcal{D}_d \subset \Sigma_d$ for each data sort d, i.e., the constants are elements of the corresponding signature. Let $\mathcal{T} \triangleq \mathcal{T}(\mathcal{D})$ denote the free Σ-model generated by $\mathcal{D}$. The satisfaction relation $\rho \models b$ between valuations ρ

and constraint formulas $b \in T_{\Sigma,Bool}(Var)$ is defined by $\rho \models b$ iff $\rho(b) = \mathcal{D}_{true}$. For simplicity, we write $true, false, 0, 1 \ldots$ instead of $\mathcal{D}_{true}, \mathcal{D}_{false}, \mathcal{D}_0, \mathcal{D}_1, \ldots$.

3. A set $\mathcal{S}$ of rewrite rules. Each rule is a pair of the form $l \wedge b \Rightarrow r$, where $l, r \in T_{\Sigma,Cfg}(Var)$ are the rule's *left-hand-side* and *right-hand-side*, respectively, and $b \in T_{\Sigma,Bool}(Var)$ is the *condition*. The formal definitions for rules and for the transition system defined by them are given below.

Remark 1. For the sake of presentation, here we consider only "pure" language definitions, where the semantics is given only by semantic rules between configurations. Some definitions may include additional functions defined by equations. For such cases the language definition may additionally includes a set of axioms A_0, e.g., associativity and/or commutativity of some functions, and a set of equations E_0. Then the model $\mathcal{T}$ is the free algebra modulo $A_0 \cup E_0$. We believe that the approach presented in this paper can be extended to these more involved definitions, but this requires more investigation and is left for future work.

We now formally introduce the notions required for defining semantic rules.

Definition 1 (pattern [12]). *A pattern is an expression of the form $\pi \wedge b$, where $\pi \in T_{\Sigma,Cfg}(Var)$ is a basic pattern and $b \in T_{\Sigma,Bool}(Var)$. If $\gamma \in T_{Cfg}$ and $\rho : Var \to \mathcal{T}$ then we write $(\gamma, \rho) \models \pi \wedge b$ iff $\gamma = \rho(\pi)$ and $\rho \models b$.*

A basic pattern π defines a set of (concrete) configurations, and the condition b gives additional constraints these configurations must satisfy.

Remark 2. The above definition is a particular case of a definition in [12]. There, a pattern is a first-order logic formula with configuration terms as sub-formulas. In this paper we keep the conjunction notation from first-order logic but separate basic patterns from constraints. Note that first-order formulas can be encoded as terms of sort *Bool*, where the quantifiers become constructors. The satisfaction relation $\models$ is then defined, for such terms, like the usual FOL satisfaction.

We identify basic patterns π with patterns $\pi \wedge true$. Sample patterns are $\langle\langle I_1 + I_2 \curvearrowright C \rangle_{\mathsf{k}} \langle Env \rangle_{\mathsf{env}} \rangle_{\mathsf{cfg}}$ and $\langle\langle I_1 / I_2 \curvearrowright C \rangle_{\mathsf{k}} \langle Env \rangle_{\mathsf{env}} \rangle_{\mathsf{cfg}} \wedge I_2 \neq_{Int} 0$.

Definition 2 (rule, transition system). *A rule is a pair of patterns of the form $l \wedge b \Rightarrow r$ (note that r is in fact the pattern $r \wedge true$). Any set $\mathcal{S}$ of rules defines a labelled transition system $(\mathcal{T}_{Cfg}, \Rightarrow_\mathcal{S})$ such that $\gamma \overset{\alpha}{\Longrightarrow}_\mathcal{S} \gamma'$ iff there exist $\alpha \triangleq (l \wedge b \Rightarrow r) \in \mathcal{S}$ and $\rho : Var \to \mathcal{T}$ such that $(\gamma, \rho) \models l \wedge b$ and $(\gamma', \rho) \models r$.*

3.2 Symbolic Execution

We briefly recap our approach to symbolic execution from [2]. The main idea is to automatically generate a new definition $(\Sigma^{\mathfrak{s}}, \mathcal{T}^{\mathfrak{s}}, \mathcal{S}^{\mathfrak{s}})$ for a language $\mathcal{L}^{\mathfrak{s}}$ from a given definition $(\Sigma, \mathcal{T}, \mathcal{S})$ of a language $\mathcal{L}$. The new language $\mathcal{L}^{\mathfrak{s}}$ has the same syntax, and its semantics extends $\mathcal{L}$'s data domains with symbolic values and adapts the semantical rules of $\mathcal{L}$ to deal with the new domains.

Let $V^{\mathfrak{s}}$ denote an infinite, data sort-wise set of *symbolic values*, disjoint from *Var* and from symbols in Σ. The data algebra is extended to $\mathcal{D}^{\mathfrak{s}}$, which is the algebra of ground terms over the signature $\Sigma^{\mathsf{Data}}(V^{\mathfrak{s}})$.

Remark 3. The approach in [2] allows some freedom in choosing the algebra $\mathcal{D}^s$, to enable the use of decision procedures for handling symbolic artifacts.

The signature Σ^s extends Σ with the symbolic values V^s as constants, a new sort Cfg^s and a constructor $\_\wedge\_ : Cfg \times Bool \to Cfg^s$. The model $\mathcal{T}^s$ is defined as being the free Σ^s-model generated by $\mathcal{D}^s$, similarly to how $\mathcal{T}$ is built over $\mathcal{D}$. The ground terms $\pi \wedge \phi \in \mathcal{T}^s_{Cfg^s}$ are called *symbolic configurations*. Let $[\![\pi \wedge \phi]\!]$ denote the set of concrete configurations $\{\gamma \mid (\exists \rho)\,(\gamma, \rho) \models \pi \wedge \phi\}$.

Thanks to the rule transformation procedure presented in [2], we make without loss of generality the assumption that the basic patterns in left-hand sides of rules do not contain operations on data, and the rules are left-linear. Concrete semantic rules $l \wedge b \Rightarrow r \in \mathcal{S}$ are then systematically transformed into rules

$$l \wedge \psi \Rightarrow r \wedge (\psi \wedge b) \tag{5}$$

where $\psi \in Var$ is a fresh variable of sort *Bool* playing the role of a path condition. This means that symbolic rules are applied like concrete rules, except for the fact that the current path condition ψ is enriched with the rule's condition b.

Then, the symbolic execution of $\mathcal{L}$ programs is the concrete execution of the corresponding $\mathcal{L}^s$ programs, i.e., the application of the rewrite rules in the semantics of $\mathcal{L}^s$. Building the definition of $\mathcal{L}^s$ amounts to extending the signature Σ to a symbolic signature Σ^s, extending the Σ-algebra $\mathcal{T}$ to a Σ^s-algebra $\mathcal{T}^s$, and turning the concrete rules $\mathcal{S}$ into symbolic rules $\mathcal{S}^s$. The transition system $(\mathcal{T}^s_{Cfg^s}, \Rightarrow_{\mathcal{S}^s})$ is defined using Definitions 1, 2 applied to $\mathcal{L}^s$. In [2] it is proved that the symbolic transition system forward-simulates the concrete one, and that the concrete transition system backward-simulates the symbolic one. These two results then imply the naturally expected properties of symbolic execution.

Theorem 1 (Coverage [2]**).** *For every concrete execution* $\gamma_0 \overset{\alpha_1}{\Longrightarrow}_{\mathcal{S}} \gamma_1 \overset{\alpha_2}{\Longrightarrow}_{\mathcal{S}}$ $\cdots \overset{\alpha_n}{\Longrightarrow}_{\mathcal{S}} \gamma_n \overset{\alpha_{n+1}}{\Longrightarrow}_{\mathcal{S}} \cdots$ *there is a symbolic execution* $\pi_0 \wedge \phi_0 \overset{\alpha_1}{\Longrightarrow}_{\mathcal{S}^s} \pi_1 \wedge \phi_1 \overset{\alpha_2}{\Longrightarrow}_{\mathcal{S}^s}$ $\cdots \overset{\alpha_n}{\Longrightarrow}_{\mathcal{S}^s} \pi_n \wedge \phi_n \overset{\alpha_{n+1}}{\Longrightarrow}_{\mathcal{S}^s} \cdots$ *such that* $\gamma_i \in [\![\pi_i \wedge \phi_i]\!]$ *for* $i = 0, 1, \ldots$.

A symbolic configuration $\pi \wedge \phi \in \mathcal{T}^s_{Cfg^s}$ is *satisfiable* if there is a valuation $\vartheta : V^s \to \mathcal{D}$ such that $\vartheta \models \phi$ (which is equivalent to $[\![\pi \wedge \phi]\!] \neq \emptyset$). We call a symbolic execution *feasible* if all its configurations are satisfiable.

Theorem 2 (Precision [2]**).** *For every feasible symbolic execution* $\pi_0 \wedge \phi_0 \overset{\alpha_1}{\Longrightarrow}_{\mathcal{S}^s}$ $\pi_1 \wedge \phi_1 \overset{\alpha_2}{\Longrightarrow}_{\mathcal{S}^s} \cdots \overset{\alpha_n}{\Longrightarrow}_{\mathcal{S}^s} \pi_n \wedge \phi_n \overset{\alpha_{n+1}}{\Longrightarrow}_{\mathcal{S}^s} \cdots$ *there is a concrete execution* $\gamma_0 \overset{\alpha_1}{\Longrightarrow}_{\mathcal{S}} \gamma_1 \overset{\alpha_2}{\Longrightarrow}_{\mathcal{S}} \cdots \overset{\alpha_n}{\Longrightarrow}_{\mathcal{S}} \gamma_n \overset{\alpha_{n+1}}{\Longrightarrow}_{\mathcal{S}} \cdots$ *such that* $\gamma_i \in [\![\pi_i \wedge \phi_i]\!]$ *for* $i = 0, 1, \ldots$.

3.3 Rewrite Theories

A rewrite theory [3] $\mathcal{R} = (\Sigma, E \cup A, R)$ consists of a signature Σ, a set of equations E, a set of axioms A, e.g., associativity, commutativity, unity or combinations of these, and a set of rewrite rules R of the form $l \to r$ **if** b, where l and r are terms with variables and b is a term of sort *Bool*. We are only interested in rewrite theories $\mathcal{R}$ that are *executable*, i.e., $(\Sigma, E \cup A, R)$ where:

1. there exists a matching algorithm modulo A;
2. $(\Sigma, E \cup A)$ is ground Church-Rosser and terminating modulo A (the equations E are seen here as rewrite rules oriented from left to right). Thus, each ground term t has a canonical form $can_{E/A}(t)$ that is unique modulo the axioms A;
3. R is *ground coherent w.r.t. E modulo A* [13]: for all $t, t_1 \in T_\Sigma$ with $t \to_{R/A} t_1$ there is $t_2 \in T_\Sigma$ s.t. $can_{E/A}(t) \to_{R/A} t_2$ and $can_{E/A}(t_1) =_A can_{E/A}(t_2)$.

The relation $\to_{R/A}$ denotes the one-step rewriting relation defined by applying a rule from R modulo axioms A: $u \to_{R/A} v$ iff there are the terms u', v', a rule $l \to r$ **if** b in R, position p in u', and substitution σ such that $u =_A u'$, $v =_A v'$, $u'|_p = \sigma(l)^1$, $v' = u[\sigma(r)]_p{}^2$, and $\sigma(b) =_A true$.

The *rewriting relation* $\to_\mathcal{R}$ defined by an executable rewrite theory $\mathcal{R}$ is: $t_1 \to_\mathcal{R} t_2$ iff $can_{E/A}(t_1) \to_{R/A} t_2'$ and $can_{E/A}(t_2') = t_2$. This is equivalent to $\to_{R/(E \cup A)}$ due to confluence and coherence. We write $t_1 \xrightarrow{\alpha}_\mathcal{R} t_2$ to emphasise that $\alpha \triangleq (l \to r$ **if** $b) \in R$ is applied in the rewriting step $can_{E/A}(t_1) \to_{R/A} t_2'$.

4   Translating Language Definitions into Rewrite Theories

This section includes the main contribution of the paper. We introduce two encodings of language definitions as rewrite theories: a faithful encoding and an approximate encoding. Since the symbolic extension of a language is also a language definition, we automatically get encodings of both concrete languages and their symbolic extensions. We investigate how the properties relating a language definition and its symbolic extension are reflected on their respective encodings.

Definition 3 (faithful encoding). *Let $\mathcal{L} = (\Sigma, \mathcal{T}, \mathcal{S})$ be a language definition. The* faithful encoding *of $\mathcal{L}$ is $\mathcal{R}(\mathcal{L}) = (\Sigma, E \cup A, R)$, where*

- *$A = \emptyset$;*
- *for each operation f in Σ^{Data} and $d_1, \ldots, d_n \in \mathcal{D}$ of corresponding sorts, E includes an equation $f(d_1, \ldots, d_n) = \mathcal{D}_f(d_1, \ldots, d_n)$;*
- *$R = \mathcal{S}$, where each rule $\pi \wedge b \Rightarrow r \in \mathcal{S}$ becomes a rewrite rule $l \to r$ **if** $b \in R$.*

Theorem 3. *Let $\mathcal{L} = (\Sigma, \mathcal{T}, \mathcal{S})$ be a language definition. Then $\mathcal{R}(\mathcal{L})$ is an executable rewrite theory satisfying $\gamma \xrightarrow{\alpha}_\mathcal{S} \gamma'$ iff $\gamma \xrightarrow{\alpha}_{\mathcal{R}(\mathcal{L})} \gamma'$, for all $\gamma, \gamma' \in T_{Cfg}$.*

Remark 4. The construction of the rewrite theory $\mathcal{R}(\mathcal{L})$, with data domain $\mathcal{D} \subseteq \Sigma^{\mathsf{Data}}$ defined by the set of equations E given in Definition 3, corresponds to the data domains $\mathcal{D}$ being *builtin sorts* in the Maude terminology. A builtin sort is a sort that is not built algebraically but one that, for efficiency reasons, is directly implemented in code (C++ code in the case of Maude). For example, natural numbers are specified by the equational specification $0 : \mathsf{Nat}, s : \mathsf{Nat} \to \mathsf{Nat}$, but using the resulting unary-notation for them would be highly inefficient. This is why natural numbers are implemented as builtins. The construction $\mathcal{R}(\mathcal{L})$

---

[1] $t|_p$ denotes subterm of t at position p.

[2] $t[u]_p$ denotes the term obtained from t by replacing the subterm at position p with u.

can, however, be extended to accomodate non-builtin sorts, i.e., sorts that are defined as the *initial model* of a finite set of equations E' that are confluent and terminating modulo a set A of axioms. For this, it is enough to ensure that $E' \cup E$ is also confluent and terminating modulo A - where E is the set of equations given in the proof of Theorem 3. This typically happens, as E and E' refer to different sorts - the builtin ones for the former, and the non-builtin ones for the latter. If this is the case then the proof of the ground coherence property in Theorem 3 still holds, because it only depends on $E' \cup E$ being confluent and terminating modulo A, not on the particular form of the equations. The proof of faithfulness of the encoding remains the same. This observation is important, since it ensures that we obtain executable Maude rewrite-theories $\mathcal{R}(\mathcal{L})$ for languages-definitions $\mathcal{L}$ whose data are specified using either bulitin sorts or non-builtin sorts. The faithfulness of the encoding then ensures that all results of reachability analyses (either positive or negative) performed on $\mathcal{R}(\mathcal{L})$, e.g., obtained using Maude's *search* command, also hold on $\mathcal{L}$.

The symbolic extension of a language definition can be encoded as a rewrite theory as well. Let $\mathcal{L}^s = (\Sigma^s, \mathcal{T}^s, \mathcal{S}^s)$ be the symbolic extension of $\mathcal{L} = (\Sigma, \mathcal{T}, \mathcal{S})$. Recall that Σ^s is Σ extended with the constructor of symbolic configurations $\_\wedge\_$ and with the symbolic values V^s seen as constants. The symbolic configurations are ground terms $\pi \wedge \phi \in \mathcal{T}^s_{Cfg^s}$. If $\mathcal{R}(\mathcal{L}^s) = (\Sigma^s, E \cup A, R)$ is the faithful encoding given by Theorem 3, then $E = A = \emptyset$ because the data algebra $\mathcal{D}^s$ we considered is the $\Sigma^{\mathsf{Data}}(V^s)$-algebra of the ground terms built over $\mathcal{D}$ and V^s. Recall that we assumed that $\mathcal{D} \subseteq \Sigma \subseteq \Sigma^{\mathsf{Data}}(V^s)$.

The relationship between a language definition $\mathcal{L}$ and its symbolic extension $\mathcal{L}^s$ can be now reflected at the level of the encodings $\mathcal{R}(\mathcal{L})$ and $\mathcal{R}(\mathcal{L}^s)$. A symbolic configuration $\pi \wedge \phi$ consists of a configuration ground term π (of sort Cfg) and a formula ground term ϕ (of sort $Bool$). The constants V^s play the role of logical variables, and the definition of satisfiability for patterns extends to their representations as symbolic configurations. Moreover, the notion of feasible execution in $\mathcal{R}(\mathcal{L}^s)$ is defined similarly to how it is defined for $\mathcal{L}^s$. The following two results are direct consequences of Theorems 3, 1, and 2, respectively.

Corollary 1 (Coverage for Encoding Rewrite Theories). *For every concrete execution* $\gamma_0 \xrightarrow{\alpha_0}_{\mathcal{R}(\mathcal{L})} \gamma_1 \xrightarrow{\alpha_2}_{\mathcal{R}(\mathcal{L})} \cdots \xrightarrow{\alpha_n}_{\mathcal{R}(\mathcal{L})} \gamma_n \xrightarrow{\alpha_{n+1}}_{\mathcal{R}(\mathcal{L})} \cdots$ *there is a symbolic execution* $\pi_0 \wedge \phi_0 \xrightarrow{\alpha_1}_{\mathcal{R}(\mathcal{L}^s)} \pi_1 \wedge \phi_1 \xrightarrow{\alpha_2}_{\mathcal{R}(\mathcal{L}^s)} \cdots \xrightarrow{\alpha_n}_{\mathcal{R}(\mathcal{L})} \pi_n \wedge$ $\phi_n \xrightarrow{\alpha_{n+1}}_{\mathcal{R}(\mathcal{L}^s)} \cdots$ *such that* $\gamma_i \in [\![\pi_i \wedge \phi_i]\!]$ *for* $i = 0, 1, \ldots$.

Corollary 2 (Precision for Encoding Rewrite Theories). *For every feasible symbolic execution* $\pi_0 \wedge \phi_0 \xrightarrow{\alpha_1}_{\mathcal{R}(\mathcal{L}^s)} \pi_1 \wedge \phi_1 \xrightarrow{\alpha_2}_{\mathcal{R}(\mathcal{L}^s)} \cdots \xrightarrow{\alpha_n}_{\mathcal{R}(\mathcal{L})}$ $\pi_n \wedge \phi_n \xrightarrow{\alpha_{n+1}}_{\mathcal{R}(\mathcal{L}^s)} \cdots$ *there is a concrete execution* $\gamma_0 \xrightarrow{\alpha_0}_{\mathcal{R}(\mathcal{L})} \gamma_1 \xrightarrow{\alpha_2}_{\mathcal{R}(\mathcal{L})}$ $\cdots \xrightarrow{\alpha_n}_{\mathcal{R}(\mathcal{L})} \gamma_n \xrightarrow{\alpha_{n+1}}_{\mathcal{R}(\mathcal{L})} \cdots$ *such that* $\gamma_i \in [\![\pi_i \wedge \phi_i]\!]$ *for* $i = 0, 1, \ldots$.

The faithful encoding thus enjoys nice theoretical properties, but it has a limited practical value when we consider actual $\mathbb{K}$ definitions of nontrivial languages:

- The heating and cooling rules, which are symmetric each other, may lead to infinite rewritings;
- The generated state space may be very large, even for small programs.

There are currently two proposals for obtaining abstractions of the rewrite theories: equational abstraction [9] or transforming some semantical rules into equations [6].

The former amounts to basically deriving a new definition, where the new model $\mathcal{T}$ is the quotient of the original one, usually requiring substantial input from the user, which is something we would like to avoid.

The latter might not be suitable for language definitions in general because, semantically, it would equate elements that are supposed to be distinct in $\mathcal{T}$. Consider a language construct `randBool` with two rules: `randBool => true` and `randBool => false`. Assume now we want to analyze a program which uses `randBool`, but who fails to satisfy a given property regardless of whether `randBool` transits to `true` or to `false`. In this case it might beneficial to collapse the state space by considering only one of the cases; however, if we transform the two rules above into equations, this will semantically identify `true` and `false` in $\mathcal{T}$, collapsing much more of the state space than desirable. An additional operational concern is that transforming certain rules into equations might destroy coherence and/or confluence, thus falling out of the executability requirements.

Two-layered rewrite theories, introduced below, allow us to preserve the benefits of the techniques above (state space reduction, efficient execution), while avoiding their semantical consequences (unnecessary collapse of states in the semantical model $\mathcal{T}$).

Definition 4. *A* two-layered rewrite theory *is a tuple* $\mathfrak{R} = (\Sigma, E \cup A, 1R \cup 2R, \varepsilon)$, *where* $(\Sigma, E \cup A, 1R \cup 2R)$ *is an executable rewrite theory,* $E \cup 1R$ *is ground terminating modulo* A, *and* $\varepsilon : T_\Sigma \rightarrow T_\Sigma$ *is a function that, for any* $t \in T_\Sigma$, *returns an element in the set of* $(E \cup 1R)/A$-irreducible terms $\{t' \in T_\Sigma \mid t \rightarrow^!_{(E \cup 1R)/A} t'\}$ *(which is nonempty precisely because* $E \cup 1R$ *is ground terminating modulo* A). *The one-step rewrite relation* $\rightarrow_{\mathcal{R}}$ *is defined by* $t_1 \rightarrow_{\mathcal{R}} t_2$ *iff* $\varepsilon(t_1) \rightarrow_{2R/A} t'_2$ *and* $can_{E/A}(t'_2) =_A t_2$.

Theorem 4. *Let* $\mathcal{L} = (\Sigma, \mathcal{T}, \mathcal{S})$ *be a language definition and* $\mathfrak{R}(\mathcal{L}) = (\Sigma, E \cup A, 1R \cup 2R, \varepsilon)$ *be a two-layered rewrite theory with* $(\Sigma, E \cup A, 1R \cup 2R)$ *built as in Definition 3 but where the set of rules is partitioned into two subsets* $1R$ *and* $2R$ *and* $E \cup 1R$ *is terminating modulo* A. *If* $\gamma \rightarrow_{\mathfrak{R}(\mathcal{L})} \gamma'$ *then* $\gamma \Rightarrow^+_{\mathcal{S}} \gamma'$.
We say that $\mathfrak{R}(\mathcal{L})$ *is an* approximate encoding *of* $\mathcal{L}$.

Corollary 3 (precision for approximate encoding). *Let* $\mathcal{L} = (\Sigma, \mathcal{T}, \mathcal{S})$ *be a language definition and* $\mathfrak{R}(\mathcal{L}^s) = (\Sigma, E \cup A, 1R \cup 2R, \varepsilon)$ *be an approximate encoding of* $\mathcal{L}^s$. *For each feasible symbolic execution* $\pi_0 \wedge \phi_0 \rightarrow_{\mathcal{R}^s} \pi_1 \wedge \phi_1 \rightarrow_{\mathfrak{R}(\mathcal{L}^s)}$ $\cdots \rightarrow_{\mathfrak{R}(\mathcal{L}^s)} \pi_n \wedge \phi_n \rightarrow_{\mathfrak{R}(\mathcal{L}^s)} \cdots$ *there is a concrete execution in* $\mathcal{L}$: $\gamma_0 \overset{\alpha_1}{\Rightarrow}^+_{\mathcal{S}}$ $\gamma_1 \overset{\alpha_2}{\Rightarrow}^+_{\mathcal{S}} \cdots \overset{\alpha_n}{\Rightarrow}^+_{\mathcal{S}} \gamma_n \overset{\alpha_{n+1}}{\Rightarrow}^+_{\mathcal{S}} \cdots$ *such that* $\gamma_i \in [\![\pi_i \wedge \phi_i]\!]$ *for* $i = 0, 1, \ldots$.

An interesting and practically relevant question is whether the coverage/precision relationships between $\mathcal{L}$ and $\mathcal{L}^s$ can be reflected on the level of the approximate encodings as two-layered rewrite theories. To investigate these relationships, we have to find a way to define an approximate two-layered rewrite theory $\mathfrak{R}(\mathcal{L}^s)$ that extends a given approximate two-layered rewrite theory $\mathcal{R}(\mathcal{L})$. A first attempt is to define $\mathfrak{R}(\mathcal{L}^s) = (\Sigma^s, E \cup A, 1R^s \cup 2R^s, \varepsilon^s)$ from $\mathcal{R}(\mathcal{L})$ in the same way $\mathcal{L}^s$ is obtained from $\mathcal{L}$, but this is not enough to have a coverage-like result. The program log in Fig. 4 is deterministic and terminating for each $\vartheta(A) \in Int$. So we may execute any instance of it with an approximate encoding $\mathcal{R}$ having no second-layer rules, i.e., $2R = \emptyset$. If $2R^s = \emptyset$, then $1R^s$ is non terminating because there is an infinite execution corresponding to the case when the value of the program variable X in the current configuration is always greater the zero. Another problem is to specify how the strategy ε is extended to ε^s. Since it is hard to give general definitions for these questions, we opted for a particular solution that can be implemented in Maude.

Definition 5 (symbolic approximate encoding). *Let $\mathcal{L}^s = (\Sigma^s, \mathcal{T}^s, \mathcal{S}^s)$ be the symbolic extension of $\mathcal{L} = (\Sigma, \mathcal{T}, \mathcal{S})$ and $\mathfrak{R}(\mathcal{L}) = (\Sigma, E \cup A, 1R \cup 2R, \varepsilon)$ an approximate encoding of $\mathcal{L}$. We assume that there is a total order relation $\prec$ over $1R$ such that:*

1. *the rewrite $t \to^!_{(E \cup 1R)/A} \varepsilon(t)$ uses the minimal rule from $1R$ w.r.t. $\prec$ whenever such a rule is applicable;*
2. *if α is unconditional and α' is conditional then $\alpha \prec \alpha'$.*

We let the approximated encoding of $\mathcal{L}^s$ be $\mathfrak{R}(\mathcal{L}^s) = (\Sigma^s, E \cup A, 1R^s \cup 2R^s, \varepsilon^s)$:

- $1R^s = \{\alpha^s \mid \alpha \in 1R, \alpha \ unconditional\}$;
- $2R^s = \{\alpha^s \mid \alpha \in 1R, \alpha \ conditional\} \cup \{\alpha^s \mid \alpha \in 2R\}$;
- $\alpha^s \prec^s \alpha'^s$ *iff* $\alpha \prec \alpha'$;
- ε^s *uses the minimal rule from $1R^s$ w.r.t. $\prec^s$.*

Theorem 5 (coverage for approximate rewrite theories). *Let $\mathcal{L} = (\Sigma, \mathcal{T}, \mathcal{S})$ be a language definition and $\mathfrak{R}(\mathcal{L}) = (\Sigma, E \cup A, 1R \cup 2R, \varepsilon)$ be an approximate encoding of $\mathcal{L}$. For every concrete execution $\gamma_0 \to_{\mathfrak{R}(\mathcal{L})} \gamma_1 \to_{\mathfrak{R}(\mathcal{L})} \cdots \to_{\mathfrak{R}(\mathcal{L})} \gamma_n \to_{\mathfrak{R}(\mathcal{L})} \cdots$ there is a symbolic execution $\pi_0 \wedge \phi_0 \to^+_{\mathfrak{R}(\mathcal{L}^s)} \pi_1 \wedge \phi_1 \to^+_{\mathfrak{R}(\mathcal{L}^s)} \cdots \to^+_{\mathfrak{R}(\mathcal{L}^s)} \pi_n \wedge \phi_n \to^+_{\mathfrak{R}(\mathcal{L}^s)} \cdots$ such that $\gamma_i \in [\![\pi_i \wedge \phi_i]\!]$ for $i = 0, 1, \ldots$.*

However, the precision relationship between $\mathfrak{R}(\mathcal{L})$ and $\mathfrak{R}(\mathcal{L}^s)$ does not hold in general. The reason is that $1R^s$ has fewer rules than $1R$ and hence the representative-selection strategy ε^s is weaker than ε. Therefore there are no guarantees that the concrete execution given by Corollary 3 will be the same with that chosen by the strategy ε. If the strategy ε^s is the "isomorphic image" of ε via the transformation $\bullet \mapsto \bullet^s$, then the precision result holds:

Theorem 6 (precision for approximate rewrite theories). *Let $\mathcal{L} = (\Sigma, \mathcal{T}, \mathcal{S})$ be a language definition and $\mathfrak{R}(\mathcal{L}) = (\Sigma, E \cup A, 1R \cup 2R, \varepsilon)$ be an* *approximated encoding of $\mathcal{L}$ such that $1R$ includes only unconditional rules (hence $1R^s = \{\alpha^s \mid \alpha \in 1R\}$). For every feasible symbolic execution $\pi_0 \wedge \phi_0 \rightarrow_{\mathfrak{R}(\mathcal{L}^s)} \pi_1 \wedge \phi_1 \rightarrow_{\mathfrak{R}(\mathcal{L}^s)} \cdots \rightarrow_{\mathfrak{R}(\mathcal{L}^s)} \pi_n \wedge \phi_n \rightarrow_{\mathfrak{R}(\mathcal{L}^s)} \cdots$ there is a concrete one $\gamma_0 \rightarrow_{\mathfrak{R}(\mathcal{L})} \gamma_1 \rightarrow_{\mathfrak{R}(\mathcal{L})} \cdots \rightarrow_{\mathfrak{R}(\mathcal{L})} \gamma_n \rightarrow_{\mathfrak{R}(\mathcal{L})} \cdots$ such that $\gamma_i \in [\![\pi_i \wedge \phi_i]\!]$ for $i = 0, 1, \ldots$.*

5 Implementing the $\mathbb{K}$ Framework in Maude

The current implementation of the $\mathbb{K}$ framework uses Maude as a rewrite engine. In [4], the framework, at that time called K-Maude, was presented as an extension of Maude consisting in several meta-transformations which gradually translate $\mathbb{K}$ modules into executable Maude modules. In the current version of $\mathbb{K}$ we use a compiler for language definitions where each of these meta-transformations is actually a separate compilation step. Through compilation, $\mathbb{K}$ definitions are translated into Maude rewrite theories which are then used for running/analysing programs. The main components of a $\mathbb{K}$ definition are the syntax declarations, the configuration and the $\mathbb{K}$ (rewrite) rules. To these, the tool adds automatically the rules generated from strictness annotations (e.g. heating/cooling rules 1–4.

The work described in this article is concerned with how the set of rules is compiled into a two-layered rewrite theory, which is then encoded into Maude by using equations for the first-layer rules and rewrite rules for the second-layer rules. By default, all $\mathbb{K}$ rules are translated into (conditional) equations, that is $1R = \mathcal{S}$ and $2R = \emptyset$. This behavior can be altered by specifying (at compile time) that certain rules are to be considered *transitions*, which will trigger their transformation into (conditional) rewrite rules in the resulted Maude module.

To specify that a rule is a transition, one must pass the rule name as an argument for the -transition option at compilation time:

```
$ kompile cink.k -transition "division"
```

The above command specifies the rule *division* as a transition; thus, the rule for division is included in $2R$. By this command we express our intent that the tool considers the rule for division as a transition when exploring an execution's transition system. By making it a rewrite rule in Maude, we can explore the non-determinism generated by the rule when using Maude's *search* command.

Another source of non-determinism arises from strictness annotations. When the *strict* attribute is given to some syntactical construct, the tool chooses by default an arbitrary, fixed order to evaluate its arguments. This optimisation has the side effect of possibly losing behaviours due to missed interleavings.

Some of these missed interleavings can be restored using the -superheat option. This option is used to instruct the $\mathbb{K}$ tool to exhaustively explore all the non-deterministic evaluation choices for the strictness of a language construct.

Once we know which rules are transitions and which are not, we can easily deduce the two sets $1R$ and $2R$, and thus we obtain the executable rewrite theory $\mathfrak{R}(\mathcal{L})$ as discussed in Sect. 4.

The following example shows how one can explore more behaviours by specifying second-layer rules at compile time. If we compile the language definition of CinK without any options, then running the program `counter` (Fig. 4) will result in a single solution, where the return value is either 1 (when the tool first evaluates `dec()` and then `inc()`) or 3 (when it first evaluates `inc()` and then `dec()`). However, if we set the operation *plus* as superheat:

```
$ kompile cink -superheat "plus"
```

then we obtain both solutions, because the heating rule for addition can be applied in two ways and the option tells the tool to explore them both.

The symbolic transformations discussed in Sect. 3.2 are implemented as compilation steps in the $\mathbb{K}$ compiler [2]. The tool uses the same translation to Maude discussed above in order to obtain the rewrite theory $\mathfrak{R}(\mathcal{L}^s)$. An important step in this process is that conditional rules whose conditions cannot be reduced to *true* are compiled as transitions, that is, they are included in *2R*. When performing search in Maude, these rules are essential in exploring all the execution paths, thereby ensuring the Coverage (Theorem 5) property. Note that none of the symbolic transformations applied by the tool to the language definition changes the initial semantics of the language.

The implementation uses a slightly modified version of Maude which includes a hook to the Z3 SMT solver [5] and a corresponding operation called *checkSat*. It receives as argument an SMTLib string, which is sent to the solver to check its satisfiability. The result returned by the solver is propagated back through the hook to Maude as a string, so *checkSat* can return "sat", "unsat", or "unknown". In practice, our tool uses checkSat to reduce the search space by slicing unfeasible execution paths, and thus being very important in preserving the precision property. To obtain $\mathfrak{R}(\mathcal{L}^s)$ from a language definition one uses the symbolic backend as follows:

```
$ kompile cink -backend symbolic
```

This command applies the symbolic transformations, moves the appropriate rules in *2R*, and generates the rewrite theory $\mathfrak{R}(\mathcal{L}^s)$. Using $\mathfrak{R}(\mathcal{L}^s)$ one can execute programs using either concrete values or symbolic ones. However, running programs with symbolic values may lead to infinite loops when the loop conditions contain symbolic values. In such cases one can bound the number of execution paths:

```
$ krun log.imp -search -bound 3 -cIN=".List" -cPC="true"
```

This executes `log` (Fig. 4) symbolically, until a number of 3 solutions is found. Each solution consists in a result configuration and a formula which constitutes the path condition. The symbolic values are represented as fresh variables with a specific sort (e.g. `A:Int`). These can also be passed as input at the command line of the tool as arguments of the `-cIN` parameter. Users can also set the initial path condition using the `-cPC` option. During the symbolic execution the tool applies a rule only if the next state is feasible: the current path condition and the new conditions imposed by the application of the rule are not "unsat".

6   Conclusion and Related Work

We presented some results that relate language definitions to different kinds of rewrite theories, which encode the language definitions both faithfully and approximately. The results show how (symbolic) analyses performed on a rewrite theory are reflected on the corresponding language definition. The general results are applied to the current implementation of $\mathbb{K}$ language definitions in Maude.

The faitfful encoding of $\mathbb{K}$ language definitions as rewrite theories is relatively simple but the resulting theory is not efficient in practice. Therefore we extended the notion of rewrite theory in order to work with under-approximations of the language definitions (and implicitly of the rewrite theories). The approximating theories are more efficient and flexible – the user has the freedom to work with various levels of approximations –, but heir use for program analysis must be done with care because they do not preserve all the behavioural properties. The coverage/precision results proved in this paper can help the user in correctly assessing which analyses hold on which representations.

Related Work. $\mathbb{K}$ started as methodology for defining the semantics of the programming languages in Maude. The first tool supporting $\mathbb{K}$ [4] was written in Maude's meta-level, as a series of transformations translating $\mathbb{K}$ definitions into Maude programs. Then the $\mathbb{K}$ compiler became a more complex tool that translates a $\mathbb{K}$ definition into an intermediate language, which is then used to generate code for various backends, including Maude. A presentation of this tool is given in [8]. There, a brief description of the semantics of $\mathbb{K}$ definitions is also included. The programming-language definition framework presented here in Sect. 3 is a specialised case of that definition.

The coverage and precision properties, which relate the faithful rewrite-theory encoding of a language and of that language's symbolic version, are analoguous to the soundness and completeness results in [10], which relate usual rewriting and rewriting modulo SMT. An interesting alternative to defining symbolic execution by as executions in a transformed language (as we do it in [2]) would be to compile a language into a rewriting-modulo-SMT Maude module.

Our construction of two-layered rewrite theories have some similarities with equational abstractions [9] and with the state-space reduction techniques obtained by transforming rules into equations presented in [6]. However, our first-layer rewrite rules do not equate states as Maude equations do; their semantics is that of transformation, not of equality. Therefore these rules do not have to satisfy the executability and property-preservation requirements of [6,9].

Acknowledgement. This work was supported by the strategic grant POSDRU/159/ 1.5/S/137750, "Project Doctoral and Postdoctoral programs support for increased competitiveness in Exact Sciences research" cofinanced by the European Social Found within the Sectorial Operational Program Human Resources Development 2007–2013.

References

1. Standard for Programming Language C++. Working Draft. http://www.open-std. org/jtc1/sc22/wg21/docs/papers/2013/n3797.pdf
2. Arusoaie, A., Lucanu, D., Rusu, V.: A generic framework for symbolic execution. In: Erwig, M., Paige, R.F., Van Wyk, E. (eds.) SLE 2013. LNCS, vol. 8225, pp. 281–301. Springer, Heidelberg (2013). (Also available as a technical report at http://hal.inria.fr/hal-00766220/)
3. Clavel, M., Durán, F., Eker, S., Lincoln, P., Martí-Oliet, N., Meseguer, J., Talcott, C.: All About Maude - A High-Performance Logical Framework. LNCS, vol. 4350. Springer, Heidelberg (2007)
4. Şerbănuţă, T.F., Roşu, G.: K-maude: a rewriting based tool for semantics of programming languages. In: Ölveczky, P.C. (ed.) WRLA 2010. LNCS, vol. 6381, pp. 104–122. Springer, Heidelberg (2010)
5. de Moura, L., Bjørner, N.S.: Z3: an efficient SMT solver. In: Ramakrishnan, C.R., Rehof, J. (eds.) TACAS 2008. LNCS, vol. 4963, pp. 337–340. Springer, Heidelberg (2008)
6. Farzan, A., Meseguer, J.: State space reduction of rewrite theories using invisible transitions. In: Johnson, M., Vene, V. (eds.) AMAST 2006. LNCS, vol. 4019, pp. 142–157. Springer, Heidelberg (2006)
7. Lucanu, D., Serbanuta, T.F.: Cink - an exercise on how to think in k. Technical Report TR 12–03, Version 2, Alexandru Ioan Cuza University, Faculty of Computer Science, December 2013
8. Lucanu, D., Şerbănuţă, T.F., Roşu, G.: K framework distilled. In: Durán, F. (ed.) WRLA 2012. LNCS, vol. 7571, pp. 31–53. Springer, Heidelberg (2012)
9. Meseguer, J., Palomino, M., Martí-Oliet, N.: Equational abstractions. Theor. Comput. Sci. 403(2–3), 239–264 (2008)
10. Rocha, C., Meseguer, J., Munoz, C.A.: Rewriting modulo SMT. In: Escobar, S. (ed.) WRLA 2014. LNCS, vol. 8663, pp. 247–262. Springer, Heidelberg (2014)
11. Roşu, G., Şerbănuţă, T.F.: An overview of the K semantic framework. J. Logic Algebraic Program. 79(6), 397–434 (2010)
12. Roşu, G., Ştefănescu, A.: Checking reachability using matching logic. In: Leavens, G.T., Dwyer, M.B. (eds) OOPSLA, pp. 555–574. ACM (2012)
13. Viry, P.: Equational rules for rewriting logic. Theor. Comput. Sci. 285(2), 487–517 (2002)

Infinite-State Model Checking of LTLR Formulas Using Narrowing

Kyungmin Bae[(✉)] and José Meseguer

Department of Computer Science, University of Illinois at Urbana-Champaign,
Urbana, IL 61801, USA
{kbae4,meseguer}@cs.uiuc.edu

Abstract. The linear temporal logic of rewriting (LTLR) is a simple
extension of LTL that adds *spatial action patterns* to the logic, expressing
that a specific instance of an action described by a rewrite rule has been
performed. Although the theory and algorithms of LTLR for finite-state
model checking are well-developed [2], no theoretical foundations have
yet been developed for infinite-state LTLR model checking. The main
goal of this paper is to develop such foundations for *narrowing-based
logical model checking* of LTLR properties. A key theme in this paper is
the systematic relationship, in the form of a simulation with remarkably
good properties, between the concrete state space and the symbolic state
space. A related theme is the use of additional state space reduction
methods, such as folding and equational abstractions, that can in some
cases yield a finite symbolic state space.

Keywords: Model checking · Infinite-state systems · LTLR · Narrowing

1   Introduction

This paper further develops previous efforts to use rewriting logic and narrowing
to perform symbolic model checking of infinite-state systems.[1] Those efforts have
gradually increased the expressiveness of the properties that can be verified, first
focusing on reachability analysis [16] and then expanding the range to general
LTL formulas [1,6]. It is by now clear that state-based temporal logics are not
expressive enough to deal with properties involving events, such as message
sends and receives; and that the temporal logic of rewriting [14] is a perfect
match—at the level of property specification—for rewriting logic—at the level of
system specification—so that both can be used seamlessly as a tandem for model
checking. For finite-state systems, the authors have developed model checkers
that demonstrate the power and usefulness of this tandem of logics [2]. The
question asked and positively answered in this paper is: can properties of a
rewrite theory $\mathcal{R}$ expressed in the *linear temporal logic of rewriting* (LTLR) [14]
be model checked symbolically by narrowing under reasonable assumptions?

---

[1] The temporal logics that can be verified by infinite-state model checking techniques
are generally less expressive than those supported by finite-state model checkers.

© Springer International Publishing Switzerland 2014
S. Escobar (Ed.): WRLA 2014, LNCS 8663, pp. 113–129, 2014.
DOI: 10.1007/978-3-319-12904-4_6

The answer to this question is nontrivial, because of a difficulty which can be best explained by briefly recalling how narrowing-based reachability analysis and LTL model checking are performed for a rewrite theory $\mathcal{R}$. For reachability analysis, *any* non-variable term t, symbolically denoting a typically infinite set of concrete state instances, can be narrowed to try to reach an instance of a goal pattern term g. However, for LTL model checking, *not all such terms t* denote states in the symbolic state space. The reason is that LTL formulas have a set AP of state propositions, but for a symbolic term t such propositions may not be defined: different term instances of t may satisfy different state propositions. The solution proposed in [1,6] is to *specialize* t to most general instances $t_1, \ldots, t_n$ for which all state propositions in AP are either true or false. If the equations defining such propositions have the finite variant property, this can be done by variant narrowing [1,6]. Therefore, narrowing-based LTL model checking symbolically explores the state space of all such *AP-instantiated symbolic terms*.

Suppose that we now want to perform not just LTL model checking but symbolic LTLR model checking, and that our formula φ involves both state propositions in AP and spatial action patterns. For example, a spatial action pattern $l(\theta)$ can appear in φ, stating that a rule $l : q \longrightarrow r$ has been performed with an instantiation that further specializes the substitution θ. As part of the model checking verification of φ we may reach a symbolic state t where we need to check whether the action specified by $l(\theta)$ can be performed. This check will succeed if t can be narrowed with a rule l and a substitution σ such that θ is an *instance* of σ. However, σ can be *incomparable* to θ in general; that is, σ may have instances for which this property holds, and other instances for which it *definitely fails*. This is analogous to the lack of AP-instantiation discussed above for narrowing-based LTL model checking. Let ACT be the set of spatial action patterns we are using, so that, say, $l(\theta) \in ACT$. Our problem is that the symbolic transitions in the LTLR state space need to be *ACT-instantiated*, while the symbolic states are *AP-instantiated*.

Lack of ACT-instantiations is a subtler problem than lack of AP-instantiation. After all, state propositions in AP are equationally defined as Boolean predicates *in both their positive and negative cases*, so that variant narrowing can automate AP-instantiation. The problem of ACT-instantiation has to do with effectively characterizing the *negative cases* in which an action pattern does *not* hold. This turns out to be closely related to the problem of computing *complement patterns* of a pattern term; e.g., for a pattern $l(\theta)$, terms $u_1, \ldots, u_k$ such that any ground term is an instance of *exactly one term* in the set

$$\{l(\theta), u_1, \ldots, u_k\}.$$

Not all terms have such complements. For example, for an unsorted signature with constant 0, unary operator s, and free binary operator f, the term $f(x, x)$ has *no* such complements. However, effective methods have been developed to check when a term t has complements and to compute them (for example, [8,9,12]). Under appropriate assumptions, they can provide a method to solve the ACT-instantiation problem.

Having identified conditions under which the state space for narrowing-based LTRL model checking can be built, the rest of the paper develops the theoretical foundations of narrowing-based LTLR model checking. A key theme in such foundations is the systematic relationship between concrete and symbolic states. This takes the form of a simulation relation from concrete to symbolic states that preserves both state propositions and spatial action patterns. A related theme is the use of additional state space reduction methods, such as folding and equational abstractions, that can in some cases yield a finite symbolic state space. How these foundations can be used in practice to prove nontrivial LTLR properties of infinite-state systems is illustrated with a running example.

2   Preliminaries

Rewriting Logic. An order-sorted signature is a triple $\Sigma = (S, \leq, \Sigma)$ with poset of sorts $(S, \leq)$ and operators $\Sigma = \{\Sigma_{w,k}\}_{(w,k) \in S^* \times S}$ typed in $(S, \leq)$. The set $\mathcal{T}_\Sigma(\mathcal{X})_s$ denotes the set of Σ-terms of sort s over $\mathcal{X}$ an infinite set of S-sorted variables, and $\mathcal{T}_{\Sigma,s}$ denotes the set of ground Σ-terms of sort s. We assume that $\mathcal{T}_{\Sigma,s} \neq \emptyset$ for each sort s in Σ. *Positions* in a term t represent tree positions when t is parsed as a tree, and the replacement in t of a subterm at a position p by another term u is denoted by $t[u]_p$. A *substitution* $\sigma : \mathcal{X} \to \mathcal{T}_\Sigma(\mathcal{X})$ is a function that maps variables to terms of the same sort, and is homomorphically extended to $\mathcal{T}_\Sigma(\mathcal{X})$ in a natural way. The *domain* of σ is a finite subset $dom(\sigma) \subseteq \mathcal{X}$, where $\sigma x = x$ for any $x \notin dom(\sigma)$. The restriction of σ to $Y \subseteq \mathcal{X}$ is the substitution $\sigma|_Y$ such that $\sigma|_Y(x) = \sigma(x)$ if $x \in Y$, and $\sigma|_Y(x) = x$ otherwise.

A rewrite theory is a formal specification of a concurrent system [13]. To apply narrowing-based methods, we consider *unconditional order-sorted rewrite theories* $\mathcal{R} = (\Sigma, E, R)$, where: (i) (Σ, E) is an equational theory with Σ an order-sorted signature and E a set of equations, specifying the system's states as the initial algebra $\mathcal{T}_{\Sigma/E}$ (i.e., each state is an E-equivalence class $[t]_E \in \mathcal{T}_{\Sigma/E}$ of ground terms); and R is a set of unconditional *rewrite rules* of the form $l : q \longrightarrow r$ with label l and Σ-terms $q, r \in \mathcal{T}_\Sigma(\mathcal{X})_s$, specifying the system's transitions as a *one-step rewrite*

$$t[l(\theta)]_p : [t[\theta q]_p]_E \longrightarrow_\mathcal{R} [t[\theta r]_p]_E$$

from a state $[t[\theta q]_p]_E \in \mathcal{T}_{\Sigma/E}$ containing a substitution instance θq of q to the corresponding state $[t[\theta r]_p]_E \in \mathcal{T}_{\Sigma/E}$ in which θq has been replaced by θr, where $t[l(\theta)]_p$ is called a *one-step proof term*.

We also require $\mathcal{R} = (\Sigma, E, R)$ being *topmost* for narrowing-based methods. That is, there is sort State at the top of one of the connected component of $(S, \leq)$ such that: (i) for each rule $l : q \longrightarrow r \in R$, both q and r have the top sort State; and no operator in Σ has State or any of its subsorts as an argument sort. This ensures that all rewrites with rules in R must take place at the top of the term. In practice, many concurrent systems, including object-oriented systems and communication protocols, can be specified by topmost rewrite theories [16].

We can associate to $\mathcal{R}$ a corresponding Kripke structure for LTL model checking. A *Kripke structure* is a 4-tuple $\mathcal{K} = (S, AP, \mathcal{L}, \longrightarrow_{\mathcal{K}})$ with S a set of states, AP a set of atomic *state propositions*, $\mathcal{L} : S \to \mathcal{P}(AP)$ a *state-labeling function*, and $\longrightarrow_{\mathcal{K}} \subseteq S \times S$ a *total transition relation* in which every state $s \in S$ has a next state $s' \in S$ with $s \longrightarrow_{\mathcal{K}} s'$. A state proposition is defined as a term of sort Prop, whose meaning is defined by equations using the auxiliary operator $\_ \models \_ :$ State Prop $\to$ Bool. By definition, $p \in \mathcal{T}_{\Sigma/E,\mathsf{Prop}}$ is satisfied on a state $[t]_E$ iff $(t \models p) =_E true$. We assume that sort Bool has two constants *true* and *false* with $true \neq_E false$ and any $t \in \mathcal{T}_{\Sigma,\mathsf{Bool}}$ is provably equal to either *true* or *false*.

Definition 1. *Given* $\mathcal{R} = (\Sigma, E, R)$ *and a set* $AP \subseteq \mathcal{T}_{\Sigma/E,\mathsf{Prop}}$ *defined by* E, *the corresponding Kripke structure is* $\mathcal{K}(\mathcal{R})_{AP} = (\mathcal{T}_{\Sigma/E,\mathsf{State}}, AP, \mathcal{L}_E, \longrightarrow_{\mathcal{R}}),$[2] *where* $\mathcal{L}_E([t]_E) = \{p \in AP \mid (t \models p) =_E true\}$.

Linear Temporal Logic of Rewriting. The *linear temporal logic of rewriting* (LTLR) is a state/event extension of LTL with *spatial action patterns* [2]. An LTLR formula φ may include spatial action patterns $\delta_1, \ldots, \delta_n$ as well as state propositions $p_1, \ldots, p_m$, and therefore may describe properties involving both states and events. Given a set of state propositions AP and a set of spatial action patterns ACT, the syntax of LTLR is defined by

$$\varphi ::= p \mid \delta \mid \neg\varphi \mid \varphi \wedge \varphi \mid \bigcirc\varphi \mid \varphi \mathbf{U} \varphi,$$

where $p \in AP$ and $\delta \in ACT$. Other operators can be defined by equivalences, e.g., $\Diamond\varphi \equiv true \mathbf{U} \varphi$ and $\Box\varphi \equiv \neg\Diamond\neg\varphi$.

Spatial action patterns describe properties of one-step rewrites by defining a set of matching one-step proof terms. For example, a pattern l describes that a rule with label l is applied, and a pattern $l(\theta)$ describes that a rule with label l is applied and the related variable instantiation is a further instantiation of the substitution θ [2,14]. In a similar way that state propositions of LTL are defined by equations, the matching relation $\models$ between a one-step proof term γ and a spatial action pattern δ can be defined by equations using the auxiliary operator $\_ \models \_ :$ ProofTerm Action $\to$ Bool, where $\gamma \models \delta \iff (\gamma \models \delta) =_E true$.

The semantics of an LTLR formula is defined on a *labeled Kripke structure* (LKS), an extension of a Kripke structure with transition labels [2,3]. An LKS is a 5-tuple $\bar{\mathcal{K}} = (S, AP, \mathcal{L}, ACT, \longrightarrow_{\bar{\mathcal{K}}})$ with S a set of *states*, AP a set of *state propositions*, $\mathcal{L} : S \to \mathcal{P}(AP)$ a *state-labeling function*, ACT a set of *spatial action patterns*, and $\longrightarrow_{\bar{\mathcal{K}}} \subseteq S \times \mathcal{P}(ACT) \times S$ a total *labeled transition relation*. A *path* (π, α) is a pair of functions $\pi : \mathbb{N} \to S$ and $\alpha : \mathbb{N} \to \mathcal{P}(ACT)$ such that $\pi(i) \xrightarrow{\alpha(i)}_{\bar{\mathcal{K}}} \pi(i+1)$, and $(\pi, \alpha)^k$ denotes the suffix of (π, α) beginning at position k such that $(\pi, \alpha)^k = (\pi \circ s^k, \alpha \circ s^k)$ with s the successor function.

We can associate to a rewrite theory $\mathcal{R}$ a corresponding LKS $\bar{\mathcal{K}}(\mathcal{R})_{AP,ACT}$ for LTLR model checking, provided that the state propositions AP and the spatial action patterns ACT are defined by its equations.

---

[2] Since $\longrightarrow_{\mathcal{R}}$ needs to be total, we also assume that $\mathcal{R}$ is deadlock-free. Note that $\mathcal{R}$ can be easily transformed into an equivalent deadlock-free theory [15].

Definition 2. *Given a rewrite theory* $\mathcal{R} = (\Sigma, E, R)$, *sets* $AP \subseteq \mathcal{T}_{\Sigma/E,\text{Prop}}$ *and* $ACT \subseteq \mathcal{T}_{\Sigma/E,\text{Action}}$ *defined by* E, *the corresponding LKS is*

$$\bar{\mathcal{K}}(\mathcal{R})_{AP,ACT} = (\mathcal{T}_{\Sigma/E,\text{State}}, AP, \mathcal{L}_E, ACT, \longrightarrow_{\bar{\mathcal{K}}(\mathcal{R})_{AP,ACT}}),$$

where $\mathcal{L}_E([t]_E) = \{p \in AP \mid (t \models p) =_E true\}$, *and* $[t]_E \xrightarrow{A}_{\bar{\mathcal{K}}(\mathcal{R})_{AP,ACT}} [t']_E$ *iff* $\gamma : [t]_E \longrightarrow_R [t']_E$ *and* $A = \{\delta \in ACT \mid (\gamma \models \delta) =_E true\}$.

Given an LTLR formula φ and an initial state $s_0 \in S$, the satisfaction relation $\bar{\mathcal{K}}, s_0 \models \varphi$ holds iff for each path (π, α) of $\bar{\mathcal{K}}$ beginning at s_0, the path satisfaction relation $\bar{\mathcal{K}}, (\pi, \alpha) \models \varphi$ holds, which is defined inductively as follows:

- $\bar{\mathcal{K}}, (\pi, \alpha) \models p$ iff $p \in \mathcal{L}(\pi(0))$
- $\bar{\mathcal{K}}, (\pi, \alpha) \models \delta$ iff $\delta \in \alpha(0)$
- $\bar{\mathcal{K}}, (\pi, \alpha) \models \neg\varphi$ iff $\bar{\mathcal{K}}, (\pi, \alpha) \not\models \varphi$
- $\bar{\mathcal{K}}, (\pi, \alpha) \models \varphi \wedge \varphi'$ iff $\bar{\mathcal{K}}, (\pi, \alpha) \models \varphi$ and $\bar{\mathcal{K}}, (\pi, \alpha) \models \varphi'$
- $\bar{\mathcal{K}}, (\pi, \alpha) \models \bigcirc\varphi$ iff $\bar{\mathcal{K}}, (\pi, \alpha)^1 \models \varphi$
- $\bar{\mathcal{K}}, (\pi, \alpha) \models \varphi \mathbf{U} \varphi'$ iff $\exists k \geq 0. \bar{\mathcal{K}}, (\pi, \alpha)^k \models \varphi', \forall 0 \leq i < k. \bar{\mathcal{K}}, (\pi, \alpha)^i \models \varphi$.

Example. We present a topmost rewrite theory $\mathcal{R} = (\Sigma, E, R)$ that specifies Lamport's bakery protocol for mutual exclusion of an unbounded number of processes (adapted from [1,6]), and its corresponding LKS $\bar{\mathcal{K}}(\mathcal{R})_{AP,ACT}$. Each state of the system has the form $n ; m ; [i_1, d_1] \ldots [i_k, d_k]$, given by the operator $\_;\_;\_ : \text{Nat Nat ProcSet} \rightarrow \text{State}$, where n is the current number in the bakery's number dispenser, m is the number currently being served, and $[i_1, d_1] \ldots [i_k, d_k]$ are a set of customer processes, each with a name i_l and in a *mode* d_l. A mode can be *idle* (not yet picked a number), *wait(n)* (waiting with number n), or *crit(n)* (being served with number n). The behavior is specified by the following *topmost* rewrite rules in the Maude language:

```
rl [wake]: N ; M ; [I,idle] PS => s N ; M ; [I,wait(N)] PS .
rl [crit]: N ; M ; [I,wait(M)] PS => N ; M ; [I,crit(M)] PS .
rl [exit]: N ; M ; [I,crit(M)] PS => N ; s M ; [I,idle] PS .
```

where natural numbers are modeled as multisets of s with the multiset union operator $\_\_$ (empty syntax) and the empty multiset 0 (e.g., $0 = 0$, and $3 = \mathbf{s\,s\,s}$).

We are interested in verifying the liveness property *"process 0 is eventually served,"* under the fairness assumption *"if process 0 can eventually pick a number forever, it must pick a number infinitely often,"* expressed as the LTLR formula

$$(\Diamond\square enabled.wake(0) \rightarrow \square\Diamond wake(0)) \rightarrow \Diamond in.crit(0),$$

where the spatial action pattern $wake(0)$ holds if the *wake* rule is applied for process 0 (i.e., the variable I in the *wake* rule is matched to the term 0), the state proposition $enabled.wake(0)$ holds in a state where process 0 is idle, and the state proposition $in.crit(0)$ holds in a state where process 0 is being served (see [1] for the mutual exclusion property).

For the set of state propositions $AP = \{in.crit(0), enabled.wake(0)\}$ and the set of spatial action patterns $ACT = \{wake(0)\}$, we can construct the related LKS $\bar{\mathcal{K}}(\mathcal{R})_{AP,ACT}$ for the bakery protocol specification $\mathcal{R}$. For example, given the initial state $0 ; 0 ; [0,idle]$, we obtain the infinite path in Fig. 1 within $\bar{\mathcal{K}}(\mathcal{R})_{AP,ACT}$ that contains an infinite number of different states. Notice that this system is infinite-state since: (i) the counters n and m are unbounded; and the number of customer processes is unbounded.

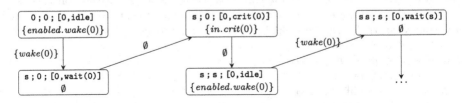

Fig. 1. A path from $0 ; 0 ; [0,idle]$ in the LKS $\bar{\mathcal{K}}(\mathcal{R})_{AP,ACT}$ for the bakery protocol.

3   Narrowing-Based LTLR Model Checking

Narrowing [10,11] generalizes term rewriting by allowing free variables in terms and by performing unification instead of matching. An *E-unifier* of $t = t'$ is a substitution σ such that $\sigma t =_E \sigma t'$ and $dom(\sigma) \subseteq vars(t) \cup vars(t')$, and $CSU_E(t = t')$ denotes a *complete set of E-unifiers* in which any E-unifier ρ of $t = t'$ has a more general substitution $\sigma \in CSU_E(t = t')$, i.e., $(\exists \eta)\ \rho =_E \eta \circ \sigma$. We assume that there exists a finitary E-unification procedure to find a *finite* complete set $CSU_E(t = t')$ of E-unifiers (e.g., there exists a finitary E-unification procedure if E has the *finite variant property* as explained in [5,7]).

Definition 3. *Given a* topmost *rewrite theory* $\mathcal{R} = (\Sigma, E, R)$, *each rewrite rule* $l : q \longrightarrow r \in R$ *specifies a topmost narrowing step* $t \leadsto_{l,\sigma,\mathcal{R}} t'$ *(or* $t \leadsto_{\mathcal{R}} t'$*) iff there exists an E-unifier* $\sigma \in CSU_E(t = q)$ *such that* $t' = \sigma r$.

For LTL model checking we can associate to $\mathcal{R} = (\Sigma, E, R)$ a corresponding *logical Kripke structure* $\mathcal{N}(\mathcal{R})_{AP}$ [6]. The states of $\mathcal{N}(\mathcal{R})_{AP}$ are AP-instantiated elements of $\mathcal{T}_{\Sigma/E}(\mathcal{X})_{\text{State}}$ and its transitions are specified by $\leadsto_{\mathcal{R}}$. A state of $\mathcal{N}(\mathcal{R})_{AP}$ is not a *concrete state*, but a *state pattern* $t(x_1, \ldots, x_n)$ with *logical variables* $x_1, \ldots, x_n$, representing the set of all concrete states $[\theta t]_E$ that are its ground instances. Such a logical Kripke structure $\mathcal{N}(\mathcal{R})_{AP}$ can be considered as an abstraction of the (possibly infinite) concrete system $\mathcal{K}(\mathcal{R})_{AP}$; that is, for an LTL formula φ and a state pattern t, we have:

$$\mathcal{N}(\mathcal{R})_{AP}, [t]_E \models \varphi \implies (\forall \theta : \mathcal{X} \to \mathcal{T}_\Sigma)\ \mathcal{K}(\mathcal{R})_{AP}, [\theta t]_E \models \varphi.$$

Generalizing such narrowing-based LTL model checking, this section presents narrowing-based LTLR model checking for infinite-state systems.

One-Step Proof Terms for Narrowing. Spatial action patterns for rewriting define their matching one-step proof terms, representing the corresponding one-step rewrites. For a topmost rewrite theory $\mathcal{R} = (\Sigma, E, R)$, one-step proof terms have the form $l(\theta)$, indicating that a rule $l : q \longrightarrow r \in R$ has been applied with a substitution θ (at the top position of the term), where $dom(\theta) \subseteq vars(q) \cup vars(r)$.

In order to define spatial action patterns for narrowing steps, we also need to have an appropriate notion of one-step proof terms for narrowing. Consider a topmost narrowing step $t \leadsto_{l,\sigma,\mathcal{R}} t'$ using a rule $l : q \longrightarrow r$. Intuitively, the rule label l and the restriction of the substitution σ to the variables in the rule[3] give the one-step proof term for the narrowing step $t \leadsto_{l,\sigma,\mathcal{R}} t'$.

Definition 4. *Given a* topmost *rewrite theory* $\mathcal{R} = (\Sigma, E, R)$, *for a topmost narrowing step* $t \leadsto_{l,\sigma,\mathcal{R}} t'$ *using a rule* $l : q \longrightarrow r$, *its one-step proof term is given by* $l(\sigma|_{vars(q) \cup vars(r)})$, *often denoted by* $l(\sigma_l)$.

The following lemma implies that a one-step proof term $l(\sigma_l)$ for narrowing faithfully captures its corresponding one-step proof terms $l(\theta)$ for rewriting, in the sense that $\theta =_E \eta \circ \sigma_l$ for some substitution η. This lemma is adapted from the soundness and completeness results of topmost narrowing in [16].

Lemma 1. *Given a topmost rewrite theory* $\mathcal{R} = (\Sigma, E, R)$, *for a non-variable term* u *and a substitution* ρ, *assuming no variable in* u *appears in the rules* R:

$$\Longleftrightarrow \quad \begin{array}{c} (\exists t', \theta)\ l(\theta) : \rho u \longrightarrow_{\mathcal{R}} t' \\[6pt] (\exists u', \sigma, \eta)\ u \leadsto_{l,\sigma,\mathcal{R}} u' \ \wedge\ \rho|_{vars(u)} =_E (\eta \circ \sigma)|_{vars(u)} \end{array}$$

where $\theta =_E (\eta \circ \sigma)|_{dom(\theta)}$ *and* $t' =_E \eta u'$.

Proof. ($\Rightarrow$) Suppose that $l(\theta) : \rho u \longrightarrow_{\mathcal{R}} t'$ for a topmost rule $l : q \longrightarrow r$, where $dom(\theta) \subseteq vars(q) \cup vars(r)$. Then, $\theta q =_E \rho u$ and $t' = \theta r$. Since *no* variable in u appears in $l : q \longrightarrow r$, we have $dom(\theta) \cap vars(u) = \emptyset$. Thus, we can define the substitution $\theta \cup \rho|_{vars(u)}$ with domain $dom(\theta) \cup vars(u)$ such that $(\theta \cup \rho|_{vars(u)})|_{dom(\theta)} = \theta$ and $(\theta \cup \rho|_{vars(u)})|_{vars(u)} = \rho|_{vars(u)}$. Since $\theta \cup \rho|_{vars(u)}$ is an E-unifier of $q = u$, there exist substitutions $\sigma \in CSU_E(u = q)$ and η' satisfying $(\theta \cup \rho|_{vars(u)})|_{vars(q) \cup vars(u)} =_E \eta' \circ \sigma$ with domain $vars(q) \cup vars(u)$. Therefore, $u \leadsto_{l,\sigma,\mathcal{R}} u'$ for $u' = \sigma r$. Next, let η be the extended substitution such that $\eta x = \eta' x$ if $x \in vars(q) \cup vars(u)$, and $\eta x = \theta x$ otherwise. Then, $\rho|_{vars(u)} =_E (\eta \circ \sigma)|_{vars(u)}$ and $\theta =_E (\eta \circ \sigma)|_{dom(\theta)}$, since $dom(\theta) \cap vars(u) = \emptyset$ and $dom(\theta) \subseteq vars(q) \cup vars(r)$. Furthermore, $t' = \theta r =_E (\eta \circ \sigma)r = \eta u'$.
($\Leftarrow$) Suppose that $u \leadsto_{l,\sigma,\mathcal{R}} u'$ and $\rho|_{vars(u)} =_E (\eta \circ \sigma)|_{vars(u)}$. Then, for a topmost rule $l : q \longrightarrow r$, $\sigma \in CSU_E(u = q)$ and $u' = \sigma r$. Since $\sigma u =_E \sigma q$ and $(vars(q) \cup vars(r)) \cap vars(u) = \emptyset$, we have $l(\sigma|_{vars(q) \cup vars(r)}) : \sigma u \longrightarrow_{\mathcal{R}} u'$. Thus, we have $l(\eta \circ \sigma|_{vars(q) \cup vars(r)}) : (\eta \circ \sigma)u \longrightarrow_{\mathcal{R}} \eta u'$, where $(\eta \circ \sigma)u =_E \rho u$, since rewrites are stable under substitutions. $\qquad\square$

---

[3] Since one-step proof terms for rewriting only contain variables in rules, we restrict one-step proof terms for narrowing in the same way.

Equational Definition of State/Event Predicates. The semantics of a spatial action pattern can be defined by means of equations using the auxiliary operator $\_ \models \_$: ProofTerm Action $\rightarrow$ Bool [2]. By definition, $\delta \in \mathcal{T}_{\Sigma/E,\text{Action}}$ is matched to a one-step proof term γ iff $(\gamma \models \delta) =_E true$. For a topmost rewrite theory $\mathcal{R}$, a one-step proof term $l(\theta)$ can be represented as a term

$$\{'l \;:\; 'x_1\backslash\theta x_1 \;;\; \ldots \;;\; 'x_m\backslash\theta x_m\}$$

of sort ProofTerm using the operator $\{\_:\_\}$: Qid Substitution $\rightarrow$ ProofTerm, where $'l, 'x_1, \ldots, 'x_m$ are quoted identifiers of sort Qid and $'x_1\backslash\theta x_1; \ldots; 'x_m\backslash\theta x_m$ is a semicolon separated set of variable assignments. For the bakery example, a topmost narrowing step from the term N ; N ; [0,idle] by the *wake* rule gives the one-step proof term {'wake : 'N \ N ; 'M \ N ; 'I \ 0 ; 'PS \ none}.

For narrowing-based model checking we further require that there exists a finitary E-unification procedure. If a spatial action pattern δ is identified by a one-step proof term *pattern* u_δ (i.e., $(\gamma \models \delta) =_E true$ iff γ is an instance of the pattern u_δ),[4] and if u_δ *has complement patterns* $u_1, \ldots, u_k$ (i.e., any ground one-step proof term is an instance of exactly one term in $\{u_\delta, u_1, \ldots, u_k\}$), then δ can be defined by the equations:

$$u_\delta \models \delta = true, \quad u_1 \models \delta = false, \quad \ldots, \quad u_k \models \delta = false.$$

Because the right-hand sides are all constants, these equations have the finite variant property [5], and therefore they provide a finitary E-unification algorithm using variant narrowing [7]. This method can also be applied for "pattern-like" state propositions (see below).

As mentioned in the introduction, effective methods have been developed to check when a term t has complements and to compute such complement patterns, not only in the free case [12], but also modulo AC and modulo permutative theories [8,9]. Therefore, for unconditional rewrite theories with axioms B such as those used in [8,9,12], we can determine if a one-step proof term pattern u_δ of δ has complements, compute such complement patterns, and define pattern satisfaction of δ by equations. For example, consider the spatial action pattern $wake(0)$ in the bakery example (which holds if the variable I in the rule is matched to 0). The positive case can be defined by the following equation, where SUBST is a variable of sort Substitution:

```
eq {'wake : 'I \ 0; SUBST} |= wake(0) = true .
```

For the negative cases, $wake(0)$ does *not* hold when the rule label is *not* 'wake or the value of 'I is *not* 0. Therefore, they can be defined by the complement patterns of 0 and 'wake as follows.

```
eq {'wake : 'I \ s J ; SUBST} |= wake(0) = false .
eq {'crit : SUBST} |= wake(0) = false .
eq {'exit : SUBST} |= wake(0) = false .
```

---

[4] Many spatial action patterns, including l and $l(\theta)$, are identified in this way [2,14].

The use of order-sorted signatures can greatly facilitate the existence of complement patterns that may not exist in an unsorted setting. For example, the unsorted term $y + 0 + 0$ for a signature with a constant 0, a unary s, and an AC symbol + is shown not to have complements in [8], but can be easily shown to have complements when the signature is refined to an order-sorted signature. We illustrate this greater ease of computing complements by using the state propositions $in.crit(0)$ and $enabled.wake(0)$, whose positive cases are defined by the following equations, where PS is a variable of sort ProcSet:

```
eq N ; M ; [0,crit(K)] PS |= in.crit(0) = true .
eq N ; M ; [0,idle] PS |= enabled.wake(0) = true .
```

In order to define the negative cases we need to find the complement patterns for [0,crit(K)] PS and [0,idle] PS. Using subsort relations, we can define sort ModeIdleWait for *idle* and *wait(n)*, ModeWaitCrit for *wait* and *crit(n)*, and ProcSet{NONat} for a set of processes with non-zero identifiers as follows:[5]

```
subsorts ModeIdle ModeWait < ModeIdleWait < Mode .
subsorts ModeWait ModeCrit < ModeWaitCrit < Mode .
subsorts NONat < Nat .
subsorts Proc{NONat} < ProcSet{NONat} Proc < ProcSet .
```

The negative cases for the above state propositions can then be defined by the following equations, where the variable DIW has sort ModeIdleWait, DWC has sort ModeWaitCrit, and NZPS has sort ProcSet{NONat}:

```
eq N ; M ; [0,DIW] NZPS |= in.crit(0) = false .
eq N ; M ; [0,DWC] NZPS |= enabled.wake(0) = false .
```

Narrowing-Based LKS. For a set $AP = \{p_1, \ldots, p_n\}$ of state propositions and a set $ACT = \{\delta_1, \ldots, \delta_m\}$ of spatial action patterns defined by the equations E, we can also associate to a topmost rewrite theory $\mathcal{R} = (\Sigma, E, R)$ a corresponding *narrowing-based logical LKS* $\bar{\mathcal{N}}(\mathcal{R})_{AP,ACT}$, where:

- each state of the LKS $\bar{\mathcal{N}}(\mathcal{R})_{AP,ACT}$ is a term in which the truth of every state proposition is decided into either *true* or *false*; and
- a transition of $\bar{\mathcal{N}}(\mathcal{R})_{AP,ACT}$ is specified by a topmost narrowing step $\leadsto_{\mathcal{R}}$, but further instantiated into possibly several transitions so that the truth b_i of each state proposition p_i, $1 \leq i \leq n$, and the truth b_{n+j} of each spatial action pattern δ_j, $1 \leq j \leq m$, are decided into either *true* or *false*.

For the bakery example, given the *logical* initial state N ; N ; [0,idle], we obtain within the logical LKS $\bar{\mathcal{N}}(\mathcal{R})_{AP,ACT}$ the infinite path in Fig. 2, which captures an infinite number of concrete paths in the concrete LKS $\bar{\mathcal{K}}(\mathcal{R})_{AP,ACT}$ starting from each ground instance of N ; N ; [0,idle]. The narrowing-based logical LKS $\bar{\mathcal{N}}(\mathcal{R})_{AP,ACT}$ of a topmost rewrite theory $\mathcal{R}$ is formally defined as follows:

---

[5] Generally, to define the negative cases for $k \in \mathbb{N}$, we can define $k + 2$ subsorts Nat0, ..., Nat$k$, NkNat of sort Nat, where NkNat denotes a number greater than k.

Definition 5. *Given a topmost rewrite theory* $\mathcal{R} = (\Sigma, E, R)$, *and* finite *sets* $AP = \{p_1, \ldots, p_n\} \subseteq \mathcal{T}_{\Sigma/E,\text{Prop}}$ *and* $ACT = \{\delta_1, \ldots, \delta_m\} \subseteq \mathcal{T}_{\Sigma/E,\text{Action}}$ *defined by its equations* E, *the narrowing-based logical LKS is*

$$\bar{\mathcal{N}}(\mathcal{R})_{AP,ACT} = (N(\mathcal{R})_{AP}, AP, \mathcal{L}_E, ACT, \longrightarrow_{\bar{N}(\mathcal{R})}),$$

where $\mathcal{L}_E([t]_E) = \{p \in AP \mid (t \models p) =_E true\}$, *and:*

- $[t]_E \in N(\mathcal{R})_{AP}$ *iff* $[t]_E \in \mathcal{T}_{\Sigma/E}(\mathcal{X})_{\text{State}} - \mathcal{X}$, *and for every state proposition* $p \in AP$, *either* $(t \models p) =_E true$ *or* $(t \models p) =_E false$.
- $[t]_E \xrightarrow{A}_{\bar{N}(\mathcal{R})} [t']_E$ *iff there exist a term* u, *a substitution* ζ, *and Boolean values* $b_1, \ldots, b_{n+m} \in \{true, false\}$ *such that*

$$t \rightsquigarrow_{l,\sigma,R} u \ \wedge \ t' = \zeta u, \ \wedge \ A = \{\delta \in ACT \mid (\zeta(l(\sigma_l)) \models \delta) =_E true\} \ \wedge$$
$$\zeta \in CSU_E\big(\bigwedge_{1 \le i \le n}(u \models p_i) = b_i \ \wedge \ \bigwedge_{1 \le j \le m}(l(\sigma_l) \models \delta_j) = b_{n+j}\big)$$

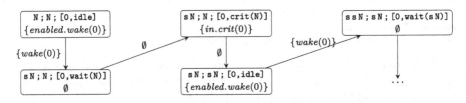

Fig. 2. A path from N ; N ; [0,idle] in the LKS $\bar{\mathcal{K}}(\mathcal{R})_{AP,ACT}$ for the bakery protocol.

A narrowing-based LKS $\bar{\mathcal{N}}(\mathcal{R})_{AP,ACT}$ captures any behavior of the related concrete LKS $\bar{\mathcal{K}}(\mathcal{R})_{AP,ACT}$, in terms of a *simulation relation*. In the following definition we extend the usual notion of a simulation for Kripke structures to one for LKSs, which also takes into account spatial action patterns.

Definition 6. *Given two LKS* $\bar{\mathcal{K}}_i = (S_i, AP, \mathcal{L}_i, ACT, \longrightarrow_{\bar{\mathcal{K}}_i})$, $i = 1, 2$, *a binary relation* $H \subseteq S_1 \times S_2$ *is a* simulation *from* $\bar{\mathcal{K}}_1$ *to* $\bar{\mathcal{K}}_2$ *iff:* (i) *if* $s_1 H s_2$, *then* $\mathcal{L}_1(s_1) = \mathcal{L}_2(s_2)$, *and if* $s_1 H s_2$ *and* $s_1 \xrightarrow{A}_{\bar{\mathcal{K}}} s'_1$, *there exists* $s'_2 \in S_2$ *such that* $s'_1 H s'_2$ *and* $s_2 \xrightarrow{A}_{\bar{\mathcal{K}}} s'_2$. *A simulation* H *is a* bisimulation *iff* H^{-1} *is also a simulation, and is* total *iff for any* $s_1 \in S_1$ *there exists* $s_2 \in S_2$ *such that* $s_1 H s_2$.

As expected, if an LKS $\bar{\mathcal{K}}_2$ simulates $\bar{\mathcal{K}}_1$, then each infinite path in $\bar{\mathcal{K}}_1$ has a corresponding path in $\bar{\mathcal{K}}_2$, as shown in the following lemma.

Lemma 2. *Given a simulation* H *from an LKS* $\bar{\mathcal{K}}_1$ *to* $\bar{\mathcal{K}}_2$, *if* $s_1 H s_2$, *then for each path* (π_1, α) *of* $\bar{\mathcal{K}}_1$ *beginning at* s_1, *there exists a corresponding path* (π_2, α) *beginning at* s_2 *such that* $\pi_1(i) H \pi_2(i)$ *for each* $i \in \mathbb{N}$.

Proof. We construct π_2 by induction. Let $\pi_2(0) = s_2$. Clearly, $\pi_1(0) H \pi_2(0)$. Next, suppose that $\pi_1(k) H \pi_2(k)$ for some $k \in \mathbb{N}$. Since $\pi_1(k) H \pi_2(k)$ and $\pi_1(k) \xrightarrow{\alpha(k)}_{\bar{\mathcal{K}}} \pi_1(k+1)$, there exists a state s'_2 such that $\pi_1(k+1) H s'_2$ and $\pi_2(k) \xrightarrow{\alpha(k)}_{\bar{\mathcal{K}}} s'_2$. Then, we choose $\pi_2(k+1) = s'_2$. □

Suppose that $s_0^1 H s_0^2$ for a simulation H from $\bar{\mathcal{K}}_1$ to $\bar{\mathcal{K}}_2$. If there exists a counterexample (π_1, α_1) in $\bar{\mathcal{K}}_1$ starting from s_0^1, then by the above lemma, there exists a corresponding counterexample (π_2, α_2) in $\bar{\mathcal{K}}_2$ starting from s_0^2 such that $\mathcal{L}_1(\pi_1(i)) = \mathcal{L}_2(\pi_2(i))$ and $\alpha_1(i) = \alpha_2(i)$ for each $i \in \mathbb{N}$. Therefore:

Corollary 1. *Given a simulation H from an LKS $\bar{\mathcal{K}}_1$ to $\bar{\mathcal{K}}_2$, if $s_0^1 H s_0^2$, then for any LTLR formula φ, $\bar{\mathcal{K}}_2, s_0^2 \models \varphi$ implies $\bar{\mathcal{K}}_1, s_0^1 \models \varphi$. In particular, if H is a bisimulation, then $\bar{\mathcal{K}}_2, s_0^2 \models \varphi$ iff $\bar{\mathcal{K}}_1, s_0^1 \models \varphi$.*

For a narrowing-based LKS $\bar{\mathcal{N}}(\mathcal{R})_{AP,ACT}$, each logical state is clearly related to a concrete state in $\bar{\mathcal{K}}(\mathcal{R})_{AP,ACT}$ in terms of the E-*subsumption* relation. The E-subsumption $t \preceq_E t'$ holds iff there exists a substitution σ with $t =_E \sigma t'$, meaning that t' is *more general* than t modulo E.

Lemma 3. *Given a topmost rewrite theory $\mathcal{R} = (\Sigma, E, R)$ and sets AP and ACT defined by E, $\preceq_E$ is a total simulation from $\bar{\mathcal{K}}(\mathcal{R})_{AP,ACT}$ to $\bar{\mathcal{N}}(\mathcal{R})_{AP,ACT}$.*

Proof. Suppose that $[t]_E \xrightarrow{A} _{\bar{\mathcal{K}}(\mathcal{R})} [t']_E$ and $t \preceq_E u$ for $u \in N(\mathcal{R})_{AP}$. Given $AP = \{p_1, \ldots, p_n\}$ and $ACT = \{\delta_1, \ldots, \delta_m\}$, fix $b_1, b_2, \ldots, b_{n+m} \in \{true, false\}$ such that $b_i =_E (t' \models p_i)$ for $1 \leq i \leq n$ and $b_{n+j} =_E (l(\theta) \models \delta_j)$ for $1 \leq j \leq m$. By definition, there is an one-step rewrite $l(\theta) : t \longrightarrow_\mathcal{R} t'$. By Lemma 1, there is a narrowing step $u \rightsquigarrow_{l,\sigma,\mathcal{R}} u'$ such that $t' =_E \eta u'$ and $\theta =_E (\eta \circ \sigma)|_{dom(\theta)}$. Thus, there exists $\zeta \in CSU_E(\bigwedge_{1 \leq i \leq n}(u' \models p_i) = b_i \wedge \bigwedge_{1 \leq j \leq m}(l(\sigma_l) \models \delta_j) = b_{n+j})$. By definition, $[u]_E \xrightarrow{A} _{\bar{\mathcal{N}}(\mathcal{R})} [\zeta u']_E$. Notice that $\bigwedge_{1 \leq i \leq n}\eta((u' \models p_i) =_E b_i)$ and $\bigwedge_{1 \leq j \leq m}\eta((l(\sigma_l) \models \delta_j) =_E b_{n+j})$. Therefore, $\eta \preceq_E \zeta$, and $t' =_E \eta u \preceq_E \zeta u'$. $\square$

By Corollary 1, this lemma implies that any LTLR formula φ satisfied in a narrowing-based LKS $\bar{\mathcal{N}}(\mathcal{R})_{AP,ACT}$ from a logical state t is also satisfied in the concrete LKS $\bar{\mathcal{K}}(\mathcal{R})_{AP,ACT}$ from each ground instance of t.

In general, $\preceq_E$ is *not* a bisimulation between $\bar{\mathcal{K}}(\mathcal{R})_{AP,ACT}$ and $\bar{\mathcal{N}}(\mathcal{R})_{AP,ACT}$. For the bakery example, although $0 \, ; \, 0 \, ; \, [\text{I},\text{wait}(0)] \preceq_E \text{N} \, ; \, \text{M} \, ; \, \text{PS}_1$ holds, there exists the transition $\text{N} \, ; \, \text{M} \, ; \, \text{PS}_1 \xrightarrow{\{wake(0)\}} _{\bar{\mathcal{N}}(\mathcal{R})} \text{s N} \, ; \, \text{M} \, ; \, \text{PS}_2 \, [0,\text{wait}(\text{N})]$, in $\bar{\mathcal{N}}(\mathcal{R})_{AP,ACT}$ with the substitution $\text{PS}_1 \backslash \text{PS}_2 \, [0,\text{idle}]$, but *no corresponding transition* exists from $0 \, ; \, 0 \, ; \, [\text{I},\text{wait}(0)]$ in $\bar{\mathcal{K}}(\mathcal{R})_{AP,ACT}$. However, any *finite* path in $\bar{\mathcal{N}}(\mathcal{R})_{AP,ACT}$ can be *instantiated* to a corresponding concrete path in $\bar{\mathcal{K}}(\mathcal{R})_{AP,ACT}$ (e.g., the above transition can be instantiated as the transition $0 \, ; \, 0 \, ; \, [0,\text{idle}] \xrightarrow{\{wake(0)\}} _{\bar{\mathcal{K}}(\mathcal{R})} \text{s} \, ; \, 0 \, ; \, [0,\text{wait}(0)]$ in $\bar{\mathcal{K}}(\mathcal{R})_{AP,ACT}$).

Lemma 4. *For a finite path $u_1 \xrightarrow{A_1} _{\bar{\mathcal{N}}(\mathcal{R})} \cdots \xrightarrow{A_{n-1}} _{\bar{\mathcal{N}}(\mathcal{R})} u_n$ of $\bar{\mathcal{N}}(\mathcal{R})_{AP,ACT}$, there is $t_1 \xrightarrow{A_1} _{\bar{\mathcal{K}}(\mathcal{R})} \cdots \xrightarrow{A_{n-1}} _{\bar{\mathcal{K}}(\mathcal{R})} t_n$ in $\bar{\mathcal{K}}(\mathcal{R})_{AP,ACT}$ with $t_i \preceq_E u_i$, $1 \leq i \leq n$.*

Proof. Since $u_1 \xrightarrow{A_1} _{\bar{\mathcal{N}}(\mathcal{R})} u_2$, by definition, there are substitutions σ_1 and ζ_1 such that $u_1 \rightsquigarrow_{l_1,\sigma_1,\mathcal{R}} u_2'$ by a topmost rule $l_1 : q_1 \to r_1 \in R$ and $u_2 = \zeta_1 u_2'$. Since $\sigma u_1 =_E \sigma q_1$ and $u_2 = \zeta_1 u_2' = (\zeta_1 \circ \sigma_1)r_1$, $(\zeta_1 \circ \sigma_1)u_1 \longrightarrow_\mathcal{R} u_2$. Similarly, $(\zeta_2 \circ \sigma_2)u_2 \longrightarrow_\mathcal{R} u_3$, etc. By composing them, $(\zeta_{n-1} \circ \sigma_{n-1} \circ \cdots \circ \zeta_2 \circ \sigma_2 \circ \zeta_1 \circ \sigma_1)u_1 \longrightarrow_\mathcal{R} \cdots \longrightarrow_\mathcal{R} (\zeta_{n-1} \circ \sigma_{n-1})u_{n-1} \longrightarrow_\mathcal{R} u_n$. Let ρ be a ground substitution instantiating every variable in the path. Then, $(\rho \circ \zeta_{n-1} \circ \sigma_{n-1} \circ \cdots \circ \zeta_2 \circ \sigma_1)u_1 \longrightarrow_\mathcal{R} \cdots \longrightarrow_\mathcal{R} (\rho \circ \zeta_{n-1} \circ \sigma_{n-1})u_{n-1} \longrightarrow_\mathcal{R} \rho u_n$ gives the desired path. $\square$

Recall that counterexamples of *safety properties* are characterized by finite sequences [4]. Therefore, the above lemma guarantees that $\bar{\mathcal{N}}(\mathcal{R})_{AP,ACT}$ does *not* generate spurious counterexamples for safety properties, since any finite counterexample in $\bar{\mathcal{N}}(\mathcal{R})_{AP,ACT}$ has a corresponding *real* counterexample in $\bar{\mathcal{K}}(\mathcal{R})_{AP,ACT}$. Together with Corollary 1 and Lemma 3, we have:

Theorem 1. *Given a topmost rewrite theory* $\mathcal{R} = (\Sigma, E, R)$, *and finite sets AP and ACT defined by* E, *for a safety LTLR formula* φ *and a pattern* $t \in N(\mathcal{R})_{AP}$:
$$\bar{\mathcal{N}}(\mathcal{R})_{AP,ACT}, [t]_E \models \varphi \iff (\forall \theta : \mathcal{X} \to \mathcal{T}_{\Sigma}) \ \bar{\mathcal{K}}(\mathcal{R})_{AP,ACT}, [\theta t]_E \models \varphi.$$

4 Abstract Narrowing-Based LTLR Model Checking

A narrowing-based LKS $\bar{\mathcal{N}}(\mathcal{R})_{AP,ACT}$ often has an infinite number of *logical* states (e.g., Fig. 2). For narrowing-based LTL model checking, the paper [1] has proposed two abstraction methods to reduce an infinite narrowing-based Kripke structure, namely, *folding abstractions* and *equational abstractions*. This section extends those abstraction techniques to narrowing-based LTLR model checking for trying to reduce an infinite *narrowing-based LKS* to a finite one.

Folding Abstractions. Given a *transition system* $\mathcal{A} = (A, \longrightarrow_{\mathcal{A}})$ with a set of states A and a transition relation $\longrightarrow_{\mathcal{A}} \subseteq A^2$, we can reduce it by collapsing each state a into a *previously seen* state b, while traversing $\mathcal{A}$ from a set of initial states $I \subseteq A$, whenever b is *more general* than a according to a folding relation $a \preccurlyeq b$ [6]. For a set of states $B \subseteq A$, let $Post_{\mathcal{A}}(B) = \{a \in A \mid \exists b \in B. \ b \longrightarrow_{\mathcal{A}} a\}$ (i.e., the *successors* of B) and $Post_{\mathcal{A}}^*(B) = \bigcup_{i \in \mathbb{N}}(Post_{\mathcal{A}})^i(B)$.

Definition 7. *Given* $\mathcal{A} = (A, \longrightarrow_{\mathcal{A}})$ *and a folding relation* $\preccurlyeq \subseteq A^2$, *the folding abstraction of* $\mathcal{A}$ *from* $I \subseteq A$ *is* $Reach_{\mathcal{A}}^{\preccurlyeq}(I) = (Post_{\mathcal{A}\preccurlyeq}^*(I), \longrightarrow_{Reach_{\mathcal{A}}^{\preccurlyeq}(I)})$, *where:*
$$Post_{\mathcal{A}\preccurlyeq}^*(I) = \bigcup_{i \in \mathbb{N}} Post_{\mathcal{A}\preccurlyeq}^i(I) \ \text{and} \ \longrightarrow_{Reach_{\mathcal{A}}^{\preccurlyeq}(I)} = \bigcup_{i \in \mathbb{N}} \longrightarrow_{\mathcal{A},i}^{\preccurlyeq} \ \text{such that:}$$

$$Post_{\mathcal{A}\preccurlyeq}^0(I) = I, \qquad \longrightarrow_{\mathcal{A},0}^{\preccurlyeq} = \emptyset,$$
$$Post_{\mathcal{A}\preccurlyeq}^{n+1}(I) = \{a \in Post_{\mathcal{A}}(Post_{\mathcal{A}\preccurlyeq}^n(I)) \mid \forall l \le n \ \forall b \in Post_{\mathcal{A}\preccurlyeq}^l(I). \ a \not\preccurlyeq b\},$$
$$\longrightarrow_{\mathcal{A},n+1}^{\preccurlyeq} = \{(a,a') \in Post_{\mathcal{A}\preccurlyeq}^n(I) \times \bigcup_{0 \le i \le n+1} Post_{\mathcal{A}\preccurlyeq}^i(I) \mid \exists b \in Post_{\mathcal{A}}(a). \ b \preccurlyeq a'\}.$$

For the bakery example, using the E-subsumption $\preccurlyeq_E$ as a folding relation, we have the *finite* folding abstraction $Reach_{\bar{\mathcal{N}}(\mathcal{R})_{AP,ACT}}^{\preccurlyeq_E}(\{\text{N ; N ; [0,idle][s,idle]}\})$ of $\bar{\mathcal{N}}(\mathcal{R})_{AP,ACT}$ from the initial state N ; N ; [0,idle][s,idle] in Fig. 3.

If a folding relation $\preccurlyeq$ is a total simulation from $\mathcal{A}$ to $\mathcal{A}$, then $Reach_{\mathcal{A}}^{\preccurlyeq}(I)$ simulates the *reachable* subsystem $Reach_{\mathcal{A}}(I) = (Post_{\mathcal{A}}^*(I), \longrightarrow_{\mathcal{A}} \cap Post_{\mathcal{A}}^*(I)^2)$ that only contains reachable states from I (i.e., $\preccurlyeq$ is a total simulation from $Reach_{\mathcal{A}}(I)$ to $Reach_{\mathcal{A}}^{\preccurlyeq}(I)$) [1]. Indeed, $\preccurlyeq_E$ for a topmost rewrite theory $\mathcal{R}$ is a total simulation from $\bar{\mathcal{N}}(\mathcal{R})_{AP,ACT}$ to $\bar{\mathcal{N}}(\mathcal{R})_{AP,ACT}$ (which can be proved in a similar way to Lemma 3). Therefore, $\preccurlyeq_E$ defines a total simulation from $Reach_{\bar{\mathcal{N}}(\mathcal{R})_{AP,ACT}}(I)$ to $Reach_{\bar{\mathcal{N}}(\mathcal{R})_{AP,ACT}}^{\preccurlyeq_E}(I)$. Consequently, by Corollary 1:

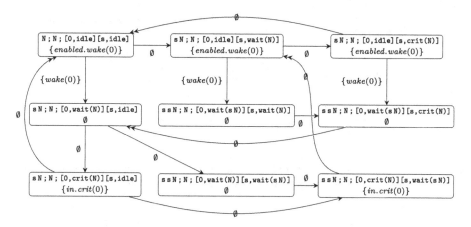

Fig. 3. A folding abstraction for the bakery protocol using the folding relation $\preccurlyeq_E$, where a double-headed arrow denotes a "folded" transition.

Theorem 2. *For an LTLR formula φ and a pattern $t \in N(\mathcal{R})_{AP}$, we have that $Reach^{\preccurlyeq_E}_{\bar{\mathcal{N}}(\mathcal{R})_{AP,ACT}}(\{[t]_E\})$, $[t]_E \models \varphi$ implies $\bar{\mathcal{N}}(\mathcal{R})_{AP,ACT}, [t]_E \models \varphi$.*

For the bakery example, the liveness property $\Diamond in.crit(0)$ under the fairness assumption $\Diamond\Box enabled.wake(0) \rightarrow \Box\Diamond wake(0)$ holds in the folding abstraction $Reach^{\preccurlyeq_E}_{\bar{\mathcal{N}}(\mathcal{R})_{AP,ACT}}(\{\texttt{N;N;[0,idle][s,idle]}\})$ of Fig. 3, because any infinite paths continuously staying in the first row violate the fairness assumption. Hence, this property is also satisfied for any related concrete system.

Equational Abstractions. In general, a folding abstraction of a narrowing-based LKS is *not* finite. For the bakery example, there exists an infinite path within the folding abstraction from N;N;[0,idle] IS in Fig. 4, which keeps incrementing the number of processes with instantiations. To further reduce an infinite logical state space, we can apply equational abstractions to eventually obtain a finite abstract narrowing-based LKS for LTLR model checking.

Given a rewrite theory $\mathcal{R} = (\Sigma, E, R)$, by adding a set of equations G such that $true \neq_{E \cup G} false$, we define an *equational abstraction* $\mathcal{R}/G = (\Sigma, E \cup G, R)$ [15]. It specifies the quotient abstraction $\bar{\mathcal{N}}(\mathcal{R}/G)_{AP,ACT}$ by the equivalence relation $\equiv_G$ on states, namely, $[t]_E \equiv_G [t']_E$ iff $t =_{E \cup G} t'$. Provided that a set of state propositions AP and a set of spatial action patterns ACT are defined by E, the condition $true \neq_{E \cup G} false$ ensures that any two states with $t =_{E \cup G} t'$ satisfy the same set of state propositions. Similarly, any two one-step proof terms with $l(\sigma_l) =_{E \cup G} l'(\sigma_{l'})$ satisfy the same set of spatial action patterns.

Similar to the cases of LTL model checking [1,15], an equational abstraction $\bar{\mathcal{N}}(\mathcal{R}/G)_{AP,ACT}$ simulates the narrowing-based LKS $\bar{\mathcal{N}}(\mathcal{R})_{AP,ACT}$.

Lemma 5. *Given a topmost rewrite theory $\mathcal{R} = (\Sigma, E, R)$, finite sets AP and ACT defined by E, and a set G of equations, if $true \neq_{E \cup G} false$, then there exists a total simulation from $\bar{\mathcal{N}}(\mathcal{R})_{AP,ACT}$ to $\bar{\mathcal{N}}(\mathcal{R}/G)_{AP,ACT}$.*

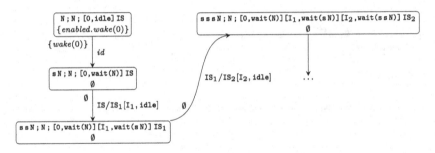

Fig. 4. An infinite path in the folding abstraction for the bakery protocol with an unbounded number of processes, where IS stands for a set of *idle* processes.

Proof. Let $H_G = \{([t]_E, [t]_{E \cup G}) \mid t \in N(\mathcal{R})_{AP}\}$. Suppose that $[t]_E \xrightarrow{A}_{\bar{\mathcal{N}}(\mathcal{R})} [t']_E$ and $t =_{E \cup G} u$. By definition, there are σ and ζ such that $t \rightsquigarrow_{l,\sigma,\mathcal{R}} t''$ by a rule $l : q \longrightarrow r \in R$ and $t' = \zeta t''$, where $\sigma \in CSU_E(t = q)$, $t'' = \sigma r$, and $\zeta \in CSU_E(\bigwedge_{1 \le i \le n}(t'' \models p_i) = b_i \wedge \bigwedge_{1 \le j \le m}(l(\sigma_l) \models \delta_j) = b_{n+j})$ for some $b_1, \ldots, b_{n+m} \in \{true, false\}$, given $AP = \{p_1, \ldots, p_n\}$ and $ACT = \{\delta_1, \ldots, \delta_m\}$. Since $\sigma \in CSU_E(t = q)$, $\exists \sigma' \in CSU_{E \cup G}(u = q)$ such that $\sigma =_{E \cup G} \sigma'$. Then, $u \rightsquigarrow_{l,\sigma',\mathcal{R}/G} u'$ using the same rule $l : q \longrightarrow r$, where $u' = \sigma' r =_{E \cup G} \sigma r = t''$. Notice that $(t'' \models p_i) =_{E \cup G} (u' \models p_i)$ and $(l(\sigma_l) \models \delta_j) =_{E \cup G} (l(\sigma'_l) \models \delta_j)$. Thus, $\exists \zeta' \in CSU_{E \cup G}(\bigwedge_{1 \le i \le n}(u' \models p_i) = b_i \wedge \bigwedge_{1 \le j \le m}(l(\sigma'_l) \models \delta_j) = b_{n+j})$ with $\zeta =_{E \cup G} \zeta'$. Thus, $[u]_{E \cup G} \xrightarrow{A}_{\bar{\mathcal{N}}(\mathcal{R}/G)} [\zeta'u']_{E \cup G}$, where $\zeta'u' =_{E \cup G} \zeta t'' = t'$. Since $true \neq_{E \cup G} false$, $[t']_E$ and $[\zeta'u']_{E \cup G}$ satisfy the same state propositions. Therefore, H_G is a total simulation from $\bar{\mathcal{N}}(\mathcal{R})_{AP,ACT}$ to $\bar{\mathcal{N}}(\mathcal{R}/G)_{AP,ACT}$. $\square$

For the bakery example, by adding the following equations that collapses extra waiting processes with non-zero identifiers, where ICPS denotes a set of *idle* or *crit* processes, and WP3 denotes *zero or at most three wait* processes:

```
eq [NZ,D] = [D] .                       --remove non-zero identifiers
eq s s s N M ; M ; ICPS WP3 [wait(s N M)] [wait(s s N M)]
 =   s s N M ; M ; ICPS WP3 [wait(s N M)] .
```

we have the folded abstract narrowing-based LKS in Fig. 5, provided with the extra spatial action pattern *wake* that holds if the *wake* rule is applied.

We can easily see that there is a counterexample of the property $\Diamond in.crit(0)$ under $\Diamond \Box enabled.wake(0) \rightarrow \Box \Diamond wake(0)$ in which the *wake* rule is continuously applied forever, which is impossible if there is a finite number of processes. Assuming the extra fairness assumption $\Box \Diamond \neg wake$, the property $\Diamond in.crit(0)$ is now satisfied since any infinite paths staying in the first column forever violate $\Diamond \Box enabled.wake(0) \rightarrow \Box \Diamond wake(0)$, and any paths staying in a self loop forever violate $\Box \Diamond \neg wake$. Consequently, under the fairness assumptions, $\Diamond in.crit(0)$ is satisfied for an unbounded number of processes.

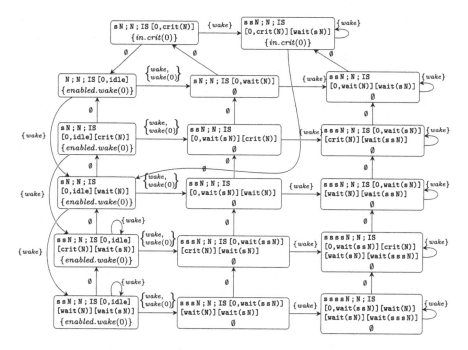

Fig. 5. An folded equational abstraction for the bakery protocol.

5   Related Work and Conclusions

A number of infinite-state model checking methods have been developed based on symbolic and abstraction techniques; see [1,6] for an overview and comparison with narrowing-based model checking. To the best of our knowledge, our work proposes the first *symbolic* model checking method to verify LTLR properties of infinite-state systems. For finite-state systems the paper [2] presents various model checking algorithms for LTLR properties. LTLR is a sublogic of TLR^* that generalizes the state-based logic CTL^* (see [14] for related work). On the topic of *complement patterns*, the most closely related work is [8,9,12]. We plan to use their ideas, as well as ongoing work by Skeirik and Meseguer on the concept of *B-linear terms* in order-sorted signatures, which are pattern terms whose syntactic structure guarantees the existence of complements modulo B, to automate the full equational definition of satisfaction of spatial action patterns.

In conclusion, this work should be understood as a contribution that increases the expressive power of infinite-state model checking methods. Specifically, the expressive power of narrowing-based infinite-state logical model checking has been extended form LTL to LTLR, allowing temporal properties that can use both state propositions and spatial action patterns. This extension is nontrivial because of the need for building a symbolic transition system where states are AP-instantiated and transitions are ACT-instantiated.

All the necessary theoretical foundations are now in place for embarking into a future implementation of a narrowing-based LTLR model checker in Maude in the spirit of the similar LTL tool described in [1]. As done in [1], for the LTLR tool we will be able to rely on the extensive body of work on efficient LTLR model checking algorithms described in [2]. Beyond these goals, the integration of constraints and SMT solving within the planned narrowing-based LTLR model checker, as well as the study of more flexible "stuttering" AP/ACT-simulations, are also exciting possibilities.

Acknowledgments. This work has been supported in part by NSF Grant CNS 13-19109 and AFOSR Grant FA8750-11-2-0084.

References

1. Bae, K., Escobar, S., Meseguer, J.: Abstract logical model checking of infinite-state systems using narrowing. In: RTA, LIPIcs, vol. 21, pp. 81–96 (2013)
2. Bae, K., Meseguer, J.: Model checking linear temporal logic of rewriting formulas under localized fairness. Sci. Comput. Program (2014). http://dx.doi.org/10.1016/j.scico.2014.02.006 (To appear)
3. Chaki, S., Clarke, E.M., Ouaknine, J., Sharygina, N., Sinha, N.: State/event-based software model checking. In: Boiten, E.A., Derrick, J., Smith, G.P. (eds.) IFM 2004. LNCS, vol. 2999, pp. 128–147. Springer, Heidelberg (2004)
4. Clarke, E.M., Grumberg, O., Peled, D.A.: Model Checking. The MIT Press (2001)
5. Comon-Lundh, H., Delaune, S.: The finite variant property: how to get rid of some algebraic properties. In: Giesl, J. (ed.) RTA 2005. LNCS, vol. 3467, pp. 294–307. Springer, Heidelberg (2005)
6. Escobar, S., Meseguer, J.: Symbolic model checking of infinite-state systems using narrowing. In: Baader, F. (ed.) RTA 2007. LNCS, vol. 4533, pp. 153–168. Springer, Heidelberg (2007)
7. Escobar, S., Sasse, R., Meseguer, J.: Folding variant narrowing and optimal variant termination. J. Algebraic Logic Program. **81**, 898–928 (2012)
8. Fernández, M.: AC complement problems: satisfiability and negation elimination. J. Symb. Comput. **22**(1), 49–82 (1996)
9. Fernández, M.: Negation elimination in empty or permutative theories. J. Symb. Comput. **26**(1), 97–133 (1998)
10. Hullot, J.M.: Canonical forms and unification. In: Bibel, W., Kowalski, R. (eds.) 5th Conference on Automated Deduction Les Arcs. LNCS. Springer, Heidelberg (1980)
11. Jouannaud, J.P., Kirchner, C., Kirchner, H.: Incremental construction of unification algorithms in equational theories. In: Diaz, J. (ed.) ICALP. LNCS, pp. 361–373. Springer, Heidelberg (1983)
12. Lassez, J.L., Marriott, K.: Explicit representation of terms defined by counter examples. J. Autom. Reasoning **3**(3), 301–317 (1987)
13. Meseguer, J.: Conditional rewriting logic as a unified model of concurrency. Theor. Comput. Sci. **96**(1), 73–155 (1992)
14. Meseguer, J.: The temporal logic of rewriting: a gentle introduction. In: Degano, P., De Nicola, R., Meseguer, J. (eds.) Concurrency, Graphs and Models. LNCS, vol. 5065, pp. 354–382. Springer, Heidelberg (2008)

15. Meseguer, J., Palomino, M., Martí-Oliet, N.: Equational abstractions. Theor. Comput. Sci. **403**(2–3), 239–264 (2008)
16. Meseguer, J., Thati, P.: Symbolic reachability analysis using narrowing and its application to verification of cryptographic protocols. Higher-Order Symbolic Comput. **20**(1–2), 123–160 (2007)

Modelling and Verifying Contract-Oriented Systems in Maude

Massimo Bartoletti[1], Maurizio Murgia[1], Alceste Scalas[1]([⊠]),
and Roberto Zunino[2]

[1] Università Degli Studi di Cagliari, Cagliari, Italy
{bart,alceste.scalas}@unica.it, murgia88@gmail.com
[2] Università Degli Studi di Trento, Trento, Italy
roberto.zunino@unitn.it

Abstract. We address the problem of modelling and verifying contract-oriented systems, wherein distributed agents may advertise and stipulate contracts, but — differently from most other approaches to distributed agents — are not assumed to always behave "honestly". We describe an executable specification in Maude of the semantics of CO_2, a calculus for contract-oriented systems [6]. The *honesty* property [5] characterises those agents which always respect their contracts, in *all* possible execution contexts. Since there is an infinite number of such contexts, honesty cannot be directly verified by model-checking the state space of an agent (indeed, honesty is an undecidable property in general [5]). The main contribution of this paper is a sound verification technique for honesty. To do that, we safely over-approximate the honesty property by abstracting from the actual contexts a process may be engaged with. Then, we develop a model-checking technique for this abstraction, we describe an implementation in Maude, and we discuss some experiments with it.

1 Introduction

Contract-oriented computing is a software design paradigm where the interaction between clients and services is disciplined through contracts [4,6]. Contract-oriented services start their life-cycle by advertising contracts which specify their required and offered behaviour. When compliant contracts are found, a session is created among the respective services, which may then start interacting to fulfil their contracts. Differently from other design paradigms (e.g. those based on the session types discipline [10]), services are not assumed to be *honest*, in that they might not respect the promises made [5]. This may happen either unintentionally (because of errors in the service specification), or because of malicious behaviour.

Dishonest behaviour is assumed to be automatically detected and sanctioned by the service infrastructure. This gives rise to a new kind of attacks, that exploit possible discrepancies between the promised and the actual behaviour. If a service does not behave as promised, an attacker can induce it to a situation where the service is sanctioned, while the attacker is reckoned honest. A crucial

© Springer International Publishing Switzerland 2014
S. Escobar (Ed.): WRLA 2014, LNCS 8663, pp. 130–146, 2014.
DOI: 10.1007/978-3-319-12904-4_7

problem is then how to avoid that a service results definitively culpable of a contract violation, despite of the honest intentions of its developer.

In this paper we present an executable specification in Maude [9] of CO_2, a calculus for contract-oriented computing [4]. Furthermore, we devise and implement a sound verification technique for honesty. We start in Sect. 2 by introducing a new model for contracts. Borrowing from other approaches to behavioural contracts [5,8], ours are bilateral contracts featuring internal/external choices, and recursion. We define and implement in Maude two crucial primives on contracts, i.e. *compliance* and *culpability testing*, and we study some relevant properties.

In Sect. 3 we present CO_2 (instantiated with the contracts above), and an executable specification of its semantics in Maude. In Sect. 4 we formalise a weak notion of honesty, i.e. when a process P is honest *in a given context*, and we implement and experiment with it through the Maude model checker.

The main technical results follow in Sect. 5, where we deal with the problem of checking honesty in *all* possible contexts. To do that, we start by defining an abstract semantics of CO_2, which preserves the transitions of a participant $A[P]$, while abstracting those of the context wherein $A[P]$ is run. Building upon the abstract semantics, we then devise an abstract notion of honesty (α-*honesty*, Definition 11), which neglects the execution context. Theorem 5 states that α-honesty correctly approximates honesty, and that — under certain hypotheses — it is also complete. We then propose a verification technique for α-honesty, and we provide an implementation in Maude. Some experiments have then been carried out; quite notably, our tool has allowed us to determine the dishonesty of a supposedly-honest CO_2 process appeared in [5] (see Example 5).

Because of space limits, we make available online the proofs of all our statements, as well as the Maude implementation, and the experiments made [2].

2   Modelling Contracts

We model contracts as processes in a simple algebra, with internal/external choice and recursion. Compliance between contracts ensures progress, until a successful state is reached. We prove that our model enjoys some relevant properties. First, in each non-final state of a contract there is exactly one participant who is *culpable*, i.e., expected to make the next move (Theorem 1). Furthermore, a participant always recovers from culpability in at most two steps (Theorem 2).

Syntax. We assume a finite set of *participant names* (ranged over by A, B, . . .) and a denumerable set of *atoms* (ranged over by a, b, . . .). We postulate an involution $co(a)$, also written as $\bar{a}$, extended to sets of atoms in the natural way. Definition 1 introduces the syntax of contracts. We distinguish between (*unilateral*) contracts c, which model the promised behaviour of a single participant, and *bilateral* contracts γ, which combine the contracts advertised by two participants.

Definition 1. Unilateral contracts *are defined by the following grammar:*

$$c, d \;::=\; \bigoplus_{i \in I} a_i \,;\, c_i \;\;\Big|\;\; \sum_{i \in I} a_i \,.\, c_i \;\;\Big|\;\; ready\; a.c \;\;\Big|\;\; rec\; X.\, c \;\;\Big|\;\; X$$

where (i) the index set $\mathcal{I}$ is finite; (ii) the "ready" prefix may appear at the top-level, only; (iii) recursion is guarded.

Bilateral contracts γ *are terms of the form* A *says* c | B *says* d, *where* A$\neq$B *and at most one occurrence of "ready" is present. The order of unilateral contracts in* γ *is immaterial, i.e.* A *says* c | B *says* d $\equiv$ B *says* d | A *says* c.

An internal sum $\bigoplus_{i\in\mathcal{I}} \mathsf{a}_i ; c_i$ allows to choose one of the branches $\mathsf{a}_i ; c_i$, to perform the action a_i, and then to behave according to c_i. Dually, an external sum $\sum_{i\in\mathcal{I}} \mathsf{a}_i . c_i$ allows to wait for the other participant to choose one of the branches $\mathsf{a}_i . c_i$, then to perform the corresponding a_i and behave according to c_i. Separators ; and . allow for distinguishing singleton internal sums $\mathsf{a} ; c$ from singleton external sums $\mathsf{a} . c$. Empty internal/external sums are denoted with 0. We will only consider contracts without free occurrences of recursion variables X.

Example 1. An online store A has the following contract: buyers can iteratively add items to the shopping cart (`addToCart`); when at least one item has been added, the client can either `cancel` the order or `pay`; then, the store can accept (`ok`) or decline (`no`) the payment. Such a contract may be expressed as c_A below:

$$c_{\mathrm{pay}} = \mathsf{pay} . (\overline{\mathsf{ok}} ; 0 \oplus \overline{\mathsf{no}} ; 0)$$
$$c_A = \mathsf{addToCart} . (\mathrm{rec}\ Z. \mathsf{addToCart} . Z + c_{\mathrm{pay}} + \mathsf{cancel} . 0)$$

Instead, a buyer contract could be expressed as:

$$c_B = \mathrm{rec}\ Z. (\overline{\mathsf{addToCart}} ; Z \oplus \overline{\mathsf{pay}} ; (\mathsf{ok} . 0 + \mathsf{no} . 0))$$

The Maude specification of the syntax of contracts is defined as follows:

```
sorts Atom UniContract Participant AdvContract BiContract
      IGuarded EGuarded IChoice EChoice Var Id RdyContract.
subsort Id < IGuarded < IChoice < UniContract < RdyContract.
subsort Id < EGuarded < EChoice < UniContract < RdyContract.
subsort Var < UniContract.
```

The sorts `IGuarded` and `EGuarded` represent singleton internal/external sums, respectively, while `IChoice` and `EChoice` are for arbitrary internal/external sums. `Id` represents empty sums, and it is a subsort of internal and external sums (either singleton or not). `RdyContract` if for contracts which may have a top-level *ready*, while `AdvContract` is a unilateral contract advertised by some participant.

```
op -_ : Atom -> Atom [ctor].
eq - - a:Atom = a:Atom.
op 0 : -> Id [ctor].
op _._ : Atom UniContract -> EGuarded [frozen ctor].
op _;_ : Atom UniContract -> IGuarded [frozen ctor].
op _+_ : EChoice EChoice -> EChoice [frozen comm assoc id: 0 ctor].
op _(+)_ : IChoice IChoice -> IChoice [frozen comm assoc id: 0 ctor].
op ready _._ : Atom UniContract -> RdyContract [frozen ctor].
op rec _._ : Var IChoice -> UniContract [frozen ctor].
op rec _._ : Var EChoice -> UniContract [frozen ctor].
op _ says _ : Participant RdyContract -> AdvContract [ctor].
op _ | _ : AdvContract AdvContract -> BiContract [comm ctor].
```

The operator − models the involution on atoms, with `eq - - a:Atom = a:Atom`. The other operators are rather standard, and they guarantee that each `UniContract` respects the syntactic constraints imposed by Definition 1.

Semantics. The evolution of bilateral contracts is modelled by $\xrightarrow{\mu}$, the smallest relation closed under the rules in Fig. 1 and under $\equiv$. The congruence $\equiv$ is the least relation including α-conversion of recursion variables, and satisfying rec $X. c \equiv c\{^{\text{rec } X. c}/X\}$ and $\bigoplus_{i \in \emptyset} a_i ; c_i \equiv \sum_{i \in \emptyset} a_i . c_i$. The label $\mu = $ A *says* a models A performing action a. Hereafter, we shall consider contracts up-to $\equiv$.

$$\text{A } says \text{ (a} ; c \oplus c') \mid \text{B } says \text{ (}\bar{a} . d + d') \xrightarrow{\text{A } says \text{ a}} \text{A } says \text{ } c \mid \text{B } says \text{ ready } \bar{a}.d \quad [\text{INTEXT}]$$

$$\text{A } says \text{ ready a. } c \mid \text{B } says \text{ } d \xrightarrow{\text{A } says \text{ a}} \text{A } says \text{ } c \mid \text{B } says \text{ } d \qquad [\text{RDY}]$$

Fig. 1. Semantics of contracts (symmetric rules for B actions omitted)

In rule [INTEXT], participant A selects the branch a in an internal sum, and B is then forced to commit to the corresponding branch $\bar{a}$ in his external sum. This is done by marking that branch with *ready* $\bar{a}$, while discarding all the other branches; B will then perform his action in the subsequent step, by rule [RDY].

In Maude, the semantics of contracts is an almost literal translation of that in Fig. 1 (except that labels are moved to configurations). The one-step transition relation is defined as follows:

```
crl [IntExt]: A says a ; c (+) c' | B says b . d + d'
=> {A says a} A says c | B says ready b . d          if a = - b.

rl [Rdy]: A says ready a.c | B says d => {A says a} A says c | B says d.
```

Compliance. Two contracts are *compliant* if, whenever a participant A wants to choose a branch in an internal sum, then participant B always offers A the opportunity to do it. To formalise compliance, we first define a partial function rdy from bilateral contracts to sets of atoms. Intuitively, if the unilateral contracts in γ do not agree on the first step, then rdy(γ) is undefined (i.e. equal to $\perp$). Otherwise, rdy(γ) contains the atoms which could be fired in the first step.

Definition 2 (Compliance). *Let the partial function* rdy *be defined as:*

$$\text{rdy}\left(\text{A } says \bigoplus_{i \in \mathcal{I}} a_i ; c_i \mid \text{B } says \sum_{j \in \mathcal{J}} b_j . c_j\right) = \{a_i\}_{i \in \mathcal{I}} \quad \begin{array}{l} if \quad \{a_i\}_{i \in \mathcal{I}} \subseteq \{\bar{b}_j\}_{j \in \mathcal{J}} \\ and \ (\mathcal{I} = \emptyset \implies \mathcal{J} = \emptyset) \end{array}$$

$$\text{rdy}(\text{A } says \text{ ready a.c} \mid \text{B } says \text{ } d) = \{a\}$$

Then, the compliance relation $\bowtie$ *between unilateral contracts is the largest relation such that, whenever* $c \bowtie d$:

(1) rdy(A *says* c | B *says* d) $\neq \perp$

(2) A *says* c | B *says* $d \xrightarrow{\mu} $ A *says* c' | B *says* $d' \implies c' \bowtie d'$

Example 2. Let $\gamma = $ A *says* c | B *says* d, where $c = $ a ; $c_1 \oplus$ b ; c_2 and $d = $ $\bar{a} . d_1 + \bar{c} . d_2$. If the participant A internally chooses to perform a, then γ will take a transition to A *says* c_1 | B *says* *ready* $\bar{a}.d_1$. Suppose instead that A chooses to perform b, which is not offered by B in his external choice. In this case, $\gamma \xcancel{\xrightarrow{\text{A } says \text{ b}}}$. We have that rdy($\gamma$) = $\perp$, which does not respect item (1) of Definition 2. Therefore, c and d are *not* compliant.

We say that a contract is *proper* if the prefixes of each summation are pairwise distinct. The next lemma states that each proper contract has a compliant one.

Lemma 1. *For all proper contracts c, there exists d such that $c \bowtie d$.*

Definition 2 cannot be directly exploited as an algorithm for checking compliance. Lemma 2 gives an alternative, model-checkable characterisation of $\bowtie$.

Lemma 2. *For all bilateral contracts $\gamma = $ A *says* c | B *says* d:*

$$c \bowtie d \iff (\forall \gamma'. \ \gamma \rightarrow^* \gamma' \implies rdy(\gamma') \neq \perp)$$

In Maude, the compliance relation is defined as suggested by Lemma 2. The predicate isBottom is true for a contract γ whenever rdy(γ) = $\perp$. The operator <> used below allows for the transitive closure of the transition relation. The relation c |X| d is implemented by verifying that the contract A *says* c | B *says* d satisfies the LTL formula $\Box \neg$ isBottom. This is done through the Maude model checker.

```
eq <{1} g> |= isBottom = is rdy(g) eq bottom.
op _|X|_ : UniContract UniContract -> Bool.
eq c |X| d = modelCheck(<A says c | B says d>, [] ~isBottom) == true.
```

Example 3. Recall the store contract c_A in Example 1. Its Maude version is:

```
op Z : -> Var.
ops addToCart pay ok no cancel : -> Atom.
ops CA CPay CB : -> UniContract.
eq CPay = pay . (- ok ; 0 (+) - no ; 0).
eq CA = addToCart . (rec Z . addToCart . Z + CPay + cancel . 0).
```

Instead, the Maude implementation of the buyer contract c_B in Example 1 is:

```
eq CB = rec Z . ( - addToCart ; Z (+) - pay ; (ok . 0 + no . 0)).
```

We can verify with Maude that CA and CB are *not* compliant:

```
red CA |X| CB.
result Bool: false
```

The problem is that CB may choose to pay even when the cart is empty. We can easily fix the buyer contract as follows, and then obtain compliance:

```
red CA |X| (- addToCart ; CB).
result Bool: true
```

Culpability. We now tackle the problem of determining who is expected to make the next step for the fulfilment of a bilateral contract. We call a participant A *culpable* in γ if she is expected to perform some actions so to make γ progress.

Definition 3. *A participant* A *is culpable in* γ *(*$A \overset{\frown}{\cdot} \gamma$ *in symbols) iff* $\gamma \xrightarrow{A \; says \; a}$, *for some* a. *When* A *is* not *culpable in* γ *we write* $A \overset{\smile}{\cdot} \gamma$.

Theorem 1 below establishes that, when starting with compliant contracts, exactly one participant is culpable in a bilateral contract. The only exception is A *says* 0 | B *says* 0, which represents a successfully terminated interaction, where nobody is culpable.

Theorem 1. *Let* $\gamma =$ A *says* c | B *says* d, *with* $c \bowtie d$. *If* $\gamma \twoheadrightarrow^* \gamma'$, *then either* $\gamma' =$ A *says* 0 | B *says* 0, *or there exists a unique culpable in* γ'.

The following theorem states that a participant is always able to recover from culpability by performing some of her duties. This requires at most two steps.

Theorem 2 (Contractual exculpation). *Let* $\gamma =$ A *says* c | B *says* d. *For all* γ' *such that* $\gamma \twoheadrightarrow^* \gamma'$, *we have that:*

(1) $\gamma' \not\twoheadrightarrow \implies A \overset{\smile}{\cdot} \gamma'$ *and* $B \overset{\smile}{\cdot} \gamma'$

(2) $A \overset{\frown}{\cdot} \gamma' \implies \forall \gamma''.\gamma' \twoheadrightarrow \gamma'' \implies \begin{cases} A \overset{\smile}{\cdot} \gamma'', \text{ or} \\ \forall \gamma'''.\gamma'' \twoheadrightarrow \gamma''' \implies A \overset{\smile}{\cdot} \gamma''' \end{cases}$

Item (1) of Theorem 2 says that, in a stuck contract, no participant is culpable. Item (2) says that if A is culpable, then she can always exculpate herself in *at most* two steps, i.e.: one step if A has an internal choice, or a *ready* followed by an external choice; two steps if A has a *ready* followed by an internal choice.

We specify culpability in Maude as follows. The formula `{1} g |= --A-->>` is true whenever g has been reached by some transitions of A. The participant A is culpable in g, written `A :C g`, if g satisfies the LTL formula `O --A-->>` (where `O` is the "next" operator of LTL). This is verified through the Maude model checker.

```
op --_-->> : Participant -> Prop .
eq {A says a} g |= -- A -->> = true .
eq {1} g |= -- A -->> = false [owise] .
op _ :C _ : Participant BiContract -> Bool .
eq A :C g = modelCheck(g, O -- A ->>) == true .
```

3   Modelling Contracting Processes

We model agents and systems through the process calculus CO_2 [3], which we instantiate with the contracts introduced in Sect. 2. The primitives of CO_2 allow agents to advertise contracts, to open sessions between agents with compliant contracts, to execute them by performing some actions, and to query contracts.

Syntax. Let $\mathcal{V}$ and $\mathcal{N}$ be disjoint sets of *session variables* (ranged over by $x, y, \ldots$) and *session names* (ranged over by $s, t, \ldots$). Let $u, v, \ldots$ range over $\mathcal{V} \cup \mathcal{N}$, and $\boldsymbol{u}, \boldsymbol{v}$ range over $2^{\mathcal{V} \cup \mathcal{N}}$.

Definition 4. *The syntax of CO_2 is given as follows:*

$$
\begin{array}{llllllll}
\textit{Systems} & S & ::= & \mathbf{0} & A[P] & s[\gamma] & S \mid S & (u)S \quad \{\downarrow_u c\}_A \\
\textit{Processes} & P & ::= & \sum_i \pi_i.P_i & P \mid P & (u)P & X(\boldsymbol{u}) & \\
\textit{Prefixes} & \pi & ::= & \tau & \mathsf{tell} \downarrow_u c & \mathsf{do}_u\, a & \mathsf{ask}_u \phi & \\
\end{array}
$$

Systems are the parallel composition of *participants* $A[P]$, *delimited systems* $(u)S$, *sessions* $s[\gamma]$ and *latent contracts* $\{\downarrow_u c\}_A$. A latent contract $\{\downarrow_x c\}_A$ represents a contract c (advertised by A) which has not been stipulated yet; upon stipulation, the variable x will be instantiated to a fresh session name. We assume that, in a system of the form $(\boldsymbol{u})(A[P] \mid B[Q]) \mid \cdots)$, $A \neq B$. We denote with K a special participant name (playing the role of contract broker) such that, in each system $(\boldsymbol{u})(A[P] \mid \cdots)$, $A \neq K$. We allow for prefix-guarded finite sums of processes, and write $\pi_1.P_1 + \pi_2.P_2$ for $\sum_{i \in \{1,2\}} \pi_i.P_i$, and $\mathbf{0}$ for $\sum_{\emptyset} P$. Recursion is allowed only for processes; we stipulate that each process identifier X has a unique defining equation $X(x_1, \ldots, x_j) \stackrel{\text{def}}{=} P$ such that $\mathrm{fv}(P) \subseteq \{x_1, \ldots, x_j\} \subseteq \mathcal{V}$, and each occurrence of process identifiers in P is prefix-guarded. We will sometimes omit the arguments of $X(\boldsymbol{u})$ when they are clear from the context.

Prefixes include silent action τ, contract advertisement $\mathsf{tell} \downarrow_u c$, action execution $\mathsf{do}_u\, a$, and contract query $\mathsf{ask}_u \phi$ (where ϕ is an LTL formula on γ). In each prefix $\pi \neq \tau$, u refers to the target session involved in the execution of π.

In Maude, we translate the syntax of CO_2 almost literally. Here we just show the sorts used; see [2] for the full details.

```
sorts System Process Prefix SessionName SessionVariable SessionIde
      GuardProc Sum IdeVec ProcIde ParamList.
subsort SessionName < SessionIde < IdeVec.
subsort Qid < SessionVariable < SessionIde < IdeVec.
subsort GuardProc < Sum < Process.
subsort SessionIde < ParamList.
```

The sort `SessionIde` is a super sort of both `SessionVariable` and `SessionName`. Session variables can be of sort `Qid`; session names can not. Sort `IdeVec` models sets of `SessionIde` (used as syntactic sugar for delimitations), while `ParamList` models vectors of `SessionIde` (used for parameters of defining equations).

Semantics. The CO_2 semantics is formalised by the relation $\xrightarrow{\mu}$ in Fig. 3, where $\mu \in \{A : \pi \mid A \neq K\} \cup \{K : \mathsf{fuse}\}$. We will consider processes and systems up-to the congruence relation $\equiv$ in Fig. 2. The axioms for $\equiv$ are fairly standard — except the last one: it collects garbage terms possibly arising from variable substitutions.

Rule [TAU] just fires a τ prefix. Rule [TELL] advertises a latent contract $\{\downarrow_x c\}_A$. Rule [FUSE] finds *agreements* among the latent contracts: it happens when there exist $\{\downarrow_x c\}_A$ and $\{\downarrow_y d\}_B$ such that $A \neq B$ and $c \bowtie d$. Once the agreement is reached, a fresh session containing $\gamma = A$ *says* $c \mid B$ *says* d is created. Rule [DO] allows a participant A to perform an action in the session s containing γ (which, commutative monoidal laws for $|$ on processes and systems

$$A[(v)P] \equiv (v)\,A[P] \qquad Z \mid (u)Z' \equiv (u)(Z \mid Z') \ \text{ if } u \notin \mathrm{fv}(Z) \cup \mathrm{fn}(Z)$$

$$(u)(v)Z \equiv (v)(u)Z \qquad (u)Z \equiv Z \ \text{ if } u \notin \mathrm{fv}(Z) \cup \mathrm{fn}(Z) \qquad \{\downarrow_s c\}_A \equiv 0$$

Fig. 2. Structural equivalence for CO_2 (Z, Z' range over systems or processes).

$$A[\tau.P + P' \mid Q] \xrightarrow{\text{A: } \tau} A[P \mid Q] \qquad\qquad [\textsc{Tau}]$$

$$A[\text{tell} \downarrow_u c.P + P' \mid Q] \xrightarrow{\text{A: tell} \downarrow_u c} A[P \mid Q] \mid \{\downarrow_u c\}_A \qquad [\textsc{Tell}]$$

$$\frac{c \bowtie d \qquad \gamma = A \text{ says } c \mid B \text{ says } d \qquad \sigma = \{s/x,y\} \qquad s \text{ fresh}}{(x,y)(S \mid \{\downarrow_x c\}_A \mid \{\downarrow_y d\}_B) \xrightarrow{\text{K: fuse}} (s)(S\sigma \mid s[\gamma])} \qquad [\textsc{Fuse}]$$

$$\frac{\gamma \xrightarrow{A \text{ says } a} \gamma'}{A[\text{do}_s\, a.P + P' \mid Q] \mid s[\gamma] \xrightarrow{\text{A: do}_s\, a} A[P \mid Q] \mid s[\gamma']} \qquad [\textsc{Do}]$$

$$\frac{\gamma \vdash \phi}{A[\text{ask}_s\, \phi.P + P' \mid Q] \mid s[\gamma] \xrightarrow{\text{A: ask}_s\, \phi} A[P \mid Q] \mid s[\gamma]} \qquad [\textsc{Ask}]$$

$$\frac{X(u) \overset{\text{def}}{=} P \qquad A[P\{v/u\} \mid Q] \mid S \xrightarrow{\mu} S'}{A[X(v) \mid Q] \mid S \xrightarrow{\mu} S'} \ [\textsc{Def}] \qquad\qquad \frac{S \xrightarrow{\mu} S'}{S \mid S'' \xrightarrow{\mu} S' \mid S''} \ [\textsc{Par}]$$

$$\frac{S \xrightarrow{\text{A: } \pi} S'}{(u)S \xrightarrow{\text{A: del}_u(\pi)} (u)S'} \ [\textsc{Del}] \qquad \text{where } \mathrm{del}_u(\pi) = \begin{cases} \tau & \text{if } u \in \mathrm{fnv}(\pi) \\ \pi & \text{otherwise} \end{cases}$$

Fig. 3. Reduction semantics of CO_2.

accordingly, evolves to γ'). Rule [Ask] allows A to proceed only if the contract γ at session s satisfies the property ϕ. The last three rules are mostly standard. In rule [Del] the label π fired in the premise becomes τ in the consequence, when π contains the delimited name/variable. This transformation is defined by the function $\mathrm{del}_u(\pi)$, where the set $\mathrm{fnv}(\pi)$ contains the free names/variables in π. For instance, $(x)\,A[\text{tell} \downarrow_x c.P] \xrightarrow{\text{A: } \tau} (x)\,(A[P] \mid \{\downarrow_x c\}_A)$. Here, it would make little sense to have the label $A:\text{tell} \downarrow_x c$, as x (being delimited) may be α-converted.

Implementing in Maude the semantics of CO_2 is almost straightforward [19]; here we show only the main rules (see [2] for the others). Rule [Do] uses the transition relation => on bilateral contracts. Rule [Ask] exploits the Maude model checker to verify if the bilateral contract g satisfies the LTL formula phi. Rule [Fuse] uses the operator |X| to check compliance between the contracts c and d, then creates the session s[A says c | B says d] (with s fresh), and finally applies the substitution {s / x}{s / y} (delimitations are dealt with as in Fig. 3).

```
crl [Do]  : A[do s a . P + P' | Q] | s[g] => {A : do s a} (A[P | Q] | s[g'])
               if g => {A says a} g'.

crl [Ask] : A[ask s phi . P + P' | Q] | s[g] => {A : ask s phi} A[P | Q]
               if g |- phi.

crl [Fuse] : (uVec , vVec) ({x c}A | {y d}B | S) => { K : fuse}
               (s , vVec) (s[A says c | B says d] | S{s / x}{s / y})
               if uVec == (x , y) / c |X| d / s := fresh(0 , S).
```

4   Honesty

A remarkable feature of CO_2 is that it allows for writing *dishonest* agents which do not keep their promises. Intuitively, a participant is honest if she always fulfils her contractual obligations, in all possible contexts. Below we formalise the notion of honesty, by slightly adapting the one appeared in [3]. Then, we show how we verify in Maude a weaker notion, i.e. honesty *in a given context*.

We start by defining the set $O_s^A(S)$ of *obligations* of A at s in S. Whenever A is culpable at some session s, she has to fire one of the actions in $O_s^A(S)$.

Definition 5. *We define the set of atoms $O_s^A(S)$ as:*

$$O_s^A(S) = \left\{ a \mid \exists \gamma, S' . S \equiv s[\gamma] \mid S' \text{ and } \gamma \xrightarrow{A \; says \; a} \right\}$$

We say that A *is* culpable *at* s *in* S *iff* $O_s^A(S) \neq \emptyset$.

The set of atoms $RD_s^A(S)$ ("Ready Do") defined below comprises all the actions that A can perform at s in one computation step within S (note that, by rule [DEL], if s is a bound name then $RD_s^A(S) = \emptyset$). The set $WRD_s^A(S)$ ("Weak Ready Do") contains all the actions that A may possibly perform at s after a finite sequence of transitions of A not involving any do at s.

Definition 6. *For all S, A and s, we define the sets of atoms:*

$$RD_s^A(S) = \left\{ a \mid \exists S' . S \xrightarrow{A: \; do_s \; a} S' \right\}$$

$$WRD_s^A(S) = \left\{ a \mid \exists S' . S \xrightarrow{A: \; \neq do_s} {}^* S' \wedge a \in RD_s^A(S') \right\}$$

where we write $S \xrightarrow{A: \; \neq do_s} S'$ *if* $\exists \pi. S \xrightarrow{A: \; \pi} S' \wedge \forall a. \; \pi \neq do_s \; a$.

A participant is *ready* if she can fulfil some of her obligations. To check if A is ready in S, we consider all the sessions s in S involving A. For each of them, we check that some obligations of A at s are exposed after some steps of A *not* preceded by other do_s of A. $A[P]$ is honest *in a given system* S when A is ready in all evolutions of $A[P] \mid S$. Then, $A[P]$ is honest when she is honest in *all* S.

Definition 7 (Honesty). *We say that:*

1. *S is A -free iff it has no latent/stipulated contracts of A, nor processes of A*
2. *A is ready in S iff $S \equiv (\boldsymbol{u})S' \wedge O_s^A(S') \neq \emptyset \implies \mathrm{WRD}_s^A(S') \cap O_s^A(S') \neq \emptyset$*
3. *P is honest in S iff $\forall A : (S$ is A -free $\wedge A[P] \mid S \to^* S') \implies A$ is ready in S'*
4. *P is honest iff, for all S, P is honest in S*

We have implemented items 2 and 3 of the above definition in Maude (item 4 is dealt with in the next section). CO_2 can simulate Turing machines [5], hence reachability in CO_2 is undecidable, and consequently WRD, readiness and honesty are undecidable as well. To recover decidability, we then restrict to finite state processes: roughly, these are the processes with neither delimitations nor parallel compositions under process definitions.

In Maude we verify readiness in a session s by searching if A can reach (with her moves only), a state which allows for a do_s a move, for some a.

```
op ready? : Participant SessionName System Module -> Bool .
eq ready?(A,s,S,M:Module) = metaSearch(M:Module, upTerm(< S > A s),
   '<_>__['S1:System , upTerm(A) , upTerm(s)],
   'S1:System => ''_'_['l:SLabel,'S2:System] /\
   '_:_[upTerm(A),'do__[upTerm(s),'a:Atom]] := 'l:SLabel,
   '*, unbounded, 0 ) =/= failure .
```

We start the search from the term < S > A s, whose meta-representation is obtained through the upTerm function. The search is performed according to the A-solo semantics of CO_2 (see Definition 10), which blocks all do at s. This is done by the operator <_>__. Then, we look for reachable systems S1 where A can fire a do at s. If the search succeeds, ready? returns true. Note that if A has no obligations at s in S, ready? returns false — uncoherently with Definition 7. To correctly check readiness, we define the function ready (see [2]), which invokes ready? only when $O_s^A(S) \neq \emptyset$.

Verifying honesty in a context is done similarly. We use metaSearch to check that A is ready in all reachable states. The operator <_> gives the CO_2 semantics.

```
op search-honest-ctx : Participant System Module -> ResultTriple? .
eq search-honest-ctx(A,S,M:Module) = metaSearch(M:Module, upTerm(< S >),
   '<_>['S:System], 'ready[upTerm(A), 'S:System,'S:System, upTerm(M:Module)]
   = 'false.Bool, '*, unbounded, 0) .
op honest-ctx : Participant System Module -> Result .
ceq honest-ctx (A , S , M:Module) = true
   if search-honest-ctx (A , S , M:Module) == failure .
ceq honest-ctx (A , S , M:Module) = downTerm (T:Term , < (0).System > )
   if {T:Term,Ty:Type,S:Substitution} := search-honest-ctx (A,S,M:Module) .
```

Example 4. A travel agency A queries in parallel an airline ticket broker F and a hotel reservation service H in order to organise a trip for some user U. The agency first requires U to pay, and then chooses either to commit the reservation or to issue a refund (contract CU). When querying the ticket broker (contract CF), the agency first receives a quotation, and then chooses either to commit and pay the ticket, or to abort the transaction. The contract CH between A and H is similar.

```
eq CU = pay . (commit ; 0 (+) refund ; 0).
eq CF = ticket . ( commitF ; payF ; 0 (+) abortF ; 0).
eq CH = hotel . ( commitH ; payH ; 0 (+) abortH ; 0).
```

In addition to the contracts above, the agency should respect the following constraints: (a) the agency refunds U only if both the transactions with F and H are aborted; (b) A pays the ticket and the hotel reservation only after it has committed the transaction with U; (c) either both the transactions with F or H are committed, or they are both aborted. A possible specification in Maude respecting the above constraints is given by the following process P:

```
eq P = ( xu , xf , xh ) ( tell xu CU . do xu pay.
       ( (tell xf CF . PF) | (tell xh CH . PH) | PU ) ).

eq PF = do xf ticket . (do xh commitH . 0 + do xf abortF . 0).
eq PH = do xh hotel  . (do xf commitF . 0 + do xh abortH . 0).

eq PU = ask xh ([] ~ payH) . do xu refund . 0 +
        t . do xu commit . (do xf payF . 0 | do xh payH . 0).
```

The process P first opens a session with U, and then advertises the contracts CF and CH, and in parallel executes PU. The process PF gets the ticket quotation, then either commits the hotel reservation, or aborts the flight reservation. Dually, PH gets the hotel quotation, then either commits the flight reservation, or aborts the hotel reservation. Note that the two choices in PF and PH ensure that constraint (c) above is satisfied: e.g., if PF fires the commitH (resp. abortF) prefix, the abortH (resp. commitF) branch in PH is disabled, and only commitF (resp. abortH) can be selected. The process PU checks if a refund is due to U. When the atom payH is no longer reachable in session xh, the ask passes, and the refund is issued. This guarantees constraint (a). In the τ-branch, PU commits the transaction with U, and then proceeds to pay both F and H. This satisfies constraint (b). Note that it may happen that PU chooses to commit even when CF or CH are not stipulated. Although this behaviour is conceptually wrong, it does not affect honesty. Indeed, honesty does not consider the domain-specific constraints among actions (e.g. (a), (b), (c) above), but only that the advertised contracts are respected.

We have experimented the function honest-ctx by inserting P in some contexts S where all the other participants U, F and H are honest (see [2] for details). The Maude model checker has correctly determined that P is honest in S.

```
red honest-ctx(A , S , ['TRAVEL-AGENCY-CTX]).
rewrites: 53950741 in 38062ms cpu (38058ms real) (1417429 rewrites/second)
result Bool: true
```

Even though we conjecture that P is honest (in all contexts), we anticipate here that the verification technique proposed in Sect. 5 does not classify P as honest. This is because the analysis is (correct but) not complete in the presence of ask: indeed, the precise behaviour of an ask is lost by the analysis, because it abstracts from the contracts of the context.

5 Model Checking Honesty

We now address the problem of automatically verifying honesty. As mentioned in Sect. 1, this is a desirable goal, because it alerts system designers before they deploy services which could violate contracts at run-time (so possibly incurring in sanctions). Since honesty is undecidable in general [5], our goal is a verification technique which safely over-approximates honesty, i.e. it never classifies a process as honest when it is not. The first issue is that Definition 7 requires readiness to be preserved in all possible contexts, and there is an *infinite* number of such contexts. To overcome this problem, we present below an *abstract* semantics of CO_2 which preserves the honesty property, while neglecting the actual context where the process $A[P]$ is executed.

The definition of the abstract semantics of CO_2 is obtained in two steps. First, we provide the projections from concrete contracts/systems to the abstract ones. Then, we define the semantics of abstract contracts and systems, and we relate the abstract semantics with the concrete one. The abstraction is always parameterised in the participant A the honesty of which is under consideration.

The abstraction $\alpha_A(\gamma)$ of a bilateral contract $\gamma = A$ *says* c | B *says* d (Definition 8 below) is either c, or $ctx.c$ when d has a *ready*.

Definition 8. *For all* γ, *we define the abstract contract* $\alpha_A(\gamma)$ *as:*

$$\alpha_A(A \; says \; c \mid B \; says \; d) \;\; = \;\; \begin{cases} c & \text{if } d \text{ is ready-free} \\ ctx \; \mathsf{a}.c & \text{if } d = ready \; \mathsf{a}.d' \end{cases}$$

We now define the abstraction α_A of concrete systems, which just discards all the components not involving A, and projects the contracts involving A.

Definition 9. *For all* A, S *we define the* abstract system $\alpha_A(S)$ *as:*

$$\alpha_A(A[P]) = A[P] \qquad \alpha_A(s[\gamma]) = s[\alpha_A(\gamma)] \qquad \alpha_A(\{\downarrow_x c\}_A) = \{\downarrow_x c\}_A$$
$$\alpha_A(S \mid S') = \alpha_A(S) \mid \alpha_A(S') \quad \alpha_A((u)S) = (u)(\alpha_A(S)) \quad \alpha_A(S) = \mathbf{0}, \; otherwise$$

Abstract semantics. For all participants A, the abstract LTSs $\xrightarrow{\ell}_A$ and $\xrightarrow{\mu}_A$ on abstract contracts and systems, respectively, are defined by the rules in Fig. 4. Labels ℓ are atoms, with or without the special prefix ctx — which indicates a contractual action performed by the context. Labels μ are either ctx or they have the form A: π, where A is the participant in $\rightarrow_A$, and π is a CO_2 prefix.

Rules for abstract contracts (first row in Fig. 4) are simple: in an internal sum, A chooses a branch; in an external sum, the choice is made by the context; in a *ready* a.c the atom a is fired. The rightmost rule handles a *ready* in the context contract. For abstract systems, some rules are similar to the concrete ones, hence we discuss only the most relevant ones. Rule [α-Do] involves the abstract transitions of contracts. The behaviour of abstract systems also considers context actions, labelled with ctx. If $c \vdash \phi$, then the ask ϕ passes, indepedently from the context (rule [α-Ask]). If $c \nvdash \neg\phi$, then the ask ϕ may pass or not, depending and the context (rule [α-AskCtx]). Rule [α-Fuse] says that a latent contract of A may always be fused (the context may choose whether this is the case or not). The context may also decide whether to perform actions within sessions ([α-DoCtx]). Unobservable context actions are modelled by rules [α-Ctx] and [α-DelCtx].

$$a \,;\, c \oplus c' \xrightarrow{a}_A ctx \ \bar{a}.c \quad a\,.\,c + c' \xrightarrow{ctx:\bar{a}}_A ready\ a.\,c \quad ready\ a.\,c \xrightarrow{a}_A c \quad ctx\ a.c \xrightarrow{ctx:a}_A c$$

$$\frac{c \xrightarrow{a}_A c'}{A[do_s\,a.P + P' \mid Q] \mid s[c] \xrightarrow{A:\,do_s\,a}_A A[P \mid Q] \mid s[c']} \qquad [\alpha\text{-Do}]$$

$$\frac{s\ fresh}{(x)(\tilde{S} \mid \{\downarrow_x c\}_A) \xrightarrow{ctx}_A (s)(s[c] \mid \tilde{S}\{s/x\})} \qquad [\alpha\text{-Fuse}]$$

$$\frac{c \vdash \phi}{A[ask_s\,\phi.P + P' \mid Q] \mid s[c] \xrightarrow{A:\,ask_s\,\phi}_A A[P \mid Q] \mid s[c]} \qquad [\alpha\text{-Ask}]$$

$$\frac{c \not\vdash \neg\phi}{A[ask_s\,\phi.P + P' \mid Q] \mid s[c] \xrightarrow{ctx}_A A[P \mid Q] \mid s[c]} \qquad [\alpha\text{-AskCtx}]$$

$$\frac{c \xrightarrow{ctx}_A c'}{s[c] \xrightarrow{ctx}_A s[c']}\ [\alpha\text{-DoCtx}] \qquad S \xrightarrow{ctx}_A S\ [\alpha\text{-Ctx}] \qquad \frac{\tilde{S} \xrightarrow{ctx}_A \tilde{S}'}{(u)\tilde{S} \xrightarrow{ctx}_A (u)\tilde{S}'}\ [\alpha\text{-DelCtx}]$$

Fig. 4. Abstract LTSs for contracts and systems (full set of rules in [2]).

To check if A[P] is honest, we must only consider those A-free contexts not already containing advertised/stipulated contracts of A. Such systems will always evolve to a system which can be split in two parts: an A-*solo* system S_A containing the process of A, the contracts advertised by A and all the sessions containing contracts of A, and an A-*free* system S_{ctx}.

Definition 10. *We say that a system S is* A-*solo iff one of the following holds:*

$$S \equiv 0 \qquad S \equiv A[P] \qquad S \equiv s[A\ says\ c \mid B\ says\ d] \qquad S \equiv \{\downarrow_x c\}_A$$

$$S \equiv S' \mid S'' \ \ where\ S'\ and\ S''\ \text{A-}solo \qquad S \equiv (u)S' \ \ where\ S'\ \text{A-}solo$$

We say that S is A-*safe iff $S \equiv (s)(S_A \mid S_{ctx})$, with S_A* A-*solo and S_{ctx}* A-*free.*

The following theorems establish the relations between the concrete and the abstract semantics of CO_2. Theorem 3 states that the abstraction is *correct*, i.e. for each concrete computation there exists a corresponding abstract computation. Theorem 4 states that the abstraction is also *complete*, provided that a process has neither ask nor non-proper contracts.

Theorem 3. *For all* A*-safe systems* S, *and for all concrete traces* η:

$$S \xrightarrow{\eta}{}^* S' \implies \exists \tilde{\eta} \, : \, \alpha_\mathsf{A}(S) \xrightarrow{\tilde{\eta}}{}_\mathsf{A}{}^* \alpha_\mathsf{A}(S')$$

Furthermore, if η *is* A*-solo and* S *is* ask*-free, then* $\eta = \tilde{\eta}$.

Theorem 4. *For all* ask*-free abstract system* $\tilde{S}$ *with proper contracts only:*

$$\tilde{S} \to_\mathsf{A}^* \tilde{S}' \implies \exists S, S' \text{ A-safe. } \alpha_\mathsf{A}(S) = \tilde{S} \, \wedge \, S \to^* S' \, \wedge \, \alpha_\mathsf{A}(S') = \tilde{S}'$$

The abstract counterparts of Ready Do, Weak Ready Do, and readiness are defined as expected, by using the abstract semantics instead of the concrete one (see [2] for details). The notion of honesty for abstract systems, namely α-*honesty*, follows the lines of that of honesty in Definition 7.

Definition 11 (α-honesty). *We say that* P *is* α-honest *iff for all* $\tilde{S}$ *such that* $\mathsf{A}[P] \to_\mathsf{A}^* \tilde{S}$, A *is ready in* $\tilde{S}$.

The main result of this paper follows. It states that α-honesty is a sound approximation of honesty, and — under certain conditions — it is also complete.

Theorem 5. *If* P *is* α-honest, then P is honest. Conversely, if P is honest, ask*-free, and has proper contracts only, then* P *is* α-honest.

In Maude, we implement abstract semantics for system and contracts for one-step transitions. We obtain their transitive closure, discarding labels, with the operator <_>. The function `ready` in `search-honest` computes abstract readiness.

```
op search-honest : Process Module -> ResultTriple?.
eq search-honest(P , M:Module) = metaSearch(M:Module, upTerm(< A[P] >),
   '<_>['S:System], 'ready['S:System,'S:System, upTerm(M:Module)]
   = 'false.Bool, '*, unbounded, 0).

op honest : Process Module -> Result.
ceq honest (P, M:Module) = true if search-honest (P,M:Module) == failure . ceq honest (P,
M:Module) = downTerm (T:Term , < (0).System > )
    if {T:Term, Ty:Type, S:Substitution} := search-honest (P , M:Module).
```

Honesty is checked by searching for states such that A is *not* ready. If the search fails, then A is honest. As in Sect. 4, this function is decidable for finite state processes, i.e. those without delimitation/parallel under process definitions. The following example shows a process which was erroneously classified as honest in [5]. The Maude model checker has determined the dishonesty of that process, and by exploiting the Maude tracing facilities we managed to fix it.

Example 5. A store A offers buyers two options: `clickPay` or `clickVoucher`. If a buyer B chooses `clickPay`, A requires a payment (`pay`) otherwise A checks the validity of the voucher with V, an online voucher distribution system. If V validates the voucher (`ok`), B can use it (`voucher`), otherwise (`no`) B must `pay`. We specify in Maude the contracts CB (between A and B) and CV (between A and V) as:

```
eq CB = clickPay . pay . 0 +
        clickVoucher . (- reject ; pay . 0 (+) - accept ; voucher . 0).
eq CV = ok . 0 + no . 0.
```

We can specify in Maude a CO_2 process for A as follows:

```
eq P = (x)(tell x CB . (do x clickPay . do x pay . 0 +
                        do x clickVoucher . ((y) tell y CV . Q))).
eq Q = do y ok . do x - accept . do x voucher . 0 +
       do y no . do x - reject . do x pay . 0     + R.
eq R = t . (do x - reject . do x pay . 0).
```

Variables x and y in P correspond to two separate sessions, where A respectively interacts with B and V. The advertisement of CV causally depends on the stipulation of the contract CB, because A must fire clickVoucher before tell y CV. In process Q the store waits for the answer of V: if V validates the voucher (first branch), then A accepts it from B; otherwise (second branch), A requires B to pay. The third branch R allows A to fire a τ action, and then reject the voucher. The intuition is that τ models a timeout, to deal with the fact that CV might not be stipulated. When we check the honesty of P with Maude, we obtain:

```
red honest(P , ['STORE-VOUCHER]).
rewrites: 31649 in 72ms cpu (77ms real) (439545 rewrites/second)
result TSystem: < ($ 0,$ 1)(A[do $ 0 - reject . do $ 0 pay . (0).Sum] |
  $ 0[- accept ; voucher . 0(+)- reject ; pay . 0] | $ 1[ready ok . 0]) >
```

This means that the process P is dishonest: actually, the output provides a state where A is not ready. There, A must do ok in session y ($1), while A is only ready to do a -reject at session x ($0). This problem occurs when the branch R is chosen. To recover honesty, it suffices to replace R with the following process R':

```
eq R' = t . (do x - reject . do x pay . 0 | (do y no . 0 + do y ok . 0)).
red honest(P' , ['STORE-VOUCHER]).
rewrites: 44009 in 32ms cpu (30ms real) (1375195 rewrites/second)
result Bool: true
```

6   Conclusions

We have described an executable specification in Maude of a calculus for contract-oriented systems. This has been done in two steps. First, we have specified a model for contracts, and we have formalised in Maude their semantics, and the crucial notions of compliance and culpability (Sect. 2). This specification has been exploited in Sect. 3 to implement in Maude the calculus CO_2 [4]. Then, we have considered the problem of honesty [5], i.e. that of deciding when a participant always respects the contracts she advertises, in all possible contexts (Sect. 4). Writing honest processes is not a trivial task, especially when multiple sessions are needed for realising a contract (see e.g. Example 4 and Example 5). We have then devised a sound verification technique for deciding when a participant is honest, and we have provided an implementation of this technique in Maude (Sect. 5).

Related work. Rewriting logic [12] has been successfully used for more than two decades as a semantic framework wherein many different programming models and logics are naturally formalised, executed and analysed. Just by restricting to models for concurrency, there exist Maude specifications and tools for CCS [17], the π-calculus [16], Petri nets [15], Erlang [14], Klaim [18], adaptive systems [7], *etc.* A more comprehensive list of calculi, programming languages, tools and applications implemented in Maude is collected in [13].

The contract model presented in Sect. 2 is a refined version of the one in [5], which in turn is an alternative formalisation of the one in [8]. Our version is simpler and closer to the notion of *session behaviour* [1], and enjoys several desirable properties. Theorem 1 establishes that only one participant may be culpable in a bilateral contract, whereas in [5] both participants may be culpable, e.g. in A *says* a ; c | B *says* ā ; d. In our model, if both participants have an internal (or external) choice, then their contracts are *not* compliant, whereas e.g. a.c and ā.d (both external choices) are compliant in [5,8] whenever c and d are compliant. The exculpation property established by Theorem 2 is stronger than the corresponding one in [5]. There, a participant A is guaranteed to exculpate herself by performing (at most) two consecutive actions *of* A, while in our model two any actions (of *whatever* participant) suffice.

As far as we know, the concept of *contract-oriented computing* (in the meaning used in this paper) has been introduced in [6]. CO_2, a contract-agnostic calculus for contract-oriented computing, has been instantiated with several contract models — both bilateral [3,5] and multiparty [4,11]. Here we have instantiated it with the contracts in Sect. 2. A minor difference w.r.t. [3,5,11] is that here we no longer have fuse as a language primitive, but rather the creation of fresh sessions is performed non-deterministically by the context (rule [FUSE]). This is equivalent to assume a contract broker which collects all contracts, and may establish sessions when compliant contracts are found. In [5], a participant A is considered honest when, in each possible context, she can always exculpate herself by a sequence of A-solo moves. Here we require that A is ready (i.e. some of her obligations are in the Weak Ready Do set) in all possible contexts, as in [3]. We conjecture that these two notions are equivalent. In [3] a type system has been proposed to safely over-approximate honesty. The type of a process P is a function which maps each variable to a *channel type*. These are behavioural types (in the form of Basic Parallel Processes) which essentially preserve the structure of P, by abstracting the actual prefixes as "non-blocking" and "possibly blocking". The type system relies upon checking honesty for channel types, but no actual algorithm is given for such verification, hence type inference remains an open issue. In contrast, here we have directly implemented in Maude a verification algorithm for honesty, by model checking the abstract semantics in Sect. 5.

Acknowledgments. This work has been partially supported by Aut. Region of Sardinia under grants L.R.7/2007 CRP-17285 (TRICS) and P.I.A. 2010 project "Social Glue", and by MIUR PRIN 2010-11 project "Security Horizons", and by EU COST Action IC1201 "Behavioural Types for Reliable Large-Scale Software Systems" (BETTY).

References

1. Barbanera, F., de'Liguoro, U.: Two notions of sub-behaviour for session-based client/server systems. In: PPDP (2010)
2. Bartoletti, M., Murgia, M., Scalas, A., Zunino, R.: Modelling and verifying contract-oriented systems in Maude. http://tcs.unica.it/software/co2-maude
3. Bartoletti, M., Scalas, A., Tuosto, E., Zunino, R.: Honesty by typing. In: Beyer, D., Boreale, M. (eds.) FORTE 2013 and FMOODS 2013. LNCS, vol. 7892, pp. 305–320. Springer, Heidelberg (2013)
4. Bartoletti, M., Tuosto, E., Zunino, R.: Contract-oriented computing in Co_2. Sci. Ann. Comp. Sci. **22**(1), 5–60 (2012)
5. Bartoletti, M., Tuosto, E., Zunino, R.: On the realizability of contracts in dishonest systems. In: Sirjani, M. (ed.) COORDINATION 2012. LNCS, vol. 7274, pp. 245–260. Springer, Heidelberg (2012)
6. Bartoletti, M., Zunino, R.: A calculus of contracting processes. In: LICS (2010)
7. Bruni, R., Corradini, A., Gadducci, F., Lluch Lafuente, A., Vandin, A.: Modelling and analyzing adaptive self-assembly strategies with maude. In: Durán, F. (ed.) WRLA 2012. LNCS, vol. 7571, pp. 118–138. Springer, Heidelberg (2012)
8. Castagna, G., Gesbert, N., Padovani, L.: A theory of contracts for web services. ACM Trans. Program. Lang. Syst. **31**(5), 1–61 (2009)
9. Clavel, M., Durán, F., Eker, S., Lincoln, P., Martí-Oliet, N., Meseguer, J., Quesada, J.F.: Maude: Specification and programming in rewriting logic. In: TCS (2001)
10. Honda, K., Vasconcelos, V.T., Kubo, M.: Language primitives and type discipline for structured communication-based programming. In: Hankin, C. (ed.) ESOP 1998. LNCS, vol. 1381, pp. 122–138. Springer, Heidelberg (1998)
11. Lange, J., Scalas, A.: Choreography synthesis as contract agreement. In: ICE (2013)
12. Meseguer, J.: Rewriting as a unified model of concurrency. In: Baeten, J.C.M., Klop, J.W. (eds.) CONCUR 1990. LNCS, vol. 458, pp. 384–400. Springer, Heidelberg (1990)
13. Meseguer, J.: Twenty years of rewriting logic. JLAP **81**(7–8), 721–781 (2012)
14. Neuhäußer, M., Noll, T.: Abstraction and model checking of core Erlang programs in Maude. ENTCS **176**(4), 143–163 (2007)
15. Stehr, M.-O., Meseguer, J., Ölveczky, P.C.: Rewriting logic as a unifying framework for Petri Nets. In: Ehrig, H., Juhás, G., Padberg, J., Rozenberg, G. (eds.) APN 2001. LNCS, vol. 2128, pp. 250–303. Springer, Heidelberg (2001)
16. Thati, P., Sen, K., Martí-Oliet, N.: An executable specification of asynchronous pi-calculus semantics and may testing in Maude 2.0. In: ENTCS 71 (2002)
17. Verdejo, A., Martí-Oliet, N.: Implementing CCS in Maude 2. In: ENTCS 71 (2002)
18. Wirsing, M., Eckhardt, J., Mühlbauer, T., Meseguer, J.: Design and analysis of cloud-based architectures with KLAIM and maude. In: Durán, F. (ed.) WRLA 2012. LNCS, vol. 7571, pp. 54–82. Springer, Heidelberg (2012)
19. Şerbănuţă, T.F., Roşu, G., Meseguer, J.: A rewriting logic approach to operational semantics. Inf. Comput. **207**(2), 305–340 (2009)

Towards Static Analysis of Functional Programs Using Tree Automata Completion

Thomas Genet[(⊠)]

INRIA/IRISA, Université de Rennes, Rennes Cedex, France
`genet@irisa.fr`

Abstract. This paper presents the first step of a wider research effort to apply tree automata completion to the static analysis of functional programs. Tree Automata Completion is a family of techniques for computing or approximating the set of terms reachable by a rewriting relation. The completion algorithm we focus on is parameterized by a set E of equations controlling the precision of the approximation and influencing its termination. For completion to be used as a static analysis, the first step is to guarantee its termination. In this work, we thus give a sufficient condition on E and $\mathcal{T}(\mathcal{F})$ for completion algorithm to always terminate. In the particular setting of functional programs, this condition can be relaxed into a condition on E and $\mathcal{T}(\mathcal{C})$ (terms built on the set of constructors) that is closer to what is done in the field of static analysis, where abstractions are performed on data.

1 Introduction

Computing or approximating the set of terms reachable by rewriting has more and more applications. For a Term Rewriting System (TRS) $\mathcal{R}$ and a set of terms $L_0 \subseteq \mathcal{T}(\mathcal{F})$, the set of reachable terms is $\mathcal{R}^*(L_0) = \{t \in \mathcal{T}(\mathcal{F}) \mid \exists s \in L_0, s \rightarrow_{\mathcal{R}}^* t\}$. This set can be computed exactly for specific classes of $\mathcal{R}$ [10] but, in general, it has to be approximated. Applications of the approximation of $\mathcal{R}^*(L_0)$ are ranging from cryptographic protocol verification [1], to static analysis of various programming languages [5] or to TRS termination proofs [15]. Most of the techniques compute such approximations using tree automata as the core formalism to represent or approximate the (possibly) infinite set of terms $\mathcal{R}^*(L_0)$. Most of them also rely on a Knuth-Bendix completion-like algorithm completing a tree automaton $\mathcal{A}$ recognizing L_0 into an automaton $\mathcal{A}^*$ recognizing exactly, or over-approximating, the set $\mathcal{R}^*(L_0)$. As a result, these techniques can be refered as *tree automata completion* techniques [4,8,9,13,19,22]. A strength of this algorithm, and at the same time a weakness, is that its precision is parameterized by a function [8] or a set of equations [13]. It is a strength because tuning the approximation function (or equations) permits to adapt the precision of completion to a specific goal to tackle. This is what made it successful for program and protocol verification. On the other hand, this is a weakness because it is difficult to guarantee its termination.

© Springer International Publishing Switzerland 2014
S. Escobar (Ed.): WRLA 2014, LNCS 8663, pp. 147–161, 2014.
DOI: 10.1007/978-3-319-12904-4_8

In this paper, we define a simple sufficient condition on the set of equations for the tree automata completion algorithm to terminate. This condition, which is strong in general, reveals to be natural and well adapted for the approximation of reachable terms when TRSs encode typed functional programs. We thus obtain a way to automatically over-approximate the set of all reachable program states of a functional program, or even restrict it to the set of all results. Thus we can over-approximate the image of a functional program.

2   Related Work

Tree automata completion. With regards to most papers about completion [4,8,9, 13,19,22], our contribution is to give the first criterion *on the approximation* for the completion to terminate. Note that it is possible to guarantee termination of the completion by inferring an approximation adapted to the TRS under concern, like in [20]. In this case, given a TRS, the approximation is fixed and unique. Our solution is more flexible because it lets the user change the precision of the approximation while keeping the termination guarantee. In [22], T. Takai have a completion parameterized by a set of equations. He also gives a termination proof for its completion but only for some restricted classes of TRSs. Here our termination proof holds for any left-linear TRS provided that the set of equations satisfy some properties.

Static analysis of functional programs. With regards to static analysis of functional programs using grammars or automata, our contribution is in the scope of data-flow analysis techniques, rather than control-flow analysis. More precisely, we are interested here in predicting the results of a function [21], rather than predicting the control flow [18]. Those two papers, as well as many other ones, deal with higher order functions using complex higher-order grammar formalisms (PMRS and HORS). Higher-order functions are not in the scope of the solution we propose here. However, we obtained some preliminary results suggesting that an extension to higher order functions is possible and gives relevant results (see Sect. 6). Furthermore, using equations, approximations are defined in a more declarative and flexible way than in [21], where they are defined by a dedicated algorithm. Besides, the verification mechanisms of [21] use automatic abstraction refinement. This can be also performed in the completion setting [3] and adapted to the analysis of functional programs [14]. Finally, using a simpler (first order) formalism, *i.e.* tree automata, makes it easier to take into account some other aspects like: evaluation strategies and built-ins types (see Sect. 6) that are not considered by those papers.

3   Background

In this section, we introduce some definitions and concepts that will be used throughout the rest of the paper (see also [2,7]). Let $\mathcal{F}$ be a finite set of symbols, each associated with an arity function, and let $\mathcal{X}$ be a countable set of *variables*.

$\mathcal{T}(\mathcal{F}, \mathcal{X})$ denotes the set of *terms* and $\mathcal{T}(\mathcal{F})$ denotes the set of *ground terms* (terms without variables). The set of variables of a term t is denoted by $\mathcal{V}ar(t)$. A *substitution* is a function σ from $\mathcal{X}$ into $\mathcal{T}(\mathcal{F}, \mathcal{X})$, which can be uniquely extended to an endomorphism of $\mathcal{T}(\mathcal{F}, \mathcal{X})$. A *position* p for a term t is a finite word over $\mathbb{N}$. The empty sequence λ denotes the top-most position. The set $\mathcal{P}os(t)$ of positions of a term t is inductively defined by $\mathcal{P}os(t) = \{\lambda\}$ if $t \in \mathcal{X}$ or t is a constant and $\mathcal{P}os(f(t_1, \ldots, t_n)) = \{\lambda\} \cup \{i.p \mid 1 \leq i \leq n \text{ and } p \in \mathcal{P}os(t_i)\}$ otherwise. If $p \in \mathcal{P}os(t)$, then $t|_p$ denotes the subterm of t at position p and $t[s]_p$ denotes the term obtained by replacement of the subterm $t|_p$ at position p by the term s.

A *term rewriting system* (TRS) $\mathcal{R}$ is a set of *rewrite rules* $l \rightarrow r$, where $l, r \in \mathcal{T}(\mathcal{F}, \mathcal{X})$, $l \notin \mathcal{X}$, and $\mathcal{V}ar(l) \supseteq \mathcal{V}ar(r)$. A rewrite rule $l \rightarrow r$ is *left-linear* if each variable of l occurs only once in l. A TRS $\mathcal{R}$ is left-linear if every rewrite rule $l \rightarrow r$ of $\mathcal{R}$ is left-linear. The TRS $\mathcal{R}$ induces a rewriting relation $\rightarrow_{\mathcal{R}}$ on terms as follows. Let $s, t \in \mathcal{T}(\mathcal{F}, \mathcal{X})$ and $l \rightarrow r \in \mathcal{R}$, $s \rightarrow_{\mathcal{R}} t$ denotes that there exists a position $p \in \mathcal{P}os(s)$ and a substitution σ such that $s|_p = l\sigma$ and $t = s[r\sigma]_p$. Given a TRS $\mathcal{R}$, $\mathcal{F}$ can be split into two disjoint sets $\mathcal{C}$ and $\mathcal{D}$. All symbols occurring at the root position of left-hand sides of rules of $\mathcal{R}$ are in $\mathcal{D}$. $\mathcal{D}$ is the set of defined symbols of $\mathcal{R}$, $\mathcal{C}$ is the set of constructors. Terms in $\mathcal{T}(\mathcal{C})$ are called *data-terms*. The reflexive transitive closure of $\rightarrow_{\mathcal{R}}$ is denoted by $\rightarrow_{\mathcal{R}}^*$ and $s \rightarrow_{\mathcal{R}}^! t$ denotes that $s \rightarrow_{\mathcal{R}}^* t$ and t is irreducible by $\mathcal{R}$. The set of irreducible terms w.r.t. a TRS $\mathcal{R}$ is denoted by $\text{IRR}(\mathcal{R})$. The set of $\mathcal{R}$-descendants of a set of ground terms I is $\mathcal{R}^*(I) = \{t \in \mathcal{T}(\mathcal{F}) \mid \exists s \in I \text{ s.t. } s \rightarrow_{\mathcal{R}}^* t\}$. A TRS $\mathcal{R}$ is sufficiently complete if for all $s \in \mathcal{T}(\mathcal{F})$, $(R^*(\{s\}) \cap \mathcal{T}(\mathcal{C})) \neq \emptyset$.

An *equation set* E is a set of *equations* $l = r$, where $l, r \in \mathcal{T}(\mathcal{F}, \mathcal{X})$. The relation $=_E$ is the smallest congruence such that for all substitution σ we have $l\sigma =_E r\sigma$. Given a TRS $\mathcal{R}$ and a set of equations E, a term $s \in \mathcal{T}(\mathcal{F})$ is rewritten modulo E into $t \in \mathcal{T}(\mathcal{F})$, denoted $s \rightarrow_{\mathcal{R}/E} t$, if there exist $s' \in \mathcal{T}(\mathcal{F})$ and $t' \in \mathcal{T}(\mathcal{F})$ such that $s =_E s' \rightarrow_{\mathcal{R}} t' =_E t$. The reflexive transitive closure $\rightarrow_{\mathcal{R}/E}^*$ of $\rightarrow_{\mathcal{R}/E}$ is defined as usual except that reflexivity is extended to terms equal modulo E, i.e. for all $s, t \in \mathcal{T}(\mathcal{F})$ if $s =_E t$ then $s \rightarrow_{\mathcal{R}/E}^* t$. The set of $\mathcal{R}$-descendants modulo E of a set of ground terms I is $\mathcal{R}_E^*(I) = \{t \in \mathcal{T}(\mathcal{F}) \mid \exists s \in I \text{ s.t. } s \rightarrow_{\mathcal{R}/E}^* t\}$.

Let $\mathcal{Q}$ be a countably infinite set of symbols with arity 0, called *states*, such that $\mathcal{Q} \cap \mathcal{F} = \emptyset$. $\mathcal{T}(\mathcal{F} \cup \mathcal{Q})$ is called the set of *configurations*. A *transition* is a rewrite rule $c \rightarrow q$, where c is a configuration and q is state. A transition is *normalized* when $c = f(q_1, \ldots, q_n)$, $f \in \mathcal{F}$ is of arity n, and $q_1, \ldots, q_n \in \mathcal{Q}$. An ϵ-*transition* is a transition of the form $q \rightarrow q'$ where q and q' are states. A bottom-up non-deterministic finite tree automaton (*tree automaton* for short) over the alphabet $\mathcal{F}$ is a tuple $\mathcal{A} = \langle \mathcal{F}, \mathcal{Q}, \mathcal{Q}_F, \Delta \rangle$, where $\mathcal{Q}_F$ is a finite subset of $\mathcal{Q}$, Δ is a finite set of normalized transitions and ϵ-transitions. The transitive and reflexive *rewriting relation* on $\mathcal{T}(\mathcal{F} \cup \mathcal{Q})$ induced by the set of transitions Δ (resp. all transitions except ϵ-transitions) is denoted by $\rightarrow_{\Delta}^*$ (resp. $\rightarrow_{\Delta}^{\not\epsilon*}$). When Δ is attached to a tree automaton $\mathcal{A}$ we also note those two relations $\rightarrow_{\mathcal{A}}^*$ and $\rightarrow_{\mathcal{A}}^{\not\epsilon*}$, respectively. A tree automaton $\mathcal{A}$ is complete if for all $s \in \mathcal{T}(\mathcal{F})$ there exists a state q of $\mathcal{A}$ such that $s \rightarrow_{\mathcal{A}}^* q$. The language (resp. $\not\!\epsilon$-language) recognized by $\mathcal{A}$ in a state q is $\mathcal{L}(\mathcal{A}, q) = \{t \in \mathcal{T}(\mathcal{F}) \mid t \rightarrow_{\mathcal{A}}^* q\}$ (resp. $\mathcal{L}^{\not\epsilon}(\mathcal{A}, q) = \{t \in \mathcal{T}(\mathcal{F}) \mid t \rightarrow_{\mathcal{A}}^{\not\epsilon *} q\}$). A state q of an automaton $\mathcal{A}$ is *reachable* (resp. $\not\!\epsilon$-reachable) if $\mathcal{L}(\mathcal{A}, q) \neq \emptyset$ (resp. $\mathcal{L}^{\not\epsilon}(\mathcal{A}, q) \neq \emptyset$). We define $\mathcal{L}(\mathcal{A}) = \bigcup_{q \in \mathcal{Q}_F} \mathcal{L}(\mathcal{A}, q)$. A set of transitions Δ is $\not\!\epsilon$-deterministic if there are no two normalized transitions in Δ with the same left-hand side. A tree automaton $\mathcal{A}$ is $\not\!\epsilon$-deterministic if its set of transitions is $\not\!\epsilon$-deterministic. Note that if $\mathcal{A}$ is $\not\!\epsilon$-deterministic then for all states q_1, q_2 of $\mathcal{A}$ such that $q_1 \neq q_2$, we have $\mathcal{L}^{\not\epsilon}(\mathcal{A}, q_1) \cap \mathcal{L}^{\not\epsilon}(\mathcal{A}, q_2) = \emptyset$.

4   Tree Automata Completion Algorithm

Tree Automata Completion algorithms were proposed in [9,13,16,22]. They are very similar to a Knuth-Bendix completion except that they run on two distinct sets of rules: a TRS $\mathcal{R}$ and a set of transitions Δ of a tree automaton $\mathcal{A}$.

Starting from a tree automaton $\mathcal{A}_0 = \langle \mathcal{F}, \mathcal{Q}, \mathcal{Q}_f, \Delta_0 \rangle$ and a left-linear TRS $\mathcal{R}$, the algorithm computes a tree automaton $\mathcal{A}'$ such that $\mathcal{L}(\mathcal{A}') = \mathcal{R}^*(\mathcal{L}(\mathcal{A}_0))$ or $\mathcal{L}(\mathcal{A}') \supseteq \mathcal{R}^*(\mathcal{L}(\mathcal{A}_0))$. The algorithm iteratively computes tree automata $\mathcal{A}_{\mathcal{R}}^1$, $\mathcal{A}_{\mathcal{R}}^2$, ... such that $\forall i \geq 0 : \mathcal{L}(\mathcal{A}_{\mathcal{R}}^i) \subseteq \mathcal{L}(\mathcal{A}_{\mathcal{R}}^{i+1})$ until we get an automaton $\mathcal{A}_{\mathcal{R}}^k$ with $k \in \mathbb{N}$ and $\mathcal{L}(\mathcal{A}_{\mathcal{R}}^k) = \mathcal{L}(\mathcal{A}_{\mathcal{R}}^{k+1})$. For all $i \in \mathbb{N}$, if $s \in \mathcal{L}(\mathcal{A}_{\mathcal{R}}^k)$ and $s \rightarrow_{\mathcal{R}} t$, then $t \in \mathcal{L}(\mathcal{A}_{\mathcal{R}}^{i+1})$. Thus, if $\mathcal{A}_{\mathcal{R}}^k$ is a fixpoint then it also verifies $\mathcal{L}(\mathcal{A}_{\mathcal{R}}^k) \supseteq \mathcal{R}^*(\mathcal{L}(\mathcal{A}_0))$. To construct $\mathcal{A}_{\mathcal{R}}^{i+1}$ from $\mathcal{A}_{\mathcal{R}}^i$, we achieve a *completion step* which consists in finding *critical pairs* between $\rightarrow_{\mathcal{R}}$ and $\rightarrow_{\mathcal{A}_{\mathcal{R}}^i}$. A critical pair is a triple $(l \rightarrow r, \sigma, q)$ where $l \rightarrow r \in \mathcal{R}$, $\sigma : \mathcal{X} \mapsto \mathcal{Q}$ and $q \in \mathcal{Q}$ such that $l\sigma \rightarrow_{\mathcal{A}_{\mathcal{R}}^i}^* q$ and $r\sigma \not\rightarrow_{\mathcal{A}_{\mathcal{R}}^i}^* q$. For $r\sigma$ to be recognized by the same state and thus model the rewriting of $l\sigma$ into $r\sigma$, it is enough to add the necessary transitions to $\mathcal{A}_{\mathcal{R}}^i$ to obtain $\mathcal{A}_{\mathcal{R}}^{i+1}$ such that $r\sigma \rightarrow_{\mathcal{A}_{\mathcal{R}}^{i+1}}^* q$. In [13,22], critical pairs are joined in the following way:

$$
\begin{array}{ccc}
l\sigma & \xrightarrow{\ \mathcal{R}\ } & r\sigma \\
{\scriptstyle \mathcal{A}_{\mathcal{R}}^i} \downarrow & & \downarrow {\scriptstyle \mathcal{A}_{\mathcal{R}}^{i+1}} \\
q & \xleftarrow[\ \mathcal{A}_{\mathcal{R}}^{i+1}\ ]{} & q'
\end{array}
$$

From an algorithmic point of view, there remains two problems to solve: find all the critical pairs $(l \rightarrow r, \sigma, q)$ and find the transitions to add to $\mathcal{A}_{\mathcal{R}}^i$ to have $r\sigma \rightarrow_{\mathcal{A}_{\mathcal{R}}^{i+1}}^* q$. The first problem, called matching, can be efficiently solved using a specific algorithm [8,10]. The second problem is solved using Normalization.

4.1   Normalization

The normalization function replaces subterms either by states of $\mathcal{Q}$ (using transitions of Δ) or by new states. A state q of $\mathcal{Q}$ is used to normalize a term t if $t \rightarrow_{\Delta}^{\not\epsilon} q$. Normalizing by reusing states of $\mathcal{Q}$ and transitions of Δ permits to preserve the $\not\!\epsilon$-determinism of $\rightarrow_{\Delta}^{\not\epsilon}$. Indeed, $\rightarrow_{\Delta}^{\not\epsilon}$ can be kept deterministic during completion though $\rightarrow_{\Delta}$ cannot.

Definition 1 (New state). *Given a set of transitions Δ, a new state (for Δ) is a state of $Q \setminus Q_f$ not occurring in left or right-hand sides of rules of Δ^1.*

We here define normalization as a bottom-up process. This definition is simpler and equivalent to top-down definitions [13]. In the recursive call, the choice of the context $C[]$ may be non deterministic but all the possible results are the equivalent modulo state renaming.

Definition 2 (Normalization). *Let Δ be a set of transitions defined on a set of states Q, $t \in T(F \cup Q) \setminus Q$. Let $C[\,]$ be a non empty context of $T(F \cup Q) \setminus Q$, $f \in F$ of arity n, and $q, q', q_1, \ldots, q_n \in Q$. The normalization function is inductively defined by:*

1. $Norm_\Delta(f(q_1, \ldots, q_n) \to q) = \{f(q_1, \ldots, q_n) \to q\}$
2. $Norm_\Delta(C[f(q_1, \ldots, q_n)] \to q) = \{f(q_1, \ldots, q_n) \to q'\} \cup$

$$Norm_{\Delta \cup \{f(q_1, \ldots, q_n) \to q'\}}(C[q'] \to q)$$

   where either $(f(q_1, \ldots, q_n) \to q' \in \Delta)$ or $(q'$ is a new state for Δ and $\forall q'' \in Q : f(q_1, \ldots, q_n) \to q'' \notin \Delta)$.

In the second case of the definition, if there are several states q' such that $f(q_1, \ldots, q_n) \to q' \in \Delta$, we arbitrarily choose one of them. We illustrate the above definition on the normalization of a simple transition.

Example 1. Given $\Delta = \{b \to q_0\}$, $Norm_\Delta(f(g(a), b, g(a)) \to q) = \{a \to q_1, g(q_1) \to q_2, b \to q_0, f(q_2, q_0, q_2) \to q\}$.

4.2 One Step of Completion

A step of completion only consists in joining critical pairs. We first need to formally define the substitutions under concern: *state substitutions*.

Definition 3 (State substitutions, $\Sigma(Q, X)$). *A state substitution over an automaton A with a set of states Q is a function $\sigma : X \mapsto Q$. We can extend this definition to a morphism $\sigma : T(F, X) \mapsto T(F, Q)$. We denote by $\Sigma(Q, X)$ the set of state substitutions built over Q and X.*

Definition 4 (Set of critical pairs). *Let a TRS R and a tree automaton $A = \langle F, Q, Q_f, \Delta \rangle$. The set of critical pairs between R and A is $CP(R, A) = \{(l \to r, \sigma, q) \mid l \to r \in R, q \in Q, \sigma \in \Sigma(Q, X), l\sigma \to_A^* q, r\sigma \not\to_A^* q\}$.*

Recall that the completion process builds a sequence $A_R^0, A_R^1, \ldots, A_R^k$ of automata such that if $s \in \mathcal{L}(A_R^i)$ and $s \to_R t$ then $t \in \mathcal{L}(A_R^{i+1})$. One step of completion, *i.e.* the process computing A_R^{i+1} from A_R^i, is defined as follows. Again, the following definition is a simplification of the definition of [13].

---

[1] Since Q is a countably infinite set of states, Q_f and Δ are finite, a new state can always be found.

Definition 5 (One step of completion). *Let $\mathcal{A} = \langle \mathcal{F}, \mathcal{Q}, \mathcal{Q}_f, \Delta \rangle$ be a tree automaton, $\mathcal{R}$ be a left-linear TRS. The one step completed automaton is $\mathcal{C}_{\mathcal{R}}(\mathcal{A}) = \langle \mathcal{F}, \mathcal{Q}, \mathcal{Q}_f, Join^{CP(\mathcal{R},\mathcal{A})}(\Delta) \rangle$ where $Join^S(\Delta)$ is inductively defined by:*

- *$Join^{\emptyset}(\Delta) = \Delta$*
- *$Join^{\{(l \to r, q, \sigma)\} \cup S}(\Delta) = Join^S(\Delta \cup \Delta')$ where*
  $\Delta' = \{q' \to q\}$ if there exists $q' \in \mathcal{Q}$ s.t. $r\sigma \to_{\mathcal{A}}^{\emptyset *} q'$, and otherwise
  $\Delta' = Norm_{\Delta}(r\sigma \to q') \cup \{q' \to q\}$ where q' is a new state for Δ

Example 2. Let $\mathcal{A}$ be a tree automaton with $\Delta = \{f(q_1) \to q_0, a \to q_1, g(q_1) \to q_2\}$. If $\mathcal{R} = \{f(x) \to f(g(x))\}$ then $CP(\mathcal{R}, \mathcal{A}) = \{(f(x) \to f(g(x)), \sigma_3, q_0)\}$ with $\sigma_3 = \{x \mapsto q_1\}$, because $f(x)\sigma_3 \to_{\mathcal{A}}^{*} q_0$ and $f(x)\sigma_3 \to_{\mathcal{R}} f(g(x))\sigma_3$. We have $f(g(x))\sigma_3 = f(g(q_1))$ and there exists no state q such that $f(g(q_1)) \to_{\mathcal{A}}^{\emptyset *} q$. Hence, $Join^{\{(f(x) \to f(g(x)), \sigma_3, q_0)\}}(\Delta) = Join^{\emptyset}(\Delta \cup Norm_{\Delta}(f(g(q_1)) \to q_3) \cup \{q_3 \to q_0\})$. Since $Norm_{\Delta}(f(g(q_1)) \to q_3) = \{f(q_2) \to q_3, g(q_1) \to q_2\}$, we get that $\mathcal{C}_{\mathcal{R}}(\mathcal{A}) = \langle \mathcal{F}, \mathcal{Q} \cup \{q_3\}, \mathcal{Q}_f, \Delta \cup \{f(q_2) \to q_3, q_3 \to q_0\} \rangle$.

4.3   Simplification of Tree Automata by Equations

In this section, we define the *simplification* of tree automata $\mathcal{A}$ w.r.t. a set of equations E. This operation permits to over-approximate languages that cannot be recognized *exactly* using tree automata completion, *e.g.* non regular languages. The simplification operation consists in finding E-equivalent terms recognized in $\mathcal{A}$ by different states and then by merging those states together. The merging of states is performed using renaming of a state in a tree automaton.

Definition 6 (Renaming of a state in a tree automaton). *Let $\mathcal{Q}, \mathcal{Q}'$ be set of states, $\mathcal{A} = \langle \mathcal{F}, \mathcal{Q}, \mathcal{Q}_f, \Delta \rangle$ be a tree automaton, and α a function $\alpha : \mathcal{Q} \mapsto \mathcal{Q}'$. We denote by $\mathcal{A}\alpha$ the tree automaton where every occurrence of q is replaced by $\alpha(q)$ in $\mathcal{Q}, \mathcal{Q}_f$ and in every left and right-hand side of every transition of Δ.*

If there exists a bijection α such that $\mathcal{A} = \mathcal{A}'\alpha$ then $\mathcal{A}$ and $\mathcal{A}'$ are said to be *equivalent modulo renaming*. Now we define the *simplification relation* which merges states in a tree automaton according to an equation. Note that it is not required for equations of E to be linear.

Definition 7 (Simplification relation). *Let $\mathcal{A} = \langle \mathcal{F}, \mathcal{Q}, \mathcal{Q}_f, \Delta \rangle$ be a tree automaton and E be a set of equations. For $s = t \in E$, $\sigma \in \Sigma(\mathcal{Q}, \mathcal{X})$, $q_a, q_b \in \mathcal{Q}$ such that $s\sigma \to_{\mathcal{A}}^{\emptyset *} q_a$, $t\sigma \to_{\mathcal{A}}^{\emptyset *} q_b$, and $q_a \neq q_b$ then $\mathcal{A}$ can be simplified into $\mathcal{A}' = \mathcal{A}\{q_b \mapsto q_a\}$, denoted by $\mathcal{A} \leadsto_E \mathcal{A}'$.*

Example 3. Let $E = \{s(s(x)) = s(x)\}$ and $\mathcal{A}$ be the tree automaton with set of transitions $\Delta = \{a \to q_0, s(q_0) \to q_1, s(q_1) \to q_2\}$. We can perform a simplification step using the equation $s(s(x)) = s(x)$ because we found a substitution $\sigma = \{x \mapsto q_0\}$ such that: $s(s(x))\sigma \to_{\mathcal{A}}^{\emptyset *} q_2$ and $s(x)\sigma \to_{\mathcal{A}}^{\emptyset *} q_1$ Hence, $\mathcal{A} \leadsto_E \mathcal{A}' = \mathcal{A}\{q_2 \mapsto q_1\}$[2]

---

[2] or $\{q_1 \mapsto q_2\}$, any of q_1 or q_2 can be used for renaming.

As stated in [13], simplification $\leadsto_E$ is a terminating relation (each step suppresses a state) and it enlarges the language recognized by a tree automaton, *i.e.* if $\mathcal{A} \leadsto_E \mathcal{A}'$ then $\mathcal{L}(\mathcal{A}) \subseteq \mathcal{L}(\mathcal{A}')$. Furthermore, no matter how simplification steps are performed, the obtained automata are equivalent modulo state renaming. In the following, $\mathcal{A} \leadsto_E^! \mathcal{A}'$ denotes that $\mathcal{A} \leadsto_E^* \mathcal{A}'$ and $\mathcal{A}'$ is irreducible by $\leadsto_E$. We denote by $\mathcal{S}_E(\mathcal{A})$ any automaton $\mathcal{A}'$ such that $\mathcal{A} \leadsto_E^! \mathcal{A}'$.

Theorem 1 (Simplified Tree Automata [13]). *Let $\mathcal{A}, \mathcal{A}'_1, \mathcal{A}'_2$ be tree automata and E be a set of equations. If $\mathcal{A} \leadsto_E^! \mathcal{A}'_1$ and $\mathcal{A} \leadsto_E^! \mathcal{A}'_2$ then $\mathcal{A}'_1$ and $\mathcal{A}'_2$ are equivalent modulo state renaming.*

4.4 The Full Completion Algorithm

Definition 8 (Automaton completion). *Let $\mathcal{A}$ be a tree automaton, $\mathcal{R}$ a left-linear TRS and E a set of equations.*

- $\mathcal{A}^0_{\mathcal{R},E} = \mathcal{A}$
- $\mathcal{A}^{n+1}_{\mathcal{R},E} = \mathcal{S}_E\left(\mathcal{C}_\mathcal{R}(\mathcal{A}^n_{\mathcal{R},E})\right)$, *for $n \geq 0$*

If there exists $k \in \mathbb{N}$ such that $\mathcal{A}^k_{\mathcal{R},E} = \mathcal{A}^{k+1}_{\mathcal{R},E}$, then we denote $\mathcal{A}^k_{\mathcal{R},E}$ by $\mathcal{A}^*_{\mathcal{R},E}$.

In practice, checking if $CP(\mathcal{R}, \mathcal{A}^k_{\mathcal{R},E}) = \emptyset$ is sufficient to know that $\mathcal{A}^k_{\mathcal{R},E}$ is a fixpoint. However, a fixpoint cannot always be finitely reached[3]. To ensure termination, one can provide a set of approximating equations to overcome infinite rewriting and completion divergence.

Example 4. Let $\mathcal{R} = \{f(x,y) \to f(s(x), s(y))\}$, $E = \{s(s(x)) = s(x)\}$ and $\mathcal{A}^0$ be the tree automaton with set of transitions $\Delta = \{f(q_a, q_b) \to q_0), a \to q_a, b \to q_b\}$, *i.e.* $\mathcal{L}(\mathcal{A}^0) = \{f(a,b)\}$. The completion ends after two completion steps on $\mathcal{A}^2_{\mathcal{R},E}$ which is a fixpoint. Completion steps are summed up in the following table. To simplify the presentation, we do not repeat the common transitions: $\mathcal{A}^i_{\mathcal{R},E}$ and $\mathcal{C}_\mathcal{R}(\mathcal{A}^i)$ columns are supposed to contain all transitions of $\mathcal{A}^0, \dots, \mathcal{A}^{i-1}_{\mathcal{R},E}$. The automaton $\mathcal{A}^1_{\mathcal{R},E}$ is exactly $\mathcal{C}_\mathcal{R}(\mathcal{A}^0)$ since simplification by equations do not apply. Simplification has been applied on $\mathcal{C}_\mathcal{R}(\mathcal{A}^1_{\mathcal{R},E})$ to obtain $\mathcal{A}^2_{\mathcal{R},E}$.

$\mathcal{A}^0$	$\mathcal{C}_\mathcal{R}(\mathcal{A}^0)$	$\mathcal{A}^1_{\mathcal{R},E}$	$\mathcal{C}_\mathcal{R}(\mathcal{A}^1_{\mathcal{R},E})$	$\mathcal{A}^2_{\mathcal{R},E}$
$f(q_a, q_b) \to q_0$	$f(q_1, q_2) \to q_3$	$f(q_1, q_2) \to q_3$	$f(q_4, q_5) \to q_6$	$f(q_1, q_2) \to q_6$
$a \to q_a$	$s(q_a) \to q_1$	$s(q_a) \to q_1$	$s(q_1) \to q_4$	$s(q_1) \to q_1$
$b \to q_b$	$s(q_b) \to q_2$	$s(q_b) \to q_2$	$s(q_2) \to q_5$	$s(q_2) \to q_2$
	$q_3 \to q_0$	$q_3 \to q_0$	$q_6 \to q_3$	

Now, we recall the lower and upper bound theorems. Tree automata completion of automaton $\mathcal{A}$ with TRS $\mathcal{R}$ and set of equations E is lower bounded by $\mathcal{R}^*(\mathcal{L}(\mathcal{A}))$ and upper bounded by $\mathcal{R}^*_E(\mathcal{L}(\mathcal{A}))$. The lower bound theorem ensures that the completed automaton $\mathcal{A}^*_{\mathcal{R},E}$ recognizes all $\mathcal{R}$-reachable terms (but not all $\mathcal{R}/E$-reachable terms). The upper bound theorem guarantees that all terms recognized by $\mathcal{A}^*_{\mathcal{R},E}$ are only $\mathcal{R}/E$-reachable terms.

---

[3] See [10], for classes of $\mathcal{R}$ for which a fixpoint always exists.

Theorem 2 (Lower bound [13]). *Let $\mathcal{R}$ be a left-linear TRS, $\mathcal{A}$ be a tree automaton and E be a set of equations. If completion terminates on $\mathcal{A}^*_{\mathcal{R},E}$ then $\mathcal{L}(\mathcal{A}^*_{\mathcal{R},E}) \supseteq \mathcal{R}^*(\mathcal{L}(\mathcal{A}))$.*

The upper bound theorem states the precision result of completion. It is defined using the $\mathcal{R}/E$-coherence property. The intuition behind $\mathcal{R}/E$-coherence is the following: in the tree automaton ϵ-transitions represent rewriting steps and normalized transitions recognize E-equivalence classes. More precisely, in a $\mathcal{R}/E$-coherent tree automaton, if two terms s, t are recognized into the same state q using only normalized transitions then they belong to the same E-equivalence class. Otherwise, if at least one ϵ-transition is necessary to recognize, say, t into q then at least one step of rewriting was necessary to obtain t from s.

Theorem 3 (Upper bound [13]). *Let $\mathcal{R}$ be a left-linear TRS, E a set of equations and $\mathcal{A}$ a $\mathcal{R}/E$-coherent tree automaton. For any $i \in \mathbb{N}$: $\mathcal{L}(\mathcal{A}^i_{\mathcal{R},E}) \subseteq \mathcal{R}^*_E(\mathcal{L}(\mathcal{A}))$ and $\mathcal{A}^i_{\mathcal{R},E}$ is $\mathcal{R}/E$-coherent.*

5   Termination Criterion for a Given Set of Equations

Given a set of equations E, the effect of the simplification with E on a tree automaton is to merge two distinct states recognizing instances of the left and right-hand side for all the equations of E. In this section, we give a sufficient condition on E and on the completed tree automata $\mathcal{A}^i_{\mathcal{R},E}$ for the tree automata completion to always terminate. The intuition behind this condition is simple: if the set of equivalence classes for E, *i.e.* $\mathcal{T}(\mathcal{F})/_{=_E}$, is finite then so should be the set of new states used in completion. However, this is not true in general because simplification of an automaton with E does not necessarily merge all E-equivalent terms.

Example 5. Let $\mathcal{A}$ be the tree automaton with set of transitions $a \to q$, $\mathcal{R} = \{a \to c\}$ and let $E = \{a = b, b = c\}$. The set of transitions of $\mathcal{C}_\mathcal{R}(\mathcal{A})$ is $\{a \to q, c \to q', q' \to q\}$. We have $a =_E c$, $a \in \mathcal{L}^q(\mathcal{C}_\mathcal{R}(\mathcal{A}), q)$ and $c \in \mathcal{L}^q(\mathcal{C}_\mathcal{R}(\mathcal{A}), q')$ but on the automaton $\mathcal{C}_\mathcal{R}(\mathcal{A})$, no simplification situation (as described by Definition 7), can be found because the term b is not recognized by $\mathcal{C}_\mathcal{R}(\mathcal{A})$. Hence, the simplified automaton is $\mathcal{C}_\mathcal{R}(\mathcal{A})$ where a and c are recognized by different states.

There is no simple solution to have a simplification algorithm merging all states recognizing E-equivalent terms (see Sect. 6). Having a complete automaton $\mathcal{A}$ solve the above problem but leads to rough approximations (see [11]). In the next section, we propose to give some simple restrictions on E to ensure that completion terminates. In Sect. 5.2, we will see how those restrictions can easily be met for "functional" TRS, *i.e.* a typed first-order functional program translated into a TRS.

5.1   General Criterion

What Example 5 shows is that, for a simplification with E to apply, it is necessary that both sides of the equation are recognized by the tree automaton. In the following, we will define a set E^c of *contracting* equations so that this property is true. What Example 5 does not show is that, by default, tree automata are not E-compatible. In particular, any non ϵ-deterministic automaton does not satisfy the reflexivity of $=_E$. For instance, if an automaton $\mathcal{A}$ has two transitions $a \to q_1$ and $a \to q_2$, since $a =_E a$ for all E, for $\mathcal{A}$ to be E-compatible we should have $q_1 = q_2$. To enforce ϵ-determinism by automata simplification, we define a set of *reflexivity equations* as follows.

Definition 9 (Set of reflexivity equations E^r). *For a given set of symbols $\mathcal{F}$, $E^r = \{f(x_1, \ldots, x_n) = f(x_1, \ldots, x_n) \mid f \in \mathcal{F}$, and arity of f is $n\}$, where $x_1 \ldots x_n$ are pairwise distinct variables.*

Note that for all set of equations E, the relation $=_E$ is trivially equivalent to $=_{E \cup E^r}$. Furthermore, simplification with E^r transforms all automaton into an ϵ-deterministic automaton, as stated in the following lemma.

Lemma 1. *For all tree automaton $\mathcal{A}$ and all set of equation E, if $E \supseteq E^r$ and $\mathcal{A} \leadsto^!_E \mathcal{A}'$ then $\mathcal{A}'$ is ϵ-deterministic.*

Proof. Shown by induction on the height of terms (see [11] for details).   □

We now define sets of contracting equations. Such sets are defined for a set of symbols $\mathcal{K}$ which can be a subset of $\mathcal{F}$. This will be used later to restrict contracting equations to the subset of constructor symbols of $\mathcal{F}$.

Definition 10 (Sets of contracting equations for $\mathcal{K}$, $E^c_\mathcal{K}$). *Let $\mathcal{K} \subseteq \mathcal{F}$. A set of equations is contracting for $\mathcal{K}$, denoted by $E^c_\mathcal{K}$, if all equations of $E^c_\mathcal{K}$ are of the form $u = u|_p$ with $u \in \mathcal{T}(\mathcal{K}, \mathcal{X})$ a linear term, $p \neq \lambda$, and if the set of normal forms of $\mathcal{T}(\mathcal{K})$ w.r.t. the TRS $\overrightarrow{E^c_\mathcal{K}} = \{u \to u|_p \mid u = u|_p \in E^c_\mathcal{K}\}$ is finite.*

Contracting equations, if defined on $\mathcal{F}$, define an upper bound on the number of states of a simplified automaton.

Lemma 2. *Let $\mathcal{A}$ be a tree automaton and $E^c_\mathcal{F}$ a set of contracting equations for $\mathcal{F}$. If $E \supseteq E^c_\mathcal{F} \cup E^r$ then the simplified automaton $\mathcal{S}_E(\mathcal{A})$ is an ϵ-deterministic automaton having no more states than terms in $\mathrm{IRR}(\overrightarrow{E^c_\mathcal{F}})$.*

Proof. First, assume for all state q of $\mathcal{S}_E(\mathcal{A})$, $\mathcal{L}^\epsilon(\mathcal{S}_E(\mathcal{A}), q) \cap \mathrm{IRR}(\overrightarrow{E^c_\mathcal{F}}) = \emptyset$. Then, for all terms s such that $s \to^{\epsilon*}_{\mathcal{S}_E(\mathcal{A})} q$, we know that s is not in normal form w.r.t. $\overrightarrow{E^c_\mathcal{F}}$. As a result, the left-hand side of an equation of $E^c_\mathcal{F}$ can be applied to s. This means that there exists an equation $u = u|_p$, a ground context C and a substitution θ such that $s = C[u\theta]$. Furthermore, since $s \to^{\epsilon*}_{\mathcal{S}_E(\mathcal{A})} q$, we know that $C[u\theta] \to^{\epsilon*}_{\mathcal{S}_E(\mathcal{A})} q$ and that there exists a state q' such that $C[q'] \to^{\epsilon*}_{\mathcal{S}_E(\mathcal{A})} q$

and $u\theta \rightarrow^{\ell*}_{\mathcal{S}_E(\mathcal{A})} q'$. From $u\theta \rightarrow^{\ell*}_{\mathcal{S}_E(\mathcal{A})} q'$, we know that all subterms of $u\theta$ are recognized by at least one state in $\mathcal{S}_E(\mathcal{A})$. Thus, there exists a state q'' such that $u|_p\theta \rightarrow^{\ell*}_{\mathcal{S}_E(\mathcal{A})} q''$. We thus have a situation of application of the equation $u = u|_p$ in the automaton. Since $\mathcal{S}_E(\mathcal{A})$ is simplified, we thus know that $q' = q''$. As mentioned above, we know that $C[q'] \rightarrow^{\ell*}_{\mathcal{S}_E(\mathcal{A})} q$. Hence $C[u|_p\theta] \rightarrow^{\ell*}_{\mathcal{S}_E(\mathcal{A})}$ $C[q'] \rightarrow^{\ell*}_{\mathcal{S}_E(\mathcal{A})} q$. If $C[u|_p\theta]$ is not in normal form w.r.t. $\overrightarrow{E^c_{\mathcal{F}}}$ then we can do the same reasoning on $C[u|_p\theta] \rightarrow^{\ell*}_{\mathcal{S}_E(\mathcal{A})} q$ until getting a term that is in normal form w.r.t. $\overrightarrow{E^c_{\mathcal{F}}}$ and recognized by the same state q. Thus, this contradicts the fact that $\mathcal{S}_E(\mathcal{A})$ recognizes no term of $\text{IRR}(\overrightarrow{E^c_{\mathcal{F}}})$.

Then, by definition of $E^c_{\mathcal{F}}$, $\text{IRR}(\overrightarrow{E^c_{\mathcal{F}}})$ is finite. Let $\{t_1, \ldots, t_n\}$ be the subset of $\text{IRR}(\overrightarrow{E^c_{\mathcal{F}}})$ recognized by $\mathcal{S}_E(\mathcal{A})$. Let $q_1, \ldots, q_n$ be the states recognizing $t_1, \ldots, t_n$ respectively. We know that there is a finite set of states recognizing $t_1, \ldots, t_n$ because $E \supseteq E^r$ and Lemma 1 entails that $\mathcal{S}_E(\mathcal{A})$ is ℓ-deterministic. Now, for all terms s recognized by a state q in $\mathcal{S}_E(\mathcal{A})$, i.e. $s \rightarrow^{\ell*}_{\mathcal{S}_E(\mathcal{A})} q$, we can use a reasoning similar to the one carried out above and show that q is equal to one state of $\{q_1, \ldots, q_n\}$ recognizing normal forms of $\overrightarrow{E^c_{\mathcal{F}}}$ in $\mathcal{S}_E(\mathcal{A})$. Finally, there are at most $card(\text{IRR}(\overrightarrow{E^c_{\mathcal{F}}}))$ states in $\mathcal{S}_E(\mathcal{A})$.   □

Now it is possible to state the Theorem guaranteeing the termination of completion if the set of equations E contains a set of contracting equations $E^c_{\mathcal{F}}$ for $\mathcal{F}$ and a set of reflexivity equations.

Theorem 4. *Let $\mathcal{A}$ be a tree automaton, $\mathcal{R}$ a left linear TRS and E a set of equations. If $E \supseteq E^r \cup E^c_{\mathcal{F}}$, then completion of $\mathcal{A}$ by $\mathcal{R}$ and E terminates.*

Proof. For completion to diverge it must produce infinitely many new states. This is impossible if E contains $E^c_{\mathcal{F}}$ and E^r (see Lemma 2).   □

5.2   Criterion for Functional TRSs

Now, we consider functional programs viewed as TRSs. We assume that such TRSs are left-linear, which is a common assumption on TRSs obtained from functional programs [2]. In this section, we will restrict ourselves to sufficiently complete TRSs obtained from functional programs and will refer to them as *functional TRSs*. For TRSs representing functional programs, defining contracting equations of $E^c_{\mathcal{C}}$ on $\mathcal{C}$ rather than on $\mathcal{F}$ is enough to guarantee termination of completion. This is more convenient and also closer to what is usually done in static analysis where abstractions are usually defined on data and not on function applications. Since the TRSs we consider are sufficiently complete, any term of $\mathcal{T}(\mathcal{F})$ can be rewritten into a data-term of $\mathcal{T}(\mathcal{C})$. As above, using equations of $E^c_{\mathcal{C}}$ we are going to ensure that the data-terms of the computed languages will be recognized by a bounded set of states. To lift-up this property to $\mathcal{T}(\mathcal{F})$ it is enough to ensure that $\forall s, t \in \mathcal{T}(\mathcal{F})$ if $s \rightarrow_R t$ then s and t are recognized by equivalent states. This is the role of the set of equations E_R.

Definition 11 ($E_\mathcal{R}$). *Let $\mathcal{R}$ be a TRS, the set of $\mathcal{R}$-equations is $E_\mathcal{R} = \{l = r \mid l \to r \in \mathcal{R}\}$.*

Theorem 5. *Let $\mathcal{A}_0$ be a tree automaton, $\mathcal{R}$ a sufficiently complete left-linear TRS and E a set of equations. If $E \supseteq E^r \cup E_\mathcal{C}^c \cup E_\mathcal{R}$ with $E_\mathcal{C}^c$ contracting then completion of $\mathcal{A}_0$ by $\mathcal{R}$ and E terminates.*

Proof. Firstly, to show that the number of states recognizing terms of $\mathcal{T}(\mathcal{C})$ is finite we can do a proof similar to the one of Lemma 2. Let $G \subseteq \mathcal{T}(\mathcal{C})$ be the finite set of normal forms of $\mathcal{T}(\mathcal{C})$ w.r.t. $\overrightarrow{E_\mathcal{C}^c}$. Since $E \supseteq E^r \cup E_\mathcal{C}^c$, like in the proof of Lemma 2, we can show that in any completed automaton, terms of $\mathcal{T}(\mathcal{C})$ are recognized by no more states than terms in G. Secondly, since $\mathcal{R}$ is sufficiently complete, for all terms $s \in \mathcal{T}(\mathcal{F}) \setminus \mathcal{T}(\mathcal{C})$ we know that there exists a term $t \in \mathcal{T}(\mathcal{C})$ such that $s \to_\mathcal{R}^* t$. The fact that $E \supseteq E_\mathcal{R}$ guarantees that s and t will be recognized by equivalent states in the completed (and simplified) automaton. Since the number of states necessary to recognize $\mathcal{T}(\mathcal{C})$ is finite, so is the number of states necessary to recognize terms of $\mathcal{T}(\mathcal{F})$. □

Finally, to exploit the types of the functional program, we now see $\mathcal{F}$ as a many-sorted signature whose set of sorts is $\mathcal{S}$. Each symbol $f \in \mathcal{F}$ is associated to a profile $f : S_1 \times \ldots \times S_k \mapsto S$ where $S_1, \ldots, S_k, S \in \mathcal{S}$ and k is the arity of f. Well-sorted terms are inductively defined as follows: $f(t_1, \ldots, t_k)$ is a well-sorted term of sort S if $f : S_1 \times \ldots \times S_k \mapsto S$ and $t_1, \ldots, t_k$ are well-sorted terms of sorts $S_1, \ldots, S_k$, respectively. We denote by $\mathcal{T}(\mathcal{F}, \mathcal{X})^\mathcal{S}$, $\mathcal{T}(\mathcal{F})^\mathcal{S}$ and $\mathcal{T}(\mathcal{C})^\mathcal{S}$ the set of well-sorted terms, ground terms and constructor terms, respectively. Note that we have $\mathcal{T}(\mathcal{F}, \mathcal{X})^\mathcal{S} \subseteq \mathcal{T}(\mathcal{F}, \mathcal{X})$, $\mathcal{T}(\mathcal{F})^\mathcal{S} \subseteq \mathcal{T}(\mathcal{F})$ and $\mathcal{T}(\mathcal{C})^\mathcal{S} \subseteq \mathcal{T}(\mathcal{C})$. We assume that $\mathcal{R}$ and E are *sort preserving*, *i.e.* that for all rule $l \to r \in R$ and all equation $u = v \in E$, $l, r, u, v \in \mathcal{T}(\mathcal{F}, \mathcal{X})^\mathcal{S}$, l and r have the same sort and so do u and v. Note that well-typedness of the functional program entails the well-sortedness of $\mathcal{R}$. We still assume that the (sorted) TRS is sufficiently complete, which is defined in a similar way except that it holds only for well-sorted terms, *i.e.* for all $s \in \mathcal{T}(\mathcal{F})^\mathcal{S}$ there exists a term $t \in \mathcal{T}(\mathcal{C})^\mathcal{S}$ such that $s \to_\mathcal{R}^* t$. We slightly refine the definition of contracting equations as follows. For all sort S, if S has a unique constant symbol we note it c^S.

Definition 12 (Set $E_{\mathcal{K},\mathcal{S}}^c$ of contracting equations for $\mathcal{K}$ and $\mathcal{S}$). *Let $\mathcal{K} \subseteq \mathcal{F}$. The set of well-sorted equations $E_{\mathcal{K},\mathcal{S}}^c$ is contracting (for $\mathcal{K}$) if its equations are of the form (a) $u = u|_p$ with u linear and $p \neq \Lambda$, or (b) $u = c^S$ with u of sort S, and if the set of normal forms of $\mathcal{T}(\mathcal{K})^\mathcal{S}$ w.r.t. the TRS $\overrightarrow{E_{\mathcal{K},\mathcal{S}}^c} = \{u \to v \mid u = v \in E_{\mathcal{K},\mathcal{S}}^c \land (v = u|_p \lor v = c^S)\}$ is finite.*

The termination theorem for completion of sorted TRSs is similar to the previous one except that it needs $\mathcal{R}/E$-coherence of $\mathcal{A}_0$ to ensure that terms recognized by completed automata are well-sorted (see [11] for proof).

Theorem 6. *Let $\mathcal{A}_0$ be a tree automaton recognizing well-sorted terms, $\mathcal{R}$ a sufficiently complete sort-preserving left-linear TRS and E a sort-preserving set* of equations. If $E \supseteq E^r \cup E^c_{\mathcal{C},\mathcal{S}} \cup E_{\mathcal{R}}$ with $E^c_{\mathcal{C},\mathcal{S}}$ contracting and $\mathcal{A}_0$ is $\mathcal{R}/E$-coherent then completion of $\mathcal{A}_0$ by $\mathcal{R}$ and E terminates.

5.3   Experiments

The objective of data-flow analysis is to predict the set of all program states reachable from a language of initial function calls, *i.e.* to over-approximate $\mathcal{R}^*(\mathcal{L}(\mathcal{A}))$ where $\mathcal{R}$ represents the functional program and $\mathcal{A}$ the language of initial function calls. In this setting, we automatically compute an automaton $\mathcal{A}^*_{\mathcal{R},E}$ over-approximating $\mathcal{R}^*(\mathcal{L}(\mathcal{A}))$. But we can do more. Since we are dealing with left-linear TRS, it is possible to build $\mathcal{A}_{\mathrm{IRR}(\mathcal{R})}$ recognizing $\mathrm{IRR}(\mathcal{R})$. Finally, since tree automata are closed under all boolean operations, we can compute an approximation of all the results of the function calls by computing the tree automaton recognizing the intersection between $\mathcal{A}^*_{\mathcal{R},E}$ and $\mathcal{A}_{\mathrm{IRR}(\mathcal{R})}$.

Here is an example of application of those theorems. Completions are performed using Timbuk. All the $\mathcal{A}_{\mathrm{IRR}(\mathcal{R})}$ automata and intersections were performed using Taml. Details can be found in [14].

Ops `append:2 rev:1 nil:0 cons:2 a:0 b:0`   **Vars** `X Y Z U Xs`
TRS R
```
append(nil,X)->X       append(cons(X,Y),Z)->cons(X,append(Y,Z))
rev(nil)->nil          rev(cons(X,Y))->append(rev(Y),cons(X,nil))
```

Automaton A0 States `q0 qla qlb qnil qf qa qb` **Final States** `q0` **Transitions**
```
rev(qla)->q0           cons(qb,qnil)->qlb     cons(qa,qla)->qla     nil->qnil
cons(qa,qlb)->qla      a->qa                  cons(qb,qlb)->qlb     b->qb
```

Equations E Rules   `cons(X,cons(Y,Z))=cons(Y,Z)`   `%%% Ec`
`%%% E_R`   `%%% E^r`
```
append(nil,X)=X                                rev(X)=rev(X)
append(cons(X,Y),Z)=cons(X,append(Y,Z))        cons(X,Y)=cons(X,Y)
rev(nil)=nil                                    append(X,Y)=append(X,Y)
rev(cons(X,Y))=append(rev(Y),cons(X,nil))      a=a  b=b  nil=nil
```

In this example, the TRS $\mathcal{R}$ encodes the classical *reverse* and *append* functions. The language recognized by automaton $\mathcal{A}_0$ is the set of terms of the form $rev([a, a, \ldots, b, b, \ldots])$. Note that there are at least one a and one b in the list. We assume that $\mathcal{S} = \{T, list\}$ and sorts for symbols are the following: $a : T$, $b : T$, $nil : list$, $cons : T \times list \mapsto list$, $append : list \times list \mapsto list$ and $rev : list \mapsto list$. Now, to use Theorem 6, we need to prove each of its assumptions. The set E of equations contains $E_{\mathcal{R}}$, E^r and $E^c_{\mathcal{C},\mathcal{S}}$. The set of Equations $E^c_{\mathcal{C},\mathcal{S}}$ is contracting because the automaton $\mathcal{A}_{\mathrm{IRR}(\overrightarrow{E^c_{\mathcal{C},\mathcal{S}}})}$ recognizes a finite language. This automaton can be computed using Taml: it is the intersection between the automaton $\mathcal{A}_{\mathcal{T}(\mathcal{C})^{\mathcal{S}}}$[4] recognising $\mathcal{T}(\mathcal{C})^{\mathcal{S}}$ and the automaton $\mathcal{A}_{\mathrm{IRR}(\{cons(X,cons(Y,Z)) \rightarrow cons(Y,Z)\})}$:

---

[4] Such an automaton has one state per sort and one transition per constructor. For instance, on our example $\mathcal{A}_{\mathcal{T}(\mathcal{C})^{\mathcal{S}}}$ will have transitions: $a \rightarrow qT$, $b \rightarrow qT$, $cons(qT, qlist) \rightarrow qlist$ and $nil \rightarrow qlist$.

States q2 q1 q0 **Final States** q0 q1 q2
Transitions b->q2 a->q2 nil->q1 cons(q2,q1)->q0

The language of $\mathcal{A}_0$ is well-sorted and E and $\mathcal{R}$ are sort preserving. We can prove sufficient completeness of $\mathcal{R}$ on $\mathcal{T}(\mathcal{F})^{\mathcal{S}}$ using, for instance, Maude [6] or even Timbuk [9] itself. The last assumption of Theorem 6 to prove is that $\mathcal{A}_0$ is $\mathcal{R}/E$-coherent. This can be shown by remarking that each state q of $\mathcal{A}_0$ recognizes at least one term and if $s \rightarrow_{\mathcal{A}_0}^{\not{\in}*} q$ and $t \rightarrow_{\mathcal{A}_0}^{\not{\in}*} q$ then $s \equiv_E t$. For instance $cons(b, cons(b, nil)) \rightarrow_{\mathcal{A}_0}^{\not{\in}*} q_{lb}$ and $cons(b, nil) \rightarrow_{\mathcal{A}_0}^{\not{\in}*} q_{lb}$ and $cons(b, cons(b, nil)) \equiv_E cons(b, nil)$. Thus, completion is guaranteed to terminate: after 4 completion steps (7 ms) we obtain a fixpoint automaton $\mathcal{A}_{\mathcal{R},E}^*$ with 11 transitions. To restrain the language to normal forms it is enough to compute the intersection with $\text{IRR}(R)$. Since we are dealing with sufficiently complete TRSs, we know that $\text{IRR}(R) \subseteq \mathcal{T}(\mathcal{C})^{\mathcal{S}}$. Thus, we can use again $\mathcal{A}_{\mathcal{T}(\mathcal{C})^{\mathcal{S}}}$ for the intersection that is:

States q3 q2 q1 q0 **Final States** q3 **Transitions** a->q0 nil->q1 b->q2 cons(q0,q1)->q3 cons(q0,q3)->q3 cons(q2,q1)->q3 cons(q2,q3)->q3

which recognizes any (non empty) flat list of a and b. Thus, our analysis preserved the property that the result cannot be the empty list but lost the order of the elements in the list. This is not surprising because the equation cons(X, cons(Y, Z)) =cons(X, Z) makes $cons(a, cons(b, nil))$ equal to $cons(a, nil)$. It is possible to refine by hand $E_{\mathcal{C},\mathcal{S}}^c$ using the following equations: cons(a,cons(a,X))=cons(a,X), cons(b,cons(b,X))=cons(b,X), cons(a,cons(b,cons(a,X)))=cons(a,X). This set of equations avoids the previous problem. Again, E verifies the conditions of Theorem 6 and completion is still guaranteed to terminate. The result is the automaton $\mathcal{A}_{\mathcal{R},E}^{\prime*}$ having 19 transitions. This time, intersection with $\mathcal{A}_{\mathcal{T}(\mathcal{C})^{\mathcal{S}}}$ gives:

States q4 q3 q2 q1 q0 **Final States** q4 **Transitions** a->q1 b->q3 nil->q0 cons(q1,q0)->q2 cons(q1,q2)->q2 cons(q3,q2)->q4 cons(q3,q4)->q4

This automaton exactly recognizes lists of the form $[b, b, \ldots, a, a, \ldots]$ with at least one b and one a, as expected. Hopefully, refinement of equations can be automatized in completion [3] and can be used here, see [14] for examples. More examples can be found in the Timbuk 3.1 source distribution.

6 Conclusion and Further Research

In this paper we defined a criterion on the set of approximation equations to guarantee termination of the tree automata completion. When dealing with, so called, functional TRS this criterion is close to what is generally expected in static analysis and abstract interpretation: a finite model for an infinite set of data-terms. This work is a first step to use completion for static analysis of functional programs. There remains some interesting points to address.

Dealing with higher-order functions. Higher-order functions can be encoded into first order TRS using a simple encoding borrowed from [17]: defined symbols become constants, constructor symbols remain the same, and an additional *application* operator '@' of arity 2 is introduced. On all the examples of [21], completion and this simple encoding produces exactly the same results [14].

Dealing with evaluation strategies. The technique proposed here, as well as [21], over-approximates the set of results for all evaluation strategies. As far as we know, no static analysis technique for functional programs can take into account evaluation strategies. However, it is possible to restrict the completion algorithm to recognize only innermost descendants [14], *i.e.* call-by-value results. If the approximation is precise enough, any non terminating program with call-by-value will have an empty set of results. An open research direction is to use this to prove non termination of functional programs by call-by-value strategy.

Dealing with built-in types. Values manipulated by *real* functional programs are not always terms or trees. They can be numerals or be terms embedding numerals. In [12], it has been shown that completion can compute over-approximations of reachable terms embedding built-in terms. The structural part of the term is approximated using tree automata and the built-in part is approximated using lattices and abstract interpretation.

Besides, there remain some interesting theoretical points to solve. In Sect. 5, we saw that having a finite $\mathcal{T}(\mathcal{F})/_{=_E}$ is not enough to guarantee the termination of completion. This is due to the fact that the simplification algorithm does not merge all states recognizing E-equivalent terms. Having a simplification algorithm ensuring this property is not trivial. First, the theory defined by E has to be decidable. Second, even if E is decidable, finding all the E-equivalent terms recognized by the tree automaton is an open problem. Furthermore, proving that $\mathcal{T}(\mathcal{F})/_{=_E}$ is finite, is itself difficult. This question is undecidable in general [23], but can be answered for some particular E. For instance, if E can be oriented into a TRS $\mathcal{R}$ which is terminating, confluent and such that $\mathrm{IRR}(\mathcal{R})$ is finite then $\mathcal{T}(\mathcal{F})/_{=_E}$ is finite [23].

Acknowledgments. Many thanks to the referees for their detailed comments.

References

1. Armando, A., et al.: The AVISPA tool for the automated validation of internet security protocols and applications. In: Etessami, K., Rajamani, S.K. (eds.) CAV 2005. LNCS, vol. 3576, pp. 281–285. Springer, Heidelberg (2005)
2. Baader, F., Nipkow, T.: Term Rewriting and All That. Cambridge University Press, Cambridge (1998)
3. Boichut, Y., Boyer, B., Genet, T., Legay, A.: Equational abstraction refinement for certified tree regular model checking. In: Aoki, T., Taguchi, K. (eds.) ICFEM 2012. LNCS, vol. 7635, pp. 299–315. Springer, Heidelberg (2012)
4. Boichut, Y., Courbis, R., Héam, P.-C., Kouchnarenko, O.: Handling non left-linear rules when completing tree automata. IJFCS **20**(5), 837–849 (2009)

5. Boichut, Y., Genet, T., Jensen, T., Le Roux, L.: Rewriting approximations for fast prototyping of static analyzers. In: Baader, F. (ed.) RTA 2007. LNCS, vol. 4533, pp. 48–62. Springer, Heidelberg (2007)

6. Clavel, M., Durán, F., Eker, S., Lincoln, P., Martí-Oliet, N., Meseguer, J., Talcott, C. (eds.): All About Maude - A High-Performance Logical Framework. LNCS, vol. 4350. Springer, Heidelberg (2007)

7. Comon, H., Dauchet, M., Gilleron, R., Jacquemard, F., Lugiez, D., Löding, C., Tison, S., Tommasi, M.: Tree automata techniques and applications (2008). http://tata.gforge.inria.fr

8. Feuillade, G., Genet, T., Viet Triem Tong, V.: Reachability analysis over term rewriting systems. J. Autom. Reason. **33**(3–4), 341–383 (2004)

9. Genet, T.: Decidable approximations of sets of descendants and sets of normal forms. In: Nipkow, T. (ed.) RTA 1998. LNCS, vol. 1379, pp. 151–165. Springer, Heidelberg (1998)

10. Genet, T.: Reachability analysis of rewriting for software verification. Université de Rennes 1 (2009). Habilitation document. http://www.irisa.fr/celtique/genet/publications.html

11. Genet, T.: Towards static analysis of functional programs using tree automata completion. Technical report, INRIA (2013). http://hal.archives-ouvertes.fr/hal-00921814/PDF/main.pdf

12. Genet, T., Le Gall, T., Legay, A., Murat, V.: A completion algorithm for lattice tree automata. In: Konstantinidis, S. (ed.) CIAA 2013. LNCS, vol. 7982, pp. 134–145. Springer, Heidelberg (2013)

13. Genet, T., Rusu, R.: Equational tree automata completion. J. Symb. Comput. **45**, 574–597 (2010)

14. Genet, T., Salmon, Y.: Tree automata completion for static analysis of functional programs. Technical report, INRIA (2013). http://hal.archives-ouvertes.fr/hal-00780124/PDF/main.pdf

15. Geser, A., Hofbauer, D., Waldmann, J., Zantema, H.: On tree automata that certify termination of left-linear term rewriting systems. In: Giesl, J. (ed.) RTA 2005. LNCS, vol. 3467, pp. 353–367. Springer, Heidelberg (2005)

16. Jacquemard, F.: Decidable approximations of term rewriting systems. In: Ganzinger, H. (ed.) RTA 1996. LNCS, vol. 1103, pp. 362–376. Springer, Heidelberg (1996)

17. Jones, N.D.: Flow analysis of lazy higher-order functional programs. In: Abramsky, S., Hankin, C. (eds.) Abstract Interpretation of Declarative Languages, pp. 103–122. Ellis Horwood, Chichester (1987)

18. Kobayashi, N.: Model checking higher-order programs. J. ACM **60**(3), 20 (2013)

19. Lisitsa, A.: Finite models vs tree automata in safety verification. In: RTA'12. LIPIcs, vol. 15, pp. 225–239 (2012)

20. Oehl, F., Cece, G., Kouchnarenko, O., Sinclair, D.: Automatic approximation for the verification of cryptographic protocols. In: Abdallah, A.E., Ryan, P.Y.A., Schneider, S. (eds.) FASec 2002. LNCS, vol. 2629, pp. 33–48. Springer, Heidelberg (2003)

21. Ong, L., Ramsay, S.: Verifying higher-order functional programs with pattern-matching algebraic data types. In: POPL'11 (2011)

22. Takai, T.: A verification technique using term rewriting systems and abstract interpretation. In: van Oostrom, V. (ed.) RTA 2004. LNCS, vol. 3091, pp. 119–133. Springer, Heidelberg (2004)

23. Tison, S.: Finiteness of the set of E-equivalence classes is undecidable (2010). Private communication

A Framework for Mobile Ad hoc Networks in Real-Time Maude

Si Liu[1]([⊠]), Peter Csaba Ölveczky[2], and José Meseguer[1]

[1] University of Illinois at Urbana-Champaign, Champaign, USA
siliu3@illinois.edu
[2] University of Oslo, Oslo, Norway

Abstract. Mobile ad hoc networks (MANETs) are increasingly popular and deployed in a wide range of environments. However, it is challenging to formally analyze a MANET, both because there are few reasonably accurate formal models of mobility, and because the large state space caused by the movements of the nodes renders straightforward model checking hard. In particular, the combination of wireless communication and node movement is subtle and does not seem to have been adequately addressed in previous formal methods work. This paper presents a formal executable and parameterized modeling framework for MANETs in Real-Time Maude that integrates several mobility models and wireless communication. We illustrate the use of our modeling framework with the Ad hoc On-Demand Distance Vector (AODV) routing protocol, which allows us to analyze this protocol under different mobility models.

1 Introduction

A *mobile ad hoc network* (MANET) is a self-configuring network of mobile devices (laptops, smart phones, sensors, etc.) that communicate wirelessly and cooperate to provide the necessary network functionality. Since MANETs can form ad hoc networks without fixed infrastructure, they are supposed to have a wide applicability, for example for providing ad hoc networks for cooperating "smart" cars, for emergency responders during accidents, during natural disasters which may disable fixed infrastructure, in battlefield areas, and so on.

Although many such applications are safety-critical and need formal analysis to ensure their correctness, the formal modeling and analysis of MANETs present a number of challenges that include:

1. The need to model node movement realistically.
2. Modeling communication. There is a subtle interaction between wireless communication, which typically is restricted to distances of between 10 and 100 m, and node mobility. For example, nodes may move into, or out of, the sender's transmission range *during* the communication delay; furthermore, the sender may itself move during the communication. Modeling communication in MANETs is therefore challenging for formal languages, which are usually based on fixed communication primitives.

© Springer International Publishing Switzerland 2014
S. Escobar (Ed.): WRLA 2014, LNCS 8663, pp. 162–177, 2014.
DOI: 10.1007/978-3-319-12904-4_9

3. Since the communication topology of the network depends on the *locations* of the nodes, such locations must be taken into account in the model. However, this leads to very large state spaces, which makes direct model checking analysis unfeasible: if there are m nodes and n locations, there are n^m different node/location-states. A 10×10 grid with four nodes would therefore lead to 100 million states just to capture all nodes and their locations.

As explained in Sect. 7, we are not aware of any formal model that provides a reasonably detailed model of both mobility and communication in MANETs. Because of its expressiveness and flexibility to define models of communication, Real-Time Maude [20] is a promising language for formally modeling MANETs. In this paper we provide, to the best of our knowledge, the first reasonably detailed formal modeling framework for MANETs. In particular, we formalize

- the most popular models for node mobility, and
- geographically bounded wireless communication, which takes into account the interplay between communication delay and mobility,

in Real-Time Maude. Furthermore, we use object-oriented techniques to make it easy to *compose* our framework with a model of a MANET protocol.

Concerning Challenge 3 above, in this paper we do not develop abstraction techniques for node mobility. Instead, to be able to perform model checking analysis, our model is parametric in aspects such as the possible velocities and directions a node can choose. However, even if a node moves slowly, it may still cover the entire area (and hence contribute to an unmanageable state space) given enough time. Another key feature of Real-Time Maude that makes some meaningful model checking analysis of MANETs possible is therefore *time-bounded* model checking, which allows us to analyze scenarios only up to a certain duration (during which the nodes may not reach most locations). Abstracting the state space caused by node mobility and the need to keep track of node locations is the *sine qua non* for serious model checking of MANETs. The point is that this paper lays the foundations for developing such abstractions by providing a first reasonably detailed formal model of location-aware MANETs.

One of the main tasks of a MANET is to maintain an (ad hoc) network, which means that the network must figure out how to route messages between nodes. In this paper we illustrate the use of our MANETs framework by modeling and analyzing the widely used *Ad hoc On-Demand Distance Vector* [22] (AODV) routing protocol for MANETs developed by the IETF MANET working group.

The rest of this paper is organized as follows. Section 2 gives a background to Real-Time Maude. Section 3 briefly introduces MANETs. Section 4 presents our Real-Time Maude modeling framework for MANETs. Section 5 shows how our framework can be used to model the AODV protocol, and Sect. 6 explains how that model of AODV can be model checked using Real-Time Maude. Finally, Sect. 7 discusses related work and Sect. 8 gives some concluding remarks.

Due to space limitations, we have to omit many details; they are all given in our accompanying longer report [14].

2   Real-Time Maude

Real-Time Maude [20] is a language and tool that extends Maude [5] to support the formal specification and analysis of real-time systems.

Specification. A Real-Time Maude module specifies a *real-time rewrite theory* $(\Sigma, E \cup A, IR, TR)$, where:

- Σ is an algebraic *signature*; that is, a set of declarations of *sorts*, *subsorts*, and *function symbols*.
- $(\Sigma, E \cup A)$ is a *membership equational logic theory* [5], with E a set of possibly conditional equations, and A a set of equational axioms such as associativity, commutativity, and identity. $(\Sigma, E \cup A)$ specifies the system's state space as an algebraic data type, and includes a specification of a sort Time.
- IR is a set of *labeled conditional rewrite rules* specifying the system's local transitions, each of which has the form[1] $[l] : t \longrightarrow t'$ if $\bigwedge_{j=1}^{m} cond_j$, where each $cond_j$ is either an equality $u_j = v_j$ or a rewrite $t_j \longrightarrow t'_j$, and l is a *label*. Such a rule specifies an *instantaneous transition* from an instance of t to the corresponding instance of t', *provided* the condition holds.
- TR is a set of *tick rules* $l : \{t\} \longrightarrow \{t'\}$ in time τ if $cond$ that advance time in the *entire* state t by τ time units.

A class declaration   class C | $att_1 : s_1, \ldots, att_n : s_n$ declares a class C with attributes att_1 to att_n of sorts s_1 to s_n. An *object* of class C in a given state is represented as a term $<O : C \mid att_1 : val_1, ..., att_n : val_n>$ of sort Object, where O, of sort Oid, is the object's *identifier*, and where val_1 to val_n are the current values of the attributes att_1 to att_n. A *message* is a term of sort Msg.

The state of an object-oriented specification is a term of sort Configuration, and is a *multiset* of objects and messages. Multiset union is denoted by an associative and commutative juxtaposition operator, so that rewriting is *multiset rewriting*. For example, the rewrite rule

```
rl [1]  :  m(O,w)    < O : C | a1 : x, a2 : O', a3 : z >
           =>
           < O : C | a1 : x + w, a2 : O', a3 : z >   dly(m'(O',x), z) .
```

defines a family of transitions in which a message m, with parameters O and w, is read and consumed by an object O of class C, the attribute a1 of object O is changed to x + w, and a new message dly(m'(O',x),z) is generated; this message will become the "ripe" message m'(O',x) after z time units. Attributes whose values do not change and do not affect the next state of other attributes or messages, such as a3, need not be mentioned in a rule. Attributes that are unchanged, such as a2, can be omitted from right-hand sides of rules.

A *subclass* inherits all the attributes and rules of its superclasses.

---

[1] An equational condition $u_i = v_i$ can also be a *matching equation*, written $u_i := v_i$, which instantiates the variables in u_i to the values that make $u_i = v_i$ hold, if any.

Formal Analysis. In this paper, we only consider Real-Time Maude's *linear temporal logic model checker*, which analyzes whether *each* behavior satisfies a temporal logic formula. *State propositions* are terms of sort `Prop`, and their semantics is defined by equations   `ceq` *statePattern* `|=` *prop* `=` *b* `if` *cond*,   for *b* a term of sort `Bool`, stating that *prop* evaluates to *b* in states that are instances of *statePattern* when the condition *cond* holds. These equations together define *prop* to hold in all states *t* where *t* `|=` *prop* evaluates to `true`. A temporal logic *formula* is constructed by state propositions and temporal logic operators such as `True`, `False`, `~` (negation), `/\`, `\/`, `->` (implication), `[]` ("always"), `<>` ("eventually"), and `U` ("until"). Real-Time Maude provides both *unbounded* and *time-bounded* LTL model checking. The time-bounded model checking command

(`mc` *t* `|=t` *formula* `in time <=` *timeLimit* `.`)

checks whether the temporal logic formula *formula* holds in all behaviors up to duration *timeLimit* starting from the initial state *t*.

3   Mobility and Communication Delay in MANETs

This section gives an overview of the main mobility models used by researchers on protocol evaluations, and of the per-hop delay in wireless communication.

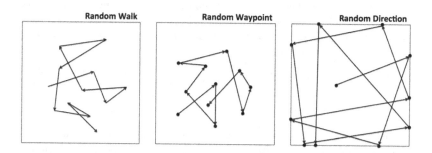

Fig. 1. Motion paths of a mobile node in three mobility models, where a bullet • depicts a pause in the movement.

Mobility Models. Different *mobility patterns* have been proposed to model node mobility in realistic scenarios. In this paper we focus on the following main *entity mobility models* [2], also illustrated in Fig. 1, in which a node's movement is independent of the movements of the other nodes:

– *Random Walk:* Each node moves in "rounds" of fixed durations. A node moves in the same direction and with the same speed throughout one round. At the end of each round, the *new speed* and the *new direction* of a node are randomly chosen, and a new moving round starts.

- *Random Waypoint:* Each node initially pauses for a fixed duration. When a pause ends, a node randomly chooses a *new destination* and a *new speed*, and then travels to that destination at the chosen speed. After arriving, the node again pauses before a new moving round starts.
- *Random Direction:* Each mobile node chooses a *random direction*, along which it travels until reaching the border of the sensing area. When a node arrives at the border, the node pauses for a given time, and then randomly selects a new direction and starts to move in that direction.

Communication Delay. To understand how node movement affects wireless communication, we must understand the messaging delays in wireless communication. In a typical wireless transmit/receive process, the per-hop communication delay from a transmitter to a receiver consists of the following five phases [24]:

Delay factor	Description
Sender processing delay	The time elapsed on the sender side from the moment a message timestamp is taken to the point the message is buffered in the device
Media access delay	The time for a message to stay in the radio device buffer; e.g., in a CSMA system, this is the delay waiting for a clear channel to transmit
Transmit delay	The time for a radio device to transmit a message over a radio link
Radio propagation delay	The time for a message to propagate through the air to a receiver
Receiver processing delay	The time spent on the receiver side to pass the received message from the device buffer to the application module

We can abstract from the radio propagation delay, since the transmission range in MANETs typically ranges from 10 to 100 m, while the radio propagation speed is approximately 3×10^8 m/s. The media access delay depends on the MAC overhead, such as collisions and waiting time.

4   Formalizing MANET Mobility and Communication

This section presents a modeling framework for MANETs with nodes that communicate wirelessly. Section 4.2 shows how mobile nodes can be specified in Real-Time Maude, Sect. 4.3 explains how the timed behavior of MANETs can be defined in a way that allows us to easily compose our model with MANET protocols, and Sect. 4.4 formalizes wireless communication for MANETs.

4.1 Some Basic Data Types

We assume a sort `Location` for the set of locations, a sort `Speed` for the different velocities with which a node can move, a set `Direction` for the different directions that a node can choose, and sorts `SpeedRange`, `DirRange`, and `DestRange` denoting *sets* of, respectively, `Speed`, `Direction`, and `Location` elements.

We also assume that nodes move in a two-dimensional square with length `areaSize`. A location is therefore represented as a pair $x.y$ of rational numbers:[2]

```
op _._ : Rat Rat ~> Location [ctor] .
cmb X . Y : Location if 0 <= X and X <= areaSize /\ 0 <= Y and Y <= areaSize .
```

We do not further specify the different powersets, whose elements could be unions of dense intervals or of single points, or both. Since the nodes need to nondeterministically select a new speed, a new next destination, and/or a new next direction, we assume for generality's sake that there is an operator `choose` that can select any value in the respective set nondeterministically, and an operator `[_]`, so that an element e can be chosen from a set S if and only if there is a rewrite (in zero or more steps) `choose(S) => [e]`. For example, if we have a discrete set of possible next directions $d_1 \; ; \; d_2 \; ; \; \ldots; \; d_n$, where the set union operator `_;_` is declared to be associative and commutative, we can specify that any value from the set can be selected, by giving the following rewrite rule:

```
var D : Direction .   var DR : DirRange .
rl [chooseDir] :  choose(D ; DR) => [D] .
```

4.2 Modeling Mobile Nodes

We model a MANET node in an object-oriented style, where a mobile node is modeled as an object instance of some subclass of the following base class `Node`:

```
class Node | currentLocation : Location .
```

The attribute `currentLocation` denotes the node's current location. A *stationary* node is an object instance of the subclass `StationaryNode` that does not add any attribute to `Node`:

```
class StationaryNode .        subclass StationaryNode < Node .
```

A mobile node is modeled as an object of a subclass of the class `MobileNode`:

```
class MobileNode | speed : Speed,  direction : Direction,  timer : TimeInf .
subclass MobileNode < Node .
```

where `speed` and `direction` denote, respectively, the node's current speed and its current movement direction. The `timer` attribute is used to ensure that a node changes its movement (or lack thereof) in a timely manner; that is, `timer` denotes the time remaining until some discrete event must take place.

---

[2] We do not show most variable declarations, but follow the Maude convention that variables are written in capital letters.

Random Walk. A node moving according to the random walk model is continuously moving, in time intervals of length `movingTime`. At the end of an interval, the node nondeterministically chooses a new speed and a new direction for its next interval. Such a node is modeled by an object of the subclass `RWNode`:

```
class RWNode | speedRange : SpeedRange, dirRange : DirRange .
subclass RWNode < MobileNode .
```

where `speedRange` and `dirRange` denote the set of possible next speeds and directions, respectively. The `timer` attribute inherited from its superclass denotes the remaining time of its current move interval. The instantaneous behavior of the mobility part of such a node can be modeled by the following rule. In this rule, the node is finishing one interval (the `timer` attribute is 0), and must select new speed and direction for its next round, and reset the timer:

```
crl [startNewMove] :
   < O : RWNode | timer : 0, speedRange : SR,  dirRange : DR >
 =>
   < O : RWNode | timer : movingTime, speed : S, direction : D >
 if choose(SR) => [S]  /\ choose(DR) => [D] .
```

The actual movement of such a node is modeled in Sect. 4.3.

Random Waypoint. In the random waypoint mobility model, a node alternates between pausing and moving. When it starts moving, it selects a new speed and a new destination and starts moving towards the destination. Such a node should be modeled by an object instance of the `RWPNode` subclass:

```
class RWPNode | speedRange : SpeedRange,   destRange : DestRange,
                status : Status .
subclass RWPNode < MobileNode .
```

The `status` attribute is either `pausing` or `moving`, and `destRange` denotes the possible next destinations.

The instantaneous behavior of this mobility model is given by the following rewrite rules. First, if the node is `pausing` and the `timer` expires, the node must get moving by selecting a new speed and desired next location, and resetting the timer so that it expires when the goal location is reached:

```
var MOVE-TIME : Time .

crl [startMoving] :
    < O : RWPNode | currentLocation : CURR-LOC, status : pausing,
                    timer : 0, speedRange : SR,  destRange : DER >
   =>
    < O : RWPNode | status : moving, speed : S,
                    direction : D, timer : MOVE-TIME >
  if choose(SR) => [S]  /\  choose(DER) => [NEXT-LOC]
    /\ D := direction(L, NEXT-LOC)
    /\ MOVE-TIME := timeBetweenLocations(CURR-LOC, NEXT-LOC, S) .
```

where `direction` gives the direction from one location to another, and `time-BetweenLocations` denotes the time it takes to travel between two locations at a given speed. The selected speed cannot be zero, unless the selected next location is also the current location, because then the last matching equation would not hold, since the traveling time between the two locations would be the infinity value `INF`, which is not a `Time` value.

The following rule applies when the timer of a *moving* node expires; then it is time to take a rest for `pauseTime` time units:

```
rl [startPausing] :
   < O : RWPNode | status : moving, timer : 0 >
   =>
   < O : RWPNode | status : pausing, timer : pauseTime, speed : 0 > .
```

Random direction nodes can be defined in the same way; see [14] for details.

4.3   Timed Behavior and Compositionality

Our model of mobile nodes must be easily *composable* with "application" protocols such as AODV to define a particular MANET system. The straightforward way of composing our model of mobility with a MANET protocol is to let the nodes in the application protocol be modeled as objects of subclasses of the classes introduced above, since a subclass "inherits" all the attributes and rewrite rules of its superclasses; in particular, such application-specific subclasses would inherit the rewrite rules modeling the movements of their nodes.

However, we must allow the user to define the *timed behavior* of her system, and compose it with the timed behavior of mobile nodes. We therefore use the following extension of the "standard" tick rule for object-oriented specifications:

```
var T : Time .    var C : Configuration .
crl [tick] : {C} => {timeEffect(timeEffectMob(C, T), T)} in time T
             if T <= min(mte(C), mteMob(C)) .
```

where `timeEffectMob` defines the effect of time elapse on the mobility-specific parts of the system, and `timeEffect` defines how the passage of time changes the state in the other parts of the composed system. Likewise, `mteMob` denotes the maximum amount of time that may elapse from a given state until some mobility action must be taken, and `mte` defines the amount of time until the application protocol must perform a discrete action. These functions distribute over the objects and messages in the configuration as explained in [14].

Since the speed is 0 when a node is pausing, we can easily define the timed behavior of both stationary and mobile nodes. First of all, time does not affect (the mobility-specific parts of) a stationary node:

```
eq timeEffectMob(< O : StationaryNode | >, T) = < O : StationaryNode | >.
```

Time affects a mobile node by moving the node and decreasing its timer value:

```
eq timeEffectMob(< O : MobileNode | currentLocation : L, speed : S,
                                    direction : D, timer : T1 >, T)
 = < O : MobileNode | currentLocation : move(L,S,D,T),
                      timer : T1 monus T > .
```

where move(l,s,d,t) denotes the location resulting from moving a node in location l for t time units in direction d and with speed s. This function also makes sure that a node does not move beyond the area under consideration.

The mobility model does not restrict the time advance for stationary nodes, whereas for mobile nodes, time can advance until the timer becomes 0:

```
eq mteMob(< O : StationaryNode | >) = INF .
eq mteMob(< O : MobileNode | timer : T >) = T .
```

4.4   Modeling Wireless Communication in Mobile Systems

Only nodes that are sufficiently close to the sender, i.e., within the sender's *transmission range*, receive a message with sufficient signal strength. However, both the sender and the potential receivers might move (possibly out of, or into, the sender's transmission range) *during* the entire communication delay.

As mentioned in Sect. 3, the total communication "delay" can be decomposed into five parts. If we abstract from the radio propagation delay, the per-hop delay can be seen to consist of two parts: the delay at the sender side (including sender processing delay, media access delay, and transmit delay) and the delay at the receiver side (including receiver processing delay). The point is that exactly those nodes that are within the transmission range of the sender *when the sending delay ends* should receive a message.

It is also worth mentioning that our model is still somewhat abstract and does not capture all network factors, most notably collisions.

In MANETs communication can be by broadcast, unicast, or groupcast, depending on which kind of message a transmitter intends to send, and who are the recipients. In our model we have three corresponding message constructors for broadcast, unicast, and groupcast, respectively:

```
msg broadcast_from_ : MsgContent Oid -> Msg .
msg unicast_from_to_ : MsgContent Oid Oid -> Msg .
msg gpcast_from_to_ : MsgContent Oid NeighborSet -> Msg .
```

When a node *sender* wants to broadcast some message content *mc*, it generates a "message" broadcast *mc* from *sender*. The following equation adds the delay on the sending side, sendDelay, to this "broadcast message:"

```
eq broadcast MC from O = dly(transmit MC from O, sendDelay) .
```

The crucial moment is when the sending delay expires and the transmit message becomes "ripe." All the nodes that are within the transmission range of the sender *at that moment* should receive the message. This distribution is performed by the function `distrMsg`, where `distrMsg(`*snd, loc, mc, conf*`)` generates a *single* message, with content *mc*, to each node in *conf* that is currently within the transmission range of location *loc*; furthermore, this single message has delay `recDelay`, modeling the delay at the receiving site:

```
eq {< O : Node | currentLocation : L > (transmit MC from O) C}
 = {< O : Node | > distrMsg(O, L, MC, C)} .

eq distrMsg(O, L, MC, < O' : Node | currentLocation : L' > C)
 = < O' : Node | currentLocation : L' > distrMsg(O, L, MC, C)
   (if L withinTransRangeOf L' then dly((MC from O to O'), recDelay)
   else none fi) .
```

Unicast and groupcast are modeled similarly.

5   Case Study: Route Discovery in AODV

This section first gives an overview of the AODV routing protocol, and then presents our Real-Time Maude model of AODV, focusing on the route discovery process. The entire executable Real-Time Maude specification is available at http://www.ifi.uio.no/RealTimeMaude/MANET/wrla2014-manets.rtmaude.

5.1   Route Discovery in AODV

AODV [22] is a widely used algorithm for routing messages between mobile nodes which dynamically form an ad hoc network. AODV allows a source node to initiate a route discovery process on an on-demand basis to establish a route to a destination node.

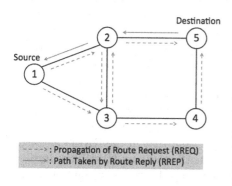

--->: Propagation of Route Request (RREQ)
——>: Path Taken by Route Reply (RREP)

Fig. 2. Route discovery process.

A source node S initiates a route discovery process by broadcasting a route request (RREQ) message to its neighbors. An intermediate node can either unicast a route reply (RREP) message back to the source if a valid route to the destination D can be found in its local routing table, or re-broadcast the received RREQ to its own neighbors. As the RREQ travels from S to D, reverse paths from all nodes back to S are automatically set up. Eventually, when the RREQ reaches D, it sends a RREP back along the previously established reverse path. After this process, a route between S and D is set up.

5.2   Modeling Route Discovery in Real-Time Maude

Modeling Nodes and Messages. We model an AODV node as an object of a subclass AODVNode of class Node. The new attributes show the identification of a node's routing request, the sequence number of a node itself, the local routing table, and the buffered routing requests sent since the beginning of the current round, respectively.

```
class AODVNode | rreqID : Nat, sequenceNumber : Sqn,
                 routingTable : RouteTable, requestBuffer : RreqBuffer .
subclass AODVNode < Node .
```

A routing table of sort RouteTable is modeled using the predefined data type MAP. It consists of routing table entries of the form Oid |-> Tuple3, mapping a destination node Oid to a 3-element tuple: the next hop towards the destination, the distance to the destination, and the local destination sequence number. A route request buffer of the sort RreqBuffer is specified as a set of requests, each of which is of the form Oid ~ Sqn, and uniquely identifies a route request by the identifier of a node and its sequence number.

In the AODV route discovery process there are mainly two kinds of messages: RREQ and RREP. They are specified in our model as rreq(...) and rrep(...) respectively. The message content will be illustrated below.

Modeling Route Discovery. A route discovery process in AODV consists of three parts: initiating route discovery, route request handling, and route reply handling. We only illustrate part of the route request handling, and refer the reader to our longer report [14] for more details.

The RREQ-handling rules specify all events that may happen when a route request is received. The receiving node first checks whether a received (OIP ~ RREQID) has already been stored locally in the request buffer. If so, the route request is ignored and the local routing table is updated by adding a routing table entry towards the sender; otherwise, the receiving node adds the new route request identifier to the request buffer, and takes further actions according to the roles played by the receiving node. In the following case, the receiving node is an intermediate node.

When receiving the RREQ message, an intermediate node either: (a) generates a route reply to the sender, or (b) re-broadcasts the received RREQ to its neighbors. For example, action (a), as the following rewrite rule shows, happens only when O's local information is fresher than that in the RREQ message (DSN <= localdsn(RT[DIP])). Then O unicasts the route reply with the fresher destination sequence number and its distance in hops from the destination along the route back to the source node.

```
crl [on-receiving-rreq-3] :
    (rreq(OIP,OSN,RREQID,DIP,DSN,HOPS,SIP) from SIP to O)
    < O : AODVNode | routingTable : RT, requestBuffer : RB >
  =>
```

```
< O : AODVNode | routingTable : RT'',
                    requestBuffer : (OIP ~ RREQID, RB) >
(msg rrep(OIP,DIP,localdsn(RT''[DIP]),hops(RT''[DIP]),O)
   from O to nexthop(RT''[OIP]))
if RT' := update(SIP,SIP,1,0,RT) /\
   RT'' := update(OIP,SIP,HOPS + 1,OSN,RT') /\
   not (OIP ~ RREQID) in RB /\ inRT(RT,DIP) /\
   DIP =/= O /\ DSN <= localdsn(RT[DIP]) .
```

6 Formal Analysis of AODV

In this section we analyze the AODV route discovery process under different mobility models. We therefore define node objects that belong to a subclass of both AODVNode and a class defining the desired mobility pattern. For example, a node moving according to the random waypoint model is an object instance of the class RWPANode, and a stationary node is an instance of the class SANode:

```
class RWPANode .        subclass RWPANode < RWPNode AODVNode .
class SANode .          subclass SANode < StationaryNode AODVNode .
```

The main objective of a routing protocol such as AODV is that a route between the desired source and the desired destination is eventually established. To analyze this property, we define a parameterized atomic proposition route-found(SRC,DEST) to hold if we can find, in the routing table of the source node SRC, a routing table entry towards the destination node DEST:

```
op route-found : Oid Oid -> Prop [ctor] .
eq {< SRC : AODVNode | routingTable : RT , (DEST |-> TP) > REST}
   |= route-found(SRC, DEST) = true .
```

The desired property of AODV can then be formalized as the temporal logic formula <> route-found(...). Given an initial state initConfig, the following command returns true if our desired property holds in the first test round (roundTime); otherwise, a trace showing a counterexample is provided.

```
(mc {initConfig} |=t <> route-found(src,dest) in time <= roundTime .)
```

Experiment Scenarios. We define the following setting for our experiments:

- The transmission range is 10m, and the test area is 100m × 100m.
- The test round is 100s. The delay at the sender and at the receiver is set to 10s and 5s, respectively.
- The range of possible velocities is the singleton set (1).
- Nodes can move right, up, left or down: the direction range is a subset of (0,90,180,270), and the destination range is a subset of four locations in the corresponding four directions based on a node's current location.

We have analyzed AODV in seven different scenarios; five of them are described below and the other cases are described in our longer report [14]:

- *Scenario (i)*, shown in Fig. 2, has five *stationary* nodes, where node 1, located at (45 . 45), wants to build a route to node 5, located at (60 . 50), and nodes 2, 3 and 4 are at (50 . 50), (50 . 40), and (60 . 40), respectively.
- *Scenario (i')*, shown in Fig. 3 (a solid circle refers to the initial location of a node, while a dashed circle refers to some point along the motion path of a node), has the same topology as Scenario (i), but now node 2 is a *random waypoint* node that can move up. We set its pause time to: (a) 10s, (b) 30s, or (c) 60s. The initial state of this scenario is specified as:

```
eq src = 1 .
eq initConfig =
    (bootstrap src)
    < 1 : SANode | currentLocation : 45 . 45 , rreqID : 10, sequenceNumber : 1,
                   routingTable : empty, requestBuffer : empty >
    < 2 : RWPANode | currentLocation : 50 . 50, speed : 0, direction : 0, timer : pauseTime,
                     speedRange : (1), destRange : (50 . 60), status : pausing, rreqID : 20,
                     sequenceNumber : 1, routingTable : empty, requestBuffer : empty >
    < 3 : SANode | currentLocation : 50 . 40, ... >
    < 4 : SANode | currentLocation : 60 . 40, ... >
    < 5 : SANode | currentLocation : 60 . 50, ... >  .
```

- *Scenario (ii)*, also shown in Fig. 3, has three nodes with both nodes 2, located at (40 . 50), and 3 (a random waypoint node located at (50 . 40)) intending to build a route to the destination node 1 located at (50 . 50).

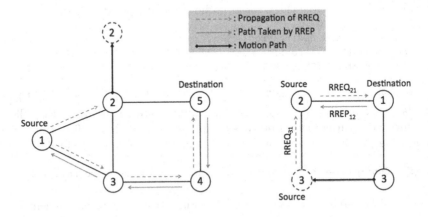

Fig. 3. Scenarios (i') and (ii)

Analysis Results. The results of the model checking show that the desired property holds in Scenarios (i), (i')-(a), and (i')-(c), but not in Scenarios (i')-(b) and (ii).

In Scenario (i')-(b), the pause time (30s) allows node 2 to forward the RREQ message from node 1 to node 5. However, node 2 cannot receive the RREP message from node 5 due to its movement (the dash circle in this case is at (50 . 60)). Meanwhile, since node 5 has already recorded node 1's RREQ from node 2, it ignores the one from node 4.

In Scenario (ii), before sending out the RREQ message, node 3 moves left to a new location (40 . 40) within the transmission range of node 2. Thus, to establish the route to node 1, node 3's RREQ message needs to be forwarded by node 2. However, the model checking counterexample shows that route discovery for node 3 fails: no route can be found between nodes 3 and 1, though obviously node 2 succeeds in building a route to node 1. This problem arises due to the discarding of the RREP message. As stated in [22], an intermediate node forwards a RREP message only if the RREP message serves to update its routing table entry towards the destination. However, in this case, node 2 has already secured an optimal route to node 1 before receiving the RREQ message from node 3. Fehnker et al. [7] also pointed out this problem, but in a static linear topology with three nodes.

7   Related Work

There are a number of formal specification and analysis efforts of MANETs in general, and AODV in particular.

Bhargavan et al. [1] use the SPIN model checker to analyze AODV. They only consider a 3-node topology with one link break, but without node movement, and communication delay is not considered. Chiyangwa et al. [4] apply the real-time model checker UPPAAL to analyze AODV. They only consider a static linear network topology. Although they take communication delay into account, the effect of mobility on communication delay is not considered, since the topology is fixed. Fehnker et al. [7] also use UPPAAL to analyze AODV. They also only considered static topologies, or simple dynamic topologies by adding or removing a link, and those topologies are based on the connectivity graph without concrete locations for nodes. Furthermore, no timing issues are considered. Höfner et al. [12] apply statistical model checking to AODV. However, mobility is simply considered by arbitrary instantaneous node jumping between zones that split the whole test grid. Although they take into account the communication delay, the combination of mobility and communication delay is not considered. None of these studies has built a generic framework for MANETs. Our modeling framework aims at the combination of wireless communication and mobility, and allows formal modeling and analysis of protocols under realistic mobility models.

On the process algebra side, CWS [17], CBS# [19], CMAN [10], CMN [15], the ω-calculus [23], RBPT [9,11], TCWS [16] and AWN [6], have been proposed as process algebraic modeling languages for MANETs. These languages feature a form of local broadcast, in which a message sent by a node could be received by other nodes "within transmission range." However, the connectivity is only considered abstractly and logically, without taking into account concrete locations and transmission range for nodes. Furthermore, [17] only considers fixed network topologies, whereas the others (except [11]) deal with arbitrary changes in topology. Godskesen et al. [11] consider realistic mobility, and propose concrete mobility models. However, no protocol application or automated analysis is given, and communication delay is not taken into account. Merro et al. [16] propose a timed calculus with time-consuming communications, and equip it with a formal semantics to analyze communication collisions.

Generally, these studies have proposed a framework for MANETs, but they lack of either mobility modeling or timing issues handling.

There are also a number of well known "ambient" calculi for mobility, such as the ambient calculus [3], the π-calculus [18], and the join-calculus [8]. However, these are very abstract models that do not take locations and geographically bounded communication into account, and are therefore not suitable to model MANETs at the level of abstraction considered in this paper.

Finally, Maude and Real-Time Maude have been applied to analyze wireless sensor networks, but the work in [13,21] does not consider node mobility (even though [13] mentions that mobility is addressed in a technical report in preparation; however, we cannot find that technical report).

8   Concluding Remarks

We have defined in Real-Time Maude what we believe is the first formal model of MANETs that provides a reasonably faithful model of popular node movement patterns and wireless communication. We have used our compositional model to specify and formally analyze the AODV routing protocol, and have shown that such Real-Time Maude analysis could easily find the known flaw in AODV.

We have abstracted from message collision, which should also be considered in our model. The price to pay for having a much more realistic model of MANETs than other formal approaches is that the state space quickly becomes too large for model checking. We should therefore develop statistical model checking techniques for MANETs. Most importantly, we should develop abstraction techniques for MANETs. The formalization presented in this paper has provided the necessary foundation for such efforts.

Acknowledgments. We thank the anonymous reviewers for helpful comments on a previous version of this paper. This work has been partially supported by AFOSR Contract FA8750-11-2-0084 and NSF Grant CNS 13-19109.

References

1. Bhargavan, K., Obradovic, D., Gunter, C.: Formal verification of standards for distance vector routing protocols. J. ACM **49**(4), 538–576 (2002)
2. Camp, T., Boleng, J., Davies, V.: A survey of mobility models for ad hoc network research. Wirel. Commun. Mob. Comput. **2**(5), 483–502 (2002)
3. Cardelli, L., Gordon, A.D.: Mobile ambients. In: Proceedings of POPL'98. ACM (1998)
4. Chiyangwa, S., Kwiatkowska, M.: A timing analysis of AODV. In: Steffen, M., Zavattaro, G. (eds.) FMOODS 2005. LNCS, vol. 3535, pp. 306–321. Springer, Heidelberg (2005)

5. Clavel, M., Durán, F., Eker, S., Lincoln, P., Martí-Oliet, N., Meseguer, J., Talcott, C. (eds.): All About Maude. LNCS, vol. 4350. Springer, Heidelberg (2007)
6. Fehnker, A., van Glabbeek, R., Höfner, P., McIver, A., Portmann, M., Tan, W.: A process algebra for wireless mesh networks used for modelling, verifying and analysing AODV. Technical report, 5513. NICTA (2012)
7. Fehnker, A., van Glabbeek, R., Höfner, P., McIver, A., Portmann, M., Tan, W.L.: Automated analysis of AODV using UPPAAL. In: Flanagan, C., König, B. (eds.) TACAS 2012. LNCS, vol. 7214, pp. 173–187. Springer, Heidelberg (2012)
8. Fournet, C., Gonthier, G.: The reflexive CHAM and the join-calculus. In: Proceedings of POPL'96. ACM (1996)
9. Ghassemi, F., Fokkink, W., Movaghar, A.: Restricted broadcast process theory. In: Proceedings of SEFM '08. IEEE (2008)
10. Godskesen, J.C.: A calculus for mobile ad hoc networks. In: Murphy, A.L., Vitek, J. (eds.) COORDINATION 2007. LNCS, vol. 4467, pp. 132–150. Springer, Heidelberg (2007)
11. Godskesen, J.C., Nanz, S.: Mobility models and behavioural equivalence for wireless networks. In: Field, J., Vasconcelos, V.T. (eds.) COORDINATION 2009. LNCS, vol. 5521, pp. 106–122. Springer, Heidelberg (2009)
12. Höfner, P., Kamali, M.: Quantitative analysis of AODV and its variants on dynamic topologies using statistical model checking. In: Braberman, V., Fribourg, L. (eds.) FORMATS 2013. LNCS, vol. 8053, pp. 121–136. Springer, Heidelberg (2013)
13. Katelman, M., Meseguer, J., Hou, J.: Redesign of the LMST wireless sensor protocol through formal modeling and statistical model checking. In: Barthe, G., de Boer, F.S. (eds.) FMOODS 2008. LNCS, vol. 5051, pp. 150–169. Springer, Heidelberg (2008)
14. Liu, S., Ölveczky, P.C., Meseguer, J.: A framework for mobile ad hoc networks in Real-Time Maude (2014). http://www.ifi.uio.no/RealTimeMaude/MANET/wrla14-manets-tech.pdf
15. Merro, M.: An observational theory for mobile ad hoc networks (full version). Inf. Comput. 207(2), 194–208 (2009)
16. Merro, M., Ballardin, F., Sibilio, E.: A timed calculus for wireless systems. Theor. Comput. Sci. 412(47), 6585–6611 (2011)
17. Mezzetti, N., Sangiorgi, D.: Towards a calculus for wireless systems. Electron. Notes Theor. Comput. Sci. 158, 331–353 (2006)
18. Milner, R.: Communicating and mobile systems - the Pi-calculus. Cambridge University Press, Cambridge (1999)
19. Nanz, S., Hankin, C.: A framework for security analysis of mobile wireless networks. Theor. Comput. Sci. 367(1), 203–227 (2006)
20. Ölveczky, P.C., Meseguer, J.: Semantics and pragmatics of Real-Time Maude. Higher-order Symb. Comput. 20(1–2), 161–196 (2007)
21. Ölveczky, P.C., Thorvaldsen, S.: Formal modeling, performance estimation, and model checking of wireless sensor network algorithms in Real-Time Maude. Theoret. Comput. Sci. 410(2–3), 254–280 (2009)
22. Perkins, C., Belding-Royer, E., Das, S.: Ad hoc on-demand distance vector (AODV) routing. RFC 3561 (experimental) (2003). http://www.ietf.org/rfc/rfc3561
23. Singh, A., Ramakrishnan, C.R., Smolka, S.A.: A process calculus for mobile ad hoc networks. Sci. Comput. Program. 75(6), 440–469 (2010)
24. Su, P.: Delay measurement time synchronization for wireless sensor networks. Intel Research Berkeley Lab (2003)

Strong and Weak Operational Termination
of Order-Sorted Rewrite Theories

Salvador Lucas[1,2]($\boxtimes$) and José Meseguer[2]

[1] DSIC, Universitat Politècnica de València, Valencia, Spain
slucas@dsic.upv.es
[2] CS Department, University of Illinois at Urbana-Champaign, Champaign, IL, USA
meseguer@cs.uiuc.edu

Abstract. This paper presents several new results on conditional term rewriting within the general framework of order-sorted rewrite theories (OSRTs) which contains the more restricted framework of conditional term rewriting systems (CTRSs) as a special case. The results uncover some subtle issues about conditional termination. We first of all generalize a previous known result characterizing the operational termination of a CTRS by the quasi-decreasing ordering notion to a similar result for OSRTs. Second, we point out that the notions of *irreducible* term and of *normal form*, which coincide for unsorted rewriting are *totally different* for conditional rewriting and formally characterize that difference. We then define the notion of a *weakly operationally terminating* (or *weakly normalizing*) OSRT, give several evaluation mechanisms to compute normal forms in such theories, and investigate general conditions under which the rewriting-based operational semantics and the initial algebra semantics of a confluent OSRT coincide thanks to a notion of *canonical term algebra*. Finally, we investigate appropriate conditions and proof methods to ensure good executability properties of an OSRT for computing normal forms.

Keywords: Conditional term rewriting · Strong and weak operational termination · Irreducible terms · Normalized terms · Rewriting logic · Maude

1 Introduction

This paper presents several new contributions to conditional term rewriting and to the semantics of declarative, rewriting-based languages. The key notion is that of an *Order-Sorted Rewrite Theory* (OSRT) $\mathcal{R} = (\Sigma, B, R)$, where (Σ, B) is an order-sorted equational theory [10] with equational axioms B, and R is a collection of rewrite rules with oriented conditions of the form: $\ell \rightarrow r \Leftarrow s_1 \rightarrow$

Research partially supported by NSF grant CNS 13-19109. Salvador Lucas' research was developed during a sabbatical year at the CS Dept. of the UIUC and was also partially supported by Spanish MECD grant PRX12/00214, MINECO project TIN2010-21062-C02-02, and GV grant BEST/2014/026 and project PROMETEO/2011/052.

© Springer International Publishing Switzerland 2014
S. Escobar (Ed.): WRLA 2014, LNCS 8663, pp. 178–194, 2014.
DOI: 10.1007/978-3-319-12904-4_10

$t_1, \ldots, s_n \to t_n$, which are applied *modulo B*. All the results are *in particular* new results for *Conditional Term Rewriting Systems* (CTRSs); that is, for order-sorted rewrite theories of the form $\mathcal{R} = (\Sigma, \varnothing, R)$, with Σ having a *single* sort. The greater generality of OSRTs is not a caprice, but an absolute necessity for making formal specification and declarative programming practical and expressive.

Our contributions consist in asking and providing detailed answers to the following, innocent-sounding questions:

1. Can the operational termination of OSRTs be characterized in terms of orders?
2. What is the right notion of *normal form* for an OSRT?
3. What is the right notion of *weak operational termination* for an OSRT?
4. Under what conditions can OSRTs be used as *declarative programs* having a well-behaved semantics? And how can we *evaluate* such programs?
5. Under what conditions does an OSRT have a *canonical term algebra* that can be effectively computed and that provides a *complete agreement* between the operational semantics of the OSRT as a functional program, and its mathematical, initial algebra semantics? How can some of these executability conditions be checked in practice?

Surprisingly enough, some of these questions seem to never have been asked. At best, the issues involved seem to have remained implicit as not well-understood, anomalous features in the literature. Consider, for example, question (2) above, which asks about the notion of normal form. For unconditional term rewriting the notion is absolutely clear and unproblematic: a normal form is a term t that is *irreducible*, that is, such that there is no t' with $t \to t'$. For an OSRT, and in particular for a CTRS, the notion of normal form is actually highly problematic. The big problem is that for an OSRT there can be terms t that are irreducible in the above sense, i.e., there is no t' with $t \to t'$, but such that when we give t to a rewrite engine for evaluation such an engine loops! For a trivial example, consider the single conditional rewrite rule $a \to b \Leftarrow a \to c$. Since the rewrite relation defined by this conditional rule is the empty set, the constant a is trivially irreducible; but the proof tree associated to the normalization of a using the CTRS inference system is *infinite* [7], and a rewrite engine that tries to evaluate a will loop when trying to satisfy the rule's condition.[1] Therefore, calling a a *normal form* is a very bad joke, since, intuitively, a term is considered to be a normal form if it is "fully normalized," that is, if it is the *result* of fully evaluating some input term by rewriting. Our answer to this puzzle is to introduce a precise distinction (fully articulated in the paper) between irreducible terms and normal forms: every normal form is irreducible, but, as the above example shows, not every irreducible term is a normal form. We call an OSRT *normal* iff every irreducible term is a normal form, and call it *abnormal* otherwise.

---

[1] For this trivial example one could find ways for an engine to detect *this* looping; but undecidability of termination makes a general loop-detecting engine an oxymoron.

Abnormal theories, like the one above, are hopeless for executablity purposes and should be viewed as monsters in the menagerie of CTRSs and OSRTs.

Termination is quite a subtle issue for OSRTs in general and CTRSs in particular. Many notions have been proposed (see e.g., [11]), but it is by now well-understood that the most satisfactory notion from a computational point of view is that of *operational termination* [7] (more on this later). Here we ask and answer two questions, further developing this notion. The first is question (1) above. For the case of deterministic 3-CTRS we proved in [7] that operational termination is *equivalent* to the order-based notion of *quasi-decreasingness*. In Sect. 3 we generalize this result to a similar result characterizing operational termination of OSRTs in terms of an (axiom-compatible) term ordering.

A second, related question, seemingly not previously addressed in the literature, is question (3), which could be rephrased as follows: what is the right notion of weak termination/normalization for OSRTs? As further explained in Sect. 4, there are in fact two possible notions, a computationally ill-behaved one (*weak termination*: every term has a terminating rewrite sequence ending in an irreducible term), and a computationally well-behaved one (*weak operational termination*: every term has a normal form).

The notions of normal OSRT and of weak operational termination are closely related to another question, namely, question (4), on executability conditions for declarative, conditional rule-based programs, and on their evaluation methods, i.e., their operational semantics. Interestingly enough, as we explain in Sect. 4, there are *several* evaluation methods, which become increasingly efficient as we impose further conditions on the OSRT which we use as our program.

For *functional* programs specified by an OSRT, the issue is not just one of having good executability conditions, but actually of *correctness*. More precisely, of *semantic agreement* between an abstract *initial algebra semantics* when the rules are viewed as equations, and an *operational semantics* based on rewriting, where the computed *values* —that is, the normal forms— give rise to a very intuitive algebra, the *canonical term algebra*, which under the assumptions of confluence, coherence, sort-decreasingness and operational termination is *isomorphic* to the initial algebra of the specification. Question (5) above asks, essentially: what is the *non plus ultra* in terms of generality to maintain this isomorphism and keeping an exact agreement between mathematical and operational semantics? That is, what are the right conditions for this semantic agreement when we drop the operational termination condition? This is also answered in Sect. 4, relating the answers to associated evaluation methods to compute normal forms. Last but not least, in Sects. 4 and 5 we investigate appropriate *conditions* and *proof methods* to ensure that a theory has good executability properties such as being normal, and evaluation to normal form defining a total recursive function.

2   Preliminaries

Order-Sorted Algebra. We summarize here material from [4,10] on order-sorted algebra. We start with a partially ordered set $(S, \leq)$ of *sorts*, where $s \leq$

s' is interpreted as *subsort inclusion*. The *connected components* of $(S, \leq)$ are the equivalence classes $[s]$ corresponding to the least equivalence relation $\equiv_\leq$ containing $\leq$. We also define $\lfloor s \rfloor = \{s' \in S \mid s' \leq s\}$, i.e., the sorts in S which are smaller than or equal to s. When $[s]$ has an upper bound, we denote it by $\top_{[s]}$. An order-sorted signature $(\Sigma, S, \leq)$ consists of a poset of sorts $(S, \leq)$ and a $S^* \times S$-indexed family of sets $\Sigma = \{\Sigma_{w,s}\}_{(w,s) \in S^* \times S}$, which are *function symbols* with a given string of argument sorts and a result sort. If $f \in \Sigma_{s_1 \ldots s_n, s}$, then we display the function symbol f as $f : s_1 \ldots s_n \longrightarrow s$. This is called a *rank declaration* for symbol f. Some of these symbols f can be *subsort-overloaded*, i.e., they can have several rank declarations related in the $\leq$ ordering [4]. Constant symbols, however, have only one rank declaration. To avoid ambiguous terms, we assume that Σ is *sensible*, meaning that if $f : s_1 \cdots s_n \to s$ and $f : s_1' \cdots s_n' \to s'$ are such that $[s_i] = [s_i']$, $1 \leq i \leq n$, then $[s] = [s']$. Throughout this paper, Σ will always be assumed *sensible*.

Given an S-sorted set $\mathcal{X} = \{\mathcal{X}_s \mid s \in S\}$ of *mutually disjoint* sets of variables, the set $\mathcal{T}_\Sigma(\mathcal{X})_s$ of terms of sort s is the least set such that (i) $\mathcal{X}_s \subseteq \mathcal{T}_\Sigma(\mathcal{X})_s$, (ii) $\mathcal{T}_\Sigma(\mathcal{X})_s \supseteq \mathcal{T}_\Sigma(\mathcal{X})_{s'}$, and (iii) for each $f : s_1 \ldots s_n \longrightarrow s$ and $t_i \in \mathcal{T}_\Sigma(\mathcal{X})_{s_i}$, $1 \leq i \leq n$, $f(t_1, \ldots, t_n) \in \mathcal{T}_\Sigma(\mathcal{X})_s$. The assumption that Σ is sensible ensures that if $[s] \neq [s']$, then $\mathcal{T}_\Sigma(\mathcal{X})_{[s]} \cap \mathcal{T}_\Sigma(\mathcal{X})_{[s']} = \varnothing$.

The set $\mathcal{T}_\Sigma(\mathcal{X})$ of order-sorted terms is $\mathcal{T}_\Sigma(\mathcal{X}) = \cup_{s \in S} \mathcal{T}_\Sigma(\mathcal{X})_s$. The family $\{\mathcal{T}_\Sigma(\mathcal{X})_s\}_{s \in S}$ together with the operations $f : (t_1, \ldots, t_n) \mapsto f(t_1, \ldots, t_n)$ define an order-sorted Σ-algebra called the *free* algebra on $\mathcal{X}$ and denoted $\mathcal{T}_\Sigma(\mathcal{X})$. When $\mathcal{X} = \varnothing$, $\mathcal{T}_\Sigma = \mathcal{T}_\Sigma(\varnothing)$ denotes the *initial* algebra. An element of any set $\mathcal{T}_\Sigma(\mathcal{X})_s$ is called a *well-formed* term. A simple syntactic condition on $(\Sigma, S, \leq)$ called *preregularity* [4] ensures that each well-formed term t has always a *least sort* possible among all sorts in S, which is denoted $LS(t)$. An order-sorted substitution σ is an S-sorted mapping $\sigma = \{\sigma : \mathcal{X}_s \to \mathcal{T}_\Sigma(\mathcal{X})_s\}_{s \in S}$ from variables to terms. The application of an OS-substitution σ to t (denoted $\sigma(t)$) consists of simultaneously replacing the variables occurring in t by a term according to the mapping σ. A specialization ν is an injective OS-substitution that maps a variable x of sort s to a variable x' of sort $s' \leq s$.

Order-Sorted Rewrite Theories. An (order-sorted) rewrite rule is an ordered pair (l, r), written $l \to r$, with $l, r \in \mathcal{T}_\Sigma(\mathcal{X})$, and $LS(l) \equiv_\leq LS(r)$. An *order-sorted conditional rewrite theory* (OSRT) is a triple $\mathcal{R} = (\Sigma, B, R)$, where Σ is an order-sorted signature, B is a set of Σ-equations, and R is a collection of conditional rewrite rules with oriented conditions of the form $\ell \to r \Leftarrow s_1 \to t_1, \ldots, s_n \to t_n$, where $\ell \to r$ and the $s_i \to t_i$ are order-sorted rewrite rules (with $\ell \notin \mathcal{X}_s$ for all $s \in S$), and where the conditions $s_i \to t_i$ are intended to express the reachability of (instances of) t_i from (instances of) s_i. Throughout this paper the equations $(u = v) \in B$ are assumed to be: (i) *regular* (i.e., $Var(u) = Var(v)$), (ii) *linear* (i.e., no repeated variables in either u or v); (iii) there is a B-matching algorithm; and (iv) *sort-preserving* (i.e., for each substitution θ, $LS(\theta(u)) = LS(\theta(v))$). Examples of axioms B satisfying (i)–(iii) include combinations of associativity and/or commutativity and/or identity axioms. Maude supports rewriting modulo such axioms and also checks

$$\text{(Refl)} \quad \frac{}{u \to^* v} \quad \text{if } u =_B v$$

$$\text{(Tran)} \quad \frac{u \to u' \qquad u' \to^* v}{u \to^* v}$$

$$\text{(Cong)} \quad \frac{u_i \to u_i'}{f(u_1, \ldots, u_i, \ldots, u_k) \to f(u_1, \ldots, u_i', \ldots, u_k)}$$
$$\text{where } f \in \Sigma \text{ and } 1 \le i \le k = ar(f)$$

$$\text{(Repl)} \quad \frac{\sigma(u_1) \to^* \sigma(v_1) \quad \cdots \quad \sigma(u_n) \to^* \sigma(v_n)}{u \to v}$$
$$\text{where } \ell \to r \Leftarrow u_1 \to v_1 \cdots u_n \to v_n \in \mathcal{R},$$
$$\sigma \text{ is an OS-substitution, } u =_B \sigma(\ell) \text{ and } v = \sigma(r)$$

Fig. 1. Inference rules for order-sorted rewrite theories

automatically property (iv) (it actually checks a somewhat weaker condition for identity axioms that still ensures a least sort for each B-equivalence class).

Rewrite rules $\ell \to r \Leftarrow c$ in OSRTs are classified according to the distribution of variables among ℓ, r, and c, as follows: type 1, if $Var(r) \cup Var(c) \subseteq Var(\ell)$; type 2, if $Var(r) \subseteq Var(\ell)$; type 3, if $Var(r) \subseteq Var(\ell) \cup Var(c)$; and type 4, if no restriction is given. An n-OSRT contains only rewrite rules of types $m \le n$. A 3-OSRT $\mathcal{R}$ is called *deterministic* if for each rule $l \to r \Leftarrow s_1 \to t_1, \ldots, s_n \to t_n$ in $\mathcal{R}$ and each $1 \le i \le n$, we have $Var(s_i) \subseteq Var(l) \cup \bigcup_{j=1}^{i-1} Var(t_j)$. If for all specializations $\nu\ LS(\nu(\ell)) \ge LS(\nu(r))$ then we say that the OS-rule $\ell \to r \Leftarrow c$ is *sort-decreasing*. We call an OSRT $\mathcal{R} = (\Sigma, B, R)$ *sort-decreasing* if all rules in R are so.

We write $t \to_\mathcal{R} u$ (resp. $t \to^*_\mathcal{R} u$) iff there is a well-formed proof tree for $t \to u$ (resp. $t \to^* u$) for $\mathcal{R}$ using the inference system in Fig. 1. As usual, $\to_\mathcal{R}$ is the *one-step* rewrite relation for the OSRT $\mathcal{R}$ and $\to^*_\mathcal{R}$ is the *zero-or-more-steps* rewrite relation for $\mathcal{R}$. We write $t \to^0_\mathcal{R} u$ if $t =_B u$; $t \to^1_\mathcal{R} u$ if $t \to_\mathcal{R} u$, and $t \to^n_\mathcal{R} u$, for some $n > 1$ if there is a term t' such that $t \to_\mathcal{R} t'$ and $t' \to^{n-1}_\mathcal{R} u$.

Operational Termination. Given a logic $\mathcal{L}$ (defined by its inference rules), one has the notion of a *theory* or *specification* $\mathcal{S}$ in such a logic, so that $\mathcal{L}$'s inference system becomes specialized to each such specification $\mathcal{S}$ to derive its provable theorems φ. Assume that we have an *interpreter* for the logic $\mathcal{L}$, that is, an *inference machine* that, given a theory $\mathcal{S}$ and a goal formula φ will try to incrementally build a proof tree for φ. Intuitively, we will call $\mathcal{S}$ *terminating* if for any φ the interpreter either finds a proof in finite time, or fails in all possible attempts also in finite time. In the same vein, we can say that a predicate π (for instance, $\to$ or $\to^*$ in the inference system of Fig. 1) is operationally terminating if for any goal φ such that $\varphi = \pi(t_1, \ldots, t_k)$ for terms $t_1, \ldots, t_k$, φ is operationally terminating. The notion of *operational termination* captures this fact, meaning that, given an initial goal, an interpreter will either succeed in finite time in producing a closed proof tree, or will fail in finite time, not being able to close or extend further any of the possible proof trees, after exhaustively searching all such proof trees [7]. In the following, according to the previous discussion, we speak about operational 1-termination of a OSRT as the operational termination of $\rightarrow$ (with respect to the inference system of Fig. 1). By operational termination of an OSRT we then mean the operational termination of $\rightarrow^*$. Similarly, we say that a term t is operationally (1-)terminating if every goal $t \rightarrow^* u$ (resp. $t \rightarrow u$) is operationally terminating for all terms u. We call $\mathcal{R}$ *ground operationally (1)-terminating* iff all $t \in \mathcal{T}_\Sigma$ are so.

One last issue important for executability purposes is (strong) B-*coherence*. This means that if $t \rightarrow^1_{\mathcal{R}} u$ and $t =_B t'$, then there exists a u' such that $t' \rightarrow^1_{\mathcal{R}} u'$ and $u =_B u'$. For axioms B such as combinations of associativity, commutativity and identity, Maude automatically completes the user-specified rules so that they become B-coherent. In this paper we will assume that *all OSRTs are B-coherent*.

3   Orderings, Quasi-Decreasingness, and (Strong) Operational Termination

A binary relation R on a set A is *terminating* (or well-founded) if there is no infinite sequence $a_1 \ R \ a_2 \ R \ a_3 \cdots$. Given $f : A^k \rightarrow A$ and $i \in \{1, \ldots, k\}$, we say that f is *i-monotonic* on its i-th argument (or that f is *i-monotone* with respect to R) if $f(x_1, \ldots, x_{i-1}, x, \ldots, x_k) \ R \ f(x_1, \ldots, x_{i-1}, y, \ldots, x_k)$ whenever $x \ R \ y$, for all $x, y, x_1, \ldots, x_k \in A$. We say that R is monotonic if, for all symbols f, f is monotonic w.r.t. R. In [7] we have shown that operational termination of deterministic 3-CTRSs (which are special deterministic 3-OSRTs where the set of sorts S contains a single sort and the set of equations B is empty) is equivalent to *quasi-decreasingness*, i.e., the existence of a well-founded partial ordering $\succ$ on terms satisfying that: (1) the one-step rewriting relation is contained in $\succ$: $\rightarrow_{\mathcal{R}} \subseteq \succ$, (2) the strict subterm relation is contained in $\succ$: $\rhd \subseteq \succ$, and (3) for every rule $\ell \rightarrow r \Leftarrow s_1 \rightarrow t_1, \ldots, s_n \rightarrow t_n$, substitution σ, and index i, $0 \leq i < n$, if $\sigma(s_j) \rightarrow^*_{\mathcal{R}} \sigma(t_j)$ for every $1 \leq j \leq i$, then $\sigma(\ell) \succ \sigma(s_{i+1})$. In the following, we generalize this result to deterministic 3-OSRTs under the assumptions on B stated in Sect. 2. We use *strong* operational termination and operational termination as synonyms. This is done to distinguish it from a notion of *weak* operational termination presented later. Now we address the problem of defining appropriate orderings for dealing with order-sorted terms and rewrite theories.

3.1   Orderings for Order-Sorted Terms

A strict ordering $\succ_s$ on terms of sort s is an irreflexive and transitive binary relation on $\mathcal{T}_\Sigma(\mathcal{X})_s$. A strict ordering $\succ_{[s]}$ on terms of sort in the connected component $[s]$ (of $S/\equiv_\leq$) is an irreflexive and transitive binary relation on $\mathcal{T}_\Sigma(\mathcal{X})_{[s]}$.

Remark 1. Order-sorted rewriting proceeds by transforming terms of the same connected component $[s] \in S/\equiv_{\leq}$. Therefore, orderings $\succ_{[s]}$ indexed by connected components of sorts, rather than by sorts, are more appropriate for compatibility with the order-sorted rewrite relation. Indeed, note that $\to_{\mathcal{R}}^+ = (\to_{\mathcal{R}[s]}^+)$ is a well-founded S-ordering if the one-step rewrite relation is terminating, an that it is monotonic if $\mathcal{R}$ is sort-decreasing. On the other hand, we can always obtain an ordering $\succ_s$ on terms of sort s as follows: $\succ_s = \succ_{[s]} \cap \mathcal{T}_{\Sigma}(\mathcal{X})_s^2$.

A strict S-ordering $\succ_S = \{\succ_{[s]}\}_{[s] \in S/\equiv_{\leq}}$ is an S-sorted strict ordering on $\mathcal{T}_{\Sigma}(\mathcal{X})$, i.e., given terms $u, v \in \mathcal{T}_{\Sigma}(\mathcal{X})$, $u \succ_S v$ if and only if $u, v \in T(\mathcal{F}, \mathcal{X})_{[s]}$ for some $[s] \in S/\equiv_{\leq}$ and $u \succ_{[s]} v$. An S-ordering $\succ_S$ is: *well-founded* if its components $\succ_{[s]}$ are well-founded for all $s \in S$; *stable* if for all S-sorted substitution σ, $s \in S$, and terms $u, v \in \mathcal{T}_{\Sigma}(\mathcal{X})_{[s]}$ $u \succ_{[s]} v$, then $\sigma(u) \succ_{[s]} \sigma(v)$; *monotonic* if for all $f : s_1 \cdots s_k \to s \in \Sigma$ and terms $u_i, v_i \in \mathcal{T}_{\Sigma}(\mathcal{X})_{[s]}$ for $1 \leq i \leq k$, if $u_i \succ_{[s_i]} v_i$, then $f(u_1, \ldots, u_i, \ldots, u_k) \succ_{[s]} f(u_1, \ldots, u_i, \ldots, u_k)$. An S-ordering $\succ_S$ on $\mathcal{T}_{\Sigma}(\mathcal{X})$ is compatible with a set of equations B on $\mathcal{T}_{\Sigma}(\mathcal{X})$ if for all terms u, u', v, whenever $u \succ_S v$ and $u' =_B u$, we have $u' \succ_S v$ (in short: $=_B \circ \succ \subseteq \succ$). The previous definitions generalize to arbitrary relations (quasi-orderings $\gtrsim$, equivalences $\approx$, etc.) on order-sorted terms.

Remark 2. S-sorted orderings cannot compare terms in different connected components. Still, S-sorted orderings are the natural ones when comparing the left- and right-hand sides of the rules of an order-sorted (conditional) rewrite system.

A term ordering $\succ$ is a strict order on $\mathcal{T}_{\Sigma}(\mathcal{X})$. An S-sorted ordering $\succ_S$ on $\mathcal{T}_{\Sigma}(\mathcal{X})$ defines a term ordering on $\mathcal{T}_{\Sigma}(\mathcal{X})$: $u \succ v$ iff $\exists [s] \in S/\equiv_{\leq}$ such that $u \succ_{[s]} v$. A term ordering which is *not* S-sorted is the subterm relation $\unrhd$: $\forall u, v \in \mathcal{T}_{\Sigma}(\mathcal{X})$, $u \unrhd v$ if either $u = v$ or $u = f(u_1, \ldots, u_k)$ for some $f : s_1 \cdots s_k \to s \in \Sigma$ and $u_i \unrhd t$ for some i, $1 \leq i \leq k$. We write $u \rhd v$ if $u \unrhd v$ and $u \neq v$.

3.2 Quasi-Decreasingness and (Strong) Operational Termination of Deterministic 3-OSRTs

After the previous discussion, we can provide a generalization to deterministic 3-OSRTs of the usual notion of quasi-decreasingness for deterministic 3-CTRSs.

Definition 1 (Quasi-decreasingness). *A deterministic 3-OSRT (Σ, B, R) is quasi-decreasing if there is a well-founded term ordering $\succ$ on $\mathcal{T}_{\Sigma}(\mathcal{X})$ satisfying: (1) $\to_{\mathcal{R}} \subseteq \succ$, (2) $=_B \circ \succ \subseteq \succ$, (3) $\rhd \subseteq \succ$, and (4) for every rule $l \to r \Leftarrow u_1 \to v_1, \ldots, u_n \to v_n$, S-sorted substitution σ, and index i, $0 \leq i < n$, if $\sigma(u_j) \to_{\mathcal{R}}^* \sigma(v_j)$ for every $1 \leq j \leq i$, then $\sigma(l) \succ \sigma(s_{i+1})$.*

Quasi-decreasingness is a sufficient condition for operational termination of deterministic 3-OSRTs.

Theorem 1. *Let $\mathcal{R}$ be a deterministic 3-OSRT. If $\mathcal{R}$ is quasi-decreasing, then it is operationally terminating.*

Quasi-decreasingness is also necessary for operational termination of order-sorted and *sort-decreasing* rewrite theories. Due to our assumption that the equations B are sort-preserving and the B-coherence assumption, sort-decreasingness is stable under B-equivalence classes.

Remark 3. Our definition of sort-decreasing conditional rule does *not* impose anything to the conditional part of the rules. In this paper, we need sort-decreasingness to ensure *monotonicity* of conditional rewriting (see Proposition 1). This holds without any further restriction on the conditions of the rules.

Thanks to the stability of sort-decreasing rules under B-equality ensured by the assumptions on B we then have:

Proposition 1. [9] *Let $\mathcal{R}$ be a sort-decreasing OSRT, $t, u, v \in \mathcal{T}_{\Sigma}(\mathcal{X})$ and $p \in \mathcal{P}os(t)$. If $t = t[u]_p$ and $u \rightarrow v$, then $t[u]_p \rightarrow t[v]_p$.*

Without sort-decreasingness, this important result does not hold (see [9]). This assumption is essential in our proof of the following result.

Theorem 2. *Let $\mathcal{R}$ be a sort-decreasing deterministic 3-OSRT. If $\mathcal{R}$ is operationally terminating, then it is quasi-decreasing.*

Thus, quasi-decreasingness characterizes operational termination of order-sorted, sort-decreasing rewrite theories.

Corollary 1. *A sort-decreasing deterministic 3-OSRT $\mathcal{R}$ is operationally terminating if and only if it is quasi-decreasing.*

4   Computing with Normal Rewrite Theories

Definition 2 (Irreducible forms and weak termination). *Let $\mathcal{R}$ be an OSRT and s, t be terms. We say that t is irreducible if, for any term u, $t \not\rightarrow_{\mathcal{R}} u$. $\mathsf{Irr}(\mathcal{R})$ (resp. $\mathsf{GIrr}(\mathcal{R})$) is the set of irreducible terms (resp. ground terms) of $\mathcal{R}$.*

If s rewrites to an irreducible term t, we say that s has a (not necessarily unique) irreducible form t, denoted $s \twoheadrightarrow t$. If every term s has an irreducible form, i.e., $s \twoheadrightarrow t$ for some irreducible term t, then $\mathcal{R}$ is called weakly terminating.

Terminating OSRTs are weakly terminating (in general, the opposite is not true).

Definition 3 (Normal form, weak normalization). *A term t is called a normal form if it is irreducible and operationally 1-terminating. Let $\mathsf{NF}(\mathcal{R})$ (resp. $\mathsf{GNF}(\mathcal{R})$) be the set of normal forms (resp. ground normal forms) of $\mathcal{R}$.*

If $s \twoheadrightarrow t$ and t is a normal form, we then write $s \rightarrow^! t$ and call t a normal form of s. If every (ground) term s has a normal form, i.e., $s \rightarrow^! t$ for some normal form t, then $\mathcal{R}$ is called weakly (ground) operationally terminating (or weakly (ground) normalizing).

Remark 4 (Notation). If $\mathcal{R}$ is confluent and weakly operationally terminating, then we write $t \rightarrow^!_{\mathcal{R}} u$ for $t \twoheadrightarrow_{\mathcal{R}} u$, denote such a u by $u = t!_{\mathcal{R}}$ or $u = can_{\mathcal{R}}(t)$, and call it *the $\mathcal{R}$-canonical form* of t which is unique up to B-equality.

Note that $\twoheadrightarrow_{\mathcal{R}/B} \supseteq \to^!_{\mathcal{R}/B}$ and $\mathsf{NF}(\mathcal{R}) \subseteq \mathsf{Irr}(\mathcal{R})$ (this inclusion can be strict!).

Example 1. The one-step rewrite relation for $a \to b \Leftarrow a \to c$ (a single rule OSRT) is empty. Hence, a is irreducible. However, a is *not* a normal form: every attempt to prove a reduction step on a starts an infinite proof tree.

There can also be *reducible* terms that are *not* operationally 1-terminating.

Example 2. Term $f(a)$ is not operationally 1-terminating in the 2-CTRS $\mathcal{R}$:

$$g(a) \to c(b) \tag{1}$$
$$b \to f(a) \tag{2}$$
$$f(x) \to x \Leftarrow g(x) \to c(y) \tag{3}$$

Since $g(a) \to c(b)$, we have $f(a) \to a$ by means of a finite proof tree. However, since the evaluation of the condition could *continue* beyond $c(b)$

$$g(a) \to c(\underline{b}) \to c(f(a))$$

and the term $f(a)$ can start a new (deep) proof tree, we also have an infinite (well-formed) proof tree for the goal $f(a) \to u$ with u arbitrary.

Remark 5. Note that $\mathcal{R}$ in Example 2 is *terminating*, i.e., there is no infinite rewrite sequence $t_1 \to_{\mathcal{R}} t_2 \to_{\mathcal{R}} \cdots$. This is easy to see, because the *underlying TRS* $\mathcal{R}_u = \{\ell \to r \mid \ell \to r \Leftarrow c \in \mathcal{R}\}$ is clearly terminating.

Definition 4 (Normal and strongly deterministic rewrite theory).
A deterministic OSRT $\mathcal{R}$ is called normal *(resp.* ground normal*) if the set* $\mathsf{Irr}(\mathcal{R})$ *(resp. the set* $\mathsf{GIrr}(\mathcal{R})$*) is operationally terminating, i.e., every irreducible (ground) term is a (ground) normal form:* $\mathsf{Irr}(\mathcal{R}) = \mathsf{NF}(\mathcal{R})$ *(resp.* $\mathsf{GIrr}(\mathcal{R}) = \mathsf{GNF}(\mathcal{R})$*).*
   A normal OSRT $\mathcal{R} = (\Sigma, B, R)$ is called strongly deterministic *if for each $\ell \to r \Leftarrow s_1 \to t_1, \ldots, s_n \to t_n$ in R, and each substitution θ such that $\theta(x) \in \mathsf{NF}(\mathcal{R})$ for each $x \in \mathcal{X}$, we have:* $\theta(t_1), \ldots, \theta(t_n) \in \mathsf{NF}(\mathcal{R})$.

The B-coherence assumption then gives us:

Proposition 2. *If a strongly deterministic 3-OSRT $\mathcal{R}$ is (ground) confluent and weakly normalizing, then $\mathcal{R}$ is (ground) normal.*

Remark 6. Ground normality is the minimum prerequisite for executability. For ground normal and ground confluent deterministic 3-OSRT $\mathcal{R}$, each ground term t has *at most* one normal form up to B-equality and the process $t \mapsto [t!_{\mathcal{R}}]_B$ defines a recursive partial function, since $\mathcal{R}$ need not even be weakly terminating.

In order to prove that a strongly deterministic OSRT $\mathcal{R} = (\Sigma, B, R)$ is ground normal, we can proceed as follows:

1. Identify a subsignature of constructors Ω with nonempty sorts such that the rules in R decompose as a disjoint union $R_{(\Sigma-\Omega)}\cup R_\Omega$, where the R_Ω have only Ω terms in their rules and conditions, and each $\ell \to r \Leftarrow s_1 \to t_1, \ldots, s_n \to t_n$ in $R_{(\Sigma-\Omega)}$ has $l = f(t_1, \ldots, t_n)$ for some $f \in \Sigma - \Omega$. We also assume that the axioms B decompose as a disjoint union $B_{(\Sigma-\Omega)} \cup B_\Omega$ with the B_Ω involving only Ω terms, and the $B_{(\Sigma-\Omega)}$ *not* Ω-equations. This yields an ORST inclusion $\mathcal{R}_\Omega \subseteq \mathcal{R}$, with $\mathcal{R}_\Omega = (\Omega, B_\Omega, R_\Omega)$.
2. Prove (by inductive theorem proving) that for all defined symbols $f \in \Sigma - \Omega$, say with rank $f : s_1 \cdots s_n \longrightarrow s$, the following inductive property holds:

$$\forall x_1 \in \mathcal{T}_{\Omega_{s_1}}, \ldots, x_n \in \mathcal{T}_{\Omega_{s_n}}, \exists y f(x_1, \ldots, x_n) \to^1_{\mathcal{R}} y$$

Then if $\mathcal{R}_\Omega$ is *operationally terminating*, $\mathcal{R}$ is *ground normal* and, furthermore, $\mathsf{GNF}(\mathcal{R}) \subseteq \mathcal{T}_\Omega$. That is, an inductive proof of ground reducibility w.r.t. the constructors shows that $t \in \mathcal{T}_\Sigma$ is a ground normal form iff:

1. $t \in \mathcal{T}_\Omega$; and
2. $t \in \mathsf{GNF}(\mathcal{R}_\Omega)$.

The assumptions on B give us:

Proposition 3. *Let* $\mathcal{R} = (\Sigma, B, R)$ *be a normal, sort-decreasing, confluent, strongly deterministic 3-OSRT such that R is finite. If $\mathcal{R}$ is weakly operationally terminating, then the function $t \mapsto [t!_{\mathcal{R}}]_B$ is* total recursive *and preserves sorts.*

Note that, otherwise, if $\mathcal{R}$ is confluent but *not* weakly operationally terminating, then the function $t \mapsto [u]_B$ with $t \twoheadrightarrow u$ *may not be recursive*, even if each t has an *irreducible* form. Implicit in Proposition 3 is the fact that, under such conditions plus the assumptions on B, when we interpret each $\ell \to r \Leftarrow s_1 \to t_1, \ldots, s_n \to t_n$ in R as a *conditional equation* $\ell = r \Leftarrow s_1 = t_1, \ldots, s_n = t_n$, normal forms define an *algebra* $\mathcal{C}_{\Sigma/R,B}$, called the *canonical term algebra* of $\mathcal{R}$. Specifically, for each sort s we define $\mathcal{C}_{\Sigma/R,B,s} = \mathsf{GNF}(\mathcal{R})/=_B \cap \mathcal{T}_{\Sigma/B}$, that is, the set of B-equivalence classes of ground normal forms of sort s, and, for each $f : s_1 \cdots s_n \longrightarrow s$ in Σ its interpretation in $\mathcal{C}_{\Sigma/R,B}$ maps each tuple $([t_1]_B, \ldots, [t_n]_B)$ with $[t_i]_B \in \mathcal{C}_{\Sigma/R,B,s_i}$ to the B-equivalence class $[f(t_1, \ldots, t_n)!_{\mathcal{R}}]_B$, which is well-defined and unique because of confluence, sort-decreasingness and B-coherence. The agreement between the operational semantics of $\mathcal{R}$ when terms are normalized by rewriting, and the mathematical semantics of $\mathcal{R}$ when its rules are interpreted as conditional equations can then be expressed for such general OSRTs as follows:

Corollary 2. *For $\mathcal{R} = (\Sigma, B, R)$ a sort-decreasing, ground confluent and weakly ground operationally terminating strongly deterministic 3-OSRT, the canonical term algebra $\mathcal{C}_{\Sigma/\mathcal{R}}$ is a computable algebra. Furthermore, $\mathcal{T}_{\Sigma/R\cup B} \simeq \mathcal{C}_{\Sigma/R,B}$.*

Computing the normal form $t!_{\mathcal{R}}$ of a term t under the assumptions of Corollary 2 is somewhat complex, and can be computationally expensive. It is therefore useful to seek conditions under which we can more efficiently compute normal forms.

We consider two such conditions, which can be executed in Maude [2] in a straight-forward manner.

The first case is that of a strongly deterministic 3-OSRT that is sort-decreasing, ground confluent, 1-terminating, and ground weakly terminating and has a finite number of rewrite rules. Under such conditions, the **search** command in Maude asking for the fully-reduced first result for the given input ground term will compute such a normal form. This assumes that the rules in the theory are expressed as *rules* in a Maude system module and *not as equations* in a functional module, even though the module does indeed have a *functional semantics*. A simple theory transformation, easily definable in Maude's **META-LEVEL** module, can transform the given functional module into its associated system module. Let us illustrate this general method with an example. Note that in this example the set B of axioms is empty. The functional module **fmod WEAK-NORM endfm** expresses the rewrite rules R as conditional equations, whereas the system module **mod WEAK-NORM endm** expresses them explicitly as rewrite rules.

```
fmod WEAK-NORM is
  protecting BOOL .
  sorts Nat Nat? .
  subsort Nat < Nat? .
  op 0 : -> Nat .              op s : Nat -> Nat .
  op _+_ : Nat Nat -> Nat .    op even : Nat -> Bool .
  ops f g : Nat? -> Nat? .
  vars N M : Nat .
  eq N + 0 = N .               eq N + s(M) = s(N + M) .
  eq even(0) = true .          eq even(s(0)) = false .
  eq even(s(s(N))) = even(N) . eq g(N) = N .
  eq f(N) = N + N .
  ceq f(N) = g(f(N)) if true := even(N) .
endfm
```

This module is sort-decreasing, weakly terminating and ground confluent. By the technique presented in Sect. 5, we can prove it normal. Giving to Maude the term f(0) for evaluation leads to non-terminating behavior. That is, the usual operational semantics for evaluating operationally terminating confluent theories cannot be relied upon to compute normal forms. This problem can be solved by transforming the above functional module into a system module, that is, by transforming equations into rules, and using Maude's **search** command:

```
mod WEAK-NORM is
  protecting BOOL .
  sorts Nat Nat? .
  subsort Nat < Nat? .
  op 0 : -> Nat .              op s : Nat -> Nat .
  op _+_ : Nat Nat -> Nat .    op even : Nat -> Bool .
  ops f g : Nat? -> Nat? .
  vars N M : Nat .
  rl N + 0 => N .              rl N + s(M) => s(N + M) .
```

```
  rl even(0) => true .              rl even(s(0)) => false .
  rl even(s(s(N))) => even(N) .     rl g(N) => N .
  rl f(N) => N + N .
  crl f(N) => g(f(N)) if even(N) => true .
endm
```

The normal form of a term can then be obtained by searching for the *first* result of a *terminating* computation from the given term. By confluence such a result is unique up to B-equality, exists by weak operational termination, and can be found by search without risk of looping thanks to 1-termination:

```
Maude> search [1] f(0) =>! N:Nat .
search in WEAK-NORM : f(0) =>! N .
Solution 1 (state 5)
states: 9  rewrites: 12 in 0ms cpu (0ms real) (44943 rewrites/second)
N --> 0
Maude> search [1] f(s(s(0))) =>! N:Nat .
search in WEAK-NORM : f(s(s(0))) =>! N .
Solution 1 (state 14)
states: 20  rewrites: 35 in 0ms cpu (0ms real) (55118 rewrites/second)
N --> s(s(s(s(0))))
Maude> search [1] f(s(s(s(s(0))))) =>! N:Nat .
search in WEAK-NORM : f(s(s(s(s(0))))) =>! N .
Solution 1 (state 27)
states: 35  rewrites: 70 in 1ms cpu (1ms real) (57189 rewrites/second)
N --> s(s(s(s(s(s(s(s(0))))))))
```

The second case where execution of a weakly operationally terminating deterministic OSRT can be achieved using execution mechanisms already available in Maude and yields again a full agreement between operational and mathematical semantics is the one of context-sensitive OSRTs under some reasonable assumptions. A *context-sensitive* [6] OSRT is a four-tuple $\mathcal{R} = (\Sigma, B, R, \mu)$, where (Σ, B, R) is an OSRT, and μ maps each $f : s_1 \cdots s_n \longrightarrow s$ in Σ to a subset $\mu(f) \subseteq \{1, \ldots, n\}$ of the argument positions of f under which rewriting is allowed. The operational semantics of context-sensitive OSRTs is defined by restricting the inference system of Fig. 1 with the single restriction that, in the (Cong) Rule, i with $1 \leq i \leq k$ must furthermore satisfy $i \in \mu(f)$.

The Lemma below states the required conditions on $\mathcal{R} = (\Sigma, B, R, \mu)$ yielding the desired agreement between operational and mathematical semantics. This result relies on the notion of μ-sufficient completeness and of the algebra $\mathcal{C}_\mathcal{R}^\mu$ of term in μ-normal form (see [5]).

Lemma 1. *If $\mathcal{R}$ is a confluent, sort decreasing and strongly deterministic context-sensitive 3-OSRT $\mathcal{R} = (\Sigma, B, R, \mu)$, which is μ-operationally terminating and μ-sufficiently complete for $\Omega \subseteq \Sigma$ a subsignature of free constructors modulo B, then:*

1. $\mathcal{R}$ is ground weakly operationally terminating.
2. $\mathcal{C}_\mathcal{R}^\mu |_\Omega = \mathcal{T}_{\Omega/B}.$

3. For each $t \in \mathcal{T}_\Sigma$, $t!_{\mathcal{R},B} = t!^\mu_{\mathcal{R},B}$, that is, the normal form and the μ-normal form of t (which can be computed by Maude's reduce command) coincide.

4. $\mathcal{T}_{\Sigma/E\cup B} \simeq \mathcal{C}^\mu_{E/B}$ (agreement between operational and denotational semantics).

Under the assumptions of Lemma 1, we compute normal forms as follows: since Maude supports the execution of confluent context-sensitive 3-OSRTs $\mathcal{R} = (\Sigma, B, R, \mu)$ specified as functional modules, we just use the reduce command to compute normal μ-forms, which under the assumptions in Lemma 1 are also ordinary normal forms in the underlying OSRT (Σ, B, R). We can illustrate these ideas with the following example of a context-sensitive 3-OSRT in Maude:

```
fmod FACTORIAL is
  protecting NAT .
  op monus : Nat Nat -> Nat .
  op _~_ : Nat Nat -> Bool [comm] .
  op [_,_,_] : Bool Nat Nat -> Nat [strat (1 0)] .
  op fact : Nat -> Nat .
  vars N M : Nat .
  eq monus(s(N),s(M)) = monus(N,M) .
  ceq monus(N,M) = N if M {:=} 0 .
  ceq monus(N,M) = 0 if N {:=} 0 .
  eq N ~ N = true .
  eq s(N) ~ s(M) = N ~ M .
  eq 0 ~ s(N) = false .
  eq [true,N,M] = N .
  eq [false,N,M] = M .
  eq fact(N) = [(N ~ 0),s(0),N * fact(monus(N,s(0)))] .
endfm
```

This theory, though ground confluent, is cleary non-terminating because of the last equation. Here, μ does not restrict any argument positions, except for the if-then-else operator $[\_, \_, \_]$, where $\mu([\_, \_, \_]) = \{1\}$, as specified by the strat attribute. It is, however, operationally μ-terminating and has 0 and s, and true, false as free constructors. Here are some evaluations:

```
Maude> red fact(2) .
reduce in FACTORIAL : fact(2) .
rewrites: 15 in 0ms cpu (0ms real) (192307 rewrites/second)
result NzNat: 2
Maude> red fact(3) .
reduce in FACTORIAL : fact(3) .
rewrites: 21 in 0ms cpu (0ms real) (10500000 rewrites/second)
result NzNat: 6
Maude> red fact(4) .
reduce in FACTORIAL : fact(4) .
rewrites: 27 in 0ms cpu (0ms real) (692307 rewrites/second)
result NzNat: 24
Maude> red fact(5) .
reduce in FACTORIAL : fact(5) .
```

```
rewrites: 33 in 0ms cpu (0ms real) (358695 rewrites/second)
result NzNat: 120
```

We end this section with the following result that, though well-known (see, e.g., [12]), has an easier proof with a rewrite theory with axioms B of associtivity and identity for strings. In some sense this result shows how wild the beasts in the general menagerie of OSRTs can be, and illustrates the need for notions such as that of normal theory to obtain reasonable computational behaviors.

Theorem 3. *There is a 2-OSRTs $\mathcal{R}$ and a sort s such that the set $\mathsf{Irr}(\mathcal{R})_s \subseteq T(\mathcal{F}, \mathcal{X})_s$ of $\mathcal{R}$-irreducible terms is* not *recursively enumerable, so it is not even semi-decidable* if *a term is $\mathcal{R}$-irreducible.*

5   Proving Order-Sorted Rewrite Theories Normal

1-operationally terminating rewrite theories are *normal*. The opposite is not true.

Example 3. The CTRS $\mathcal{R}$ in Example 2 is *not* 1-operationally terminating. However, $\mathcal{R}$ is normal: assume that there is a minimal irreducible term s having an infinite well-formed proof tree whose strict subterms are normal forms. Since f is the only symbol defined by a conditional rule, $s = f(t)$ for some normal form t. Since $f(t)$ is irreducible, the evaluation of the condition in the rule cannot succeed, i.e., $g(t)$ must be irreducible. Since t is a normal form, $g(t)$ cannot start any infinite well-formed tree. Contradiction.

Remark 7. As noticed in Remark 5, $\mathcal{R}$ in Example 2 is terminating. Since $\mathcal{R}$ is *not* 1-operationally terminating and a fortiori not operationally terminating, it follows from Example 3 that neither 1-operational termination nor operational termination of $\mathcal{R}$ follow from the termination and normality of $\mathcal{R}$.

An interesting feature in the treatment of innermost termination problems using the dependency pair approach [1] is that, since the variables in the right-hand side of the dependency pairs are in normal form, the rules which can be used to connect contiguous dependency pairs are usually a proper subset of the rules in the TRS. This leads to the notion of *usable rules* [1, Definition 32] which simplifies the proofs of innermost termination of rewriting.

In our analysis of normal rewrite theories we have a similar situation: when an irreducible term $t = f(t_1, \ldots, t_k)$ is tested to see whether it is a normal form, we know that all possible reductions derived from a proof $t \to x$ (for a fresh variable x) cause the evaluation of the conditional part c of some conditional rule $f(\ell_1, \ldots, \ell_k) \to r \Leftarrow c$. Therefore, if we single out those rules that *can be* involved in any attempt to evaluate $\sigma(c)$ for some σ such that $t = \sigma(f(\ell_1, \ldots, \ell_k))$, we can obtain a more precise analysis. The notion of usable rule provides an upper, purely syntactic, approximation to the set of rules that eventually apply to a term t during any possible rewriting on t. We keep the original flavor of the original, unsorted notion in the following definition.

Definition 5 (Usable rules for a rewrite theory). *Let* $\mathcal{R} = (\Sigma, B, R)$ *be an OSRT. Let* $RULES(\mathcal{R}, t)$ *be the set of rules defining symbols occurring in* t:

$$RULES(\mathcal{R}, t) = \{\ell \to r \Leftarrow c \in R \mid \exists p \in \mathcal{P}os(t), root(\ell) = root(t|_p)\}$$

Then, the set of usable rules *of* $\mathcal{R}$ *for* t *is:*

$$\mathcal{U}(\mathcal{R}, t) = RULES(\mathcal{R}, t) \cup \bigcup_{l \to r \Leftarrow c \in RULES(\mathcal{R}, t)} \mathcal{U}(\mathcal{R}', r) \cup \bigcup_{s_i \to t_i \in c} \mathcal{U}(\mathcal{R}', s_i)$$

where $\mathcal{R}' = \mathcal{R} - RULES(\mathcal{R}, t)$.

That is: we consider both unconditional and conditional rules and add the rules that could be *used* to evaluate the conditions in the rules. Since we are dealing with OSRTs $\mathcal{R} = (\Sigma, B, R)$, rewriting happens *modulo B*. This raises the issue of whether the above definition of usable rules is overly syntactic, that is, not stable under B-equality. The key issue is whether in the (Repl) rule in the inference system of Fig. 1 the top symbol of the redex u coincides with that of the lefthand side l. This is the case by requiring the axioms B to be as follows:

$$B = \bigcup_{f:[s_1]\cdots[s_n]\to[s]\in\Sigma} B_f$$

where B_f is a set of equations $u = v$ with $u, v \in \mathcal{T}_{\{f\}}(\mathcal{X}) - \mathcal{X}$, i.e., only symbol f is allowed (and must) to occur in the equations belonging to B_f. Associativity and commutativity axioms satisfy this requirement, which can even be made to work for identity axioms by performing the semantics-preserving transformation described in [3]. Now we can give the main result of this section. For an OSRT $\mathcal{R} = (\Sigma, B, R)$, we say that B *preserves* the $\mathcal{R}$-normal forms if for all $\mathcal{R}$-normal forms t, if $t =_B u$, then u is an $\mathcal{R}$-normal form. *B-coherence*, which is a usual requirement for working OSRTs, implies this property. By $\mathcal{R}_C$ we denote the OSRT obtained as the union of $\mathcal{U}(\mathcal{R}, s)$ for all *lhs*'s conditions in the rules of $\mathcal{R}$:

$$\mathcal{R}_C = \bigcup_{\ell \to r \Leftarrow c} \bigcup_{s \to t \in c} \mathcal{U}(\mathcal{R}, s)$$

Theorem 4. *A deterministic 3-OSRT* $\mathcal{R} = (\Sigma, B, R)$ *is normal if B preserves the $\mathcal{R}$-normal forms and $\mathcal{R}_C$ is operationally terminating.*

Example 4. Consider the functional module WEAK-NORM in Sect. 4. Here, $\mathcal{R}_C$ is the unconditional subOSRT consisting of the rules defining **even**. Note that $\mathcal{R}_C$ has no conditional rule and is clearly terminating, hence operationally terminating. We conclude that, as claimed, WEAK-NORM is a normal OSRT.

Now we show that Theorem 4 does *not* characterize normality of OSRTs:

Example 5. Consider the following deterministic 1-CTRS:

$$a \to b \qquad f(x) \to x \Leftarrow c \to d, a \to c$$
$$b \to a$$

Every term $f(t)$ is *irreducible* and also a normal form because the unsatisfiable condition $c \to d$ prevents the looping evaluation of the condition $a \to c$. However, $\mathcal{R}_C = \{a \to b, b \to a\}$ is not (operationally) terminating.

6   Conclusions and Future Work

The results presented in this paper can be viewed from two complementary perspectives: one more theoretical, and another more practical. At the theoretical level, we have investigated parts of the *terra incognita* of conditional term rewriting by asking and providing precise answers to innocent-sounding questions such as: what is a normal form? How can normal forms be effectively computed? How should the notion of weakly normalizing system be understood in the conditional case? How can good executability properties be ensured for a theory? There is, however, a more practical aspect to all these results. It consists in taking to heart the idea that rewrite theories are an excellent framework for declarative programming and formal specification and verification. From this second perspective, the questions asked and answered include: what is the most general notion possible of a conditional rule-based program for which normal forms can be computed? What is the appropriate term normalization operational semantics? How can it be made more efficient? What are the most general possible requirements under which conditional functional programs can be given an initial algebra semantics which *fully agrees* with their operational semantics?

Future work should further investigate proof methods and supporting tools for all the properties discussed here. For example, although the characterization of the operation termination of an OSRT in terms of quasi-decreasingness offers in principle a complete proof method, we are currently investigating a far-reaching generalization to the conditional case of the dependency pair method that seems considerably more effective for mechanizing actual proofs. In general, the development of *intrinsic methods* for proving both strong and weak operational termination of OSRTs seems both quite attractive and sorely needed.

With regard to checking normality of OSRTs, Example 5 shows that the notion of operational termination of OSRTs is perhaps too strong to capture normality of some OSRTs. In [8] we have introduced the *weaker* notion of V-termination for CTRSs, which captures the absence of infinite computations involving an infinite number of failed attempts to issue a *single* rewriting step (which we associate to a *vertical* dimension of nontermination in [8]). The definition of V-termination of CTRSs is based on the Dependency Pairs for CTRSs (2D DPs) described in [8]. The interesting feature is that V-termination can be *independently* proved in the 2D DP Framework. Unfortunately, V-termination does not yield a valid criterion to prove CTRSs normal.

Example 6. The following variant $\mathcal{R}'$ of $\mathcal{R}$ in Example 5

$$a \to b \qquad f(x) \to x \Leftarrow a \to c$$
$$b \to a$$

is *not* normal because terms $f(t)$ are *irreducible* (since $a \to^* c$ cannot be satisfied), but they are *not* normal forms because $f(t) \to u$ starts an infinite well-formed tree (i.e., $\mathcal{R}'$ is *not* 1-terminating). However, by using the methods in [8] it is easy to prove that $\mathcal{R}'$ is V-terminating.

Since 1-termination implies V-termination, the following hierarchy of properties

$$Operational\ termination \Rightarrow 1\text{-termination} \Rightarrow V\text{-termination}$$
$$\Downarrow$$
$$Normal\ theory$$

suggests now the development of techniques for proving 1-termination as an important topic for further research.

References

1. Arts, T., Giesl, J.: Termination of term rewriting using dependency Pairs. Theor. Comput. Sci. **236**(1–2), 133–178 (2000)
2. Clavel, M., Durán, F., Eker, S., Lincoln, P., Martí-Oliet, N., Meseguer, J., Talcott, C. (eds.): All About Maude. LNCS, vol. 4350. Springer, Heidelberg (2007)
3. Durán, F., Lucas, S., Meseguer, J.: Termination modulo combinations of equational theories. In: Ghilardi, S., Sebastiani, R. (eds.) FroCoS 2009. LNCS, vol. 5749, pp. 246–262. Springer, Heidelberg (2009)
4. Goguen, J., Meseguer, J.: Order-sorted algebra I: equational deduction for multiple inheritance, overloading, exceptions and partial operations. Theor. Comput. Sci. **105**, 217–273 (1992)
5. Hendrix, J., Meseguer, J.: On the completeness of context-sensitive order-sorted specifications. In: Baader, F. (ed.) RTA 2007. LNCS, vol. 4533, pp. 229–245. Springer, Heidelberg (2007)
6. Lucas, S.: Context-sensitive computations in functional and functional logic programs. J. Funct. Logic Program. **1998**(1), 1–61 (1998)
7. Lucas, S., Marché, C., Meseguer, J.: Operational termination of conditional term rewriting systems. Inf. Process. Lett. **95**, 446–453 (2005)
8. Lucas, S., Meseguer, J.: 2D dependency Pairs for proving operational termination of CTRSs. In: Escobar, S. (ed.) WRLA 2014. LNCS, vol. 8663, pp. 195–212. Springer, Heidelberg (2014)
9. Lucas, S., Meseguer, J.: Order-sorted dependency Pairs. In: Proceedings of PPDP'08, pp. 108–119. ACM Press (2008)
10. Meseguer, J.: Membership algebra as a logical framework for equational specification. In: Parisi-Presicce, Francesco (ed.) WADT 1997. LNCS, vol. 1376, pp. 18–61. Springer, Heidelberg (1998)
11. Ohlebusch, E.: Advanced Topics in Term Rewriting. Springer, New York (2002)
12. TeReSe: Term Rewriting Systems, Cambridge University Press (2003)

2D Dependency Pairs for Proving Operational Termination of CTRSs

Salvador Lucas[1,2]([✉]) and José Meseguer[2]

[1] DSIC, Universitat Politècnica de València, València, Spain
[2] Computer Science Department, University of Illinois at Urbana-Champaign, Champaign, IL, USA
slucas@dsic.upv.es

Abstract. The notion of *operational termination* captures nonterminating computations due to subsidiary processes that are necessary to issue a *single* 'main' step but which often remain 'hidden' when the main computation sequence is observed. This highlights *two dimensions* of nontermination: one for the infinite sequencing of computation steps, and the other that concerns the proof of some single steps. For conditional term rewriting systems (CTRSs), we introduce a new *dependency pair framework* which exploits the *bidimensional* nature of conditional rewriting (rewriting steps + satisfaction of the conditions as reachability problems) to obtain a powerful and more expressive framework for proving operational termination of CTRSs.

Keywords: Conditional term rewriting · Dependency pairs · Program analysis · Operational termination

1 Introduction

Assume that we have an *interpreter* for a logic $\mathcal{L}$, i.e., an *inference machine* that, given a theory $\mathcal{S}$ and a goal formula φ, will try to incrementally build a proof tree for φ. Intuitively, we call $\mathcal{S}$ *terminating* if for any φ the interpreter either finds a proof in finite time, or fails in all possible attempts also in finite time. The notion of *operational termination* captures this idea, meaning that, given an initial goal, an interpreter will either succeed in finite time in producing a closed proof tree, or will fail in finite time, not being able to close or extend further any of the possible proof trees, after exhaustively searching all such proof trees [12]. In particular, operational termination captures a *'vertical' dimension* of the termination behavior which is missing in the usual definition of termination of relations as *well-founded*, i.e., "without infinite reduction sequences" (the 'horizontal' dimension).

Research partially supported by NSF grant CNS 13-19109. Salvador Lucas' research was developed during a sabbatical year at the CS Dept. of the UIUC and was also partially supported by Spanish MECD grant PRX12/00214, MINECO project TIN2010-21062-C02-02, and GV grant BEST/2014/026 and project PROMETEO/2011/052.

© Springer International Publishing Switzerland 2014
S. Escobar (Ed.): WRLA 2014, LNCS 8663, pp. 195–212, 2014.
DOI: 10.1007/978-3-319-12904-4_11

Available tools for proving operational termination of conditional rewriting (APROVE [10] or VMTL [16]) rely on *transformations* $\mathcal{U}$ that map each operational termination problem for the CTRS $\mathcal{R}$ into a termination problem for a TRS $\mathcal{U}(\mathcal{R})$. Then, available methods for proving termination of $\mathcal{U}(\mathcal{R})$ are used. However, this transformational approach has substantial limitations.

Example 1. Consider the following CTRS $\mathcal{R}$ [15, Example 8]

$$h(d) \rightarrow c(a) \tag{1}$$

$$h(d) \rightarrow c(b) \tag{2}$$

$$f(k(a), k(b), x) \rightarrow f(x, x, x) \tag{3}$$

$$g(x) \rightarrow k(y) \Leftarrow h(x) \rightarrow d, h(x) \rightarrow c(y) \tag{4}$$

As reported in [15, Example 8], $\mathcal{U}(\mathcal{R})$ is *not* terminating. However, our methods in this paper will show that $\mathcal{R}$ is operationally terminating (Example 19).

Most termination tools for proving termination of (variants of) rewriting with TRSs implement extensions or generalizations of the *Dependency Pair Framework* [7,8]. The main idea is the following: the rules $\ell \rightarrow r$ that are able to produce infinite sequences are those whose right-hand side r contains (possibly recursive) *function calls*. The calls associated to $\ell \rightarrow r$ are represented as new rules $u \rightarrow v$, that are collected in a new TRS DP($\mathcal{R}$) of *dependency pairs* (DPs); $\mathcal{R}$ and DP($\mathcal{R}$) determine *dependency chains* whose finiteness characterize termination of $\mathcal{R}$ [1].

In this paper we generalize this approach to *deterministic 3-CTRSs*, which are the basis of rewriting-based languages like CafeOBJ [5] or Maude [3]. In Sect. 3 we show that computations starting from *minimal* operationally nonterminating terms can always follow a precise path where two sources of nontermination can be identified: infinite sequences of rewriting steps (an *horizontal* dimension), and infinitely many attempts to check the satisfaction of the conditions in the rules (a *vertical* dimension). Section 4 introduces a definition of dependency pairs that makes such a bidimensional nature of infinite computations explicit (we call them *2D DPs*). The corresponding notion of chain of dependency pairs permits a completely *independent* treatment of both dimensions of the termination problems. For 2-CTRSs (a subclass of 3-CTRSs), we characterize *termination* (i.e., the absence of infinite rewrite sequences) in terms of the "horizontal" component of our 2D DPs only. In Sect. 5, we adapt the *Dependency Pair Framework* [7,8] to mechanize proofs of operational termination of deterministic 3-CTRSs using 2D DPs. The framework can also be used to prove *termination* of 2-CTRSs which are *not* operationally terminating.

Example 2. The following deterministic 2-CTRS $\mathcal{R}$:

$$g(a) \rightarrow c(b) \tag{5}$$

$$b \rightarrow f(a) \tag{6}$$

$$f(x) \rightarrow x \Leftarrow g(x) \rightarrow c(y) \tag{7}$$

$$\text{(Refl)} \qquad \overline{t \to^* t}$$

$$\text{(Tran)} \qquad \frac{s \to u \qquad u \to^* t}{s \to^* t}$$

$$\text{(Cong)} \qquad \frac{s_i \to t_i}{f(s_1, \ldots, s_i, \ldots, s_k) \to f(s_1, \ldots, t_i, \ldots, s_k)}$$
$$\text{for all } f \in \mathcal{F} \text{ and } 1 \leq i \leq k = ar(f)$$

$$\text{(Repl)} \qquad \frac{\sigma(s_1) \to^* \sigma(t_1) \quad \ldots \quad \sigma(s_n) \to^* \sigma(t_n)}{\sigma(\ell) \to \sigma(r)}$$
$$\text{for all rules } \ell \to r \Leftarrow s_1 \to t_1 \cdots s_n \to t_n \in \mathcal{R}$$
$$\text{and substitutions } \sigma.$$

Fig. 1. Inference rules for conditional rewriting

is *not* operationally terminating. However, it is *terminating*. We can prove *both things* in our framework (see Examples 13 and 15), illustrating its expressiveness.

Section 6 develops the framework by introducing a number of *processors* and illustrating their use. Section 7 discusses related work and concludes.

2   Preliminaries

Recall from [14] the usual notions and notations regarding term rewriting and CTRSs. An (*oriented*) CTRS $\mathcal{R}$ is a pair $\mathcal{R} = (\mathcal{F}, R)$ where $\mathcal{F}$ is a signature and R a set of rules $\ell \to r \Leftarrow s_1 \to t_1, \cdots, s_n \to t_n$, where the conditions $s_i \to t_i$ for $1 \leq i \leq n$ are intended to express the reachability of (instances of) t_i from (instances of) s_i. As usual, ℓ and r are called the left- and right-hand sides of the rule, and the sequence $s_1 \to t_1, \cdots, s_n \to t_n$ (often abbreviated to c) is the *conditional part* of the rule. Rewrite rules $\ell \to r \Leftarrow c$ are classified according to the distribution of variables among $l, r,$ and $c,$ as follows: type 1, if $\mathcal{V}ar(r) \cup \mathcal{V}ar(c) \subseteq \mathcal{V}ar(\ell)$; type 2, if $\mathcal{V}ar(r) \subseteq \mathcal{V}ar(\ell)$; type 3, if $\mathcal{V}ar(r) \subseteq \mathcal{V}ar(\ell) \cup \mathcal{V}ar(c)$; and type 4, if no restriction is given. An n-CTRS contains only rewrite rules of type $m \leq n$. An oriented 3-CTRS $\mathcal{R}$ is called *deterministic* if for each rule $\ell \to r \Leftarrow s_1 \to t_1, \ldots, s_n \to t_n$ in $\mathcal{R}$ and each $1 \leq i \leq n,$ we have $\mathcal{V}ar(s_i) \subseteq \mathcal{V}ar(l) \cup \bigcup_{j=1}^{i-1} \mathcal{V}ar(t_j).$ Given $\mathcal{R} = (\mathcal{F}, R)$, we consider $\mathcal{F}$ as the disjoint union $\mathcal{F} = \mathcal{C} \uplus \mathcal{D}$ of symbols $c \in \mathcal{C}$ (called *constructors*) and symbols $f \in \mathcal{D}$ (called *defined functions*), where $\mathcal{D} = \{root(l) \mid (l \to r \Leftarrow c) \in R\}$ and $\mathcal{C} = \mathcal{F} - \mathcal{D}$. Terms $t \in \mathcal{T}(\mathcal{F}, \mathcal{X})$ such that $root(t) \in \mathcal{D}$ are called *defined* terms. $Pos_{\mathcal{D}}(t)$ is the set of positions p of subterms $t|_p$ such that $root(t|_p) \in \mathcal{D}$.

A conditional rewrite $s \to^* t$ with a CTRS $\mathcal{R}$ exists if and only if it has a closed proof tree using the inference system in Fig. 1. We say that a proof tree T is *closed* whenever it is finite and contains no open goals; it is *well-formed* if it is either an open goal, or a closed proof tree, or a derivation tree of the form $\frac{T_1 \quad \cdots \quad T_n}{G}$ where, for each j, T_j is itself well-formed, and there is $i \leq n$ such that T_i is not closed, for any $j < i$ T_j is closed, and each of the $T_{i+1},\ldots,T_n$ is an open goal [12]. An infinite proof tree is *well-formed* if it is an ascending chain of well-formed finite proof trees. Intuitively, well-formed trees are the trees that an interpreter would incrementally build when trying to solve one condition at a time from left to right. We write $s \rightarrow_{\mathcal{R}} t$ (resp. $s \rightarrow_{\mathcal{R}}^* t$) iff there is a well-formed proof tree for $s \rightarrow t$ (resp. $s \rightarrow^* t$). The CTRS $\mathcal{R}$ is called *operationally terminating* if no infinite well-formed tree for a goal $s \rightarrow_{\mathcal{R}} t$ or $s \rightarrow_{\mathcal{R}}^* t$ exists. The CTRS $\mathcal{R}$ is called *terminating* if there is no infinite sequence $t_1 \rightarrow_{\mathcal{R}} t_2 \rightarrow_{\mathcal{R}} \cdots$.

3   Minimal Operationally Nonterminating Terms in CTRSs

Given a proof tree T, $root(T)$ is the formula (goal) at the root of the tree, and $left(G)$ is the left-hand side s of goal G, where G is $s \rightarrow t$ or $s \rightarrow^* t$ for some terms s and t.

Definition 1 (Operationally Nonterminating Term). *Let $\mathcal{R}$ be a CTRS. A term t such that $left(root(T)) = t$ for an infinite well-formed proof tree T is called* operationally nonterminating. *If there is no infinite well-formed proof tree T such that $left(root(T)) = t$, then we call t* operationally terminating.

Definition 2 (Minimality). *Let $\mathcal{R}$ be a CTRS. An operationally nonterminating term t is called* minimal *if every strict subterm u of t (i.e., $t \rhd u$) is operationally terminating. Let $\mathcal{T}_{op\text{-}\infty}$ be the set of minimal operationally nonterminating terms associated to $\mathcal{R}$.*

The following lemma shows that operationally nonterminating terms always contain a *minimal* operationally nonterminating term.

Lemma 1. *Let $\mathcal{R} = (\mathcal{F}, R)$ be a CTRS and $s \in \mathcal{T}(\mathcal{F}, \mathcal{X})$. If s is operationally nonterminating, then there is a subterm t of s ($s \trianglerighteq t$) such that $t \in \mathcal{T}_{op\text{-}\infty}$.*

Proposition 1 below establishes that, for $t \in \mathcal{T}_{op\text{-}\infty}$, there is a precise way for an infinite computation to proceed. Roughly speaking, a rule $\ell \rightarrow r \Leftarrow \bigwedge_{i=1}^{n} s_i \rightarrow t_i$ must be used to try a *root-step* on a reduct of t. Then, there is a minimal operationally nonterminating subterm which is either (1) an instance of a non-variable subterm of the *right-hand side* r of the rule (so that the infinite computation continues through the *horizontal* dimension), or (2) an instance of a non-variable subterm of one of the *left-hand sides* s_i of a condition $s_i \rightarrow t_i$ (the infinite computation continues through the *vertical* dimension). Given a term t, $\mathcal{D}Subterm(\mathcal{R}, t) = \{t|_p \mid p \in \mathcal{P}os_{\mathcal{D}}(t)\}$ is the set of defined subterms of t with respect to rules in $\mathcal{R}$. Let $DRules(\mathcal{R}, t)$ be the set of (possibly conditional) rules in $\mathcal{R}$ defining $root(t)$ which *depend* on other defined symbols in $\mathcal{R}$:

$$DRules(\mathcal{R}, t) = \{\ell \rightarrow r \Leftarrow c \in \mathcal{R} \mid root(\ell) = root(t), r \notin \mathcal{T}(\mathcal{C}, \mathcal{X})\}.$$

The *dependency* is captured as $r \notin \mathcal{T}(\mathcal{C}, \mathcal{X})$ in the above definition.

Example 3. For $\mathcal{R}$ in Example 1, $DRules(\mathcal{R}, h(x)) = \emptyset$ (because $c(a), c(b) \in \mathcal{T}(\mathcal{C}, \mathcal{X})$), $DRules(\mathcal{R}, g(x)) = \emptyset$ (again $k(y) \in \mathcal{T}(\mathcal{C}, \mathcal{X})$) and $DRules(\mathcal{R}, f(x, x, x)) = \{(3)\}$.

For each $v \in DSubterm(\mathcal{R}, r)$, $DRules(\mathcal{R}, v)$ contains the rules that *will (eventually) be used* in root steps $\sigma(\ell) \to \sigma(r)$ for some $\ell \to r \Leftarrow c \in DRules(\mathcal{R}, v)$ in the *immediate* continuation of the infinite computation in the *horizontal* dimension (starting from an instance $\sigma(v)$ of v). With regard to the *vertical* dimension, given a term t, the set of 'proper' conditional rule defining $root(t)$ is:

$$Rules_C(\mathcal{R}, t) = \{\ell \to r \Leftarrow \bigwedge_{i=1}^{n} s_i \to t_i \in \mathcal{R} \mid root(\ell) = root(t), n > 0\}.$$

These are the rules involved in transitions of computations to *upper* levels. We let $URules(\mathcal{R}, t) = DRules(\mathcal{R}, t) \cup Rules_C(\mathcal{R}, t)$ to be the set of used rules.

Example 4. For $\mathcal{R}$ in Example 1, $URules(\mathcal{R}, h(x)) = DRules(\mathcal{R}, h(x))$ and $URules(\mathcal{R}, f(x, x, x)) = DRules(\mathcal{R}, f(x, x, x))$. However $URules(\mathcal{R}, g(x)) = DRules(\mathcal{R}, g(x)) \cup Rules_C(\mathcal{R}, g(x)) = \{(4)\}$.

Proposition 1. *Let $\mathcal{R}$ be a deterministic 3-CTRS. Then, for all $t \in \mathcal{T}_{op\text{-}\infty}$, there exist $\alpha : \ell \to r \Leftarrow \bigwedge_{i=1}^{n} s_i \to t_i$ and a substitution σ such that $t \xrightarrow{>\Lambda}{}^{*} \sigma(\ell)$, and there is a term v such that $\ell \not\trianglerighteq v$, $\sigma(v) \in \mathcal{T}_{op\text{-}\infty}$ and either*

1. $\alpha \in DRules(\mathcal{R}, t)$, *for all $1 \leq i \leq n$, $\sigma(s_i)$ is operationally terminating and $\sigma(s_i) \to^{*} \sigma(t_i)$, and $v \in DSubterm(\mathcal{R}, r)$ is such that $URules(\mathcal{R}, v) \neq \emptyset$, or*
2. $\alpha \in Rules_C(\mathcal{R}, t)$, *there is i, $1 \leq i \leq n$ such that $\sigma(s_j)$ is operationally terminating and $\sigma(s_j) \to^{*} \sigma(t_j)$ for all j, $1 \leq j < i$, and $v \in DSubterm(\mathcal{R}, s_i)$ is such that $URules(\mathcal{R}, v) \neq \emptyset$.*

Remark 1. In the following we do *not* impose that the domain of the substitutions be finite. This is usual practice in the dependency pair approach, where a single substitution is used to instantiate an infinite number of variables coming from renamed versions of the dependency pairs (see below).

The next result formalizes a *bidimensional* view of infinite computations starting from minimal operational nonterminating terms: they can be viewed as a path over $\mathbb{N} \times \mathbb{N}$, where each bidimensional point (x_i, y_i) is labeled with a rule α_i.

Theorem 1. *Let $\mathcal{R} = (\mathcal{F}, R)$ be a deterministic 3-CTRS and $t \in \mathcal{T}_{op\text{-}\infty}$. There is a substitution σ and an infinite sequence $\{(x_i, y_i, \alpha_i)\}_{i \in \mathbb{N}}$ of triples $(x_i, y_i, \alpha_i) \in \mathbb{N} \times \mathbb{N} \times R$ such that, for all $i \geq 0$, $x_{i+1} + y_{i+1} = x_i + y_i + 1$ and*

1. $x_0 = y_0 = 0$, $\alpha_0 \in URules(\mathcal{R}, t)$ *and $t \xrightarrow{>\Lambda}{}^{*} \sigma(\ell_0)$.*
2. *For all $i \geq 0$, and $\alpha_i : \ell_i \to r_i \Leftarrow \bigwedge_{j=1}^{n_i} s_j^i \to t_j^i \in R$, we have $\sigma(\ell_i) \in \mathcal{T}_{op\text{-}\infty}$; furthermore, there is a term v_i such that $\ell_i \not\trianglerighteq v_i$, $\sigma(v_i) \in \mathcal{T}_{op\text{-}\infty}$, $\sigma(v_i) \xrightarrow{>\Lambda}{}^{*} \sigma(\ell_{i+1})$, $\alpha_{i+1} \in URules(v_i)$, and*

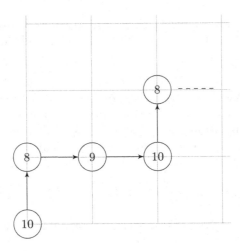

Fig. 2. Computations starting with $f(a)$ for $\mathcal{R}$ in Example 5

(a) If $x_{i+1} = x_i + 1$, then $v_i \in \mathcal{D}Subterm(\mathcal{R}, r_i)$ and $\alpha_i \in \mathcal{D}Rules(\mathcal{R}, \ell_i)$.
(b) If $y_{i+1} = y_i + 1$, then there is j, $1 \leq j \leq n_i$ s.t. $v_i \in \mathcal{D}Subterm(\mathcal{R}, s_j^i)$ and $\alpha_i \in Rules_C(\mathcal{R}, \ell_i)$.

Example 5. Consider the following deterministic 3-CTRS $\mathcal{R}$ which is obtained from the 2-CTRS in Example 2 by a small change in rule (7) to yield (10):

$$g(a) \to c(b) \tag{8}$$
$$b \to f(a) \tag{9}$$
$$f(x) \to y \Leftarrow g(x) \to c(y) \tag{10}$$

Figure 2 shows the representation of computation starting from $f(a) \in \mathcal{T}_{\text{op-}\infty}$ according to Theorem 1, where the coordinates (x_i, y_i) have been left implicit.

Remark 2. The *minimal* sequence $f(a) \to_{(10)} b \to_{(9)} f(a) \to_{(10)} b \to \cdots$ is also possible for $\mathcal{R}$ in Example 5. This is because $\sigma(g(x)) \to^* \sigma(c(y))$ for rule (10) is satisfied *without any reduction on b* if $\sigma(x) = a$ and $\sigma(y) = b$. The implicit assumption in the computation model of Proposition 1 is that only reachability conditions $\sigma(s_i) \to^* \sigma(t_i)$ that are free of any infinite computation are important to decide the application of a rule. This makes real sense in practice. And, of course, it is harmless for the correctness or completeness of our approach.

According to our discussion, the following definition establishes the subsets of rules that play a special role in computations starting from minimal terms.

Definition 3. *The* dependent usable rules *for a CTRS $\mathcal{R}$ and $t \in \mathcal{T}(\mathcal{F}, \mathcal{X})$ are:*

$$\mathcal{D}\mathcal{U}(\mathcal{R}, t) = \mathcal{D}Rules(\mathcal{R}, t) \cup \bigcup_{(l \to r \Leftarrow c) \in \mathcal{D}Rules(\mathcal{R}, t)} \bigcup_{v \in \mathcal{D}Subterm(\mathcal{R}, r)} \mathcal{D}\mathcal{U}(\mathcal{R}^\bullet, v)$$

where $\mathcal{R}^{\bullet} = \mathcal{R} - DRules(\mathcal{R}, t)$. The set of minimal usable rules of $\mathcal{R}$ for t is:

$$MU(\mathcal{R}, t) = URules(\mathcal{R}, t) \cup \bigcup_{(l \to r \Leftarrow c) \in DRules(\mathcal{R}, t)} \bigcup_{v \in \mathcal{D}Subterm(\mathcal{R}, r)} MU(\mathcal{R}^{\bullet}, v).$$

Let $\overline{MU}(\mathcal{R}, t) = \emptyset$ if $MU(\mathcal{R}, t)$ is a TRS and $\overline{MU}(\mathcal{R}, t) = MU(\mathcal{R}, t)$ otherwise.

Example 6. For $\mathcal{R}$ in Example 1, $\mathcal{D}U(\mathcal{R}, h(x)) = MU(\mathcal{R}, h(x)) = \emptyset$; $\mathcal{D}U(\mathcal{R}, g(x)) = \emptyset$ but $MU(\mathcal{R}, g(x)) = \overline{MU}(\mathcal{R}, g(x)) = \{(4)\}$, and $\mathcal{D}U(\mathcal{R}, f(x, x, x)) = MU(\mathcal{R}, f(x, x, x)) = \{(3)\}$, but $\overline{MU}(\mathcal{R}, f(x, x, x)) = \emptyset$.

Example 7. For $\mathcal{R}$ in Example 5, $DRules(\mathcal{R}, f(a)) = \emptyset$ (because the right-hand side y in rule (10) defining f is a variable), $\mathcal{D}U(\mathcal{R}, g(x)) = \{(8), (9)\}$ and $MU(\mathcal{R}, g(x)) = \overline{MU}(\mathcal{R}, g(x)) = \mathcal{R}$.

The following result shows that an infinite computation starting from a minimal operationally nonterminating term can either start an infinite (*horizontal*) *rewrite* sequence (possibly as part of the evaluation of one of the conditions of a rule) or else climb infinitely many '*vertical*' steps over the conditions in the rules.

Corollary 1. *Let $\mathcal{R}$ be a deterministic 3-CTRS and $t \in \mathcal{T}_{op\text{-}\infty}$. Then, the sequence $\{(x_i, y_i, \alpha_i)\}_{i \geq 0}$ associated to t according to Theorem 1 satisfies one of the following conditions. Either*

1. *There is $k \geq 0$, $\ell_k \to r_k \Leftarrow c_k \in \mathcal{R}$, and an infinite 'horizontal' sequence $\{(x_i, y_k, \alpha_i)\}_{i \geq k}$ such that for all $i \geq k$, $x_{i+1} = x_i + 1$ and $\alpha_i \in \bigcup_{v_k \in \mathcal{D}Subterm(\mathcal{R}, r_k)} \mathcal{D}U(\mathcal{R}, v_k)$, or*
2. *For each $i \in \mathbb{N}$ such that $y_i > 0$ and $y_i = y_{i-1} + 1$, there is $k_i > i$ such that $y_{k_i} = y_i + 1$, and there is j_i, $1 \leq j_i \leq n_i$ such that $\alpha_{k_i - 1} \in \bigcup_{v_i \in \mathcal{D}Subterm(\mathcal{R}, s_{ij_i})} \overline{MU}(\mathcal{R}, v_i)$, with $n_{k_i - 1} > 0$ conditions in the conditional part of the rule.*

In the following, we use *Dependency Pairs* to capture the nontermination behavior of computations with CTRSs.

4   2D Dependency Pairs for CTRSs

Given a signature $\mathcal{F}$ and $f \in \mathcal{F}$, we let $f^{\sharp}$ (often just capitalized, e.g., F) be a fresh symbol associated to f [1]. Let $\mathcal{F}^{\sharp} = \{f^{\sharp} \mid f \in \mathcal{F}\}$. For $t = f(t_1, \ldots, t_k) \in \mathcal{T}(\mathcal{F}, \mathcal{X})$, we write $t^{\sharp}$ to denote the *marked* term $f^{\sharp}(t_1, \ldots, t_k)$. Our Dependency Pairs for CTRSs are organized into two blocks. The *horizontal* block contains those pairs that correspond to rules issuing root steps in infinite rewrite sequences (Proposition 1, item 1):

$$\mathsf{DP}_H(\mathcal{R}) = \{\ell^{\sharp} \to v^{\sharp} \Leftarrow c \mid \ell \to r \Leftarrow c \in R, r \trianglerighteq v, \ell \ntrianglerighteq v, DRules(\mathcal{R}, v) \neq \emptyset\}$$

Example 8. For $\mathcal{R}$ in Example 1, $\mathsf{DP}_H(\mathcal{R}) = \{F(k(a), k(b), x) \to F(x, x, x)\}$. For $\mathcal{R}$ in Example 5 (and also for $\mathcal{R}$ in Example 2), $\mathsf{DP}_H(\mathcal{R}) = \{G(a) \to B\}$.

The *vertical* block contains pairs for shifting the infinite computation to the conditions of the rules (Proposition 1, item 2):

$$\mathsf{DP}_V(\mathcal{R}) = \{\ell^\sharp \to v^\sharp \Leftarrow \bigwedge_{j=1}^{k-1} s_j \to t_j \mid \ell \to r \Leftarrow \bigwedge_{i=1}^{n} s_i \to t_i \in R,$$
$$\exists k, 1 \leq k \leq n, s_k \trianglerighteq v, \ell \ntrianglerighteq v, URules(\mathcal{R}, v) \neq \emptyset\}.$$

Example 9. For $\mathcal{R}$ in Example 1, $\mathsf{DP}_V(\mathcal{R}) = \emptyset$. For $\mathcal{R}$ in Example 2 and $\mathcal{R}$ in Example 5), $\mathsf{DP}_V(\mathcal{R}) = \{F(x) \to G(x)\}$.

The subterms in the conditions of the rules that originate the pairs in $\mathsf{DP}_V(\mathcal{R})$ are collected in the following set, which we use below:

$$\mathsf{V}_C(\mathcal{R}) = \{v \mid \ell \to r \Leftarrow \bigwedge_{i=1}^{n} s_i \to t_i \in R, \exists k, 1 \leq k \leq n, s_k \trianglerighteq v, \ell \ntrianglerighteq v, URules(\mathcal{R}, v) \neq \emptyset\}.$$

Example 10. For $\mathcal{R}$ in Example 1, $\mathsf{V}_C(\mathcal{R}) = \emptyset$. For $\mathcal{R}$ in Example 2 and $\mathcal{R}$ in Example 5, $\mathsf{V}_C(\mathcal{R}) = \{g(x)\}$.

We also have pairs to *connect* pairs in $\mathsf{DP}_V(\mathcal{R})$ (Corollary 1, item 1):

$$\mathsf{DP}_{VH}(\mathcal{R}) = \bigcup_{w \in \mathsf{V}_C(\mathcal{R})} \{\ell^\sharp \to v^\sharp \Leftarrow c \mid \ell \to r \Leftarrow c \in \overline{\mathcal{MU}}(\mathcal{R}, w),$$
$$r \trianglerighteq v, \ell \ntrianglerighteq v, URules(\mathcal{R}, v) \neq \emptyset\}.$$

Example 11. For $\mathcal{R}$ in Example 1, $\mathsf{DP}_{VH}(\mathcal{R}) = \emptyset$. For $\mathcal{R}$ in Example 2 and $\mathcal{R}$ in Example 5, $\mathsf{DP}_{VH}(\mathcal{R}) = \{G(a) \to B, B \to F(a)\}$.

Here is the definition of 2D-Dependency Pairs for a CTRS.

Definition 4 (2D-Dependency Pairs). *The triple of* 2D-dependency pairs *(2D DPs) for the CTRS $\mathcal{R}$ is* $\mathsf{DP}_{2D}(\mathcal{R}) = (\mathsf{DP}_H(\mathcal{R}), \mathsf{DP}_V(\mathcal{R}), \mathsf{DP}_{VH}(\mathcal{R}))$.

Example 12. Consider the following 3-CTRS $\mathcal{R}$ in [14, Example 7.1.5]

$$\mathsf{less}(x, 0) \to \mathsf{false} \tag{11}$$
$$\mathsf{less}(0, \mathsf{s}(x)) \to \mathsf{true} \tag{12}$$
$$\mathsf{less}(\mathsf{s}(x), \mathsf{s}(y)) \to \mathsf{less}(x, y) \tag{13}$$
$$\mathsf{minus}(0, \mathsf{s}(y)) \to 0 \tag{14}$$
$$\mathsf{minus}(x, 0) \to x \tag{15}$$
$$\mathsf{minus}(\mathsf{s}(x), \mathsf{s}(y)) \to \mathsf{minus}(x, y) \tag{16}$$
$$\mathsf{quotrem}(0, \mathsf{s}(y)) \to \mathsf{pair}(0, 0) \tag{17}$$
$$\mathsf{quotrem}(\mathsf{s}(x), \mathsf{s}(y)) \to \mathsf{pair}(0, \mathsf{s}(x)) \Leftarrow \mathsf{less}(x, y) \to \mathsf{true} \tag{18}$$
$$\mathsf{quotrem}(\mathsf{s}(x), \mathsf{s}(y)) \to \mathsf{pair}(\mathsf{s}(q), r) \tag{19}$$
$$\Leftarrow \mathsf{less}(x, y) \to \mathsf{false}, \mathsf{quotrem}(\mathsf{minus}(x, y), \mathsf{s}(y)) \to \mathsf{pair}(q, r)$$

The set $\mathsf{DP}_H(\mathcal{R})$ consists of the rules:

$$\mathsf{LESS}(\mathsf{s}(x), \mathsf{s}(y)) \to \mathsf{LESS}(x, y) \tag{20}$$
$$\mathsf{MINUS}(\mathsf{s}(x), \mathsf{s}(y)) \to \mathsf{MINUS}(x, y) \tag{21}$$

The set $\mathsf{DP}_V(\mathcal{R})$ consists of the rules:

$$\mathsf{QUOTREM}(\mathsf{s}(x), \mathsf{s}(y)) \to \mathsf{LESS}(x, y) \tag{22}$$
$$\mathsf{QUOTREM}(\mathsf{s}(x), \mathsf{s}(y)) \to \mathsf{QUOTREM}(\mathsf{minus}(x, y), \mathsf{s}(y)) \Leftarrow \mathsf{less}(x, y) \to \mathsf{false} \tag{23}$$
$$\mathsf{QUOTREM}(\mathsf{s}(x), \mathsf{s}(y)) \to \mathsf{MINUS}(x, y) \Leftarrow \mathsf{less}(x, y) \to \mathsf{false} \tag{24}$$

Finally, $\mathsf{DP}_{VH}(\mathcal{R}) = \emptyset$.

4.1 Characterizing Operational Termination of CTRSs Using 2D DPs

An essential property of the dependency pair method is that it provides a *characterization* of termination of a TRS $\mathcal{R}$ as the absence of infinite (minimal) *chains of dependency pairs* [1,8]. As we prove below, this is also true for deterministic 3-CTRSs when 2D DPs are considered. First, we have to introduce a suitable notion of chain that can be used with 2D DPs.

Definition 5 (Chain of Pairs - Minimal Chain). *Let $\mathcal{P}, \mathcal{Q}, \mathcal{R}$ be CTRSs. A $(\mathcal{P}, \mathcal{Q}, \mathcal{R})$-chain is a finite or infinite sequence of pairs $u_i \to v_i \Leftarrow \bigwedge_{j=1}^{n_i} s_{ij} \to t_{ij} \in \mathcal{P}$, together with a substitution σ satisfying that, for all $i \geq 1$,*

1. $\sigma(s_{ij}) \to_{\mathcal{R}}^* \sigma(t_{ij})$ for all j, $1 \leq j \leq n_i$ and

2. $\sigma(v_i)(\to_{\mathcal{R}}^* \circ \xrightarrow{\Lambda}{=}_{\mathcal{Q}})^* \sigma(u_{i+1})$, where given a rule $\ell \to r \Leftarrow \bigwedge_{j=1}^{n} s_j \to t_j \in \mathcal{Q}$, we write $s \xrightarrow{\Lambda}{=}_{\mathcal{Q}} t$ if either $s = t$ or there is a substitution θ such that $s = \theta(\ell)$, $t = \theta(r)$ and $\theta(s_i) \to_{\mathcal{R}}^* \theta(t_i)$ for all j, $1 \leq j \leq n$ (note that the satisfaction of reachability constraints involves rewritings with $\mathcal{R}$).

As usual, we assume that different occurrences of pairs do not share any variable (renaming substitutions are used if necessary). A $(\mathcal{P}, \mathcal{Q}, \mathcal{R})$-chain is called minimal if for all $i \geq 1$, $\sigma(v_i)$ is $\mathcal{R}$-operationally terminating.

Remark 3. Note that, if $\mathcal{P}$ and $\mathcal{R}$ are TRSs (without conditional rules) and $\mathcal{Q} = \emptyset$, Definition 5 specializes to the standard definition of chain of pairs in the Dependency Pair Framework for TRSs [8, Definition 3].

We now provide a new characterization of operational termination of CTRSs.

Theorem 2 (Operational Termination of CTRSs). *A deterministic 3-CTRS $\mathcal{R}$ is operationally terminating if and only if there is no infinite (minimal) $(\mathsf{DP}_H(\mathcal{R}), \emptyset, \mathcal{R})$-chain and there is no infinite (minimal) $(\mathsf{DP}_V(\mathcal{R}), \mathsf{DP}_{VH}(\mathcal{R}), \mathcal{R})$-chain.*

Example 13. Consider again the $\mathcal{R}$ in Examples 2 and 5 and $\mathsf{DP}_V(\mathcal{R})$ and $\mathsf{DP}_{VH}(\mathcal{R})$ (that coincide for both CTRSs) as given in Examples 9 and 11. There is an infinite $(\mathsf{DP}_V(\mathcal{R}), \mathsf{DP}_{VH}(\mathcal{R}), \mathcal{R})$-chain:

$$B \to_{\mathsf{DP}_{VH}(\mathcal{R})} F(a) \to_{\mathcal{R}}^* F(a) \to_{\mathsf{DP}_V(\mathcal{R})} G(a) \to_{\mathcal{R}}^* G(a) \to_{\mathsf{DP}_{VH}(\mathcal{R})} B$$

witnessing that *both* CTRSs are *not* operationally terminating.

For the sake of brevity, in the following we often call H-chains to the $(\mathsf{DP}_H(\mathcal{R}), \emptyset, \mathcal{R})$-chains. And we call V-chains to the $(\mathsf{DP}_V(\mathcal{R}), \mathsf{DP}_{VH}(\mathcal{R}), \mathcal{R})$-chains. The following result, involving chains of a simpler type (closer to the usual ones, where pairs are connected by rewritings with $\mathcal{R}$ only, see Remark 3), also characterizes operational termination of deterministic 3-CTRSs.

Theorem 3 (Operational Termination of CTRSs II). *A deterministic 3-CTRS $\mathcal{R}$ is operationally terminating if and only if there is no infinite (minimal) $(\mathsf{DP}_H(\mathcal{R}) \cup \mathsf{DP}_V(\mathcal{R}) \cup \mathsf{DP}_{VH}(\mathcal{R}), \emptyset, \mathcal{R})$-chain.*

In the following section, though, we further motivate the explicit and *independent* use of the H-chains and V-chains to prove termination properties of CTRSs.

4.2   Termination of 2-CTRSs

The existence of infinite H-chains witnesses *nontermination* of deterministic 3-CTRSs, i.e., the absence of infinite *rewrite sequences.*

Theorem 4 (Non-termination of CTRSs). *Let $\mathcal{R}$ be a deterministic 3-CTRS. If there is an infinite $(\mathsf{DP}_H(\mathcal{R}), \emptyset, \mathcal{R})$-chain, then $\mathcal{R}$ is not terminating.*

The CTRS $\mathcal{R}$ in Example 5 shows that Theorem 4 provides a sufficient but *not necessary* criterion for termination of CTRSs.

Example 14. For $\mathcal{R}$ in Example 5, we have $\mathsf{DP}_H(\mathcal{R}) = \{G(a) \to B\}$ (Example 8). There is no infinite H-chain. However, $\mathcal{R}$ is *not* terminating (see Remark 2).

However, the following result holds:

Theorem 5 (Termination of 2-CTRSs.) *A 2-CTRS $\mathcal{R}$ is terminating if and only if there is no infinite minimal $(\mathsf{DP}_H(\mathcal{R}), \emptyset, \mathcal{R})$-chain.*

Example 15. For the deterministic 2-CTRS $\mathcal{R}$ in Example 2, $\mathsf{DP}_H(\mathcal{R}) = \{G(a) \to B\}$ and there is no infinite H-chain. By Theorem 5, $\mathcal{R}$ is *terminating.*

Therefore, for CTRSs with extra variables in the right-hand sides of conditional rules, the vertical and horizontal dimensions of operational termination are *not* completely independent. Theorem 5 suggests the following.

Definition 6. (V-termination of CTRSs). *A CTRS $\mathcal{R}$ is V-terminating if there is no infinite $(\mathsf{DP}_V(\mathcal{R}), \mathsf{DP}_{VH}(\mathcal{R}), \mathcal{R})$-chain.*

As a consequence of Theorems 2 and 5, we have the following.

Corollary 2. *A deterministic 2-CTRS is operationally terminating if and only if it is terminating and V-terminating.*

5   Mechanizing Proofs of Operational Termination with 2D DPs

In the following, we speak of $(\mathcal{P}, \mathcal{Q}, \mathcal{R}, (\mathsf{ctrs}, \gamma))$-chains, for $\gamma = \mathsf{a}$ (or $\gamma = \mathsf{m}$) if arbitrary (resp. only minimal) chains are considered. Similarly, according to Remark 3, we speak of $(\mathcal{P}, \mathcal{Q}, \mathcal{R}, (\mathsf{trs}, \gamma))$-chains if $\mathcal{P}$ and $\mathcal{R}$ are TRSs and $\mathcal{Q} = \emptyset$.

Definition 7 (CTRS Problem). *A* CTRS problem τ *is a tuple* $\tau = (\mathcal{P}, \mathcal{Q}, \mathcal{R}, e)$, *where* $\mathcal{P}$, $\mathcal{Q}$ *and* $\mathcal{R}$ *are CTRSs, and* $e \in \{\mathsf{ctrs}, \mathsf{trs}\} \times \{\mathsf{a}, \mathsf{m}\}$ *is a flag. The CTRS problem* τ *is* finite *if there is no infinite minimal* $(\mathcal{P}, \mathcal{Q}, \mathcal{R}, e)$-*chain. The CTRS problem* τ *is* infinite *if* $\mathcal{R}$ *is non-operationally terminating or there is an infinite minimal* $(\mathcal{P}, \mathcal{Q}, \mathcal{R}, e)$-*chain.*

Definition 8 (CTRS Processor). *A* CTRS processor P *is a mapping from CTRS problems into sets of CTRS problems. Alternatively, it can also return* "no". *A CTRS processor* P *is*

– sound *if for all CTRS problems* τ, *we have that* τ *is finite whenever* $\mathsf{P}(\tau) \neq \mathsf{no}$ *and all CTRS problems in* $\mathsf{P}(\tau)$ *are finite.*
– complete *if for all CTRS problems* τ, *we have that* τ *is infinite whenever* $\mathsf{P}(\tau) = \mathsf{no}$ *or when* $\mathsf{P}(\tau)$ *contains an infinite CTRS problem.*

A (sound) processor transforms CTRS problems into (hopefully) *simpler* ones, in such a way that the existence of an infinite chain in the original CTRS problem implies the existence of an infinite chain in the transformed one. Here, 'simpler' usually means that fewer pairs are involved. Soundness is essential for proving *operational termination*; completeness for proving *non-operational termination*.

Processors are used in a *divide and conquer* scheme to incrementally simplify the original CTRS problem as much as possible, possibly decomposing it into (a tree of) smaller pieces which are independently treated in the same way. The trivial case comes when the set of pairs $\mathcal{P}$ becomes empty. Then, no infinite chain is possible, and the CTRS problem is finite. Such *positive* answer is propagated upwards in the decision tree. In some cases, a witness of an infinite chain is obtained; then a *negative* answer "no" can be provided and propagated upwards.

Theorem 6 (2D DP Framework). *Let* $\mathcal{R}$ *be a deterministic 3-CTRS. We construct two trees whose nodes are labeled with CTRS problems* τ *or* "yes" *or* "no". *The roots are* $\tau_H = (\mathsf{DP}_H(\mathcal{R}), \emptyset, \mathcal{R}, (\mathsf{ctrs}, \gamma))$ *and* $\tau_V = (\mathsf{DP}_V(\mathcal{R}), \mathsf{DP}_{VH}(\mathcal{R}), \mathcal{R}, (\mathsf{ctrs}, \gamma))$, *respectively (for* $\gamma \in \{\mathsf{a}, \mathsf{m}\}$*). For every node which is a CTRS problem* τ, *there is a sound processor* P *satisfying one of the following conditions:*

1. $\mathsf{P}(\tau) = \mathsf{no}$ *and the node has just one child that is labeled with* "no".
2. $\mathsf{P}(\tau) = \emptyset$ *and the node has just one child that is labeled with* "yes".
3. $\mathsf{P}(\tau) \neq \mathsf{no}$, $\mathsf{P}(\tau) \neq \emptyset$, *and the children of the node are labeled with the CTRS problems in* $\mathsf{P}(\tau)$.

If all leaves of both trees are labeled with "yes", then $\mathcal{R}$ is operationally terminating. If a leaf is labeled with "no" in some of the trees and all processors used on the path from the root to this leaf are complete, then $\mathcal{R}$ is operationally nonterminating.

Remark 4. By Theorem 3, an alternative to the twofold proof starting from an H-problem and a V-problem is to start the proof of operational termination of $\mathcal{R}$ from a *single* CTRS problem $(\mathsf{DP}_H(\mathcal{R}) \cup \mathsf{DP}_V(\mathcal{R}) \cup \mathsf{DP}_{VH}(\mathcal{R}), \emptyset, \mathcal{R}, (\mathsf{ctrs}, \gamma))$.

Remark 5. In order to prove (or disprove) *termination* of a deterministic CTRS $\mathcal{R}$, we would use Theorem 6 with a *single* problem: $\tau_H = (\mathsf{DP}_H(\mathcal{R}), \emptyset, \mathcal{R}, e)$. The procedure is analogous and the conclusion of a positive analysis (i.e., "yes" in all leaves of the tree) is *termination* of $\mathcal{R}$ (if it is a 2-CTRS). Similarly, a leaf labeled with "no" witnesses nontermination of $\mathcal{R}$ (if it is a 3-CTRS).

6   Processors for the 2D DP Framework

The first processor *moves* rules from $\mathcal{Q}$ to $\mathcal{P}$ in CTRS problems.

Theorem 7 (Moving $\mathcal{Q}$-rules). *Let $\mathcal{P}$, $\mathcal{Q}$, and $\mathcal{R}$ be TRSs. Then,*

$$\mathsf{P}_{\mathsf{Q2P}}(\mathcal{P}, \mathcal{Q}, \mathcal{R}, (\mathsf{ctrs}, \gamma)) = \{(\mathcal{P} \cup \mathcal{Q}, \emptyset, \mathcal{R}, (\mathsf{ctrs}, \mathsf{a}))\}$$

is a sound processor.

In general, $\mathsf{P}_{\mathsf{Q2P}}$ is not complete nor preserves minimality.

Example 16. Let $\mathcal{P} = \{a \to b, c \to a\}$, $\mathcal{Q} = \{b \to c\}$, and $\mathcal{R} = \{c \to c\}$. There is an infinite $(\mathcal{P}, \mathcal{Q}, \mathcal{R})$-chain Γ: $a \to b, c \to a, a \to b, c \to a, \ldots$ due to $b \to_{\mathcal{Q}} c$. Note that Γ is minimal because b and a are $\mathcal{R}$-terminating. However, Γ requires the use of the (only) pair in $\mathcal{Q}$ to become an infinite $(\mathcal{P} \cup \mathcal{Q}, \emptyset, \mathcal{R})$-chain

$$a \to b, b \to c, c \to a, a \to b, b \to c, c \to a, \ldots$$

which is, however, *not* minimal now because c is *not* $\mathcal{R}$-terminating.

The following processor *transfers* any proof of finiteness of 2D DP problems to the DP Framework for TRSs. In this way, all existing processors for the DP Framework are now available for the 2D DP framework.

Theorem 8 (Shift to DP-Framework). *Let $\mathcal{P}$ and $\mathcal{R}$ be TRSs. Then,*

$$\mathsf{P}_{TRS}(\mathcal{P}, \emptyset, \mathcal{R}, (\mathsf{ctrs}, \gamma)) = \{(\mathcal{P}, \emptyset, \mathcal{R}, (\mathsf{trs}, \gamma))\}$$

is a sound and complete processor.

6.1 Graph of a CTRS Problem

Given a CTRS problem $(\mathcal{P}, \mathcal{Q}, \mathcal{R}, e)$, we provide a notion of graph that is able to represent all infinite (*minimal*) chains of pairs as given in Definition 5.

Definition 9 (Graph of a CTRS Problem). *Let $\mathcal{P}$, $\mathcal{Q}$ and $\mathcal{R}$ be CTRSs. The CTRS-graph $G(\mathcal{P}, \mathcal{Q}, \mathcal{R}, e)$ where $e = (\text{ctrs}, \gamma)$ and $\gamma \in \{\text{a}, \text{m}\}$ has $\mathcal{P}$ as the set of nodes. Given $\alpha : u \rightarrow v \Leftarrow c, \alpha' : u' \rightarrow v' \Leftarrow c' \in \mathcal{P}$, there is an arc from α to α' if α, α' is a minimal $(\mathcal{P}, \mathcal{Q}, \mathcal{R}, e)$-chain for some substitution σ.*

In general, CTRS graphs are *not* computable due to the reachability conditions $\sigma(v)(\rightarrow_{\mathcal{R}}^{*} \circ \xrightarrow{\Lambda}_{\mathcal{Q}})^{*}\sigma(u')$ (for $u \rightarrow v \Leftarrow c \in \mathcal{P}$). Since the reachability problem for (conditional) rewriting is undecidable, we *approximate* it. Following [9], we approximate the CTRS-dependency graph as follows. Let $\text{TCAP}_{\mathcal{R}}$ be:

$$\text{TCAP}_{\mathcal{R}}(x) = y \quad \text{if } x \text{ is a variable, and}$$

$$\text{TCAP}_{\mathcal{R}}(f(t_1, \ldots, t_k)) = \begin{cases} f([t_1], \ldots, [t_k]) & \text{if } f([t_1], \ldots, [t_k]) \text{ does not unify} \\ & \text{with } \ell \text{ for any } \ell \rightarrow r \Leftarrow c \text{ in } \mathcal{R} \\ y & \text{otherwise} \end{cases}$$

where y is a new, fresh variable that has not yet been used, and given a term s, $[s] = \text{TCAP}_{\mathcal{R}}(s)$. We assume that ℓ shares no variable with $f([t_1], \ldots, [t_k])$ (rename if necessary). With $\text{TCAP}_{\mathcal{R}}$ we approximate reachability problems as *unification*. According to Definitions 5 and 9, we have the following.

Definition 10 (Estimated connection). *Let $\mathcal{Q}$ and $\mathcal{R}$ be CTRSs, θ be a substitution, and $\alpha : u \rightarrow v \Leftarrow c$ to $\alpha' : u' \rightarrow v' \Leftarrow c'$ be two conditional rules. There is a $(\mathcal{Q}, \mathcal{R}, \theta)$-connection from α to α' if*

1. $\text{TCAP}_{\mathcal{R}}(\theta(v))$ *and u' unify, or*
2. $\text{TCAP}_{\mathcal{R}}(\theta(v))$ *and u'' unify with mgu θ' for some $\alpha'' : u'' \rightarrow v'' \Leftarrow c'' \in \mathcal{Q}$ and there is a $(\mathcal{Q} - \{\alpha''\}, \mathcal{R}, \theta')$-connection from α'' to α'.*

Definition 11 (Estimated Graph). *Let $\mathcal{P}$, $\mathcal{Q}$ and $\mathcal{R}$ be CTRSs. The estimated CTRS-graph $EG(\mathcal{P}, \mathcal{Q}, \mathcal{R}, e)$ has $\mathcal{P}$ as the set of nodes. There is an arc from α to α' if there is a $(\mathcal{Q}, \mathcal{R}, \epsilon)$-connection from α to α'.*

Remark 6. If $\mathcal{Q} = \emptyset$ and $\mathcal{P}, \mathcal{R}$ are TRSs, Definitions 9 and 11 specialize to the standard ones for TRSs [8, Definition 7] (and [9, Definition 12]).

The following processor decomposes a CTRS problem $(\mathcal{P}, \mathcal{Q}, \mathcal{R}, e)$ with graph $G(\mathcal{P}, \mathcal{Q}, \mathcal{R}, e)$ according to the *strongly connected components* (SCCs) of the graph, i.e., cycles in $G(\mathcal{P}, \mathcal{Q}, \mathcal{R}, e)$ that are not contained in any other cycle.

Theorem 9 (SCC Processor). *Let $\mathcal{P}$, $\mathcal{Q}$ and $\mathcal{R}$ be CTRSs. Then,*

$$\mathsf{P}_{SCC}(\mathcal{P}, \mathcal{Q}, \mathcal{R}, e) = \{(\mathcal{P}', \mathcal{Q}, \mathcal{R}, e) \mid \mathcal{P}' \subseteq \mathcal{P} \text{ is an SCC in} G(\mathcal{P}, \mathcal{Q}, \mathcal{R}, e)\}$$

is a sound and complete processor.

With P_{SCC}, we can *separately* work with the strongly connected components of $G(P, Q, R, e)$, disregarding other parts of the graph.

Example 17. For R in Example 12, $\tau_H = (DP_H(R), \emptyset, R, e)$ and $\tau_V = (DP_V(R), DP_{VH}(R), R, e)$; $EG(\tau_H)$ and $EG(\tau_V)$ are:

We have $P_{SCC}(\tau_H) = \{\tau_{H1}, \tau_{H2}\}$, where $\tau_{H1} = (\{(20)\}, \emptyset, R, e)$ and $\tau_{H2} = (\{(21)\}, \emptyset, R, e)$. For τ_V we get $P_{SCC}(\tau_V) = \{\tau_{V1}\}$, where $\tau_{V1} = (\{(23)\}, \emptyset, R, e)$.

6.2   Use of Orderings and Argument Filterings

A CTRS problem (P, Q, R, e) can be *simplified* by *removing* rules with a *decrease* with respect to a well-founded relation $\sqsupset$. In order to be more precise, in the following we say that a relation S is *compatible* with R if $S \circ R \subseteq R$ or $R \circ S \subseteq R$.

Definition 12 (Removal Triple). *A removal triple* $(\gtrsim, \succeq, \sqsupset)$ *consists of relations* $\gtrsim, \succeq, \sqsupset$ *on terms such that* $\sqsupset$ *is well-founded; for all* $R \in \{\gtrsim, \succeq\}$, *R is compatible with* $\sqsupset$; *and* $\gtrsim \circ \succeq \subseteq \gtrsim$ *or* $\gtrsim \circ \succeq \subseteq \succeq$.

An *argument filtering* π for a signature $\mathcal{F}$ is a mapping that assigns to each k-ary function symbol $f \in \mathcal{F}$ an argument position $i \in \{1, \ldots, k\}$ or a (possibly empty) list $[i_1, \ldots, i_m]$ of argument positions $1 \le i_1 < \cdots < i_m \le k$ [11]. The *trivial* argument filtering $\pi_T(f) = [1, \ldots, k]$ (for each k-ary symbol $f \in \mathcal{F}$) does nothing. The signature $\mathcal{F}_\pi$ of symbols with filtered arguments consists of all function symbols $f \in \mathcal{F}$ such that $\pi(f) = [i_1, \ldots, i_m]$; the arity of f in $\mathcal{F}_\pi$ is m but we do not change the name. An argument filtering π induces a mapping from $\mathcal{T}(\mathcal{F}, \mathcal{X})$ to $\mathcal{T}(\mathcal{F}_\pi, \mathcal{X})$, also denoted by π, which removes subterms:

$$\pi(t) = \begin{cases} t & \text{if } t \text{ is a variable} \\ \pi(t_i) & \text{if } t = f(t_1, \ldots, t_k) \text{ and } \pi(f) = i \\ f(\pi(t_{i_1}), \ldots, \pi(t_{i_m})) & \text{if } t = f(t_1, \ldots, t_k) \text{ and } \pi(f) = [i_1, \ldots, i_m] \end{cases}$$

And if R is a relation on terms, we let $\pi(R) = \{(\pi(s), \pi(t)) \mid (s, t) \in R\}$. Argument filterings provide a simple way to *remove* parts of the syntactic structure of a rule. In this way, we obtain simpler rules that are easier to compare. In the following, given (possibly empty) set of rules R, S and a rule $\alpha : \ell \to r \Leftarrow c$, we define the (possible) *replacement* of α in R by the rules S as follows:

$$R[S]_\alpha = \begin{cases} (R - \{\alpha\}) \cup S & \text{if } \alpha \in R \\ R & \text{otherwise} \end{cases}$$

Theorem 10 (Removal Triple Processor). *Let $\mathcal{P}$, $\mathcal{Q}$, and $\mathcal{R}$ be CTRSs, π be an argument filtering and $(\gtrsim, \succeq, \sqsupset)$ be a removal triple such that $\pi(\to_{\mathcal{R}}^{*}) \subseteq \gtrsim$ and for all $\ell \to r \Leftarrow c \in \mathcal{P} \cup \mathcal{Q}$ and substitutions σ, if for all $s \to t \in c$, $\sigma(s) \to_{\mathcal{R}}^{*} \sigma(t)$ holds, then $\pi(\sigma(\ell)) \bowtie \pi(\sigma(r))$ holds for some $\bowtie \in \{\gtrsim, \succeq, \sqsupset\}$. Let $\alpha : u \to v \Leftarrow c \in \mathcal{P} \cup \mathcal{Q}$ be such that, for all substitutions σ, if for all $s \to t \in c$, $\sigma(s) \to_{\mathcal{R}}^{*} \sigma(t)$ holds, then $\pi(\sigma(u)) \sqsupset \pi(\sigma(v))$ holds. Then,*

$$\mathsf{P}_{RT}(\mathcal{P}, \mathcal{Q}, \mathcal{R}, e) = \{(\mathcal{P}[\emptyset]_{\alpha}, \mathcal{Q}[\emptyset]_{\alpha}, \mathcal{R}, e)\}$$

is a sound and complete processor.

Example 18. For τ_{H1}, τ_{H2} and τ_{V1} in Example 17, we apply P_{RT} to those problems with $\pi_{\top}$ (which we do not make explicit here, as it does nothing) and using the same removal triple $(\geq, \geq, >)$ induced by the polynomial interpretation

$$
\begin{aligned}
[\mathsf{false}] &= 0 & [\mathsf{true}] &= 0 & [0] &= 0 & [\mathsf{s}](x) &= x + 1 \\
[\mathsf{less}](x) &= 0 & [\mathsf{minus}](x, y) &= x & [\mathsf{pair}](x, y) &= 0 & [\mathsf{quotrem}](x, y) &= 0 \\
[\mathsf{LESS}](x, y) &= x & [\mathsf{MINUS}](x, y) &= x & [\mathsf{QUOTREM}](x, y) &= x &
\end{aligned}
$$

over the naturals $\mathbb{N}$ by $s \geq t$ if $[s] \geq [t]$ and $s > t$ if $[s] > [t]$. We have:

$$
\begin{aligned}
[\mathsf{less}(x, 0)] &= & 0 & \geq 0 = [\mathsf{false}] \\
[\mathsf{less}(0, \mathsf{s}(x))] &= & 0 & \geq 0 = [\mathsf{true}] \\
[\mathsf{less}(\mathsf{s}(x), \mathsf{s}(y))] &= & 0 & \geq 0 = [\mathsf{less}(x, y)] \\
[\mathsf{minus}(0, \mathsf{s}(y))] &= & 0 & \geq 0 = [0] \\
[\mathsf{minus}(x, 0)] &= & x & \geq x = [x] \\
[\mathsf{minus}(\mathsf{s}(x), \mathsf{s}(y))] &= x + 1 & \geq x = [\mathsf{minus}(x, y)] \\
[\mathsf{quotrem}(0, \mathsf{s}(y))] &= & 0 & \geq 0 = [\mathsf{pair}(0, 0)] \\
[\mathsf{quotrem}(\mathsf{s}(x), \mathsf{s}(y))] &= & 0 & \geq 0 = [\mathsf{pair}(0, \mathsf{s}(x))] \\
[\mathsf{quotrem}(\mathsf{s}(x), \mathsf{s}(y))] &= & 0 & \geq 0 = [\mathsf{pair}(\mathsf{s}(q), r)]
\end{aligned}
$$

$$
\begin{aligned}
[\mathsf{LESS}(\mathsf{s}(x), \mathsf{s}(y))] &= x + 1 > x = [\mathsf{LESS}(x, y)] \\
[\mathsf{MINUS}(\mathsf{s}(x), \mathsf{s}(y))] &= x + 1 > x = [\mathsf{MINUS}(x, y)] \\
[\mathsf{QUOTREM}(\mathsf{s}(x), \mathsf{s}(y))] &= x + 1 > x = [\mathsf{QUOTREM}(\mathsf{minus}(x, y), \mathsf{s}(y))]
\end{aligned}
$$

Since $\geq$ is monotonic, stable, reflexive and transitive, the first nine inequalities prove $\to_{\mathcal{R}}^{*} \subseteq \geq$ (we do not really need to pay attention to the conditional part of the rules). Similarly, since $\sqsupset$ is stable, the last three strict inequalities prove $\sigma(u) \sqsupset \sigma(v)$ for all $u \to v \Leftarrow c \in \mathcal{P}$ (in the corresponding CTRS problem) and substitution σ, again without paying attention to the conditional part of the rules. This proves τ_{H1}, τ_{H2} and τ_{V1} finite, and $\mathcal{R}$ operationally terminating.

Theorem 11 (Unsatisfiable Rules). *Let $\mathcal{P}$, $\mathcal{Q}$, and $\mathcal{R}$ be CTRSs, π be an argument filtering, $\gtrsim$ and $\sqsupset$ be relations on terms such that $\gtrsim$ is compatible with $\sqsupset$, $\pi(\to_{\mathcal{R}}^{*}) \subseteq \gtrsim$, and $\sqsupset$ is well-founded. Let $\alpha : \ell \to r \Leftarrow c \in \mathcal{P} \cup \mathcal{Q} \cup \mathcal{R}$ and $s_i \to t_i \in c$ be such that for all substitutions σ, $\pi(\sigma(t_i)) \sqsupset \pi(\sigma(s_i))$ holds. Then,*

$$\mathsf{P}_{UR}(\mathcal{P}, \mathcal{Q}, \mathcal{R}, e) = \{(\mathcal{P}[\emptyset]_{\alpha}, \mathcal{Q}[\emptyset]_{\alpha}, \mathcal{R}[\emptyset]_{\alpha}, e)\}$$

is a sound and (if $\alpha \notin \mathcal{R}$ or $e = (\rho, \mathsf{a})$) complete processor.

Example 19. For $\mathcal{R}$ in Example 1, $\mathsf{DP}_H(\mathcal{R}) = \{F(k(a), k(b), x) \rightarrow F(x, x, x)\}$, and $\mathsf{DP}_V(\mathcal{R}) = \mathsf{DP}_{VH}(\mathcal{R}) = \emptyset$. For $\tau_H = (\mathsf{DP}_H(\mathcal{R}), \emptyset, \mathcal{R}, (\mathsf{ctrs}, \mathsf{m}))$, we use

$$[a] = [b] = [c](x) = [g](x) = [h](x) = [k](x) = [f](x, y, z) = 0 \quad \text{and} \quad [d] = 1$$

to generate $\geq$ and easily show (as in Example 18) that $\rightarrow_{\mathcal{R}}^* \subseteq \geq$. Since $[h(x)] = 0$ and $[d] = 1$, we have $[d] > [h(x)]$. With P_{UR}, we remove (4) from $\mathcal{R}$ to obtain $\tau_{H1} = (\mathsf{DP}_H(\mathcal{R}), \emptyset, \mathcal{R}-\{(4)\}, (\mathsf{ctrs}, \mathsf{m}))$ that satisfies the conditions for a shift with P_{TRS} to a DP problem $\tau_{\mathsf{trs}} = (\mathsf{DP}_H(\mathcal{R}), \emptyset, \mathcal{R}-\{(4)\}, (\mathsf{trs}, \mathsf{m}))$ that can then be solved by using any processor for TRSs. For instance, the forward instantiation processor [8, Definition 28] can be used to prove finiteness of τ_{trs}.

Theorem 12 (Unsatisfiable Rules II). *Let $\mathcal{P}$, $\mathcal{Q}$, and $\mathcal{R}$ be CTRSs, π be an argument filtering, $\gtrsim$ and $\sqsupseteq$ be relations on terms such that $\gtrsim$ is compatible with $\sqsupseteq$, $\sqsupseteq$ is well-founded, and $\pi(\rightarrow_{\mathcal{R}}) \subseteq \sqsupseteq$. Let $\alpha : \ell \rightarrow r \Leftarrow c \in \mathcal{P} \cup \mathcal{Q} \cup \mathcal{R}$ and $s_i \rightarrow t_i \in c$ be such that $\pi(s_i)$ and $\pi(t_i)$ do not unify and for all substitutions σ, $\pi(\sigma(t_i)) \gtrsim \pi(\sigma(s_i))$ holds. Then,*

$$\mathsf{P}_{UR}(\mathcal{P}, \mathcal{Q}, \mathcal{R}, e) = \{(\mathcal{P}[\emptyset]_\alpha, \mathcal{Q}[\emptyset]_\alpha, \mathcal{R}[\emptyset]_\alpha, e)\}$$

is a sound and (if $\alpha \notin \mathcal{R}$ or $e = (\rho, \mathsf{a})$) complete processor.

Example 20. Consider the following CTRS $\mathcal{R}$ [6, p. 46]:

$$a \rightarrow b \qquad f(a) \rightarrow b \qquad g(x) \rightarrow g(a) \Leftarrow f(x) \rightarrow x$$

$\mathsf{DP}_H(\mathcal{R})$ consists of a single rule: $G(x) \rightarrow G(a) \Leftarrow f(x) \rightarrow x$ and $\mathsf{DP}_V(\mathcal{R}) = \mathsf{DP}_{VH}(\mathcal{R}) = \emptyset$. We use the relations $\geq$ and $>$ generated by

$$[a] = 1 \qquad [b] = 0 \qquad [f](x) = [g](x) = [G(x)] = x$$

(over $\mathbb{N}$), and P_{UR} to remove the rule in $\mathsf{DP}_H(\mathcal{R})$ from $\tau_H = (\mathsf{DP}_H(\mathcal{R}), \emptyset, \mathcal{R}, e)$, thus proving operational termination of $\mathcal{R}$. Note that $>$ is monotonic, stable, transitive, and well-founded, and we have $\rightarrow_{\mathcal{R}} \subseteq >$ (and also $\rightarrow_{\mathcal{R}}^+ \subseteq >$); the crucial point is that no substitution σ satisfies $\sigma(f(x)) \rightarrow_{\mathcal{R}}^* \sigma(x)$ for the conditional rules: since $f(x)$ and x do not unify, we should have $\sigma(f(x)) \rightarrow_{\mathcal{R}}^+ \sigma(x)$ and hence $\sigma(f(x)) > \sigma(x)$. But $[\sigma(f(x))] = \sigma(x) \not> \sigma(x) = [\sigma(x)]$. Thus, we do not need to ensure that $[\sigma(g(x))] > [\sigma(g(a))]$ holds! However, $[x] = x \geq x = [f(x)]$.

7 Related Work and Conclusions

To the best of our knowledge, this is the first correct and complete characterization of operational termination of deterministic 3-CTRS which is based on the notion of dependency pair. The notion of minimal operationally nonterminating term and the properties explored here (Sect. 3) are also new in the literature. Furthermore, our treatment of the problem provides a *bidimensional* method that we have shown useful to simplify the analysis of operational termination itself and also to prove other termination properties like nontermination of 3-CTRSs and termination of 2-CTRSs. The analysis of termination of 2-CTRSs can also be accomplished as termination of the *underlying TRS* (i.e., the TRS $\mathcal{R}_u$ which is obtained by just dropping the conditional part of the rules). However, in contrast to our Theorem 5, the analysis of termination of 2-CTRSs $\mathcal{R}$ as termination of the underlying TRS $\mathcal{R}_u$ provides a *sufficient* condition only; it may fail in those cases where taking into account the conditions of the rules is essential to prove termination. For instance the one rule 2-CTRS $a \to a \Leftarrow a \to b$ is terminating but $\mathcal{R}_u$ is *not*. We prove $(\mathsf{DP}_H(\mathcal{R}), \emptyset, \mathcal{R}, e) = (\{A \to A \Leftarrow a \to b\}, \emptyset, \mathcal{R}, e)$ finite (and hence $\mathcal{R}$ terminating) using P_{UR} with the removal triple $(\geq, \geq, >)$ generated by the interpretation $[a] = 0$ and $[b] = 1$ to remove $A \to A \Leftarrow a \to b$.

The recent *Conditional Dependency Pairs* (CDPs) by Nakamura et al. [13] apply to a subclass of *1-CTRSs* where the conditions c in 1-rules ($\ell \to r \Leftarrow c$) are *terms* instead of sequences $s_1 \to t_1, \ldots, s_n \to t_n$. An instance $\sigma(c)$ of c is satisfied if and only if $\sigma(c) \to^* \mathsf{true}$. We generate a (usually strict) *subset* of the pairs considered in [13, Definition 3.1]: $\mathsf{DP}_H(\mathcal{R}) \cup \mathsf{DP}_V(\mathcal{R}) \cup \mathsf{DP}_{VH}(\mathcal{R}) \subseteq CDP(\mathcal{R})$. Their chains [13, Definition 3.2] are also different to ours (Definition 5).

As remarked in the introduction, existing tools for proving termination of conditional TRSs currently use transformation techniques. We are not aware of any implementation of *direct* methods. The transformation which is typically used for this purpose is $\mathcal{U}$ in [14, Definition 7.2.48]. This transformation is not complete, however. For instance, $\mathcal{U}(\mathcal{R})$ is not terminating for $\mathcal{R}$ in Examples 1 and 20, but we proved them operationally terminating in Examples 19 and 20. Furthermore, when $\mathcal{U}(\mathcal{R})$ is terminating, tools may fail to find a proof. This is often due to the loss of information introduced by transformations, and also to the presence of new symbols and rules that prevent the search process from finding a proof. The techniques presented in this paper have been incorporated in the latest version of the tool MU-TERM[1] [2]. The first benchmarks of existing examples in the literature are very positive and show that the 2D DP framework permits simple and fast proofs like the ones in the examples of this paper. This makes these techniques available to tools like MTT [4], which use MU-TERM as a backend for achieving proofs of operational termination of more general theories like membership equational programs or order-sorted rewrite theories. Direct termination methods for these wider logics will require extending the techniques presented here to the case of order-sorted conditional rewrite theories with types and subtypes, and where rewriting is context-sensitive and can take place modulo axioms B. This is envisaged as an interesting subject for future work.

References

1. Arts, T., Giesl, J.: Termination of term rewriting using dependency pairs. Theor. Comput. Sci. **236**(1–2), 133–178 (2000)
2. Alarcón, B., Gutiérrez, R., Lucas, S., Navarro-Marset, R.: Proving termination properties with MU-TERM. In: Johnson, M., Pavlovic, D. (eds.) AMAST 2010. LNCS, vol. 6486, pp. 201–208. Springer, Heidelberg (2011)

---

[1] We thank Raúl Gutiérrez for the implementation of the 2D DP Framework.

3. Clavel, M., Durán, F., Eker, S., Lincoln, P., Martí-Oliet, N., Meseguer, J., Talcott, C. (eds.): All About Maude - A High-Performance Logical Framework. LNCS, vol. 4350. Springer, Heidelberg (2007)

4. Durán, F., Lucas, S., Meseguer, J.: MTT: the Maude termination tool (system description). In: Armando, A., Baumgartner, P., Dowek, G. (eds.) IJCAR 2008. LNCS (LNAI), vol. 5195, pp. 313–319. Springer, Heidelberg (2008)

5. Futatsugi, K., Diaconescu, R.: CafeOBJ Report. AMAST Series. World Scientific, Singapore (1998)

6. Giesl, J., Arts, T.: Verification of Erlang processes by dependency pairs. Appl. Algebra Eng. Commun. Comput. **12**, 39–72 (2001)

7. Giesl, J., Thiemann, R., Schneider-Kamp, P.: The dependency pair framework: combining techniques for automated termination proofs. In: Baader, F., Voronkov, A. (eds.) LPAR 2004. LNCS (LNAI), vol. 3452, pp. 301–331. Springer, Heidelberg (2005)

8. Giesl, J., Thiemann, R., Schneider-Kamp, P., Falke, S.: Mechanizing and improving dependency pairs. J. Autom. Reason. **37**(3), 155–203 (2006)

9. Giesl, J., Thiemann, R., Schneider-Kamp, P.: Proving and disproving termination of higher-order functions. In: Gramlich, B. (ed.) FroCos 2005. LNCS (LNAI), vol. 3717, pp. 216–231. Springer, Heidelberg (2005)

10. Giesl, J., Schneider-Kamp, P., Thiemann, R.: APRoVE 1.2: automatic termination proofs in the dependency pair framework. In: Furbach, U., Shankar, N. (eds.) IJCAR 2006. LNCS (LNAI), vol. 4130, pp. 281–286. Springer, Heidelberg (2006)

11. Kusakari, K., Nakamura, M., Toyama, Y.: Argument filtering transformation. In: Nadathur, G. (ed.) PPDP 1999. LNCS, vol. 1702, pp. 47–61. Springer, Heidelberg (1999)

12. Lucas, S., Marché, C., Meseguer, J.: Operational termination of conditional term rewriting systems. Inf. Process. Lett. **95**, 446–453 (2005)

13. Nakamura, M., Ogata, K., Futatsugi, K.: On proving operational termination incrementally with modular conditional dependency pairs. Int. J. Comput. Sci. **40**, 2 (2013)

14. Ohlebusch, E.: Advanced Topics in Term Rewriting. Springer, New York (2002)

15. Schernhammer, F., Gramlich, B.: Characterizing and proving operational termination of deterministic conditional term rewriting systems. J. Logic Algebr. Program. **79**, 659–688 (2010)

16. Schernhammer, F., Gramlich, B.: VMTL–a modular termination laboratory. In: Treinen, R. (ed.) RTA 2009. LNCS, vol. 5595, pp. 285–294. Springer, Heidelberg (2009)

FunKons: Component-Based Semantics in K

Peter D. Mosses and Ferdinand Vesely[✉]

Swansea University, Swansea SA2 8PP, UK
{p.d.mosses,csfvesely}@swansea.ac.uk

Abstract. Modularity has been recognised as a problematic issue of programming language semantics, and various semantic frameworks have been designed with it in mind. Reusability is another desirable feature which, although not the same as modularity, can be enabled by it. The K Framework, based on Rewriting Logic, has good modularity support, but reuse of specifications is not as well developed.

The PLanCompS project is developing a framework providing an open-ended collection of reusable components for semantic specification. Each component specifies a single fundamental programming construct, or 'funcon'. The semantics of concrete programming language constructs is given by translating them to combinations of funcons. In this paper, we show how this component-based approach can be seamlessly integrated with the K Framework. We give a component-based definition of CinK (a small subset of C++), using K to define its translation to funcons as well as the (dynamic) semantics of the funcons themselves.

1 Introduction

Even very different programming languages often share similar constructs. Consider OCaml's conditional 'if E_1 then E_2 else E_3' and the conditional operator 'E_1 ? E_2 : E_3' in C. These constructs have different concrete syntax but similar semantics, with some variation in details. We would like to exploit this similarity when defining formal semantics for both languages by reusing commonalities between the OCaml and C specifications. With traditional approaches to semantics, reuse through 'copy-paste-and-edit' is usually the only option that is available to us. By default, this is also the case with the K Framework [9,13]. This style of specification reuse is not systematic, and prone to error.

The semantic framework currently being developed by the PLanCompS project[1] provides *fundamental constructs* (funcons) that address the issues of reusability in a systematic manner. Funcons are small semantic entities which express essential concepts of programming languages. These formally specified components can be composed to capture the semantics of concrete programming language constructs. A specification of Caml Light has been developed as an initial case study [3] and a case study on C# is in progress.

---

[1] http://www.plancomps.org/

© Springer International Publishing Switzerland 2014
S. Escobar (Ed.): WRLA 2014, LNCS 8663, pp. 213–229, 2014.
DOI: 10.1007/978-3-319-12904-4_12

For example, the funcon if-true can be used to specify OCaml's conditional expression. Semantics is given by defining a translation from the concrete construct to the corresponding funcon term:

$$[\![\text{if } E_1 \text{ then } E_2 \text{ else } E_3]\!] = \text{if-true}([\![E_1]\!], [\![E_2]\!], [\![E_3]\!])$$

Since the conditional operator in C uses integer valued expressions as the condition, its translation will reflect this:

$$[\![E_1 \text{ ? } E_2 \text{ : } E_3]\!] = \text{if-true}(\text{not}(\text{equal}([\![E_1]\!], 0)), [\![E_2]\!], [\![E_3]\!])$$

We could also define an if-non-zero funcon that would match the C-conditional semantics exactly. However, the translation using if-true is so simple that there wouldn't be much advantage in doing so. We can reuse the if-true funcon, and with it, its semantic definition. This way, we also make the difference between the OCaml and C conditional construct explicit. Section 2 provides more information on funcons.

PLanCompS uses MSOS [10], a modular variant of structural operational semantics [11], to formally define individual funcons. However, the funcon approach can be seamlessly integrated with other sufficiently modular specification frameworks. We have tested the use of funcons with the K Framework by giving a specification of CinK [8,9], a pedagogical subset of C++. We have defined both the translation of CinK to funcons and the semantics of the funcons using K's rewrite rules. The complete prototyped specification is available online, together with the CinK test programs which we have used to test our specification.[2] Interested readers may run these programs themselves using the K tool.

In this paper, we present our specification of the CinK translation (Sect. 3) and illustrate the definition of the semantics of funcons involved in it (Sect. 4). Section 5 offers an overview of related work and alternative approaches. We conclude and suggest directions of future work in Sect. 6.

2   Fundamental Constructs

As mentioned in the Introduction, the PLanCompS project is developing an open-ended collection of fundamental programming constructs, or 'funcons'. Many funcons correspond closely to simplified programming language constructs. However, each funcon has *fixed* syntax and semantics. For example, the funcon written assign(E1,E2) has the effect of evaluating *E1* to a variable, *E2* to a value (in any order), then assigning the value to the variable; it is well-typed only if *E1* is of type variables(T) and *E2* is of type *T*. In contrast, the language construct written '*E1* = *E2*' may be interpreted as an assignment or as an equality test (and its well-typedness changes accordingly) depending on the language.

The syntax or *signature* of a funcon determines its name, how many arguments it takes (if any), the sort of each argument, and the sort of the result. The following *computation sorts* reflect fundamental conceptual and semantic distinctions in programming languages.

---

[2] http://cs.swan.ac.uk/~csfvesely/wrla2014/

- The sort Comm (commands) is for funcons (such as assign(E1,E2)) that are executed only for their effects; on normal termination, a command computes the fixed value skip.
- The sort Expr (expressions) is for funcons (such as stored-value(E) and bound-value(I)) that compute values of sort Values.
- The sort Decl (declarations) is for funcons (such as bind-value(I,E)) that compute values of sort Environments, which represent sets of bindings between identifiers and values.

All computation sorts include their sorts of computed values as subsorts: a value takes no steps at all to compute itself.

One of the aims of the PLanCompS project is to establish an online repository of funcons (and data types) for anybody to use 'off-the-shelf' as components of language specifications. The project is currently testing the reusability of existing funcons and developing new ones in connection with some major case studies (including Caml Light, C#, and Java). Because individual funcons are meant to represent *fundamental* concepts in programming languages, many funcons (expressing, e.g., sequencing, conditionals, variable lookup and dereferencing) have a high potential for reuse. In fact, many funcons used in the Caml Light case study appear in the semantics of CinK presented in the following section.

The nomenclature and notation for the existing funcons are still evolving, and they will be finalised only when the case studies have been completed, in connection with the publication of the repository. Observant readers are likely to notice some (minor) differences between the funcon names used in this paper and in previous papers (e.g. [3]).

Regardless of the details of funcon notation, funcons can be algebraically composed to form funcon terms, according to their argument and result sorts (strictly lifted to corresponding computation sorts). Well-*formedness* of funcon terms is context-free: assign(E1,E2) is a well-formed funcon term whenever E1 and E2 are well-formed funcon terms of sort Expr. In contrast, well-*typedness* of funcon terms is generally context-sensitive. For example, the funcon term assign(bound-value(I),42) is well-typed only in the scope of a declaration that binds I to an integer variable. Dynamic semantics is defined for all well-formed terms; execution of ill-typed terms may fail.

The composability of funcons does *not* depend on features such as whether they might have side effects, terminate abruptly, diverge, spawn processes, interact, etc. This is crucial for the reusability of the funcons. The semantics of each funcon has to be specified without regard to the context in which it might be used, which requires a highly modular specification framework. Funcon specifications have previously been given in MSOS, Rewriting Logic, ASF + SDF, and action notation. Here, we explore specifying funcons in K, following Roşu.[3]

A component-based semantics of a programming language is specified by a context-free grammar for an abstract syntax for the language, together with a family of inductively specified functions translating abstract syntax trees to

---

[3] k/examples/funcons in the stable K distribution at http://www.kframework.org.

funcon terms. The static and dynamic semantics of a program is given by that of the resulting funcon term. As mentioned above, funcons have fixed syntax and semantics. Thus, evolution of a language is expressed as changes to translation functions. If the syntax or semantics of the programming language changes, the definition of the translation function has to be updated to reflect this.

Tool support for translating programs to funcon terms, and for executing the static and dynamic semantics of such terms, has previously been developed in Prolog [2], Maude [1] and ASF + SDF. We now present our experiment with K, focusing on dynamic semantics.

3   A Funcon Specification of CinK

This section presents an overview of our CinK specification using funcons. We include examples from the K sources of the specification. A selection of definitions of funcons involved in the specification can be found in Sect. 4.

CinK is a pedagogical subset of C++ [8,9] used for experimentation with the K Framework. The original report [8] presents the language in seven iterations. The first specifies a basic imperative language; subsequent iterations extend it with threads, model-checking, references, pointers, and uni-dimensional and multi-dimensional arrays. Our specification starts with only an expression language which we extend with declarations, statements, functions, threads, references, pointers, and arrays. The extensions follow the order of the CinK iterations; however, we omit support for model-checking.

The grammar which we have used for our specification is a simplified grammar matching CinK derived from the C++ grammar found in the standard [7, Appendix A].

We invite the reader to compare our specification by translation to funcons with the original K specification of CinK in [8]. Our hope is that our translation functions, together with the suggestive naming of funcons, give a rough understanding of the semantics of language constructs, even before looking at the semantics of funcons themselves.

3.1   Simple Expressions

To give semantics for expressions we use the translation function evaluate$[\![\_]\!]$: Expression $\rightarrow$ Expr. It produces a funcon term (of sort Expr) which, when executed, evaluates the argument expression.

Definitions for arithmetic expressions in CinK can be given very straightforwardly using data operations, which all extend to strict funcons on Expr. For example, semantics of the multiplication operator is expressed as the application of the operation int-times to translations of operand expressions (numeric types in CinK are limited to integers with some common operations):

```
rule evaluate[[ E1:Expression * E2:Expression ]] ⇒
    int-times(evaluate[[ E1 ]], evaluate[[ E2 ]])
```

The 'short-circuit and' operator can be readily expressed using a conditional funcon, which is strict only in its first argument. The (obvious) K definition for if-true can be found in Sect. 4.

rule evaluate⟦ *E1*:Expression && *E2*:Expression ⟧ ⇒
    if-true(evaluate⟦ *E1* ⟧, evaluate⟦ *E2* ⟧, false)

We will use the generic if-true funcon later in this section to define the conditional statement.

3.2 Variables, Blocks and Scope

Bindings and Variables. Semantics of declarations are given using the translation function elaborate⟦_⟧ : DeclarationSeq → Decl. The bind-value(*I*,*V*) funcon binds the identifier *I* to the value *V*, producing a 'small' environment containing only the newly created binding. To allocate a new variable of a specified type we use allocate. In Caml Light, bind-value was used for individual name-value bindings in let-expressions, and allocate for reference data types (e.g. '**ref** int').

rule elaborate⟦ *T*:TypeSpecifier *I*:Id ; ⟧ ⇒
    bind-value(*I*, allocate(variables(type⟦ *T* ⟧)))

In relation to variables, CinK (following C++) distinguishes between two general categories of expressions: *lvalue-* and *rvalue*-expressions. We express this distinction by having different translation functions for expressions in lvalue and rvalue contexts: in addition to evaluate⟦_⟧, we define evaluate-lval⟦_⟧ and evaluate-rval⟦_⟧. The default function evaluate⟦_⟧ produces terms evaluating lvalue and rvalue expressions according to their category. When an expression is expected to evaluate to an *lvalue*, we use evaluate-lval⟦_⟧. When an *rvalue* is expected, we use evaluate-rval⟦_⟧ which produces terms evaluating all expressions into rvalues. For lvalue expressions it returns the corresponding stored value, i.e., it serves as an lvalue-to-rvalue conversion.

The addition of variables also affects our translations of simple expressions and we need to update them. For example, numeric operations expect an rvalue and thus the operands are now translated using evaluate-rval⟦_⟧.

To obtain the variable bound to an identifier in the current environment we use bound-value. A variable is dereferenced using stored-value. The semantics for an identifier appearing in an lvalue or rvalue context is thus:

rule evaluate-lval⟦ *I*:Id ⟧ ⇒ bound-value(*I*)
rule evaluate-rval⟦ *I*:Id ⟧ ⇒ stored-value(evaluate-lval⟦ *I* ⟧)

Blocks and Controlling Scope. We distinguish between declaration statements and other statements within a block using funcons scope and seq. The funcon scope(*D*,*X*) evaluates *X* in the current environment overridden with the environment computed by *D*. A declaration statement within a block produces a new environment that is valid until the end of the block:

rule execute⟦ *BD*:BlockDeclaration *SS*:StatementSeq ⟧ ⇒
    scope(elaborate⟦ *BD* ⟧, execute⟦ *SS* ⟧)

The function execute⟦_⟧ : StatementSeq → Comm translates statements to fun-con commands.

For all other kinds of statements in a block we use the simple sequencing funcon seq(C,X) which executes the command C for side effects, then executes X.

rule execute⟦ *BS*:BlockStatement *SS*:StatementSeq ⟧ ⇒
    seq(execute⟦ *BS* ⟧, execute⟦ *SS* ⟧)

To accumulate multiple declarations into one environment we use the accum funcon. The funcon accum($D1$,$D2$) is similar to scope, except its result is the environment produced by elaborating declaration $D2$ and overriding the environment computed by $D1$ with it. This matches the semantics of a multi-variable declaration:

rule elaborate⟦ *T*:TypeSpecifier *ID*:InitDeclarator ,
                          IDL:InitDeclaratorList ; ⟧ ⇒
    accum(elaborate⟦ *T ID* ; ⟧, elaborate⟦ *T IDL* ; ⟧)

Note that accum is strict only in its first argument, so the correct order of evaluation is enforced.

Although Caml Light and CinK are quite different languages, all the funcons we needed here so far for CinK are reused from [3].

3.3   Assignment and Control Statements

The basic construct for updating variables in CinK/C++ is the assignment expression '$E1$ = $E2$', where the expression $E1$ is expected to evaluate to an lvalue, to which the rvalue of $E2$ will be assigned. The value of the whole expression is the lvalue of $E1$. Semantics of assignment is a rather simple translation using the assign-giving-variable funcon (defined in Sect. 4.4):

rule evaluate-lval⟦ *E1*:Expression = *E2*:Expression ⟧ ⇒
    assign-giving-variable(evaluate-lval⟦ *E1* ⟧, evaluate-rval⟦ *E2* ⟧)

The funcon assign-giving-variable is strict in both arguments but not sequentially, so the arguments are evaluated in an unspecified order. The funcon assigns the value given as its second argument to the variable given as its first argument and returns this variable as result.

CinK has boolean-valued conditions and the translations of while- and if-statements are trivial:

rule execute⟦ while (*E*:Expression) *S*:Statement ⟧ ⇒
    while-true(evaluate-rval⟦ *E* ⟧, execute⟦ *S* ⟧)
rule execute⟦ if (*E*:Expression) *S*:Statement ⟧ ⇒
    execute⟦ if (*E*) *S* else { } ⟧
rule execute⟦ if (*E*:Expression) *S1*:Statement else *S2*:Statement ⟧ ⇒
    if-true(evaluate-rval⟦ *E* ⟧, execute⟦ *S1* ⟧, execute⟦ *S2* ⟧)

3.4 Function Definition and Calling

We represent functions as *abstraction values* which wrap any computation as a value. An abstraction can be passed as a parameter, bound to an identifier, or stored like any other value. To turn a funcon term into an abstraction, we use the `abstraction` value constructor. The funcon `apply` applies an abstraction to a value and the abstraction may refer to the passed value using `given`. Multiple parameters can be passed as a tuple constructed using tuple value constructors.

A function call expression simply applies the abstraction to translated arguments:

rule evaluate-rval⟦ *E1*:Expression (*E2*:Expression) ⟧ ⇒
  apply(evaluate-rval⟦ *E1* ⟧, evaluate-params⟦ tuple(*E2*) ⟧)

At this stage the language only supports call-by-value semantics and so each parameter is evaluated to an *rvalue* before being passed to a function. The translation function evaluate-params⟦_⟧ (defined in terms of evaluate-rval⟦_⟧) recurses through the parameter expressions and constructs a tuple.

rule evaluate-params⟦ tuple(*E1*:Expression , *E2*:Expression) ⟧ ⇒
   tuple-prefix(evaluate-rval⟦ *E1* ⟧, evaluate-params⟦ tuple(*E2*) ⟧)
rule evaluate-params⟦ tuple(*E*:Expression) ⟧ ⇒
   tuple-prefix(evaluate-rval⟦ *E* ⟧, tuple(.))

We have introduced the auxiliary abstract syntax `tuple(E)` to ensure that parameters separated by commas are not interpreted as a comma-operator expression.

We use *patterns* as translations of function parameters. Patterns themselves are abstractions which compute an environment when applied to a matching value. The pattern for passing a single parameter by value allocates a variable of the corresponding type and binds it to an identifier; then it assigns the parameter value to the variable and returns the resulting environment.

rule pattern⟦ *T*:TypeSpecifier *I*:Id ⟧ ⇒
   abstraction(
    accum(bind-value(*I*, allocate(variables(type⟦ *T* ⟧))),
     decl-effect(assign(bound-value(*I*), given))))

Here we use the funcon `decl-effect(C)`, which allows using a command *C* as a declaration. It is an abbreviation for `seq(C,bindings(.))`.

Roughly, the semantics of a function definition is to allocate storage for an abstraction of the corresponding type, bind it to the function name, and use it to store an abstraction of the function body. Looking closer, the definition has to deal with some more details:

rule elaborate⟦ *T*:TypeSpecifier *I*:Id (*PDL*:ParameterDeclarationList)
        CS:CompoundStatement ⟧ ⇒
   decl-effect(assign(bound-value(*I*),
    close(abstraction(
     scope(match-compound(pattern-tuple⟦ *PDL* ⟧, given),
      catch(seq(execute⟦ *CS* ⟧, throw(variant(returned, null))),
       abstraction(original(returned, given)))))))))

Within the abstraction we use match-compound to match the passed value against the pattern tuple constructed from individual parameter patterns. The translation of the function body is evaluated in the environment produced by this matching (scope). Since a return statement abruptly terminates a function returning a value, we represent return statements as exceptions containing a value tagged with the atom 'returned' and wrap the function body in a handler. The catch funcon catches the exception and the handling abstraction retrieves the value tagged with 'returned', making it the return value of the whole function. In case there was no return statement in the body of the function, we throw a 'returned' with null. Using close we form a closure of the abstraction with respect to the definition-time environment, to ensure static scopes for bindings.

As mentioned above, an explicit return statement translates to throwing a value tagged with 'returned'. A parameterless return throws a null.

rule execute$[\![$ return E:Expression; $]\!]$ $\Rightarrow$
  throw(variant(returned, evaluate-rval$[\![$ E $]\!]$))
rule execute$[\![$ return ; $]\!]$ $\Rightarrow$ throw(variant(returned, null))

As a simple way of allowing self- and mutually recursive function definitions, we pre-allocate function variables and bind all function names declared at the top-level in a global environment using evaluate-forwards$[\![$_$]\!]$. Then we combine this environment with the elaboration of full function definitions and other declarations. The main function is called in the scope of the global environment.

rule translate$[\![$ DS:DeclarationSeq $]\!]$ $\Rightarrow$
  scope(accum(elaborate-forwards$[\![$ DS $]\!]$, elaborate$[\![$ DS $]\!]$),
    effect(apply(evaluate-rval$[\![$ main $]\!]$, tuple(.)))))

Because function identifiers are already bound when the full function definition is elaborated, the full definition only assigns the abstraction to the pre-allocated variable.

3.5   Threads

The second iteration in the original CinK report adds very basic thread support to the language. Spawning a thread in CinK mimics the syntax of using the std::thread class from the C++ standard library. However, instead of referring to the standard library, semantics is given to the construct directly.

rule elaborate$[\![$ std::thread $I1$:Id ($I2$:Id , E:Expression) ; $]\!]$ $\Rightarrow$
  decl-effect(effect(spawn(close(abstraction(evaluate$[\![$ $I2$ (E) $]\!]$)))))

The funcon spawn(A) creates a new thread in which the abstraction A will be applied. In our case the abstraction contains a function call corresponding to the parameters given to the thread constructor.

3.6   References

A reference in C++ is an alias for a variable, i.e., it introduces a new name for an already existing variable.

rule elaborate⟦ *T*:TypeSpecifier & *I*:Id = *E*:Expression ⟧ ⇒
    bind-value(*I*, evaluate-lval⟦ *E* ⟧)

The expression *E* is expected to compute an lvalue and we bind the resulting variable to identifier *I*. We are assuming that the input program is statically correct and thus the variable will have the right type.

A reference parameter pattern simply binds *I* to the given variable.

rule pattern⟦ *T*:TypeSpecifier & *I*:Id ⟧ ⇒
    abstraction(bind-value(*I*, given))

Before introducing references, we evaluated function parameters to an rvalue. Now the function evaluate-param⟦_⟧ has to be *redefined* in terms of evaluate⟦_⟧ instead of evaluate-rval⟦_⟧. Dereferencing is handled conditionally inside the parameter pattern.

rule pattern⟦ *T*:TypeSpecifier *I*:Id ⟧ ⇒
    abstraction(
      accum(bind-value(*I*, allocate(variables(type⟦ *T* ⟧))),
        decl-effect(assign(bound-value(*I*), current-value(given)))))

The funcon current-value dereferences its argument if it is a variable (lvalue), otherwise it returns the parameter itself.

3.7 Pointers

Pointer variables either hold a reference to another variable or are null otherwise. In this iteration we introduce auxiliary syntax for types, which we use to extract type information from declarations. Our type syntax is not part of the original language. It mostly resembles the original C++ syntax, except for function types which are expressed using a functional (arrow) notation. Here we extract types from a pointer declaration and a function declaration:

rule type⟦ *FT*:FunType (∗ *D*:Declarator) ⟧ ⇒ type⟦ (*FT* ∗) *D* ⟧
rule type⟦ *FT*:FunType (*D*:Declarator
            (*PDL*:ParameterDeclarationList)) ⟧ ⇒
    type⟦ ((*PDL*) --> *FT*) *D* ⟧

We translate these intermediate types into funcon types (just as we do with simple types). The funcon type pointers(*T*) is the type of pointers to variables of type *T*:

rule type⟦ (*FT*:FunType ∗):FunType ⟧ ⇒ pointers(type⟦ *FT* ⟧)

To illustrate, consider the pointer declaration **int** ∗∗ppi; which declares ppi to be a pointer to a pointer to an integer variable. The type of this variable in our auxiliary syntax is ((**int** ∗) ∗) and the analysed type is pointers(pointers(variables(integers))).

Pointer variables are allocated in the same manner as other variables: we simply pass the type of the pointer variable as the argument to the allocate funcon.

Explicit dereferencing of a pointer variable in an expression amounts to retrieving the value stored in the pointer. This value is the location to which the pointer is pointing. This is expressed in our translation:

rule evaluate-lval⟦ * *E*:Expression ⟧ ⇒ evaluate-rval⟦ *E* ⟧

If the pointer is null, dereferencing it or assigning to it will result in a stuck computation.

3.8 Arrays

This extension adds uni-dimensional and multi-dimensional array declarations and expressions to the specification. We analyse CinK arrays, which are indexed from zero, in terms of vectors. Similarly to pointers, we use auxiliary syntax for array types.

rule type⟦ *FT*:FunType (*D*:Declarator [*E*:Expression]) ⟧ ⇒
   type⟦ ([*E*] *FT*) *D* ⟧
rule type⟦ ([*E*:Expression] *FT*:FunType):FunType ⟧ ⇒
   vectors(evaluate⟦ *E* ⟧, type⟦ *FT* ⟧)

The arguments of the type constructor **vectors** are the length of the vector and the type of its elements. To allocate an array of a given type, we use the allocate-vector funcon:

rule elaborate⟦ ([*E*:Expression] *FT*:FunType) *I*:Id ; ⟧ ⇒
   bind-value(*I*, allocate-vector(type⟦ ([*E*] *FT*) ⟧))

Vectors allocated in this way are composed of the appropriate number of individual variables. These are read from and assigned to separately.

The semantics of accessing an array element via its index is given using the vector-select funcon. An array access expression in an lvalue position has the following semantics:

rule evaluate-lval⟦ *E1*:Expression [*E2*:Expression] ⟧ ⇒
   vector-select(evaluate-lval⟦ *E1* ⟧, evaluate-rval⟦ *E2* ⟧)

In CinK, multi-dimensional arrays are specified as vectors of vectors. As an illustration of translating array types, consider the declaration statement **int** x[2][3]; in C++. Expressing the type of x using our auxiliary syntax gives us ([2] ([3] **int**)). The translated type is vectors(2, vectors(3, variables(integers))). The construct allocate-vector properly allocates variables for such multi-dimensional vectors and returns a compound value of the appropriate type.

A Note on Reuse. The complete funcon definition of CinK available online uses 27 funcons. Of these, 19 have been previously used in the specification of Caml Light and only 8 were introduced in the present work, 3 of which are just abbreviations for longer funcon terms. It is thus possible to conclude that the degree of reuse of funcons between the Caml Light and CinK specifications is high, even if the languages are quite different.

3.9 Configuration

The configuration of the final iteration of our specification is as follows:

```
configuration
  <T>
    <threads>
      <thread multiplicity="*">
        <name> main:Threads </name>
        <k> translate[[ $PGM:TranslationUnit ]] </k>
        <xstack> .List </xstack>
        <context>
          <env> .Map </env>
          <given> no-value </given>
        </context>
      </thread>
    </threads>
    <store> .Map </store>
    <output stream="stdout"> .List </output>
    <input stream="stdin"> .List </input>
  </T>
```

It appears that this configuration could be generated from the K rules defining the funcons used in our specification of CinK. It is unclear to us whether inference of K configurations from arbitrary K rules is possible, and whether it would be consistent with the K configuration abstraction algorithm.

3.10 Sequencing of Side Effects

Following the C++ standard [7], CinK decouples side effects of some constructs to allow delaying memory writes to after an expression value has been returned. This gives compilers more freedom for performing optimisations and during code generation. The newest C++ standard uses a relation *sequenced before* to define how side effects are to be ordered with respect to each other and to value evaluation. The original CinK specification in K [8] uses auxiliary constructs for side effects and uses a bag to collect side effects. An auxiliary sequence point construct forces finalisation of side effects in the bag.

We have experimented with funcons to express decoupled side effects and have developed a preliminary K specification of the relevant funcons. Our solution is based on a pair of funcons. The first funcon encapsulates an expression, which can potentially request to defer side effects. It also maintains a set of deferred side effects which are computed interleaved with the encapsulated expression. Finally, it ensures that all side effect computations have finished before returning the value of the original expression. The other funcon serves to defer a side effect: it signals to the encapsulating funcon that a computation is to be interleaved with the evaluation of the original expression.

4   Funcons in K

We now illustrate our K specification of the syntax and semantics of the funcons and value types used in our component-based analysis of CinK. We specify each funcon and value type in a separate module, to facilitate selective reuse. Since modularity is a significant feature of our specifications, we show some of the specified imports. The complete specifications are available online, together with the K specification of the translation of CinK programs to funcons.

4.1   Expressions

Expressions compute values:

```
module EXPR  imports VALUES
   syntax Expr ::= Values
   syntax KResult ::= Values
```

Our specifications of value types lift the usual value operations to expression funcons, each of which is strict in all its arguments:

```
module INTEGERS  imports EXPR ...
   syntax Expr ::= "int-times" "(" Expr "," Expr ")" [strict]
               | ...
   syntax Values ::= Int
   rule int-times(I1:Int, I2:Int) ⇒ I1 *Int I2
   rule ...
```

In contrast, the conditional expression funcon if-true(E1,E2,E3) is strict only in E1, and its rules involve unevaluated expression arguments:

```
module IF-TRUE-EXPR  imports EXPR ...
   syntax Expr ::= "if-true" "(" Expr "," Expr "," Expr ")" [strict(1)]
   rule if-true(true, E:Expr, _) ⇒ E
   rule if-true(false, _, E:Expr) ⇒ E
```

We specify a corresponding funcon for conditional commands separately, since it appears that K modules cannot have parametric sorts (although the rules above could be generalised to arbitrary K arguments).

4.2   Declarations

```
module DECL  imports BINDINGS
   syntax Decl ::= Bindings
   syntax KResult ::= Bindings
```

Bindings are values corresponding to environments (mapping identifiers to values), and come equipped with some operations that can be used to compose declarations:

```
module BINDINGS  imports DECL
   syntax Bindings ::= bindings(Map)
   syntax Decl ::= "bindings-union" "(" Decl "," Decl ")" [strict]
   rule bindings-union(bindings(M1:Map), bindings(M2:Map)) ⇒
      bindings(M1 M2)
```

We could have included the funcon bind-value(*I*,*E*) as an operation in the above module, since it is strict in its only expression argument:

```
module BOUND-VALUE  imports ...
  syntax Expr ::= "bound-value" "(" Id ")"
  rule <k> bound-value(I:Id) ⟹ V:Values ...</k>
      <env>... I |-> V ...</env>
```

In contrast, the following funcons involve inspecting or (temporarily) changing the current environment, which is assumed to be in an accompanying cell:

```
module BOUND-VALUE  imports ...
  syntax Expr ::= "bound-value" "(" Id ")"
  rule <k> bound-value(I:Id) ⟹ V:Values ...</k>
      <env>... I |-> V ...</env>

module SCOPE-COMM  imports ...
  syntax Comm ::= "scope" "(" Decl "," Comm ")" [strict(1)]
  rule <k> scope(bindings(Env:Map), C:Comm) ⟹
          reset-env(Env', C) ...</k>
      <env> Env':Map ⟹ Env'[Env] </env>

module ACCUM  imports ...
  syntax Decl ::= "accum" "(" Decl "," Decl ")" [strict(1)]
  rule <k> accum(bindings(Env:Map), D:Decl) ⟹
          reset-env(Env', bindings-union(bindings(Env), D)) ...</k>
      <env> Env':Map ⟹ Env'[Env] </env>
```

The auxiliary operation reset-env(*M*,*K*) preserves the result of *K* when resetting the current environment to *M*:

```
module RESET-ENV
  syntax K ::= "reset-env" "(" Map "," K ")" [strict(2)]
  rule <k> reset-env(Env:Map, V':KResult) ⟹ V' ...</k>
      <env> _:Map ⟹ Env </env>
```

The *K* argument could be of sort Expr, Decl or Comm. Since we do not use reset-env directly in the translation of CinK to funcons, the fact that reset-env(*M*,*K*) is (semantically) of the same sort as *K* is irrelevant.

4.3   Commands

```
module COMM  imports SKIP
  syntax Comm ::= Skip
  syntax KResult ::= Skip
```

In contrast to the usual style in K specifications, commands compute the unique value skip:Skip on normal termination, rather than dissolving. However, this difference does not affect the translation of programs to funcons.

```
module SEQ-DECL  imports ...
  syntax Decl ::= "seq" "(" Comm "," Decl ")" [strict(1)]
  rule seq(skip, D:Decl) ⟹ D
```

As with if-true, the funcon seq(*C*,*X*) is essentially generic in *X*, but its syntax needs to be specified separately for each sort of *X*. In contrast, the sort of effect(*X*) is independent of the sort of *X*, and we can specify it generically:

```
module EFFECT imports COMM
  syntax Comm ::= "effect" "(" K ")" [strict]
  rule effect(_:KResult) ⇒ skip
```

The specification of **while-true** illustrates reuse *between* funcon specifications:

```
module WHILE-TRUE
  imports COMM
  imports EXPR
  imports IF-TRUE-COMM
  imports SEQ-COMM
  syntax Comm ::= "while-true" "(" Expr "," Comm ")"
  rule while-true(E:Expr, C:Comm) ⇒
          if-true(E, seq(C, while-true(E, C)), skip)
```

4.4   Variables

Variables are themselves treated as values:

```
module VARIABLES imports ...
  syntax Variables ::= "no-variable"
  syntax Values ::= Variables
```

The specifications of the funcons for allocating, assigning to, and inspecting the values stored in variables are much as usual. For example, the funcon **assign-giving-variable** assigns a value to a variable and then returns the variable:

```
module ASSIGN-GIVING-VARIABLE imports ...
  syntax Expr ::=
      "assign-giving-variable" "(" Expr "," Expr ")" [strict]
  rule <k> assign-giving-variable(Var:Variables, V:Values) ⇒
              Var ...</k>
        <store>... Var |-> ( _ ⇒ V ) ...</store>
```

4.5   Vector Allocation

The funcon **allocate-vector** serves to allocate a vector of variables. It uses the **allocate** funcon for allocation of element variables.

```
module ALLOCATE-VECTOR imports ...
  syntax Expr ::= "allocate-vector" "(" Expr ")" [strict]
  rule allocate-vector(vectors(1, T:Types):Types) ⇒
          vector-prefix(allocate-vector(T), vector(.))
  rule allocate-vector(vectors(I:Int, T:Types):Types) ⇒
          vector-prefix(allocate-vector(T),
                        allocate-vector(vectors(int-minus(I, 1), T)))
      when I >Int 1
  rule allocate-vector(T:Types) ⇒ allocate(variables(T))
    when is-vector-type(T) =/=K true
```

4.6 Functions

```
module FUNCTIONS imports ...
  syntax Functions ::= "abstraction" "(" Expr ")"
  syntax Values ::= Functions
```

The operation **abstraction(E)** constructs a value from an *unevaluated* expression *E*. It can then be closed to obtain static bindings for identifiers in *E* (the K specification of the funcon **close(E)** is unsurprising, and omitted here).

```
module APPLY imports ...
  syntax Expr ::= "apply" "(" Expr "," Expr ")" [strict]
  rule apply(abstraction(E:Expr), V:Values) ⇒ supply(V, E)
```

The funcon **supply(E1,E2)** makes the value of *E1* available as 'given' in the evaluation of *E2*:

```
module SUPPLY-EXPR imports ...
  syntax Expr ::= "supply" "(" Expr "," Expr ")" [strict(1)]
  rule <k> supply(V:Values, E:Expr) ⇒ reset-given(V', E) ...</k>
        <given> V' ⇒ V </given>
```

```
module GIVEN imports ...
  syntax Expr ::= "given"
  rule <k> given ⇒ V:Values ...</k> <given> V </given>
```

The specifications of the funcons **throw** and **catch** assume that all cells used to represent the current context of a computation are grouped under a unique context cell. This gives improved modularity: the specification remains the same when further contextual cells are required. In other respects, the specification follows the usual style in the K literature, using a stack of exception handlers:

```
module THROW imports ...
  syntax Comm ::= "throw" "(" Expr ")" [strict]
  rule <k> (throw(V':Values) ~> _) ⇒ (apply(F, V') ~> K) </k>
        <xstack> (F:Functions, K:K, B:Bag) ⇒ . ...</xstack>
        <context> _ ⇒ B </context>
```

```
module CATCH imports ...
  syntax Expr ::= "catch" "(" Comm "," Expr ")" [strict(2)]
  rule <k> (catch(C:Comm, F:Functions) ⇒ (C ~> popx)) ~> K </k>
        <xstack> . ⇒ (F, K, B) ...</xstack>
        <context> B:Bag </context>
  syntax K ::= "popx"
  rule <k> popx ⇒ . </k> <xstack> _:ListItem ⇒ . ...</xstack>
```

Funcons **throw** and **catch** have the most complicated definitions of all, yet they are still modest in size and complexity.

5 Related Work

The work in this paper was inspired by a basic specification of the IMP example language in funcons using K by Roşu. IMP contains arithmetic and boolean expressions, variables, if- and while-statements, and blocks. The translation to funcons is specified directly using K rewrite rules without defining sorted translation functions. The example can be found in the stable K distribution.[4]

CinK, the sublanguage of C++ that we use as a case study in this paper, is taken from a technical report by Lucanu and Șerbănuță [8]. We have limited ourselves to the same subset of C++.

SIMPLE [12] is another K example language which is fairly similar to CinK. The language is presented in two variants: an untyped and a typed one. The definition of typed SIMPLE uses a different syntax and only specifies static semantics. With the component-based approach, we specify a single translation of language constructs to funcons. The MSOS of the funcons defines separate relations for typing and evaluation; in K, it seems we would need to provide a separate static semantics module for each funcon, since the strictness annotations and the computation rules differ.

K specifications scale up to real-world languages, as illustrated by Ellison's semantics of C [4]. The PLanCompS project is currently carrying out major case studies (C#, Java) to examine how the funcon-based approach scales up to large languages, and to test the reusability of the funcon specifications.

Specification of individual language constructs in separate K modules was proposed by Hills and Roșu [6] and further developed by Hills [5, Chap. 5]. They obtained reusable rules by inferring the transformations needed for the rules to match the overall K configuration. The reusability of their modules was limited by their dependence on language syntax, and by the fact that the semantics of individual language constructs is generally more complicated than that of individual funcons.

6   Conclusion

We have given a component-based specification of CinK, using K to define the translation of CinK to funcons as well as the (dynamic) semantics of the funcons themselves. This experiment confirms the feasibility of integrating component-based semantics with the K Framework.

The K specification of each funcon is an independent module. Funcons are significantly simpler than constructs of languages such as CinK, and it was pleasantly straightforward to specify their K rules. However, we would have preferred the K configurations for combination of funcons to be generated automatically.

Many of the funcons used here for CinK were introduced in the component-based specification of Caml Light [3], demonstrating their reusability. The names of the funcons are suggestive of their intended interpretation, so the translation specification alone should convey a first impression of the CinK semantics. Readers are invited to browse the complete K specifications of our funcons online, then compare our translation of CinK to funcons with its direct specification in K [8].

In the future, we are aiming to define the static semantics of funcons in K, so our translation would induce a static semantics for CinK.

---

[4] http://www.kframework.org

References

1. Chalub, F., Braga, C.: Maude MSOS tool. In: WRLA 2006, ENTCS, vol. 176, pp. 133–146. Elsevier (2007)
2. Churchill, M., Mosses, P.D.: Modular bisimulation theory for computations and values. In: Pfenning, F. (ed.) FOSSACS 2013 (ETAPS 2013). LNCS, vol. 7794, pp. 97–112. Springer, Heidelberg (2013)
3. Churchill, M., Mosses, P.D., Torrini, P.: Reusable components of semantic specifications. In: Proceedings of the 13th International Conference on Modularity, MODULARITY '14, pp. 145–156. ACM, New York (2014)
4. Ellison, C., Roşu, G.: An executable formal semantics of C with applications. In: Proceedings of the 39th Annual ACM SIGPLAN-SIGACT Symposium on Principles of Programming Languages, POPL '12, pp. 533–544. ACM, New York (2012)
5. Hills, M.: A Modular Rewriting Approach to Language Design, Evolution and Analysis. Ph.D. thesis, University of Illinois at Urbana-Champaign (2009)
6. Hills, M., Roşu, G.: Towards a module system for K. In: Corradini, A., Montanari, U. (eds.) WADT 2008. LNCS, vol. 5486, pp. 187–205. Springer, Heidelberg (2009)
7. ISO International Standard ISO/IEC 14882:2011(E) – Programming Language C++ (2011). http://isocpp.org/std/the-standard
8. Lucanu, D., Şerbănuţă, T.F.: CinK – an exercise on how to think in K. Technical report TR 12-03 (v2), Faculty of Computer Science, A. I. Cuza University, December 2013. https://fmse.info.uaic.ro/publications/181/
9. Lucanu, D., Şerbănuţă, T.F., Roşu, G.: K framework distilled. In: Durán, F. (ed.) WRLA 2012. LNCS, vol. 7571, pp. 31–53. Springer, Heidelberg (2012)
10. Mosses, P.D.: Modular structural operational semantics. J. Log. Algebr. Program. **60–61**, 195–228 (2004)
11. Plotkin, G.D.: A structural approach to operational semantics. J. Log. Algebr. Program. **60–61**, 17–139 (2004)
12. Roşu, G., Şerbănuţă, T.F.: K overview and SIMPLE case study. In: Proceedings of the Second International Workshop on the K Framework and Its Applications (K 2011), ENTCS, vol. 304, pp. 3–56. Elsevier (2014)
13. Şerbănuţă, T.F., Arusoaie, A., Lazar, D., Ellison, C., Lucanu, D., Roşu, G.: The K primer (v3.3). In: Proceedings of the Second International Workshop on the K Framework and its Applications (K 2011), ENTCS, vol. 304, pp. 57–80. Elsevier (2014)

An Integration of CafeOBJ into Full Maude

Adrián Riesco[✉]

Facultad de Informática, Universidad Complutense de Madrid, Madrid, Spain
ariesco@fdi.ucm.es

Abstract. We present in this paper an integration of CafeOBJ into Full Maude. We have developed a grammar to parse any CafeOBJ specification, an intermediate language to store it, and a translation from this representation into Maude specifications. This integration enhances CafeOBJ functionality in many ways: our intermediate representation has been developed mirroring Maude metalevel, and hence it allows CafeOBJ users to analyze, modify, and execute them; CafeOBJ specifications can use Maude commands, including the LTL model checker; other Full Maude tools can be straightforwardly combined with this extension; and we provide an alternative implementation for CafeOBJ that can be easily modified and extended. We present here the ideas for parsing and translating CafeOBJ specifications, and illustrate with examples the features listed above.

Keywords: CafeOBJ · Full Maude · Integration · Metalevel

1 Introduction

CafeOBJ [9] is a language for writing formal specifications of models for wide varieties of software and systems, and verifying properties of them. CafeOBJ implements equational logic by rewriting and can be used as a powerful interactive theorem proving system. Specifiers can write proof scores [10] also in CafeOBJ and perform proofs by executing these proof scores. CafeOBJ provides several features to ease the specification of systems. These features include a flexible mix-fix syntax, powerful and clear typing system with ordered sorts, parameterized modules and views for instantiating the parameters, module expressions, operators for defining terms, and equations for defining the (possibly conditional) equalities between terms and (possibly conditional) transitions for specifying how a system evolves, among others. However, only a subset of the CafeOBJ specifications, the equational part, is executable, where the operational semantics is given by a conditional order-sorted term rewriting system.

Maude modules are executable rewriting logic specifications. Maude functional modules [1, Chap. 4] are executable membership equational specifications

Research partially supported by Japanese project Kakenhi 23220002, MICINN Spanish project *StrongSoft* (TIN2012-39391-C04-04), and Comunidad de Madrid program *PROMETIDOS* (S2009/TIC1465).

S. Escobar (Ed.): WRLA 2014, LNCS 8663, pp. 230–246, 2014.
DOI: 10.1007/978-3-319-12904-4_13

that allow the definition of sorts; subsort relations between sorts; operators for building values of these sorts, giving the sorts of their arguments and result, and which may have attributes such as being associative or commutative, for example; memberships asserting that a term has a sort; and equations identifying terms. Both memberships and equations can be conditional. Maude system modules [1, Chap. 6] are executable rewrite theories. A system module can contain all the declarations of a functional module and, in addition, declarations for rules and conditional rules. An important feature of rewriting logic is that it is reflective, that is, it can be faithfully interpreted in terms of itself. This feature is efficiently implemented in Maude by means of the META-LEVEL module [1, Chapt. 14], which allows us to use Maude modules and terms as usual data.

Full Maude [1, Part II] is an extension of Maude written in Maude itself. Full Maude provides an even more powerful module algebra than the one available in Core Maude, features for parsing and printing Maude modules, and an explicit module database. This database, combined with the meta-level features explained above, allows us to introduce, remove, modify, and analyze the modules introduced by the user. Moreover, it is also possible to change the syntax of existing features and add new kinds of modules and commands. Full Maude is built on top of the Loop Mode [1, Chapt. 17], which provides a mechanism to read the modules and commands introduced by the user enclosed in parentheses, and to show him the results generated by these commands. For these reasons, Full Maude has been traditionally used as a basis for further extensions, either for extra syntactic constructs, like the support for Real-Time modules [14], or for new commands, like the narrowing search currently available for symbolic execution [2, Chap. 16].

We present in this paper an extension of Full Maude to parse CafeOBJ modules. The advantages obtained by using this tool, publicly available at http://maude.sip.ucm.es/cafe/, are:

- Maude modules can be imported by CafeOBJ modules, and vice versa. The former is specially useful because Maude provides the predefined modules SATISFACTION, LTL-SIMPLIFIER, and MODEL-CHECKER [1, Chapt. 12], which allow the user to define and prove LTL properties on CafeOBJ specifications. We can also use the Loop Mode [1, Chapt. 17] to develop interactive tools. Moreover, we have defined an intermediate representation of CafeOBJ specifications that mirrors Maude metalevel, and have included functions to execute terms using these modules. That is, CafeOBJ modules can use CafeOBJ modules and terms as standard data, just as several Maude applications have been designed during the last years.
- Maude commands can be used on CafeOBJ specifications. This allows the user to use, among others, the rew command to apply transitions (and normalization via equations) to CafeOBJ terms (which cannot be done in the current release of CafeOBJ) [1, Chapt. 6]; the search command to perform searches to check invariants [1, Chapt. 12]; or the narrowing command for symbolic execution [2, Chap. 16].

- It provides a new implementation of CafeOBJ. Our interface parses any CafeOBJ module and accepts `open-close` environments, required to execute proof scores. We also process behavioral specifications, although the current version of the tool does not distinguish between behavioral and non-behavioral statements in the translation.

  Moreover, this new implementation is more powerful in the sense that any CafeOBJ programmer can add new syntax and commands. Although this extension would require modifying the Maude code used by the interface, it is so similar to CafeOBJ code that it can be easily understood. Actually, the code has been designed with this feature in mind, so the syntax and parsing modules are carefully distinguished and documented.

  As an example of the syntax that can be added to CafeOBJ specifications, our parser allows the user to use matching and rewrite conditions, as well as using the `nonexec` and `metadata` attributes in equations and transitions. Some of these features are available in the latest release of CafeOBJ, while others are only supported by our implementation.
- It allows an easy integration of CafeOBJ specifications with any tool implemented on top of Full Maude. We have currently integrated the Maude Declarative Debugger and Test-case Generator [16] and the Constructor-based Inductive Theorem Prover [11]. Our goal when integrating these tools was to provide a minimum framework where CafeOBJ functions can be tested, fixed when a wrong behavior is found, and proved correct with respect to some properties, once we have confidence in the soundness of the implementation. However, many other interesting tools can be integrated using our approach.
- Finally, we provide a script to connect CafeOBJ with Full Maude in a transparent way. We have implemented a Java class that transforms the source code to meet the format required by Full Maude, which includes enclosing the modules in parentheses, adding the ' to escape characters such as [,], or ,, and removing CafeOBJ comments, among others. In this way, it is not necessary to modify the original CafeOBJ specifications to use the interface.

The rest of the paper is organized as follows: Sect. 2 briefly introduces the related work, while Sect. 3 presents the basic notions used throughout the paper. Section 4 describes the parsing and translation process. Section 5 illustrates how to use the tool. Finally, Sect. 6 presents the concluding remarks and outlines some lines of future work.

2   Related Work

The most similar examples to the present work are Full Maude itself [1, Part II], Real-Time Maude [14], and the Maude Strategy Language [7]. The former defines a complete syntax for Maude, extends it with support for object-oriented modules, and provides commands to execute them. Similarly, Real-Time Maude defines real-time modules and timed commands to execute them, while the Strategy Language extends Maude modules with syntax for defining execution strategies, as well as rewrite commands using these strategies. Our work follows the same steps: it requires to define the syntax of our modules and commands, parse them, translate them into Maude (in Full Maude this is only the case for object-oriented modules, since standard modules do not require translation), and execute the commands. Nonetheless, we take advantage of many features developed for Full Maude and reused later [5], which greatly ease the parsing task.

Besides these tools, Maude has been used as a semantical framework to specify the semantics of several languages, such as LOTOS [17], CCS [17], or C [8]. These researches, as well as several other efforts to describe a methodology to represent the semantics of programming languages in Maude, led to the *rewriting logic semantics project* [12], which presents a comprehensive compilation of these works.

Another translation from CafeOBJ to Maude can be found in [18]. There, the authors translate a subset of CafeOBJ specifications (more specifically, specifications of state machines standing for asynchronous distributed systems) into Maude to perform model checking. Although they follow an approach similar to the one in the current paper, it is focused in just one kind of specification, and hence it lacks scalability.

3   Preliminaries

We present in this section some basic notions required throughout the rest of the paper. First, we describe CafeOBJ and Maude by means of an example. Then, we give some details about the Maude metalevel and Full Maude.

3.1   CafeOBJ and Maude

CafeOBJ (on the lefthand side) can define modules with loose semantics by using the syntax mod*. For example, we can define a module ELT requiring the existence of a sort Elt and an element of this sort, called mt, which is a constructor. This kind of behavior is specified in Maude (on the righthand side) as a theory:

```
mod* ELT {                        fth ELT is
  [Elt]                             sort Elt .
  op mt : -> Elt {constr}           op mt : -> Elt [ctor] .
}                                 endfth
```

We can use this module to define a parameterized module with tight semantics, with syntax mod!. The module LIST below indicates that it receives a parameter X fulfilling the requirements stated by ELT. This module first defines the sort List for lists. Similarly, we define a parameterized system module LIST in Maude with syntax mod:

```
mod! LIST(X :: ELT) {             mod LIST{X :: ELT} is
  [List]                            sort List .
```

The constructors are defined, as shown above, with the keyword op and the constr attribute. In this case the constructors are nil for empty lists and the juxtaposition operator __ for placing an element of sort Elt in front of a list. Note the different syntax for the sort Elt, qualified by the parameter X:

```
op nil : -> List {constr}              op nil : -> List [ctor] .
op __ : Elt.X List -> List {constr}    op __ : X$Elt List -> List [ctor] .
```

We can also define functions for lists. For example, composition of lists is defined by distinguishing constructors on the first argument. Note that both CafeOBJ and Maude follow the same syntax, although CafeOBJ allows some extra syntactic sugar, including just-once on-the-fly declaration of variables:

```
var E : Elt.X      var L : List    var E : X$Elt . var L : List .
op _@_ : List List -> List         op _@_ : List List -> List .
eq [c1] : nil @ L = L .            eq [c1] : nil @ L = L .
eq [c2] : (E L) @ L':List =        eq [c2] : (E L) @ L':List =
          E (L @ L') .                       E (L @ L':List) .
```

Similarly, we can define the reverse function. This function uses the constant mt from module ELT as the reverse of the empty list,[1] while the reverse for bigger lists is defined as usual by using the composition above:

```
op reverse : List -> List          op reverse : List -> List .
eq [r1] : reverse(nil) = mt nil .  eq [r1] : reverse(nil) = mt nil .
eq [r2] : reverse(E L) =           eq [r2] : reverse(E L) =
          reverse(L) @ (E nil) .             reverse(L) @ (E nil) .
```

We can also define non-deterministic transitions. For example, we can combine two lists by using the commutative operator mix and two transitions to indicate that the next element is the first one of any of the lists (thanks to the matching modulo commutativity):

```
op mix : List List -> List {comm}  op mix : List List -> List [comm] .
trans [m1] : mix(nil, L) => L .    rl [m1] : mix(nil, L) => L .
trans [m2] : mix(E L, L')          rl [m2] : mix(E L, L')
           => E mix(L, L') .                => E mix(L, L') .
}                                  endm
```

Finally, in CafeOBJ we can use an on-the-fly view to instantiate LIST with natural numbers:

```
mod! NAT-LIST {
  pr(LIST(view to NAT {sort Elt -> Nat, op mt -> 0}))
}
```

On the other hand, we need to define an explicit view in Maude, and then use this view to instantiate the module:

---

[1] This is a wrong definition that will be detected and fixed in Sect. 5.3.

```
view Nat from Elt to NAT is
 sort Elt to Nat .
 op mt to 0 .
endv

mod NAT-LIST is
 pr LIST{Nat} .
endm
```

3.2 Maude Metalevel and Full Maude

Exploiting the fact that rewriting logic is reflective [3], an important feature of Maude is its systematic and efficient use of reflection through its predefined META-LEVEL module [1, Chapt. 14], a characteristic that allows many advanced metaprogramming and metalanguage applications. In this work, we take advantage of this feature to parse, store, transform, and execute CafeOBJ modules.

Full Maude [1, Part II] is an extension of Maude written in Maude itself. Full Maude is built on top of the LOOP-MODE module [1, Chapt. 17]. This module allows input/output interaction by means of the [_,_,_] operator, which builds terms of sort System and where the first argument corresponds to the input introduced by the user, which must be enclosed in parentheses to be recognized; the second one is a term of sort State that can be defined by the user for each application; and the third one the output shown to the user.

In Full Maude this State is defined by using a class Database, which has an attribute db standing for the Full Maude database. It also has attributes for the current input, the output not processed yet, and the default module. Essentially, the Loop Mode transforms the data introduced by the user into a list of quoted identifiers; this list is then meta-parsed by Full Maude by using the GRAMMAR module, which includes the syntax for modules and commands. If this parsing is successful, then the term thus obtained is placed in the input attribute. Different inputs are treated by using rules: modules and views are processed to check whether they fulfill the semantic constraints required by Maude, and then introduced into the database, while commands are executed by using this database. The results must be placed in the output attribute; a rule will move this data to the third component of the system.

Hence, our aims in this paper are to extend GRAMMAR to include CafeOBJ syntax, process the new terms obtained from the parsing, and define commands (and the appropriate rules) to deal with these new features.

4 Introducing CafeOBJ Modules into the Full Maude Database

We present in this section the basic ideas to introduce CafeOBJ modules into the Full Maude database. First, we describe how CafeOBJ modules are parsed. Then we show how the obtained modules can be translated into Maude and used by other tools implemented in Full Maude.

4.1   Parsing CafeOBJ Modules and Commands

As explained in the previous section, in order to parse CafeOBJ modules we have
to define its syntax, which will be used by Full Maude to create a term that will
be processed to obtain the actual module. We use the metarepresentation of
this module to extend the `GRAMMAR` metamodule from Full Maude, providing the
metamodule `CafeGRAMMAR`. It can be used to parse both Maude and CafeOBJ
modules and commands.

Basically, the syntax follows the CafeOBJ grammar in [13], although we
have extended it with some features that will be available in the next release of
CafeOBJ, such as the `nonexec` attribute or matching conditions. Following the
standard approach, we define a sort for each syntactic category in the grammar,
and operator declarations for each production rule. In this way, we specify a module `CafeMETA-SIGN` where this information is contained. For example, the sort
`@CafeTransDecl@`[2] stands for the definition of transitions in CafeOBJ syntax:

```
op trans_=>_. : @CafeBubble@ @CafeBubble@ -> @CafeEqDecl@ [ctor] .
op ctrans_=>_if_. : @CafeBubble@ @CafeBubble@ @CafeBubble@
                         -> @CafeTransDecl@ [ctor] .
op ctrns_=>_if_. : @CafeBubble@ @CafeBubble@ @CafeBubble@
                         -> @CafeTransDecl@ [ctor] .
```

Note that we use a special sort `@CafeBubble@` to encapsulate terms that can
take any form. Basically, a bubble is any list of quoted identifiers, which must
be later parsed to obtain a valid term in the current module.

These declarations, as well as the rest of declarations for the statements
available in a CafeOBJ module, are defined as a subsort of a `@CafeDeclList@`,
which are composed by means of a juxtaposition operator:

```
subsorts @CafeImportDecl@ ... @CafeTransDecl@ < @CafeDeclList@ .
op __ : @CafeDeclList@ @CafeDeclList@ -> @CafeDeclList@ [assoc] .
```

For example, the transition m1 from Sect. 3 would be parsed as:

```
'trans_=>_.['CafeBubble['__[''[.Qid, ''m1.Qid, ''], ':, ''mix.Qid,
     ''(.Qid, ''nil.Qid, '',, ''L.Qid, '').Qid]], 'CafeBubble[''L.Qid]]
```

Note that the label is included in the bubble for the lefthand side; it must be
extracted before processing this side (analogously, attributes might appear in
the bubble for the righthand side). This term must be now parsed again in order
to check whether it fulfills the semantics constraints, e.g., the terms only use
variables previously defined, they are bound either in the lefthand side or in a
matching condition, and terms are built using existing operators. This second
phase returns, when the module is correct, a term of sort `CafeModule`:

```
op mod*_{__[_]____} : CafeHeader CafeImportList HiddenSortDecl SortSet
                      CafeSubsortDeclSet CafeOpDeclSet CafeEqSet
                      CafeTransSet -> CafeModule [ctor] .
```

---

[2] We follow the Full Maude convention and enclose sorts for parsing in @.

Our definition of CafeOBJ modules uses the sorts `Qid`, `Term`, and `Condition` from Maude metalevel to define the sorts used here. For example, transitions are declared as follows:

```
op trans_=>_{_}. : Term Term CafeAttrSet -> CafeTrans [ctor] .
op ctrans_=>_if_{_}. : Term Term Condition CafeAttrSet -> CafeTrans [ctor] .
```

In this way, the transition `m1` is represented as:

```
trans 'mix['nil.List, 'L:List] => 'L:List {label:('m1)} .
```

Once the final module has been obtained, it is stored in a database, which is just a partial function from quoted identifiers (of sort `Qid`) to `CafeModule`. This modules can be retrieved, modified, executed, and stored again, as we will see in Sect. 5. Note that the current version of the tool does not support metasyntax for views; they are just introduced as Maude views.

Regarding commands, we provide the syntax for **open**...**close** environments, which combine operator declarations (mainly constants) and equation definitions with **red** commands to define proof scores [10], and specific commands for dealing with CafeOBJ modules. In this case we create an on-the-fly module where the reductions take place.

4.2 Translating the Modules

Taking advantage of the similarities between the syntax and the semantics of CafeOBJ and Maude, most of the transformations performed by our tool are straightforward. Both languages have modules with loose semantics (called *theories* in Maude), modules with tight semantics, parameterized modules, views to instantiate these modules, equations, and transitions (*rules* in Maude) as main features. From the Maude point of view there are some features that cannot be translated into CafeOBJ, being the main one the membership axioms stating the members of a sort, because Maude implements membership equational logic while the CafeOBJ type system is based on order sorted algebra. However, the differences in this case are not important because we are interested in the translation from CafeOBJ to Maude.

There are two important features in CafeOBJ that cannot be translated into Maude. Both of them are related to the importation of modules with loose semantics: (i) these modules can be imported by any module, while in Maude they can only be imported by other theories, and (ii) these modules can be imported in any mode (being the modes **protecting**, indicating that no junk and no confusion is added to the sorts; **extending**, denoting that no confusion is allowed; and **including**, indicating that there are no restrictions, see [1, Chapt. 8] for details), while Maude theories can only be imported in **including** mode. We have dealt with these restrictions in a conservative way. First, we translate these modules, that should be Maude theories, as modules (i.e., they have tight semantics), and a warning message is shown. This change is harmless if our aim is to execute them or to use any of the tools currently integrated (the declarative debugger and the CITP), but has two disadvantages: (a) it might fail later, if this module is used as the target of a view, and (b) other tools, not integrated yet, might distinguish between the different kinds of modules. Similarly, we always translate the importation modes for these modules as `including`, which is also fine in our case (the tools integrated thus far use flattened modules) but might produce problems with other tools. The user can force the tool to translate the modules without modifications with the `(strict translation on.)` command.

There are also some other complex features that require a non-straightforward translation. More specifically, the CafeOBJ syntax for views is much more flexible than the one used by Maude: they can be defined on-the-fly and can be used in an order different from the one specified in the parameterized module by using the parameter name. The former is solved by creating explicit views with fresh view identifiers, while the latter requires to manipulate the parameterized module from the database to reorder the views.

Basically, our implementation defines a function `cafe2maude`, which takes a `CafeModule` and returns a Maude `Module`:

```
op cafe2maude : CafeModule -> Module .
```

It uses auxiliary functions to translate each element in a CafeOBJ module. For instance, transitions are translated into rules as follows:

```
op cafe2maude : CafeTrans -> Rule .
eq cafe2maude(trans T => T' {AtS} .) = rl T => T' [cafe2maude*(AtS)] . .
eq cafe2maude(ctrans T => T' if C {AtS} .) = crl T => T'
                                    if C [cafe2maude*(AtS)] . .
```

where `cafe2maude*` is an auxiliary function that translates the attributes.

As explained in Sect. 3.2, the connection between the Loop Mode and the behavior of the tool is implemented by rules. We have defined a new class `CafeDatabase`, subclass of `Database`, to take care of the translation and the new commands:

```
sort CafeDatabaseClass .
subsort CafeDatabaseClass < DatabaseClass .
op CafeDatabase : -> CafeDatabaseClass [ctor] .
```

This class defines two new attributes: `strict`, which indicates whether the translation is strict or not, and `cafeDB`, which contains the CafeOBJ database:

```
op strict :_ : Bool -> Attribute [ctor] .
op cafeDB :_ : CafeDB -> Attribute [ctor] .
```

4.3   Combining CafeOBJ and Other Full Maude Tools

Using the modules described in the previous sections, it is easy to modify any tool built in Full Maude for Maude specifications and make it work with CafeOBJ modules, given that they follow two standard principles:[3]

---

[3] Note that these changes will allow us to execute the tools. However, some theoretical considerations may be required to prove that this execution is correct.

- They use a module extending GRAMMAR to parse their modules/commands. In this case, it is enough to extend CafeGRAMMAR instead, and CafeOBJ modules will be parsed.
- They define a subclass of Database to process their modules/commands. We have to modify this definition to extend CafeDatabase. It is also required to initialize the attributes strict and cafeDB, so they can be used later.

To test the benefits of this approach we have already worked with the Maude declarative debugger and test-case generator [16] and the Constructor-based Inductive Theorem Prover (CITP) [11]. Note that a potential problem of any integration is that the output provided by the tool refers to the transformed Maude code. Although this might be fine in some cases (e.g. the debugger refers to the label of the wrong statement, so it is safe to use it, see Sect. 5.3 for details), in some others it is interesting to refer to the original CafeOBJ module or just use commands which are specifically defined for CafeOBJ users. In this case, some extra changes are required, as shown in the next section for the CITP.

5   Connecting CafeOBJ and Maude

We present in this section how to use the most important features of our implementation. We first show how to use the metalevel representation of CafeOBJ. Then, we describe the basic commands provided in the interface and how to use the Maude Declarative Debugger and the Constructor-based Inductive Theorem Prover. All the modules, scripts, and examples shown here are available at http://maude.sip.ucm.es/cafe/.

5.1   Metaprogramming in CafeOBJ

We provide in the META-CAFE-SYNTAX module the syntax for CafeOBJ modules. It follows the syntax in the predefined module META-LEVEL for Maude modules, but uses specific syntax to follow CafeOBJ conventions. These modules are retrieved from and inserted into the database with the functions getTopModule and setTopModule. Note that, since these modules are stored in a specific attribute of the CafeDatabase class, specifications using the database are not completely transparent from Maude syntax:

```
op getTopModule : CafeDB Qid ~> CafeModule .
op setTopModule : CafeDB Qid CafeModule -> CafeDB .
```

Finally, these modules can be modified and executed by using the functions in CAFE-META-LEVEL. It includes functions for accessing the different components of a module, update them, and for executing terms in a given module. The current version of the tool provides the functions metaReduce, for applying equations until a normal form is reached; metaRewrite, for applying transitions given a bound in the number of transitions applied; and metaFrewrite, for fair application of transitions given a bound in the number of transitions applied and the maximum number of rewrites at each entitled position on each traversal of a subject term (see [1, Chapt. 14] for details):

```
op metaReduce : Qid Term CafeDB Database -> ResultPair .
op metaRewrite : Qid Term Bound CafeDB Database -> ResultPair .
op metaFrewrite : Qid Term Bound Nat CafeDB Database -> ResultPair .
```

Note that these functions require the Maude database, since they might import some Maude modules. They are implemented by building the corresponding flat Maude module and then using the appropriate built-in Maude functions.

For example, we could define a function getCommOps extracting the commutative operators from a CafeOBJ module by using an auxiliary function filterCommOps that keeps the commutative operators from a set:

```
op getCommOps : CafeModule -> CafeOpDeclSet
eq getCommOps(CM) = filterCommOps(getOps(CM)) .
op filterCommOps : CafeOpDeclSet -> CafeOpDeclSet
eq filterCommOps(none) = none .
eq filterCommOps(COD CODS) = if isComm?(COD) then COD
                             else none fi filterCommOps(CODS) .
```

where isComm? is an auxiliary function that checks whether an operator is commutative. Note that we allow operators with both the op definition and the pred keyword. This function uses another auxiliary function containsComm? which just traverses the attributes looking for comm:

```
pred isComm? : CafeOpDecl
eq isComm?(op Q : TyL -> Ty {AtS}) = containsComm?(AtS) .
eq isComm?(pred Q : TyL {AtS}) = containsComm?(AtS) .
pred containsComm? : CafeAttrSet
eq containsComm?(none) = false .
eq containsComm?(A AtS) = A == comm or containsComm?(AtS) .
```

5.2 Basic Commands

Once the files in the webpage have been downloaded and the paths have been configured, and assuming the modules above are saved in a file called wrla.cafe, we can start the tool by typing:

```
$ ./cafe2maude wrla.cafe
```

The cafe2maude script creates a temporary file generated by a Java application. This file contains the original CafeOBJ modules modified in order to be accepted by Full Maude (e.g. adding the parentheses enclosing modules and views, removing CafeOBJ comments, and adding the ' character to the escape characters such as { or }). Once the script is executed, the modules are introduced into the Full Maude database and we can use any Maude command on them. For example, the rew command uses transitions to evaluate terms. Note that this command, as well as the one below, is not available in CafeOBJ:

```
Maude> (rew mix(1 3 nil, 2 4 nil) .)
result List : 1 2 3 4 nil
```

We can also use symbolic search to start with terms with variables and look for substitutions that fulfill the conditions imposed by the search. For example, we can look for the term required in the `mix` operator to obtain the result from the `rew` command:

```
Maude> (search [1] mix(L:List, 2 4 nil) ~>! 1 2 3 4 nil .)
Solution 1
L:List --> 1 3 nil
No more solutions.
```

where the `!` option indicates that we are looking for *final* terms and `>!` distinguishes the symbolic search from the standard one, performed with `=>!`. In this case we obtain the substitution `L:List --> 1 3 nil`, indicating that we needed this list to obtain the result.

Besides using Maude commands, we can also work with CafeOBJ specifications. For example, we can see the original module and execute proof scores. Basically, proof scores are scripts defining an inductive proof, where constants can be declared by means of operators and hypothesis by using equations. The base and the inductive steps are proved by using the `red` command. For example, we can prove the associativity of the `_+_` function as follows:

```
open NAT + BOOL
ops i j k : -> Nat
red (0 + j) + k == 0 + (j + k) .       -- base step
eq (i + j) + k = i + (j + k) .         -- induction hypothesis
red (s(i) + j) + k == s(i) + (j + k) . -- inductive step
close
```

Once we load the file with this `open-close` environment, Maude executes the `red` commands and provides the following result:

```
Processing open-close environment:
reduce(0 + j)+ k == 0 + j + k .
Result: true : Bool
reduce(s i + j)+ k == s i + j + k .
Result: true : Bool
```

5.3   Using the Declarative Debugger and Test-Case Generator

To start this tool it is enough to download the script `cdd`, configure the paths, and execute it with the files we want to test and debug. Then, we can use all the commands described in http://maude.sip.ucm.es/debugging/ to test and debug our CafeOBJ modules. For example, we can test the `reverse` function by using the so called *function coverage* criterium, which generates ground test cases that must use all the equations defined for `reverse` (`r1` and `r2`) in all the calls (the single call to this function is located in `r2`). This is done by using:

```
Maude> (function coverage .)
Function Coverage selected
Maude> (test in NAT-LIST : reverse .)
1 test cases have to be checked by the user:
   1. The term reverse(0 0 nil) has been reduced to 0 0 0 nil
All calls were covered.
```

That is, the call `reverse(0 0 nil)` uses both `r1` and `r2` for the recursive call (`r2` for the first call and `r1` for the second one). Note that the result of this call is unexpected, because it should also be `0 0 nil`. Hence, this function is buggy and must be debugged. We can do it by typing:

```
Maude> (invoke debugger with user test case 1 .)
Declarative debugging of wrong answers started.
```

This command starts the declarative debugger. Declarative debuggers find bugs in programs by asking questions to the user, that must answer `yes` or `no` (check the webpage above for more possible answers) until the bug is found. Hence, the debugger presents the following question:

```
Is this reduction (associated with the equation r2) correct?
reverse(0 nil) -> 0 0 nil
Maude> (no .)
```

This result is erroneous for the same reasons explained above, so the user answers `no` and the debugging session continues with the following questions:

```
Is this reduction (associated with the equation com2) correct?
(0 nil) @ 0 nil -> 0 0 nil
Maude> (yes .)
Is this reduction (associated with the equation r1) correct?
reverse(nil) -> 0 nil
Maude> (no .)
```

We answer `yes` for a correct composition but `no` for another application of `reverse`. With this information the debugger is able to find the bug:

```
The buggy node is: reverse(nil) -> 0 nil
with the associated equation: r1
```

In fact, the equation `r1` should return just `nil`. The questions asked during the session correspond to the nodes of a tree representing the wrong computation. This tree, which might be useful to the user to check the relations between the calls, can also be shown.

Finally, it is also possible to use a property and a correct module to test the functions. For example, we can define in the module PROP-LIST the property `prop` stating that applying `reverse` twice returns the same list, while in CORRECT-PROP-LIST we state that this property must be always `true`:

```
mod! PROP-LIST {                          mod! CORRECT-PROP-LIST {
  pr(NAT-LIST)                              pr(NAT-LIST)
  op prop : List -> Bool                    op prop : List -> Bool .
  eq [p1] : prop(L:List) =                  eq prop(L) = true .
      reverse(reverse(L:List)) == L:List .
}                                         }
```

Now we can set the correct module and generate test cases:

```
Maude> (correct test module CORRECT-PROP-LIST .)
CORRECT-PROP-LIST selected as correct module for testing.
Maude> (test in PROP-LIST : prop .)
10 test cases are incorrect with respect to the correct module.
```

Once the test cases have been generated, they can be displayed and debugged as shown above.

5.4 Using the Constructor-Based Inductive Theorem Prover

We have extended the CITP to work with CafeOBJ-like commands, hence obtaining a tool fully customized for CafeOBJ. This has been done by adding an extra attribute **language** to the tool, which allows us to distinguish between interfaces, while the underlying modules dealing with proofs are left unmodified.

The CITP allows the user to prove properties on CafeOBJ specifications. It is started by the **citp** script. Since we want to prove properties on CafeOBJ specifications, we have to indicate it with a specific command, which sets the **language** attribute explained above to **cafeOBJ**, hence modifying the syntax and the display options to work with CafeOBJ specifications:

```
Maude> (cafeOBJ language .)
CafeOBJ selected as current specification language.
```

Now we can introduce goals, which are depicted as equations or transitions. For example, we can prove the associativity of list composition, using on-the-fly declaration of variables from CafeOBJ, by typing:

```
Maude> (goal NAT-LIST |- eq L1:List @ (L2:List @ L3:List) =
                        (L1 @ L2) @ L3 ;)
============================ GOAL 1-1 ============================
< Module NAT-LIST is concealed ... end,
  eq L1:List @(L2:List @ L3:List) = (L1:List @ L2:List)@ L3:List . >
unproved
INFO: an initial goal generated!
```

This goal can be easily proved by using induction on L1 and then applying the default tactic with the **auto** command:

```
Maude> (set ind on L1:List .)
INFO: Induction will be conducted on L1:List
Maude> (auto .)
INFO: Goal 1-1 was successfully proved by applying tactic: SI CA CS TC IP
INFO: PROOF COMPLETED
```

It is also possible to state goals involving transitions. For example, we can define the following trivial goal, which just uses the commutativity attribute:

```
Maude> (goal NAT-LIST |- trans mix(L:List, nil) => L ;)
=========================== GOAL 1-1 ===========================
< Module NAT-LIST is concealed ... end,
  trans mix(L:List,nil) => L:List . >
unproved
INFO: an initial goal generated!
```

Note that CafeOBJ syntax is used for both the goal and the displayed information. This simple goal can be discarded by just using `auto`:

```
Maude> (auto .)
INFO: Goal 1-1 was successfully proved by applying tactic: SI CA CS TC IP
INFO: PROOF COMPLETED
```

Much more information on the CITP, including several other commands, all of them now customized for CafeOBJ specifications, is described at http://www.jaist.ac.jp/~danielmg/citp.html.

6   Concluding Remarks and Ongoing Work

We have presented in this paper a tool to introduce CafeOBJ specifications into the Full Maude database. This tool allows us to use Maude modules and commands with CafeOBJ specifications, provides an implementation of a CafeOBJ metalevel, and eases the task of connecting CafeOBJ specifications with tools implemented on top of Full Maude. Using this feature we provide an environment where CafeOBJ specifications can be tested, debugged, and proved correct by integrating the Maude Declarative Debugger and Test-case Generator and the Constructor-based Inductive Theorem Prover.

We want to improve the implementation of the metalevel in two different ways: first, we want to define the syntax for representing views, in such a way that they can also be analyzed and modified. On the other hand, we are interested in defining more execution commands: currently only `metaReduce`, `metaRewrite`, and `metaFrewrite` are available, but several others can be implemented using our translation for CafeOBJ specifications and the built-in commands in Maude metalevel. Another interesting topic would be distinguish between behavioral and non-behavioral specifications when translating and executing the modules.

We are currently working to extend our framework with the Maude Formal Environment (MFE) [6]. This environment allows to check properties such as termination, confluence, and coherence on Maude specifications. It also includes the Inductive Theorem Prover [4], a tool to prove inductive properties on equational Maude specifications. Integrating this environment with CafeOBJ specifications would allow us to check that the executability requirements hold.

We are also interested in integrating Real-Time Maude [14] in our framework. This integration would be specially interesting for CafeOBJ users, since several protocols, such as [15], has already been specified in CafeOBJ. However, this integration is not straightforward, since it requires to extend the syntax of CafeOBJ specifications with timed transitions, as originally implemented for Maude.

Besides connecting more tools, we are also interested in extending the commands for CafeOBJ. More specifically, we are interested in the `t1 =(m,n)=> t2` predicate, which indicates that the term `t2` is reachable from `t1`, with `m` the number of searched terms and `n` the depth of the search (both numbers can be set to `*` to indicate that it is unbounded). This predicate, that is not documented and allows several extra conditions to constrain the states, is similar to the `search` command in Maude. It is interesting to implement this predicate, since it would increment the amount of CafeOBJ commands supported by our interface while providing a documented version in terms of Maude.

References

1. Clavel, M., Durán, F., Eker, S., Lincoln, P., Martí-Oliet, N., Meseguer, J., Talcott, C.: A hierarchy of data types: from trees to sets. In: Clavel, M., Durán, F., Eker, S., Lincoln, P., Martí-Oliet, N., Meseguer, J., Talcott, C. (eds.) All About Maude - A High-Performance Logical Framework. LNCS, vol. 4350, pp. 119–129. Springer, Heidelberg (2007)
2. Clavel, M., Durán, F., Eker, S., Lincoln, P., Martí-Oliet, N., Meseguer, J. Talcott, C.: Maude Manual (Version 2.6), January 2011. http://maude.cs.uiuc.edu/maude2-manual
3. Clavel, M., Meseguer, J., Palomino, M.: Reflection in membership equational logic, many-sorted equational logic, Horn logic with equality, and rewriting logic. Theor. Comput. Sci. **373**(1–2), 70–91 (2007)
4. Clavel, M., Palomino, M., Riesco, A.: Introducing the ITP tool: a tutorial. J. Univ. Comput. Sci. **12**(11), 1618–1650 (2006). Programming and Languages. Special Issue with Extended Versions of Selected Papers from PROLE 2005: The 5th Spanish Conference on Programming and Languages
5. Durán, F., Ölveczky, P.C.: A guide to extending full maude illustrated with the implementation of real-time Maude. In: Roşu, G. (ed), Proceedings of the 7th International Workshop on Rewriting Logic and its Applications, WRLA 2008, vol. 238(3), Electronic Notes in Theoretical Computer Science, pp. 83–102. Elsevier (2009)
6. Durán, F., Rocha, C., Álvarez, J.M.: Towards a Maude formal environment. In: Agha, G., Danvy, O., Meseguer, J. (eds.) Formal Modeling: Actors, Open Systems, Biological Systems. LNCS, vol. 7000, pp. 329–351. Springer, Heidelberg (2011)

7. Eker, S., Martí-Oliet, N., Meseguer, J., Verdejo, A.: Deduction, strategies, and rewriting. In: Archer, M., de la Tour, T.B., Muñoz, C.A. (eds.) Proceedings of the 6th International Workshop on Strategies in Automated Deduction (STRATE-GIES 2006), vol. 174, Electronic Notes in Theoretical Computer Science, pp. 3–25. Elsevier (2007)

8. Ellison, C., Roşu, G.: An executable formal semantics of C with applications. In: Proceedings of the 39th Symposium on Principles of Programming Languages, POPL 2012, pp. 533–544. ACM (2012)

9. Futatsugi, K., Diaconescu, R.: CafeOBJ Report. World Scientific, AMAST Series (1998)

10. Futatsugi, K., Gâinâ, D., Ogata, K.: Principles of proof scores in CafeOBJ. Theor. Comput. Sci. **464**, 90–112 (2012)

11. Găină, D., Zhang, M., Chiba, Y., Arimoto, Y.: Constructor-based inductive theorem prover. In: Heckel, R., Milius, S. (eds.) CALCO 2013. LNCS, vol. 8089, pp. 328–333. Springer, Heidelberg (2013)

12. Meseguer, J., Roşu, G.: The rewriting logic semantics project. Theor. Comput. Sci. **373**(3), 213–237 (2007)

13. Nakagawa, A.T., Sawada, T., Futatsugi, K.: CafeOBJ User's Manual (version 1.4.8), July 2010. http://www.comp.dit.ie/pbrowne/compfund2/manual.pdf

14. Ölveczky, P.C., Meseguer, J.: Semantics and pragmatics of real-time Maude. High. Order Symbolic Comput. **20**, 161–196 (2007)

15. Ouranos, I., Ogata, K., Stefaneas, P.: Formal analysis of TESLA protocol in the timed OTS/CafeOBJ method. In: Margaria, T., Steffen, B. (eds.) ISoLA 2012, Part II. LNCS, vol. 7610, pp. 126–142. Springer, Heidelberg (2012)

16. Riesco, A., Verdejo, A., Martí-Oliet, N., Caballero, R.: Declarative debugging of rewriting logic specifications. J. Logic Algebraic Program. **81**(7–8), 851–897 (2012)

17. Verdejo, A., Martí-Oliet, N.: Executable structural operational semantics in Maude. J. Logic Algebraic Program. **67**, 226–293 (2006)

18. Zhang, M., Ogata, K.: Modular implementation of a translator from behavioral specifications to rewrite theory specifications. In: Choi, B. (ed.) Proceedings of the 9th International Conference on Quality Software, QSIC 2009, pp. 406–411. IEEE Computer Society (2009)

Rewriting Modulo SMT and Open System Analysis

Camilo Rocha[1]([✉]), José Meseguer[2], and César Muñoz[3]

[1] Escuela Colombiana de Ingeniería, Bogotá, Colombia
`camilo.rocha@escuelaing.edu.co`
[2] University of Illinois at Urbana-Champaign, Urbana, IL, USA
[3] NASA Langley Research Center, Hampton, VA, USA

Abstract. This paper proposes *rewriting modulo SMT*, a new technique that combines the power of SMT solving, rewriting modulo theories, and model checking. Rewriting modulo SMT is ideally suited to model and analyze infinite-state *open systems*, i.e., systems that interact with a non-deterministic environment. Such systems exhibit both internal non-determinism, which is proper to the system, and external non-determinism, which is due to the environment. In a reflective formalism, such as rewriting logic, rewriting modulo SMT can be reduced to standard rewriting. Hence, rewriting modulo SMT naturally extends rewriting-based reachability analysis techniques, which are available for closed systems, to open systems. The proposed technique is illustrated with the formal analysis of a real-time system that is beyond the scope of timed-automata methods.

1 Introduction

Symbolic techniques can be used to represent possibly infinite sets of states by means of symbolic constraints. These techniques have been developed and adapted to many other verification methods such as SAT solving, Satisfiability Modulo Theories (SMT), rewriting, and model checking. A key open research issue of current symbolic techniques is extensibility. Techniques that combine different methods have been proposed, e.g., decision procedures [28,29], unifications algorithms [7,11], theorem provers with decision procedures [1,10,32], and SMT solvers in model checkers [3,18,27,36,38]. However, there is still a lack of general extensibility techniques for symbolic analysis that simultaneously combine the power of SMT solving, rewriting- and narrowing-based analysis, and model checking.

This paper proposes a new symbolic technique that seamlessly combines rewriting modulo theories, SMT solving, and model checking. For brevity, this technique is called *rewriting modulo SMT*, although it could more precisely be called *rewriting modulo SMT+B*, where B is an equational theory having a

---

© Springer International Publishing Switzerland 2014 (outside the US)
S. Escobar (Ed.): WRLA 2014, LNCS 8663, pp. 247–262, 2014.
DOI: 10.1007/978-3-319-12904-4_14

matching algorithm. It complements another symbolic technique combining narrowing modulo theories and model checking, namely narrowing-based reachability analysis [8,26]. Neither of these two techniques subsumes the other.

Rewriting modulo SMT can be applied to increase the power of equational reasoning, e.g., [16,17,21], but its full power, including its model checking capabilities, is better exploited when applied to concurrent open systems. Deterministic systems can be naturally specified by equational theories, but specification of concurrent, non-deterministic systems requires rewrite theories [24], i.e., triples $\mathcal{R} = (\Sigma, E, R)$ with (Σ, E) an equational theory describing system states as elements of the initial algebra $\mathcal{T}_{\Sigma/E}$, and R rewrite rules describing the system's local concurrent transitions. An *open system* is a concurrent system that interacts with an external, non-deterministic environment. When such a system is specified by a rewrite theory $\mathcal{R} = (\Sigma, E, R)$, it has two sources of non-determinism, one internal and the other external. Internal non-determinism comes from the fact that in a given system state different instances of rules in R may be enabled. The local transitions thus enabled may lead to completely different states. What is peculiar about an open system is that it also has external, and often infinitely-branching, non-determinism due to the environment. That is, the state of an open system must include the state changes due to the environment. Technically, this means that, while a system transition in a closed system can be described by a rewrite rule $t \rightarrow t'$ with $vars(t') \subseteq vars(t)$, a transition in an open system is instead modeled by a rule of the form $t(\overrightarrow{x}) \rightarrow t'(\overrightarrow{x}, \overrightarrow{y})$, where $\overrightarrow{y}$ are fresh new variables. Therefore, a substitution for the variables $\overrightarrow{x} \uplus \overrightarrow{y}$ decomposes into two substitutions, one, say θ, for the variables $\overrightarrow{x}$ under the control of the system and another, say ρ, for the variables $\overrightarrow{y}$ under the control of the environment. In rewriting modulo SMT, such open systems are described by conditional rewrite rules of the form $t(\overrightarrow{x}) \rightarrow t'(\overrightarrow{x}, \overrightarrow{y})$ **if** ϕ, where ϕ is a constraint solvable by an SMT solver. This constraint ϕ may still allow the environment to choose an infinite number of substitutions ρ for $\overrightarrow{y}$, but can exclude choices that the environment will never make.

The non-trivial challenges of modeling and analyzing open systems can now be better explained. They include: (1) the enormous and possibly infinitary non-determinism due to the environment, which typically renders finite-state model checking impossible or unfeasible; (2) the impossibility of executing the rewrite theory $\mathcal{R} = (\Sigma, E, R)$ in the standard sense, due to the non-deterministic choice of ρ; and (3) the, in general, undecidable challenge of checking the rule's condition ϕ, since without knowing ρ, the condition $\phi\theta$ is non-ground, so that its E-satisfiability may be undecidable. As further explained in the paper, challenges (1)–(3) are all met successfully by rewriting modulo SMT because: (1) states are represented not as concrete states, i.e., ground terms, but as symbolic constrained terms $\langle t; \varphi \rangle$ with t a term with variables ranging in the domains handled by the SMT solver and φ an SMT-solvable formula, so that the choice of ρ is avoided; (2) rewriting modulo SMT can symbolically rewrite such pairs $\langle t; \varphi \rangle$ (describing possibly infinite sets of concrete states) to other pairs $\langle t'; \varphi' \rangle$; and (3) decidability of $\phi\theta$ (more precisely of $\varphi \wedge \phi\theta$) can be settled by invoking an SMT solver.

Rewriting modulo SMT can be integrated with model-checking by exploiting the fact that rewriting logic is reflective [15]. Hence, rewriting modulo SMT can be reduced to standard rewriting. In particular, all the techniques, algorithms, and tools available for model checking of closed systems specified as rewrite theories, such as Maude's search-based reachability analysis [14], become directly available to perform symbolic reachability analysis on systems that are now infinite-state.

The technique proposed in this paper is illustrated with the formal analysis of the CASH scheduling protocol [13]. This protocol specifies a real-time system whose formal analysis is beyond the scope of timed-automata [2].

2   Preliminaries

Notation on terms, term algebras, and equational theories is used as in [6,19].

An *order-sorted signature* Σ is a tuple $\Sigma = (S, \leq, F)$ with a finite poset of sorts $(S, \leq)$ and set of function symbols F. The binary relation $\equiv_\leq$ denotes the equivalence relation generated by $\leq$ on S and its point-wise extension to strings in S^*. The function symbols in F can be subsort-overloaded and satisfy the condition that, for $w, w' \in S^*$ and $s, s' \in S$, if $f : w \longrightarrow s$ and $f : w' \longrightarrow s'$ are in F, then $w \equiv_\leq w'$ implies $s \equiv_\leq s'$. A *top sort* in Σ is a sort $s \in S$ such that if $s' \in S$ and $s \equiv_\leq s'$, then $s' \leq s$. For any sort $s \in S$, the expression $[s]$ denotes the connected component of s, that is, $[s] = [s]_{\equiv_\leq}$.

The symbol X denotes an S-indexed family $X = \{X_s\}_{s \in S}$ of disjoint variable sets with each X_s countably infinite. Expressions $T_\Sigma(X)_s$ and $T_{\Sigma,s}$ denote, respectively, the *set of terms of sort s* and the *set of ground terms of sort s*; accordingly, $T_\Sigma(X)$ and T_Σ denote the corresponding order-sorted Σ-term algebras. All order-sorted signatures are assumed *preregular* [19], i.e., each Σ-term t has a *least sort* $ls(t) \in S$ s.t. $t \in T_\Sigma(X)_{ls(t)}$. For $S' \subseteq S$, a term is called S'-*linear* if no variable with sort in S' occurs in it twice. The *set of variables* of t is written $vars(t)$.

A *substitution* is an S-indexed mapping $\theta : X \longrightarrow T_\Sigma(X)$ that is different from the identity only for a finite subset of X. The identity substitution is denoted by id and $\theta|_Y$ denotes the restriction of θ to a family of variables $Y \subseteq X$. Expression $dom(\theta)$ denotes the domain of θ, i.e., the subfamily of X for which $\theta(x) \neq x$, and $ran(\theta)$ denotes the family of variables introduced by $\theta(x)$, for $x \in dom(\theta)$. Substitutions extend homomorphically to terms in the natural way. A substitution θ is called *ground* iff $ran(\theta) = \emptyset$. The application of a substitution θ to a term t is denoted by $t\theta$ and the composition of two substitutions θ_1 and θ_2 is denoted by $\theta_1\theta_2$. A *context* C is a λ-term of the form $C = \lambda x_1, \ldots, x_n.c$ with $c \in T_\Sigma(X)$ and $\{x_1, \ldots, x_n\} \subseteq vars(c)$; it can be viewed as an n-ary function $C(t_1, \ldots, t_n) = c\theta$, where $\theta(x_i) = t_i$ for $1 \leq i \leq n$ and $\theta(x) = x$ otherwise.

A Σ-*equation* is an unoriented pair $t = u$ with $t \in T_\Sigma(X)_{s_t}$, $u \in T_\Sigma(X)_{s_u}$, and $s_t \equiv_\leq s_u$. A *conditional Σ-equation* is a triple $t = u$ **if** γ, with $t = u$ a Σ-equation and γ a finite conjunction of Σ-equations; it is called *unconditional* if γ is the empty conjunction. An *equational theory* is a tuple (Σ, E), with Σ an order-sorted signature and E a finite collection of (possibly conditional) Σ-equations. It is assumed that $T_{\Sigma,s} \neq \emptyset$ for each $s \in S$. An equational theory

$\mathcal{E} = (\Sigma, E)$ induces the congruence relation $=_{\mathcal{E}}$ on $T_{\Sigma}(X)$ defined for $t, u \in T_{\Sigma}(X)$ by $t =_{\mathcal{E}} u$ iff $\mathcal{E} \vdash t = u$ by the deduction rules for order-sorted equational logic in [25]. Similarly, $=_{\mathcal{E}}^{1}$ denotes provable $\mathcal{E}$-equality in *one step* of deduction. The $\mathcal{E}$-*subsumption* ordering $\ll_{\mathcal{E}}$ is the binary relation on $T_{\Sigma}(X)$ defined for any $t, u \in T_{\Sigma}(X)$ by $t \ll_{\mathcal{E}} u$ iff there is a substitution $\theta : X \longrightarrow T_{\Sigma}(X)$ such that $t =_{\mathcal{E}} u\theta$. A set of equations E is called *collapse-free* for a subset of sorts $S' \subseteq S$ iff for any $t = u \in E$ and for any substitution $\theta : X \longrightarrow T_{\Sigma}(X)$ neither $t\theta$ nor $u\theta$ map to a variable for some sort $s \in S'$. The expressions $\mathcal{T}_{\mathcal{E}}(X)$ and $\mathcal{T}_{\mathcal{E}}$ (also written $\mathcal{T}_{\Sigma/E}(X)$ and $\mathcal{T}_{\Sigma/E}$) denote the quotient algebras induced by $=_{\mathcal{E}}$ on the term algebras $\mathcal{T}_{\Sigma}(X)$ and $\mathcal{T}_{\Sigma}$, respectively; $\mathcal{T}_{\Sigma/E}$ is called the *initial algebra* of (Σ, E). A theory inclusion $(\Sigma, E) \subseteq (\Sigma', E')$, with $\Sigma \subseteq \Sigma'$ and $E \subseteq E'$, is called *protecting* iff the unique Σ-homomorphism $\mathcal{T}_{\Sigma/E} \longrightarrow \mathcal{T}_{\Sigma'/E'}|_{\Sigma}$ to the Σ-reduct *of the initial algebra* $\mathcal{T}_{\Sigma'/E'}$ is a Σ-isomorphism, written $\mathcal{T}_{\Sigma/E} \simeq \mathcal{T}_{\Sigma'/E'}|_{\Sigma}$. A set of equations E is called *regular* iff $vars(t) = vars(u)$ for any equation $(t = u \text{ if } \gamma) \in E$.

Appropriate requirements are needed to make an equational theory $\mathcal{E}$ *admissible*, i.e., *executable* in rewriting languages such as Maude [14]. In this paper, it is assumed that the equations of $\mathcal{E}$ can be decomposed into a disjoint union $E \uplus B$, with B a collection of structural axioms (such as associativity, and/or commutativity, and/or identity) for which there exists a *matching algorithm modulo B* producing a finite number of B-matching solutions, or failing otherwise. Furthermore, it is assumed that the equations E can be oriented into a set of (possibly conditional) sort-decreasing, operationally terminating, and confluent conditional rewrite rules $\overrightarrow{E}$ modulo B. The conditional rewrite system $\overrightarrow{E}$ is *sort decreasing* modulo B iff for each $(t \rightarrow u \text{ if } \gamma) \in \overrightarrow{E}$ and substitution θ, $ls(t\theta) \geq ls(u\theta)$ if $(\Sigma, B, \overrightarrow{E}) \vdash \gamma\theta$. The system $\overrightarrow{E}$ is *operationally terminating* modulo B iff there is no infinite well-formed proof tree in $(\Sigma, B, \overrightarrow{E})$. Furthermore, $\overrightarrow{E}$ is *confluent* modulo B iff for all $t, t_1, t_2 \in T_{\Sigma}(X)$, if $t \rightarrow^{*}_{E/B} t_1$ and $t \rightarrow^{*}_{E/B} t_2$, then there is $u \in T_{\Sigma}(X)$ such that $t_1 \rightarrow^{*}_{E/B} u$ and $t_2 \rightarrow^{*}_{E/B} u$. The term $t\downarrow_{E/B} \in T_{\Sigma}(X)$ denotes the *E-canonical form* of t modulo B so that $t \rightarrow^{*}_{E/B} t\downarrow_{E/B}$ and $t\downarrow_{E/B}$ cannot be further reduced by $\rightarrow_{E/B}$. Under the above assumptions $t\downarrow_{E/B}$ is unique up to B-equality.

A Σ-*rule* is a triple $l \rightarrow r \text{ if } \phi$, with $l, r \in T_{\Sigma}(X)_s$, for some sort $s \in S$, and $\phi = \bigwedge_{i \in I} t_i = u_i$ a finite conjunction of Σ-equations. A *rewrite theory* is a tuple $\mathcal{R} = (\Sigma, E, R)$ with (Σ, E) an order-sorted equational theory and R a finite set of Σ-rules. The rewrite theory $\mathcal{R}$ induces a rewrite relation $\rightarrow_{\mathcal{R}}$ on $T_{\Sigma}(X)$ defined for every $t, u \in T_{\Sigma}(X)$ by $t \rightarrow_{\mathcal{R}} u$ iff there is a rule $(l \rightarrow r \text{ if } \phi) \in R$ and a substitution $\theta : X \longrightarrow T_{\Sigma}(X)$ satisfying $t =_E l\theta$, $u =_E r\theta$, and $E \vdash \phi\theta$. The relation $\rightarrow_{\mathcal{R}}$ is undecidable in general, unless conditions such as coherence [37] are given. A key point of this paper is to make such a relation decidable when E decomposes as $\mathcal{E}_0 \uplus B_1$, where $\mathcal{E}_0$ is a built-in theory for which formula satisfiability is decidable and B_1 has a matching algorithm. A *topmost rewrite theory* is a rewrite theory $\mathcal{R} = (\Sigma, E, R)$, such that for some top sort *State*, no operator in Σ has *State* as argument sort and each rule $l \rightarrow r \text{ if } \phi \in R$ satisfies $l, r \in T_{\Sigma}(X)_{State}$ and $l \notin X$.

3 Rewriting Modulo a Built-In Subtheory

This section introduces the concept of rewriting modulo a built-in equational subtheory and presents its main properties. Detailed proofs can be found in [33, 34].

Definition 1 (Signature with Built-ins). *An order-sorted signature* $\Sigma = (S, \leq, F)$ *is a signature with* built-in subsignature $\Sigma_0 \subseteq \Sigma$ *iff* $\Sigma_0 = (S_0, F_0)$ *is many-sorted,* S_0 *is a set of minimal elements in* $(S, \leq)$, *and if* $f : w \longrightarrow s \in F_1$, *then* $s \notin S_0$ *and* f *has no other typing in* F_0, *where* $F_1 = F \backslash F_0$.

The notion of built-in subsignature in an order-sorted signature Σ is modeled by a many-sorted signature Σ_0 defining the built-in terms $T_{\Sigma_0}(X_0)$. The restriction imposed on the sorts and the function symbols in Σ w.r.t. Σ_0 provides a clear syntactic distinction between built-in terms (the only ones with built-in sorts) and all other terms.

If $\Sigma \supseteq \Sigma_0$ is a signature with built-ins, then an *abstraction of built-ins* for t is a context $\lambda x_1 \cdots x_n.t^\circ$ such that $t^\circ \in T_{\Sigma_1}(X)$ and $\{x_1, \ldots, x_n\} = vars(t^\circ) \cap X_0$, where $\Sigma_1 = (S, \leq, F_1)$ and $X_0 = \{X_s\}_{s \in S_0}$. Lemma 1 shows that such an abstraction can be chosen so as to provide a canonical decomposition of t with useful properties.

Lemma 1. *Let* Σ *be a signature with built-in subsignature* $\Sigma_0 = (S_0, F_0)$. *For each* $t \in T_\Sigma(X)$, *there exist an abstraction of built-ins* $\lambda x_1 \cdots x_n.t^\circ$ *for* t *and a substitution* $\theta^\circ : X_0 \longrightarrow T_{\Sigma_0}(X_0)$ *such that (i)* $t = t^\circ \theta^\circ$ *and (ii)* $dom(\theta^\circ) = \{x_1, \ldots, x_n\}$ *are pairwise distinct and disjoint from* $vars(t)$; *moreover, (iii)* t° *can always be selected to be* S_0-*linear and with* $\{x_1, \ldots, x_n\}$ *disjoint from an arbitrarily chosen finite subset* Y *of* X_0.

In the rest of the paper, for any $t \in T_\Sigma(X)$ and $Y \subseteq X_0$ finite, the expression $abstract_{\Sigma_1}(t, Y)$ denotes the choice of a triple $\langle \lambda x_1 \cdots x_n.t^\circ ; \theta^\circ ; \phi^\circ \rangle$ such that the context $\lambda x_1 \cdots x_n.t^\circ$ and the substitution θ° satisfy the properties (i)–(iii) in Lemma 1 and $\phi^\circ = \bigwedge_{i=1}^n (x_i = \theta^\circ(x_i))$.

Under certain restrictions on axioms, matching a Σ-term t to a Σ-term u can be decomposed modularly into Σ_1-matching of the corresponding λ-abstraction and Σ_0-matching of the built-in subterms. This is described in Lemma 2.

Lemma 2. *Let* $\Sigma = (S, \leq, F)$ *be a signature with built-in subsignature* $\Sigma_0 = (S_0, F_0)$. *Let* B_0 *be a set of* Σ_0-*axioms and* B_1 *a set of* Σ_1-*axioms. For* B_0 *and* B_1 *regular, linear, collapse free for any sort in* S_0, *and sort-preserving, if* $t \in T_{\Sigma_1}(X_0)$ *is linear with* $vars(t) = \{x_1, \ldots, x_n\}$, *then for each* $\theta : X_0 \longrightarrow T_{\Sigma_0}(X_0)$:

(a) *if* $t\theta =_{B_0}^1 t'$, *then there exist* $x \in \{x_1, \ldots, x_n\}$ *and* $w \in T_{\Sigma_0}(X_0)$ *such that* $\theta(x) =_{B_0}^1 w$ *and* $t' = t\theta'$, *with* $\theta'(x) = w$ *and* $\theta'(y) = \theta(y)$ *otherwise;*
(b) *if* $t\theta =_{B_1}^1 t'$, *then there exists* $v \in T_{\Sigma_1}(X_0)$ *such that* $t =_{B_1}^1 v$ *and* $t' = v\theta$; *and*
(c) *if* $t\theta =_{B_0 \uplus B_1} t'$, *then there exist* $v \in T_{\Sigma_1}(X_0)$ *and* $\theta' : X_0 \longrightarrow T_{\Sigma_0}(X_0)$ *such that* $t' = v\theta'$, $t =_{B_1} v$, *and* $\theta =_{B_0} \theta'$ *(i.e.,* $\theta(x) =_{B_0} \theta'(x)$ *for each* $x \in X_0$).

Definition 2 introduces the notion of rewriting modulo a built-in subtheory.

Definition 2 (Rewriting Modulo a Built-in Subtheory). *A rewrite theory modulo the built-in subtheory $\mathcal{E}_0$ is a topmost rewrite theory $\mathcal{R} = (\Sigma, E, R)$ with:*

(a) *$\Sigma=(S, \leq, F)$ a signature with built-in subsignature $\Sigma_0=(S_0, F_0)$ and top sort State$\in S$;*

(b) *$E = E_0 \uplus B_0 \uplus B_1$, where E_0 is a set of Σ_0-equations, B_0 (resp., B_1) are Σ_0-axioms (resp., Σ_1-axioms) satisfying the conditions in Lemma 2, $\mathcal{E}_0 = (\Sigma_0, E_0 \uplus B_0)$ and $\mathcal{E} = (\Sigma, E)$ are admissible, and the theory inclusion $\mathcal{E}_0 \subseteq \mathcal{E}$ is protecting;*

(c) *R is a set of rewrite rules of the form $l(\overrightarrow{x_1}, \overrightarrow{y}) \to r(\overrightarrow{x_2}, \overrightarrow{y})$ if $\phi(\overrightarrow{x_3})$ such that $l, r \in T_\Sigma(X)_{State}$, l is $(S \setminus S_0)$-linear, $\overrightarrow{x_i}:\overrightarrow{s_i}$ with $\overrightarrow{s_i} \in S_0^*$, for $i \in \{1, 2, 3\}$, $\overrightarrow{y}:\overrightarrow{s}$ with $\overrightarrow{s} \in (S \setminus S_0)^*$, and $\phi \in QF_{\Sigma_0}(X_0)$, where $QF_{\Sigma_0}(X_0)$ denotes the set of quantifier-free Σ_0-formulas with variables in X_0.*

Note that no assumption is made on the relationship between the built-in variables x_1 in the left-hand side, x_2 in the right-hand side, and x_3 in the condition ϕ of a rewrite rule. This freedom is key for specifying open systems with a rewrite theory because, for instance, x_2 can have more variables than x_1. On the other hand, due to the presence of conditions ϕ in the rules of $\mathcal{R}$ that are general quantifier-free formulas, as opposed to a conjunction of atoms, properly speaking $\mathcal{R}$ is more general than a standard rewrite theory as defined in Sect. 2.

The binary rewrite relation induced by a rewrite theory $\mathcal{R}$ modulo $\mathcal{E}_0$ on $T_{\Sigma, State}$ is called the *ground rewrite relation* of $\mathcal{R}$.

Definition 3 (Ground Rewrite Relation). *Let $\mathcal{R} = (\Sigma, E, R)$ be a rewrite theory modulo $\mathcal{E}_0$. The relation $\to_\mathcal{R}$ induced by $\mathcal{R}$ on $T_{\Sigma, State}$ is defined for $t, u \in T_{\Sigma, State}$ by $t \to_\mathcal{R} u$ iff there is a rule $l \to r$ if ϕ in R and a ground substitution $\sigma : X \longrightarrow T_\Sigma$ such that (a) $t =_E l\sigma$, $u =_E r\sigma$, and (b) $T_{\mathcal{E}_0} \models \phi\sigma$.*

The ground rewrite relation $\to_\mathcal{R}$ is the topmost rewrite relation induced by R modulo E on $T_{\Sigma, State}$. This relation is defined even when a rule in R has extra variables in its right-hand side: the rule is then non-deterministic and such extra variables can be arbitrarily instantiated, provided that the corresponding instantiation of ϕ holds. Also, note that non-built-in variables can occur in l, but $\phi\sigma$ is a *variable-free formula* in $QF_{\Sigma_0}(\emptyset)$, so that either $T_{\mathcal{E}_0} \models \phi\sigma$ or $T_{\mathcal{E}_0} \not\models \phi\sigma$.

A rewrite theory $\mathcal{R}$ modulo $\mathcal{E}_0$ always has a canonical representation in which all left-hand sides of rules are S_0-linear Σ_1-terms.

Definition 4 (Normal Form of a Rewrite Theory Modulo $\mathcal{E}_0$). *Let $\mathcal{R} = (\Sigma, E, R)$ be a rewrite theory modulo $\mathcal{E}_0$. Its normal form $\mathcal{R}^\circ = (\Sigma, E, R^\circ)$ has rules:*

$$R^\circ = \{l^\circ \to r \text{ if } \phi \wedge \phi^\circ \mid (\exists l \to r \text{ if } \phi \in R)\langle \lambda \overrightarrow{x}.l^\circ ; \theta^\circ ; \phi^\circ \rangle = abstract_\Sigma(l, vars(\{l, r, \phi\}))\}.$$

Lemma 3 (Invariance of Ground Rewriting under Normalization). *Let $\mathcal{R} = (\Sigma, E, R)$ be a rewrite theory modulo $\mathcal{E}_0$. Then $\to_\mathcal{R} = \to_{\mathcal{R}^\circ}$.*

By the properties of the axioms in a rewrite theory modulo built-ins $\mathcal{R} = (\Sigma, E_0 \uplus B_0 \uplus B_1)$ (see Definition 2), B_1-matching a term $t \in T_\Sigma(X_0)$ to a left-hand side l° of a rule in R° provides a complete unifiability algorithm for ground B_1-unification of t and l°.

Lemma 4 (Matching Lemma). *Let $\mathcal{R} = (\Sigma, E_0 \uplus B_0 \uplus B_1, R)$ be a rewrite theory modulo $\mathcal{E}_0$. For $t \in T_\Sigma(X_0)_{State}$ and l° a left-hand side of a rule in R° with $vars(t) \cap vars(l^\circ) = \emptyset$, $t \ll_{B_1} l^\circ$ iff $GU_{B_1}(t = l^\circ) \neq \emptyset$ holds, where $GU_{B_1}(t = l^\circ) = \{\sigma : X \longrightarrow T_\Sigma \mid t\sigma =_{B_1} l^\circ\sigma\}$.*

4   Symbolic Rewriting Modulo a Built-In Subtheory

This section explains how a rewrite theory $\mathcal{R}$ modulo $\mathcal{E}_0$ defines a symbolic rewrite relation on terms in $T_{\Sigma_0}(X_0)_{State}$ constrained by formulas in $QF_{\Sigma_0}(X_0)$. The key idea is that, when $\mathcal{E}_0$ is a decidable theory, transitions on the symbolic terms can be performed by rewriting modulo B_1, and satisfiability of the formulas can be handled by an SMT decision procedure. This approach provides an efficiently executable symbolic method called *rewriting modulo SMT* that is sound and complete with respect to the ground rewrite relation of Definition 3 and yields a complete symbolic reachability analysis method. Detailed proofs of the theorems presented in this section can be found in [34].

Definition 5 (Constrained Terms and their Denotation). *Let $\mathcal{R} = (\Sigma, E, R)$ be a rewrite theory modulo $\mathcal{E}_0$. A constrained term is a pair $\langle t; \varphi \rangle$ in $T_\Sigma(X_0)_{State} \times QF_{\Sigma_0}(X_0)$. Its denotation $[\![t]\!]_\varphi$ is defined as $[\![t]\!]_\varphi = \{t' \in T_{\Sigma,State} \mid (\exists \sigma : X_0 \longrightarrow T_{\Sigma_0}) \, t' = t\sigma \wedge T_{\mathcal{E}_0} \models \varphi\sigma\}$.*

The domain of σ in Definition 5 ranges over all built-in variables X_0 and consequently $[\![t]\!]_\varphi \subseteq T_{\Sigma,State}$ for any $t \in T_\Sigma(X_0)_{State}$, even if $vars(t) \not\subseteq vars(\varphi)$. Intuitively, $[\![t]\!]_\varphi$ denotes the set of all ground states that are instances of t and satisfy φ.

Before introducing the symbolic rewrite relation on constrained terms induced by a rewrite theory $\mathcal{R}$ modulo $\mathcal{E}_0$, auxiliary notation for variable renaming is required. In the rest of the paper, the expression $fresh\text{-}vars(Y)$, for $Y \subseteq X$ finite, represents the choice of a variable renaming $\zeta : X \longrightarrow X$ satisfying $Y \cap ran(\zeta) = \emptyset$.

Definition 6 (Symbolic Rewrite Relation). *Let $\mathcal{R} = (\Sigma, E, R)$ be a rewrite theory modulo built-ins $\mathcal{E}_0$. The symbolic rewrite relation $\leadsto_\mathcal{R}$ induced by $\mathcal{R}$ on $T_\Sigma(X_0)_{State} \times QF_{\Sigma_0}(X_0)$ is defined for $t, u \in T_\Sigma(X_0)_{State}$ and $\varphi, \varphi' \in QF_{\Sigma_0}(X_0)$ by $\langle t; \varphi \rangle \leadsto_\mathcal{R} \langle u; \varphi' \rangle$ iff there is a rule $l \rightarrow r$ if ϕ in R and a substitution $\theta : X \longrightarrow T_\Sigma(X)$ such that (a) $t =_E l\zeta\theta$ and $u = r\zeta\theta$, (b) $\mathcal{E}_0 \vdash (\varphi' \Leftrightarrow \varphi \wedge \phi\zeta\theta)$, and (c) φ' is $T_{\mathcal{E}_0}$-satisfiable, where $\zeta = fresh\text{-}vars(vars(t, \varphi))$.*

The symbolic relation $\leadsto_\mathcal{R}$ on constrained terms is defined as a topmost rewrite relation induced by R modulo E on $T_\Sigma(X_0)$ with extra bookkeeping of constraints. Note that φ' in $\langle t; \varphi \rangle \leadsto_\mathcal{R} \langle u; \varphi' \rangle$, when witnessed by $l \rightarrow r$ if ϕ and

θ, is *semantically equivalent* to $\varphi \wedge \phi\zeta\theta$, in contrast to being *syntactically* equal. This extra freedom allows for simplification of constraints if desired. Also, such a constraint φ' is satisfiable in $\mathcal{T}_{\mathcal{E}_0}$, implying that φ and $\phi\theta$ are both satisfiable in $\mathcal{T}_{\mathcal{E}_0}$, and therefore $[\![t]\!]_\varphi \neq \emptyset \neq [\![u]\!]_{\varphi'}$. Note that, up to the choice of the semantically equivalent φ' for which a fixed strategy is assumed, the symbolic relation $\rightsquigarrow_{\mathcal{R}}$ is deterministic because the renaming of variables in the rules is fixed by *fresh-vars*. This is key when executing $\rightsquigarrow_{\mathcal{R}}$, as explained in Sect. 5.

The important question to ask is whether this symbolic relation soundly and completely simulates its ground counterpart. The rest of this section affirmatively answers this question in the case of *normalized* rewrite theories modulo built-ins. Thanks to Lemma 3, the conclusion is therefore that $\rightsquigarrow_{\mathcal{R}^\circ}$ soundly and completely simulates $\rightarrow_{\mathcal{R}}$ for any rewrite theory $\mathcal{R}$ modulo built-ins $\mathcal{E}_0$.

The soundness of $\rightsquigarrow_{\mathcal{R}^\circ}$ w.r.t. $\rightarrow_{\mathcal{R}^\circ}$ is stated in Theorem 1.

Theorem 1 (Soundness). *Let $\mathcal{R} = (\Sigma, E, R)$ be a rewrite theory modulo built-ins $\mathcal{E}_0$, $t, u \in T_\Sigma(X_0)_{State}$, and $\varphi, \varphi' \in QF_{\Sigma_0}(X_0)$. If $\langle t; \varphi \rangle \rightsquigarrow_{\mathcal{R}^\circ} \langle u; \varphi' \rangle$, then $t\rho \rightarrow_{\mathcal{R}^\circ} u\rho$ for all $\rho : X_0 \longrightarrow T_{\Sigma_0}$ satisfying $\mathcal{T}_{\mathcal{E}_0} \models \varphi'\rho$.*

The completeness of $\rightsquigarrow_{\mathcal{R}^\circ}$ w.r.t. $\rightarrow_{\mathcal{R}^\circ}$ is stated in Theorem 2. Intuitively, completeness states that a symbolic relation yields an over-approximation of its ground rewriting counterpart.

Theorem 2 (Completeness). *Let $\mathcal{R} = (\Sigma, E, R)$ be a rewrite theory modulo built-ins $\mathcal{E}_0$, $t \in T_\Sigma(X_0)_{State}$, $u' \in T_{\Sigma,State}$, and $\varphi \in QF_{\Sigma_0}(X_0)$. For any $\rho : X_0 \longrightarrow T_{\Sigma_0}$ such that $t\rho \in [\![t]\!]_\varphi$ and $t\rho \rightarrow_{\mathcal{R}^\circ} u'$, there exist $u \in T_\Sigma(X_0)_{State}$ and $\varphi' \in QF_{\Sigma_0}(X_0)$ such that $\langle t; \varphi \rangle \rightsquigarrow_{\mathcal{R}^\circ} \langle u; \varphi' \rangle$ and $u' \in [\![u]\!]_{\varphi'}$.*

Although the above soundness and completeness theorems, plus Lemma 3, show that $\rightarrow_{\mathcal{R}}$ is characterized symbolically by $\rightsquigarrow_{\mathcal{R}^\circ}$, for any rewrite theory $\mathcal{R}$ modulo $\mathcal{E}_0$, because of Condition (c) in Definition 6, the relation $\rightsquigarrow_{\mathcal{R}^\circ}$ is in general undecidable. However, $\rightsquigarrow_{\mathcal{R}^\circ}$ becomes decidable for built-in theories $\mathcal{E}_0$ that can be extended to a *decidable theory* $\mathcal{E}_0^+$ (typically by adding some inductive consequences) such that

$$(\forall \phi \in QF_{\Sigma_0}(X_0))\ \phi \text{ is } \mathcal{E}_0^+\text{-satisfiable} \iff (\exists \sigma : X_0 \longrightarrow T_{\Sigma_0})\ \mathcal{T}_{\mathcal{E}_0} \models \phi\sigma. \quad (1)$$

Many decidable theories $\mathcal{E}_0^+$ of interest are supported by SMT solvers satisfying this requirement. For example, $\mathcal{E}_0$ can be the equational theory of natural number addition and $\mathcal{E}_0^+$ Pressburger arithmetic. That is, $\mathcal{T}_{\mathcal{E}_0}$ is the *standard model* of both $\mathcal{E}_0$ and $\mathcal{E}_0^+$, and $\mathcal{E}_0^+$-satisfiability coincides with satisfiability in such a standard model. Under such conditions, satisfiability of $\varphi \wedge \phi\zeta\theta$ (and therefore of φ') in a step $\langle t; \varphi \rangle \rightsquigarrow_{\mathcal{R}^\circ} \langle u; \varphi' \rangle$ becomes decidable by invoking an SMT-solver for $\mathcal{E}_0$, so that $\rightsquigarrow_{\mathcal{R}^\circ}$ can be naturally described as *symbolic rewriting modulo SMT* (and modulo B_1).

The symbolic reachability problems considered for a rewrite theory $\mathcal{R}$ modulo $\mathcal{E}_0$ in this paper, are existential formulas of the form $(\exists \overrightarrow{z})\ t \rightarrow^* u \wedge \varphi$, with $\overrightarrow{z}$ the variables appearing in t, u, and φ, $t \in T_\Sigma(X_0)_{State}$, $u \in T_\Sigma(X)_{State}$, and $\varphi \in QF_{\Sigma_0}(X_0)$. By abstracting the Σ_0-subterms of u, the ground solutions of

such a reachability problem are those witnessing the model-theoretic satisfaction
relation

$$\mathcal{T}_{\mathcal{R}} \models (\exists \overrightarrow{x} \uplus \overrightarrow{y}) \, t(\overrightarrow{x}) \rightarrow^* u^{\circ}(\overrightarrow{y}) \wedge \varphi_1(\overrightarrow{x}) \wedge \varphi_2(\overrightarrow{x}, \overrightarrow{y}), \qquad (2)$$

where $\mathcal{T}_{\mathcal{R}} = (\mathcal{T}_{\Sigma/E}, \rightarrow_{\mathcal{R}}^*)$ is the initial reachability model of $\mathcal{R}$ [12], $t \in T_{\Sigma}(X_0)$
and $u^{\circ} \in T_{\Sigma_1}(X)$ are S_0-linear, $vars(t) \subseteq \overrightarrow{x} \subseteq X_0$, and $\overrightarrow{y} \subseteq X$. Thanks to the
soundness and completeness results, Theorem 1, and Theorem 2, the solvability
of Condition (b) for $\rightarrow_{\mathcal{R}}$ can be achieved by reachability analysis with $\leadsto_{\mathcal{R}^{\circ}}$, as
stated in Theorem 3.

Theorem 3 (Symbolic Reachability Analysis). *Let $\mathcal{R} = (\Sigma, E, R)$ be a
rewrite theory modulo built-ins $\mathcal{E}_0$. The model-theoretic satisfaction relation in (2)
has a solution iff there exist a term $v \in T_{\Sigma}(X)_{State}$, a constraint $\varphi' \in QF_{\Sigma_0}(X_0)$,
and a substitution $\theta : X \longrightarrow T_{\Sigma}(X)$, with $dom(\theta) \subseteq \overrightarrow{y}$, such that (a) $\langle t; \varphi_1 \rangle \leadsto_{\mathcal{R}^{\circ}}^*$
$\langle v; \varphi' \rangle$, (b) $v =_{B_1} u^{\circ}\theta$, and (c) $\varphi' \wedge \varphi_2\theta$ is $\mathcal{T}_{\mathcal{E}_0}$-satisfiable.*

In Theorem 3, since $dom(\theta) \subseteq \overrightarrow{y}$, and $\overrightarrow{x}$ and $\overrightarrow{y}$ are disjoint, the variables
of $\overrightarrow{x}$ in $\varphi_2\theta$ are left unchanged. Therefore, $\varphi_2\theta$ *links* the requirements for the
variables $\overrightarrow{x}$ in the initial state and $\overrightarrow{y}$ in the final state according to both φ_1
and φ_2. Also note that the inclusion of formula φ_1 as a conjunct in the formula
in Condition (c) of Theorem 3 is superfluous because $\langle t; \varphi_1 \rangle \leadsto_{\mathcal{R}^{\circ}} \langle v; \varphi' \rangle$ implies
that φ_1 is a semantic consequence of φ'.

5   Reflective Implementation of $\leadsto_{\mathcal{R}^{\circ}}$

This section discusses the design and implementation of a prototype that offers
support for symbolic rewriting modulo SMT in the Maude system. The prototype
relies on Maude's meta-level features, that implement rewriting logic's reflective
capabilities, and on SMT solving for $\mathcal{E}_0^+$ integrated in Maude as CVC3's decision
procedures. The extension of Maude with CVC3 is available from the Matching
Logic Project [35]. In the rest of this section, $\mathcal{R} = (\Sigma, E_0 \uplus B_0 \uplus B_1, R)$ is a
rewrite theory modulo built-ins $\mathcal{E}_0$, where $\mathcal{E}_0$ satisfies Condition (1) in Sect. 4.
The theory mapping $\mathcal{R} \mapsto \mathbf{u}(\mathcal{R})$ removes the constraints from the rules in R.

In Maude, reflection is efficiently supported by its *META-LEVEL* module [14], which provides key functionality for rewriting logic's *universal the-
ory* $\mathcal{U}$ [15]. In particular, rewrite theories $\mathcal{R}$ are meta-represented in $\mathcal{U}$ as terms
$\overline{\mathcal{R}}$ of sort *Module*, and a term t in $\mathcal{R}$ is meta-represented in $\mathcal{U}$ as a term $\overline{t}$ of
sort *Term*. The key idea of the reflective implementation is to reduce symbolic
rewriting with $\leadsto_{\mathcal{R}^{\circ}}$ to *standard rewriting* in an associated reflective rewrite theory extending the universal theory $\mathcal{U}$. This is specially important for formal
analysis purposes, because it makes available to $\leadsto_{\mathcal{R}^{\circ}}$ some formal analysis features provided by Maude for rewrite theories such as reachability analysis by
search. This is illustrated by the case study in Sect. 6.

The prototype defines a parametrized functional module $SAT(\Sigma_0, E_0 \uplus B_0)$ of
quantifier-free formulas with Σ_0-equations as atoms. In particular, this module
extends $(\Sigma_0, E_0 \uplus B_0)$ with new sorts *Atom* and *QFFormula*, and new *constants*

$var(X_0)$ identifying the variables X_0. It has, among other functions, a function $sat : QFFormula \longrightarrow Bool$ such that for ϕ, $sat(\phi) = \top$ if ϕ is $\mathcal{E}_0^+$-satisfiable, and $sat(\phi) = \bot$ otherwise.

The process of computing the one-step rewrites of a given constrained term $\langle t; \varphi \rangle$ under $\rightsquigarrow_{\mathcal{R}\circ}$ is decomposed into two conceptual steps using Maude's metalevel. First, all possible triples $\langle u; \theta; \phi \rangle$ such that $t \rightarrow_{\mathbf{u}(\mathcal{R}\circ)} u$ is witnessed by a matching substitution θ and a rule with constraint ϕ are computed[1]. Second, these triples are filtered out by keeping only those for which the quantifier-free formula $\varphi \wedge \phi\theta$ is $\mathcal{E}_0^+$-satisfiable.

The first step in the process is mechanized by function $next$, available from the parametrized module $NEXT(\overline{\mathcal{R}}, \overline{State}, \overline{QFFormula})$ where $\overline{\mathcal{R}}$, $\overline{State}$, and $\overline{QFFormula}$ are the metalevel representations, respectively, of the rewrite theory module $\mathcal{R}$, the state sort $State$, and the quantifier-free formula sort $QFFormula$. Function $next$ uses Maude's $meta\text{-}match$ function and the auxiliary function $new\text{-}vars$ for computing fresh variables (see Sect. 4). In particular, the call $next$ $(((S, \leq, F \uplus var(X_0)), E_0 \uplus B_0 \uplus B_1, R^\circ), \overline{t}, \overline{\varphi})$ computes all possible triples $\langle \overline{u}; \overline{\theta'}; \overline{\phi'} \rangle$ such that $t \rightsquigarrow_{\mathcal{R}\circ} u$ is witnessed by a substitution θ' and a rule with constraint ϕ'. More precisely, such a call first computes a renaming $\zeta = fresh\text{-}vars(vars(t, \varphi))$ and then, for each rule($l^\circ \rightarrow r$ if ϕ), it uses the function $meta\text{-}match$ to obtain a substitution $\overline{\theta} \in meta\text{-}match(\overline{((S, \leq, F \uplus var(X_0))}, B_0 \uplus B_1)$, $\overline{t\downarrow_{E_0/B_0\uplus B_1}}, \overline{l^\circ\zeta})$, and returns $\langle \overline{u}; \overline{\theta'}; \overline{\phi'} \rangle$ with $\overline{u} = \overline{r\zeta\theta}$, $\overline{\theta'} = \overline{\zeta\theta}$, and $\overline{\phi'} = \overline{\phi\zeta\theta}$. Note that by having a $deterministic$ choice of fresh variables (including those in the constraint), function $next$ is actually a $deterministic$ function.

Using the above-mentioned infrastructure, the parametrized module $NEXT$ implements the symbolic rewrite relation $\rightsquigarrow_{\mathcal{R}\circ}$ as a $standard$ $rewrite$ $relation$ in the theory $NEXT$, extending $META\text{-}LEVEL$, by means of the following conditional rewrite rule:

ceq $\langle X{:}State; \varphi{:}QFFormula \rangle \rightarrow \langle Y{:}State; \varphi'{:}QFFormula \rangle$

if $\langle \overline{Y}; \overline{\theta}; \overline{\phi} \rangle$ $S := next(\overline{\mathcal{R}^\bullet}, \overline{X}, \overline{\varphi}) \wedge sat(\varphi \wedge \phi) = \top \wedge \varphi' := \varphi \wedge \phi$

where $\mathcal{R}^\bullet = ((S, \leq, F \uplus var(X_0)), B, R^\circ)$. Therefore, a call to an external SMT solver is just an invocation of the function sat in $SAT(\Sigma_0, E_0 \uplus B_0)$ in order to achieve the above functionality more efficiently and in a built-in way.

Given that the symbolic rewrite relation $\rightsquigarrow_{\mathcal{R}\circ}$ is encoded as a standard rewrite relation, symbolic search can be $directly$ $implemented$ in Maude by its $search$ command. In particular, for terms t, u°, constraints φ_1, φ_2, F a variable of sort $QFFormula$, the following invocation solves the inductive reachability problem in Condition (2):

$$search \; \langle t; \varphi_1 \rangle \rightarrow^* \langle u^\circ; F \rangle \;\; such \; that \; sat(F \wedge \varphi_2).$$

---

[1] Note that in $\mathbf{u}(\mathcal{R}^\circ)$ variables in X_0 are interpreted as $constants$. Therefore, the number of matching substitutions θ thus obtained is finite.

6   Analysis of the CASH Algorithm

This section presents an example, developed jointly with Kyungmin Bae, of a real-time system that can be symbolically analyzed in the prototype tool described in Sect. 5. The analysis applies model checking based on *rewriting modulo SMT*. Some details are omitted. Full details and the prototype tool can be found in [9].

The example involves the symbolic analysis of the CASH scheduling algorithm [13], which attempts to maximize system performance while guaranteeing that critical tasks are executed in a timely manner. This is achieved by maintaining a queue of unused execution budgets that can be reused by other jobs to maximize processor utilization. CASH poses non-trivial modeling and analysis challenges because it contains an unbounded queue. Unbounded data types cannot be modeled in timed-automata formalisms, such as those of UPPAAL [22] or Kronos [39], which assume a finite discrete state.

The CASH algorithm was specified and analyzed in Real-Time Maude by *explicit-state model checking* in an earlier paper by Ölveczky and Caccamo [30], which showed that, under certain variations on both the assumptions and the design of the protocol, it could miss deadlines. Explicit-state model checking has intrinsic limitations which the new analysis by rewriting modulo SMT presented below overcomes. The CASH algorithm is parametrized by: (i) the number N of servers in the system, and (ii) the values of a maximum budget b_i and period p_i, for each server $1 \leq i \leq N$. Even if N is fixed, *there are infinitely many initial states* for N servers, since the maximum budgets b_i and periods p_i range over the natural numbers. Therefore, explicit state model checking cannot perform a full analysis. If a counterexample for N servers exists, it may be found by explicit-state model checking for some chosen initial states, as done in [31], but it could be missed if the wrong initial states are chosen.

Rewriting modulo SMT is useful for symbolically analyzing infinite-state systems like CASH. Infinite sets of states are symbolically described by terms which may involve user-definable data structures such as queues, but whose only variables range over decidable types for which an SMT solving procedure is available. For the CASH algorithm, the built-in data types used are the Booleans (sort iBool) and the integers (sort iInt). Integer built-in terms are used to model discrete time. Boolean built-in terms are used to impose constraints on integers.

A symbolic state is a pair {iB,Cnf} of sort Sys consisting of a Boolean constraint iB, with *and* denoted ^, and a multiset configuration of objects Cnf, with multiset union denoted by juxtaposition, where each object is a record like-structure with an object identifier, a class name, and a set of attribute-value pairs. In each object configuration there is a global object (of class global) that models the time of the system (with attribute name time), the priority queue (with attribute name cq), the availability (with attribute name available), and a deadline missed flag (with attribute name deadline-miss). A configuration can also contain any number of server objects (of class server). Each server object models the maximum budget (the maximum time within which a given job will be finished, with attribute name maxBudget), period (with

attribute name `period`), internal state (with attribute name `state`), time executed (with attribute name `timeExecuted`), budget time used (with attribute
name `usedOfBudget`), and time to deadline (with attribute name `timeTo`
`Deadline`). The symbolic transitions of CASH are specified by 14 conditional
rewrite rules whose conditions specify constraints solvable by the SMT decision
procedure. For example, rule [`deadlineMiss`] below models the detection of a
deadline miss for a server with non-zero maximum budget.

```
vars AtSG AtS : AttributeSet .   var iB : iBool .        var Cnf : Configuration .
vars iT iT' iNZT : iInt .        var St : ServerState .  vars G S : Oid .  var B : Bool .

crl [deadlineMiss] :
    { iB, < G : global | dead-miss |-> B, AtSG >
      < S : server | state |-> St, usedOfBudget |-> iT, timeToDeadline |-> iT',
                     maxBudget |-> iNZT, AtS > Cnf }
=> {iB ^ iT >= c(0) ^ iNZT > c(0) ^ iT' >  c(0) ^ iNZT > iT + iT',
      < G : global | dead-miss |-> true, AtSG >
      < S : server | state |-> St, usedOfBudget |-> iT, timeToDeadline |-> iT',
                     maxBudget |-> iNZT, AtS > Cnf }
if St =/= idle /\ check-sat(iB ^ iT >= c(0) ^ iNZT > c(0) ^ iT' >  c(0) ^ iNZT > iT + iT') .
```

That is, the protocol misses a deadline for server S whenever the value
of attribute `maxBudget` exceeds the addition of values for `usedOfBudget` and
`timeToDeadline` (i.e., `iNZT > iT + iT'`), so that the allocated execution time
cannot be exhausted before the server's deadline.

The goal is to verify *symbolically* the existence of missed deadlines of the
CASH algorithm for the *infinite set of initial configurations* containing two server
objects s_0 and s_1 with maximum budgets b_0 and b_1 and periods p_0 and p_1 as
unspecified natural numbers, and such that each server's maximum budget is
strictly smaller than its period (i.e., $0 \le b_0 < p_0 \wedge 0 \le b_1 < p_1$). This infinite set
of initial states is specified symbolically by the equational definition (not shown)
of term `symbinit`. Maude's `search` command can then be used to symbolically
check if there is a reachable state for any ground instance of `symbinit` that
misses the deadline:

```
search in SYMBOLIC-FAILURE : symbinit =>*
    { iB:iBool, Cnf:Configuration < g : global | AtS:AttributeSet, deadline-miss |-> true > } .
Solution 1 (state 233)
states: 234 rewrites: 60517 in 2865ms cpu (2865ms real) (21118 rewrites/second)
iB:iBool --> ((i(0) <= c(0) ^ i(1) <= c(0)) v i(0) <= c(0) + i(1) ^ ...
Cnf:Configuration -->
< s1 : server | maxBudget |-> i(0), period |-> i(1), state |-> waiting, usedOfBudget |-> c(0),
                timeToDeadline |-> ((i(1) -- c(1)) -- c(1)), timeExecuted |-> c(0) >
< s2 : server | maxBudget |-> i(2), period |-> i(3), state |-> executing, usedOfBudget |-> c(2),
                timeToDeadline |-> ((i(3) -- c(1)) -- c(1)), timeExecuted |-> c(2) >
AtS:AttributeSet --> time |-> c(2), cq |-> emptyQueue, available |-> false
```

A counterexample is found at (modeling) time two, after exploring 233 symbolic states in less than 3 seconds. By using a satisfiability witness of the constraint iB computed by the search command, a concrete counterexample is found
by exploring only 54 ground states. This result compares favorably, in both
time and computational resources, with the ground counterexample found by
explicit-state model checking in [30], where more that 52,000 concrete states
were explored before finding a counterexample.

7   Related Work and Concluding Remarks

The idea of combining term rewriting/narrowing techniques and constrained data structures is an active area of research, specially since the advent of modern theorem provers with highly efficient decision procedures in the form of SMT solvers. The overall aim of these techniques is to advance applicability of methods in symbolic verification where the constraints are expressed in some logic that has an efficient decision procedure. In particular, the work presented here has strong similarities with the narrowing-based symbolic analysis of rewrite theories initiated in [26] and extended in [8]. The main difference is the replacement of narrowing by SMT solving and the decidability advantages of SMT for constraint solving.

M. Ayala-Rincón [5] investigates, in the setting of many-sorted equational logic, the expressiveness of conditional equational systems whose conditions may use built-in predicates. This class of equational theories is important because the combination of equational and built-in premises yield a type of clauses which is more expressive than purely conditional equations. Rewriting notions like confluence, termination, and critical pairs are also investigated. S. Falke and D. Kapur [16] studied the problem of termination of rewriting with constrained built-ins. In particular, they extended the dependency pairs framework to handle termination of equational specifications with semantic data structures and evaluation strategies in the Maude functional sublanguage. The same authors used the idea of combining rewriting induction and linear arithmetic over constrained terms [17]. Their aim is to obtain equational decision procedures that can handle semantic data types represented by the constrained built-ins. H. Kirchner and C. Ringeissen proposed the notion of constrained rewriting and have used it by combining symbolic constraint solvers [20]. The main difference between their work and rewriting modulo SMT presented in this paper is that the former uses narrowing for symbolic execution, both at the symbolic 'pattern matching' and the constraint solving levels. In contrast, rewriting modulo SMT solves the symbolic pattern matching task by rewriting while constraint solving is delegated to an SMT decision procedure. More recently, C. Kop and N. Nishida [21] have proposed a way to unify the ideas regarding equational rewriting with logical constraints. More generally, while the approaches in [5,16,17,20,21] address symbolic reasoning for *equational* theorem proving purposes, none of them addresses the kind of non-deterministic rewrite rules, which are needed for open system modeling. More recently, A. Arusoaie et al. [4] have proposed a language-independent symbolic execution framework, within the K framework [23], for languages endowed with a formal operational semantics based on term rewriting. There, the built-in subtheories are the datatypes of a programming language and symbolic analysis is performed on constrained terms (called "patterns"); unification is also implemented by matching for a restricted class of rewrite rules and uses SMT solvers to check constraints.

This paper has presented rewrite theories modulo built-ins and has shown how they can be used for *symbolically* modeling and analyzing concurrent open systems, where non-deterministic values from the environment can be represented by built-in terms [33,34]. In particular, the main contributions of this paper can be summarized as follows: (1) it presents rewriting modulo SMT as a new symbolic technique combining the powers of rewriting, SMT solving, and model checking; (2) this combined power can be applied to model and analyze systems outside the scope of each individual technique; (3) in particular, it is ideally suited to model and analyze the challenging case of *open systems*; and (4) because of its reflective reduction to standard rewriting, current algorithms and tools for model checking closed systems can be *reused* in this new symbolic setting without requiring any changes to their implementation.

Under reasonable assumptions, including decidability of $\mathcal{E}_0^+$, a rewrite theory modulo is executable by term rewriting modulo SMT. This feature makes it possible to use, for symbolic analysis, state-of-the-art tools already available for Maude, such as its space search commands, with no change whatsoever required to use such tools. We have proved that the symbolic rewrite relation is sound and complete with respect to its ground counterpart, have presented an overview of the prototype that offers support for rewriting modulo SMT in Maude, and have presented a case study on the symbolic analysis of the CASH scheduling algorithm illustrating the use of these techniques.

Future work on a mature implementation and on extending the idea of rewriting modulo SMT with other symbolic constraint solving techniques such as narrowing modulo should be pursued. Also, the extension to symbolic LTL model checking, together with state space reduction techniques, should be investigated. The ideas presented here extend results in [33] and have been successfully applied to the symbolic analysis of NASA's PLEXIL language to program open cyber-physical systems [33]. Future applications to PLEXIL and other languages should also be pursued.

Acknowledgments. The authors would like to thank the anonymous referees for their comments that helped to improve the paper. This work was partially supported by NSF Grant CNS 13-19109. The first author would like to thank the National Institute of Aerospace for a short visit supported by the Assurance of Flight Critical System's project of NASA's Aviation Safety Program at Langley Research Center under Research Cooperative Agreement No. NNL09AA00A.

References

1. Althaus, E., Kruglov, E., Weidenbach, C.: Superposition modulo linear arithmetic SUP(LA). In: Ghilardi, S., Sebastiani, R. (eds.) FroCoS 2009. LNCS, vol. 5749, pp. 84–99. Springer, Heidelberg (2009)
2. Alur, R., Dill, D.L.: A theory of timed automata. Theor. Comput. Sci. **126**(2), 183–235 (1994)
3. Armando, A., Mantovani, J., Platania, L.: Bounded model checking of software using SMT solvers instead of SAT solvers. In: Valmari, A. (ed.) SPIN 2006. LNCS, vol. 3925, pp. 146–162. Springer, Heidelberg (2006)
4. Arusoaie, A., Lucanu, D., Rusu, V.: A generic framework for symbolic execution. In: Erwig, M., Paige, R.F., Van Wyk, E. (eds.) SLE 2013. LNCS, vol. 8225, pp. 281–301. Springer, Heidelberg (2013)

5. Ayala-Rincón, M.: Expressiveness of conditional equational systems with built-in predicates. Ph.D. thesis, Universität Kaiserslauten (1993)
6. Baader, F., Nipkow, T.: Term Rewriting and All That. Cambridge University Press, Cambridge (1998)
7. Baader, F., Schulz, K.: Unification in the union of disjoint equational theories: combining decision procedures. J. Symb. Comput. **21**, 211–243 (1996)
8. Bae, K., Escobar, S., Meseguer, J.: Abstract logical model checking of infinite-state systems using narrowing. In: van Raamsdonk, F. (ed.) RTA. LIPIcs, vol. 21, pp. 81–96. Schloss Dagstuhl - Leibniz-Zentrum fuer Informatik, Wadern (2013)
9. Bae, K., Rocha, C.: A note on symbolic reachability analysis modulo integer constraints for the CASH algorithm (2012). http://maude.cs.uiuc.edu/cases/scash
10. Bonacina, M.P., Lynch, C., de Moura, L.M.: On deciding satisfiability by theorem proving with speculative inferences. J. Autom. Reason. **47**(2), 161–189 (2011)
11. Boudet, A.: Combining unification algorithms. J. Symb. Comp. **16**(6), 597–626 (1993)
12. Bruni, R., Meseguer, J.: Semantic foundations for generalized rewrite theories. Theor. Comput. Sci. **360**(1–3), 386–414 (2006)
13. Caccamo, M., Buttazzo, G.C., Sha, L.: Capacity sharing for overrun control. In: IEEE Real-Time Systems Symposium, pp. 295–304. IEEE Computer Society (2000)
14. Clavel, M., Durán, F., Eker, S., Lincoln, P., Martí-Oliet, N., Meseguer, J., Talcott, C. (eds.): All About Maude - A High-Performance Logical Framework. LNCS, vol. 4350. Springer, Heidelberg (2007)
15. Clavel, M., Meseguer, J., Palomino, M.: Reflection in membership equational logic, many-sorted equational logic, horn logic with equality, and rewriting logic. Theor. Comput. Sci. **373**(1–2), 70–91 (2007)
16. Falke, S., Kapur, D.: Operational termination of conditional rewriting with built-in numbers and semantic data structures. ENTCS **237**, 75–90 (2009)
17. Falke, S., Kapur, D.: Rewriting induction + linear arithmetic = decision procedure. In: Gramlich, B., Miller, D., Sattler, U. (eds.) IJCAR 2012. LNCS, vol. 7364, pp. 241–255. Springer, Heidelberg (2012)
18. Ganai, M., Gupta, A.: Accelerating high-level bounded model checking. In: ICCAD, pp. 794–801. ACM (2006)
19. Goguen, J.A., Meseguer, J.: Order-sorted algebra I: equational deduction for multiple inheritance, overloading, exceptions and partial operations. Theor. Comput. Sci. **105**(2), 217–273 (1992)
20. Kirchner, H., Ringeissen, C.: Combining symbolic constraint solvers on algebraic domains. J. Symb. Comput. **18**(2), 113–155 (1994)
21. Kop, C., Nishida, N.: Term rewriting with logical constraints. In: Fontaine, P., Ringeissen, C., Schmidt, R.A. (eds.) FroCoS 2013. LNCS, vol. 8152, pp. 343–358. Springer, Heidelberg (2013)
22. Larsen, K.G., Pettersson, P., Yi, W.: Uppaal in a nutshell. STTT **1**(1–2), 134–152 (1997)
23. Lucanu, D., Şerbănuţă, T.F., Roşu, G.: K framework distilled. In: Durán, F. (ed.) WRLA 2012. LNCS, vol. 7571, pp. 31–53. Springer, Heidelberg (2012)
24. Meseguer, J.: Conditional rewriting logic as a unified model of concurrency. Theor. Comput. Sci. **96**(1), 73–155 (1992)
25. Meseguer, J.: Membership algebra as a logical framework for equational specification. In: Parisi-Presicce, F. (ed.) WADT 1997. LNCS, vol. 1376, pp. 18–61. Springer, Heidelberg (1998)

26. Meseguer, J., Thati, P.: Symbolic reachability analysis using narrowing and its application to verification of cryptographic protocols. High.-Order Symb. Comput. **20**(1–2), 123–160 (2007)
27. Milicevic, A., Kugler, H.: Model checking using SMT and theory of lists. In: Bobaru, M., Havelund, K., Holzmann, G.J., Joshi, R. (eds.) NFM 2011. LNCS, vol. 6617, pp. 282–297. Springer, Heidelberg (2011)
28. Nelson, G., Oppen, D.C.: Simplification by cooperating decision procedures. ACM Trans. Program. Lang. Syst. **1**(2), 245–257 (1979)
29. Nieuwenhuis, R., Oliveras, A., Tinelli, C.: Solving SAT and SAT modulo theories: from an abstract Davis-Putnam-Logemann-Loveland procedure to DPLL(t). J. ACM **53**(6), 937–977 (2006)
30. Ölveczky, P.C., Caccamo, M.: Formal simulation and analysis of the CASH scheduling algorithm in real-time Maude. In: Baresi, L., Heckel, R. (eds.) FASE 2006. LNCS, vol. 3922, pp. 357–372. Springer, Heidelberg (2006)
31. Ölveczky, P.C., Meseguer, J.: Semantics and pragmatics of real-time Maude. High.-Order Symb. Comput. **20**(1–2), 161–196 (2007)
32. Owre, S., Rushby, J.M., Shankar, N.: PVS: a prototype verification system. In: Kapur, D. (ed.) 11th International Conference on Automated Deduction (CADE). LNCS (LNAI), vol. 607, pp. 748–752. Springer, Saratoga, NY (1992)
33. Rocha, C.: Symbolic reachability analysis for rewrite theories. Ph.D. thesis, University of Illinois at Urbana-Champaign (2012)
34. Rocha, C., Meseguer, J., Muñoz, C.: Rewriting modulo SMT. Technical Memorandum NASA/TM-2013-218033, NASA, Langley Research Center, Hampton, VA, 23681-2199, USA, August 2013
35. Roşu, G., Ştefănescu, A.: Matching logic: a new program verification approach (NIER Track). In: ICSE'11: Proceedings of the 30th International Conference on Software Engineering, pp. 868–871. ACM (2011)
36. Veanes, M., Bjørner, N.S., Raschke, A.: An SMT approach to bounded reachability analysis of model programs. In: Suzuki, K., Higashino, T., Yasumoto, K., El-Fakih, K. (eds.) FORTE 2008. LNCS, vol. 5048, pp. 53–68. Springer, Heidelberg (2008)
37. Viry, P.: Equational rules for rewriting logic. TCS **285**, 487–517 (2002)
38. Walter, D., Little, S., Myers, C.J.: Bounded model checking of analog and mixed-signal circuits using an SMT solver. In: Namjoshi, K.S., Yoneda, T., Higashino, T., Okamura, Y. (eds.) ATVA 2007. LNCS, vol. 4762, pp. 66–81. Springer, Heidelberg (2007)
39. Yovine, S.: Kronos: a verification tool for real-time systems. STTT **1**(1–2), 123–133 (1997)

Formal Specification of Button-Related Fault-Tolerance Micropatterns

Mu Sun$^{(\boxtimes)}$ and José Meseguer

University of Illinois at Urbana-Champaign, Champaign, IL, USA
{musun,meseguer}@illinois.edu

Abstract. Fault tolerance has been a major concern in the design of computing platforms. However, currently, fault tolerance has been done mostly with just heuristics, high level probabilistic analysis and extensive testing. In this work, we explore how we can use formal patterns to achieve fault-tolerance designs and methods. In particular, we look at faults that occur in mechanical button interfaces such as button bounce, button stuck, and phantom button faults. Our primary goal is the safety of such interfaces for medical devices [7], but the methods are more widely applicable. We formally describe corresponding patterns to address these faults including button debouncing, button stuck detection, and phantom press filtering. We prove stuttering-bisimulation results for some patterns showing their fault-masking capabilities. Furthermore, for patterns where fault-masking is not possible, we prove fault-detection properties. We also instantiate these patterns to a simple instance of a button-press counter and perform execution and model checking as further validation.

1 Introduction

Idealized abstractions of computing systems allow us to build more complex applications and for more complex scenarios. One can think in terms of binary values instead of continuous voltages, and in terms of objects and messages instead of assembly-level instructions. Given the complexities of the real world, it is remarkable how accurate these abstractions can be. However, sometimes the real world behavior violates the expectation of idealized models and we refer to this type of behavior as faults.

In order to maintain the behavior of ideal models in the presence of faults, fault tolerance techniques are essential. We would like faults to be completely contained within the lower levels of design and never be exposed to the upper layers; this is the notion of *fault masking*. However, there are many cases where fault masking is impossible. In these cases, faults will inevitably be exposed to the upper layers, either by explicit fault detection or as behavioral anomalies such as extra delays and nondeterminism.

In this paper, we explore *fault-tolerance micropatterns* for button related faults including button bounce, phantom button presses, and stuck buttons.

Research partially supported by NSF Grant 13-19109.

© Springer International Publishing Switzerland 2014
S. Escobar (Ed.): WRLA 2014, LNCS 8663, pp. 263–279, 2014.
DOI: 10.1007/978-3-319-12904-4_15

These micropatterns provide specific levels of safety for medical device interfaces in the presence of faults [7], and can be likewise applied to devices in other areas. All of these faults and fault-tolerance patterns are quite well known, but our contribution is in the formalization of these fault-tolerance models including:

(1) defining a model for button interfaces;
(2) modeling faults as a relation from ideal environments to faulty environments;
(3) describing fault tolerance methods as a design transformation pattern using parameterized modules;
(4) proving fault-tolerance results about our models using appropriate bisimulation relations; and
(5) validating of our models with execution and model checking.

Since we are dealing with faults on the interface, we mainly focus on faults in the environment. There are also other classes of faults such as internal faults (e.g. bit flips, memory corruption, computation errors). However, environmental faults and internal faults are generally handled orthogonally in the design of a system, so we focus only on environmental faults. The fault tolerance patterns that we describe in this paper all have a similar structure that is captured in Fig. 1. All fault tolerance designs have a goal, an ideal abstraction that it is trying to provide (left-hand side of Fig. 1). An ideal environment, and the ideal design will give the correct behavior of the system. However, the challenge comes when we have a faulty environment (right-hand side of Fig. 1). Just using an ideal design with a faulty environment will most likely lead to undesirable deviations in the behavior of the system. The goal then is to provide a design transformation for the system along with the fault model that will have behavior similar to the ideal. The notion of *correspondence in behavior* is an important one. In this paper, this correspondence is expressed as a *bisimulation*.

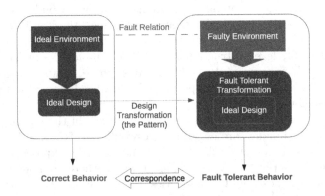

Fig. 1. Fault Modeling

The rest of the paper is organized as follows. Section 2 covers the basics of rewriting logic and the subset of Maude that we use to describe our models.

Section 3 describes how we model buttons in order to describe button-related faults. Sections 4, 5, and 6 describe in detail our patterns to handel button bounce, phantom button presses, and stuck buttons respectively. We conclude in Sect. 7 with a summary and a discussion of potential future work.

2   Background on Parameterized Formal Specifications and Real-Time Maude

We use the Maude rewriting logic language [2] to define formal specifications for our fault-tolerance wrappers for medical systems. We present some of the basic concepts behind rewriting logic, its real-time extensions, and parametrization.

2.1   Membership Equational Logic and Rewriting Logic

Membership equational logic (MEL) [5] describes the most general form of the equational components of a Maude rewrite theory. These are called functional modules in Maude [2].

A MEL signature is a tuple (K, F, S) where S is a set of sorts (i.e. types), K is a set of kinds (i.e. super types or error types for data), and F is a set of typed function symbols (and constants). A MEL theory is a pair (Σ, E) where Σ is a MEL signature, and E a set of sentences (equations and memberships) expressing (possibly conditional) membership or equality constraints. If an MEL theory is convergent (satisfies properties of confluence, termination, and sort-decreasingness), Maude provides efficient execution of its initial model semantics.

Rewriting logic [1] describes the most general form of modules defined in Maude. A rewrite theory in Maude is defined in the form of a tuple: (Σ, E, ϕ, R), where (Σ, E) is an underlying MEL theory, ϕ defines the frozen positions of operators (positions where no rewrites are allowed to occur below), and R is a set of rewrite sentences (possibly conditional on equality and membership sentences). If a rewrite theory satisfies the properties of coherence, and the underlying MEL theory of a rewrite theory is convergent, then Maude provides efficient execution of the initial model semantics for the rewrite theory. This includes efficient execution for simulation, searching and LTL model checking.

2.2   Full Maude and Real-Time Maude

Full Maude [3] is a Maude interpreter written in Maude, which in addition to the Core Maude constructs provides syntactic constructs such as object oriented modules. Object oriented modules implicitly add in sorts `Object` and `Msg`. Furthermore, OO-modules add a sort called `Configuration` which consists of a multiset of terms of sort `Object` or `Msg`. Objects are represented as records:

```
< objectID : classID | Attribute 1 : Value 1, ... Attribute n :  Value n >
```

Rewriting logic rules are then used to describe state transitions of objects based on consumption of messages. For example, the following rule expresses the fact that a surgical-laser object consumes a message to set the power to 50 Watts:

```
rl setPower(sl1, 50) < sl1 : SurgeryLaser | power : P >
=> < sl1 : SurgeryLaser | power : 50 > .
```

Real-time Maude [6] is a real-time extension for Maude developed on top of Full Maude. It adds syntactic constructs for defining timed modules. Timed modules automatically import the TIME module, which defines the sort Time (which can be instantiated as discrete or continuous) along with various arithmetic and comparison operations on Time. Timed modules also provide a sort System which encapsulates a Configuration and implicitly associates with it a time stamp of sort Time. After defining a time-advancing strategy, Real-time Maude provides timed execution (trew), timed search (tsearch), which performs search on a term of sort System based on the time advancement strategy, and timed and untimed LTL model checking commands.

Real-time Maude provides useful constructs for specifying real-time systems, including basic semantics of time and time advancement. We use the model of linear time provided by Real-Time Maude. For time advancement, we have used the conventional best practice where only one timed rewrite rule is used and is fully determined by the operators *tick* and *mte* [6].

The *tick* operator advances time over a configuration by some time duration. For example, with timer (and time units being seconds): $tick(timer(10), 3) = timer(7)$. That is, a timer with 10 sec remaining ticked by 3 sec will become a timer with 7 sec remaining.

The *mte* operator computes the maximum time that can elapse in a system before an interesting event occurs. Interesting events include all state transitions in which messages are generated in a configuration. Again, with the timer example, we assume that components only react when the timers expire, so the maximum time elapsable for a timer would be the time it takes the timer to expire: $mte(timer(10)) = 10$.

Real-Time Maude also includes models of time that have infinity, INF, as a possible time value. Although, INF will never be used to advance time in any system, it is useful to have INF to describe unbounded time. For example, $mte(\text{stableSys}) = \text{INF}$.

2.3 Parameterized Modules

Modules in Maude have an *initial model semantics*. Maude also supports *theories* which have a *loose semantics* (that is, not just the initial mode, but all the models of the theory are allowed). Theories can be instantiated by *views* (i.e., theory interpretations) to other theories or modules. In particular, a theory can be instantiated by a view to any module whose initial model satisfies all equational, membership, and rewrite sentences of the theory.

Parametrized modules [2] are modules which take theories as input parameters and define operations (parametrically) in terms of the input theory. Parametrized modules are instantiated by providing views to concrete modules for the corresponding input theories. Once instantiated, the parametrized module is given the free extension semantics for the initial models of the targets of the input views. Core Maude, Full Maude, and Real-Time Maude all support parameterized modules. For our pattern, we will exploit in particular the Real-Time Maude parameterization mechanisms.

3   Modeling Buttons

Before we describe specific patterns, we should describe the problem domain that we are addressing. Many cyber-physical systems, including many medical devices, use buttons as an input interface. We need a general abstraction that can capture the important details of any button interaction with the system. This abstraction must be detailed enough to model faulty button behavior.

For the cases that we are considering, it is sufficient to use a 2-state button abstraction. A button model can be in one of two states, either *pressed* or *not pressed*, at any instant in time. Button behavior is then a function $button_{state} : Time \rightarrow \{on, off\}$. Here, $Time$ is some ideal continuous physical time, which can be represented by the positive real numbers $\mathbb{R}_{\geq 0}$. $Time$ can also be reasoned about from the perspective of a system clock that ticks (advances time) in discrete intervals, in which case we can model it using the natural numbers $\mathbb{N}$. It is desirable to prove results about our system using continuous time as it is more general. However, some of our proved results later use a discrete time model as it allows for cleaner proofs using induction and is still general enough to cover the behaviors of systems running on a system clock.

Realistic button press behaviors will have additional constraints such as buttons cannot toggle faster than a certain frequency, and we can also make some mathematical simplifications such as making all the button press intervals left-closed [7]. With these assumptions, we can model continuous button behavior with a discrete timed model, since in each finite interval of time, given a button function, b, there are only a finite number of press and release events in b. For example, if the button behavior is $b(t) = on$ for $t \in [0,1) \cup [2,5)$ and $b(t) = off$ otherwise. This can be represented discretely without any loss of information as a list of pairs describing when a button gets pressed and released, e.g., $(press, 0).(release, 1).(press, 2).(release, 5)$. We can easily specify this type of list structure in Maude with its expressive typing system [7].

3.1   Button Behavior Semantics in a System

The behavior of a button we have just defined is a purely mathematical one. By itself, it has no behavior semantics. To capture the behavior of the list of button press events over time, we simply convert the list of press and release events over time into a set of delayed messages:

```
op to-msgs : PressReleaseList Oid -> Configuration .
msgs press release : Oid -> Msg .
```

The `to-msgs` operator homomorphically maps each element of the list to a message.

```
eq to-msgs(nil, O) = none .
eq to-msgs(L press(T), O) = to-msgs(L,O) delay(press(O), t(T)) .
eq to-msgs(L release(T), O) = to-msgs(L,O) delay(release(O), t(T)) .
```

The object reacting to this button press event will then receive each button-related message at the appropriate time according to the semantics of the delay operator.

4   A Pattern to Address Button Bounce Faults

With our current model of the environment (button presses as delayed messages), we are now ready to discuss how to model faults. Faults essentially add additional behavior to the environment or system. In general, we would like to capture a fault in full generality in order to check all cases, but we also need to make enough assumptions to restrict in a realistic way the faulty behavior. Otherwise, it may become impossible to correctly design a fault-tolerant system.

4.1   Button Bounce

When a button is pressed, the button may "bounce." A button bounce is a mechanical phenomenon that occurs due to oscillations when a button is pressed. The contact voltages of the button may oscillate between high and low thresholds multiple times before stabilizing. This results in multiple erroneous button press events for only one intended button press event. Since oscillatory phenomena are usually dampened pretty quickly, there is a short time window, T_{bounce}^{max}, within which a button may bounce after it is pressed.

Of course, the basic model of button bouncing behavior can be described in the continuous time model as a relation $F_{bounce} \subseteq I_{valid} \times I_{valid}$ (implicitly parameterized by a maximum bounce time T_{bounce}^{max}) where $(b, b_f) \in F_{bounce}$ means that given an ideal input b, the faulty input b_f could result from the button bouncing fault [7]. However, with proper assumptions on the spacing of events to avoid zeno behavior, we can use F_{bounce} to define a corresponding relation on the discrete list-like representation of button press and release events. This is represented as the binary predicate `bounce-fault`. The first argument is the ideal input, and the second argument is the nonideal faulty input. The predicate returns true iff the faulty model is a possible result of button bounce faults applied to the ideal model.

```
op bounce-fault : Input Input -> Bool .
eq bounce-fault(nil,nil) = true .
```

If the last press events match, then we can remove it and look for earlier faults.

```
eq bounce-fault(I press(T), I' press(T)) = bounce-fault(I,I') .
```

If a press event occurs in the faulty model, which is later than the corresponding press event in the ideal model, then it is possibly a bounce event if it is within the T_{bounce}^{max} duration, **bounce-duration**. We can remove this event and analyze the earlier times for more faults.

```
ceq bounce-fault(I press(T), I' press(T'))
   = bounce-fault(I press(T), I')
    if T' le (T plus bounce-duration) /\ T' gt T .
```

Release events should match the ideal ones, but there might be extraneous release events generated by the bounce fault, which we can just remove and reason about the corresponding press event earlier (using the equations above). Anything that does not match the patterns described above could not have been generated by a bounce fault.

```
eq bounce-fault(I release(T),I' release(T)) = bounce-fault(I,I') .
ceq bounce-fault(I press(T), I' release(T')) = bounce-fault(I
press(T),I')
if T lt T' .
eq bounce-fault(I,I') = false [owise] .
```

The current fault model is purely declarative. It is a binary relation that can be used to check whether one button input is a faulty version of another. However, this gives no means for generating a faulty model directly from a nonfaulty one. In order to have some degree of completeness in model checking analysis later, we need to have a more executable fault model; one that specifies faults as transitions and not just by a predicate. Of course, if we choose *Time* to be the real numbers, we have no hope of obtaining a set of possible faults manageable for execution purposes as there are uncountably many. However, for most practical purposes, we can obtain a fairly complete analysis just by using discrete time, mostly because systems operate based on discrete clocks anyway. Assuming a natural number model of time, a more executable fault model can be defined [7].

4.2   A Button Debouncer Pattern

Finally, we come to the most important part of our specification, namely, a formal pattern for correctly handling faulty button bounce behavior. Figure 2 shows the intuitive structure of the button debouncer. Essentially, all button inputs are filtered through a wrapper, and by properly timing button press events, we can ignore exactly the faulty bounced button press events (assuming proper spacing between normal button press events).

We must first describe the input theory **oth DEBOUNCED** that is required for a button debouncer. This includes the original class that the button debouncer will modify, and also parameters of the system and of the fault in order to adjust the pattern's behavioral parameters accordingly. The parameters of the theory **DEBOUNCED** can be intuitively described as follows. The class **Wrapped** is

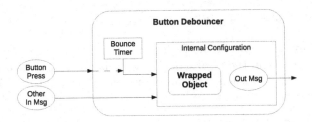

Fig. 2. The Button Debouncer Pattern

the class for the internal object that is wrapped by the button debouncer. An operator |dest| needs to be provided in order to know whether a message should be forwarded outside of the wrapped configuration. The constant |t-bounce| should be mapped to an appropriately measured constant T_{bounce}^{max}. Furthermore, another constant t-space is required to define the minimal time spacing between two intentional button presses. The message press is of course the special button press message that we want to debounce. We also add an equation in the theory specifying that time should not be allowed to advance when a press message has not yet been handled.

```
class |Wrapped| .
op |dest| : Msg -> Oid .
op |t-bounce| : -> Time .
op |t-space| : -> Time .
eq |t-bounce| lt |t-space| = true .
msg |press| : Oid -> Msg .
eq mte(|press|(O:Oid)) = zero .
```

Now, the actual pattern itself is quite straightforward. The debouncer pattern is a wrapper enclosing an object that modifies its behavior by filtering messages. Besides the internal configuration, it also adds a timer attribute, which is needed to filter the debouncing actions correctly. Note that we use parameter |O| as the parameter label of the theory DEBOUNCED.

```
(tomod DEBOUNCER{|O| :: DEBOUNCED} is
  pr RT-COMP .
  pr DELAY-MSG .

  class !Debouncer{|O|} |
      inside : NEConfiguration,
      timer : Timer .
```

The tick and mte equations are the intuitive ones, where we must tick the internal configuration according to its defined semantics as well as the timer stored in the wrapper object.

```
eq tick(< O : !Debouncer{|O|} | inside : C, timer : TM >, T)
   = < O : !Debouncer{|O|} | inside : tick(C, T), timer : tick(TM, T) > .
eq mte(< O : !Debouncer{|O|} | inside : C, timer : TM >)
   = minimum(mte(C), mte(TM)) .
```

Finally, we have the behavioral rules for the object. For receiving messages, all messages that are not a button press message are forwarded to the internal configuration. Also, all messages output from the internal object are forwarded to the external wrapper:

```
crl [forward-in] : IM < O : !Debouncer{|O|} | inside : C >
  => < O : !Debouncer{|O|} | inside : IM C >
  if |dest|(IM) == O /\ IM =/= |press|(O) .
crl [forward-out] : < O : !Debouncer{|O|} | inside : OM C >
  => < O : !Debouncer{|O|} | inside : C > OM
  if |dest|(OM) =/= O .
```

When a button press message is received, the behavior will differ based on the timer. If the timer is not set, then we have an initial button press event, which is immediately forwarded to the internal configuration. Furthermore, the timer is set for the maximum bounce duration.

```
rl [set-timer] : |press|(O) < O : !Debouncer{|O|} | timer : no-timer, inside : C >
  => < O : !Debouncer{|O|} | timer : t(|t-space|), inside : |press|(O) C > .
```

If the timer is set, then the system is within a bounce duration, and the incoming button press event is ignored.

```
crl [ignore-press] : |press|(O) < O : !Debouncer{|O|} | timer : TM, inside : C >
  => < O : !Debouncer{|O|} | inside : C >
  if TM =/= timerO /\ TM =/= no-timer .
```

Finally, when the timer expires, the timer is removed. This is a model-specific construct that allows the time to advance.

```
crl [reset-timer] : < O : !Debouncer{|O|} | timer : TM >
  => < O : !Debouncer{|O|} | timer : no-timer >
  if TM == timerO .
endtom)
```

4.3 Proof of Correctness of the Debouncer Pattern

The button debouncer should essentially mitigate button bounce faults, but we must make clear this notion and what it means. We essentially need to define a correspondence between ideal behavior and the debounce pattern behavior under a faulty input. We must define the two transition systems of interest and express their correspondence. First, we define appropriate projection operations. We need a message filter and a wrapper remover. π_{nf} only projects the nonfaulty messages. π_w projects the object on the inside of the wrapper. In Maude, they can be defined as follows:

```
vars C C' : NEConfiguration .
eq pi-nf(C) = pi-nonpress(C) pi-press(C, get-time(C)) .

eq pi-w(< I:Oid : PressDebouncer | inside : C >) = C .
eq pi-w(C C') = pi-w(C) pi-w(C') .
eq pi-w(C) = C [owise] .
```

Here all these operators are frozen. **pi-nonpress** projects all the components of the configuration that are not **press** messages, and **pi-press** filters all press messages that are not faulty using the defined times **T-bounce** and **T-space**, and also the timer set on the debounce wrapper to filter initial times.

Definition 1. *States of the transition system S_{ideal} are system configurations with a single instance of a wrapped object, and such that the input button press messages are spaced by at least the assumed minimal time spacing.*

States of the transition system $S_{wrapped}$ are system configurations with a single instance of a wrapped object in a wrapper object, and such that input button press messages are related to an ideal button press configuration by the button press fault F_{bounce}.

We define a relation $H \subseteq S_{ideal} \times S_{wrapped}$ by the equivalence $s_i H s_f$ iff $\pi_{nf}(\pi_w((s_f))) = s_i$ and $time(s_f) = time(s_i)$.

We now come to the theorem that shows that H defines a bisimulation between an ideal system and a faulty system with our pattern applied. Since H preserves all the states of the object, this theorem essentially states that our pattern fully masks button bounce faults for our model of input (with proper spacing between successive button presses). The full proof of the theorem can be found in [7].

Theorem 1. *The relation H is a well-founded bisimulation, and thus H defines a stuttering bisimulation between S_{ideal} and $S_{wrapped}$ when considering natural number time.*

Note that if we do not have natural number time, then it is not guaranteed that we have a bisimulation. A simple counter-example would be one where a button bounces an infinite number of times in a finite time period. Of course, this is due to Zeno behavior. In order to remove Zeno behavior, we can make the assumption that all events are spaced at least Δt apart. This means that if we convert all times t into the natural number $\lceil t/\Delta t \rceil$, then the relation is still well founded, and the bisimulation result would still hold.

Notice that any atomic proposition AP defined on a state s_i can be lifted to a property of s_f by labelling s_f according to $\pi_{nf}(\pi_w((s_f)))$.

In addition to proving these theorems, we have also performed some model checking for simple instantiations of this pattern as an extra level of validation [7].

5   A Pattern to Address Phantom Faults

5.1   Phantom Faults

Slight disturbances in the environment (e.g. EMI, moving parts, etc.) can lead to a button being unintentionally pressed for a very short time.

The domain model is exactly the same as that for button bounce. We consider button inputs that we model as discrete messages, and an object that reacts to button inputs by consuming these messages.

A phantom button fault is a relation $F_{phantom} \subseteq I_{valid} \times I_{valid}$ (implicitly parameterized by a phantom press duration $T_{phantom}$) where faulty button presses of very short durations may occur. More precisely, $(b, b_f) \in F_{phantom}$ iff

1. $b(t) = 1 \implies b_f(t) = 1$ (an intentional button press is always registered)
2. if $b_f(t) = 1$ and $b(t) = 0$, then $t - init(b_f, t) < T_{phantom}$ (the duration of all phantom presses are bounded by $T_{phantom}$)

We can similarly construct the discrete definition of the $F_{phantom}$ relation and also the executable fault generation definitions when we are working in discrete time.

5.2   Dephantom Pattern

The pattern for handling phantom button events first requires describing the necessary parameters to fully define its behavior in the parameter theory PHANTOMABLE.

Like the button debouncer pattern, the dephantomizer pattern is parameterized, in this case by the PHANTOMABLE input theory that describes the nature of the phantom button press fault and the object which will be wrapped by the pattern. This includes a class |Wrapped| which specifies which object is subject to the phantom press fault. The |dest| operator which is again used to find which messages to forward to the outside configuration. The |press| and |release| messages which describe the actual button press events subject to phantom press faults.

```
(oth PHANTOMABLE is pr TICK-MTE-SEM .

    class |Wrapped| .
    op |dest| : Msg -> Oid .
    op |t-phantom| : -> Time .

    msg |press| : Oid -> Msg .
    msg |release| : Oid -> Msg .

    var O : Oid .
    eq mte(|press|(O)) = zero .
endoth)
```

The dephatomizer pattern takes a PHANTOMABLE theory as input and describes a wrapper pattern to mitigate phantom button press faults. The wrapper structure is very similar to the button debouncer, except for the logic of handling button presses, which is of course necessary since the fault behavior is different for the pattern.

```
(tomod DEPHANTOMIZER{|O| :: PHANTOMABLE} is
    pr RT-COMP .
    pr DELAY-MSG .

    class !PhantomIgnore{|O|} |
        inside : NEConfiguration,
        timer : Timer .

    op init-timer : -> Timer .
    eq init-timer = no-timer .

    vars T : Time .
    var O : Oid .
    var TM : Timer .
    var C : Configuration .
```

The equations below define the wrapper class and the time advancement semantics. This is exactly the same as in the button debouncer case. However, here the timer is used slightly differently to eliminate a different set of faults. The logic for the timer will be shown later.

```
eq tick( < 0 : !PhantomIgnore{|0|} | inside : C, timer : TM >, T)
= < 0 : !PhantomIgnore{|0|} | inside : tick(C, T), timer : tick(TM, T) > .

eq mte( < 0 : !PhantomIgnore{|0|} | inside : C, timer : TM >)
= minimum(mte(C), mte(TM)) .
```

The rule **set-timer** below sets the timer whenever a button press event is received. The timer is then used to make sure that the button is pressed for sufficiently long before it is actually recognized as an intentional button press event. The rule **non-phantom-release** decides the behavior when the system receives a release after sufficient time has elapsed, and hence the timer is disabled to **no-timer**. The rule **phantom-release** is applied when a release message is received before the timer expires. This means that insufficient time has elapsed before a button is released and it is considered a phantom event. Thus, the button press and the release events are hidden from the internal object. Furthermore, the timer is reset. The last rule **reset-timer** is specified when the timer expires. This means that the button press duration has just passed the threshold to be registered as a valid press. The press event is forwarded to the internal configuration.

```
rl [set-timer] : |press|(0) < 0 : !PhantomIgnore{|0|} | timer : no-timer >
=> < 0 : !PhantomIgnore{|0|} | timer : t(|t-phantom|) > .

rl [non-phantom-release] : |release|(0) < 0 : !PhantomIgnore{|0|} |
   timer : no-timer, inside : C >
=> < 0 : !PhantomIgnore{|0|} | inside : |release|(0) C > .

crl [phantom-release] : |release|(0) < 0 : !PhantomIgnore{|0|} | timer : TM >
=> < 0 : !PhantomIgnore{|0|} | timer : no-timer >
if TM =/= timer0 /\ TM =/= no-timer .

crl [reset-timer] : < 0 : !PhantomIgnore{|0|} | timer : TM, inside : C >
=> < 0 : !PhantomIgnore{|0|} | timer : no-timer, inside : |press|(0) C >
if TM == timer0 .
```

The last two rules for forwarding messages in and out from the internal configuration are similar to the forwarding rules for the debouncer pattern. Indeed, any wrapper that selectively filters certain messages will have forward rules of this form.

```
var IM OM : Msg .
crl [forward-in] : IM < 0 : !PhantomIgnore{|0|} | inside : C >
   => < 0 : !PhantomIgnore{|0|} | inside : IM C >
   if |dest|(IM) == 0 /\ IM =/= |press|(0) /\ IM =/= |release|(0) .
crl [forward-out] : < 0 : !PhantomIgnore{|0|} | inside : OM C >
   => < 0 : !PhantomIgnore{|0|} | inside : C > OM
   if |dest|(OM) =/= 0 .
endtom)
```

5.3   Proof of Correctness of the Dephantomizer Pattern

As with the button debouncer, we would like to establish a correspondence between the execution of an ideal system and that of a system with input faults but with the pattern applied. Again, the key is to define a projection relation between the two systems. However, in this case, in addition to the projection operations, we also need to define a *time translation* on button press messages to capture the delays of the pattern.

The first transformation operation of interest is the `delay-press`, which delays all press messages by a time duration T. This is useful as the dephantom pattern introduces delays in processing the press messages. Because of this, a delay transformation is required to show an equivalent execution between an ideal system and a delayed system. The projection $\pi_{phantom}$ from a phantom input system with a wrapper to an ideal input system with no wrapper would be the composition `remove-small` ; `remove-wrapper` ; `delay-press`. Where `remove-small` is applied first and removes all messages whose durations are too small; `remove-wrapper` removes the pattern wrapper and exposes the internal object; and `delay-press` shifts the time of all button press events by a specific duration. Full details about each of these operator definitions can be found in [7].

Again, we use the same definitions as with the button bounce case defining the states of systems S_{ideal} and $S_{wrapped}$, but this time using the phantom fault $F_{phantom}$ to provide faulty button inputs.

Definition 2. *Define a relation $H \subseteq S_{ideal} \times S_{wrapped}$ such that $s_i H s_f$ iff $\pi_{phantom}(s_f) = s_i$ and $time(s_f) = time(s_i)$.*

We again have a bisimulation result, for which the full proof can be found in [7].

Theorem 2. *The relation H is a well-founded bisimulation, and thus H defines a stuttering bisimulation between S_{ideal} and $S_{wrapped}$ when considering natural number time.*

Notice that in this case, H still preserves all the attributes of objects but only by making the button press delivery times later in the ideal model. This means that H adds a delay into the system, which is to be expected as detecting for faulty short button presses requires the system to wait before registering the button press event.

6   A Pattern to Address Stuck Faults

6.1   Stuck Faults

When a button is pressed, it may become stuck. This may be caused by deterioration in the spring or sudden increase in friction due to deformation or adhesives. This results in a persistent logical 1 signal, even though the button was already released.

We again have another device-button interaction, and the model is entirely similar to the button bounce and phantom press cases.

A button stuck fault is a relation $F_{stuck} \subseteq I_{valid} \times I_{valid}$ such that a faulty button may be held down for longer durations than intended, or more precisely, $(b, b_f) \in F_{stuck}$ iff:

1. $b(t) = 1 \implies b_f(t) = 1$ (a button appears pressed when it is physically pressed, regardless of being stuck)
2. If $b_f(t) = 1$ and $b(t) = 0$, then there is a $t' < t$ s.t. $b(t') = 1$ and $b_f(t'') = 1$ for all $t'' \in [t', t]$ (a button can only become stuck after it has been pressed, and stays stuck for a continuous time interval).

6.2 Stuck Detection Pattern

Like the button debouncer pattern, the stuck detector pattern takes an input theory that describes the nature of the stuck button press fault. This includes a class Wrapped which specifies which object is subject to the stuck button press fault. The dest operator is again used to find which messages to forward to the outside configuration. The press and release messages describe the actual button press events subject to stuck button press faults. Furthermore, we have t-stuck to describe the minimal time that the button will remain stuck. The input theory for the stuck detector pattern is given as follows.

```
(oth STUCKABLE is
   pr TICK-MTE-SEM .

   class |Wrapped| .
   op |dest| : Msg -> Oid .
   op |t-stuck| : -> Time .

   msg |press| : Oid -> Msg .
   msg |release| : Oid -> Msg .

   var O : Oid .
   eq mte(|press|(O)) = zero .
endoth)
```

The stuck detector pattern is defined in the STUCK-DETECT module below. It takes a STUCKABLE theory as input and describes a wrapper pattern to detect stuck button press faults. The wrapper structure is again very similar to the button debouncer wrapper.

```
(tomod STUCK-DETECT{|O| :: STUCKABLE} is
   pr RT-COMP .
   pr DELAY-MSG .

   class !StuckDetect{|O|} |
      inside : NEConfiguration,
      timer : Timer,
      stuck-err : Bool .

   op init-timer : -> Timer .
   eq init-timer = no-timer .
   op init-stuck-err : -> Bool .
   eq init-stuck-err = false .
```

We first define the necessary attributes of the wrapper object. Besides the internal configuration, we have a timer for keeping track of when the button has been pressed passed its stuck duration. The `stuck-err` bit, when set to true represents detection of the error. The other constants define initialization values for each of the attributes.

The tick and mte rules are again similar to those for the other patterns and work by propagating the operations homomorphically to the internal configuration and timers. Their behavior on objects are defined by the equations below.

```
eq tick( < 0 : !StuckDetect{|0|} | inside : C, timer : TM >, T)
= < 0 : !StuckDetect{|0|} | inside : tick(C, T), timer : tick(TM, T) > .

eq mte( < 0 : !StuckDetect{|0|} | inside : C, timer : TM >)
= minimum(mte(C), mte(TM)) .
```

The rules for the behavior under button press events is just forwarding all button press and release messages normally, but setting and resetting the timers appropriately. The last rule, `stuck-event`, is applied whenever a button press event is not followed by a release within `t-stuck` time units. When this happens, the `stuck-err` is set to true to indicate detection.

```
rl [set-timer] : |press|(0) < 0 : !StuckDetect{|0|} | timer : no-timer, inside : C >
=> < 0 : !StuckDetect{|0|} | timer : t(|t-stuck|), inside : |press|(0) C > .

rl [release-event] : |release|(0) < 0 : !StuckDetect{|0|} | inside : C >
=> < 0 : !StuckDetect{|0|} | inside : |release|(0) C, timer : no-timer, stuck-err : false > .

crl [stuck-event] : < 0 : !StuckDetect{|0|} | timer : TM >
=> < 0 : !StuckDetect{|0|} | timer : no-timer, stuck-err : true >
if TM == timer0 .
```

The forward in and out rules are again similar to the previous two patterns.

```
var IM OM : Msg .
crl [forward-in] : IM < 0 : !StuckDetect{|0|} | inside : C >
    => < 0 : !StuckDetect{|0|} | inside : IM C >
    if |dest|(IM) == 0 /\ IM =/= |press|(0) /\ IM =/= |release|(0) .
crl [forward-out] : < 0 : !StuckDetect{|0|} | inside : OM C >
    => < 0 : !StuckDetect{|0|} | inside : C > OM
    if |dest|(OM) =/= 0 .
endtom)
```

6.3   Proof of Correctness of the Stuck Detection Pattern

The stuck fault is inherently lossy, so the correctness of the pattern is shown in two parts. First, if no stuck faults occur then we show that the behavior with the pattern is bisimilar to the ideal system. Second, if a stuck fault occurs, we can no longer guarantee any correspondence in behavior to the ideal case, but we can guarantee *detection* of the fault within a certain time bound.

The projection π_{stuck} from a wrapped system for stuck detection to an ideal input system with no wrapper is just simply a function `remove-wrapper`, which removes the pattern wrapper and exposes the internal object to the external configuration.

Again, we use definitions analogous to those for the button bounce case for states of S_{ideal} and $S_{wrapped}$. Although stuck faults will ruin any possibility of behavioral correspondence (since the system becomes unresponsive), we can still show that without faults our pattern does not alter the behavior of the system.

Definition 3. *Define a relation* $H \subseteq S_{ideal} \times S_{wrapped}$ *such that* $s_i H s_f$ *iff* $\pi_{stuck}(s_f) = s_i$ *and* $time(s_f) = time(s_i)$.

We can show that under a strict relation H that does not allow for differences in the faulty model (i.e. no stuck faults occur), then the behavior of the wrapped system in a faulty environment is bisimilar to that of the ideal system, that is, the added wrapper does not essentially change to the behavior of the system. Proof in [7].

Theorem 3. *The relation H is a well-founded bisimulation, and thus H defines a stuttering bisimulation between S_{ideal} and $S_{wrapped}$ when considering natural number time.*

However when a button does become stuck, we can no longer give any guarantees about correct behavior, but we can still detect a fault. The following theorem proves that any stuck faults will be detected by our pattern. Proof in [7].

Theorem 4. *Consider a system in $S_{wrapped}$. If we have a stuck fault such that there exist two consecutive press and release events on the input* delay(press, t) delay(release, t') *such that* $t' - t > T_{stuck}$ *then the wrapper attribute* stuck-err *will be set after* $t + T_{stuck}$ *time units.*

7 Conclusion and Future Work

The goal of this work has been to define *formal patterns*, as parameterized real-time rewrite theories, that provide provably correct guarantees of fault tolerance for commonly occuring faults in button interfaces of manually-operated devices, including medical equipment. The general technique of well-founded bisimulations [4] has been used to obtain the desired guarantees for each pattern. Since the formal specifications are executable, formal analysis by model checking has also been performed.

For future work, an important next step is to analyze the compositional behavior of multiple patterns together. Although each of the patterns have bisimulation results which is by itself composable, some of the bisimulations are conditional (such as introducing delays or adding additional fault-detection messages). In these cases the order of pattern composition can result in different system behaviors. This highly nontrivial problem of pattern composition is one of the major challenges that must be addressed before these patterns can be used for larger scale systems.

References

1. Bruni, R., Meseguer, J.: Semantic foundations for generalized rewrite theories. Theor. Comput. Sci. **360**(1), 386–414 (2006)
2. Clavel, M., Durán, F., Eker, S., Lincoln, P., Martí-Oliet, N., Meseguer, J., Talcott, C.: All About Maude - A High-Performance Logical Framework. LNCS. Springer, Heidelberg (2007)
3. Durán, F., Meseguer, J.: The Maude specification of Full Maude. Technical report, SRI International (1999)
4. Meseguer, J., Palomino, M., Martí-Oliet, N.: Algebraic simulations. J. Log. Algebr. Program **79**(2), 103–143 (2010)
5. Meseguer, J.: Membership algebra as a logical framework for equational specification. In: Parisi-Presicce, Francesco (ed.) WADT 1997. LNCS, vol. 1376, pp. 18–61. Springer, Heidelberg (1998)
6. Ölveczky, P.C., Meseguer, J.: Semantics and pragmatics of Real-Time Maude. Higher-Order Symbolic Comput. **20**(1–2), 161–196 (2007)
7. Sun, M.: Formal patterns for medical device safety. Doctoral Dissertation, Department of Computer Science, University of Illinois at Urbana-Champaign (2013). https://dl.dropboxusercontent.com/u/54321762/mu-thesis.pdf

A Formal Semantics of the OSEK/VDX Standard in $\mathbb{K}$ Framework and Its Applications

Min Zhang[1]([⊠]), Yunja Choi[2], and Kazuhiro Ogata[1]

[1] Research Center for Software Verification, Japan Advanced Institute of Science and Technology (JAIST), Nomi, Japan
{zhangmin,ogata}@jaist.ac.jp
[2] School of Computer Science and Engineering, Kyungpook National University, Daegu, South Korea
yuchoi76@knu.ac.kr

Abstract. The OSEK/VDX is an international standard of automobile operating systems. Such systems are safety-critical and require extensive safety analysis and verification. Formal methods have been shown useful and effective to verify the safety of both the OSEK/VDX-based operating systems and applications. Using formal methods requires formal semantics of the OSEK/VDX standard. In this paper, we present a formal semantics of the standard using $\mathbb{K}$, a rewrite-based formal semantics framework. With the formal semantics, we can (1) verify user-defined applications by model checking, and (2) automatically generate test cases for testing of the OSEK/VDX-based operating systems. Features of the formal semantics are its executability and flexibility. Compared with existing formal semantics of the standard, the formal semantics defined in $\mathbb{K}$ is more flexible and generic. This work also shows that $\mathbb{K}$ is not only used for formalizing the semantics of programming languages, but also for automobile operating systems.

1 Introduction

The OSEK/VDX is an international standard of developing automobile operating systems [1]. An automobile operating system is a piece of safety-critical software to manage resources and applications which run on the system to control electrical devices in automobiles. Its safety should be extensively analyzed and verified. To implement an OSEK/VDX-based operating system, the traditional approach is to develop both the kernel and applications following the standard, and compile them together to generate an executable system. The system must be tested extensively for safety [2]. This approach is effort-consuming and prone to errors in that modification to source code usually requires recompilation and testing requires complete suite of test cases, which usually are difficult to build.

This research was supported by Kakenhi 23220002, Japan, and by the MSIP(Ministry of Science, ICT and Future Planning), Korea, under the ITRC(Information Technology Research Center) support program (NIPA-2013-H0301-13-5004) supervised by the NIPA(National IT Industry Promotion Agency).

© Springer International Publishing Switzerland 2014
S. Escobar (Ed.): WRLA 2014, LNCS 8663, pp. 280–296, 2014.
DOI: 10.1007/978-3-319-12904-4_16

Our previous work [3] and the work [4] have shown that using formal methods is an effective approach to both safety verification of OSEK/VDX systems and applications, which is complementary to the traditional testing-based approach. Using formal methods requires formal semantics of the OSEK/VDX standard. In this paper, we present an executable formal semantics of the standard, which is defined in $\mathbb{K}$, a rewrite-based formal framework [5]. We choose $\mathbb{K}$ for its executability, flexibility, simplicity and tool-support. $\mathbb{K}$ allows user-defined data types and supports formalization of infinite-state systems. Especially, $\mathbb{K}$ provides tool-support to automatically generate interpreter and state-space explorer based on the defined semantics. Another advantage of using $\mathbb{K}$ is that it does not require extra effort to transform user-defined applications into corresponding formal definition in $\mathbb{K}$ in order to use the formal semantics. In this sense, the formal semantics of the standard in $\mathbb{K}$ is more flexible and generic than those formalized in Promela [6] and NuSMV [4], which have restriction on the number of tasks, resources, events in OSEK/VDX-based operating systems, and also need extra effort to instantiate the semantics with user-defined applications, though the number of tasks, resources and events must be fixed when the formal semantics is used for model checking.

The benefit from this formal semantics is multifold. Firstly, it can be used to model check user-defined OSEK/VDX applications with a fixed number of tasks, resources and events by integrating the formal semantics with the semantics of the language in which the applications are implemented. Secondly, it can be used to generate test cases for the testing of OSEK/VDX-based operating systems. This work shows that $\mathbb{K}$ is also well suited to the formalization of automobile operating systems besides the formalization of semantics of programming languages [7–9].

Organization of the paper: Sect. 2 introduces the background and our overall approach. Sections 3 and 4 describe the OSEK/VDX standard and $\mathbb{K}$. Section 5 shows the formalization of OSEK/VDX in $\mathbb{K}$. Section 6 demonstrates two applications of the formal semantics, i.e., model checking and test case generation. Sections 7 and 8 mention some related work and conclude the paper.

2   Background and Overall Approach

The OSEK/VDX standard is a generic description which is mandatory for any implementation of an OSEK/VDX operating system. It concerns the general description of the strategy and functionality, standardized application programming interface (API), resource management, event mechanism, etc. Figure 1 depicts the traditional process of implementing OSEK/VDX-based operating systems [10]. An OSEK/VDX-based operating system is built out of a kernel which includes basic functionality described in the standard such as scheduler, APIs, etc., and a group of applications which interact with the kernel through APIs. An application includes a configuration of resources, tasks, and events that are defined in OIL (OSEK Implementation Language) and source code for each task of the application. They are compiled together and an executable operating

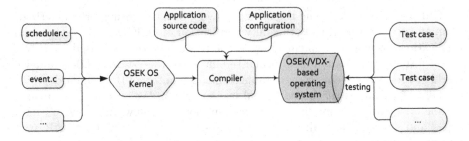

Fig. 1. Traditional approach to the implementation of OSEK/VDX operating systems

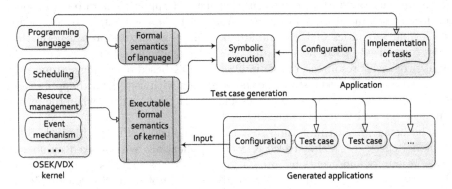

Fig. 2. The framework of our formal approach

system is developed. The system is then extensively tested for safety. There are two major problems with the traditional approach. One is that the whole system must be re-compiled and re-tested due to every change to either the kernel or applications. It is costly in terms of both effort and time. Another problem is that it is prone to errors due to the ambiguity of the standard which in written in natural language and the lack of test cases. A suite of comprehensive test cases are necessary to detect potential errors in a system, but it is not an easy task to build such a suite of test cases.

Using formal methods is an effective means of developing reliable OSEK/ VDX-based operating systems, complementary to the traditional one. Figure 2 shows the overview of our formal approach to the verification of OSEK/VDX-based applications and automatic generation of test cases for the testing of OSEK/VDX-based operating systems. The OSEK/VDX standard, including features such as task scheduling, resource management, or event mechanism is formalized. To verify user-defined applications, the semantics of the programming language in which tasks are implemented should also be formalized. User-defined applications can be model checked with the integration of the two formal semantics. By model checking, we can detect potential errors such as deadlock in applications. For test case generation, users only need to provide a configuration of tasks, resources and events, and the constraints that generated test cases should satisfy, such as the number of APIs for each task. Test cases are automatically generated based on the formal semantics of the kernel. Generated test cases can be used for conformance checking of OSEK/VDX-based operating systems by checking whether the result obtained by running each test case on practical system is the same as the expected one.

3   The OSEK/VDX Standard and OIL

As mentioned earlier, the OSEK/VDX standard generically describes all mandatory requirements of an OSEK/VDX-based operating system. In our current formalization we only consider some fundamental parts in the standard such as task scheduling, resource management, event mechanism, error handling, and leave others such as interruption and real-time feature as future work.

Task and Task Scheduling. Task is the basic building block of an OSEK/VDX application. Multitask is one of the basic requirements of OSEK/VDX-based operating systems. The OSEK/VDX standard specifies two kinds of tasks, i.e., *basic task* and *extended task*. Figure 3 shows the state transitions of basic tasks and extended tasks. A basic task has three states, i.e., *ready*, *running* and *suspended*, while an extended task has a *waiting* state besides the three. The difference between them is that the extended tasks can wait for events during execution by using the system call *WaitEvent*, while the basic tasks cannot. Calling *WaitEvent* may result in a *waiting* state, and the release of the processor. The processor can be reassigned to a lower-priority task without the need to terminate the running extended task.

Tasks are controlled by the scheduler. The scheduler decides on the basis of the task priority which is the next of the *ready* tasks to be transferred into the *running* state. The OSEK/VDX standard provides two scheduling policies, i.e., *full preemptive* and *non-preemptive* scheduling. By full preemptive scheduling, a running task may be rescheduled at any instruction by the occurrence of trigger conditions pre-set by the operating system, such as successful termination of a task, and activating a task. The running task is put into the ready state, as soon as a higher priority task gets ready.

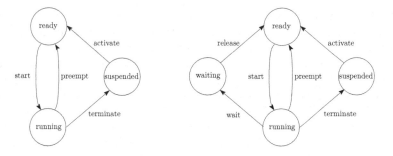

Fig. 3. The state model of basic task (left) and extended task (right)

Resource Management and Priority Ceiling Protocol. Resource management is used to co-ordinate concurrent accesses of several tasks with different priorities to shared resources. It ensures that two tasks can never occupy the same resource at the same time, deadlocks will never occur by use of these resources, and access to resources never results in a *waiting* state.

There are some restrictions when using resources. When occupying a resource, the task should not call some APIs such as *TerminateTask*, which may cause rescheduling after they are called. If a task is occupying multiple resources, these resources must be released in LIFO order.

However, under these restrictions it is possible that a lower-priority task may delay the execution of higher-priority task, which is called *priority inversion*. An example about it can be found in [1]. To avoid priority inversion, OSEK prescribes the OSEK Priority Ceiling Protocol (PCP). The protocol requires that each resource has a *ceiling priority* which is statically assigned at the system generation. Basically, the priority shall be set at least to the highest priority of all tasks that can access that resource. If a task requires a resource, and its current priority is lower than the ceiling priority of the resource, the priority of the task is dynamically raised to the ceiling priority of the resource. If the task releases a resource, the priority of the task is reset to the one before it requires that resource.

Event Mechanism. Tasks in OSEK/VDX-based operating systems are synchronized by events. Events are the criteria for the transition of extended tasks from the *waiting* state to the *ready* state (see Fig. 3). Events are not independent objects, but assigned to extended tasks. An event can be assigned to multiple extended tasks, and each extended task has a definite number of events. It should be statically declared that which events can be assigned to an extended task in OSEK/VDX applications.

When activating an extended task from the *suspended* state, its events are cleared by the system. An extended task goes into *waiting* state when it is running and the events that it is waiting for are not set. The task keeps in the *waiting* state and goes into *ready* state until any event is set by another task. All tasks can set any event of any non-suspended extended task, but only the owner can clear its events. Details about event mechanism can be referred to [1].

OSEK Implementation Language (OIL). OIL is used to configure tasks, resources, events and their relations in an OSEK/VDX-based operating system [10]. Figure 4 shows an example of how to declare resources, events and tasks in OIL. It says that in the corresponding application there is a resource named r1, an event named e1, and a task named t1. Resource r1 is declared as a standard resource. Event e1 is declared with a mask as AUTO. Event mask is an integer number. If a mask is set AUTO, one bit is assigned to it. The statements in the configuration of task t1 say that the task should be automatically started (put into *ready* state) after the initialization of operation system. The priority of the task is 3, and it is preemptable (indicated by FULL). The last two statements in t1 mean that task t1 can access resource r1, and it has the event e1.

```
RESOURCE r1 {                          TASK t1{
   RESOURCEPROPERTY = STANDARD;           AUTOSTART = true;
};                                        PRIORITY = 3;
                                          SCHEDULE = FULL;
EVENT e1 {                                RESOURCE = r1;
   MASK = AUTO;                           EVENT = e1;
};                                     };
```

Fig. 4. An example of OSEK/VDX application configuration in OIL

4   The $\mathbb{K}$ Framework

$\mathbb{K}$ is a rewrite-based semantics definitional framework, in which programming languages, calculi, as well as type systems or formal analysis tools can be defined or formalized [5]. A $\mathbb{K}$ definition of a semantics is automatically translated into Maude [11] rewrite theories, which are efficiently executable and can be used for state-exploration by exhaustive behavior analysis such as model checking [11]. The $\mathbb{K}$ framework has been used to formalize some practical programming languages such as C [7], Scheme [9], Python [8]. Some analysis tools have also been defined in $\mathbb{K}$ for type checking and type inference [5].

Semantics is defined in $\mathbb{K}$ by using labeled and potentially nested cell structures and $\mathbb{K}$ (rewrite) rules. The cell structure is called a *configuration*, which is used to represent system or program state. In this paper, we call it $\mathbb{K}$ configuration to differ from the configuration of OSEK/VDX-based applications. There are two types of $\mathbb{K}$ rules: *computational rules*, which count as computational steps, and *structural rules*, which do not count as computational steps. The role of structural rules is to rearrange the configuration so that computational rules can match and apply. They correspond to the equations and rewrite rules respectively in rewriting logic [12].

The formal definition of a programming language in $\mathbb{K}$ can automatically yield an interpreter for the language, and program analysis tools such as a statespace explorer by model checking, with which we can verify programs in that language by exhaustively explore all possible results under the condition that the state space is finite and reasonably small.

5   Formalizing the OSEK/VDX Standard in $\mathbb{K}$

In this section, we explain our approach to formalizing the OSEK/VDX standard in the $\mathbb{K}$ framework[1].

5.1 $\mathbb{K}$ Configuration of the OSEK/VDX

The $\mathbb{K}$ configuration of a running OSEK/VDX-based operating system consists of over 40 nested cells. Figure 5 shows part of them. Each cell has a label. The

---

[1] Some details are omitted due to the limitation of space. The complete formalization, $\mathbb{K}$ source code and the examples mentioned in Sect. 6 are available at the webpage http://www.jaist.ac.jp/~zhangmin/osek-formal.html.

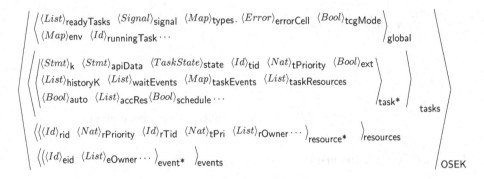

Fig. 5. $\mathbb{K}$ configuration of the OSEK/VDX standard

label ended with * indicates that there can be multiple such cells. A cell that does not have nested cells is a unit cell, storing a term which represents a piece of information of a state. In the brackets is the type of the terms in Fig. 5.

We take the task cell for example. There is both static and dynamic information of a task represented by the nested cells in task. Static information is that configured by users such as task ID in cell tid, priority in cell tPriority, its source code in cell apiData, whether the task is an extended one in cell ext, etc. Dynamic information is that which changes during the execution of operating system such as the next statement to be executed in cell k, the list of events which the task is waiting for in cell waitEvents, the events owned by the task and their status (*set* or *clear*) in cell taskEvents, etc. We do not explain all the cells due to the space limitation. Some will be explained later when needed.

5.2 Formalization of the Scheduler

In our formalization, we only consider *full preemptive* scheduling. As mentioned earlier, the occurrence of trigger conditions such as termination of a task will cause operating system to reschedule tasks. We define a type `Signal` and a constant `schedule` of it. We use a cell with label signal to store the occurrence of such trigger conditions. When there is a signal `schedule` in the signal cell, it indicates that some trigger condition has just occurred. Operating system must first handle it before executing any task. We define a set of $\mathbb{K}$ rules to specify the scheduler. The main one is as follows:

```
rule <signal> schedule => .</signal> <runningTask> I' => I </runningTask>
     <readyTasks> (< I,N >, L) => add2Head(I',N',L) </readyTasks>
     <task> <schedule> FULL </schedule> <state> running => ready </state>
            <tid> I' </tid> <tPriority> N' </tPriority> ... </task>
     <task> <tid> I </tid> <state> ready => running </state> ... </task>
when N >Int N' [transition]
```

The rule specifies how a $\mathbb{K}$ configuration changes before and after scheduling. Before scheduling, there is a signal `schedule` in cell signal. In cell readyTasks there is the list of ready tasks in a descend order by their priority. If there are two or more ready tasks with the same priority, they are ordered by the time when they get ready. However, the task which is preempted from running is considered as the oldest one among the ready tasks of the same priority [1]. In the cell readyTasks, $< I, N >, L$ represents that task I is the oldest one with the highest priority N among the ready tasks. The cells nested in the first task represent that task I' is the present running task with priority N' and it is preemptable, indicated by the value FULL in the cell schedule. If task I has a higher priority than task I', i.e., $N >Int N'$, I' is preempted, and I becomes running. After being preempted, I' is changed into ready state. It is added to the head of the sub-list of the ready tasks which have the same priority as I in the list of ready tasks by function add2Head.

5.3 Formalization of Resource Management

As depicted in Fig. 5, each resource is represented as a cell with label resource, which consists of unit cells for the resource identifier, ceiling priority, and a list of tasks that can access the resource. It also contains two unit cells which are dynamically created when the resource is allocated to a task. The two unit cells are used to store the identifier of the task to which the resource is allocated, and the priority of the task before it gets the resource.

Tasks access resources by two APIs, i.e., *GetResource* and *ReleaseResource*. As mentioned earlier, there are restrictions when accessing resources. Such restrictions together with the Priority Ceiling Protocol should be reflected by the formal semantics of the two APIs. For instance, the main rule defined for *GetResource* is as follows:

```
rule <signal> schedule => .</signal> <runningTask> I' => I </runningTask>
     <readyTasks> (< I,N >, L) => add2Head(I',N',L) </readyTasks>
     <task> <schedule> FULL </schedule> <state> running => ready </state>
          <tid> I' </tid> <tPriority> N' </tPriority> ... </task>
     <task> <tid> I </tid> <state> ready => running </state> ... </task>
when N >Int N' [transition]
```

In the cell k, there is a list of APIs to be executed by task I. The API to be executed next in the list is GetResource(R), where R is a resource ID. The cell tPriority stores the present priority of task I, and the cell accRes stores the list L of resources which task I is accessing. Resource R has a ceiling priority N2. L' in the cell rOwner represents the list of tasks that can access resource R. The condition (following the keyword when) is true when task I can access but is not accessing resource R. When the condition is true, R is allocated to I. According to the Priority Ceiling Protocol, if the present priority of task I is lower than the resource's ceiling priority, it is raised to the ceiling priority, as defined in the cell tPriority. R is added to the head of the list of resources being accessed by I. In the cell resource for R, two cells rTid and tPri are created, storing the task's ID and present priority, i.e., I and N', respectively. The present priority should be stored because when task I releases the resource by *ReleaseResource*, its priority should be reset to the one before it gets the resource. The semantics of *ReleaseResource* can be defined likewise. We omit the details of it in the paper.

5.4 Formalization of Event Mechanism

Each event is represented by an event cell as shown in Fig. 5. An event cell only consists of two sub-cells, storing the static information of the event, i.e., the event name in cell labeled by eid, and a list of owners (tasks) to which the event can be accessed in cell labeled by eOwner. Because event is not an independent object, but is assigned to extended tasks. We declare a new cell with label taskEvents for each extended task, storing the status of events that are assigned to the task. The status of an event is either *set* or *clear*, indicating that the event is set or cleared respectively. We declare a type EventStatus and two constants SET and CLEAR of it to represent the two corresponding status.

There are four APIs associated to events, i.e., *GetEvent*, *SetEvent*, *WaitEvent* and *ClearEvent*, with which tasks can get, set, wait and clear specific events. We take *SetEvent* for example to show how to define its semantics in $\mathbb{K}$. *SetEvent* takes a task ID and an event name. The state of the task specified in the API is transferred to *ready* state, if the event specified in the API is one of the events which the task was waiting for. This can be formalized by the following $\mathbb{K}$ rule:

```
rule <task> <state> running </state> <k> SetEvent(I,E); => . ...</k>
...</task> <task> <tid> I </tid> <state> waiting => ready </state>
<waitEvents> L => . </waitEvents> <tPriority> N </tPriority>
<taskEvents>... (E |-> (CLEAR => SET)) ...</taskEvents> ...</task>
<readyTasks> L' => add2Tail(I,N,L') </readyTasks>
<signal> . => schedule </signal>  when (E in L)  [transition]
```

The rule says that SetEvent(I,E); is the next API to be executed by a running task, where I is a task ID and E is an event name. Task I is in the *waiting* state, and is waiting for a list L of events. If E is in the list, task is transferred to *ready* state, and it does not wait for any events. Thus, the list L is changed into an empty one, represented by L => . in the cell waitEvents. The status of event E is changed into SET in the cell taskEvents. Task I is added to the tail of the sub-list of ready tasks which have the same priority as I in the list of ready tasks by function add2Tail. At the same time, the schedule signal is fired to invoke the scheduler.

If task I is not waiting for the event E, the event is simply set after the API is called. We omit the formal definition of it and those of other three event-related APIs in the paper.

5.5 Formalization of Error Handling

There are pre-defined errors in the OSEK/VDX standard. Such errors should be handled correctly when an operating system is implemented. For instance, an error will occur when a task tries to terminate itself while occupying some resources, which is strictly forbidden. If an error is raised, a specific error code should be returned. However, the standard does not specify how to handle such errors, and it is up to system developers.

We formalize errors by a specific function called Error, which takes four arguments, i.e., an error code, the identifier of the task which causes the error, the API that causes the error, and a string to provide detailed information of the error. When an error occurs, an error cell errorCell as shown in Fig. 5 is created with a term constructed by the **Error** function in it. At the same time, an error signal is inspired and put in the signal cell. The following rule shows an example of the formalization of the error which is caused when a task tries to terminate while still occupying resources.

```
rule <task> <state> running </state> <k> TerminateTask(); </k>
     <tid> I </tid> <accRes> ListItem(R) ... </accRes> ... </task>
     <signal> . => stop </signal>
     (.Bag => <errorCell> Error(E_OS_RESOURCE, I, TerminateTask();,
     "Task cannot terminate when occupying resources!") </errorCell>)
[transition]
```

The term in cell accRes is the list of resources that are currently occupied by the task. In the above rule the list is not empty when the API TerminateTask(); is to be executed in the next step. In the cell errorCell, E_OS_RESOURCE is an error code which is pre-defined in the standard.

5.6   Formalization of OIL

We formalize OIL in $\mathbb{K}$ in order to support user-defined configurations. $\mathbb{K}$ is well suited to formalize programming languages. OIL can also be naturally formalized in $\mathbb{K}$ like other languages such as C. One difference is that the semantics of OIL is formalized as structural rules, instead of computational rules. That is because OIL is a configuration language, which is used for configuring resources, tasks, events, etc. in a system, but not for computation or execution. Thus, we declare a set of structural rules which are used to construct an initial $\mathbb{K}$ configuration according to an input OIL program.

Given an OIL program, a $\mathbb{K}$ configuration is instantiated based on the declarations of resources, tasks, and events in the program. For instance, for each resource which is declared as shown in Fig. 4, a resource cell is created, which consists of four unit cells for resource identifier, its ceiling priority (0 at initial), the resource property, and the list of tasks that can access it (empty at initial). The following rule specifies the creation of a resource cell according to a declaration of a resource. The condition means that I is not used as an identifier for other tasks, events and resources.

```
rule <k> (RESOURCE I:Id { RESOURCEPROPERTY = RP; } ; => .) ... </k>
     <resources>(. => <resource> <rid> I </rid> <rPriority> 0 </rPriority>
        <rProperty> RP </rProperty> <rOwner> .List </rOwner> </resource>)
     ... </resources> <types> M:Map => (I |-> resource) M </types>
     <signal> . </signal> when notBool $hasMapping(M,I) [structural]
```

The ceiling priority of the resource and the list of tasks are calculated when tasks are initialized. If a task is declared to own a resource as shown in Fig. 4, it is added to the list. If the current ceiling priority (initially 0) is less than the priority of the task, it is raised to the priority of the task. The corresponding structural rules can be defined likewise. We omit the details in the paper.

6   Applications of the Formal Semantics

In this section, we demonstrate two applications of the formal semantics of the OSEK/VDX standard, i.e., to verify the properties of OSEK/VDX applications by model checking, and to generate test cases for the testing of OSEK/VDX operating systems.

6.1   Verification of OSEK/VDX Applications by Model Checking

There may be multiple tasks running in an OSEK/VDX application. It is necessary to verify that tasks can correctly synchronize and deadlock should never happen. Suppose that there are only two tasks t_1, t_2 in an application and two events e_1, e_2. Task t_1 is waiting for e_1 in order to set event e_2, while t_2 is waiting for e_2 in order to set event e_1. Both the two tasks are in *waiting* state, leading to deadlock.

An OSEK/VDX application consists of two parts: one is application configuration which describes the basic information of resources, tasks, events, etc., in the application, and implementation of each task. Application configurations are defined by OIL, and tasks are implemented in some programming language such as C. Thus, it requires formalizing the semantics of a specific programming language in which tasks are implemented, as shown in Fig. 2. As mentioned in Sect. 4, $\mathbb{K}$ can be easily used to define the operational semantics of programming languages. In this paper, we use a simple C-like imperative programming language whose semantics has been formally defined in $\mathbb{K}$ [13], to demonstrate the feasibility of verifying OSEK/VDX-based applications. We integrate the semantics of the language and the semantics of the OSEK/VDX standard. With the integrated semantics, we verify the OSEK/VDX applications that are implemented in the simplified language.

Figure 6 shows a simplified application which is used to monitor tire pressure [14]. There are four tasks with different priorities. Task MT is used to repeatedly activate task RT (line 34), which collects data from tire sensor and then activates task ST. Task ST puts the collected data into buffer (line 47) and activate task PT to process the data (line 49). The synchronization between task RT and ST is achieved by an event evt. Task ST has to wait for the event until the event is set by RT (line 45, 41).

The application is supposed to run repeatedly. We verify if the application is free of deadlock by searching all possible execution results of the application using the formal semantics of the standard and the simplified programming language. The command is as follows:

```
krun tire-app.osek --search-final
```

krun is a $\mathbb{K}$ command, used to run a program with the formal semantics which is predefined in $\mathbb{K}$ for the language in which the program is implemented. In this example, the program is saved as a file named tire-app.osek. The option search-final means that krun will return all possible final states of the program. With the command, krun returns a final state, which means that the

```
 1 EVENT evt {
 2     MASK = AUTO;
 3 };
 4 RESOURCE BUFF{
 5     RESOURCEPROPERTY = STANDARD;
 6 };
 7 TASK MT {
 8     PRIORITY = 4;
 9     AUTOSTART = true;
10     SCHEDULE = FULL;
11 };
12 TASK RT{
13     PRIORITY = 6;
14     AUTOSTART = false;
15     SCHEDULE = FULL;
16 };
17 TASK ST{
18     PRIORITY = 8;
19     AUTOSTART = false;
20     SCHEDULE = FULL;
21     EVENT = evt;
22     RESOURCE = BUFF;
23 };
24 TASK PT{
25     PRIORITY = 10;
26     AUTOSTART = false;
27     SCHEDULE = FULL;
28     RESOURCE = BUFF;
29 };
```

```
30 int data;
31 int buff;
32
33 TASK MT{
34     while(true){ActivateTask(RT);}
35 };
36 //Terminate
37 TASK RT{
38     //get data from tire sensor
39     ActivateTask(ST);
40     if(data!=0)
41         {SetEvent(ST,evt);   }
42     TerminateTask();
43 };
44 TASK ST{
45     WaitEvent(evt);
46     GetResource(BUFF);
47     buff=data;
48     ReleaseResource(BUFF);
49     ChainTask(PT);
50 };
51 TASK PT{
52     //Read data from buff
53     GetResource(BUFF);
54     // process data
55     buff=0;
56     ReleaseResource(BUFF);
57     TerminateTask();
58 };
```

a. Configuration   b. Implementation of tasks

Fig. 6. The configuration and source code of an OSEK/VDX application

program cannot proceed from that state. The returned state shows that all the four tasks cannot be executed. In the state, task RT is in *running* state, and the statement it executes next is ActivateTask(ST) (line 39). However, task ST is in *waiting* state. According to the OSEK/VDX standard, there is a maximum number of task activation. If the number of activation times exceeds the maximum number, an error occurs. In our experiment, we assume the maximal number is 1. In this case, an error occurs because it violates the maximum activation count.

We found the reason why the *running* task called the *waiting* task in the application by checking the execution path from the initial state to the returned state. 4 The execution path shows that after RT activates ST (line 39), ST starts to run because it has a higher priority than RT. However, ST goes to *waiting* state because evt is not set (line 45). The scheduler selects RT to run because among the ready tasks, i.e., RT and MT, RT's priority is the highest. However, RT does not set the event because evt data is 0 (line 40). It just terminates itself (line 42). MT is the only ready task, which is selected to run by the scheduler. It activates RT (line 34), and RT tries to activate ST (line 39). However, ST is in the *waiting* state, leading to the deadlock. The problem is caused by the code at line 40 and 41 because evt cannot be always set after ST is activated. We can fix it by moving ActivateTask(ST); to the block of if condition. We execute the revised application by *searching* with the same command. No solution is found, which means that there is no deadlock state from which the system cannot proceed further. Namely, the program is free of deadlock.

OSEK/VDX-based applications are implemented usually in C. The semantics of C has been formalized in $\mathbb{K}$ [7]. We believe that by integrating the semantics of C and the standard we can verify more complicated OSEK/VDX-based applications implemented in C, which is one piece of our future work.

6.2 Using the Formal Semantics for Test Case Generation

In this section, we show that the formal semantics of the standard in $\mathbb{K}$ can be used to generate test cases for the conformance checking of OSEK/VDX-based operating systems. Testing is still the main approach to conformance checking of OSEK/VDX-based operating systems. For example, an automobile operating system must pass a set suite distributed by a certification agency in order to get a certificate for the compliance of the system with the OSEK/VDX standard. However, it is practically impossible to test all possible combinations of APIs. One solution is to analyze the constraints among APIs and to generate automatically test cases that satisfy these constraints [4,6]. Given some constraints and a configuration of tasks, resources, and events, we would like to generate a sequence of APIs for each task and the generated sequence of APIs satisfies the specified constraints. Specifically, we provide an initial state where an OSEK/VDX application is configured, i.e., events, resources and tasks are defined. Tasks are not implemented, that is, there are no statements defined for tasks. We specify the target states which the operating system can reach from the given initial state by executing the application with a sequence of APIs for each task. Test case generation problem is to generate such API sequence for each task.

The formal semantics of the OSEK/VDX standard in $\mathbb{K}$ can also be used for generating such test cases. The basic idea is as follows. The input is the configuration part of an OSEK/VDX application. After the configuration is loaded by the $\mathbb{K}$ tool, a task cell is instantiated for each task according to their corresponding setting in the configuration and the task is in the *suspended* state. Only the task whose AUTOSTART property is true becomes ready and then is scheduled to run. In the initial state, all the tasks do not have any API to execute. We define a set of $\mathbb{K}$ rules which randomly generate an API for the currently running task based on the state of the task. The generated API is then executed based on its formal semantics that is predefined, and the state of the running task is changed correspondingly.

Generated APIs must satisfy some built-in constraints. These constraints are also specified in $\mathbb{K}$ rules. For instance, we define a rule which generates the API ReleaseResource with a resource R where R is predefined in the configuration of an application. Namely, the statement to be generated is ReleaseResource(R);. For the task that is go to execute the generated statement, the resource R must be the latest one that is allocated to the task, i.e., the resource R must be at the head of the list of resources in the cell taskResources. The corresponding $\mathbb{K}$ rule is defined as follows:

```
rule <task> <tid> I </tid> <state> running </state> <apiData> . </apiData>
  <k> . => ReleaseResource(R); </k> <taskRes> ListItem(R) ... </taskRes>
  ... </task> <tcgMode> true </tcgMode> <signal> . </signal>  [transition]
```

The rule also represents three conditions when API can be generated, i.e., the
system is running in the test case generation mode as indicated by the cell
tcgMode, the running task is undefined as indicated by an empty cell apiData,
and no signal is waiting for handling as indicated by the empty cell signal.

If the randomly generated API is `TerminateTask` or `ChainTask`, a sequence
of APIs are completed for the running task. That is because there is a constraint
that `TerminateTask` and `ChainTask` must be the last API in a task. After the
API is executed, the task is terminated and the scheduler selects another task to
run according to the scheduling policy. After each task has a generated sequence
of APIs, a test case is generated.

As an example, we explain how to generate test cases with the configuration
defined in Fig. 6. Each test case consists of four sequences of APIs for the tasks
in the configuration. We feed the configuration into the $\mathbb{K}$ tool and a pattern
to which expected results should match. The pattern specifies the constraints
to the target states such as the number of APIs for each task. There are two
optional parameters specifying the maximal searching depth and the number of
test cases. The following command is an example used for test case generation.

```
krun tire-conf.osek -c TCG=true --search --pattern="<task> <historyK> I1:
  ListItem I2:ListItem </historyK> <done> true </done> BG1:Bag </task>
  <task> <historyK> J1:ListItem J2:ListItem </historyK> <done> true </done>
  BG2:Bag </task> <task> <done> true </done> BG3:Bag </task> <task> <done>
  true </done> BG4:Bag </task>" --depth=30 --bound=100
```

It takes the configuration of the tire monitor application as input. TCG is an
argument which is used to initialize the cell tcgMode as true so that the rules
defined for test case generation can be executed. The pattern in the command
specifies that in the target states there are at least two tasks which have exactly
two APIs. The last two optional arguments means that the maximal searching
depth is 30 and the bound of solutions is 100. By the above command, the $\mathbb{K}$
tool returns a set of $\mathbb{K}$ configurations that match the specified pattern. In each
configuration, every task is assigned with a sequence of APIs. All the tasks with
assigned sequences of APIs constitute a test case.

Table 1. Experimental result of generating two classes of test cases with pattern A
(the left table) and B (the right table).

Depth	Solution	Test case	Time (sec)	Depth	Solution	Test cases	Time (sec)
16	0	0	6	20	0	0	16
17	92	23	10	21	176	44	23
20	1024	132	30	25	1320	186	76
21	1468	163	43	26	1572	209	97
22	1748*	200*	65	27	1736*	234*	146

The number of test cases may be infinite, leading to the non-termination of generation. For instance, a task can infinitely repeat the process of getting and releasing a resource, making the process of test case generation non-terminating. We can solve this problem by setting upper bounds to the number of generated test cases and the number of APIs in each task respectively. In the experiment, we defined two patterns denoted by A and B, specifying that in each generated test case there must be at least two tasks which have exactly two and three APIs, respectively. The experimental result is shown in Table 1. Solutions are the configurations returned by $\mathbb{K}$, and they match the specified pattern. We extract the generated APIs in cell apiData from the configurations returned by the $\mathbb{K}$ tool, and obtain a number of test cases. The numbers with $*$ mean that they are the upper bound at the corresponding depth. The $\mathbb{K}$ tool runs out of memory once the upper bound exceeds that numbers.

7   Related Work

There is some formalization in different formal languages of the OSEK/VDX standard. In [15], the semantics of APIs in the standard is formalized using Hoare-logic. The purpose is to verify the correctness of the APIs that are implemented in concrete OSEK/VDX-based operating systems, which is different from ours. The semantics of the standard is formalized using Promela in [6] and NuSMV in [4], with the purpose of test case generation. Compared with their formalization, our formal semantics in $\mathbb{K}$ is more flexible and generic in that they have to assume that the list of ready tasks in system is finite because the languages requires the system specified must be of finite-state, while in our formalization we do not have that restriction. Their formalization also requires extra effort to be instantiated according to concrete user-defined applications, while our formalization directly accepts user-defined applications as input without any transformation. Their approaches to test case generation are different from the one described in this paper. For instance, in [4] they use automata to control what is the next possible API to call based on user-given constraints. This can improve the efficiency by avoiding unnecessary trial of those APIs that violate the constraints if they are called. We have tried implementing the automata-based approach in Maude and evaluated that Maude can be used as an efficient test case generator [3]. Since Maude is the underlying rewrite engine of $\mathbb{K}$, we believe that this approach can also be implemented in $\mathbb{K}$ based on our formal semantics of the OSEK/VDX standard. As a piece of future work, we also consider integrating the automata-based approach into our formalization to improve the efficiency of test case generation.

The OSEK/VDX standard is also formalized in CafeOBJ [16] with the purpose of defining a formal specification of the standard so that we can verify the conformance of an automobile operating system to the standard by verifying whether it conforms to the formal standard. However, it is still a challenging problem to check the formal specification contains no contradiction as the authors mentioned [16]. The standard is also formalized using Event-B in [17].

However, in their work they do not explain how to use their formalization for verification. The common problem with the two existing formalization is how they can be used for formal verification. Our work shows that the formalization of the standard in $\mathbb{K}$ can be effectively used for the verification of concrete OSEK/VDX-based applications and operating systems.

8   Conclusion and Future Work

We have presented a formal semantics of the OSEK/VDX standard, which is defined in the $\mathbb{K}$ framework. We demonstrated two applications of using the formal semantics, i.e., verification of OSEK/VDX-based applications by model checking and generation of test cases for the testing of OSEK/VDX-based operating system. Compared with the existing formalization of the standard, the formal semantics in $\mathbb{K}$ is more flexible and generic in that there is no restriction to the number of tasks, resources and events in the formalization, and it does not need extra effort to instantiate the formal semantics with user-defined applications. Another advantage of the formal semantics is that it can be integrated with the semantics of other prevalent programming languages such as C in order to verify OSEK/VDX-based applications which are implemented in those languages. This work also shows that $\mathbb{K}$ is not only a semantics framework for the definition and formalization of programming languages, but for automobile operating systems such as OSEK/VDX-based operating systems.

In our current formalization, we do not consider some functionality in the standard such as interruption and real-time feature, which are also equally important to task scheduling, etc. As one piece of our future work, we will formalize them based on the current work and develop a tool for the formal analysis of OSEK/VDX applications with interruption and real-time features. Another piece of future work is to improve the efficiency of test case generation by integrating the automata-based approach proposed in [3] into our formalization and to support user-defined constraints for test case generation by formalizing the OSEK constraints specification language defined in [4]. We also consider integrating the formal semantics of C in $\mathbb{K}$ with the formal semantics of the standard for the verification of more complicated OSEK/VDX-based applications that are developed in C.

References

1. OSEK Group, et al.: OSEK/VDX Operating System Specification (2009)
2. John, D.: OSEK/VDX conformance testing-MODISTARC. In: Proceedings of OSEK/VDX Open Systems in Automotive Networks, IET (1998)
3. Choi, Y., Zhang, M., Ogata, K.: Evaluation of Maude as a test generation engine for automotive operating systems, pp. 1–15 (2013) (Manuscript)
4. Choi, Yunja: Constraint specification and test generation for OSEK/VDX-based operating systems. In: Hierons, Robert M., Merayo, Mercedes G., Bravetti, Mario (eds.) SEFM 2013. LNCS, vol. 8137, pp. 305–319. Springer, Heidelberg (2013)

5. Roşu, G., Şerbănută, T.F.: An overview of the $\mathbb{K}$ semantic framework. J. Log. Algebr. Program. **79**(6), 397–434 (2010)

6. Yatake, Kenro, Aoki, Toshiaki: Automatic generation of model checking scripts based on environment modeling. In: van de Pol, Jaco, Weber, Michael (eds.) Model Checking Software. LNCS, vol. 6349, pp. 58–75. Springer, Heidelberg (2010)

7. Ellison, C., Roşu, G.: An executable formal semantics of C with applications. In: Proceedings of the 39th POPL, pp. 533–544. ACM (2012)

8. Guth, D.: A formal semantics of Python 3.3, Master thesis (2013)

9. Meredith, P., Hills, M., Roşu, G.: An executable rewriting logic semantics of $\mathbb{K}$-Scheme. In: Workshop on Scheme and Functional Programming, vol. 1 (2007)

10. Zahir, A.: OIL-OSEK implementation language. In: OSEK/VDX Open Systems in Automotive Networks (Ref. No. 1998/523), IEE Seminar, IET, pp. 1–8 (1998)

11. Clavel, M., Durán, F., Eker, S., Lincoln, P., Martí-Oliet, N., Meseguer, J., Talcott, C. (eds.): All About Maude - A High-Performance Logical Framework. LNCS, vol. 4350. Springer, Heidelberg (2007)

12. Meseguer, J.: Twenty years of rewriting logic. J. Log. Algebr. Program. **81**(7–8), 721–781 (2012)

13. Roşu, G., Şerbănută, T.F.: $\mathbb{K}$ overview and simple case study. In: Proceedings of International K Workshop (K'11), ENTCS. Elsevier (2013) (to appear)

14. Zhang, H., Aoki, T., Yatake, K., Zhang, M., Lin, H.H.: An approach for checking OSEK/VDX applications. In: Proceedings of the 13th QSIC, IEEE CSP, pp. 113–116 (2013)

15. Huang, Y., Zhao, Y., Zhu, L., Li, Q., Zhu, H., Shi, J.: Modeling and verifying the code-level osek/vdx operating system with csp. In: Proceedings of the 5th TASE, IEEE CSP, pp. 142–149 (2011)

16. Yatsu, H., Ando, T., Kong, W., Hisazumi, K., Fukuda, A., Aoki, T., Futatsugi, K.: Towards formal description of standards for automotive operating systems. In: Proceedings of 6th ICSTW, IEEE CSP, pp. 13–14 (2013)

17. Vu, D.H., Aoki, T.: Faithfully formalizing OSEK/VDX operating system specification. In: Proceedings of the 3rd SoICT, pp. 13–20. ACM (2012)

Author Index

Printed in the United States
By Bookmasters